THE CERTIFIED
SOFTWARE QUALITY
ENGINEER HANDBOOK

Also available from ASQ Quality Press:

The Software Audit Guide
John Helgeson

Fundamental Concepts for the Software Quality Engineer, Volume 2
Sue Carroll and Taz Daughtrey, editors

Safe and Sound Software: Creating an Efficient and Effective Quality System for Software Medical Device Organizations
Thomas H. Faris

Quality Audits for Improved Performance, Third Edition
Dennis R. Arter

The ASQ Auditing Handbook, Third Edition
J.P. Russell, editing director

The Internal Auditing Pocket Guide: Preparing, Performing, Reporting, and Follow-Up, Second Edition
J.P. Russell

Root Cause Analysis: Simplified Tools and Techniques, Second Edition
Bjørn Andersen and Tom Fagerhaug

The Certified Manager of Quality/Organizational Excellence Handbook, Third Edition
Russell T. Westcott, editor

The Certified Quality Engineer Handbook, Third Edition
Connie M. Borror, editor

Six Sigma for the New Millennium: A CSSBB Guidebook, Second Edition
Kim H. Pries

The Certified Quality Process Analyst Handbook
Eldon H. Christensen, Kathleen M. Coombes-Betz, and Marilyn S. Stein

Enabling Excellence: The Seven Elements Essential to Achieving Competitive Advantage
Timothy A. Pine

To request a complimentary catalog of ASQ Quality Press publications, call 800-248-1946, or visit our Web site at http://www.asq.org/quality-press.

THE CERTIFIED SOFTWARE QUALITY ENGINEER HANDBOOK

Linda Westfall

ASQ Quality Press
Milwaukee, Wisconsin

American Society for Quality, Quality Press, Milwaukee 53203
© 2010 by Linda Westfall
All rights reserved. Published 2009
Printed in the United States of America
17 16 15 14   5 4

Library of Congress Cataloging-in-Publication Data

Westfall, Linda, 1954–
  The certified software quality engineer handbook / Linda Westfall.
      p. cm.
  Includes bibliographical references and index.
  ISBN 978-0-87389-730-3 (hard cover : alk. paper)
    1. Electronic data processing personnel—Certification. 2. Computer software—
Examinations—Study guides. 3. Computer software—Quality control. I. Title.

  QA76.3.W466 2009
  005.1'4—dc22   2009030360

ISBN: 978-0-87389-730-3

Publisher: William A. Tony
Acquisitions Editor: Matt T. Meinholz
Project Editor: Paul O'Mara
Production Administrator: Randall Benson

ASQ Mission: The American Society for Quality advances individual, organizational, and
community excellence worldwide through learning, quality improvement, and knowledge
exchange.

Attention Bookstores, Wholesalers, Schools, and Corporations: ASQ Quality Press books,
videotapes, audiotapes, and software are available at quantity discounts with bulk purchases
for business, educational, or instructional use. For information, please contact ASQ Quality
Press at 800-248-1946, or write to ASQ Quality Press, P.O. Box 3005, Milwaukee, WI 53201-3005.

To place orders or to request a free copy of the ASQ Quality Press Publications Catalog,
including ASQ membership information, call 800-248-1946. Visit our Web site at www.asq.org
or http://www.asq.org/quality-press.

Printed in the United States of America

 Printed on acid-free paper

CMM, CMMI, and Capability Maturity Model are registered in the US Patent & Trademark Office
by Carnegie Mellon University.

Quality Press
600 N. Plankinton Avenue
Milwaukee, Wisconsin 53203
Call toll free 800-248-1946
Fax 414-272-1734
www.asq.org
http://www.asq.org/quality-press
http://standardsgroup.asq.org
E-mail: authors@asq.org

For Robert Westfall, my husband, my partner, my best friend, and my playmate. Thank you for all of your support and patience while I wrote this book and as I volunteered countless hours to ASQ and other organizations over the years. Thank you for sharing your life with me, making me laugh out loud, cooking all of those fantastic meals, and sharing your passion for fireworks with me. Life with you continues to be a blast!!!

Table of Contents

Part I   General Knowledge

Part II   Software Quality Management

Part III   Systems and Software Engineering Processes

Part VII   Software Configuration Management

CD-ROM Contents

PracticeExam1.pdf

PracticeExamAnswers1.pdf

PracticeExam2.pdf

PracticeExamAnswers2.pdf

PracticeExam3.pdf

PracticeExamAnswers3.pdf

List of Figures and Tables

Preface

Continuous improvement is a mantra implicit to the quality profession. So as software quality engineers, we should not be surprised our own discipline has continued to evolve and change. By 'practicing what we preach' in our own field, adopting 'lessons learned' from implementing software quality principles and practices, and proactively staying involved in managerial, procedural, and technological advances in software engineering and the quality arena, software quality engineers have learned to increase the value they add to the end software products.

One of the primary roles of a software quality engineer is to act as a management information source that keeps software quality as visible to software management as cost and schedule are when business plans and decisions need to be made. In order to fulfill this role, software quality engineers must continuously improve their skill and knowledge sets. The software quality profession has moved beyond the limits of using only testing or auditing as the primary tools of our trade. Software quality has emerged into a multi-faceted discipline that requires us, as software quality engineers, to be able to understand and apply knowledge that encompasses:

- *Software quality management.* The processes and activities involved in setting the organization's strategic quality goals and objectives, establishing organizational, project, and product quality planning, and providing the oversight necessary to ensure the effectiveness and efficiency of the organization's quality management system. Software quality management provides leadership and establishes an integrated, cross-functional culture where producing high-quality software is "just the way we do things around here."

- *Software quality engineering.* The processes and activities needed to define, plan, and implement the quality management system for software-related processes, projects, and products. This includes defining, establishing, and continuously improving software-related systems, policies, processes, and work instructions that help prevent defects and build quality into the software.

- *Software quality assurance.* The planned and systematic set of all actions and activities needed to provide adequate confidence that the:

  – Software work products conform to their standards of workmanship and that quality is being built into the products

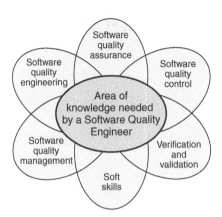

  – Organization's quality management system (or each individual
    process) is adequate to meet the organization's quality goals and
    objectives, is appropriately planned, is being followed, and is effective
    and efficient.

  • *Software quality control.* The planned and systematic set of all actions
    and activities needed to monitor and measure software projects,
    processes, and products to ensure that special causes have not introduced
    unwanted variation into those projects, processes, and products.

  • *Software verification and validation.* The processes and activities used to
    ensure that software products meet their specified requirements and
    intended use. It helps ensure that the "software was built right" and
    the "right software was built."

  • *Soft skills.* A software quality engineer also needs what are referred to
    as the "soft skills" to be effective in influencing others toward quality.
    Examples of "soft skills" include leadership, team building, facilitation,
    communication, motivation, conflict resolution, negotiation, and more.

The ASQ Certified Software Quality Engineer (CSQE) Body of Knowledge (BoK)
is a comprehensive guide to the "common knowledge" software quality engineers
should possess about these knowledge areas. To keep the CSQE BoK current with
industry and practitioner needs, a modernized version of the CSQE BoK is released
every five years. This handbook contains information and guidance that supports
all of the topics of the 2008 version of the CSQE BoK (included in Appendix A)
upon which the CSQE exam is based. Armed with the knowledge presented in
this handbook to complement the required years of actual work experience, qualified software quality practitioners may feel confident they have taken appropriate
steps in preparation for the ASQ CSQE exam.

    However, my goals for this handbook go well beyond it being a CSQE exam
preparation guide. I designed this handbook not only to help the software quality engineers, but as a resource for software development practitioners, project
managers, organizational managers, other quality practitioners, and other professionals who need to understand the aspects of software quality that impact their

work. It can also be used to benchmark their (or their organization's) understanding and application of software quality principles and practices against what is considered a cross-industry "good practice" baseline. After all, taking stock of our strengths and weaknesses we can develop proactive strategies to leverage software quality as a competitive advantage.

New software quality engineers can use this handbook to gain an understanding of their chosen profession. Experienced software quality engineers can use this handbook as a reference source when performing their daily work. I also hope that trainers and educators will use this handbook to help propagate software quality engineering knowledge to future software practitioners and managers. Finally, this handbook strives to establish a common vocabulary that software quality engineers, and others in their organizations can use to communicate about software and quality. Thus increasing the professionalism of our industry and eliminating the wastes that can result from ambiguity and misunderstandings.

For me, personally, obtaining my CSQE certification, participating in the development of the ASQ CSQE program and even the writing this book were more about the journey than the destination. I have learned many lessons from my colleagues, clients and students over the years since I first became involved with the ASQ CSQE effort in 1992, as well as during my 30 plus year career in software. I hope that you will find value in these 'lessons learned' as they are embodied in this handbook. Best wishes for success in your software quality endeavors!

Linda Westfall
lwestfall@westfallteam.com

Acknowledgments

I would like to thank all of the people who helped review this book as I was writing it: Zigmund Bluvband, Dan Campo, Sue Carroll, Carolee Cosgrove-Rigsbee, Margery Cox, Ruth Domingos, Robin Dudash, Scott Duncan, Eva Freund, Tom Gilchrist, Steven Hodlin, Theresa Hunt, James Hutchins, Yvonne Kish, Matthew Maio, Patricia McQuaid, Vic Nanda, Geree Streun, Ponmurugarajan Thiyagarajan, Bill Trest, Rufus Turpin, and Cathy Vogelsong.

I would like to thank Jay Vogelsong for the cartoons and character clip art used in this book.

I would like to express my appreciation to the people at ASQ Quality Press, especially Matt Meinholz and Paul O'Mara, for helping turn this book into reality. I would also like to thank the staff of New Paradigm Prepress and Graphics for their copyediting skills, for creating the table of contents, list of figures, and index, and for turning my manuscript into a format worthy of being published.

Finally, I would like to thank all of the people who volunteered their time, energy, and knowledge to work with the ASQ and the Software Division to turn the Certified Software Quality Engineer (CSQE) exam into reality and who continue to support the ongoing body of knowledge and exam development activities.

Part I

General Knowledge

Part I

Chapter 1

A. Quality Principles

Since this is a book about software quality engineering, it would be appropriate to start with a definition of *quality*. However, the industry has not, and may never, come to a single definition of the term *quality*. For example, the ISO/IEC *Systems and Software Engineering—Vocabulary* (ISO/IEC 2009) has the following set of definitions for quality:

1. The degree to which a system, component, or process meets specified requirements

2. Ability of a product, service, system, component, or process to meet customer or user needs, expectations, or requirements

3. The totality of characteristics of an entity that bear on its ability to satisfy stated and implied needs

4. Conformity to user expectations, conformity to user requirements, customer satisfaction, reliability, and level of defects present

5. The degree to which a set of inherent characteristics fulfills requirements.

Based on his studies of how quality is perceived in various domains (for example, philosophy, economics, marketing, operations management), Garvin (Schulmeyer 1998) concluded, "Quality is a complex and multifaceted concept." Garvin describes quality from five different perspectives:

- *Transcendental perspective.* Quality is something that can be recognized but not defined. As stated by Kan (2003), "to many people, quality is similar to what a federal judge once said about obscenity: 'I know it when I see it.'" This perspective of quality takes the viewpoint of the individual into consideration. What is "obscenity" to one person may be "art" to another. What one customer considers good software quality may not be high enough quality for another customer. Tom Peters cites the customer's reaction as the only appropriate measure for the quality of a product. This requires that product developers keep in touch with their customers to ensure that their specifications accurately reflect the customer's real (and possibly changing) needs.

- *Manufacturing perspective.* Philip Crosby defines quality in terms of conformance to the specification. His point is that an organization does not want a variety of people throughout the development of a product trying to make judgments about what the customer needs or wants. A well-written specification is the cornerstone for creating a quality product. For software, however, this perspective of quality may not be sufficient since according to Wiegers (2003), errors made during the requirements stage account for 40 percent to 60 percent of all defects found in a software project. From another viewpoint, this perspective refers to the ability to manufacture (replicate) a product to that specification over and over within accepted tolerances. W. Edwards Deming talks about quality needing "precision of effort." Before an organization adjusts its processes to improve them, it must let them run long enough to understand what is really being produced. Then it needs to design its specifications to reflect the real process capabilities. While the primary focus of software quality is on the design and development activities, this manufacturing and "precision of effort" quality perspective reminds software organizations that the replication process can not be completely ignored.

- *User perspective.* Joseph M. Juran cites fitness for use as the appropriate measure for quality. Software practitioners can all probably relate stories of software products that conformed to their specifications but did not function adequately when deployed into operations. This perspective of quality not only considers the viewpoints of the individual users but their context of use as well. For example, what a novice user might consider a "quality" user interface might drive a power user to distraction with pop-up help and warning messages that require responses. What is a secure-enough interface for a software database used for personal information at home might be woefully inadequate in a business environment.

- *Product perspective.* Quality is tied to inherent characteristics of the product. These characteristics are the quality attributes, also called the "ilities" of the software product. Examples include reliability, usability, availability, flexibility, maintainability, portability, installability, and adaptability. Of course they don't all end in "ility." Functionality, correctness, fault tolerance, integrity, efficiency, security, and safety are also examples of quality attributes. The more the software has high levels of these characteristics, the higher its quality is considered to be. The ISO/IEC 25000 *Software Engineering—Software Product Quality Requirements and Evaluation* (SQuaRE) standard series (transition from the previous ISO/IEC 9126 and 14598 series of standards) provides a reference model and definitions for external and internal quality attributes and quality-in-use attributes. This standards series also provides guidance for specifying requirements, planning and managing, measuring, and evaluating quality attributes.

- *Value-based perspective.* Quality is dependent on the amount a customer is willing to pay for it. This perspective leads to considerations of "good enough" software quality. Are people willing to pay as much for high-quality video game software as they are for high-quality software in biomedical devices or the high-quality software for airplane navigation systems?

1. BENEFITS OF SOFTWARE QUALITY

> Describe the benefits that software quality engineering can have at the organizational level. (Understand)
>
> **Body of Knowledge I.A.1**

At its most basic, increasing the quality of the software typically means reducing the number of *defects* in the software. Defects can result from *mistakes* that occurred during the development process that introduced *faults* into the software work products. Defects can also be missing, ambiguous, or incorrect requirements that result in the development of software that does not match the needs of its stakeholders. The most cost-effective way of handling a defect is to prevent it. In this case, software quality is accomplished through process improvement, increasing staff knowledge and skill, and through other defect prevention techniques that keep defects out of the software. Every defect that is prevented eliminates *rework* to correct that defect and the effort associated with that rework.

If a defect does get interjected into the software, the shorter the period of time between when that defect is introduced and when it is identified and corrected, the less rework effort is typically required to correct that defect. Eliminating the waste of rework allows organizations to use the saved effort hours to produce additional value-added software. In this case, software quality is accomplished through techniques that improve defect detection techniques and find the defects earlier. Both defect prevention and detection help keep software defects from being delivered into operations.

The elimination or reduction of rework can also be used to shorten the cycle time required to produce a software product, and it can directly translate into reductions in costs. For example, as illustrated in Figure 1.1, when using traditional software development methods, if a requirements defect is found during the requirements phase and it costs one unit to fix (for example, three engineering hours of effort, or $500), that same defect will typically increase exponentially in cost to fix as it is found later and later in the life cycle. In fact, studies show that it can cost 100-plus times more to fix a requirements defect if it is not found until after the software is released into operations. The main point here is that the development of software is a series of dependencies, where each subsequent step

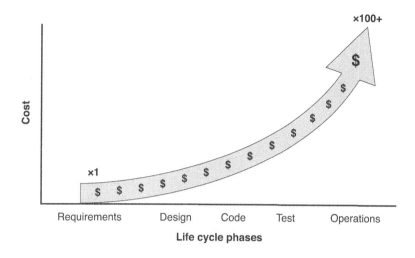

Figure 1.1   Cost of fixing defects.

builds on and expands the products of the previous step. For example, a single requirement could result in four design elements that expand into seven code units. All of these have supporting documentation and/or tests. A defect that is prevented or found early keeps the entire tree from needing to be backtracked, investigated, and potentially reworked. Agile methods specifically attack these costs by significantly shortening the development cycle using incremental development and through other techniques that shorten defect interjection to correction cycle times.

If fewer software defects are delivered into operations, there is a higher probability of failure-free operations. Unlike hardware, software does not wear out with time. If a defect is not encountered during operations, the software performs reliably. Reliable software can increase the effectiveness and efficiency of work being done using that software. Reliable software reduces both failure and maintenance costs to the software's customers and thus reduces the overall cost of ownership of the software product.

Taking a broader view, high-quality software is software that has been specified correctly and that meets its specification. If the software meets the stakeholder's needs and expectations and is value-added, it is more likely to be used instead of ending up as "shelfware."

If the customers and users receive software that has fewer defects, that is more reliable, and that performs to their needs and expectations, then those customers and users will be more satisfied with the software. This is illustrated in Figure 1.2, which depicts Noritaki Kano's model of the relationship between customer satisfaction and quality.

- *Basic quality.* There is a basic level of quality that a customer expects the product to have. These are quality requirements that are assumed by the customer and are typically not explicitly stated or requested. For example,

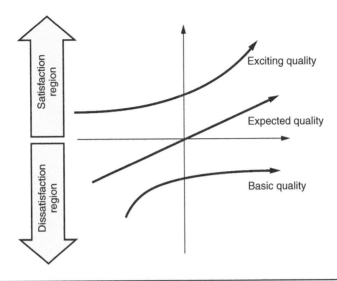

Figure 1.2 Kano model.

customers expect a car to have four tires, a windshield, windshield wipers, and a steering wheel. They will not ask for these items when purchasing a new car, but they expect them to be there. This level of quality does not satisfy the customer. (Note that the entire "basic quality" line is in the dissatisfaction region.) However, absence of quality at this level will quickly increase a customer's dissatisfaction.

- *Expected quality.* The "expected quality" line on the graph in Figure 1.2 represents those quality requirements that the customer explicitly considers and requests. For example, they will state their preferences for the make, model, and options when shopping for a car. The customer will be dissatisfied if this level of quality is not met and increasingly satisfied as this quality level increases.

- *Exciting quality.* This is the innovative quality level and represents unexpected quality items. These are items that the customer doesn't even know they want, but they will love them when they see them, for example, when cup holders were introduced in cars. Note that the entire "exciting quality" line is in the satisfaction region. It should be remembered, however, that today's innovations are tomorrow's expectations. If fact, most customers now consider a cup holder as part of the basic requirements for a car.

An increase in the quality of the software can also increase the satisfaction of the software practitioners. For most software engineers, their favorite activity is not burning the midnight oil trying to debug critical problems reported from operations. By producing a high-quality product, engineers can also take pride in what they are doing, which increases their satisfaction.

2. ORGANIZATIONAL AND PROCESS BENCHMARKING

> Use benchmarking at the organizational, process, and project levels to identify and implement best practices. (Apply)
>
> **Body of Knowledge I.A.2**

Benchmarking is the process used by an organization to identify, understand, adapt, and adopt outstanding practices and processes from others, anywhere in the world, to help that organization improve the performance of its processes, projects, products, and/or services. Benchmarking can provide management with the assurance that quality and improvement goals and objectives are aligned with best-in-class practices of other organizations. At the same time it helps ensure that those goals and objectives are obtainable because others have obtained them. The use of benchmarking can help an organization "think outside the box," and can result in breakthrough improvements.

Figure 1.3 illustrates the steps in the benchmarking process. The first step is to determine what to benchmark, that is, which process, project, product, or services the organization wants to analyze and improve. This step involves assessing the effectiveness and efficiencies, strengths, and weaknesses of the organization's current practices, identifying areas that require improvement, prioritizing those areas, and selecting the area to benchmark first. *The Certified Manager of Quality/ Organizational Excellence Handbook* (Westcott 2006) says, "examples of how to select what to benchmark include systems, processes, or practices that:

- Incur the highest costs

- Have a major impact on customer satisfaction, quality, or cycle time

- Strategically impact the business

- Have the potential of high impact on competitive position in the marketplace

- Present the most significant area for improvement

- Have the highest probability of support and resources if selected for improvement"

The second step in the benchmarking process is to establish the infrastructure for doing the benchmarking study. This includes identifying a sponsor to provide necessary resources and championship for the benchmarking activities within the organization. This also includes identifying the members of the benchmarking team who will actually perform the benchmarking activities. Members of this team should include individuals who are knowledgeable and involved in the area being benchmarked, and others who are familiar with benchmarking practices.

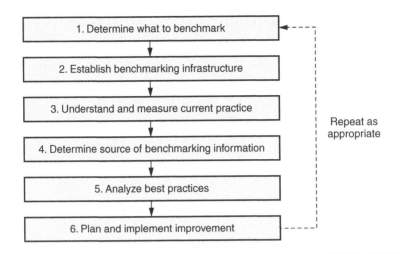

Figure 1.3   Steps in the benchmarking process.

In order to do an accurate comparison, the benchmarking team must obtain a thorough, in-depth understanding of current practice in the selected area. Key performance factors for the current practice are identified, and the current values of those key factors are measured during this third step in the benchmarking process. Current practices are studied, mapped as necessary, and analyzed.

The fourth step is to determine the source of benchmarking best-practice information. A search and analysis is performed to determine the best-practice leaders in the selected area of study. There are several choices that can be considered:

- *Internal benchmarking*. Looks at other teams, projects, functional areas, or departments within the organization for best-practice information.

- *Competitive benchmarking*. Looks at direct competitors, either locally or internationally, for best-practice information. This information may be harder to obtain than internal information, but industry standards, trade journals, competitor's marketing materials, and other sources can provide useful data.

- *Functional benchmarking*. Looks at other organizations performing the same functions or practices but outside the same industry. For example, an information technology (IT) team might look for best practices in other IT organizations in other industries. IEEE and ISO standards and the Software Engineering Institute's Capability Maturity Model Integration (CMMI) for Development are likely sources of information in addition to talking directly to individual organizations.

- *Generic benchmarking*. Looks outside the box. For example, an organization that wants to improve on-time delivery practices might look to FedEx, or an organization that wants to improve just-in-time, lean inventory practices might look to Wal-Mart or Toyota, even if the organization is not in the shipping, retail, or automotive arena.

In the fifth step of the benchmarking process, the best-practices information is gathered and analyzed. There are many mechanisms for performing this step including site visits to targeted benchmark organizations, partnerships where the benchmark organization provides coaching and mentoring, research studies of industry standards or literature, evaluations of best-practice databases, Internet searches, attending trade shows, hiring consultants, customer surveys, and other activities. The objective of this study is to:

- Collect information and data on the performance of the identified benchmark leader and/or on best practices

- Evaluate and compare the organization's current practices with the benchmark information and data

- Identify performance gaps between the organization's current practices and the benchmark information and data in order to identify areas for potential improvement and lessons learned

This comparative analysis is used to determine where the benchmark is better and by how much. The analysis then determines why the benchmark is better. What specific practices, actions, or methods result in the superior performance?

For benchmarking to be useful, the lessons learned from the best-practice analysis must be used to improve the organization's current practices. This final step in the benchmarking process involves:

- Obtaining management buy-in and acceptance of the findings from the benchmarking study.

- Incorporating the benchmarking findings into business analysis and decision making.

- Creating a plan of specific actions and assignments to adapt (tailor) and adopt the identified best practices to fill the performance gaps.

- Piloting those improvement actions and measuring the results against the initial values of identified key factors to monitor the effectiveness of the improvement activities.

- For successful improvement activities, propagating those improvements throughout the organization. For unsuccessful pilots or propagations, appropriate corrective action must be taken.

Once the selected area has been successfully improved, lessons learned from the benchmarking activities should be leveraged into the improvement of future benchmarking activities. The benchmarking process can also be repeated to consider improvements for other areas from the prioritized list created in the first step of the benchmarking process, and of course this prioritized list should be updated as additional information is obtained over time. Benchmarking must be a continuous process that not only looks at current performance but also continues to monitor key performance indicators into the future as industry practices change and improve.

Chapter 2

B. Ethical and Legal Compliance

The author of this book is not an ethicist or lawyer, nor has she received any legal training. All ethical and legal issues and risks that arise within an organization, on any software project or with any contract, should be referred to a lawyer or other legal professional. The descriptions below should be used as general information and summaries for no other purpose than as refresher materials for the ASQ Certified Software Quality Engineer (CSQE) exam.

1. ASQ CODE OF ETHICS

> Determine appropriate behavior in situations requiring ethical decisions, including identifying conflicts of interest, recognizing and resolving ethical issues, etc. (Evaluate)
>
> **Body of Knowledge I.B.1**

ASQ requires its members and certification holders to comply with the ASQ Code of Ethics. The ASQ Code of Ethics documents and communicates the behaviors that ASQ considers to be acceptable for quality professionals. It is intended to define the general principles and specific actions that quality professionals should employ during their interactions with the public, employers and clients, and peers in order to ensure ethical behavior.

Quality professionals can also use the ASQ Code of Ethics as a model to help their own organizations define acceptable and ethical behaviors. This is important so that people in the organization know and understand what is expected of them when ethical issues arise.

Conflicts of Interest

A *conflict of interest* occurs when an individual in a position of trust, like a quality professional, has competing professional or personal interests that may make

---

ASQ Code of Ethics

Fundamental Principles

ASQ requires its members and certification holders to conduct themselves ethically by:

   I. Being honest and impartial in serving the public, their employers, customers, and clients

   II. Striving to increase the competence and prestige of the quality profession, and

   III. Using their knowledge and skill for the enhancement of human welfare

Members and certification holders are required to observe the tenets set forth below:

Relations with the Public

Article 1—Hold paramount the safety, health, and welfare of the public in the performance of their professional duties.

Relations with Employers and Clients

Article 2—Perform services only in their areas of competence.

Article 3—Continue their professional development throughout their careers and provide opportunities for the professional and ethical development of others.

Article 4—Act in a professional manner in dealings with ASQ staff and each employer, customer, or client.

Article 5—Act as faithful agents or trustees and avoid conflict of interest and the appearance of conflicts of interest.

Relations with Peers

Article 6—Build their professional reputation on the merit of their services and not compete unfairly with others.

Article 7—Assure that credit for the work of others is given to those to whom it is due.

---

it difficult for that individual to perform his/her duties in an impartial or unbiased manner. A conflict of interest exists when a quality professional is in a position that can be exploited in some way for personal gain. A conflict of interest can create the appearance of unethical behavior, even if no unethical behavior results from that conflict. Examples where conflicts of interest can occur include:

- Previous employment, regardless of reason for separation
- Multiple jobs or clients where the interests of one job or client conflict with another's
- Holding a significant amount of stocks or bonds
- Previous or current close working relationship
- Desire to be hired
- Close friendship or family tie

- Offer of money, goods, or services in the nature of a bribe, kickback, or secret commission

- Acceptance of gifts

As stated in Article 5 of the ASQ Code of Ethics, the best way to mitigate conflicts of interest is to *"avoid conflict of interest and the appearance of conflicts of interest."* There are cases, however, where this may not be possible. In these cases, the quality professional can also mitigate the conflict of interest through disclosing the actual or potential conflicts of interest to all parties so that informed decisions can be made about how to proceed.

2. LEGAL AND REGULATORY ISSUES

> Define and describe the impact that issues such as copyright, intellectual property rights, product liability, data privacy, the Sarbanes-Oxley Act, etc., can have on software development. (Understand)
>
> **Body of Knowledge I.B.2**

Contracts

Contracts are agreements that are legally binding. To be legally binding, the promises made in the contract must be exchanged for appropriate consideration. In other words, there has to be something of value received by both parties. If a legal contract is breached, the parties to the contract can seek legal remedies. When selecting the type of contract to be used, consideration should be given to minimizing the risks for both parties and to motivating the suppliers to perform optimally. There are many different contract types, including fixed-price, cost-reimbursement, incentive-based, time and materials, and indefinite-delivery contracts.

Intellectual Property Rights

Intellectual property is a legal area that includes inventions and ideas of the human mind, such as books, music, artwork, and software. Intellectual property rights give the creators of these works exclusive rights to their creations. Software intellectual property rights deal with legal issues involving the copyrighting, patenting, and licensing of software products, as well as trademarks.

According to Futrell, et al. (2002), "*Patents* protect ideas and are exclusive rights for novel inventions for a limited period of time." A patent owner has the right to exclude others from manufacturing, selling, or using products that are based on the patented idea or underlying concept for a specific period of time after the patent is issued.

Copyrights protect original written works, such as software, from being copied without permission. Owning a copyright on a software product means that the owners are protected under the law from other people copying, distributing, or making adaptations to their software products without their permission. Unlike a patent, a copyright does not protect the underlying idea or concept but only protects the tangible expression of that idea or concept. Fair use is a defense to copyright infringement. Most software in the United States is sold under a licensing agreement rather than just depending on copyrights for protection. Other countries also have copyright laws that are applied to software.

A typical software *license* grants the license holder the right to either use or redistribute one or more copies of copyrighted software without breaking copyright law. Proprietary software licenses grant limited rights to the end user to use of one or more copies of the software while the ownership of that software remains with the software development organization. Typically, proprietary software licenses have a well-defined list of restrictions on what the end users can do with the software. The end user is required to accept the terms of the proprietary software license in order to use the software. In contrast, the ownership of the specific copy of the software is transferred to the end user with an open source license. However, the copyright ownership remains with the software developer. The end user may use the software without accepting the open source license, or the end user can optionally accept the license, in which case the end user is typically granted additional privileges.

Trademarks are devices that are used to "brand" products or services and distinguish them from other similar products or services in the marketplace. Examples of trademarks can include words, names, slogans, logos, symbols, and even sounds or colors. A service mark is similar to a trademark except that it identifies and distinguishes a service rather than a product. In the United States (U.S.), the symbols "TM" for trademark and "SM" for service mark can be used "as soon as one intends to make a claim to the public as to the exclusive right to use a mark" (Vienneau 2008). However, there is a formal process for registering trademarks and service marks with the U.S. federal government if additional protection is desired. An example of a software trademark is the Software Engineering Institute's (SEI's) Capability Maturity Model Integration (CMMI®), where the "®" symbol identifies it as a U.S. registered trademark.

Tort

Black's Law Dictionary (Futrell 2002) defines a *tort* as "a wrongful act other than a breach of contract that injures another and for which the law imposes civil liabilities." There are five types of tort lawsuits that might be applied to software:

1. *Conversion.* Conversion is involved if the software was intentionally designed to steal from the customer or destroy property. Conversion only involves tangible personal property. For example, conversion might apply if the software was intentionally designed to round transactions downward to the nearest penny and then deposit the fractions of a penny into someone's personal bank account.

2. *Negligence.* If the developer of a software system failed to take steps that a reasonable software developer would take, and because of this failure the software caused personal injury or property damage, that developer might be liable to damages under tort law. There are four aspects to any negligence lawsuit:

   • Duty to behave in a way that does not reduce public safety by creating an unreasonable risk of injury or property damage

   • Negligent breach of duty means that reasonable precautions were not taken to make sure that duty is satisfied

   • Causation means that the software had to cause the injury or property damage

   • Actual damages had to result from the negligence (the award may include compensatory damages to make up for the actual damages suffered, as well as punitive damages to punish the offending party)

3. *Strict product liability.* This type of tort lawsuit might be appropriate if the software caused injury or property damage because it is dangerously defective.

4. *Malpractice.* The software's author (or the program itself) provides unreasonably poor professional services. For example, if an accounting software application did not apply the generally accepted accounting principles (GAAP), or if an income tax package did not implement the tax laws.

5. *Fraud.* Fraud exists if the seller of the software knowingly misrepresented the capabilities of the product.

Data Privacy

Data privacy issues exist whenever personal information is collected, transmitted, and/or stored by the software. This personal information can include financial or credit information (including credit card information), medical records, personal identification information (for example, social security numbers or mailing addresses), lifestyle information (religion, organizational or political affiliations, sexual preferences), and so on. Data privacy also applies to encryption and how it applies to export, tort, and criminal laws. Privacy laws around the world vary greatly, so the software development team must be aware of the laws that apply to their product and market. The privacy risk is that this information will be revealed to or obtained by unauthorized parties. One of the intents of software security measures is to prevent unauthorized access to private information.

Sarbanes-Oxley Act

The *Sarbanes-Oxley Act*, also known as the Public Company Accounting Reform and Investor Protection Act of 2002, or SOX, is financial legislation that focuses on:

- Integrity in reporting of financial and other information

- Independence of auditors and board members

- Proper oversight of compliance by all levels of management

- Executive accountability

- Strong internal governance and control system

- Transparent operations

- Deterrents to discourage noncompliant and unacceptable behavior (Anand 2006)

Even though the Sarbanes-Oxley Act is financial regulation, the organization's information systems have a major role in recording, tracking, protecting, and reporting corporate data. These information systems need to implement processes and controls that facilitate compliance to the Sarbanes-Oxley Act.

Part I.B.2

Chapter 3

C. Standards and Models

> Define and describe the following standards
> and assessment models: ISO 9000 standards,
> IEEE software standards, and the SEI
> Capability Maturity Model Integration
> (CMMI). (Understand)
>
> **Body of Knowledge I.C**

The Software Engineering Institute (SEI) defines a *standard* as "the formal mandatory requirements developed and used to prescribe consistent approaches to development," (SEI 2006). A standard specifies a disciplined, consistent approach to software development and other activities through the specification of rules, requirements, guidelines, or characteristics. Standards aim at promoting optimum community or organizational benefit and should be based on the combined results of science, technology, and practical experience.

A standard is used as a basis for comparison (for example when specifying, developing, reviewing, auditing, assessing, or testing a system, process, or product). An organization and its people comply with standards—a comparison between what the standard says should be done and what people are actually doing. Products (including services) conform to standards—a comparison between what the standard requires and the actual characteristics or status of the product. A standard is usually specified by standard practice or is defined by a designated standards body (for example, ISO or IEEE). A standard can specify requirements for an item or activity, including:

- *Size.* For example, an external interface standard might specify a communication packet size of 32 bytes.

- *Content.* For example, the IEEE Standard for Project Management Plans (IEEE 1998) specifies the format and content of what should be in a software project management plan.

- *Value.* For example, an external interface standard might specify values for the communications packet size or values for error codes transmitted across that interface.

- *Quality*. For example, the ISO 9001 standard (ISO 2008) specifies the requirements for the effective implementation of a quality management system (QMS).

At the organizational level, software standards make it easier for professionals to move between projects and products within the organization and reduce the effort required for training. The fact that everyone involved knows and understands the standard way of developing and/or maintaining the software products permits a uniform method for reviewing the status of the product and the project.

At the industry level, standards can increase the professionalism of a discipline by providing access to good practices as defined by the experienced practitioners in the software industry. For example, many companies benchmark the ISO and IEEE standards as a basis for improving their processes and practices. Standards can also help introduce new technologies and methods into the software industry. For example, the Unified Modeling Language Standards from the Object Management Group (OMG) helped to introduce a consistent methodology for modeling object-oriented requirements and design across the software industry.

It should be noted that *guidelines* (guides) are different from standards. Both standards and guides are typically issued by some body of authority. However, standards define requirements while guides define suggested practices, advice, methods, or procedures that are considered good practice but are not mandatory.

Regulations are also different from standards. Regulations are rules or laws established by a legislative or regulatory body. Typically, there are penalties for nonconformance to regulations, which can include fines or even jail time for organizational officers.

A *model* is an abstract representation of an item or process from a particular point of view. A model expresses the essentials of some aspect of an item or process without giving unnecessary detail. The purpose of a model is to enable the people involved to think about and discuss these essential elements without getting sidetracked by excessive or complex details. Unlike standards, models are communication vehicles and not mandatory requirements. The SEI's Capability Maturity Model Integration (CMMI) for Development (SEI 2006) and life cycle models (for example, waterfall, V, or spiral) are examples of models.

ISO 9000 STANDARDS

The "International Organization for Standardization (ISO) is a worldwide federation of national standards bodies (ISO member bodies)" (ISO 2008). ISO developed the 9000 family of standards to define good practice in the area of quality management systems.

Within the ISO 9000 family, the ISO 9001 standard defines the specific set of quality management system requirements. ISO 9001 is the standard that organizations can be certified against. Figure 3.1 illustrates a model of the major clauses of ISO 9001:2008.

Other core standards in the ISO 9000 family include:

- ISO 9000:2005 *Quality management systems—Fundamentals and vocabulary*

- ISO 9004:2000 *Quality management systems—Guidelines for performance improvements*

- ISO 90002:2004 *Guidelines for the application of ISO 9001:2000 to computer software*

- ISO 19011:2002 *Guidelines for quality and/or environmental management systems auditing*

Other documents in the ISO 9000 family cover specific aspects of quality management including guidelines related to activities and areas such as customer satisfaction, quality planning, quality management in projects, configuration management, statistical techniques, measurement, training, and selecting consultants.

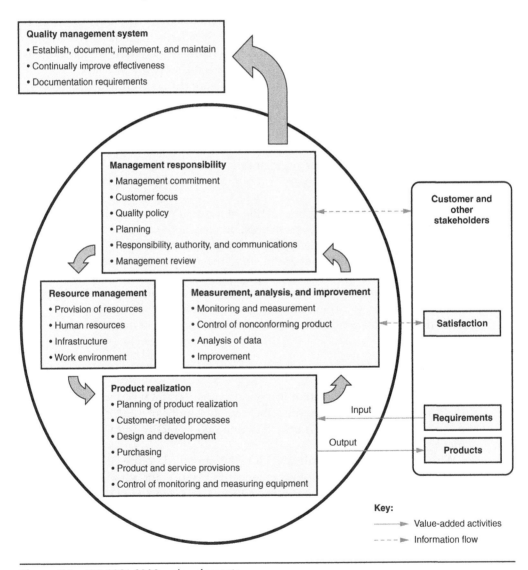

Figure 3.1   ISO 9001:2008 major elements.

IEEE SOFTWARE ENGINEERING STANDARDS

The Software and Systems Engineering Standards Committee of the IEEE Computer Society develops and maintains a set of software engineering standards that are available individually, as a set on CD, or through online subscription access. While many organizations don't use this IEEE standards set verbatim, they are used extensively as benchmarks, templates, and examples of industry good practices that organizations tailor to their own specific requirements. For organizations defining their software processes, these standards can provide guidance that minimizes time and effort. They can also serve as checklists that help ensure that important items are not overlooked. The ISO 9001 standard and the SEI's CMMI for Development provide road maps for what should occur in a good software engineering environment while the IEEE Software Engineering Standards provide more detailed "how-to" information and guidance. As of this publication, the current list of IEEE Software Engineering Standards includes (IEEE 2008):

- 730-2002 *Standard for Software Quality Assurance Plans*

- 828-2005 *Standard for Software Configuration Management Plans*

- 829-2008 *Standard for Software and System Test Documentation*

- 830-1998 *Recommended Practice for Software Requirements Specifications*

- 982.1-2005 *Standard Dictionary of Measures of the Software Aspect of Dependability*

- 1008-1987 (reaffirmed 2002) *Standard for Software Unit Testing*

- 1012-2004 *Standard for Software Verification and Validation*

- 1016-1998 *Recommended Practice for Software Design Descriptions*

- 1028-2008 *Standard for Software Reviews and Audits*

- 1044-1993 (reaffirmed 2002) *Standard Classification for Software Anomalies*

- 1058-1998 *Standard for Software Project Management Plans*

- 1061-1998 (reaffirmed 2004) *Standard for a Software Quality Metrics Methodology*

- 1062a-1998 (reaffirmed 2002) *Recommended Practice for Software Acquisition*

- 1063-2001 (reaffirmed 2007) *Standard for Software User Documentation*

- 1074-2006 *Standard for Developing Software Project Life Cycle Process*

- 1175.1-2002 *Guide for CASE Tool Interconnections—Classification and Description*

- 1175.2-2006 *Recommended Practice for CASE Tool Interconnections—Classification and Description*

- 1175.3-2004 *Standard for CASE Tool Interconnections—Reference Model for Specifying Software Behavior*

- 1220-2005 *Standard for the Application and Management of the Systems Engineering Process*

- 1228-1994 (reaffirmed 2002) *Standard for Software Safety Plans*

- 1233-1996 (reaffirmed 2002) *Guide for Developing System Requirements Specifications*

- 1320.1-1998 (reaffirmed 2004) *Standard for Functional Modeling Language Syntax and Semantics for IDEF0*

- 1320.2-1998 (reaffirmed 2004) *Standard for Conceptual Modeling Language Syntax and Semantics for IDEF1X97 (IDEFobject)*

- 1362-1998 (reaffirmed 2007) *Guide for Information Technology—System Definition—Concept of Operations (ConOps) Document*

- 1362a-1998 (reaffirmed 2007) *Guide for Information Technology—System Definition—Concept of Operations Document: Content Map for IEEE 12207:1*

- 1462-1998 (reaffirmed 2004) *Adoption of International Standard ISO/IEC 14102: 1995—Information Technology—Guideline for the Evaluation and Selection of CASE Tools*

- 1465-1998 (reaffirmed 2004) *Standard—Adoption of International Standard ISO/IEC 12119: 1994(E)—Information Technology—Software Packages Quality Requirements and Testing*

- 1471-2000 *Recommended Practice for Architectural Description of Software Intensive Systems*

- 1490-2003 *Guide Adoption of PMI Standard—A Guide to the Project Management Body of Knowledge*

- 1517-1999 (reaffirmed 2004) *Standard for Information Technology—Software Life Cycle Processes—Reuse Processes*

- 2001-2002 *Recommended Practice for Internet Practices—Web Site Engineering, Web Site Management and Web Site Life Cycle*

- 12207-2008 *Systems and Software Engineering—Software Life Cycle Processes*

- 12207.1-1997 *Guide for Information Technology—Software Life Cycle Processes—Life Cycle Data*

- 12207.2-1997 *Guide for Information Technology—Software Life Cycle Processes—Implementation Considerations*

- 14143.1-2000 (reaffirmed 2005) *ISO/IEC 14143-1:1998 Information Technology—Software Measurement—Functional Size Measurement—Part 1: Definition of Concepts*

- 14764-2006 *ISO/IEC 14764:2006 Standard for Software Engineering—Software Life Cycle Processes—Maintenance*

- 15288-2008 *Systems and Software Engineering—System Life Cycle Processes*

- 16085-2006 *ISO/IEC 16085:2006 Standard for Software Engineering—Software Life Cycle Processes—Risk Management*

SEI CAPABILITY MATURITY MODEL INTEGRATION (CMMI)

The SEI promotes the evolution of software engineering from an ad hoc, labor-intensive activity to a discipline that is well managed and supported by technology. According to the SEI Web site, principal areas of work for the SEI include:

- "Software engineering management practices: This work focuses on the ability of organizations to predict and control quality, schedule, cost, cycle time, and productivity when acquiring, building, or enhancing software systems."

- "Software engineering technical practices: This work focuses on the ability of software engineers to analyze, predict, and control selected properties of software systems. Work in this area involves the key choices and trade-offs that must be made when acquiring, building, or enhancing software systems."

The SEI's CMMI is intended to be a set of models for use by organizations pursuing enterprise-wide process improvement. The resulting CMMI framework allows for the generation of multiple CMMI models depending on the representation (staged or continuous) and the disciplines:

- Capability Maturity Model Integration (CMMI) for Development (SEI 2006).

- Capability Maturity Model Integration (CMMI) for Acquisition (SEI 2007).

- In addition there is a People Capability Maturity Model (P-CMM) (SEI 2002).

The staged representation SEI CMMI for Development is a five-level model that includes a four-level structure of best practices designed to be a road map to improving software quality and project performance. When most people talk about the CMMI it is typically the CMMI for Development model to which they are referring. Each level from 2 to 5 of the CMMI for Development is made up of process areas, with defined "objectives" that must be met to achieve that level of process maturity. These process areas are cumulative. For example, to achieve level 3 maturity, an organization must satisfy all of the process areas from level 2 and level 3.

As illustrated in Figure 3.2, each process area of the staged representation of the CMMI for Development includes one or more specific goals. In addition, the CMMI for Development has generic goals that are applicable to all process areas. A goal is a required component that must be achieved to consider the process area satisfied. Each goal of the staged representation CMMI for Development includes one or more practices. A practice is an expected component where each practice or

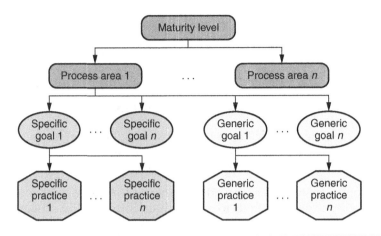

Figure 3.2 SEI CMMI for Development staged representation.

an equivalent alternative must be achieved to consider the process area satisfied. The SEI CMMI for Development staged representation levels and process areas are listed in Table 3.1.

The SEI CMMI for Development continuous representation provides a recommended order for approaching process improvement within each process area. As illustrated in Figure 3.3, instead of the entire organization achieving a maturity level, as in the staged representation, in the continuous representation each process area achieves an individual capability level ranging from level 0 to level 5 (SEI 2006). For example, an organization could have a level 4 capability in project planning, a level 3 capability in configuration management, and a level 1 capability in risk management. Capability levels include:

- *Level 0.* A process area has a level 0 capability if it is either not performed or only partially performed.

- *Level 1.* A process area has a level 1 capability if it satisfies all the level 1 goals and practices:

  - GP 1.1—Identify work scope

  - GP 1.2—Perform base practices: a performed process satisfies all the specific goals of the process area

- *Level 2.* A process area has a level 2 capability if it satisfies all the level 1 goals above and the level 2 goals and practices:

  - GP 2.1—Establish an organizational policy

  - GP 2.2—Plan the process

  - GP 2.3—Provide resources

  - GP 2.4—Assign responsibility

  - GP 2.5—Train people

Table 3.1 SEI CMMI for Development staged representation levels and process areas (SEI 2006).

Level	CMMI for Development staged representation—process areas
1	Initial
2	Repeatable: • Project planning • Configuration management • Project monitoring and control • Requirements management • Supplier agreement management • Measurement and analysis • Process and product quality assurance
3	Defined: • Organizational process focus • Requirements development • Organizational process definition • Technical solution • Organizational training • Product integration • Integrated project management • Risk management • Verification • Decision analysis and resolution • Validation
4	Quantitatively managed: • Organizational process performance • Quantitative project management
5	Optimizing: • Organizational innovation and • Causal analysis and resolution deployment

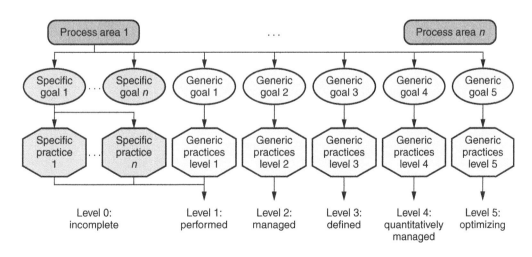

Figure 3.3 SEI CMMI for Development continuous representation.

  - GP 2.6—Manage configurations

  - GP 2.7—Identify and involve relevant stakeholders

  - GP 2.8—Monitor and control the process

  - GP 2.9—Objectively evaluate adherence

  - GP 2.10—Review status with higher-level management

- *Level 3.* A process area has a level 3 capability if it satisfies all the level 1 and 2 goals above and the level 3 goals and practices:

  - GP 3.1—Establish a defined process

  - GP 3.2—Collect improvement information

- *Level 4.* A process area has a level 4 capability if it satisfies all the level 1, 2, and 3 goals above and the level 4 goals and practices:

  - GP 4.1—Establish quality objectives

  - GP 4.2—Stabilize subprocess performance

- *Level 5.* A process area has a level 5 capability if it satisfies all the level 1, 2, 3, and 4 goals above and the level 5 goals and practices:

  - GP 5.1—Ensure continuous process improvement

  - GP 5.2—Correct common causes of problems

Chapter 4

D. Leadership Skills

Defining *leadership*, like defining quality, can be a challenge. Example definitions from the literature include:

- "Leadership is the process of influencing others to willingly work toward common, shared goals" (unknown).

- "Leadership is the privilege to have the responsibility to direct the actions of others in carrying out the purpose of the organization, at varying levels of authority and with accountability for both successful and failed endeavors" (Roberts 1987).

- "Leadership is the art of liberating people to do what is required of them in the most effective and humane way possible" (DePree 1989).

- "Leadership is the set of qualities that cause people to follow" (Loeb 1999).

- "Leadership focuses on doing the right things, management focuses on doing things right" (Covey in Westcott 2006).

Effective leaders have many qualities and characteristics that help them influence others to follow them. Some of these qualities and characteristics may include:

- *Vision.* Ability to create and nurture a vision, the ability to communicate that vision, and to inspire others to follow them toward the realization of that vision.

- *Courage.* Must not balk at the sight of obstacle, or fear failure; leaders must have the courage to act with confidence and take risks.

- *Decisiveness.* Ability to make decisions and know when to act and when not to act—postponing decisions can decrease project productivity and effectiveness.

- *Emotional stamina.* Ability to recover quickly from disappointment and bounce back from discouragement—the ability to laugh and be happy.

- *Empathy.* An appreciation for and understanding of the values and needs of others.

- *Self-confidence.* An assuredness with which the leader meets the inherent challenges of leadership—also the ability to expect and accept criticism.

- *Accountability.* Ability to accept responsibility for one's actions and the actions of the team.

- *Credibility.* The leader's actions and words must be trusted and believed.

- *Persistence.* Ability to stick to a task or project until it is completed.

- *Dependability.* Ability to meet commitments.

- *Stewardship.* Ability to coach, guide, and develop team members and effectively and efficiently utilize project resources.

- *Knowledge.* Ability to apply their knowledge about the business domain, the technical domain, management techniques, change management, and interpersonal skills to aid their followers in performing the tasks at hand.

- *Ability to learn.* A leader must also be a perpetual student, learning about new systems, processes, techniques, methods, tools, and other changes to the business and technical domains in which they work.

1. ORGANIZATIONAL LEADERSHIP

> Use leadership tools and techniques, such as organizational change management, knowledge-transfer, motivation, mentoring and coaching, recognition, etc. (Apply)
>
> **Body of Knowledge I.D.1**

Organizational Change Management

Organizational change management is the mechanism that organizations use to grow and improve in order to stay competitive. There are two major types of change. *Incremental change* improves the existing systems, processes, and/or products to make them better. For example, many incremental changes have improved the Model T into the modern car. *Evolutionary change* replaces the existing systems, processes, and/or products with better ones. For example, evolutionary change moved us from trains as the primary cross-country mode of transportation to airplanes.

During the first step in the change process, the organizational leaders must identify and communicate the underlying need for change so that the people involved in and impacted by the change will buy into the fact that the change is necessary. This creates a sense of urgency to make the change.

The next step is to initiate a change project and assemble a core team to lead the change effort. This includes identifying:

- *Official change agent.* An individual or team assigned the primary responsibility to plan and manage the change process.

- *Sponsor.* A senior leader/manager who has the position and authority to legitimize and champion the change. This individual ensures that resources and staff are assigned to accomplish the change.

- *Advocates.* People who see the need for the change and help sell it to the sponsor and to the organization. Look to the "early adopters" for potential advocates.

- *Informal change agents.* People other than the official change agent who will help plan, manage, and implement the change process (based on Pyzdek 2001).

This core team establishes and communicates a vision of what the organization, systems, processes, or products will look like after the change is implemented. This vision is the destination on the road map to change. The need for continuous and active communications throughout the change process can not be overemphasized. Change involves modifying the way people think and modifying the norms of the organization. "All change begins with the individual, at a personal level. Unless the individual is willing to change his behavior, no real change is possible" (Pyzdek 2001).

In order to change, people must be empowered to change. That means providing them with the resources, tools, knowledge, skills, and motivation they need in order to do things in a different way. To paraphrase Einstein, one definition of insanity is "doing things the way we have always done them and expecting the outcome to be different." To accomplish this, the change effort should be treated as a planned project. This includes creating a plan of small, short-term steps toward accomplishing the long-term goal (vision). Doing this has several advantages. First, the organization can see progress more easily and celebrate its successes. Secondly, the organization can learn from what has been accomplished and leverage these achievements into momentum toward future process improvement. During this effort, forces that enable the change and make it more likely to occur should be identified and leveraged. Forces that act as barriers to the change should also be identified, and proactive actions should be taken to remove or minimize the impacts of these barriers. Figure 4.1 illustrates a force field analysis diagram showing some of the forces that may drive an organization toward change and forces that may act as potential barriers to change.

The final step is to institutionalize the change within the organization. This requires changing organizational norms that guide people's behavior so that the change becomes "just the way business is conducted." This may involve changing standards, control systems, patterns of behavior, and reward systems.

The *Satir change model*, shown in Figure 4.2, illustrates the relationship between change and productivity. Within a certain level of variation, the existing way of doing things has a set level of productivity (old status quo). When change is first introduced, it causes a period of chaos in productivity where variation increases. Some individuals are trying the new way and being successful, others are not as successful. Assuming that the change was positive, a learning curve then occurs

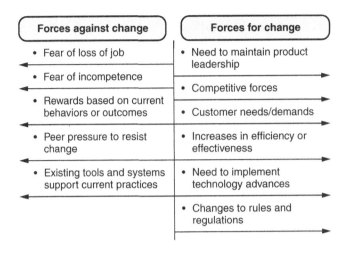

Figure 4.1   Change force field analysis.

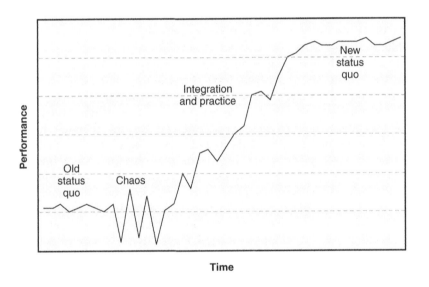

Figure 4.2   Satir change model (based on Weinberg [1997]).

where people learn the new ways of doing things. During this learning curve, productivity generally increases, and the amount of variation in productivity starts decreasing. Finally, a new status quo is reached when the change is institutionalized and productivity levels out at a new higher level.

Knowledge Transfer

Takeuchi (1995) talks about the transfer of two different types of knowledge, tacit knowledge and explicit knowledge. *Tacit knowledge* is gained through experience

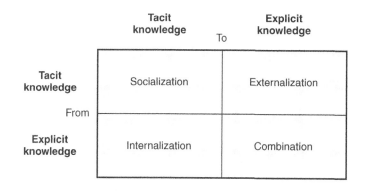

Figure 4.3   Knowledge transfer.
Source: H. Takeuchi and I. Nonaka, *The Knowledge Creating Company* (New York: Oxford University Press, 1995).

rather than through formal reading or education. This knowledge is learned by "being there," seeing, participating, and experiencing. Software development methods rely on the tacit knowledge gained by participating in the project and through on-the-job experience. *Explicit knowledge* is transmitted in a formal manner through various documents, artifacts, or books. As illustrated in Figure 4.3, different mechanisms are needed when transferring between these different types of knowledge.

Transferring tacit knowledge to tacit knowledge happens through socialization, the sharing of experience. For example, socialization occurs when an experienced member of the team explains coding standards to a new team member, or when two people pass knowledge back and forth about a code module during pair programming.

Transferring tacit knowledge to explicit knowledge happens through externalization, for example, when a business analyst documents the customer's requirements, or when a project formally documents its lessons learned.

Transferring from explicit knowledge to tacit knowledge happens through internalization, for example, when an individual reads a book on software testing and uses that knowledge to define a systematic set of test cases for a software system.

Transferring from explicit knowledge to explicit knowledge happens through combination. For example, the author of this book read multiple books and other references on software quality engineering and combined that information into this text.

Motivation, Recognition, and Rewards

According to Blohowiak (1992), "if people believe that what they are doing has meaning—that it makes a contribution, that someone appreciates it—then they are motivated." *Motivation* requires two key elements. First, for people to be motivated, they must have a clear understanding of what is expected of them. The second key element is that meeting that expectation (or not meeting it) must be reinforced.

Part I.D.1

There are two types of motivation. In *extrinsic motivation*, the reinforcement comes from the satisfaction of psychological or material needs by others through incentives or rewards. *Intrinsic motivation* is a self-motivating process where an individual obtains reinforcement through personally valuing characteristics of the situation itself. For example, in intrinsic motivation, the reinforcement might come from gaining a sense of achievement or power, feeling creative, feeling a sense of belonging, having the satisfaction of making a contribution, or from self-actualization.

Different types of extrinsic and intrinsic forces motivate different people. Therefore, "one size does not fit all" when it comes to using *recognition* and *rewards* as reinforcement. Examples of different types of recognition and rewards include:

- Public praise and appreciation

- Thank-you letters or notes

- Compliments from important people while receiving the undivided attention of those people

- Gifts and other tokens of appreciation

- Conference or training opportunities

- Teaching or mentoring opportunities

- Special project or time for pet projects

- Time away from work

- More independence or autonomy

- Money, promotions, better office

As illustrated in Figure 4.4, Maslow defined a hierarchy of needs that he believed prioritized the types of rewards that motivated people. For example, if people's basic physiological needs for food, water, air, and shelter are not met, they will be motivated to fulfill those needs first. People will put themselves in danger or

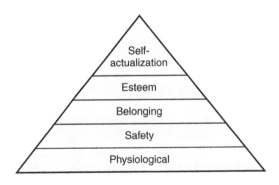

Figure 4.4   Maslow's hierarchy of needs.

leave their social groups if necessary to meet those basic physiological needs. At the next level, people need to feel physically and economically safe. Once physiological and safety needs are met, people will be motivated by the need to belong, to be accepted by family and friends. Higher-level needs include self-esteem and self-actualization (the need to perform at one's best and self-improve).

Westcott (2006), discusses three motivational theories specifically related to rewards:

- *Equity theory.* For rewards to be motivational, people have to believe that rewards (and punishments) are being equally distributed as desired. People seek equity between the amount of effort (input) they put into a task and the rewards (output) they receive for doing it. For example, if everyone on the team gets the same reward no matter how much or little they contributed, then those rewards can actually de-motivate team members.

- *Expectancy theory.* A person will be motivated to perform an activity based on his or her belief that:

  - Putting in the effort will actually lead to better results

  - The extra effort will be noticed and that those better results will actually lead to personal rewards

  - Those personal rewards are valuable

- *Reinforcement theory.* People will be motivated to perform an activity based on their perception of a trigger (a signal to initiate the behavior) and the historic consequences of that behavior.

Mentoring and Coaching

Mentoring is the act of more-experienced individuals forming relationships with less-experienced individuals in order to help those individuals develop or improve their skill sets, performance, knowledge, or other capabilities. According to the Software Engineering Institute's People Capability Maturity Model (P-CMM) (SEI 2002), "*coaching* is a form of mentoring that involves expert knowledge and skill in the subject matter being coached." Mentoring and coaching are all about people's performance and capabilities.

When mentoring to establish performance expectation, the mentor tells the individuals being mentored what to do and how to do it. The mentor describes the job in terms of major outcomes and how it aligns with higher-level goals and objectives. Measurable performance objectives and priorities are agreed to, and necessary skills, resources, and guidelines are mutually identified. The mentor reviews and verifies the understanding and commitments of the individuals being mentored. Dates are then set for early progress reviews. Mentoring is used to establish performance expectation when the mentored individuals:

- Are unclear about what is expected

- Need help sorting out priorities because they have taken on more than they can handle

- Are acting on inaccurate advice from coworkers about job procedures or standards

- Produce substandard work because they don't seem to fully understand what's expected

- Are exceeding expectation and need new challenges

When mentoring to transfer job skills, the mentor explains the why as well as the how of the job skill. The mentor shows the individuals being mentored how to do the work then lets the mentored individuals perform the work under the mentor's guidance. The mentored individuals then perform the work on their own, but the mentor stays available to answer questions if necessary. Mentoring is used to transfer job skills when the mentored individuals:

- Need help learning to do a new task or assignment

- Seem confused about how to do a job

- Resist taking on or doing a job because they don't have the right skills

- Ask to take on an assignment for which they are not adequately skilled

- Are seeking career paths or advancements that require new skills

Mentoring to improve job performance involves the mentor describing the performance issues and why corrective action is important. The mentor seeks the opinions of the individuals being mentored about the root cause of the performance issues and ways in which performance can be improved. The mentor provides feedback on those opinions and adds their own. The mentor and mentored individuals jointly create and commit to an action plan to improve performance, and set follow-up dates. The mentor expresses confidence and support in the mentored individuals' ability to correct the performance issue. Mentoring is used to improve job performance when the mentored individuals:

- Are not meeting performance expectation

- Are meeting expectation but want to continue to improve

- Are meeting expectation, but the mentor believes that more effective or efficient ways to perform the work exist

- Are faced with an important career opportunity

Situational Leadership

The concept behind *situational leadership* is that the style of leadership that is needed depends on the situation and the "readiness" of the followers to be led. As illustrated in Figure 4.5, the leadership style dictates the amount of relationship/supportive behaviors and the amount of task/directive behavior the leaders use in a given situation. Relationship/supportive behaviors include:

- Two-way or multi-way communications

- Listening

High relationship/supportive behavior

Participating style	Selling style
• Followers are able	• Followers are unable
• Followers are unwilling or insecure	• Followers are willing or confident
• Sharing ideas and facilitating in making decisions	• Explain decisions and provide opportunity for clarification
Delegating style	Directing style
• Followers are able	• Followers are unable
• Followers are willing or confident	• Followers lack confidence or motivation
• Turn over responsibility for decisions and implementation	• Provide specific instructions and closely supervise performance

(Left axis: Low task/directive behavior; Right axis: High task/directive behavior)

Low relationship/supportive behavior

Figure 4.5   Situational leadership styles (based on Hersey [1984]).

- Encouraging
- Facilitating/coaching
- Socio-emotional support

Task/directive behaviors include:

- One-way communications from leader to follower
- Spelling out of duties and responsibilities
- Telling people what to do
- Telling people how, when, where, and with whom to do it
- Telling people who is to do it

According to Hersey (1984), a directing leadership style, with high levels of task/directive behavior and low levels of relationship/supportive behaviors, should be used when the followers are unable to do the job and also lack the confidence to do it. For example, this directing style would be used for a new software practitioner fresh from the university who requires more supervision performing tasks like configuration management or requirements analysis if they are not trained in these skills. In the selling style of leadership, with high levels of both task/directive behaviors and relationship/supportive behaviors, decisions are explained and opportunities are provided to ask questions and clarify instructions. For example, the selling style would be used for newly training a tester who is trying to apply new skills but who does not understand the need to follow the steps in the prescribed test development process. The participating leadership style, with low levels of task/directive behaviors and high levels of relationship/

supportive behaviors, emphasizes the sharing of ideas and responsibilities and provides encouragement to the participants. For example, the participative style is appropriate when practitioners obtain the needed level of skills but are reluctant to take on total responsibility for the work because they feel unsure themselves. Finally, once practitioners are both able and willing to perform their work, the delegating style of leadership may be most appropriate, where responsibility for decisions and implementation is turned over to the practitioners. The self-organized teams used in scrum projects are examples of the delegating style of leadership.

2. FACILITATION SKILLS

> Use various approaches to manage and resolve conflict. Use negotiation techniques and identify possible outcomes. Use meeting management tools to maximize performance. (Apply)
>
> **Body of Knowledge I.D.2**

A *facilitator* is an individual who creates an environment in which a team can direct its own work. An effective facilitator structures the activities of the team and guides the team through its problem-solving activities. However, the team prioritizes issues, evaluates and judges the alternatives, makes the decisions, and solves the problems. The facilitator helps stimulate discussion, makes sure everyone is participating, asks questions, and helps clarify key points. An effective facilitator helps the team reflect, expand, and summarize its discussions, options, alternatives, and decisions. The facilitator does not spend most of the time leading the meeting or talking; in fact, if the team is performing effectively, the facilitator simply sits back and lets the team direct and control their own activities. However, the facilitator does watch closely just in case problems arise that need attention. For example, the facilitator keeps the team focused on the processes and problems and does not allow the team to focus on people and personalities. The facilitator never presents himself or herself as a subject matter expert—the team members are the experts. The only thing the facilitator is an expert on is the team tools that they may recommend to the team to help them solve a problem.

Conflict Management and Resolution

The traditional view of *conflict* is that it is caused by troublemakers and that it should be avoided or suppressed. The contemporary view of conflict is that it is inevitable and that it is often beneficial because it is necessary for creativity and innovation. However, conflict should be appropriately managed.

Positive conflict can be beneficial. Problems can not be fixed if the team is not aware that those problems exist. Sometimes it takes a conflict to bring problems to the forefront and make them visible. Discussing different points of view and digging down into the issues help create collaborative solutions that take the needs of a diverse set of stakeholders into consideration. Conflict can create insight and innovation through combining multiple conflicting solutions into a single, better-integrated solution. Managing positive conflict can help remove roadblocks to productivity by eliminating "brooding" and other negative feelings that sap motivation. Conflict creates incentives to challenge and change outmoded policies, methods, processes, and assignments. By making it all right to talk about and manage conflict instead of squelching it, people become aware of how behaviors and actions affect others so that they can correct or avoid similar behaviors in the future. Conflict resolution also increases interpersonal skills as people practice and become proficient at understanding the viewpoints of others in order to seek win–win outcomes. All creativity comes from conflict. If everything is good, there is no reason to do anything new or different. Discussion and problem solving help people release stress. Finding solutions to problems and getting them resolved also increases morale. When managed correctly, conflict can present a fun challenge and a break from the normal routine, for example, in a rousing debate or challenging competition.

The facilitator should watch for cues that there is too much conformity and not enough positive conflict, including:

- Most issues are decided with little or no discussion.

- Certain members of the team give opinions, others nod, and the decision is considered made.

- Instant and silent "agreement" with opinions of leader or other influential members.

- Controversial issues receive little or no open discussion—all sides of the controversy are not raised.

- Rejection of the minority opinion without consideration.

The facilitator should help the team take corrective action if too much conformity exists in the team. Steps to corrective action can include:

- Openly rewarding divergent points of view

- Asking outright for other points of view

- Encouraging conflict and controversy arising from opposing ideas and opinions

- Making sure the team stays focused on products and processes, not on personalities

- Protecting or giving equal weight to minority opinions

- Asking for opinions from silent team members

- Ensuring that power and influence are approximately equal

- Creating a devil's advocate role and valuing that role highly

- Having leaders hold their opinions until other team members have had an opportunity to be heard

On the other hand, managing conflict is a balancing act. Too much negative conflict can be damaging to the team synergy and inhibit the team's ability to accomplish its objectives. The facilitator should watch for cues that there is too much negative conflict, including:

- Team members start avoiding each other to the detriment of work progress.

- Team members withholding important information or resources from each other making it difficult to work effectively and efficiently.

- Emotions running high and unproductive tension between team members.

- Some team members show that they are unwilling to work together.

- Team members are complaining that their work is being adversely affected by conflict between other team members.

When faced with a conflict, it is easy to respond with emotion or instinct. Team members must learn to move to the logical, thinking part of their brains in order to handle the conflict productively. One way to recognize the potential signs of conflict before it erupts is to recognize "provocative" statements. This can help people avoid lighting the match when the others are presenting them with powder kegs. It can also help people avoid using the same types of statements in their own interactions. Examples of these provocative statements include (Bernstein 1990):

- "I just want to tell you my *real* feelings about . . ."

- "You always . . ."

- "You never . . ."

- "I checked with Joe and Mary, and we *all* feel . . ."

- "Why wasn't I consulted about . . .?"

- "How come some people are allowed to . . .?"

- "I thought I was in charge . . ."

- "In this company we do things a certain way . . ."

- "In the good old days . . ."

The facilitator should help the team take corrective action if too much negative conflict exists on the team. Steps to corrective action can include:

- Promptly letting the people involved know how their conflict is affecting performance

- Setting up a joint problem-solving approach to resolve the conflict

- Asking the people involved to present their viewpoints objectively

- Searching for areas of agreement and common goals

- Getting agreement on the problem that needs to be solved

- Refocusing the team members on process and product issues and away from personalities

- Having each person involved in the conflict generate possible solutions

- Getting commitment on what each person will do to solve the problem

- Summarizing and setting a follow-up date to make sure the conflict has been resolved

Negotiation Techniques

Negotiation involves two or more parties who each have something the other wants reaching a mutually acceptable agreement through a process of bargaining. People do lots of negotiation in their business lives as well as their personal lives. For example, on the job:

- Salaries and benefits are negotiated between organizations and employees.

- Requirements, prices, and schedules are negotiated between customers and suppliers.

- Job assignments, priorities, and deliverables are negotiated between project managers and project team members and/or functional managers.

One of the keys to successful negotiation is to realize that each party to the negotiation must give in order to receive. Each party must also gain something of value to them in compensation for any concessions that they make.

Core skills required for a successful negotiation include the ability to:

- Prepare well

- Define a range of objectives and prioritize them clearly

- Remain flexible

- Identify the other person's needs

- Separate people from the process

- Explore a wide range of options

- Focus on common interests

- Communicate (listening, questioning, verbal communication)

Figure 4.6 illustrates the basic steps in the formal negotiation process. During the preparation step of negotiation, objectives for the negotiation are established and prioritized. This includes establishing ideal objectives (if the negotiators could get everything they want, what would it look like), realistic objectives (what the negotiators expect to be able to get), and minimum objectives (the minimum the negotiators will accept without walking away). Preparing also includes doing research to obtain as much advance information as possible to help the negotiators

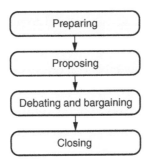

Figure 4.6 Formal negotiation process.

understand the people they are negotiating with and their needs. Using their objectives and the gathered information, the negotiators can then plan and prepare a strategy for what they believe to be the possible paths the negotiation might take.

The negotiators should begin the actual negotiation session with uncontroversial, general points and stress the need for agreement from the outset. Depending on who presents the initial proposal:

- If the negotiators make the initial proposal, they should start with their ideal objectives and leave themselves room to maneuver and not give away everything up front.

- If the other party makes the initial proposal, the negotiators need to listen carefully; they may be closer to agreement than they think.

The negotiators should wait for the other party to finish before responding. The debating and bargaining step then begins with asking clarifying questions as necessary—the more information the negotiators have, the better job they can do in negotiations. It may also be a good idea to summarize the other party's proposal—"what I understand you to be asking for is . . ."—in order to verify understanding. The negotiators should look for similarities in their negotiating positions as starting points to build agreement. They should then look for areas where they can counteroffer by trading-off their low-priority objectives that match up with what are higher priorities to the other party in exchange for receiving their high-priority objectives. The negotiators should not concede one of their objectives without receiving something in return.

The negotiation closes with the documentation of a written record of the final agreement, including definitions of any words that may be ambiguous. If the negotiators can not come to a mutually beneficial agreement, then everyone just walks away.

Meeting Management

For a meeting to be productive, the facilitator should determine specific objectives for the meeting. The meeting objectives are basically the requirements statement for the meeting. Why is the team holding a meeting? What is the purpose? What is the expected outcome? As a checkpoint, the meeting planner should always determine if there is a better way to accomplish these objectives other than holding a meeting.

Once the objectives are established, the facilitator must plan how the team is going to accomplish those objectives during the meeting. This is the design stage for the meeting. Who needs to be at the meeting in order to accomplish the objectives? Who should not be at the meeting? What methods or tools are going to be used during the meeting? An agenda is then created that outlines the meeting plan and assigns specific responsibilities for each section of the meeting. The facilitator needs to make sure that the meeting logistics are handled in advance as well. This includes deciding where and when to hold the meeting and making reservations for the meeting room. It also means handling any special logistical arrangements. For example, arranging for equipment (flip charts, projectors), making copies of materials needed in the meeting, or ordering special meeting supplies. Finally, the meeting objective and agenda need to be distributed to the meeting attendees. If there are any instructions for preparing for the meeting or any materials that need to be reviewed before the meeting or brought to the meeting, these requirements need to be made clear to the attendees.

When starting a productive meeting, the facilitator should arrive early for the meeting and make sure that everything is set up as required, for example, checking to ensure that any equipment is in working order. Arriving early also gives the facilitator the opportunity to select an appropriate position in the room from which to run the meeting. If the facilitator wants to take control of the meeting and direct it, an authority position at the head of the table should be selected. If the facilitator wants to join the group in an open discussion, a seat in the middle of the table should be selected.

The facilitator should establish a reputation as someone who starts meetings on time. Don't waste the team's time reviewing for latecomers. Ask them to stay after the meeting, and review with them then. The objective is to get people in the habit of coming to meetings on time.

The meeting itself should start with reviewing and confirming the meeting's objectives and expected outcomes, followed by a review of the meeting's agenda. This will help focus the team on the meeting's goals and how those goals are going to be accomplished. It is also a good idea to review any ground rules for the meeting if problems have occurred in prior meetings. The facilitator should confirm with the participants that all required preparation has been accomplished. This may require postponing the meeting until a later date if key preparation has not been accomplished.

During the meeting, the facilitator should help the team stick to the agenda and ensure that everyone is participating. Using a "parking lot" to record off-topic ideas or items for later discussion can aid the team in staying focused on the meeting objectives. A record (meeting minutes) should also be kept during the meeting to document important information, action items, and decisions.

At the end of the meeting, the list of action items should be reviewed to ensure that they have been adequately captured and assigned. The facilitator should help the team summarize its accomplishments and evaluate the meeting. The next meeting should also be planned as necessary. Productive meetings also end on or before schedule. If all of the objectives have not been met, follow-up meetings can be scheduled.

After the meeting, the meeting record (meeting minutes) should be completed and distributed. As appropriate, that record should also be archived as a quality record. The facilitator should follow up with team members that are assigned to action items to ensure that those items are being addressed. The facilitator then starts the meeting planning process over again for the next meeting.

3. COMMUNICATION SKILLS

> Use various communication elements (e.g., interviewing and listening skills) in oral, written, and presentation formats. Use various techniques for working in multi-cultural environments, and identify and describe the impact that culture and communications can have on quality. (Apply)
>
> **Body of Knowledge I.D.3**

Software practitioners spend a large portion of their time working with and communicating with other individuals. Strong *communications* skills are needed to ensure that these interactions are effective.

One-way communication occurs when the sender of a message communicates that message to the receiver without obtaining feedback. Examples of one-way communications include speeches and written documents. Figure 4.7 illustrates a one-way communication model. In one-way communications, the sender has a message they want to convey. This message is encoded using the sender's filters. These filters include the sender's:

- Paradigms about how things are (the way the sender sees the world)

- Experiences and vocabulary about the specific subject of the message

- Feelings and emotions about the receiver of the message, about the subject, and about life in general at the time the message is being encoded

The sender's encoded message is then interpreted through the receiver's filters. Because of these filters, what the receiver thinks the message is may be very different than what the sender actually intended to communicate.

Two-way communication occurs when the sender of a message communicates that message to the receiver and obtains feedback. Examples of two-way communications include discussions and interviews. Figure 4.8 illustrates a two-way communication model. The first half of the two-way communication model is identical to the one-way communication model. However, the two-way model includes the receiver providing feedback that is encoded through the receiver's filters and interpreted through the sender's filters (which includes their belief about what the content of the original message was).

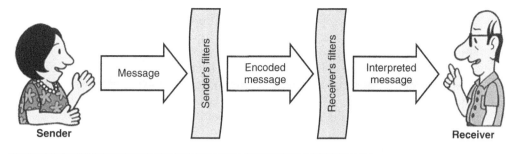

Figure 4.7   One-way communication model.

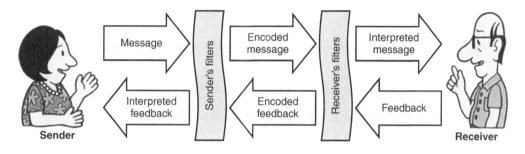

Figure 4.8   Two-way communication model.

Typically, message problems include:

- The message was misinterpreted

- The message was considered unimportant and was ignored

- The message arrived too late to be effective

- The message ended up in the hands (or ears) of the wrong person (Baker 1998)

Does this sound familiar? The manager gives detailed instructions to an employee. The manager asks, "Do you have any questions?" and the employee responds, "No." The manager asks, "Do you understand what needs to be done?" and the employee responds, "Yes." Later, the manager finds out that the employee has done something completely different than the manager intended. Whose fault is it?—the answer is, the manager's. Lewis (1995) says, "the responsibility for communications rests with the communicator—not the other person." In this case the manager did not obtain adequate feedback to ensure that their instructions were correctly interpreted. The manager should have asked open-ended questions and/or had the employee restate or summarize the instructions in their own words to ensure successful communications. If a message is misinterpreted, it may mean that the tone, word choice, medium, or timing (or any combination of these) used to convey the message were deficient. It may also mean that the sender's and receiver's filters were different enough to cause communications to break down, in which case the sender may need to try a different approach to ensure that their message is received, for example, get a third party to act as an interpreter. An interpreter may be necessary even if both parties to the communications speak the same language, but are using very different vocabularies. For example, a business analyst may act as an interpreter to facilitate communications between the customer who is speaking in the vocabulary of the business domain and the software engineer who is speaking in the vocabulary of the technical domain.

Oral Communication

Table 4.1 lists examples of various types of oral communications and the advantages and disadvantages of each type.

Table 4.1   Oral communication techniques.

Informal verbal interchanges—quality by walking around	
Advantages	**Disadvantages**
• Great way to see the action and keep in touch with what is happening • Immediate feedback on current problems • Can discuss wide range of topics in detail • Two-way communications	• Might be perceived as nosy if quality engineers are not genuine in their interest or if they visit too often • Can be disruptive • No permanent record • If unfocused, can waste time
Formal meetings	
Advantages	**Disadvantages**
• Allows multiple people to express opinions and issues • Creates team synergy • Can discuss wide range of topics and issues in detail • Two-way communications	• Can degrade into time-wasters • Some people may feel uncomfortable offering opinions in public • All topics may not be relevant to all people, or needed people may be missing from meeting • Difficult when people are at remote locations (solution—teleconferencing)
Telephone calls	
Advantages	**Disadvantages**
• Good for short, focused communications that need personal touch • Easy to reach people in remote locations • Two-way communications	• Phone tag • Disruptive to receiver • No permanent record • Loss of nonverbal communications

Continued

Table 4.1 *Continued.*

Voice mail	
Advantages	**Disadvantages**
• Good for short, focused messages • Quick way to reach people in remote locations • Can be broadcast to multiple people • Receiver can listen to message at their convenience	• Messages can be lost without sender or receiver knowing there is a problem • Some people don't check their messages regularly • No permanent record • One-way communications

Formal presentations	
Advantages	**Disadvantages**
• Great for presenting complex status reports or new training materials to audiences of various sizes • If done professionally, can have lasting positive impression on the audience • Limited two-way communications with questions and answers	• Requires considerable planning and skill to achieve a positive impression • Time-consuming • Poorly presented materials can negatively affect attitudes toward an otherwise successful project

Written Communication

Table 4.2 lists examples of various types of written communications and the advantages and disadvantages of each type.

Effective Listening

Dr. Ralph Nichols, who pioneered the study of listening, says that bad listening is the true cause of lost sales and lost customers, most accidents and production breakdowns, personality clashes and poor morale, bad communications, and misguided management. So how do people listen more effectively? Toastmasters recommends the following nine techniques:

1. *Like to listen.* The listeners must show a willingness to listen and enjoy what (and whom) they are listening to.

2. *Ignore distractions.* Listeners must learn to ignore distractions and visually and mentally focus on the speaker and what he or she is saying. Listeners need to listen with their eyes as well as their ears.

3. *Summarize.* Listeners can mentally summarize what the speaker is saying as they speak. Summarization techniques include:

   • Picking out main points, concepts, or/and key words.

Table 4.2   Written communication techniques.

Formal reports and memos	
Advantages	**Disadvantages**
• Provide permanent record • Good for communicating updates, important procedures, or major changes	• Require precise wording to ensure desired message is conveyed • Can not be easily taken back if a problem or misinterpretation arises • One-way communications

E-mail	
Advantages	**Disadvantages**
• Provides written record without generating paper • Allows the attachment of other documents • Quick way to reach people in remote and distributed locations • We can find out if mail has been received (return receipt) • Messages can be forwarded to others	• Lose the "personal touch,"—tone of voice, and so on • Not good for sensitive issues • Some people don't read their messages regularly • Lack of privacy—can be forwarded easily to almost anyone • One-way communications

Handwritten, short notes	
Advantages	**Disadvantages**
• Good for kudos and thanks • Personal touch • Quick, simple, friendly, cheap	• Can get lost in the shuffle • Some people's handwriting is illegible • Difficult if people not in the same location • One-way communications

- Mental outlining or taking notes.

- Comparing and contrasting what the speaker says with what the listeners already know.

- Thinking ahead of the speaker and trying to predict their next point. If listeners are right, it will reinforce their memory of what was said. If the listener's prediction is incorrect, they will remember what was said because it was unexpected.

- Numbering the points as listeners hear them.

4. *Tame emotions.* If listeners have negative feelings about what is being said or about the speaker, they can throw up mental barriers that make listening difficult. Listeners must control their mental attitude and listen objectively.

5. *Eliminate hasty judgments.* Listeners must work to ignore any biases they may have based on a person's appearance, accent, or even title. Listeners should listen with empathy by trying to place themselves in the speaker's shoes and attempt to listen from his or her point of view. Listeners should remind themselves to hear the speaker out before making judgments.

6. *Never interrupt.* There are many ways to interrupt a speaker besides speaking up while he or she is talking:

   • Arguing mentally with the speaker

   • Continuing to ponder something that was said while another point is being made

   • Mentally questioning, at length, a statistic that was presented

   • Disagreeing as a point is being made

   • Not remaining open to reasons, arguments, and data

7. *Inspire openness.* Listeners should look at the speaker. Listeners can also nod in agreement or smile when they hear something they like, look friendly, and react positively to the speaker. Listeners can also communicate their receptivity and be aware of their own body language.

8. *Need to listen.* Listeners can acknowledge that they need to listen. This makes listening a conscious decision.

9. *Generate conclusions.* As listeners listen, they can decide what it is they are going to accept from the speaker and what they will reject. Conclusions are different from hasty judgment because they are thought out and reasoned using logic (Toastmasters 1990).

Verbal listening involves listening for and analyzing word choice and the direct and implied meanings of the words being chosen by the speaker. It also means listening for and analyzing tone of voice, emphasis, and inflection, and the pacing of the communications. *Nonverbal listening* involves watching for and analyzing the eye contact, facial expressions, and body language of the speaker.

Interviews

Interviews are an excellent mechanism for obtaining detailed information from another person. For example, interviews are used in selecting candidates for open positions (job interviews), for obtaining data for an audit, in identifying risks, eliciting requirements, and in determining the level of customer satisfaction.

Interviews are used to gather information from interviewees through their answers to questions. The intent of interview questions is to prompt the interviewee to do most of the talking. In order to accomplish this, the interviewer should ask open-ended, context-free interview questions. Table 4.3 includes examples of open-ended versus closed-ended questions. *Open-ended questions* include "what-," "when-," "where-," "who-," and "how"-type questions. Interviewers should be very careful when using "why"-type questions because they may sound

Table 4.3   Open–ended versus closed-ended questions—examples.

Open-ended question	Closed-ended question
What procedures do you follow when performing your work?	Do you follow the XYZ procedure when you do your work?
What reviews and approvals are involved in releasing your work products?	Do you perform a peer review on your work products?
	Does the software lead approve your work products?
How do you communicate the problems you encounter?	Do you record the problems you find in the defect-tracking tool?

Table 4.4   Context-free questions—examples.

Ask this	Not this
What documentation do you use when performing this task?	How do you use the Statement of Work template when performing this task?
How do you verify the quality, completeness, and consistency of your work products?	What steps do you use when conducting unit testing of your work product?
How do you track your project's progress?	How do you use Microsoft Project to track your project's progress?

accusatory when interpreted through the filters of the interviewee. The interviewer might be intending to ask a neutral question like, "Why are you doing it that way?" but based on the interviewee's past experiences and emotions, their interpretation of the message might come across as, "Why would anyone ever want to do it that way, you idiot!" To avoid these problems the interviewer might want to rephrase "why" questions, for example, as "what are the reasons behind . . .?"

Context-free questions remove most of the context from the question itself and therefore do not put limitations on the scope of the answers the interviewee might give. Table 4.4 includes examples of context-free questions. Preparing interview questions in advance helps ensure that good, open-ended, context-free questions will be asked during the interview. Preparing the questions in advance also allows the interviewer to arrange the questions in a logical flow of topics rather than jumping around from topic to topic.

When asking an interview question, the interviewer should know what the "right," or expected, answer is. For example, if an audit interviewer is asking the question, "How do you communicate the problems you encounter?" that interviewer should know, based on the process requirements and procedure documentation, that problems are reported by entering them into a specific problem-reporting tool.

During the interview, the interviewer should start by introducing himself or herself and explaining the purpose and process of the interview. The interviewer should put the interviewee at ease and then ask questions and actively listen to the responses provided by the interviewee. However, preparing questions in advance does not lock the interviewer into just using those questions. Some prepared questions may need to be supplemented with follow-up questions to adequately cover an area, and some prepared questions may become unnecessary depending on the responses the interviewee gives to other questions. At the end of the interview the interviewer should handle any administrative matters and explain any next steps. The interviewer should also thank the interviewee for their time.

After the interview, the interviewer should take time to further document the interview. Notes taken during the interview may be sketchy and need to be expanded on while the interview is still fresh in the interviewer's mind. The interviewer should also take any follow-up action that is necessary as a result of conducting the interview.

Working in Multicultural Environments

Working closely together as teams or one-on-one with others brings up humanity issues including personality types and personal preferences, cultural differences and diversity issues, and even political correctness concerns. The internationalization of the software industry has expanded our horizons but also brings even more differences in culture, norms, and expectations into the workforce. Increasing focus on these human differences and cultural issues may be new or even uncomfortable to software practitioners who are used to working as individual contributors.

Communication filter differences can be particularly strong in a multicultural setting. Humanity issues are also more extreme in a multicultural setting. Extra care must be taken to ensure that communications are effective. Proactive steps should be taken to become aware of the cultural differences and expectations of the people individuals interact with in the workplace. This awareness coupled with a willingness to learn about other people's needs and preferences will help avoid misunderstandings and allow people to work together effectively within a diverse work environment. Mutual respect and understanding is essential in handling any issues as they arise.

Chapter 5

E. Team Skills

Teams are an important part of any quality system. Management teams establish, implement, and monitor the quality management system. Other teams are formed to improve the performance of interdependent processes and tasks. Team assignments are made to integrate complementary skills and knowledge to create synergy where the strength of the team as a whole is greater than the sum of its individual members. The team approach stimulates innovation and creativity by creating an environment that encourages people to try new approaches. Newer team members benefit from the mentoring of more-experienced members. Teamwork promotes trade-offs in problem solving and helps individual members accept the challenges of change.

Teams also have weaknesses. For example, team goals can become misaligned with the goals of the organization. Time is needed to build and maintain high-performance teams. Decision making is also typically slower using a team because of the time it takes to get the team to make a decision by consensus. There is also negative synergy where time is wasted simply because of the effort it takes to work with other people or because teams get distracted with off-task activities, including social interactions.

There are many different types of teams at various levels in the organization that have roles in the quality of software processes and products. The *quality council* may be called by many different names, but whatever name is used this team is made up of high-level executive management charged with setting the strategic quality direction and establishing the quality policies for the organization. This team is responsible for establishing, implementing, and monitoring the quality management system at the organizational level to ensure its effectiveness.

Under the quality council, multiple *quality management teams* are made up of mid-level management. These teams are responsible for the implementation of the quality management system and quality policies for individual departments, projects, or teams within the organization.

Cross-functional teams are typically established to deal with quality areas or issues that cross organizational boundaries. For example, a cross-functional team charged with system reliability may include members from hardware, software, manufacturing, customer service, and quality. Their role is to take a systemwide perspective of the area or issue and to ensure that one department or team does not optimize their part of the process to the detriment of overall process performance.

Quality action teams, also called *quality circles, quality improvement teams*, or *Six Sigma teams*, are typically established to improve a targeted process or product.

They analyze and prioritize improvement ideas, plan improvement actions, ensure the implementation of those plans, and evaluate the results of that implementation. They then repeat the process for the next-highest priority improvement idea.

Unlike a quality action team, which is typically established with a goal of continuous improvement of a process or set of processes, a *tiger team* is typically established to deal with a specific quality issue. After that issue is satisfactorily resolved, the tiger team is usually disbanded.

A *engineering process group* (EPG) is typically a team of process experts that act as consultants to help document and implement standardized processes across the organization. The EPG then aids individual departments, projects, or teams in tailoring those standardized processes to their individual needs. The EPG also acts as a focal point for identifying lessons learned and best practices and propagating them to the benefit of the entire organization.

While the EPG is a set of process experts, they don't actually own the processes. The processes are owned by the *process owner teams,* which include representatives of the individuals that implement those processes as part of their daily work. For example, the testers own the system testing process while the coders own the coding process and associated coding standards. In large organizations, where many individuals share each process, process owner teams may be formed for each major process to act as users' groups or process change control boards. One of the roles of these process owner teams is to share lessons learned and improvement ideas. Another role may be to evaluate the impact of proposed process changes that come from quality action teams, EPGs, or other groups or individuals. The process owner teams then act as the final authority to accept or reject the proposed changes to the organization's standardized processes and ensure it's the implementation of the changes that are accepted.

1. TEAM MANAGEMENT

> Use various team management skills, including assigning roles and responsibilities, identifying the classic stages of team development (forming, storming, norming, performing, adjourning), monitoring and responding to group dynamics, and working with diverse groups and in distributed work environments. (Apply)
>
> **Body of Knowledge I.E.1**

Team Roles and Responsibilities

Different team roles have specific responsibilities associated with them. The *team champion* is typically a senior member of management who selects and defines the team's mission, scope, and goals, setting the vision and chartering the team.

The champion is responsible for establishing the team and selecting the team leader and/or facilitator and works with them to identify team members. The champion reviews the team's progress, provides ongoing support and direction, represents the team to upper management, and runs interference for the team with the rest of the organization and other stakeholders. The team escalates issues to the their champion that can not be resolved by the team itself. The champion maintains overall executive-level responsibility for the success of the team's efforts.

The team champion may also act as the team sponsor, or another member of management may sponsor the team. The team sponsor provides ongoing funding and other necessary resources to the team.

The *team leader* is the person responsible for managing the team, which includes:

- Focusing the team on its objectives and monitoring team progress toward accomplishing those objectives

- Calling, arranging, and chairing for team meetings

- Handling or assigning administrative details

- Directing the team, including making assignments and taking follow-up action as required

- Managing and directing the utilization of team resources

- Overseeing the preparation and presentation of team reports and presentations

- Representing the team to the rest of the organization, including interacting with the team champion and sponsor

The *team facilitator* is someone who has experience in working with teams and can guide the team in their work and in the use of team tools. The facilitator is responsible for keeping the team running smoothly, including ensuring that all team members have an opportunity to participate and express their ideas, and handling nonproductive behaviors and other issues of team dynamics, including helping the team resolve negative conflict.

The members of the team are responsible for working together to accomplish the objectives of the team. This includes:

- Actively participating in team activities

- Offering ideas, alternatives, and suggestions

- Actively listening to other team members and leveraging their inputs to create synergistic solutions and improvements

- Completing assigned tasks and action items on schedule

- Eliciting information from the groups or organizational units they represent and adequately representing those groups/units during team activities and discussions

The *recorder,* also called the *scribe,* is the person responsible for generating, publishing, and maintaining minutes from team meetings, including tracking action items and team decisions. The recorder may be a temporary or rotating position within the team.

Stages of Team Development

Teams typically move through a set of predictable stages of development as they move from formation through the execution of their assigned responsibilities, as illustrated in Figure 5.1. These stages can vary in duration and intensity depending on the makeup and personalities of the team membership, the organizational culture and environment, and the effectiveness and skills of the team leader and/or facilitator. Sometimes a team can move through forming, storming, and norming into performing in just a meeting or two. Other teams may take a much longer time to become a cohesive unit and move to high performance. If enough problems exist, a team may never make it out of the storming stage and therefore never accomplish their mission. Reorganizing the team or other issues can also cause it to regress one or more stages and then have to progress back through the team development stages. Team reorganization occurs when one or more team members leave the team, new members are added to the team, or major changes in work assignments occur.

The *forming* stage occurs when a new team is first created or when an existing team encounters a major reorganization. The forming stage is a period where the team members start to get to know each other and understand each other's values, priorities, work preferences, and abilities. The team leader and facilitator work with a team in the forming stage to clarify the mission and scope of the team, and to collaborate in the definition of specific objectives and tasks needed to achieve the team's mission. The facilitator also works to establish an environment of openness and trust between team members and to train team members in the tools and methods that the team will use.

The forming stage is typically followed by the *storming* stage. During the storming stage, team members become aware that they are personally going to have to change in order to work together effectively, and there is a period of resistance to that change. During this stage, team members are vacillating between working toward individual goals and working as part of the team. The phase is

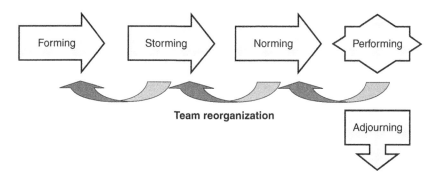

Figure 5.1   Stages of team development.

marked with arguments, frustration, anxiety, and the testing of the authority of the team leaders. During this stage, the team leader may need to take a primary role in guiding the team and reinforcing the mission of the team. The facilitator understands that tension and negative conflict are normal during this stage and helps the team learn to identify and manage the resulting issues. The facilitator also ensures that all of the team members are participating and have a voice in defining how the team will accomplish its mission.

The team then progresses to a *norming* stage where the team members work out their differences and come together and start acting as a cohesive unit that cooperates to perform their work. The team establishes agreed-to methods of operation and ground rules (norms) for conducting business. During the norming stage, the team leader starts sharing more responsibility with the team and allows the team to begin to self-organize. The facilitator supports team members as they take on more responsibility for conducting their own meetings and as they start identifying, analyzing, and solving their own problems. "The key to this stage is to build the team's confidence in their ability to resolve differences without anyone feeling left out or discounted" (Scholtes 2003).

Truly effective teams then move into the *performing* stage of high performance where everyone knows how to work together effectively and efficiently. The team leader shifts from an authority position to more of a coaching role. The main role of the facilitator during the performing stage is one of monitoring team interactions for issues that may require intervention. The facilitator continues to mentor the team by recommending tools and providing training as necessary

When a team completes one assignment, they may move on to the next assignment or the next priority. However, at some point the team may complete all of its work and enter an *adjourning* phase where the team accomplishes its mission, shuts down its efforts, and disbands.

Group Dynamics

Teams are collections of individuals, each with their own styles, personalities, cultures, work preferences, and personal goals. These differences can cause group dynamics problems to occur that threaten the cohesion and synergy of the team. Table 5.1 lists examples of these problems and their potential solutions.

Working with Diverse Groups

Teams need diversity to perform effectively. They need leaders and followers. They need people who focus on strategies and those who emphasize tactics. They need people with different skills and knowledge (for example, domain knowledge, technical knowledge, tool skills, interpersonal skills, analysts, programmers, testers, technical writers). Teams also need people with different personality types (for example, socializer, timekeeper, persuader, big-picture people, and people who are good at taking care of all the details). Without diversity, teams may not have enough of the positive conflict necessary to be creative and innovative.

Table 5.1   Team problems and potential solutions.

Problem	Potential solution
Problems starting or ending a task or activity	• Review mission statement • Review the action plan
Dominating participant	• Utilize structured participation technique (for example, the nominal group technique) • Proactively ask for opinions from other team members • Use a round-robin technique by going around the team and letting each person take a turn talking • Talk to the dominating person outside the meeting to discuss the behavior
Reluctant participants	• Utilize structured participation technique or round-robin technique • Divide agenda into tasks with individual or small-group assignments and reports (some people are shy about participating in larger groups) • Proactively seek out the opinions of reluctant members • Talk to the reluctant person outside the meeting to discuss the behavior

Participant attempting to use position or authority to direct team decisions	• Utilize structured participation technique
	• Talk to authority figures off-line and ask them to:
	  – Hold their opinions until other team members have had an opportunity to be heard
	  – Use questions when stating their views (for example, "What does the team think about . . .")

Using opinions rather than facts	• Stress the importance of basing decisions on facts as part of the team norms • Ask if there is supporting data or who could collect the data • Ask how the team can confirm or verify the facts
Rushing to solutions or completion	• Provide an opportunity for everyone's views to be heard • Provide the team with constructive feedback on this behavior • Utilize structured problem-solving techniques • Openly ask for alternatives or other opinions • Create a "devil's advocate" role

Continued

Table 5.1 *Continued.*

Problem	Potential solution
Digression and tangents	• Use a written agenda • Restate the topic being discussed and redirect the conversation back on track • Review mission statement and/or objectives • Use a "parking lot" to capture ideas or issues but postpone their discussion to a later time
Feuding team members	• Refocus group on process and products, not on people • Develop or restate ground rules • Utilize conflict resolution techniques • Adjourn meeting and talk to offending parties off-line
Too much conformity	• Openly reward divergent points of view • Ask outright for other points of view • Encourage positive conflict and controversy arising from opposing ideas and opinions • Protect or give equal weight to minority opinions • Create a "devil's advocate" role

On the other hand, in today's multicultural, global economy diversity also brings the potential for misunderstandings and miscommunication that can lead to negative conflict and other issues. For example, in Asia a business card represents the person and should be treated with the utmost respect. A business card is presented and accepted with both hands, it is read and acknowledged when presented, and it should never be written on or stuck in a hip pocket. Words, phrases, and hand gestures that are commonly used in the United States may have derogatory meanings in other countries. Humor is very different between cultures. Praise and criticism can be handled very differently. Even different colors have different meanings. In order to avoid these potential "land mines," team leaders, facilitators, and members must proactively learn about and seek to understand differences in the language and culture of their team members and other stakeholders.

Working in Distributed Work Environments

When people need to work together in distributed work environments, virtual teams can form by using technology to support communications when face-to-face interactions are limited by distance. These technologies can include Web-based meetings, videoconferencing, teleconferencing, shared intranet areas, e-mail, and other mechanisms.

2. TEAM TOOLS

> Use decision-making and creativity tools, such as brainstorming, nominal group technique (NGT), multi-voting, etc. (Apply)
>
> **Body of Knowledge I.E.2**

Brainstorming

Brainstorming is a team technique for generating lots of creative ideas or suggestions in a short period of time. The basic steps in brainstorming include:

Step 1: For brainstorming to be effective, the team must share a common understanding of exactly what is being brainstormed. This can be accomplished through team consensus on a single statement. For example, "we are brainstorming ideas for improving our peer review process" or "we are brainstorming a list of risks that exist for project ABC."

Step 2: Team members then offer up their ideas. This can be accomplished in an ad hoc manner with each member calling out their ideas as they come up with them, or it can be done in a round-robin manner with each member taking a turn to verbalize an idea or passing. The objective during this step is to get the creative juices flowing. Each team member should use the ideas that other members have suggested as a catalyst for new ideas of their own. Even the most off-the-wall suggestion may spark a really brilliant idea in someone else. Therefore, during this step of brainstorming, all the team members should refrain from analyzing or critiquing any of the ideas. Judgment is set aside during this step in order to let creativity flow.

Step 3: As each suggestion is made, the facilitator or recorder records that idea on a flip chart or in some other manner so that everyone in the group can read all of the ideas. This helps team members utilize those ideas to generate more new ideas.

Steps 2 and 3 are repeated over and over until the team runs out of new ideas. If the team gets bogged down too quickly, the facilitator may want to prompt participants for more ideas. The facilitator might pick one idea from the list and ask for more ideas similar to that idea or more ideas that expand on a similar theme. For example, if the team is brainstorming a risk list, the facilitator may pick a suggested risk that states, "We have never used Java before and don't have any real experts." The facilitator might ask, "What else are we doing on this project that we don't have a lot of experience with?"

Step 4: At the end of the brainstorming session, participants must put their analytical skill back to work and use their judgment to discuss, clarify, combine, categorize, and prioritize the items on the list to make them useful.

Nominal Group Technique

The *nominal group technique* (NGT) is a more structured way of generating and analyzing creative ideas. Steps in the NGT process include:

Step 1: State the purpose of the session and describe the process and rules for an NGT session. The team leader or facilitator usually performs this step.

Step 2: As with brainstorming, for NGT to be effective the team must share a common understanding of exactly what question they are trying to answer. A specific problem statement or question must be communicated to the participating team members either before or during the team meeting.

Step 3: The team members each generate a list of ideas in silence, writing down his or her ideas for solving the problem or answering the question. One way of doing this is to have them write one idea per sticky note or index card so that each idea can easily be handled separately. By doing this step in silence, members do not overly influence each other. This can result in more different and diverse ideas. This step can be done during the meeting or it can even be done as a preparation step prior to bringing the team together.

Step 4: The ideas are then presented to the team in round-robin fashion. This allows team members to present and explain each idea to the team. By using a round-robin technique, everyone is actively participating and one member does not dominate at any given time. In a similar manner to brainstorming, there should be no discussion or critique of the ideas at this point. However, participants should consider the ideas as they are being presented and use them to stimulate additional ideas that are then added to their personal lists. They can also cross ideas off their list if another team member has already presented that idea.

Step 5: After all of the ideas are presented (or time runs out), the facilitator then opens the floor for questions, discussion, and clarification of the ideas.

Step 6: Participants then put their analytical and judgmental skills back to work. Ideas are grouped, simplified, and/or combined as appropriate. Other ideas may be removed from the list.

Step 7: During this final step, the ideas are ranked through the use of a multivoting process or other prioritization process.

Nominal group technique can be used when:

- The group is new or has several new members
- The topic under consideration is controversial
- Team members are unable to resolve a disagreement
- Group decisions need to be made without the impact of authority or personal influence
- Problems need to be thought through thoroughly
- Participants are reluctant to participate in group discussion

Affinity Diagram

After a brainstorming session or as part of the NGT process, an *affinity diagram* can be used to organize the ideas into categories. Affinity diagrams can also be used with defect data, customer quality requirements, audit observations, or any other set of data that needs to be organized into categories. The steps in constructing an affinity diagram include:

Step 1: Writing each idea (or data item) in the set to be sorted on pieces of paper (for example, on sticky notes or index cards).

Step 2: The team works in silence, moving the ideas around and collecting similar ideas into groups (categories). New ideas can also be added to the set of ideas during the generation of the affinity diagram. For example, once a group is created, new ideas may be generated because something is missing from that group (additional details may also be added to existing ideas). If an idea fits into multiple categories, additional copies of that idea can be generated. In Figure 5.2

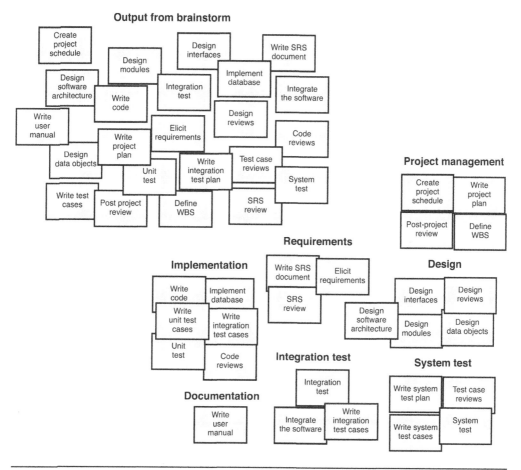

Figure 5.2   Affinity diagram technique—example.

for example, the original "write test case" idea fits under implementation, integration test, and system test. The idea was rewritten as three ideas: write unit test cases, write integration test cases, and write system test cases.

Step 3: After a few minutes have elapsed without additional changes, the team breaks the silence and starts a discussion of the final configuration. At this time, short labels (one to five words in length) should be assigned to each group to describe that category (Pyzdek 2000).

Multivoting

In the *multivoting* method each participant is given a specific number of votes to distribute among the ideas. For example, if there are 50 ideas, each person might be given eight votes. A participant can give one idea all eight votes, distribute their votes between a few ideas, or give one vote to each of eight different ideas. The facilitator collects the votes and uses them to score and rank the ideas by priority. The group then reviews and discusses the results. A variation on this is to give each participant one sticker for each vote to place next to the ideas they are voting for.

An alternative to multivoting is the *ranked-choice method*, in which each participant is asked to select and rank their top *n* choices. For example, if there are 30 ideas, each participant is given six index cards. The participants then write their choices and the rank of that choice (6 = first choice to 1 = last choice) on the index cards, one choice per card. The facilitator collects the cards, scores (for example if an idea was ranked 6, 3, 1, and 4 by four different participants, it would get a score of 14), and ranks the ideas based on their scores. The group then reviews and discusses the results.

Prioritization Matrix

A *prioritization matrix* is used to rank items in order of priority based on a set of criteria. Each of these criteria can also be assigned a weight. For example, in the prioritization matrix in Table 5.2, four criteria have been selected to prioritize a set of process improvement suggestions:

- *Bottom line.* The impact of implementing the improvement suggestion on the profits of the company is weighted at .25

- *Easy.* How easy the improvement suggestion will be to implement is weighted at .15

- *Staff acceptance.* How accepting the software engineering staff will be to the implementation of the improvement suggestion is weighted at .20

- *Customer satisfaction.* The impact of implementing the improvement suggestion on the satisfaction levels of the customer is weighted at .40

Each of the process improvement ideas is then rated on a scale of 1 to 4 for each of these criteria, and a total score is calculated. In this example, the total score for

Table 5.2 Prioritization matrix—example.

	Criteria and weights				
	Bottom line (.25)	Easy (.15)	Staff acceptance (.20)	Customer satisfaction (.40)	Total
Process improvement 1	1	3	2	4	2.7
Process improvement 2	4	1	4	3	3.15
Process improvement 3	2	2	2	1	1.6
Process improvement 4	2	4	3	2	2.5

Inspection metrics

1. Number of defects found
2. Defect discovery rate
3. Number of inspectors
4. Defect density versus inspection rate
5. Inspection rate control chart
6. Phase containment
7. Post-release defect trends
8. Return on investment

Importance: 1 = not important, 5 = very important

Ease of implementation: 1 = very difficult, 5 = very easy

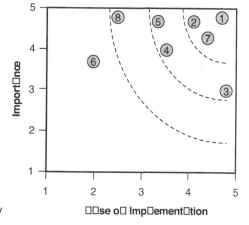

Figure 5.3 Prioritization graph—example.

process improvement suggestion 1 = $(1 \times .25) + (3 \times .15) + (2 \times .20) + (4 \times .40) = 2.7$. These total scores are then used to rank the improvements for implementation.

Prioritization Graph

When only two criteria are being used to rank items by priority, another tool that can be used is a *prioritization graph*. To use this method, each item is rated on a scale (for example, 1 to 5 where 5 is the highest priority) on each of the two criteria. The ratings for each item are then plotted on an *x–y* graph as a bubble. Figure 5.3 shows an example of a prioritization graph used to prioritize possible software inspection metrics by the importance of the information they provide and by their ease of implementation. Items with the highest priority will be in the upper right-hand corner (both important and easy to implement). One of the advantages

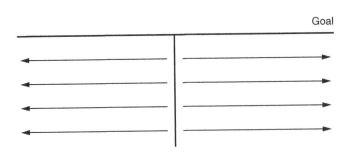

Figure 5.4   Force field analysis template.

of this method is that it is easy to view the relationships between the items and understand the impacts of the criteria on the priority.

Force Field Analysis

In *force field analysis,* the team identifies factors (forces) that will help move them toward the goal they are trying to accomplish (for example, the idea they are trying to implement) and factors that will inhibit movement toward that goal. Figure 5.4 shows an example of a force field analysis template, and Figure 4.1 showed an example of a completed force field analysis for analyzing change. The information from the force field analysis can then be used to identify activities needed as part of the plan to implement the goal. Activities that will leverage or enhance the factors that help move toward the goal should be planned. Activities should also be planned to handle or eliminate factors that will inhibit or move away from the goal.

Part II

Software Quality Management

Part II

Chapter 6

A. Quality Management System

The primary purpose of a *quality management system* (QMS) is to implement an organization's chosen quality strategy by focusing on areas that are critical to successfully achieving quality objectives, providing high-quality products and services, and satisfying customers. A QMS is the aggregate of the organization's quality-related organizational structure, policies, processes, work instructions, plans, supporting tools, and infrastructure. The QMS provides the guidance, techniques, and mechanisms needed to plan, implement, maintain, and improve the activities and actions related to quality planning, quality assurance, quality engineering, quality improvement, and verification and validation.

1. QUALITY GOALS AND OBJECTIVES

> Design quality goals and objectives for programs, projects, and products that are consistent with business objectives. Develop and use documents and processes necessary to support software quality management systems. (Create)
>
> **Body of Knowledge II.A.1**

Quality Goals and Objectives

The primary goal of establishing a QMS is to institutionalize quality-related activities into every aspect of the organization and its key business practices. This starts at the highest levels of management where *quality goals* or targets are established and integrated into the strategic plans of the organization. These quality goals should align with the organizational business goals and objectives, the mission of the organization, and the needs of its customers.

Specific, measurable, achievable, realistic, and time-framed *quality objectives* are then planned to achieve these quality goals. As part of the organizational-level quality plans, organizational "quality objectives are set to specify what specific actions will be taken, within a given time period, to achieve a measurable quality outcome" (Westcott 2006). Examples of software quality objectives include:

- The organization will be formally assessed and achieve level 3 maturity on the Software Engineering Institute's (SEI's) Capability Maturity Model Integration (CMMI) for Development version 1.2 by the end of the second quarter of 2010.

- Software developers will be cross-trained so that 90 percent of software source code modules currently under active development or maintenance are supported by at least two developers by the end of the second quarter of 2009.

- The percentage of development dollars currently being spent on rework activities will be reduced to less than a maximum of 15 percent per project by the end of the fourth quarter of 2009.

- The average percentage of the total test cases that have been automated for a project will be increased from 20 percent to 50 percent by the end of the third quarter of 2009.

- Customer satisfaction levels will be increased to 90 percent of the responses scored in the top two boxes by the end of 2009.

- The number of defects reported post-release will be decreased by 20 percent from levels measured for the previous release of the same product for each new version release of the product until the total defect containment effectiveness measure for the product reaches 98 percent.

These organizational-level quality objectives should be propagated down into lower-level division, team, and individual objectives and into program, project, product, and process objectives that support them. Specific responsibilities for the quality objectives need to be assigned at all levels of the organization. These objectives need to be communicated so that individual employees are aware of their responsibilities and how their work impacts progress toward achieving the objectives.

Quality Management System Documentation

The QMS documentation hierarchy defines the organization's strategy and tactics for achieving its quality objectives. Figure 6.1 illustrates the different levels and types of documentation in the QMS documentation hierarchy.

At the highest level, the organization's QMS is typically based on a framework of one or more industry standards or models. There are a variety of software industry standards and models that can be used, for example, ISO 9001, ISO 15504, the IEEE standards, or the SEI's CMMI for Development. Using one or more of these industry standards and models can provide guidance that helps the organization share the good practices discovered through trial and error by other organizations and defined by the industry experts. This can also help keep the organization from wasting time by "reinventing the wheel."

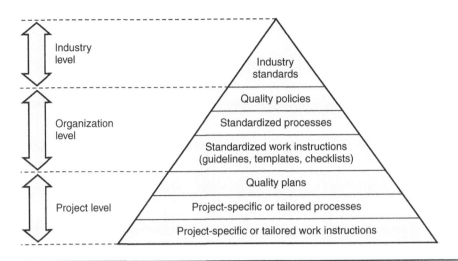

Figure 6.1   QMS documentation hierarchy.

Quality Policies

At the organizational level, *quality policies* are formally established to define the overall direction and principles to be followed when making decisions and performing activities that impact quality. Upper-level management usually establishes quality policies to communicate the intent of the QMS and its objectives. A document, such as a quality manual, is typically used to document the quality policies.

Standardized Processes

Standardized processes define the mechanics of what is required to implement the QMS activities at the organizational level. A *process* is a definable, repeatable, measurable sequence of tasks used to produce a quality product. By standardizing and documenting software processes, an organization can describe and communicate what usually works best. This can help the organization:

- Ensure that important steps in the processes aren't forgotten

- Facilitate the propagation of lessons learned from one project to the next so the organization can repeat its successes and stop repeating actions that lead to problems

- Eliminate the need to "reinvent the wheel" with each new project while providing a foundation for tailoring the processes to the specific needs of that project

Documented processes provide the structured basis for creating metrics that can be used to understand process capabilities and analyze process results to identify areas for improvement. Standardized software processes are necessary for training, management review, and tools support. They provide the basis for organizational learning and continual process improvement.

There are many different methods for mapping processes. One simple way of documenting processes is to use the *ETVX* (Entry criteria, Tasks, Verification steps, eXit criteria) method, illustrated in Table 6.1. The *entry criteria* are specific, measurable conditions that must be met before the process can be started. The *tasks* are the individual steps or activities that must be performed to implement the process and create the resulting product. The task definitions should also include responsibility assignments for each step. *Verification steps* describe the mechanisms used to ensure that the tasks are performed as required and that the deliverables meet required quality levels. Typical verification steps include reviews, tests, or sign-offs. The *exit criteria* are specific, measurable conditions that must be met before the process can be completed. Examples of entry and exit criteria include:

- Other processes or activities that must be satisfactorily completed

- Plans or documents that must be in place or must be updated

- Reviews, tests, or other evaluations that must be satisfactorily completed or approvals that must be obtained

- Specific measured values that must be obtained

- Staff with appropriate levels of expertise that must be available to perform the process

- Other resources that must be available and/or ready for use during the process

The SEI (2006) expands on the ETVX method and states that "a defined process clearly states the purpose, inputs, entry criteria, activities, roles, measures, verification steps, outputs, and exit criteria."

The process's purpose is a statement of the value-added reason for the process. The purpose defines what the organization is attempting to accomplish by executing the steps in that process. For example, the purpose of a software testing process might be to validate the software system against the approved requirements and identify product defects before the product is released to the customer.

Inputs are the tangible, physical objects that are input into and utilized during the process. These inputs may be work products created as part of other processes or they may be purchased items or other items supplied by sources external to the organization (for example, customers, subcontractors). Example inputs to the software testing process might include the test cases and procedures, the software build, and the user manual. Some individuals find the separation of inputs from entry criteria confusing. For example, are the test cases an input into the process or is the fact that the test cases have been reviewed, approved, and placed under configuration management an entry criteria into the process? To remove this confusion, some process definition templates combine inputs and entry criteria into a single section.

A simple flow diagram of a process can make that process easier to understand by showing the relationships between the various tasks, verification steps, and deliverables and by showing who (what role) is responsible for each task or verification step. The first step in creating a *process flow diagram* is to define the various *roles* of the process. These are the individuals or groups responsible for

Table 6.1   ETVX method–example.

System test execution process		
Entry criteria:	**Tasks:**	**Exit criteria:**
• System Test Plan approved and under CM control • System Test Cases and System Test Procedures approved and under CM control • User documentation and software installation procedures approved and under CM control • Software build promoted to System Test state • System Test Lab ready and available for use • Integration Test successfully complete • Testing staff available with the appropriate levels of expertise	T1. Execute System Tests and Report Anomalies: The system tester executes a selected set of test cases for each system test load. If system test is suspended and restarted, these selected test cases will include cases to test all corrections and to regression test the software as appropriate. Any anomalies identified during system test are reported by the tester in accordance with the Anomaly Reporting process. T2. Debug and Correct Defects: The owner(s) (for example, software development, technical publications) of each work product that is suspected to have caused the anomaly debugs that work product and corrects any identified defect(s) in accordance with the Problem Resolution process. T3. Build and Freeze Next Revision of System Test Work Products: Configuration management builds any updated revision of the software product(s) (for example, software load, user manual, and installation instructions) that include the identified corrected components in accordance with the Software Build Process. T4. Write System Test Report: At the end of the final cycle of System Test execution, the tester writes a System Test Report that includes a summary of the results from all of the System Test cycles. T5. Promote Work Products: After the final test report is approved, all of the system test work products are promoted to the acceptance test status in accordance with the Configuration Management Promotion Process.	• System test completion criteria are met (as specified in the system test plan). • System Test Report is approved by test management. • Final System Test software work products are promoted to beta test status.
	Verification:	
	V1. Conduct Periodic Test Status Reviews: System test status review meetings are held on a periodic basis (as specified in the system test plan) during system test. If at any time it is determined that the suspension criteria (as specified in the system test plan) are met, system test execution is halted until the resumption criteria (as specified in the system test plan) are met and new revisions of the software work products are built and/or frozen. These meetings are also used to determine when system test is complete based on the system test completion criteria (as specified in the system test plan). V2. Peer Review Test Report: the testers peer review the system test report in accordance with the Peer Review process. V3. Review and Approve Test Report: test management reviews and approves the final test report for distribution.	

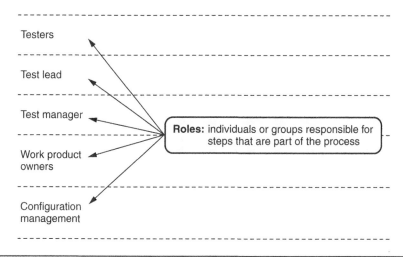

Figure 6.2   Roles in a process flow diagram—example.

Part II.A.1

the steps that are part of the process. Their roles are listed in the "swim lanes" along the left side of the process flow diagram, as illustrated in Figure 6.2.

In order to make standardized processes as adaptable as possible, these roles should be labeled in generic terms (for example, project manager, developer, tester, test manager, SQE, SCM librarian) rather than by using specific organizational titles or the actual names of individuals or groups. This keeps the organization from being forced to update the process documentation every time there is a reorganization, someone gets a promotion or title change, or there is staff turnover. This also allows individual projects of various sizes to use the processes without the need for tailoring. For example, on very large projects an entire team might be assigned to one of the process roles, but on very small projects a single individual might be assigned several roles.

A flowchart can then be drawn across the swim lanes that illustrates the various tasks, verification steps, decisions, and deliverables of the process. For example, the system test process is illustrated in Figure 6.3. This example process starts at step *T1: Execute system tests and report anomalies* and follows the process flow through to end at step *T5: Promote work products*. This method makes it easy for an individual assigned to a role to read across their "swim lane" and identify their responsibilities. If more than one role is responsible for a step, the box for that step simply spans multiple swim lanes (for example, verification step V2 in Figure 6.3). Occasionally, a task needs to span more than one swim lane, but the order of the swim lanes does not allow for a single solid box to be used. This can be illustrated using a split box (for example, verification step V3 in Figure 6.3).

For each task or verification step defined in the process flow diagram, a textual description should be included that describes the task or verification step in detail. These descriptions may include:

- Pointers to the detailed work instructions that describe how to accomplish the task or verification steps.

- Additional descriptions of specific responsibilities. For example, "the Test Manager is responsible for conducting periodic test status reviews with

Part II.A.1

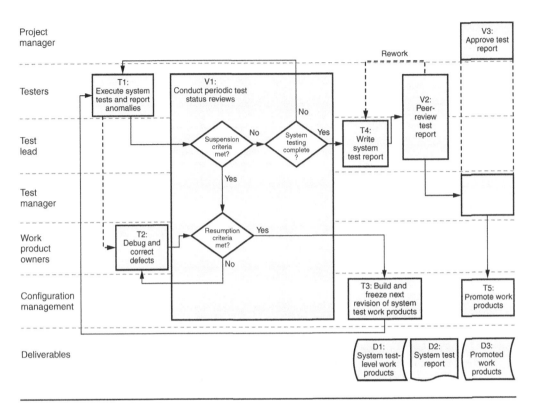

Figure 6.3   Process flow diagram—example.

the review participants including Testers, the Test Lead, the Work Product
Owners, and Configuration Management."

- Required levels of expertise (or pointers to the descriptions of required
  levels of expertise) that must be possessed by those responsible for the
  task or verification step. For example, "Testers must be proficient on the
  XYZ testing tools set and the use of the ABC simulator."

- Pointers to standards to be used when conducting the step or when
  creating the output. For example, standards for the system testing process
  might including formal inspection process standards and work product
  workmanship standards.

- Pointers to standardized templates for creating the outputs of the task
  or verification step. For example, document, report, or meeting agenda
  templates.

- Other resources, for example, tools or hardware, that should be used in
  the task or verification step.

The expanded process description might also include descriptions of (or pointers
to the descriptions of) specific metrics collected and/or used as part of the process
or to measure the quality of its products.

The expanded process description might separate outputs from the existing criteria or combine these into the same section. The outputs from the process

include both deliverables and quality records. *Deliverables* are the tangible, physical objects or specific, measurable accomplishments that are the outcomes of the tasks or verification steps. *Quality records* are secondary outputs that provide the evidence that the appropriate activities took place and that the execution of those activities met the required standards. Examples of quality records include meeting minutes, logs, change requests, completed forms or checklists, formal sign-off or approval pages, reports, and metrics.

It is also useful to define the high-level *process architecture* in order to understand the ordering of the individual processes, their interactions and interdependencies, work product flows between the processes, and their interfaces to external processes. Figure 6.4 illustrates an example of a process architecture flow diagram. Note that the System Test process defined in detail in the above example is just one box in this higher-level architecture.

Standardized Work Instructions

Standardized processes define the "what to do" requirements, but the "how to do it" should be left to the lower-level standardized *work instructions*.

One type of work instructions is a *guideline*. For example, a testing process might have a task for "opening a problem report in the problem reporting database." By leaving this generic, the same process document can be used no matter which problem-reporting tool a project selects. To support this process there may be several guideline-type work instructions, each that tell how to open a problem report in a different tool, which fields to complete, and with guidance for entering data in each field.

Another type of work instructions is a *template*. For example, a project planning process typically has a task for "documenting the project plans." To support this process there may be several template-type work instructions that provide guidance on what to document in the project plans for each of several different project types (for example, large projects, small projects, maintenance projects). Templates allow the software practitioners to concentrate on content rather than format and at the same time help ensure that needed information isn't forgotten because the guidelines act as an outline of the needed information with instructions on what to document in each area. Utilizing a hierarchy of documentation templates similar to the process hierarchy illustrated in Figure 6.4 can also help reduce redundancy of content across the documentation set by defining where each type of information will be documented. For example, should each different planning document (project plan, software quality plan, verification and validation plan, and so on) have its own risk management section defining specific risks associated with each plan, or should a separate comprehensive risk management plan be used instead? With separate risk sections, the templates for each type of plan would include a risk management section. If a separate risk management plan is used, it would have its own template.

Another type of work instructions is a *checklist*. Checklists are tools used to ensure that all of the important items for a process, product, or service are considered. Examples of different uses for checklists include:

- A checklist that includes all the steps in an activity is used to ensure that none of the steps are skipped

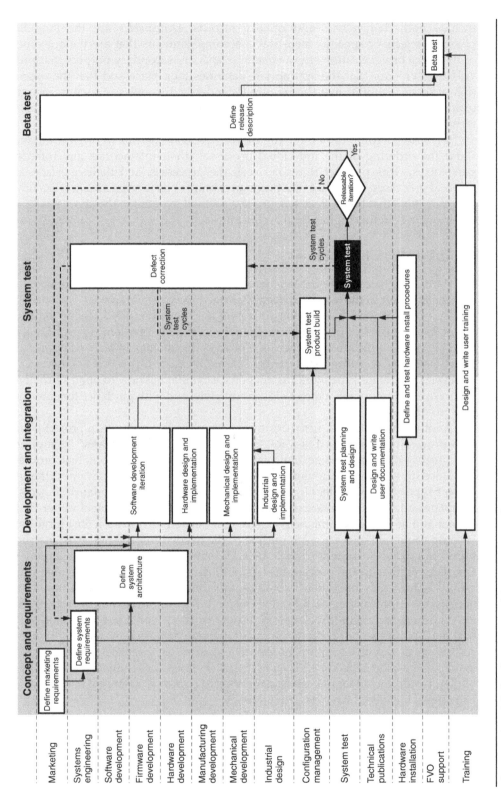

Figure 6.4 High-level process architecture—example.

- A checklist that includes a list of all the factors and attributes that should be considered when performing an activity (for example, a checklist of the different types of testing to be performed, including performance, security, safety, usability, load/volume/stress, resource usage, and so on)

- A checklist of common defects that should be checked for when conducting a peer review or test

- A checklist used by an auditor to ensure that they remember to ask all the questions they planned to ask or investigate all the areas they planned to examine

Checklists typically need to be either process- or product-specific. For example, a different checklist would be used to audit the configuration management process than would be used for the requirements development process. A different checklist would also be used for peer reviewing a design document than would be used for a code review, and a different checklist would be used for a Java code review than for a code review of C code. Checklists can be created from standards and guidelines but should then evolve over time as lessons are learned.

Project-Level Quality Plans

Quality plans define the specifics of how a project intends to implement the organization's QMS in order to meet the quality goals and objectives of the organization and of that project. The software quality plans can be a defined in a stand-alone software *quality plan* document or incorporated into the project plans. Other quality plans, including the *verification and validation plan,* the *configuration management plan, supplier management plan,* and the *risk management plan,* can also be incorporated as subplans in either the project plan or software quality plan or they may be documented as stand-alone planning documents. In other words, the format of the plans is not what is important. The important thing is that quality planning takes place and that it is documented. There may also be higher-level program- or product-level quality plans that the project-level quality plans are based on.

Project-Specific or Tailored Processes

While the standardized processes define what "usually works best," they don't always match the exact needs of a specific project (program or product). One way of handling this situation is to tailor the standardized processes. Tailoring a process alters or adapts that process to a specific end and allows standardized processes to be implemented appropriately for the needs of the project. Tailoring may also elaborate the process description to provide additional details so that project personnel can perform the resulting defined process. For example, on a project that is smaller than the typical project, the standardized processes may be tailored to remove unnecessary reviews or approval levels because the same person is assigned to multiple roles. On projects that are larger than typical, additional steps may need to be added to the standardized processes to allow for additional communications channels or levels of management. Process tailoring for a project may be defined as part of the project plans or in separate process tailoring documentation.

Another way to handle the process requirements of a project is to create project-specific processes. For example, a project that is a joint venture with another organization may require processes that are significantly different enough from the standard organizational processes that tailoring would be laborious and confusing. In this case, writing project-specific processes could be the best solution.

Project-Specific or Tailored Work Instructions

As with process documentation, based on the needs of the project (program or product), there may be a need to tailor standard, organizational-level work instructions. For example, checklists for audits might need to be tailored to include any tailoring that was done to the processes being audited. The project may also need to create project-specific work instructions. For example, a joint venture project might use a completely different problem-reporting tool than is typically used by the organization. In this case, project-specific guidelines on how to open a problem report using the new tool would be created.

2. CUSTOMERS AND OTHER STAKEHOLDERS

> Describe and distinguish between various stakeholder groups, and analyze the effect their requirements can have on software projects and products. (Analyze)
>
> **Body of Knowledge II.A.2**

Stakeholders are individuals or groups who affect or are affected by a software product, project, or process and therefore have some level of influence over the requirements for that software product, project, or process.

Product Stakeholders

As illustrated in Figure 6.5, there are three main categories of product stakeholders: the suppliers of the software, the acquirers of the software, and other stakeholders.

The *acquirer*-type stakeholders can be divided into two major groups. First there are the *customers* who select, request, purchase, and/or pay for the software in order to meet their business objectives. The second group is the *users* who actually use the software directly or use the software indirectly by receiving reports, outputs, or other information generated by the software. There may also be many different types of users. For example, there may be novice users, occasional users, and power users of a software product. There may also be users with different levels of knowledge or skill, different roles or objectives, different access privileges, or different motivations. For example, some of the users of a "pay at the

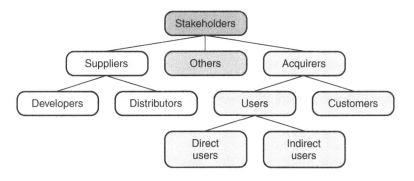

Figure 6.5 Categories of product stakeholders.

pump" system include the manager of the gas station, the attendant, car owners purchasing gas, eighteen-wheeler drivers, credit card thieves, people with expired credit cards, illiterate people, and people that don't speak English. Each of these stakeholder groups may place different requirements on the software.

The suppliers of the software include developers—the individuals and groups that are part of the organization that develops and/or maintains the software—and distributors—the individuals and groups that distribute the software. Examples of distributors include the office supply store that sells a word processor software package or a construction firm that installs an energy management and building automation system in the high-rise they are building.

Other stakeholders that don't belong to either the supplier or acquirer groups but still may have some level of influence over the software include:

- Lawmakers or regulatory agencies that create laws, regulations, and standards that impact the software product

- Organizations that create industry standards or guidelines or define industry best practices for the software product

- Other groups or individuals that are impacted by the actions or decisions of the product's acquirers or suppliers

- Even society at large can have a vested interest in the software

Project Stakeholders

The Project Management Institute (PMI) (2008) defines project stakeholders as "persons and organizations . . . that are actively involved in the project, or whose interests may be positively or negatively affected by the execution or completion of the project." Project stakeholders include the individuals funding, initiating, and/ or championing the project, customers of the project, or individuals supporting the project, as well as anyone on the project team and the stakeholders of the products produced by that project. Project stakeholders may also include individuals from other projects or programs that must interface or coordinate with the project (for example, other projects in the same program or individuals in the project management office).

Process Stakeholders

Process stakeholders are individuals who affect or are affected by a software process or its outcome. Process stakeholders include the individuals funding the process activities, defining, documenting, and improving the process, or championing the process, as well as anyone directly involved in the execution of the process activities or steps and the stakeholders of the products produced by that process. Process stakeholders may also include individuals from other processes that must interface or coordinate with the process, as well as individuals responsible for auditing or assessing the process.

Benefits of Identifying and Involving Stakeholders

There are many benefits to identifying and involving stakeholders in decisions about software products, processes, and projects. Identifying and considering the needs of all of the different stakeholders can help prevent requirements from being overlooked. For example, if a project is creating a payroll system and they don't consider charities as one of the stakeholders, they might not include the requirements for the software to withhold, handle, track, and report charitable payroll deductions. As Wiegers (2003) puts it in his discussion about product requirements, getting stakeholders involved eliminates the need for two of the most ineffective requirements elicitation techniques: clairvoyance and telepathy.

Product, process, or project specialists can never know as much about a stakeholder's work as that stakeholder knows. Identifying and involving key stakeholders provides access to the stakeholder's experience base and domain knowledge. The specialist's job is then to analyze, expand on, synthesize, resolve conflicts in, and combine the inputs from all the stakeholders into an organized set of product requirements, process definitions, or project plans. Identifying the different stakeholders and getting them involved also brings different perspectives to the table that can aid in a more complete view of the work to be accomplished.

Many people are uncomfortable with and therefore resist change. New or improved software products, processes, and projects typically mean changing the way some stakeholders will perform part or all of their jobs. Obtaining stakeholder input and participation gets them involved in the change based on their needs. Involved stakeholders are more likely to buy in to the completed work, which can create "ownership" and make them champions for the change within their stakeholder community. This can be beneficial in the transition of the new product, process, or project into the stakeholder's environment.

Stakeholder Participation Plans

When developing a software product, designing, implementing, and/or improving a process, or planning and managing a project, it is almost impossible to take into consideration the needs of all of the potential stakeholders. The needs of stakeholders may also contradict or conflict with each other. For example, the need to keep unfriendly hackers from breaking into the payroll software conflicts with the accountant's need for quick and easy access to the software. Therefore, decisions need to be made about how to determine which stakeholders have higher priorities so that appropriate trade-offs can be made. Once all of the stakeholders have been identified, the first-level cut at this prioritization is to sort those stakeholders into categories of:

- *Must include*—this stakeholder must be included

- *Like to include*—this stakeholder will only be included if time allows

- *Ignore*—this stakeholder will not be directly included

For each stakeholder group that is included, a decision must be made about who will represent that stakeholder group in the product, process, or project activities. There are three main choices:

- *Representative*. Select a stakeholder champion to represent the group of stakeholders. For example, if there are multiple testers who will be testing the product, the lead tester might be selected to represent this stakeholder group. The lead tester would then participate in the activities and be responsible for gathering inputs from other testers and managing communication with them.

- *Sample*. For large stakeholder groups or for groups where direct access is limited for some reason, sampling may be appropriate. In this case, it would be necessary to devise a sampling plan for obtaining inputs from a representative set of stakeholders in that particular group. For example, if the company has several thousand employees, it may decide to take a sample set of employees to interview about their needs for the new accounting system.

- *Exhaustive*. If the stakeholder group is small or if it is critical enough to success, it may be necessary to obtain input from every member of that stakeholder group. For example, if the software product has a small set of customers, it might be important to obtain input from each of the customers.

The second decision is to determine when and how each included stakeholder group needs to participate in the activities. Are they going to participate throughout the entire product life cycle, process, or project, or only at specific times? What activities are they going to participate in? For example, a stakeholder's input may be gathered during the definition of the process, but that stakeholder might not be involved in the peer review of that definition or be part of the ongoing process change approval authority. For product requirements development, one stakeholder might just be interviewed during requirements elicitation activities while another key stakeholder is considered part of the requirements development team and participates in:

- Requirements elicitation as an active participant in facilitated requirements workshops

- Requirements analysis by evaluating use cases and requirements models

- Requirements specification by documenting part of the requirements

- Requirements verification by peer reviewing the requirements specification

- Requirements management as a member of the requirements change control board

The final decision is to establish the second level of priority of each included stakeholder group based on their relative importance to the success of the software product, process, or project. As conflicts arise between the needs of various stakeholders, priorities help determine whose voice to listen to.

Stakeholder Needs and Motivations

Individual stakeholders have different needs and motives that must be identified and understood for a product, process, or project to be successful. One method for accomplishing this is to meet with each stakeholder representative individually to encourage open communication and sharing of both positive and negative perspectives of the product, process, or project.

Stakeholders typically have commonly acknowledged business needs that they can easily identify. However, stakeholders may also have unacknowledged motives (hidden agendas) that might drive the direction of their influence on the effort. Both the acknowledged business needs and these less obvious motives need to be uncovered and understood to effectively plan the product, process, or project. Table 6.2 illustrates an example of business needs and motives for the development of a payroll software package.

3. PLANNING

Design program plans that will support software quality goals and objectives.
(Evaluate)

Body of Knowledge II.A.3

At the organizational level, quality plans need to be incorporated into the annual operating plans for the organization. These plans should include the definition of quality goals and objectives for the coming fiscal year.

At the project (program or product) level, planning should include quality plans that define the specifics for how each project intends to implement the organization's QMS. Project-level quality plans must be aligned with both organizational-level and project-level quality goals and objectives, as well as with other project plans. According to the IEEE Standard for Software Quality Assurance Plans (IEEE 2002), the software quality plan should include:

Table 6.2 Business needs and motives—example.

Key stakeholder	Business needs and motives
Accounting	• Convenient mechanisms for capturing time worked, vacations, and so on, for each employee • Track, reconcile, manage, and report payroll • Eliminate the need to "chase" employees and supervisors for completed/approved time sheets each pay period • Keep jobs (don't automate people out of employment)
HR	• Automate and track employee-elected deductions, contributions, savings, and so on • Eliminate the tedious task of dealing with paper forms from their workload
Employees	• Convenient mechanisms for reporting time worked, vacations, and so on • Detailed statement of earnings, deductions, contributions, savings, and so on • On-time delivery of accurate paychecks and automatic deposit of payroll checks to banks • Elimination of many different, complicated (sometimes hard-to-obtain) forms for requesting/changing deductions, contributions, insurance benefits, savings plans, and so on
IRS, Social Security, and state tax offices	• Ability to automate wage garnishment, reporting, and funds transfers for taxes owed • Ability to collect taxes owed on or before due date • Eliminate labor-intensive paperwork
Insurance companies	• Ability to automate premium payments through payroll deduction • Ability to sell more policies and options to employees
Charities	• Ability to establish and automate long-term contributions through payroll deduction
Employee's bank	• Automated transfer of payroll into employee bank accounts • Get payroll check into employee bank account sooner • Eliminate labor-intensive paperwork and need for human interaction with paycheck
Company's bank	• Automated transfer of payroll into employee bank accounts • Automated transfer of withheld taxes from company account • Keep the company's money in their bank accounts as long as possible • Eliminate labor-intensive paperwork and need for human interaction with paycheck

- Plans for managing the quality function and activities, including the organizational structure, quality tasks, and quality-related roles and responsibilities.

- A definition of the minimum required set of quality-related documentation and the identification of the "reviews or audits to be conducted and the criteria by which adequacy is to be confirmed" (IEEE 2002).

- Specification of the specific quality-related standards, practices, conventions, and metrics (for example, documentation standards, logic and coding standards, test standards, a selected software quality product, and process metrics). This can simply point to the standard organizational-level standards, practices, conventions, and metrics or it may include (or point to) tailoring of those standard organizational-level documents or to project-specific standards, practices, conventions, and metrics.

- Plans for all of the reviews and audits (or pointers to separate plan documents) that will be held as part of this project.

- Identification of any tests to be performed and the testing methods to be used (or pointers to separate plan documents). This may also be a pointer to the verification and validation plan or separate test plans if they exist and define this information.

- Plans for problem reporting and corrective action (or pointers to separate plan documents) for reporting, tracking, and resolving any product or process problems or issues identified during software development and maintenance.

- Definitions of the specific quality-related tools, techniques, and methodologies the project will use.

- Plans for media control (or pointers to separate plan documents) including the definition of the methods and facilities used to identify and protect the media used to store internal and external software work products and deliverables.

- Plans for supplier management and control (or pointers to separate plan documents) used to ensure that suppler-provided software products and deliverables meet requirements including quality standards and requirements.

- Plans for quality record collection, maintenance, and retention (or pointers to separate plan documents).

- Plans for quality-related training (or pointers to separate plan documents).

- Quality-related risk management plans (or pointers to separate plan documents).

4. OUTSOURCING

> Determine the impact that acquisitions, multi-supplier partnerships, outsourced services, and other external drivers can have on organizational goals and objectives, and design appropriate criteria for evaluating suppliers and subcontractors. (Analyze)
>
> **Body of Knowledge II.A.4**

In today's fast-paced software industry where customers demand larger, more complex software products with high quality, lower costs, and faster times to market, software organizations are forced to seek whatever competitive advantages they can. *Outsourcing* the development or maintenance of all or part of a software product to a supplier outside the organization can sometimes provide an advantage. Outsourcing can be accomplished in a number of ways: on site where the supplier is colocated with the acquirer, off site where the supplier is located in the same city, state, or country as the acquirer, or offshore where the supplier is located in a different country than the acquirer.

Depending on the circumstances, outsourcing can provide several different competitive advantages, including:

- Reducing staff by taking advantage of less expensive but equally competent outsourced personnel.

- Reducing operating costs through reduced overhead and facilities costs in other parts of the country or in other countries. For example, costs per square foot of office space are lower in Plano, Texas, than in Manhattan, New York.

- Providing availability to additional skilled people and other resources without the time and expense required to hire and train individuals or to purchase nonhuman resources.

- Reducing time to market by providing more staff and resources with reduced lead time and thus allowing more work to be accomplished on a shorter schedule. Remember that these additions must be appropriately planned and integrated into the project. As Brooks (1995) notes in *The Mythical Man-Month,* "adding manpower to a late software project makes it later."

- Improving quality by working with suppliers that have more expertise in a particular area or more mature processes than are available within the organization.

- Taking advantage of innovations available from the supplier.

- Allowing the organization to focus on core competencies while obtaining the expertise needed to create software requiring additional expertise. For example, a telecommunications company might outsource their relational database development to an organization with more expertise in that area.

- Mitigating or sharing risks by transferring some of the risk to the supplier.

While many potential outsourcing benefits exist, outsourcing can also be risky. As stated in the SEI's CMMI for Acquisition, "according to recent studies, 20 to 25 percent of large information technology (IT) acquisition projects fail within two years and 50 percent fail within five years. Mismanagement, the inability to articulate customer needs, poor requirements definition, inadequate supplier selection and contracting processes, insufficient technology selection procedures, and uncontrolled requirements changes are factors that contribute to project failure" (SEI 2007).

Acquisition Process

Acquisition is the process of obtaining software. Acquisition may be accomplished through in-house development or outsourcing or a combination of these methods. Outsourcing can include the purchase of commercial off-the-shelf (COTS) software, development of custom-built software by a third-party supplier, or both. Figure 6.6 illustrates the basic steps in the software acquisition process.

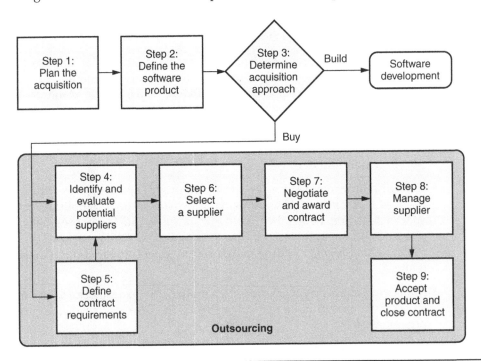

Figure 6.6   Acquisition process.

Plan the Acquisition

Step 1: Planning for the software acquisition begins when the idea or need is established for acquiring a software product. In this first step of the acquisition process key acquisition roles are assigned, the business need for the software is described in terms of technical and functional needs, quality attributes, project constraints, and acceptance and completion criteria, and the acquisition plans are documented.

Responsibilities for key acquisition roles must be assigned. These roles include the acquisition sponsor, acquisition manager, and members of the acquisition team. The role of the acquisition sponsor is to provide organizational influence to help justify and sell the acquisition within the acquirer's organization. The acquisition manager is the project manager for the acquisition project. The role of each individual acquisition team member is to adequately represent their stakeholder organization and to perform assigned tasks. Acquisition roles may also include representatives from the customer and/or user community and other key stakeholders that will work with the acquisition team to define the business needs and software requirements.

The business need defines the "why" behind the software acquisition. A business need could be a problem that needs to be addressed or it could be an opportunity that the business wants to take advantage of through software acquisition. It is important to precisely specify the business need so that people will clearly understand what action is to be taken and avoid addressing the wrong need. The business need also includes the description of any assumptions on which the project is based or any constraints on the project factors such as schedule, budget, resources, software to be reused, technology to be employed, and product interfaces to other products.

Acquisition plans are established to detail the methods to be employed throughout the acquisition project's life cycle. The time spent up front defining the acquisition strategy early will pay off in the long run by assuring stability throughout the acquisition process and the life of the software. The acquisition planning process should link acquisition objectives and tasks to resources (time, people, funds, and technology). The acquisition plans must organize these resources and define a method for achieving the approval of all stakeholders to guarantee the adoption of the acquisition plan. The acquisition plans should define the acquisition activities and provide for the integration of the effort. Acquisition plans should also specify the reviews and key measurement indicators that will be used to track and control that acquisition project. Software acquisition activities are sensitive to the same risks that occur in any project and require the same level of project and risk planning and management.

Define the Software Product

Step 2: The next step in the acquisition process is to define the software product. This typically includes defining the business- and stakeholder-level requirements. This step defines the scope of the acquisition. The desired product must be adequately analyzed and its business objectives, stakeholder functional requirements, business rules, and quality attributes determined and documented. The acquisition team should prioritize the requirements and separate needs from wants. Successful acquisition projects are dependent on clearly defining the required product.

Step 3: The acquisition team must determine the mechanism for acquiring the software. If the choice is to develop the software internally, then the acquisition project becomes a software development project and is not considered outsourcing.

Identify and Evaluate Potential Suppliers

Step 4: In this step the acquisition team performs a market search to identify possible suppliers. The data collected during the market search can be used as feedback to reassess the original product definition and to determine whether modification to that definition will result in greater overall value in terms of cost, performance, availability, reliability, and other attributes. The market analysis should also cover maintenance and support, test results, and user satisfaction analyses. Using the information from the market search, the acquisition team narrows the list of all available suppliers down to the few potential suppliers that best match the business needs and product definition in order to target the evaluation and keep evaluation costs to a minimum. In this step the acquisition team then evaluates these selected potential suppliers by performing an examination of their capabilities, quality systems, and products. Another method for accomplishing this is to start with a preferred supplier list of prequalified suppliers.

The depth required for this analysis is dependent on the needs and characteristics of the acquisition. However, care should be taken to obtain enough information to compare the qualifications of each potential supplier in order to make an informed decision. For example, a formal *request for proposal* (RFP) process is typically used only for larger projects involving customized software to be developed by the supplier. It is a very formal process where specific proposal requirements and questions are outlined by the acquirer in the RFP and responded to by the supplier in a proposal. Advertising an upcoming RFP may not only identify unknown suppliers but it may also encourage suppliers to offer technological input and business advice. They may be able to suggest new technologies and capabilities not previously known about or considered by the acquirer as possible alternatives. An RFP should include quantifiable, measurable, and testable tasks to be performed by the supplier, specifications and standards used for the project, acquirer-furnished equipment, information, and/or software to be used, and requirements for the products and services to be produced (GSAM 2000).

Other mechanisms for obtaining information and evaluating potential COTS suppliers include:

- *Supplier demonstration.* For COTS software, holding supplier demonstrations provides an excellent opportunity to see the product firsthand and ask questions. Actually seeing the features of different software in a live demonstration provides a context for comparison. Perhaps the basic functionality is comparable, but one product has a more intuitive user interface. The level of product knowledge and confidence of the supplier representative and their willingness to answer tough questions can be an indicator of the acquirer's future relationship with them. Another indicator of future support is whether the supplier presents a "canned" demo or has spent the time to customize their demo to specifically address the acquirer's business needs and requirements.

- *Evaluation copies.* For many COTS products, evaluation copies are available as mechanisms for demonstrating the software functions and capabilities and for eliciting user buy-in.

- *References.* Evaluating references and past product performance can provide useful information that can be used to evaluate the functionality and quality of the software.

Other mechanisms for obtaining information and evaluating potential suppliers to develop custom software include:

- *Past performance.* Evaluating references and past project performance can provide useful information. A supplier who has a consistent history of successfully providing software is more likely to perform effectively in the future. Past performance is a strong indicator of whether the supplier has the capability and ability to successfully complete delivery within schedule, on budget, and with the required level of functionality and quality. Previous experience with successfully developing similar products is also a credible indicator of the likelihood that a supplier can successfully perform in the future.

- *Prototypes.* For custom-built software, prototyping can be used to determine the supplier's understanding of the requirements or as proofs of concept.

Define Contract Requirements

Step 5: This step of the acquisition process is typically only necessary for suppliers who will be building custom-build software. The contract or agreement type is selected and the contents of the desired contract or agreement are defined. The contents of the contract will be based not only on the original requirements but also on the products and capabilities that are available and identified as potential suppliers are identified and evaluated. Trade-offs between cost, schedule, and scope will also impact the contents of the contract. Steps 4 and 5 of the acquisition process are thus done iteratively as they impact each other.

Select a Supplier

Step 6: In this step of the acquisition process, the results of the supplier evaluation are judged against established selection criteria, risks associated with each supplier are identified and analyzed, and a cost/benefit analysis is conducted. Based on this information, the final supplier of the COTS package is selected.

One or more supplier evaluation scorecards can be created to summarize all of the evaluation criteria information and scores for individual cost, schedule, product, and process attributes. Care should be taken that all information is gathered and the suppliers are scored in a way that eliminates variances in the scoring. This is best performed in a group-scoring meeting where participants have all of

Attribute	Max score	Supplier 1	Supplier 2	Supplier 3
Ability to deliver by date needed	10	10	7	8
Purchase price/licensing costs	10	7	5	10
Licensing restrictions	5	5	4	5
Operating costs	15	12	15	5
Maintenance costs	10	5	10	7
Process capability	10	10	8	5
Product functionality matches needs	20	18	16	8
Product quality	20	20	15	15
Ease of integration with existing systems	5	3	5	3
Ease of integration with our business processes	10	10	7	10
Ability to customize product	5	5	4	5
Technical support	5	5	3	2
Training availability	10	10	5	5
Total score	135	120	104	88

← Ability to deliver by date needed = 10 points minus one point for each week past needed date

← Product functionality meets needs = (Number requirements met ÷ Total requirements) × 20

Figure 6.7 Supplier score card–calculated scoring examples.

the gathered information available to assist in their scoring decisions. Using these forms and evaluating scores as a group can assist in maintaining momentum and assuring consistency. Different techniques can be used for assigning a score to each attribute or criterion. For example:

- The calculated scoring method where scores are assigned to each attribute based on predefined formulas as illustrated in Figure 6.7.

- A weighted scoring method where a numerical weight is assigned to each of the evaluation criteria and that weight is multiplied by the grade given to each prospective supplier to obtain a score for the individual criterion. Individual scores are then summed to give a total score as illustrated in Figure 6.8.

- The indexed scoring method where specific predefined criteria are used to select each score as illustrated in Figure 6.9.

Once the primary supplier candidate has been selected, a supplier qualification audit may be used as a final in-depth evaluation of that supplier's quality system and capability to produce the required software, prior to final selection.

Negotiate and Award Contract

Step 7: Once the supplier has been selected, the contract or agreement terms are negotiated and the contract is awarded. Now is the time to do the final negotiation with the preferred supplier. Depending on the type of acquisition, this step may be as simple as issuing a purchase order for the COTS software or as complex as negotiating a formal legal contract.

When a formal contract is needed, a well-written contract minimizes the probability of misunderstandings and is a major contributor to a congenial relationship between the acquirer and the supplier. Experience has shown that when the contract is unambiguous and clearly defines the duties and responsibilities of

Attribute	Max score	Supplier 1	Supplier 2	Supplier 3
Ability to deliver by date needed	10	10	7	8
Purchase price/licensing costs	10	7	5	10
Licensing restrictions	5	5	4	5
Operating costs	15	12	15	5
Maintenance costs	10	5	10	7
Process capability	10	10	8	5
Product functionality matches needs	20	18	16	8
Product quality	20	20	15	15
Ease of integration with existing systems	5	3	5	3
Ease of integration with our business processes	10	10	7	10
Ability to customize product	5	5	4	5
Technical support	5	5	3	2
Training availability	10	10	5	5
Total score	135	120	104	88

Process capability	Grade	Weight	Score
Software quality	1	×1	1
Project management	1	×2	2
Configuration management	1	×1	1
Requirements management	0	×1	0
Systems and software engineering	1	×2	2
Verification and validation	1	×2	2
Risk management	0	×1	0
Total score:			8

Grade: 1 = Meets or exceeds requirements
0 = Does not meet requirements

Figure 6.8 Supplier score card–weighted scoring examples.

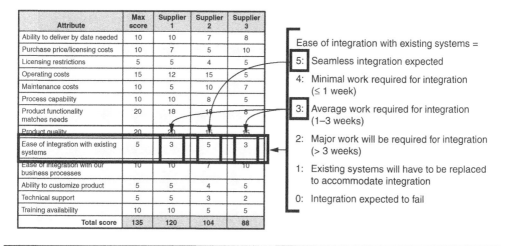

Attribute	Max score	Supplier 1	Supplier 2	Supplier 3
Ability to deliver by date needed	10	10	7	8
Purchase price/licensing costs	10	7	5	10
Licensing restrictions	5	5	4	5
Operating costs	15	12	15	5
Maintenance costs	10	5	10	7
Process capability	10	10	8	5
Product functionality matches needs	20	18	16	8
Product quality	20	20	15	15
Ease of integration with existing systems	5	3	5	3
Ease of integration with our business processes	10	10	7	10
Ability to customize product	5	5	4	5
Technical support	5	5	3	2
Training availability	10	10	5	5
Total score	135	120	104	88

Ease of integration with existing systems =

5: Seamless integration expected

4: Minimal work required for integration (≤ 1 week)

3: Average work required for integration (1–3 weeks)

2: Major work will be required for integration (> 3 weeks)

1: Existing systems will have to be replaced to accommodate integration

0: Integration expected to fail

Figure 6.9 Supplier score card–indexed scoring examples.

each party, the animosity that arises from quibbling over performance obligations usually can be avoided. The contract should be customized to consider both the acquirer's and supplier's strengths and weaknesses.

Supplier Management

Step 8: This step includes monitoring the supplier's performance throughout the execution of the acquisition project to ensure successful completion of the contract. Again, the level of rigor in this step depends on the type of acquisition. For example, it may be as simple as monitoring to ensure that the order of COTS software arrived and is properly installed without problems, or it may be as complex as managing the supplier over a multiyear development project.

For acquisitions that involve software development, ongoing formal evaluations and metrics should be used to monitor the supplier's progress against baselined budget, schedule, and quality standards and to manage the risks associated with the acquisition. For example, this may include ongoing supplier audits, joint project or product reviews, and partnering for joint process improvement actions. The goal is to provide the acquirer with enough visibility into the supplier's work activities to have confidence that the contractual obligations and product requirements are being met, or to identify issues that need corrective action. "When the supplier's performance, processes, or products fail to satisfy established criteria as outlined in the supplier agreement, the acquirer may take corrective action" (SEI 2007).

For an acquisition project of any length, change will occur. Therefore, this step involves managing and maintaining the requirements throughout the execution of the acquisition project. Requirements management mechanisms must be implemented to manage and control changes to those requirements and to ensure that approved changes are integrated into the acquisition plans, software products, and activities. This step can also involve managing any needed changes to the contract during the project.

When the final software product will include software developed in-house integrated with software from one or more suppliers, an effective mechanism for establishing communications between the acquirer and their suppliers is to form an *integrated product team* (IPT). An IPT, as illustrated in Figure 6.10, is a

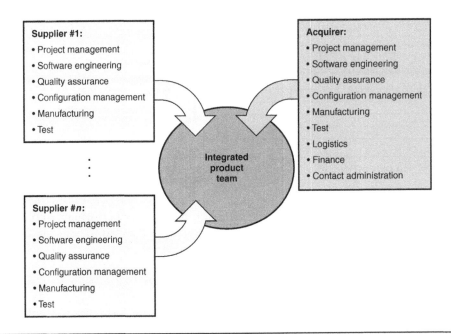

Figure 6.10   Integrated product team.

cross-functional team formed for the specific purpose of delivering an integrated product. An IPT is composed of representatives from all appropriate organizations and functional disciplines working together with a team leader to plan and implement a successful program (interrelated set of acquirer and suppliers' development projects), identify and resolve cross-functional issues, and make sound and timely decisions. IPT members should have complementary skills and be committed to a common purpose, performance objectives, and approach for which they hold themselves mutually accountable.

Accept the Product and Close the Contract

Step 9: Throughout the software development process the supplier should be performing *verification and validation* (V&V) activities. The acquirer should monitor these activities as part of the supplier management process. As part of product acceptance, the acquirer should also conduct V&V activities of their own on the delivered products. Example V&V activities may include alpha, beta, or acceptance testing and physical and functional configuration audits. These V&V activities should be conducted against negotiated acceptance criteria that are included in the contract to ensure that the delivered products meet all agreed-to requirements. The supplier should correct any identified product problems.

The accepted software is delivered and either used as delivered or incorporated into the acquirer's software as one of its components. If the software is being integrated into a larger product, integration and system testing should also be performed on that larger product as well.

As with any other project, an acquisition project will end and need to be closed. This includes transitioning the product into operations and its support into maintenance mode. For example, if the acquiring company has not purchased the rights to the software source code, that code may be transitioned into escrow so that if the supplier goes out of business, the acquirer is not substantially harmed because the acquirer can obtain the source code from escrow and still support its products. This step also includes the completing and closing of the contract and any other related activities.

Preferred Supplier Relationship

One way of minimizing the effort in selecting and monitoring suppliers is to create preferred supplier relationships. Suppliers are evaluated and rated against standardized criteria (for example, quality management systems and past performance). Suppliers who meet or exceed the standards are identified and recognized as preferred suppliers who are entitled to additional benefits. Those benefits may include selection preference, reduced inspections, and additional business opportunities.

These preferred suppliers may also be considered for strategic partnership across multiple acquisition projects. A strategic partnership is a corporate strategy for teaming up with one or more suppliers that have complementary resources to achieve a mutual business objective. Benefits of preferred suppliers and strategic partnership can include:

- The leveraging of competencies
- Reducing costs and improving service
- Freeing-up in-house resources
- Reducing the number of suppliers to manage
- Sharing of best practices and process improvement initiatives to provide mutual benefit

Chapter 7

B. Methodologies (for Quality Management)

An organization's quality management system (QMS) focuses on the strategies and tactics necessary to allow that organization to successfully achieve its quality objectives and provide high-quality products and services. As part of the QMS, methodologies need to exist that:

- Monitor the effectiveness of those strategies and tactics (cost of quality)

- Continually improve those strategies and tactics (process improvement models)

- Deal with problems identified during the implementation and performance of those strategies and tactics (corrective action procedures)

- Prevent problems from occurring during the implementation and performance of those strategies and tactics (defect prevention)

1. COST OF QUALITY (COQ)

> Analyze COQ categories (prevention, appraisal, internal failure, external failure) and their impact on products and processes. (Evaluate)
>
> **Body of Knowledge II.B.1**

Cost of quality is a technique used by organizations to attach a dollar figure to the costs of not producing high-quality products and services. In other words, the cost of quality is the cost of defects (nonconformances to the requirements). The costs of quality represent the money that would not be spent if the product was developed or the service was provided perfectly the first time. According to Krasner (1998), "cost of software quality is an accounting technique that is useful to enable our understanding of the economic trade-offs involved in delivering good-quality software." There are four major categories of cost of quality: prevention, appraisal, internal failure costs, and external failure costs.

Prevention cost of quality is the total cost of all the activities used to prevent defects from getting into products or services. Examples of prevention cost of quality include the costs of:

- Quality training and education
- Quality planning
- Supplier qualification and supplier quality planning
- Root cause analysis
- Process capability evaluations
- Process definition and process improvement

Appraisal cost of quality is the total cost of analyzing the products and services to identify any defects that do make it into those products and services. Examples of appraisal cost of quality include the costs of:

- Peer reviews and other technical reviews focused on defect detection
- Testing
- Review and testing tools, databases, and test beds
- Qualification of supplier's products, including software tools
- Process, product, and service audits
- Other verification and validation activities
- Measuring product quality

Internal failure cost of quality is the total cost of handling and correcting failures that were found internally before the product or service was delivered to the customer and/or users. Examples of internal failure cost of quality include the costs of:

- Scrap—the costs of software that was created but never used
- Recording failure reports and tracking them to resolution
- Debugging the failure to identify the defect
- Correcting the defect
- Rebuilding the software to include the correction
- Re–peer reviewing the product or service after the correction is made
- Testing the correction and regression testing other parts of the product or service

External failure cost of quality is the total cost of handling and correcting failures that were found after the product or service has been made available externally to the customer and/or users. Examples of external failure cost of quality include many of the same correction costs that were included in the internal failure costs of quality:

- Recording failure reports and tracking them to resolution

- Debugging the failure to identify the defect

- Correcting the defect

- Rebuilding the software to include the correction

- Re–peer reviewing the product or service after the correction is made

- Testing the correction and regression testing other parts of the product or service

In addition, external failure costs of quality include the costs of the failure's occurrence in operations. Examples of these costs include the costs of:

- Warranties, service level agreements, performance penalties, and litigation

- Losses incurred by the customer and/or users because of lost productivity or revenues due to product or service downtime

- Product recalls

- Corrective releases

- Customer support services, including help desks and field service

- Loss of reputation or goodwill

- Customer dissatisfaction and lost sales

The costs of building the product perfectly the first time do not count as costs of quality. Therefore, the costs of performing activities including requirements development, architectural and detailed design, coding, creating the initial build, and shipping and installing the initial version of a product into operations do not count as costs of quality.

In order to reduce the costs of internal and external failures, an organization must typically spend more on prevention and appraisal. As illustrated in Figure 7.1, the classic historic view of cost of quality is that there is a theoretical optimal cost-of-quality balance where the total cost of quality is at its lowest point. However, this point may be very hard to determine because many of the external failure costs such as the cost of customer dissatisfaction or lost sales can be extremely hard to measure or predict.

Figure 7.2 illustrates a more modern model of the optimal cost of quality. This view reflects the increasing empirical evidence that process improvement activities and loss prevention techniques are also subject to increasing cost-effectiveness. This evidence seems to indicate that near-perfection can be reached for a finite cost (Campanella 1990). For example, Krasner (1998) quotes a study of 15 projects over three years at Raytheon Electronic Systems (RES) as they implemented the Software Engineering Institute's (SEI) Capability Maturity Model (CMM). At maturity level 1 the total cost of software quality ranged from 55 to 67 percent of the total development costs. As maturity level 3 was reached, the total cost of software

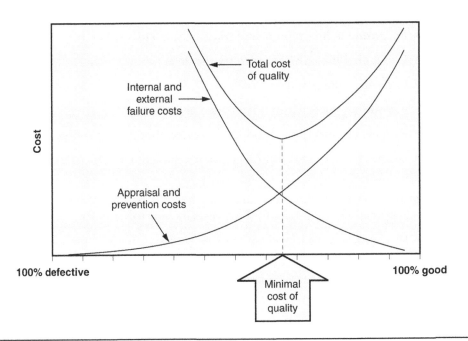

Figure 7.1   Classic model of optimal cost-of-quality balance (based on Campanella [1990]).

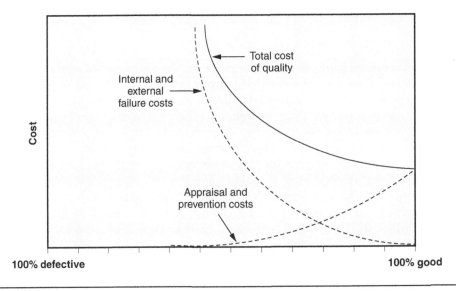

Figure 7.2   Modern model of optimal cost of quality (based on Campanella [1990]).

quality dropped to an average of 40 percent of the total development costs. By the end of three years, the total cost of software quality dropped to approximately 15 percent of the total development costs.

Cost-of-quality information can be collected for the current implementation of a project and/or process. These values can then be compared with historic, baselined, or benchmark values, or trended over time and considered with other quality data to:

- Identify areas of inefficiency, ineffectiveness, and waste as process improvement opportunities to reduce overall costs of software development and ownership.

- Evaluate the impacts of process improvement activities. For example, did the implementation of more formality in the peer review process have a positive impact by reducing the overall cost of quality?

- Provide information for future risk-based trade-off decisions between costs and product integrity requirements.

2. PROCESS IMPROVEMENT MODELS

> Define and describe elements of lean tools and the six sigma methodology, and use the plan–do–check–act (PDCA) model for process improvement. (Apply)
>
> **Body of Knowledge II.B.2**

Plan–Do–Check–Act (PDCA) Model

There are many different models that describe the steps to process improvement. One of the simplest models is the classic *plan–do–check–act* (PDCA) *model,* also called the the *Deming circle,* or the *Shewhart cycle.* In this model, illustrated in Figure 7.3, process improvement is viewed as a cycle that starts with the *plan* step. The plan step includes studying the current state and determining what process improvements are needed. A plan is then created to define the specific actions, assignments, and resources needed to implement the identified improvements. That plan is then implemented during the *do* step of the model.

The *check* step of the model analyzes the resulting process after the plan is implemented to determine if the expected improvements actually occurred and if any new problems were created. In other words, did the plan and its implementation work? During the *act* step the knowledge gained during the check step is acted on. If the plan and implementation worked, action is taken to institutionalize the process improvement throughout the organization, and the cycle is started over by repeating the plan step for the next improvement. If the plan and implementation did not result in the desired improvement, or if other problems were created, the act step identifies the root causes of the resulting issues and determines the needed corrective actions. In this case, the cycle is started over by repeating the plan step to plan the implementation of those corrective actions. The act step can also involve the abandoning of the change.

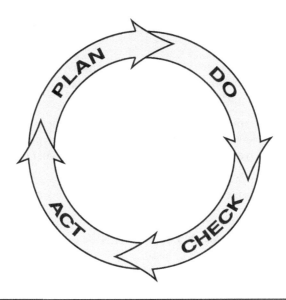

Figure 7.3   Plan–do–check–act model.

Six Sigma

The Greek letter *sigma* (σ) is the statistical symbol for *standard deviation*. As illustrated in Figure 7.4, assuming a normal distribution, ±six standard deviations from the mean (average) would include 99.99999966 percent of all items in the sample. This leads to the origin of the term *six sigma*, which is a near-perfection goal of no more than 3.4 defects per million opportunities. *Six Sigma* is a data-driven methodology for eliminating defects in processes through focusing on understanding customer needs, continual improvement of processes, and the reduction in the amount of variation in those processes. As a business management strategy, Six Sigma has evolved into "a comprehensive and flexible system for achieving, sustaining, and maximizing business success" (Pande 2000).

The Six Sigma *DMAIC model* (define, measure, analyze, improve, control) is used to improve existing processes that are not performing at the required level through incremental improvement. The *define* step in the DMAIC model identifies the customers, defines the problem, determines the requirements, and sets the goals for process improvement that are consistent with customer needs and the organization's strategy. A team is formed that is committed to the improvement project and provided with management support (a champion) and the required resources.

During the *measure* step in the DMAIC model, the current process is mapped (if a process map doesn't already exist) and the critical-to-quality (CTQ) characteristics of the process being improved are determined. Metrics to measure those CTQ characteristics are then selected, designed, and agreed upon. A data collection plan is defined, and data is collected to determine the baselines and levels of variation for each selected metric. This information is used to determine the

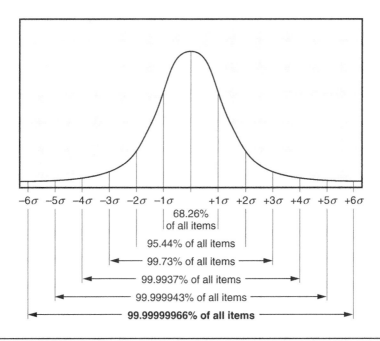

Figure 7.4   Standard deviations versus area under a normal distribution curve.

current sigma level and to define the benchmark performance levels of the current process.

During the *analyze* step in the DMAIC model, statistical tools are used to analyze the data from the measure step and the current process to fully understand the influences that each input variable has on the process and its results. Gap analysis is performed to determine the differences between the current performance of the process and the desired performance. Based on these evaluations the root cause(s) of the problem and/or variation in the process are determined and validated. The objective of the analyze step is to understand the process well enough that it is possible to identify alternative improvement actions during the improve step.

During the *improve* step in the DMAIC model, alternative approaches (improvement actions) to solving the problem and/or reducing the process variation are considered. The team then assesses the costs and benefits, impacts, and risks of each alternative and performs trade-off studies. The team comes to consensus on the best approach and creates a plan to implement the improvements. The plan should contain the appropriate actions needed to meet the customer's requirements. Appropriate approvals for the implementation plan are obtained. A pilot is conducted to test the solution, and CTQ metrics from that pilot are collected and analyzed. If the pilot is successful, the solution is propagated to the entire organization and CTQ metrics are again collected and analyzed. If the pilot is not successful, appropriate DMAIC steps are repeated as necessary.

During the *control* step in the DMAIC model, the newly improved process is standardized and institutionalized. A control plan is defined to put tools in place to ensure that the improvement gains are sustained into the future. Key metrics are selected, defined, and implemented to monitor the process and identify any future "out of control" conditions. The team develops a strategy for project hand-off to the process owners. This strategy includes propagating lessons learned, creating documented procedures and training materials, and any other mechanisms necessary to guarantee ongoing maintenance of the improvement solution. The current Six Sigma project is closed, and the team identifies next steps for future process improvement opportunities.

The Six Sigma *DMADV model* (define, measure, analyze, design, verify), also known as *design for Six Sigma* (DFSS), is used to define new processes and products at Six Sigma quality levels. The DMADV model is used when the existing process or product has been optimized but still does not meet required quality levels. In other words, it is used when evolutionary (radically redesigned) rather than incremental change is needed. Figure 7.5 illustrates the differences between the DMAIC and DMADV models.

During the *define* step in the DMADV model, the goals of the design activity are determined based on customer needs and aligned with the organizational strategy.

During the *measure* step in the DMADV model, critical-to-quality (CTQ) characteristics of the new product or process are determined. Metrics to measure those

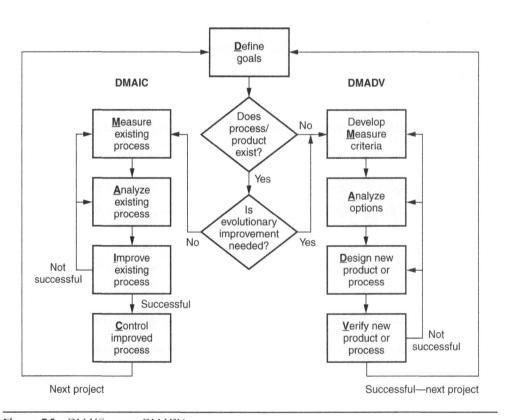

Figure 7.5   DMAIC versus DMADV.

CTQ characteristics are then selected, designed, and agreed upon. A data collection plan is defined for each selected metric.

During the *analyze* step in the DMADV model, alternative approaches to designing the new product or process are considered. The team then assesses the costs and benefits, impacts, and risks of each alternative and performs trade-off studies. The team comes to consensus on the best approach.

During the *design* step in the DMADV model, high-level and detailed designs are developed and those designs are implemented and optimized. Plans are also developed to verify the design.

During the *verify* step in the DMADV model, the new product or process is verified to ensure that it meets the customer requirements. This may include simulations, pilots, or tests. The design is then implemented into production. The team develops a strategy for project handoff to the process owners. The current Six Sigma project is closed and the team identifies next steps for future projects.

Lean Techniques

While *lean principles* originated in manufacturing, the Poppendiecks have applied these ideas to software development (Poppendieck 2003). There are seven lean principles:

1. Eliminate waste

2. Amplify learning

3. Decide as late as possible

4. Deliver as fast as possible

5. Empower the team

6. Build integrity in

7. See the whole system

Waste is anything that does not add, or gets in the way of adding, value as perceived by the customer. In order to be able to eliminate waste, any wastes in the software development process must be identified. The sources of those wastes must then be determined and removed. Examples of wastes in software development include:

- *Incomplete work.* If work is left in various stages of being completed (but not complete) it can result in waste. If a task is worth starting, it should be completed before moving on to other work.

- *Extra processes.* The process steps should be optimized to eliminate any unnecessary work, bureaucracy, or extra non-value-added activities.

- *Extra features or code.* It is a fundamental software quality engineering principle that one should avoid "gold plating," that is, avoid adding extra features or "nice to have" functionality that are not in the current development plan/cycle. Everything extra adds cost, both direct and hidden, due to increased testing, complexity, difficulty in making changes, potential failure points, and even obsolescence.

- *Task switching.* Belonging to multiple teams causes productivity losses due to task switching and other forms of interruption (DeMarco 2001). Surprisingly, "the fastest way to complete two projects that use the same resources is to do them one at a time" (Poppendieck 2003).

- *Waiting.* If something or someone must wait for output from some predecessor task, organizations need to look for a more effective way to produce that output to reduce the delay getting to the step or person that is waiting. Anything interfering with progress is waste since it delays the early realization of value by the customer and development organization.

- *Unnecessary motion* (to find answers, information). Interrupts concentration and causes extra effort and waste. It is important to determine just how much effort is truly required to learn something useful in moving ahead with a project.

- *Defects.* Another fundamental software quality engineering principle is that rework to correct defects is waste. The goal should be to prevent as many defects a possible. For those defects that do get into the product, the goal is to find those defects as early as possible while they are the least expensive to correct.

Value stream mapping is a lean technique used to trace a product from raw materials to use. The first step in this technique is to identify the product or service to be studied. The current value stream is then mapped by identifying all of the inputs, steps, and information flows required to develop and deliver that product or service. This current value stream is analyzed to determine areas where wastes can be eliminated. Value stream maps are then drawn for the optimized process and that new process is implemented.

Learning is amplified through providing feedback mechanisms. For example, developing a large product using shorter iterations allows multiple feedback cycles as iterations are reviewed with the customer. The continuous use of metrics and retrospective reviews throughout the project and process implementation also creates additional opportunities for feedback. The team should be taught to use the scientific method to establish hypotheses, conduct rapid experiments, and implement the best alternatives. *Set-based development* is a constraint-focused approach to making decisions, for example, asking people for their constraints on meeting times and selecting a time to accommodate the most people based on the constraints rather than suggesting a time and then going round and round modifying it until the team hits on a time everyone finds acceptable.

The principle of deciding as late as possible helps address the difficulties that can result from making irrevocable decisions when uncertainty is present. Making decisions at the "last responsible moment" means delaying decisions until failing to do so would eliminate an important alternative and cause decisions to be made by default. Gathering as much additional information as possible as progress is made allows better, more informed decisions to be made.

The product should be delivered as fast as possible because the sooner the product is delivered the sooner feedback from the customer and users can be obtained.

"Empower the team" means creating teams of engaged, thinking people who are motivated to design their own work rather than just waiting for others to order them to do things. Motivation provides people with a clear, compelling, achievable purpose, gives them access to customers, and allows them to make their own commitments. The manager provides the vision and resources to the team and helps them when needed without taking over.

"Building integrity in" means the developers focus on perceived and conceptual integrity as they implement, refactor, and test the software. Perceived integrity involves how the whole experience with a product affects a customer both now and as time passes. Conceptual integrity comes from system concepts working together as a smooth, cohesive whole. Refactoring involves adopting the attitude that internal structure will require continual improvement as the system evolves. Testing is even more critical after a product goes into production because greater than 50 percent of product change occurs when the product is in production. Having a healthy test suite both helps maintain product integrity and helps document the system.

"Seeing the whole" is all about systems thinking. Winning is not about being ahead at every stage (optimizing/measuring every task). It is possible to optimize an individual process and actually suboptimize the entire system. All decisions and changes should be made in reference to their impacts on the entire system, as well as their alignment with organizational and customer goals.

3. CORRECTIVE ACTION PROCEDURES

> Evaluate corrective action procedures related to software defects, process nonconformances, and other quality system deficiencies. (Evaluate)
>
> **Body of Knowledge II.B.3**

Product Problem Resolution

The product problem resolution process deals with correcting specific instances of a problem in one or more software products. This process starts when a customer, tester, or other internal originator identifies a problem in a software product. The steps in the problem resolution process are then dependent on whether that specific product is a baselined configuration item, as illustrated in Figure 7.6.

For example, if a problem has been identified in a product that is not an identified configuration item or that has not yet been baselined, that problem is simply communicated to the responsible author (the software practitioner currently assigned to that product) and the author corrects the problem as needed. Depending on where the problem was identified in the life cycle, it may be closed after unit testing or other levels of testing. On the other hand, if a problem has been identified in a product that has been baselined, a formal change request must be

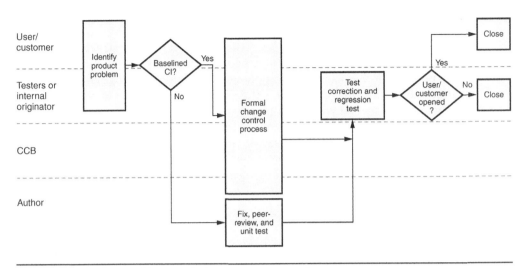

Figure 7.6 Product problem resolution process—example.

originated. One mechanism for accomplishing this is to open a problem report in a problem report database or other change request tracking system.

For problems identified in one or more baselined configuration items that are under change control, the appropriate *configuration control board* (CCB) reviews the change request and ensures that an impact analysis is performed. The CCB can make one of three decisions. The CCB can defer the change request to a later release, in which case the request is put on hold and re-reviewed with that release. If the CCB rejects the change request, the originator of the change request is informed. If the CCB approves the change, the responsible manager assigns an author to debug the problem and make the corrections. The changed product(s) are then peer reviewed and/or unit tested as appropriate. The changed product(s) then progresses through the appropriate levels of testing where the correction(s) are tested and the software product and/or system is regression tested to ensure that the change(s) didn't cause any other problems in the software. If a tester or other internal originator opened the change request, the change request is closed when the testing cycle is complete. If a customer opened the change request, it may not be closed until the customer receives the changed software and agrees to the closure, depending on the organization's problem resolution process.

For problems identified in one or more baselined configuration items that are under document control, the primary difference in the problem resolution process is that the CCB decision is made after the product is changed instead of before. Chapter 28 provides more information about change control, document control, and the CCB processes.

When evaluating the effectiveness of the product problem resolution process, examples of factors to consider include:

- How many problem reports were returned to the originator because not enough information was included to replicate or identify the associated defect?

- How many problem reports were not actual defects in the product (for example, operator errors, works as designed, could not duplicate)?

- What is the fix-on-fix ratio (where testing or future operations determines that all or part of the problem was not corrected)?

- Are identical problems being identified later in other products or other versions of the same product?

- Are unauthorized corrections being made to baselined configuration items?

- Are individuals involved in the process adequately trained in and following the process?

When evaluating the efficiency of the product problem resolution process, examples of factors to consider include:

- What are the cycle times for the entire process or individual steps in the process? (Are problems being corrected in a timely manner?)

- Are there any bottlenecks or excessive wait times in the process?

- Are there any wastes in the process? (Are problems being corrected in a cost-effective manner?)

Corrective Action Process

While the product problem resolution process deals with correcting a particular occurrence of a specific problem, the *corrective action process* addresses the underlying *root causes* to ensure that similar problems do not reoccur in the future. Corrective action is intended to address the underlying process problems or other quality system deficiencies that result in the product problems, process issues, and/or ineffective or inefficient activities. According to SEI (2006), "corrective action is taken when special causes of process variation are identified." One of the generic goals of the SEI's Capability Maturity Model Integration (CMMI) for Development is to monitor and control each process, which involves "measuring appropriate attributes of the process or work products produced by the process" and taking appropriate "corrective action when requirements and objectives are not being satisfied, when issues are identified, or when progress differs significantly from the plan for performing the process." The plan–do–check–act and Six Sigma models discussed previously in this chapter, as well as other models such as the Software Engineering Institute's IDEAL model (McFeeley 1996), are all examples of models that can be used for corrective action.

Problems or weaknesses in current processes or systems can be identified through a variety of sources. For example, they can be identified as nonconformances or other negative observations during audits, through suggestion systems, by quality action teams, through lessons learned during project, process, or system implementation, through the performance of root cause analysis on one or more product problems, or through the identification of unstable trends or out-of-control states using metrics. Whatever the source, the first step in the corrective action process is to identify and document the problem. For example, this can be accomplished by opening a corrective action request (CAR) as shown in Figure 7.7, which illustrates an example of a corrective action process.

The second step in the corrective action process is to assign a champion to sponsor the corrective action and assemble a corrective action team. The team determines if remedial action is necessary to stop the problem from affecting the quality of the organization's products and services until a longer-term solution can be implemented. For example, if the problem is that the code being produced does not meet the coding standard, a remedial action might be for team leads to review all newly written or modified code against the coding standard prior to it being baselined. While this is not a permanent solution and may in fact cause a bottleneck in the process, it helps prevent any more occurrences until a long-term solution can be reached. If remedial action is needed it is implemented as appropriate.

In the third step, the corrective action team researches the problem and identifies its root cause through the use of statistical techniques, data gathering metrics, and/or other means. This avoids simply eliminating the symptoms of the problem, which may allow the problem to recur in the future. For the coding standard example, the root cause might be that the coding standard is out of date because a newer coding language is now in use, or that new hires have not been trained on the coding standard, or that management has not enforced the coding standard and therefore the engineers consider it optional. Based on their research, the team develops alternative approaches to solving the identified root cause. The team analyzes the cost and benefits, risks, and impacts of each alternative solution and performs trade-off studies to come to consensus on the best approach. The corrective action plan should address improvements to the control systems

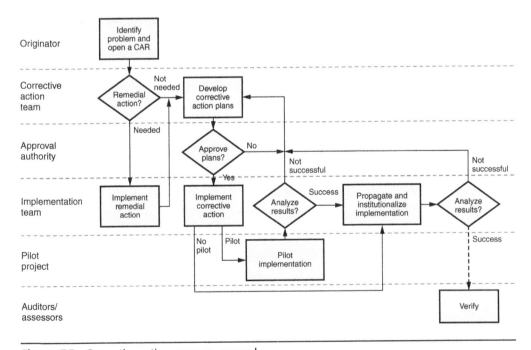

Figure 7.7 Corrective action process—example.

that will avoid potential reoccurrence of the problem in the future. For example, if the team determines that the root cause is lack of training, not only must the current staff be trained, but controls must be put in place to ensure that all future staff members (for example, new hires, transfers, outsourced personnel) receive the appropriate training in the coding standard as well.

The corrective action team must also analyze the effects that the problem had on past products and services. Does the organization need to take any action to correct the products or services created while the problem existed? For example, assuming that training was the root cause of not following the coding standard, all of the modules written by the untrained coders need to be reviewed against the coding standard to understand the extent of the problem. Then a decision needs to be made about whether to correct those modules or simply accept them with a waiver.

The output of this third step is corrective action plans, developed by the corrective action team, that:

- Define specific actions to be taken

- Assign a person responsible for ensuring that each action is performed

- Estimate effort and cost for each action

- Determine due dates for completion of each action

- Select mechanisms or measures to determine if desired results are achieved

In the fourth step, the corrective action plans are reviewed and approved by whomever has the authority as defined in the corrective action process. For example, if changes are recommended to the organization's quality management system (QMS), approval for those changes may need to come from senior management. If individual organizational-level processes or work instructions need to be changed, there may be an *engineering process group* (EPG) or *process change control board* (PCCB) made up of process owners that form the approval body. On the other hand, if the action plans recommend training, the managers of the individuals needing that training may need to approve those plans. During this step, any affected stakeholders should be informed of the plans and given an opportunity to provide input into their impact analysis and approval. The approval/disapproval decision from the approval authority should also be communicated to impacted stakeholders. If the corrective action plans are not approved, the corrective action team determines what appropriate future actions to take (replanning).

In the fifth step of the corrective action process, the implementation team executes the corrective action plan. Depending on the actions to be taken, the implementation team may or may not include members from the original corrective action team. If appropriate, the implementation of the corrective action may also include a pilot project to test whether the corrective action plan works in actual application. If a pilot is held, the implementation team analyzes the results of that pilot to determine the success of the implementation. If a pilot is not needed or if it is successful, the implementation is propagated to the entire organization and institutionalized. Results of that propagation are analyzed, and any issues are reported to the corrective action team. If the implementation and/or pilot didn't correct the problem or resulted in new problems, then the results may be sent back to the corrective action team to determine what appropriate future actions to take (replanning). Successful propagation and institutionalization closes the corrective action. However, at some point in the future, auditors, assessors, or other individuals may perform an evaluation of the completeness, effectiveness, and efficiency of that implementation to verify its continued success.

Evaluating the success of the corrective action implementation or verifying its continued success over time requires the determination of the CTQ characteristics of the process being corrected (as discussed in the DMAIC Six Sigma process earlier in this chapter). Metrics to measure those CTQ characteristics should be selected, designed, and agreed upon as part of the corrective action plans. Examples of CTQs that might be evaluated as part of corrective action include:

- Positive impacts on total cost of quality, cost of development, or overall cost of ownership

- Positive impacts on development and/or delivery schedules or cycle times

- Positive impacts on product functionality, performance, reliability, maintainability, technical leadership, or other quality attributes

- Positive impacts on team knowledge, skills, or abilities

- Positive impacts on customer satisfaction or stakeholder success

4. DEFECT PREVENTION

> Design and use defect prevention processes such as technical reviews, software tools and technology, special training, etc. (Evaluate)
>
> **Body of Knowledge II.B.4**

Unlike corrective action, which is intended to eliminate the future repetition of problems that have already occurred, *preventive actions* are taken to eliminate the possibility of problems that have not yet occurred. For example, an organization's supplier, Acme, experienced a problem because they were not made aware of the organization's changing requirement. As a result, the organization established a supplier liaison for Acme whose responsibility it was to communicate all future requirements changes to Acme in a timely manner. This is corrective action because the problem had already occurred. However, the organization also established supplier liaisons for all of its other key vendors. This is preventive action because those suppliers had not yet experienced any problems. The SEI's CMMI for Development specifically addresses corrective and preventive actions in its Causal Analysis and Resolution process area (SEI 2006).

Preventive action is proactive in nature; like risk management for projects, preventive actions identify potential problems and address them before they occur. Once a potential problem is identified, the preventive action process is very similar to the corrective action process discussed above. The primary difference is that instead of analyzing the actual root cause of an existing problem, the action team researches potential causes of a potential problem.

Since software is knowledge work, one of the most effective forms of preventive action is to provide individuals with the knowledge and skills they need to perform their work with fewer mistakes. If people make mistakes and don't have the knowledge and skill to catch their own mistakes, those mistakes can lead to defects in the work products. Training and on-the-job mentoring can be very effective techniques for propagating necessary knowledge and skills. For example, this can include training or mentoring in the following areas:

- In the customer/user's business domain so that requirements are less likely to be missed or defined incorrectly

- In coding language, coding standards, and naming conventions so that defects are less likely to be inserted into the code

- In the tool set so that misuse of tools and techniques do not cause the inadvertent interjection of defects

- In the quality management system, processes, and work instructions so people know what to do and how to do it so they are less likely to make mistakes

Technical reviews, including peer reviews and inspections, can not only be used to identify defects but also as a mechanism for promoting the common understanding of the work product under review. For example, if the designers and testers participate in the peer review of requirements, they may obtain a more complete understanding of the requirements that prevents future product problems and rework.

Software tools and technologies can also help prevent problems. For example, modern build tools may automatically initialize memory to zero so that missing variable initialization code does not cause product problems. Defined, repeatable processes prevent problems arising from doing activities incorrectly. When people understand what to do, when to do it, how to do it, and who is supposed to do it, they are less likely to make mistakes. Standardized templates can also act as a tool for preventing future problems. For example, if one project forgot to list activities in their work breakdown, those activities can be added to the template to prevent future projects from missing those activities. Checklists can also prevent problems that might arise from missed steps or activities.

Prevention also comes from benchmarking and identifying good practices in the industry and propagating them into improved practices within the organization. This allows the organization to learn from the problems encountered by others without having to make the mistakes and solve the problems themselves.

Evaluating the success of the preventive action implementation or verifying its continued success over time again requires the determination of the CTQ characteristics of the process being improved. Metrics to measure those

CTQ characteristics should be selected, designed, and agreed upon as part of the preventive action plans. Examples of CTQs that might be evaluated as part of preventive action include:

- Positive trends showing decreases in total cost of quality, cost of development, or overall cost of ownership

- Positive trends showing decreases in development and/or delivery cycle times

- Positive trends showing increased first-pass yields (work product making it though development without needing correction because of defects) and reductions in defect density

- Positive impacts on team knowledge, skills, or abilities

- Positive impacts on customer satisfaction or stakeholder success

Chapter 8

C. Audits

The ASQ Audit Division (Russell 2005) defines an *audit* as "a systematic, independent and documented process for obtaining audit evidence and evaluating it objectively to determine the extent to which the audit criteria are fulfilled." IEEE (2008a) includes a similar definition of an audit as "an independent examination of a software product, software process, or set of software processes performed by a third party to assess compliance with specifications, standards, contractual agreements, or other criteria." According to ISO (2008), internal audits are a required part of a quality management system. The Software Engineering Institute's Capability Maturity Model Integration (CMMI) for Development includes formal audits as one of the ways to perform objective evaluations in the Process and Product Assurance process area. The CMMI for Development also includes the performance of configuration audits as a specific practice in the Configuration Management process area (SEI 2006). The IEEE *Standard for Software Reviews and Audits* (IEEE 2008a) includes the process required for the execution of audits.

Software audits are planned activities—there are no surprise software audits. Software audits aren't trying to "catch" anyone at their worst. The people involved in a software audit should be aware of the audit's scope, objectives, and schedule and their roles and responsibilities during the audit. Individuals who are independent of the area being audited conduct the software audits. This independence helps ensure that an objective evaluation is conducted. Software audits have documented plans and reports. In addition, corrective action plans are documented, as required, for any nonconformances discovered during the audit. Software audits evaluate some aspect of a software system, process, project, product, or supplier and provide management with information from which fact-based decisions can be made. Software audits use a set of agreed-to criteria to conduct these evaluations.

AUDIT OBJECTIVES

Software audits should be value-added activities conducted to provide information based on an evaluation of whether the:

- Organization's standards, processes, systems, and/or plans are adequate to enable the organization to meet its policies, requirements, and objectives

107

- Organization complies with those documented standards, processes, systems, and/or plans during the execution of its work activities

- Organization's standards, processes, systems, and/or plans and their implementation are effective, in other words, the policies, requirements, and objectives are actually being met

- Resources, including people and other nonhuman resources, are being efficiently and effectively utilized

- Products conform to their required specifications and workmanship standards and are actually fit for use for their intended audience

Software audits also help identify areas for continual improvement and identify best practices within the organization that need to be propagated to other areas. In fact, this is one of the primary objectives of audits in more mature organizations where few or no nonconformances exist.

AUDIT PROGRAM

An overarching internal *audit program* should be planned as part of an organization's quality management system to ensure that required audits are performed regularly and audits of critical functions are performed frequently. The audit program also ensures that only trained, qualified, and independent auditors perform audits, and that audit processes are standardized and continually improved. Audits within the audit program should be scheduled so that they closely align with the organization's strategies, customer's requirements, and senior management's concerns and risks. Within the audit program schedule, individual audits should be scheduled to minimize the inconvenience for the auditee. For example, an in-process audit of a project's release management system should not be scheduled to coincide with the release of a major new feature package. A better time to schedule such an audit might be while that release is in development.

CONSEQUENCES OF AUDITS

Audit findings must be based on facts. However, since humans are identifying and interpreting those "facts," the audit staff must be as independent as possible in order to ensure objectivity. Objectivity is the absence of any bias that will influence the results of the audit. While total independence on the part of an internal auditor is impossible (at some level of the organization everyone reports to the same management), the goal is still to maintain enough independence so that the auditor can objectively evaluate and analyze the evidence and produce unbiased audit results.

Conducting an audit consumes resources, including money and time. Auditors need to be able to spend time with and talk to software managers and individual contributors in order to perform an effective audit. This can take time away from the business of developing and maintaining software, which is the primary mission of a software organization. Care should be taken to ensure that the value of the information received from the audit is worth more than the expected cost of the audit. In other words, audits should be value-added activities. This means that the audit information must have a client (customer), someone who is going to use the information to make decisions, even if that decision is "everything is great—no action is necessary."

An audit will typically result in one or more findings. This means that more resources will be needed to perform root cause analysis of any identified non-conformance and take corrective action, or to plan and implement improvement actions or the propagation of best practices. Things will improve, but in the mean-time more resources will be consumed.

The mere act of conducting an audit establishes expectations in the partici-pants' minds that management is going to act on the information and make things better. If the results of the audit are not adequately followed up on, the entire audit process may be perceived as a waste of time and energy. Unless everything is per-fect, value-added audits result in actions and follow-through.

Based on past experience with pure conformance-type audits, people may perceive audits in a negative light as "policing actions." This may lead to reluc-tance to cooperate with the audit or suspicions that the audit results will be used against them. Care should be taken by management to focus the audits on process and product improvement and not on people issues.

1. AUDIT TYPES

> Define and distinguish between various
> audit types, including process, compliance,
> supplier, system, etc. (Understand)
>
> **Body of Knowledge II.C.1**

Audits are typed either by who conducts the audit (internal versus external audits or first-, second-, and third-party audits) or by what is being audited (systems audits, process audits, product audits, project audits, or supplier audits). There are also special-purpose audits including follow-up audits and desk audits.

Internal or First-Party Audits

An *internal audit*, also known as a *first-party audit*, is an audit that an organization performs on itself. As illustrated in Figure 8.1, in a first-party audit the people con-ducting the audit (auditors), the people being audited (auditees), and the client (the person or organization that requested the audit) are all members of the same orga-nization. The audit criteria for an internal audit can come from inside the organi-zation (for example, the organization's quality management system, individual processes, or plans). The audit criteria can also come from outside the organiza-tion. For example, the standards or requirements of the organization's customers can be used as audit criteria.

Part II.C.1

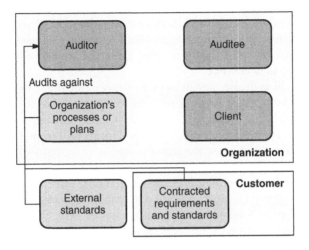

Figure 8.1   Internal first-party audit.

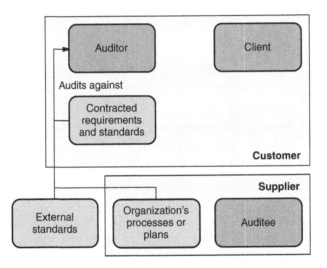

Figure 8.2   External second-party audit.

In some cases, an organization can hire or outsource their internal audits to an external firm or team of consultants. This is still considered a first-party audit because the hired organization is simply a temporary part of the organization.

External Second-Party Audits (Supplier Audits)

A *second-party audit*, also known as a *supplier audit*, is an external audit where a customer or an organization contracted by a customer performs an audit on its supplier. As illustrated in Figure 8.2, in a second-party audit the auditor and clients are in the customer's organization and the auditee is in the supplier's organization. The audit criteria for an external second-party audit can come from inside the supplier's organization. For example, the supplier's systems, processes, or plans can be used as audit criteria. The audit criteria can also come from the customer's organization. For example, standards or requirements from the customer's organization can be used as audit criteria. In a second-party audit, the supplier can also be audited to external standards, but only if the customer has contractually required adherence to those standards.

An example of a second-party audit would be a *supplier qualification audit* where a customer audits a potential supplier prior to awarding a contract to ensure that the supplier has the capability and capacity necessary to produce products of the required quality level. Another example would be a *supplier surveillance audit* where a customer performs audits of its suppliers as part of ongoing supplier monitoring activities during the execution of a contract. Of course, the requirements for these audits should be documented in the contracts or other agreements with the supplier.

External Third-Party Audits

A *third-party audit* is an audit performed on an auditee by an external auditor other than their customer. In a third-party audit, the client may be the organization being audited or it may be a third-party organization. As illustrated in Figure 8.3, the audit criteria for a third-party audit may be the audited organization's own internal systems, processes, or plans, or external standards may be used as the audit criteria.

An example of a third-party audit would be government regulators auditing an organization to ensure that all required external regulations (standards) are being met. Another example would be a registrar conducting an audit prior to granting registration to ISO 9001. Even though the registrar's fees are paid by the organization being audited, they are considered an independent third party because they report to an accreditation board.

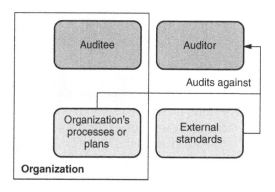

Figure 8.3   External third–party audit.

System Audits

System audits are audits conducted on management systems that evaluate all of the policies, processes, and work instructions, supporting plans and activities, training, and other components of those systems. A system audit can be thought of as a mega-process audit because it looks at all of the processes in the system.

For example, a quality management system audit evaluates an organization's existing quality management system's adequacy, conformance, and effectiveness. Examples of other systems that might be audited include an organization's environmental system or safety system.

Process Audits

A *process audit* evaluates a single process (or small set of processes) to determine if the process is defined, deployed, and adequate to meet the required quality objectives, if the process is being implemented correctly and with due diligence, and to determine if the process really works. A process audit only covers a sample portion of an entire system.

An example of a process audit would be an organization auditing its requirements specification inspection process to evaluate conformance to its documented peer review process and the effectiveness of that process. Another example might be auditing the software configuration management process or just one of its subprocesses such as the configuration identification process.

Product Audits

A *product audit* looks at a product and evaluates conformance to the product specifications, performance requirements, and workmanship standards or the customer's requirements. A product audit may look at the results of software peer reviews and testing quality records or it may actually include a sampling of rereview or retest activities.

An example of a product audit would be an organization auditing a sampling of source code to determine the level of conformance to internal coding standards. Another example would be to audit a finished subsystem to evaluate its compliance to its allocated functional requirements.

Project Audits

A *project audit* looks at the processes and activities used to initiate, plan, execute, track, control, and close a project. It evaluates the processes' conformance to documented instructions or standards. A project audit also looks at the effectiveness of the project management process in meeting the intended goals and objectives of the project, and the adequacy and effectiveness of the project's controls.

Follow-Up Audits

Any audit may produce findings that require corrective action. When those corrective actions are completed at some future date, a *follow-up audit* is one of the mechanisms that can be used to verify the completeness and effectiveness of their implementation. A follow-up audit can also be combined with the next scheduled audit of the area in order to minimize time and expense.

Desk Audits

A *desk audit*, also called a *document audit*, is limited to the evaluation of the organization's documentation, including quality records. These audits can be conducted at the auditor's desk since no on-site visit, where people are interviewed and activities are observed, is required. A desk audit may also be conducted as part of the preparation step for other types of audits.

2. AUDIT ROLES AND RESPONSIBILITIES

> Identify roles and responsibilities for audit participants: client, lead auditor, audit team members and auditee. (Understand)
>
> **Body of Knowledge II.C.2**

Client

The *client,* also called the *initiator* or *customer* of the audit, is the person or organization requesting the audit. The client determines the need for the audit and provides the authority to initiate the audit. The client defines the purpose (objectives) and scope of the audit, determines the audit criteria, and selects the auditing organization. The client is the main customer of the audit report and defines its distribution. The client also acts as the final arbitrator for any audit-related issues that can not be handled at a lower level.

Auditor Management

The *auditor management* is the management of the auditing organization. The auditor management is responsible for assigning a lead auditor to each audit and working with that lead auditor to select any additional members for the audit team. The auditor management ensures that the selected lead auditor and other auditors have appropriate training, knowledge, skill level, and independence. The auditor management provides the funding and other resources required to plan, prepare for, execute, report and follow up on, and manage the audit.

In the case of internal audits, the auditor management may also be responsible for establishing an effective audit program, including supporting procedures, processes, and tools, and for evaluating the performance of that audit program and the performance of the individual auditors. The auditor management may also plan the audit program, which includes setting priorities for audits and defining the organization's audit program schedule. An organization may have a full-time team of internal auditors or a group of part-time, trained auditors that perform audits as just one of their work activities. Either way, while performing their auditing duties the internal auditors should be responsible to a manager within the organization with enough authority to:

- Promote the independence of auditors and audits and maintain the operational freedom necessary to conduct audits

- Ensure that the audit program has a broad focus that includes all of the functions within the organization that impact the quality of the products and services produced

- Provide adequate resources to conduct the audits and train the auditors

- Authorize access to records, personnel, and physical properties relevant to the performance of audits

- Ensure that the management of the audited organization adequately considers and addresses the audit findings

- Ensure that the management of the audited organization takes the appropriate actions to correct the root cause of any problems or nonconformances found during the audit

Lead Auditor

The *lead auditor,* also called the *audit team lead,* is designated to manage the individual audit and its audit team and is responsible for the overall conduct and success of that audit. In addition to fulfilling the responsibilities of an auditor, the lead auditor:

- Plans the audit and documents the audit plan, including assigning responsibilities to audit team members and working with the auditee management to plan the schedule and logistics for the audit

- Manages the audit team, including assisting in the selection of the team, ensuring that the auditors have the skills, knowledge, and information they need to successfully conduct the audit, making team assignments, mentoring and evaluating the auditors on the team, and providing feedback on their performance

- Makes decisions about how the audit will be conducted, including controlling conflict and handling any difficult situations that may arise during the audit

- Acts as a focal point for communications to the auditee management, including negotiating with the auditee management over issues that arise during the audit or disagreements about the content of the audit report

- Coordinates the activities and logistics of the audit, including conducting the opening, daily feedback, and closing meetings

- Reviews the findings and observations found during the document review and audit execution and prepares and distributes the audit report

- Coordinates the review of the corrective action plans

- Verifies the implementation of the corrective action plans

Auditors

The *auditors* are the individuals conducting the audit. For larger audits there may be an audit team made up of a group of auditors. For small audits, the lead auditor may be the only auditor. The auditors are responsible for:

- Preparing for the audit by:

  - Understanding the purpose and scope of the audit and the audit criteria

  - Reviewing the audit plan and requirements

  - Creating checklists, interview questions, and other audit tools

  - Performing the documentation review

- Gathering objective evidence during audit execution

- Evaluating evidence against audit criteria to determine audit findings

- Attending opening, closing, and daily audit team meetings

- Reporting audit findings to the lead auditor as input to the audit report

- Maintaining confidentiality and professionalism

Auditee Management

The *auditee management* is the manager of the organization being audited who has been assigned to coordinate with the lead auditor on matters related to the audit. The auditee management is responsible for:

- Working with the lead auditor to plan the schedule and logistics for the audit

- Informing employees of the audit and its purpose and scope

- Providing access to auditee people, facilities, and resources

- Attending the opening, daily feedback, and closing meetings of the audit

- Providing all appropriate information requested by the auditors

- Providing a liaison/escort to the auditors as needed

- Responding to findings with corrective action plans and working with the lead auditor to resolve any issues that arise during the review of the corrective action plans

- Ensuring implementation of corrective actions

- Providing the lead auditor with evidence of successful implementation of corrective action

Auditee

The *auditees* are the individuals being interviewed or observed during the execution of the audit. The auditees are responsible for providing appropriate and accurate answers to the auditors' questions and for providing all appropriate information requested by the auditors.

Escort

For external audits or for audits where the auditors are unfamiliar with the auditees' organization or physical location, escorts from the auditee organization may be assigned to each auditor or group of auditors. The *escort* accompanies the auditor during data gathering and serves as liaison between the audit team and the auditee and the auditee management. The escort is responsible for:

- Introducing auditee personnel to the auditor

- Providing clarifying information as necessary; for example, this might include interpreting terminology or acronyms

- Providing or requesting supplies, records, and so on, needed by the auditor

- Acting as a guide for the auditor

- Ensuring that the auditor complies with company rules

3. AUDIT PROCESS

> Define and describe the steps in conducting an audit, developing and delivering an audit report, and determining appropriate follow-up activities. (Apply)
>
> **Body of Knowledge II.C.3**

The basics steps in the audit process are illustrated in Figure 8.4 and include:

- *Initiation.* A software audit starts with the formal initiation of the audit by the client of that audit.

- *Planning.* The audit must then be planned and that plan must be documented and communicated to the audit stakeholders.

- *Preparation.* During the audit preparation step, the lead auditor and other auditors prepare for the audit by gathering, sifting through, and analyzing as much of the information as possible before actually executing the audit. By the time the auditors actually conduct the audit, they should be familiar with the auditee's organization, the audit criteria, and the

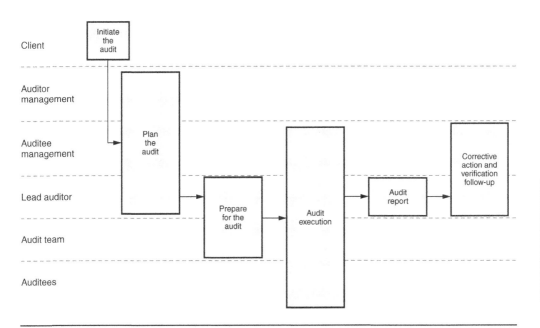

Figure 8.4   Audit process.

Part II.C.3

systems, processes, procedures, and/or project being audited. During this step, the audit inputs are evaluated against the audit criteria. Audit checklists, interview questions, and other tools are also prepared during this step.

- *Execution.* The audit execution, also called the audit performance or audit implementation, is the actual on-site fieldwork of the audit. It is the data- and information-gathering portion of the audit. During the execution step, the audit plans are implemented and the audit tools are utilized to gather objective evidence, which can then be analyzed to produce the audit results.

- *Reporting.* During audit reporting, the results of the audit are formally documented in the audit report, and all of the records associated with the audit are collected and appropriately stored.

- *Corrective action and follow-up.* The auditee management is responsible for creating and implementing corrective actions for any nonconformances identified during the audit. The auditee management may also choose to implement process improvement and best-practice propagation actions. Verification follow-up ensures the effective implementation of those actions.

Audit Initiation

The frequency of audits varies based on an organization's goals, objectives, and contractual requirements. Audits may be initiated when:

- Defined criteria in the audit program establish the need for the audit:

  – Every area should be periodically scheduled for an audit to ensure a comprehensive evaluation. Critical areas may be scheduled for audits more frequently than less critical areas.

  – When major milestones in the software development project are completed. For example, an audit of the requirements specification process might be held at the end of the requirements phase of the development life cycle.

  – When measured values reach specified targets. For example, an audit of the project management process might be held if the project goes over budget by more than 20 percent. Another example would be to audit the problem resolution process if more than 10 non-fixed major field-reported problems are over 30 days old.

  – When a major discrepancy or problem is identified, an audit may be conducted to determine what factors led up to the problem or to identify improvements that will prevent similar issues from occurring in the future.

- An initiator requests an audit. For example, an internal manager requests an audit of their area or an external customer requests an audit based on contractual requirements.

- Regulatory or governmental audit requirements must be met. For example, a regulatory agency may require that a certain type of audit be conducted annually or when a major milestone is met.

- Contractual audit requirements must be met. For example, a supplier may be required to conduct internal audits of their processes and systems and report the results to their customers, or the customer may require second-party audits where they audit the supplier's processes and systems.

- A major organizational change has occurred and the new management is seeking information about the current status of the organization.

During the initiation steps, the client selects the auditing organization, defines the purpose, scope, and objectives of the audit, and designates the audit criteria. This includes defining why the audit is being conducted and what organizations, processes, or products will be audited. All of the required inputs to the audit must also be available before the audit can start.

The *audit purpose statement* acts as a mission statement for the audit. It should define the purpose (reason) and major objectives for the audit. Examples of audit purpose statements include:

- *Internal first-party audit example.* To ensure continued implementation of the peer review process, to evaluate its effectiveness, and to identify improvement opportunities at the Northeast site

- *External second-party audit example.* To evaluate Acme subcontractor's software development processes to determine if they should be qualified as a preferred supplier for the GUI interface designs

- *External third-party audit example.* To perform a gap analysis of the software quality management system to determine the readiness for an ISO 9001:2008 registration audit

The *audit scope* defines the boundaries of the audit by identifying the exact items, groups, locations, and/or activities to be examined. While the client of the audit is responsible for defining the purpose and scope of the audit, for internal audits it many times falls to the lead auditor to formally document the purpose and scope statement as part of the audit plan. The scope of the audit is also used to focus the auditors' attention on what they are supposed to be evaluating. Auditors should not actively seek to identify problems outside the scope of the audit. However, if problems outside the scope are identified, they should be reported to the auditee management. If they are serious or systemic problems that could have major impact on the quality of the software products or services or that could have legal ramifications if not corrected, they should also be reported to the client as a negative observation in the audit report.

The major documents that will be reviewed during the audit should be available as input to the audit. This allows the auditors to perform a documentation review prior to the actual execution of the audit. For example, if an internal audit is being conducted for a project using the organization's *software configuration management* (SCM) process as the audit criteria, major audit-related documents might include the project's SCM plans and project-specific SCM processes or work instructions (or tailoring of organizational-level processes or work instructions). Note that the level of these input documents depends on the scope of the audit. For example, while the project-level audit in the example above looked at project-level documentation as inputs, for a system-level audit the input documents would include system-level documentation (project-level documentation might be sampled during the audit execution but would not be requested as input documentation). Quality records are typically not considered inputs to audit at any level, but again may be sampled as appropriate during audit execution.

Other inputs to the audit may include background information about the auditee's organization and information from prior audits. Background information can help the auditor understand the context in which the audit is taking place. This can include information about the business strategies and objectives, product information, domain information, and information about the industry (for example, competitive factors, regulatory environment). If prior audits have been conducted for the organization, the system, or processes being audited, then the audit reports, corrective action plans, and follow-up from those audits are also inputs to the current audit.

Audit criteria provide the objective requirements against which conformance and compliance are evaluated. Examples of audit evaluation criteria include:

- Written organizational quality policies

- Documented objectives (for example, budgets, programs, contracts)

Part II.C.3

- Customer or organizational quality specifications, standards, processes, or plans

- Product requirements

- Governmental or regulatory requirements

- Industry standards

Audit Planning

During the planning step the lead auditor selects the appropriate strategy for the audit. The *element method* audit strategy organizes the audit into manageable tasks based on the various elements of the audit requirements. For example, an audit against the ISO 9001 standard might be divided into elements based on the various requirements such as document control, control of records, quality policy, quality planning, management review, and so on. The auditors then examine each element across all organizations or locations being audited.

The *departmental* audit strategy organizes the audit into manageable tasks based on the departmental or functional structure of the organization being audited or by physical location. For example, that same ISO 9001 audit could also be structured by departments such as project management, systems engineering, software development, software testing, software quality assurance, software configuration management, and so on. The auditors then examine all of the elements of the standard for each department.

In the *discovery method* audit strategy, also called *random* or *exploratory* auditing, the auditors go into an area and investigate whatever is currently going on in that area. For example, if the auditors visit a software engineering group and that group is currently conducting a peer review, then the auditors evaluate that peer review. If instead they are doing unit testing or writing a requirements specification, then that is what the auditors evaluate. While discovery method auditing does examine current work practices and finds just-in-time issues, it does not lend itself to systematic auditing or complete audit coverage.

Based on the strategy selected the lead auditor estimates effort and staffing needs for the audit. The lead auditor works with the auditor management to provide funding, resources, and staffing for the audit. The lead auditor then coordinates with the auditee management to establish the detailed audit schedule, make arrangements to obtain audit-related input documents and information about the auditee organization, and coordinate the audit logistics.

The lead auditor documents the *audit plan* to formally communicate the details of the audit to auditor and auditee management and to the audit team. The audit plan is the primary communication vehicle to inform audit stakeholders of the impending audit. According to IEEE (2008a), the audit plan describes the:

- Purpose and scope of the audit

- Audited organization (location[s] and management), including units to be audited

- Software systems, processes, products, projects, or suppliers to be audited

- Audit evaluation criteria

- Auditor responsibilities

- Examination activities (for example, document reviews, interviews, activities being observed, records being examined)

- Resource requirements

- Audit schedule

- Requirements for confidentiality

- Checklists (and tools)

- Audit report formats

- Audit report distribution

- Required follow-up activities

The audit plan is a living document and should be updated and/or progressively elaborated as information is gathered during the audit. According to IEEE (2008), the audit plans and changes to those plans should be reviewed and approved by the client.

Audit Preparation

Auditors prepare for the audit by studying the input documentation prior to audit execution. The purpose of the document review is to evaluate the audit input documents against the audit criteria in order to assess them for compliance, completeness, consistency, and effectiveness. The subsequent execution step will then determine if the system, processes, and/or plans defined in those documents have been implemented as documented and are functioning effectively and efficiently. During the preparation step, the auditors use information from the input documents and audit criteria to prepare checklists, interview questions, and other tools for use during the audit. Standardized checklists, interview questions, or other tools may be used but should be tailored to the needs of each specific audit.

"An audit checklist is the primary tool for bringing order to quality audits" (Russell 2005). Checklists are lists of yes or no questions that correspond to the audit requirements. Each audit criterion can be translated into one or more checklist items. Checklists are used to bring order and structure to the audit and to ensure complete coverage within the audit scope. Each item in the checklist should be precise, measurable (it is possible to gather objective evidence to determine if that item is being met), and factual. The purpose of a checklist is to guide the gathering of information during the execution step of the audit. Checklists help the auditor remember what to look for and observe in a particular area. The information recorded on the checklists can then be analyzed and used to substantiate audit findings and conclusions. Checklists are simply tools, however, and should not be used to limit or restrict the execution of the audit. Checklists can be modified or even abandoned during the audit execution as appropriate.

In addition to preparing for the audit as an auditor, the lead auditor also prepares the audit team by ensuring that they have received orientation and any necessary training required by the audit. The lead auditor continues to work with the auditee management to keep communication lines open, answer questions, and handle ongoing logistical issues.

Audit Execution

The audit execution step is the actual on-site fieldwork of the audit. As illustrated in Figure 8.5, the audit execution is the data- and information-gathering (objective evidence–gathering) portion of the audit that starts when the auditors arrive at the auditee's location and hold the opening meeting and ends with the closing meeting.

The execution step of the audit starts with an *opening meeting* between the audit team and the auditee organization. The lead auditor conducts this meeting, and at least one member of the auditee management should attend the opening meeting. However, additional members of the auditee management and other auditees and interested parties may attend at the discretion of the auditee management.

The objectives of this meeting include introducing the audit team, reviewing the conduct of the audit, reviewing audit schedule and logistics, and making sure the auditee understands what to expect from the audit. Any known issues, problems, or adjustments that need to be made to the audit schedule or logistics should be handled at this meeting through consensus between the auditee management and the audit team. For example, if interviewees are not available at the scheduled time, the audit schedule can be adjusted. If there are any disagreements, required clarifications, or questions from the auditees, these should also be addressed at this time.

Most of the time and effort of the audit execution step is spent gathering objective evidence. "The job of the auditors is to collect factual information, analyze and evaluate it in terms of the specified requirements, draw conclusions from this comparison, and report results to management" (Arter 1994). The ASQ Audit Division defines *objective evidence* as "information which can be proven true, based on

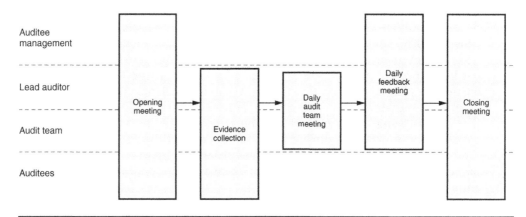

Figure 8.5   Audit execution process.

facts obtained through observation, measurement, test or other means" (Russell 2005). One of the reasons that the independence of the auditor is so important to the audit is that it helps ensure that the observed or documented evidence is uninfluenced by prejudice, emotion, or bias. Techniques for gathering objective evidence include:

- *Examining quality records.* Quality records provide the evidence that:

  - The products conform to requirements

  - Appropriate activities or processes took place

  - The execution of those activities met required standards

  Examples of quality records include: meeting minutes, reports, engineering notebooks, action item lists, problem reports, corrective action plans, metrics, memos, status reports, completed checklists or forms, formal sign-off/approval pages, and logs.

- *Reviewing documents.* If the documents were supplied as audit inputs, examination of those documents was accomplished during the preparation step. Based on information obtained during audit execution, it may be necessary to do additional reviews of those documents supplied as input or to examine other documents requested during the audit execution.

- *Witnessing an event or process.* An auditor can witness or observe work-in-progress events taking place or a process being implemented to see if what is actually happening meets the audit criteria and/or the documentation. This involves witnessing how work is actually being performed by watching or being present without participating actively in the event or process. The auditor observes to determine that:

  - The product was made or activity performed according to documented procedures or work instructions

  - Activities were performed by the designated responsible person

  - The proper equipment and/or tools were used

  - Participants were familiar with policies and procedures and they knew their roles and responsibilities (based on Russell 2005)

- *Finding patterns.* The auditor can examine data or software metrics and look for patterns or trends. For example, the auditor could look at problem report data and look for error-prone components or common root causes.

- *Interviewing auditees.* The auditor can interview auditees to obtain information. However, one person saying something is true does not make it objective evidence. The auditor must seek corroboration through more than one interviewee saying the same thing, or through quality records, documentation, observation, or other methods.

- *Examining physical properties.* The technique of examining physical properties for gathering objective evidence is used most often in product-type audits. While this technique is used widely in manufacturing, hardware, and some service industry audits where physical products or outputs are more prevalent, it is less applicable to software-type audits. It could, however, still be used to examine the properties of items such as screen displays or media labeling.

There is never time to look at all possible objective evidence during an audit. For example, there may be hundreds of source code modules or thousands of sets of meeting minutes (from peer reviews, status meetings, and change control board meetings, and so on) or other quality records. Audits are always based on sampling from all of the possible objective evidence that is available.

Tracing is an example of one approach for gathering samples of objective evidence. Tracing follows the chronological progress of an item as it is being processed. Tracing begins by selecting to start at the beginning, middle, or end of the process, choosing an action, and sampling work products from that action. For example, the auditor could start in the middle of the software development process and select the action of coding a module. The auditor then selects one or more specific modules from the list of modules that have been coded. The auditor gathers information about the sampled item(s) in five areas:

- *Labor.* Information about who coded the module(s), how much effort was expended, or what the estimated effort was for each module

- *Equipment.* Information about the development platform and tools

- *Methods.* Information about coding standards, code inspection processes, naming conventions, or source control processes used

- *Environment.* Information about the quality of the environment where the coders work (for example, noise level, interruptions)

- *Measurements.* Information about what measurements were collected

The auditor can then trace the module(s) forward into integration test, system test, and release, looking at items such as the integration methods, change control, and problem reports against the module(s). The auditor can also choose to trace the module(s) backward and ask to see the associated detailed design for each module or the higher-level design that specified each module, or examine the tracing of each module back to its associated requirements. The benefit of tracing is that if a random sampling of items can be traced forward or backward through the process, there is a high confidence level that all of the items can be traced.

Each day of the audit, the audit team should get together in a *daily audit team meeting* to share gathered objective evidence, tentative conclusions, and problems. Based on the progress that has been made during audit execution, these meetings may also be used to replan the audit activities. For example, the team may decide that additional data need to be gathered to clarify incomplete or contradictory results, or delays in one area of the audit can result in the shifting of assigned activities between auditors. Even if there is only a single auditor performing the audit, that auditor should take time each day to consolidate information and plan further activities as appropriate. During the last day of the audit, the daily team meeting is used to create the draft audit report that will be presented during the closing meeting. Utilizing the objective evidence obtained during the execution phase allows audit conclusions and results to be fact-based.

After the audit team meeting each day, a *daily feedback meeting* (also called a *daily briefing*) is held to update the auditee management on the information that has been collected so far and on any potential nonconformances, problems, or areas of concern. The goal here is "no surprises." These meetings also give the auditee management an opportunity to provide additional objective evidence to clarify misconceptions and prevent incorrect information from being included in the audit report.

Holding a *closing meeting* completes the audit execution step. The auditee management should attend this meeting along with members of the audit team and other interested stakeholders, including auditees. The lead auditor conducts the closing meeting by starting with a summary of the audit and then presenting the audit results in detail. This presentation is followed by an open discussion about the results. The lead auditor or a member of the audit team responds to any questions and clarifies information as necessary. This discussion also gives the auditee management a final opportunity to "point out any mistakes with respect to the facts that have been collected" (Juran 1999). During the closing meeting, the lead auditor also explains the requirements for the auditee management's corrective action response to any nonconformances identified and the associated follow-up activities. The objective of the closing meeting is to ensure that the auditee management clearly understands the results of the audit so they can start working on corrective actions.

Audit Reporting

During the reporting step, the results of the audit are formally documented in the audit report. The *audit report* contains a summary of the audit results, including a synopsis of the findings, and the audit team's evaluations of the extent of the auditee's compliance to the audit criteria and their ability to achieve their objectives based on the current systems, processes, and/or plans. The report also contains the detailed audit findings, including major and minor nonconformances, other observations, process improvement opportunities, and/or best practices that were identified. A *major nonconformance* is a major breakdown of a system, control, or process, a nonfulfillment of specified requirements or audit criteria, or a number of minor nonconformances all related to the same requirement that are summarized into a single major nonconformance. A *minor nonconformance* is an isolated or single observed lapse in a requirement or audit criterion or part of a requirement or audit criterion not being met. Nonconformances are always within the scope of the audit. *Observations* are anything else that was observed by the auditors that is important enough to be communicated to the client but that is not a nonconformance. Positive observations contribute to the quality of the product, system, process, or project. Negative observations detract from the quality of the product, system, process, or project, and if not addressed may result in a future issue. Any observed potential nonconformance outside the scope of the audit is also reported as a negative observation. *Process improvement opportunities* are identified areas where proactive steps can be taken to prevent future issues or improve the effectiveness or efficiency of a system, process, or product. *Best practices* are identified areas where the auditee's practices are worthy of being brought forth as examples that other teams, groups, or projects within the organization could use as benchmarks to improve their practices.

Audit Corrective Action and Follow-Up

For each nonconformance in the audit report, the auditee management needs to ensure that *corrective actions* are planned and implemented. The auditee management may also decide that corrective actions need to be planned and implemented for negative observations and process improvement opportunities. The auditee management may either do this planning and implementation themselves or delegate those activities to others. The completed corrective action plan should include specific actions with schedules and responsibility assignments for each action. If actions have already been taken to correct the nonconformance or problem, these should also be documented in the corrective action plans. If the auditee management determines that corrective action is not appropriate after additional review of the audit findings, they should document the reasons why no action is necessary in their response to the lead auditor.

Upon receipt of the auditee management's response, the lead auditor coordinates the review of the corrective action plans. This may be accomplished by the lead auditor reviewing the corrective action plans, by the audit team reviewing those plans, or, if necessary, by using a technical expert to review those plans. This review can help prevent the auditee organization from wasting time and resources implementing corrective actions that will not eliminate the nonconformance or solve the problem.

If the corrective action plans or justifications for why no corrective actions were needed are acceptable, the lead auditor informs the auditee. If one or more of the proposed corrective actions or justifications is not acceptable, the lead auditor contacts the auditee management and resolves the issue. If the issues can not be resolved between the lead auditor and auditee management, they can be escalated to the client.

As the auditees complete the implementation of each corrective action, they inform the lead auditor. The lead auditor then coordinates the verification of each implemented corrective action:

- Through written communications with the auditee

- By reviewing the revised documentation or new quality records

- By conducting a follow-up audit or by re-auditing against the associated findings during a future audit

If the corrective action is completed before the end of the audit, the follow-up on that corrective action's implementation may be completed as part of that same audit and the audit report can include both the reporting of the nonconformance and the fact that a correction was implemented and verified.

The lead auditor ensures that the actions that were taken to verify the corrective action are documented. This documentation becomes part of the quality records for the audit.

Each corrective action is closed as its successful implementation is verified. Each nonconformance is closed when all of its associated corrective actions are verified and closed. The audit is closed when all nonconformances for that audit are closed.

Audits, like any other process, should be auditable. This means that quality records related to the audit must be collected and retained. Based on the needs of the auditing organization, the required quality records for an audit should be defined in the audit process definition. Examples of quality records maintained for an audit might include:

- The audit plan

- Opening and closing meeting minutes, including attendance lists

- Completed working papers such as checklists and auditor notes

- The audit report

- Corrective action, follow-up, and closeout documentation for each nonconformance

Part II.C.3

Part III

Systems and Software Engineering Processes

Part III

Chapter 9

A. Life Cycles and Process Models

> Evaluate various software development
> life cycles (iterative, waterfall, etc.) and
> process models (V-model, Feature Driven
> Development, Test Driven Development,
> etc.) and identify their benefits and when
> they should be used. (Evaluate)
>
> **Body of Knowledge III.A**

Software development *life cycles* and *process models* are high-level representations of the software development process. These models define the stages (phases) through which software development moves and the activities performed in each of those phases. Each of these models covers the life of the software project (one iteration or increment) from conception until that version of product is completed and/or released. They provide the framework for the detailed definitions of the processes for individual life cycle activities and depicts interrelationships between major milestones, baselines, and project deliverables. Life cycle models can also help project managers plan activities and track progress by breaking the development effort into phases, each with a defined set of activities, including phase transition reviews.

Software product life cycle models cover the life of the software product from conception until the product is retired from use. For successful software products, product life cycles usually encompass multiple passes through software development. Incremental and evolutionary development models are examples of software product life cycle models.

WATERFALL MODEL

The *waterfall model* is the most basic of all software life cycle models. It is based on the concept that software development can be thought of as a simple sequence of phases. Each phase proceeds from start to finish before the next phase is started. The work products produced in one phase in the waterfall model are typically the inputs into subsequent phases. The waterfall model is based on the premise that a project can be planned before it is started and that it will progress in a reasonably orderly manner through development. In the waterfall model, a well-defined set of requirements is specified before design begins, design is complete before coding begins, and the product is tested after it is built.

Figure 9.1 illustrates an example of the waterfall model. This example shows six phases, but on an actual project the number of phases chosen for the model depends on the needs of that project and the organization conducting the project. Some waterfall models only include the downward arrows, depicting the flow of activities downward through the development project. This example also includes upward arrows to indicate that iteration is allowed in the development activities.

Many critics of the waterfall model say that it is antiquated and does not reflect what truly goes on in software development. It should be remembered, however, that a model is an abstract representation of an item or process from a particular point of view. The aim of a model is to express the essentials of some aspect of the item or process without giving unnecessary detail. The purpose of a model is to enable the people involved to think about and discuss these essential elements without getting sidetracked by all of the detail. In this respect, the waterfall model is still a useful tool because it is an easy model to understand and discuss. Even the most unsophisticated stakeholder can understand the basic concepts of the waterfall model. It is true that the waterfall model removes almost all of the detail, including most of the iterations that typically occur during development, but many of those details may be accounted for in lower-level process definitions under the model.

The waterfall model was the first model to define a disciplined approach to software development. It has been well studied and is well understood and well defined. Another strength of the waterfall model is that it maps well to the deliverables of software development, which can aid in project management activities. Many tools exist to support this model.

A major weakness of the waterfall model is the fact that most, if not all, requirements must be known up front at the beginning of development. The waterfall model does not readily accommodate change. The software is also not available for use until the project is completed or nearly complete so there is no provision for intermediate feedback from stakeholders, although prototypes may be used to provide early feedback during waterfall model–based development.

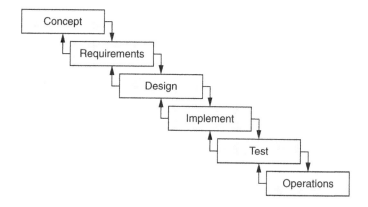

Figure 9.1   Waterfall model–example.

Part III.A

The waterfall model is most appropriate for projects where the requirements are expected to be stable and the development process is expected to progress in an orderly, disciplined manner. For example, a project to port an existing product to a new platform, environment, or language where the constraints are well known might be a candidate for using the waterfall model. Other examples might include enhancement projects to update the software to adhere to new government regulations or to automate a report that is currently being implemented manually. The waterfall life cycle model may also be appropriate for projects with only a few experienced programmers and many junior programmers, or new development projects in very mature domains where yet another software product, just like the last one, is being built. The waterfall model would typically not be appropriate for projects where the requirements are fuzzy or expected to have high volatility or projects that are not expected to progress in a linear manner. For large, high-risk projects, a more risk-based approach such as the spiral model or incremental development may be more appropriate than using the waterfall model.

V-MODEL

The *V-model* is a variation on the waterfall model that highlights the relationship between the testing phases and the products produced in the early life cycle phases, as illustrated in Figure 9.2. For example, *acceptance test* evaluates the software against the user needs as defined in the *concept* phase, and *system test* evaluates the software against the requirements specified during the *requirements* phase, and so on.

W-MODEL

Another variation on the waterfall model is the *W-model*, as illustrated in Figure 9.3. The W-model has two paths (or crossing V's), each one representing the life cycle for a separate organization or team during development. The first path represents the development organization that is responsible for developing requirements,

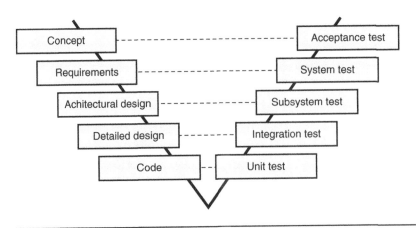

Figure 9.2   V–model–example.

design, and code. The second path represents the independent verification and validation organization that is responsible for independently analyzing, reviewing, and testing the work products of each phase of the software life cycle.

SPIRAL MODEL

The *spiral model*, originally defined by Boehm (1988), is a risk-based model that expands on the structure of the waterfall model with details including the exploration of alternatives, prototyping, and planning. As illustrated in Figure 9.4, the

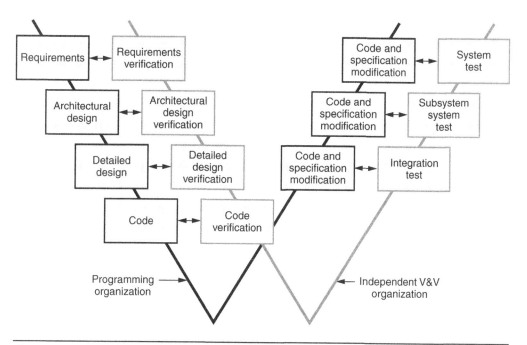

Figure 9.3   W-model—example.

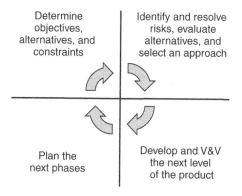

Figure 9.4   Spiral model steps.

spiral model segregates each of the initial phases of software development into four steps. In the first step the development team determines the objectives, alternatives, and constraints for that phase. During the second step, each alternative is evaluated and its risks are identified and analyzed, and prototyping is done in order to select the approach that is the most suitable for the project. The third step involves the actual development of the next level of software products and the verification and validation (V&V) of those products. This may also include creating simulations, models, or benchmarks if appropriate. During these first three steps, decisions are made and additional information is obtained that will impact the project plans. Therefore, in the fourth step of the spiral model the project plans are progressively elaborated with additional details for subsequent phases. This fourth step typically ends with a phase review.

The life cycle phases are then incorporated into the four quadrants created by these four steps in a spiral fashion, as illustrated in the example in Figure 9.5. The spiral starts in the middle with step 1 of the concept phase. For example, this step of the concept phase might include exploring buy versus build alternatives or determining which business- or stakeholder-level requirements should be addressed during the project. The second step of the concept phase activities might include the risk identification and analysis for the buy versus build option, a cost/benefit analysis of the alternatives, and prototyping to evaluate the choices in order to determine that building the software in-house is the appropriate deci-

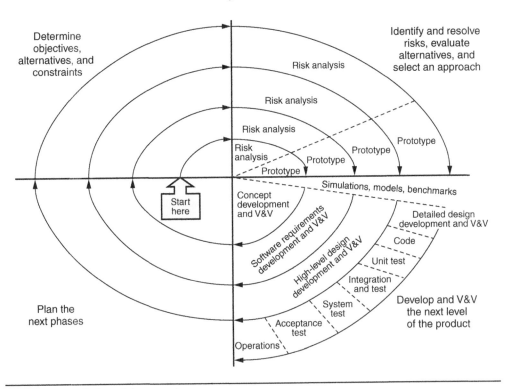

Figure 9.5 Spiral model—example.

Source: "A Spiral Model of Software Development and Enhancement" by Barry W. Boehm, *IEEE Computer*, May 1988. Copyright IEEE 1988.

sion. During the third step of the concept phase, the business-level and stake-holder-level requirements are elicited, analyzed, and specified (for example, in a concept of operations document, marketing specification, or in a set of user cases). V&V activities are performed to analyze those requirements. In the fourth step the information and decisions from the first three steps are used to update the project plans for the requirements phase and other subsequent phases. This cycle of four steps is then repeated for the requirements phase and the high-level (architectural) design phase. The fourth cycle through the spiral determines the detailed design and implementation objectives, alternatives, and constraints in the first step. The second step chooses the detailed design and implementation approaches that will be used for the project. At this point most of the major decisions for the project have been made, and the spiral model finishes with a waterfall-like third step that includes detailed design, code, unit test, integration and test, system test, acceptance test, and operations. As with all of the other software development life cycle models, the spiral model should be tailored to the needs of the project and organization.

The spiral model shifts emphasis from product development to risk analysis and avoidance. The strengths of the spiral model include the fact that it accommodates good features of other models while its risk-driven approach avoids many of their shortcomings. The spiral model focuses attention on exploring options early by obtaining feedback through prototyping to ensure that the right product is being built in the most appropriate way. The spiral model also includes mechanisms for handling change through the iteration of any given cycle as many times as necessary before moving on to the next cycle. The spiral model also incorporates good project management by emphasizing project plan updates as more information is obtained.

Weaknesses of the spiral model include the fact that it does not map as well as the waterfall model does to the needs of software development done under contract (for example, mapping to controls, checkpoints, and intermediate deliveries). The spiral model requires a high level of risk management skills and analysis techniques, which makes it more people-dependent than other models. This also means that the spiral model requires a strong, skilled project manager. Because of the extensive flexibility and freedom built into the spiral model, fixed-cost or fixed-schedule projects may not be good candidates for using this model. The spiral model is also a complex model and is not well understood or as easily grasped by some managers or other stakeholders. These individuals may find the spiral model difficult to communicate about and use. Further elaboration of the model may also be needed, especially in the activities from detailed design onward, which fall back to the basic waterfall flow. These details are often defined in lower-level process definitions.

The spiral model is appropriate for large, high-risk projects where the requirements are fuzzy or are expected to have a high level of volatility. Projects where the software development approach is nonlinear or contains multiple alternative approaches that need to be explored are also candidates for the spiral model.

For smaller, low-risk, straightforward projects, the extra risk management, analysis, and planning steps may add an unnecessary additional cost and/or effort. The spiral model may also not be an appropriate choice for projects done under fixed-price or fixed-schedule contracts or with less-experienced staff.

Part III.A

ITERATIVE MODEL

The *iterative model* is an iterative software development model where steps or activities are repeated multiple times. This may be done to add more and more detail to the requirements, design, code, or tests, or it may be done to implement small pieces of new functionality one after another. There are many different iterative models. For example, the spiral model discussed above can be implemented as an iterative model and the test-driven development and feature-driven development methods described below are also iterative models. Figure 9.6 illustrates another example of the iterative development model demonstrating the extreme programming (XP) principle of flow. In this example, a development cycle starts with a short-term, focused plan, which defines the functionality to be implemented in that cycle. The cycle itself consists of a little design, a little test writing, a little code development, a little testing, integration of successfully developed code into the "baseline" for that cycle, and then more design, more test writing, and so on, iterating through the loop. This continues with feedback (from other developers, the customer, and the software itself) occurring at all points until the functionality is completed within the time frame allocated to the increment. The functionality is then released to the customer who may try it out and put it into production or just provide feedback for the next development cycle (iteration).

TEST-DRIVEN DEVELOPMENT

Test-driven development (TDD), also known as *test-driven design*, is an agile iterative development methodology. TDD implements software functionality based on writing the test cases that the code must pass. Those test cases become the requirements and design documentation used as the basis for implementing the code. These test cases are then run often to verify that changes have not broken any existing capability (regression testing). Extreme programming (XP) takes this idea "to the extreme" by suggesting that developers should write a test that the current software can not pass (because they have not yet written the corresponding code), then write the code that will pass that test. Using *refactoring*, the developers

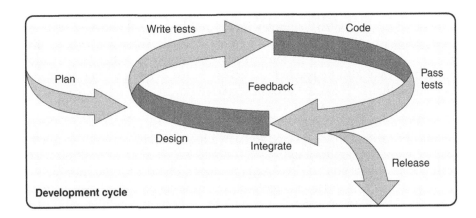

Figure 9.6   Iterative model–example.

then improve the quality of that code, eliminating any duplication, complexity, or awkward structure. This establishes what Beck (2005) calls a natural and efficient "rhythm" of test–code–refactor, test–code–refactor, and so on, as illustrated in Figure 9.7.

TDD requires the maintenance of a set of automated test cases written by the developer to exhaustively test the existing code before it goes to the customers for their testing (and potentially into production). As illustrated in Figure 9.8, the software is considered in the "green" state when it passes all of these programmer test cases. When new functionality is identified, the first step in TDD is to write test cases for that new functionality. Since code does not yet exist to implement these test cases, they fail, and the software goes into the "red" state. The developer then writes just enough code to pass these new test cases and moves the software back to the green state. According to Astels (2003), "that means you do the simplest thing that could possibly work." Refactoring is then done on the changed code as

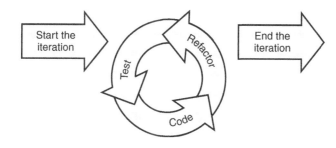

Figure 9.7   Test–code–refactor rhythm.

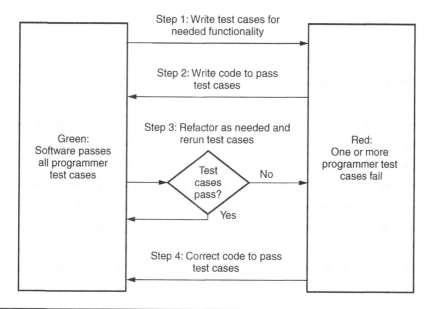

Figure 9.8   Test-driven development.

Part III.A

necessary to improve the quality of that new code. If changes made during the refactoring cause test cases to fail, the code is corrected until the software returns to the green state (all test cases pass).

FEATURE-DRIVEN DEVELOPMENT

Feature-driven development (FDD) is another agile development methodology for implementing software functionality. It is based on breaking the requirements down into small client-valued pieces of functionality and iteratively implementing them. The FDD process includes five steps, as illustrated in Figure 9.9.

During the first step—"develop an overall model"—the domain experts become familiar with the scope, context, and requirements of the system. FDD does not address the initial creation or management of documented requirements and assumes that requirements development has been accomplished in a supporting process. The domain experts conduct a walk-through where they inform team members and the chief architect of the high-level system description. The system domain is divided into different domain areas and a more detailed walk-through is held for each area. The development team then works in small groups to produce object models for each domain area. The development team discusses and decides on the appropriate models for each area, and these individual models are merged into an overall model.

During step 2—"build a features list"—the information from the walk-throughs, object models, and existing requirements documentation are used as the basis for building a system features list. This list defines each of the client-valued features to be included in the system. The team defines features for each domain area and groups them into major feature sets. The team then divides the

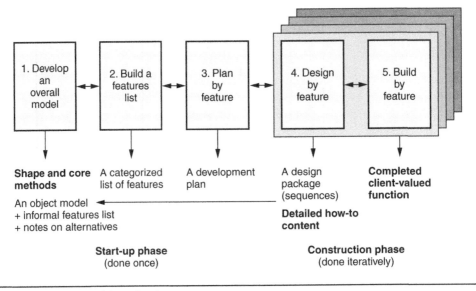

Figure 9.9 Feature-driven development process.

Source: Based on "Feature Driven Development (FDD) and Agile Modeling," an essay by Scott W. Ambler, http://www.agilemodeling.com/essays/fdd.htm.

major feature sets into lower-level feature sets representing different business activities within specific domain areas. The domain experts review the completed feature list for validity and completeness.

The team should keep features small, splitting them if necessary. When a business activity step looks longer than two weeks of effort, the activity is broken into smaller steps that in turn become features. For large systems (500-plus features), variance in complexity, presence of duplicates, and missed features all balance out. For medium systems (100 to 500 features), the team needs to take more care to ensure balance between features. For small systems (less than 100 features), a couple of the chief programmers and a domain expert usually work together to create the feature list (instead of using a full feature team).

Step 3—"plan by feature"—includes creating a high-level plan, which sequences feature sets by priority and dependencies. The feature sets are assigned to chief programmers, and classes identified in step 1 of the process (develop an overall model) are assigned to individual class owners. At this point, it is appropriate for the project manager, development manager, and chief programmers to set the initial schedule and major milestones for the feature sets. The development sequence is based on considerations such as the client value level, client dissatisfaction level, and risk-reduction impact.

Step 4—"design by feature"—begins with the scheduling of a small group of features, called *chief programmer work packages*, selected from the feature set(s) by combining features that use the same classes. Feature teams, who will do the software development, are formed from the class owners involved in the selected feature(s). The feature teams produce sequence diagrams for assigned features. Based on those diagrams, the domain experts refine the object models created in step 1. Each feature team then writes the class and method prologues and holds design inspections.

Step 5—"build by feature"—includes coding, code inspection, and unit testing. The chief programmer uses feedback from the class owners to track the promoted classes. In this role, the chief programmer acts as an integration point between the feature team and other teams working on the same iteration. After a successful iteration, completed features are available for integration into the regular build.

As a set, the design by feature (step 4) and build by feature (step 5) steps create the iteration. During this iteration, multiple feature teams concurrently design and build their assigned set of features. The quality gate between the design by feature and build by feature steps is the design inspection. An individual iteration should take no more than two weeks. At the completion of the iteration, the next iteration begins by starting a new design by feature step if there are still unimplemented features in the feature list.

To obtain full benefit from the FDD methodology, the project must use all of the following FDD core practices:

- *Domain object modeling.* Describes the structure and behavior of the problem domain through the use of class diagrams and high-level sequence diagrams.

- *Developing by feature.* Provides for focusing on small, client-valued pieces of functionality and tracking progress through the functionally decomposed pieces.

Part III.A

- *Individual class (code) ownership.* A scaleable practice that protects conceptual integrity and increases the chance of a concise, consistent, public class interface, or *application programming interface* (API). Each class has one person responsible for its consistency, performance, and conceptual integrity. FDD takes the opposite view of XP on code ownership. FDD believes that if the team owns all the code, individual responsibility, authority, and accountability are lost.

- *Feature teams.* These are small, dynamically formed teams under the guidance of a chief programmer. These teams are formed based on the features selected and the people most capable of implementing them.

- *Inspections.* FDD considers inspections to be the best defect detection technique. Inspections also spread good practices and enforce project standards across more than one developer.

- *Regular builds.* FDD integrates and builds frequently so that there is always a testable, demonstrable system. Regular builds form the baseline to which new features are added.

- *Configuration management.* Allows the identification of the latest versions of each completed source file and the tracking of their change history. A configuration management tool stores the finished code used to provide the input to the regular build.

- *High visibility and reporting of results.* Reporting describes where the team is, where the team is going, and how fast the team is getting there. All organizational levels receive progress reports based on completed work as necessary.

INCREMENTAL DEVELOPMENT

Incremental development is the process of constructing increasingly larger subsets of the software's requirements through the use of multiple passes through software development. In incremental development, after the requirements have been determined they are prioritized and allocated to planned increments (one pass through software development), as illustrated in Figure 9.10. Each subsequent delivery is usable but only has part of the functionality (except the last delivery, which includes all of the requirements). Each increment can have its own software development life cycle model (for example, waterfall, V, iterative) but there is no requirement to use the same model for each increment. For example, the first two increments could use the waterfall model, and the next increment could switch to the spiral model.

Incremental development can be done sequentially where one increment is completed before the next increment is started, as illustrated in increments 1 and 2 in Figure 9.11. The increments may also be done in parallel, as illustrated by increments 2 and 3 in this figure. For example, once the development team has completed the coding process and turned the software over to the test team for increment 2, they can start development of increment 3.

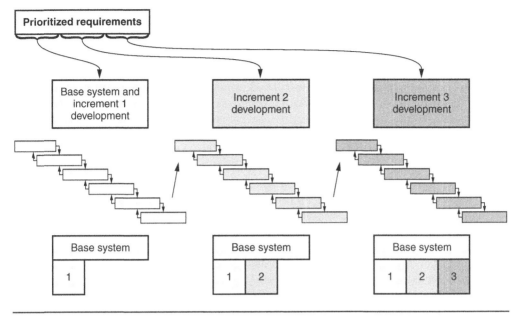

Figure 9.10   Incremental development process—example.

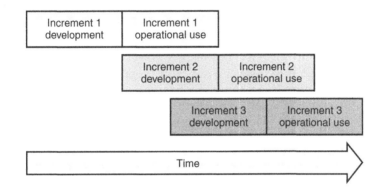

Figure 9.11   Incremental development over time—example.

One of the major strengths of incremental development results from the fact that building smaller subsets is less risky than building one large system. This allows customers and users to receive and/or evaluate early versions of product containing their highest priority operational needs, thus providing opportunities for validation and feedback of the delivered software much earlier than traditional waterfall-based projects. Incremental development also accommodates change very well. If new or changed requirements are discovered during the development of an increment, they can be allocated to future increments without disrupting the schedules and plans for the current development cycle. However, if the new or changed requirements are of high enough priority that they must be added

Part III.A

to the current release, then the project plans must be revisited. Either unimplemented requirements with lower priorities can be slipped to the next increment or updated schedules and other plans may need to be renegotiated.

Weaknesses of the incremental development model include the fact that most of the requirements must still be known up front. Depending on the system and the development methodology the project is using, additional work may be needed to create initial architecture that can support the entire system and is open enough to accept the new functionality as it is added. Incremental development is also sensitive to how content of a specific increment is selected. This is especially true if the increment is intended for release (for use in operations). Each released increment must be a complete working system even though it does not include all of the intended functionality. For example, it would not be feasible to release an inventory control system increment that allowed the checking-in of inventory if the functionality of checking-out inventory is not scheduled for development until the next release. Incremental development also places portions of the product under configuration control earlier, thereby requiring formal change procedures, with the associated increased overhead, to start earlier. Finally, one of the benefits of incremental development is the ability to get high-priority software functionality into the hands of users faster and thus get their feedback earlier. This may also be a weakness, however, if the software that is delivered is of poor quality. In other words, the development organization may be so busy fixing defects in the last increment that they have no time to work on new development for the next increment.

Iterative development does not require an incremental product life cycle, but they are often used together. In practice, however, the two terms are merging, and the terms "iterative development" and "iteration" are being used, especially in the agile community, to generally mean any combination of an incremental product life cycle and iterative development life cycle. For example, as illustrated in Figure 9.12, the XP principle of flow combines iterative development cycles with incremental development where the outputs of one iteration become the inputs into the next.

RAPID APPLICATION DEVELOPMENT

Rapid application development (RAD) is a variation on incremental development that achieves an extremely shortened development cycle through parallel development of multiple increments. The RAD approach requires a software product that can be modularized into small, independent increments that can be assigned to separate teams to develop in parallel, as illustrated in Figure 9.13. This requires sufficient staff to create multiple independent RAD teams. For example, RAD will not work if there is only one chief architect being shared across multiple teams. RAD also requires developers and customers who are committed to the rapid-fire activities necessary for these shortened cycle times.

The RAD approach is risky in and of itself, so it is therefore not an appropriate choice for projects that have a high level of technical risk (for example, heavy use of new technology or a high degree of interoperability with existing software). RAD is also not appropriate for projects that are building software that has high performance requirements that necessitate system-level tuning.

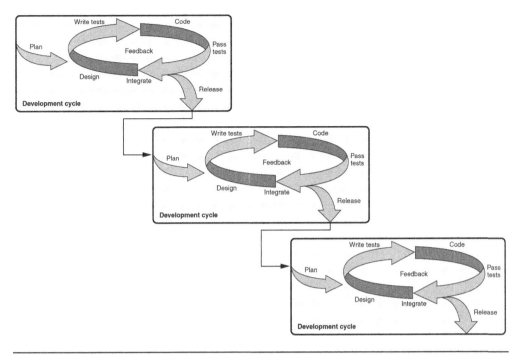

Figure 9.12   Combination of iterative and incremental models—example.

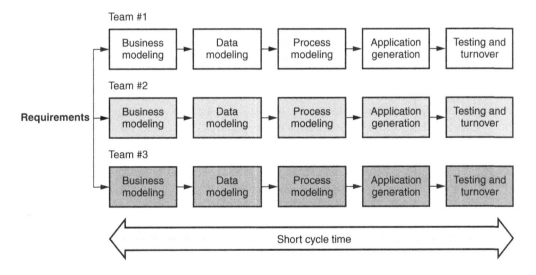

Figure 9.13   Rapid application development—example.

EVOLUTIONARY DEVELOPMENT

Evolutionary development is what happens when a software product is successful. If the customers and users like the product and find it useful, they will use it over time in operations. Things are not static: technologies change, customer and user needs and priorities change, business domains change, standards and regulations change. Therefore, smart organizations plan their software strategies to consider these potential changes. The primary difference between evolutionary and incremental development is that in evolutionary development the complete system with all of its requirements has been in operational use for some period of time, as illustrated in Figure 9.14. Evolutionary development happens when an existing software product is updated to implement perfective, adaptive, or preventive maintenance.

Like incremental development, evolutionary development builds a series of successively different versions of the software. However, with evolutionary development all of the original requirements are built into the first evolution of the software delivered into operations using some type of software development model (for example, waterfall, V, iterative). Incremental development techniques could also be used to build any of the software evolutions. Some time later, the next set of requirements is defined, and a new software development project is started using the legacy software as input. Each evolution can use the same or a different software development model from its predecessor evolutions, as illustrated in Figure 9.15.

A strength of the evolutionary model is that it focuses on the long-term success of the software as it changes and adapts to its customer/user needs and any other changes that occur over time. Only the requirements for the current evolution are known, but this approach provides opportunities for user validation and feedback as releases are delivered. Product evolutions can be sold to fund further development and provide profit to the organization. In fact, these evolutions are many times "cash cows" for the development organization as they receive funding for new and updated software without the investment necessary to create an entirely new system from scratch.

Weaknesses of the evolutionary development model include the fact that the longer the span of time between evolutions, the higher the probability that knowledgeable people have moved on to other projects or even other organizations. Effort and other project attributes can typically be estimated only for the current

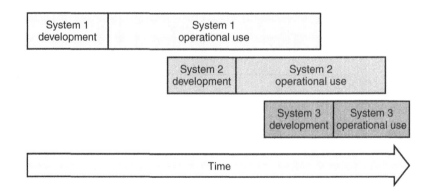

Figure 9.14   Evolutionary development over time—example.

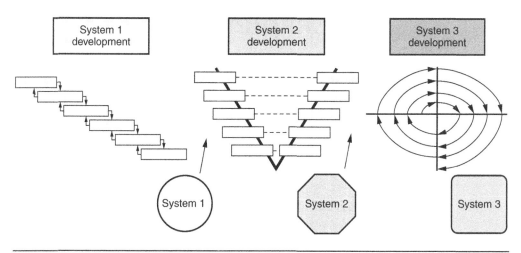

Figure 9.15 Evolutionary development process—example.

development project, and it can be very difficult to estimate long-term support and future development needs for requirements that the organization won't even know about for months or even years. Evolutionary development will not be successful without strong customer and user involvement and input. There is also the risk (and potential benefit) of never-ending evolutions. For example, it is not unusual for software that was built in the 1970s or even the 1960s to still be operational. At some point it may become difficult to find staff with the appropriate skill sets or to find the hardware and other technologies to support these very old software systems. For example, one company is still supporting an old legacy payroll system written in COBOL. Their product support team consists of programmers all with ages ranging from their late 50s to mid-60s. It fact, many of them are getting ready for retirement. The management of this company can not find any younger programmers who want to learn COBOL. Of course, the answer to this dilemma is reengineering, but that is a major investment that management doesn't want to make for software that still works and meets the customer's needs.

Part III.A

Chapter 10

B. Systems Architecture

Any *system architecture* is composed of system-level components (including subsystems), interfaces between those components, and the allocation of system-level requirements to those components and interfaces. The architectural design of a system may also consider timing and bandwidth of those interfaces. System-level components will typically consist of software, hardware, and humans (who implement processes and manual operations). Good systems architectures address higher-level concepts and abstractions for the system. Lower-level details are dealt with during the detailed design activities, which define the internals of each component at the hardware/software/process engineering level. Users of the systems architecture should be able to:

- Understand what the system does

- Understand how the system works

- Be able to work on one piece of the system, independent of other pieces

- Extend the system

- Reuse one or more components or parts of the system to build another system

"Architecture is what remains when you can not take away any more things and still understand the system and explain how it works" (Kruchten 2000).

EMBEDDED SYSTEM

An *embedded system* is typically a system where the software is embedded as part of a complete device that includes hardware and mechanical components. The software in an embedded system is referred to as firmware and is stored in read-only memory (ROM) or in a flash memory chip.

Embedded systems can vary widely in capability. Many embedded systems are limited to the performance of one or a limited number of dedicated functions or tasks, as opposed to a personal computer or mainframe. Digital watches, microwaves, mobile phones, traffic lights, and handheld calculators are just a few of the many examples of embedded systems. A modern automobile has multiple embedded systems controlling everything from the antilock brakes, to fuel injection, to the radio, to the airbags, and so on. Medical devices and weapons systems are other examples of embedded systems that are complex and multifunctional. Embedded systems can range from having no user interface to a complex graphical user interface similar to a personal computer desktop. Many embedded systems are also restricted by real-time constraints.

n-TIER

In an *n-tier architecture*, also called a *multitier architecture*, the system is logically decomposed into two or more layers (levels), each with independent processing capability creating a modularized approach to the architecture. The "n" in an n-tier architecture implies any number, such as two-tier, four-tier, five-tier, and so on.

Well-defined interfaces and information hiding (abstraction) characterize a tiered or layered architectural style. As illustrated in Figure 10.1, each tier interfaces with the tiers just above and/or below it and performs part of the functionality of the whole system. That way if communication is severed between two tiers, partial independent functionality within each tier or between non-severed tiers is still possible. For example, the telecommunications network is a classic

Part III.B

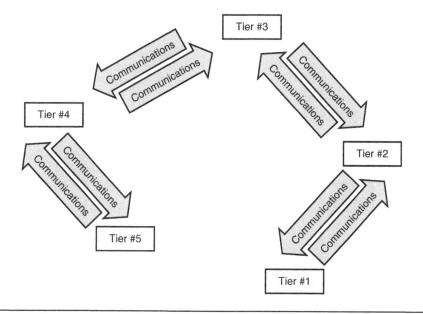

Figure 10.1   Five-tier architecture—example.

tiered architecture. If the private branch exchange (PBX) inside a company loses connections with the local switch, employees can not make outside phone calls but they may still be able to call other employees using the same PBX. If, however, the local switch has good connection to the PBX, but loses connection with the class 5 switch, employees can still call each other and may also have limited outside calling capacity with others sharing the same local switch.

The tiers provide abstraction because a tier doesn't need to know how the operations of the layer above or below it are implemented. In a tiered architecture, layers can be added, upgraded, or replaced independently without major impact to other parts of the system.

CLIENT–SERVER

Client–server architectures are a specific type of two-tier architecture, as illustrated in Figure 10.2. For example, most computer networks within businesses are based on client–server architectures. Each computer or device on the network is either a client or a server. Central server computers/devices on a network provide services, manage network resources (for example, the sharing of software licenses), and centralize all (or most) of the data.

The client is the requester of services and typically runs on a decentralized access terminal, computer, or workstation. These clients download or access the centralized data, share the network resources, and utilize centralized processing capability available from the server. A *thin client*, also referred to as a *slim* or *lean client*, primarily focuses on the user interface and on sending and receiving inputs/outputs from the server. A thin client depends on the server for most or all of the processing activities. Typically, the only software that is installed on a thin client is the user interface, networked operating system, and possibly a limited number of frequently used applications. In contrast, a *fat client*, also referred to as a *rich* or *thick client*, typically has a large number of applications installed and

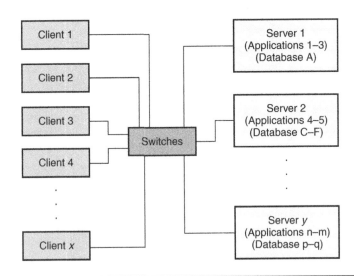

Figure 10.2 Client–server architecture–example.

performs most of the processing functionality locally, depending on the server mostly for shared data. A thick client can run much more independently. In fact, a thick client may be able to run without connectivity to the server for some period of time, requiring only periodic connection for data refreshing.

Advantages of a client–server architecture include the distribution of roles and responsibilities across the network, the sharing of resources and data, easy systems management (for example, easier propagation of new/updated software and easier backups), and easy entry/modification of that shared data with the ability to have increased security protection at the server level. Another advantage may include lower costs, especially if software licenses can be economically shared or if lower-cost equipment can be utilized (for example, for thin clients).

Disadvantages can include degraded performance or resource unavailability under high network traffic conditions, limitations on the level of processing available to the client if connection with the server is severed, and potential issues with backing up organizational assets that are not uploaded to the servers.

WEB

There are three major types of web architectures, as illustrated in Figure 10.3: the Internet, intranets, and extranets.

The *Internet* is a global network connecting millions of computers. The Internet is characterized by business-to-consumer (B to C) architectures where

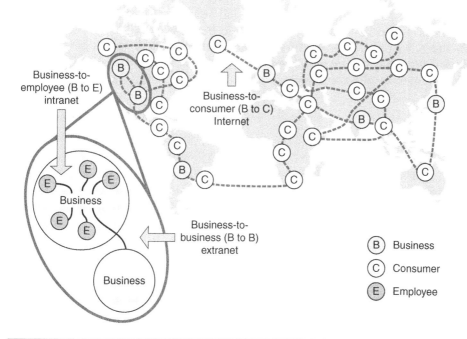

Figure 10.3 Web architecture–examples.

Internet pages are created by businesses, organizations, or individuals to provide open access to consumers. The intent is to create a community that consumers will revisit because of dynamic content-delivery capabilities.

An *intranet* resides behind the firewall of an organization and is only accessible to people within the organization. Intranets typically implement a business-to-employee (B to E) architecture where intranet pages integrate and consolidate enterprise information and make that information available to employees from a single point of access (self-service access). There can be many portals within a single organization for different departments, projects, geographic locations, and so on. The objective is to allow employees to access and utilize existing information more effectively, facilitate the capturing and sharing of new information, reduce data overload, and ensure that only current, up-to-date information is utilized.

Extranets refer to intranets that have various levels of accessibility (through various security protections) available to authorized outsiders. An extranet allows organizational partners to exchange information based on a business-to-business (B to B) architecture. Extranet pages provide business information and application functionality to external partners, including real-time access to important data. This can decrease the costs of partner support activities. Each portal has the ability to be customized and personalized to the needs of individual partners.

WIRELESS

In today's environment, many individuals need to take their computer processing power with them as they travel, without being tethered via cabling to a network. People need *wireless* access to the Internet, to telecommunications, to stored information and data, and so on, as they travel from site to site. For example, a doctor or nurse might use a personal digital assistant (PDA) to store medical or drug information that can be accessed from the hospital rooms of each of their patients. Sales people, consultants, law enforcement offices, students, and many others need to stay in contact while traveling, which can be accomplished through wireless access on their laptop computers.

MESSAGING

Messaging system architectures are designed to accept messages from or deliver messages to other systems. An e-mail system is an example of a messaging system. In its simplest form a messaging architecture should accept messages from external systems, determine the internal recipients, and route those messages appropriately. Messaging systems should also accept messages from internal sources, determine their destination systems, and route them as required.

COLLABORATION PLATFORMS

According to Wikipedia, "*Collaboration platforms* offer a set of software components and software services that enable individuals to find each other and the information they need and to be able to communicate and work together to achieve common business goals." A collaboration platform helps individuals and teams work together regardless of how geographically dispersed they are. Examples of key components of a collaboration platform include:

- Messaging via e-mail, databases or lists of contacts or customers, and coordinated calendars and scheduling tools

- Virtual meeting tools, including instant messages, Web-based meetings, audio or video conferencing, and desktop sharing

- Information sharing via shared files and data refreshing, document repositories with search capabilities, and mechanisms for sharing ideas and notes

- Blogs, wikis, and other social computing tools

Chapter 11

C. Requirements Engineering

Part III.C

A *requirement* is a capability, attribute, or design constraint of the software that provides value to or is needed by a stakeholder. The requirements are what the customers, users, software product supplier, and other relevant stakeholders must determine and agree on before that software can be built. The requirements define the "what" of a software product:

- *What the software must do to add value for its stakeholders.* These functional requirements define the capabilities of the software product.

- *What the software must be to add value for its stakeholders.* These nonfunctional (product attribute) requirements define the characteristics, properties, or qualities that the software product must possess. They define how well the product performs its functions.

- *What limitations exist on the choices that the developers have when implementing the software.* The external interface definitions and design constraints define these limitations.

The task of eliciting, analyzing, and writing good requirements is the most difficult part of software engineering. However, to quote Fredrick Brooks (1995), "The hardest part of building a software system is deciding precisely what to build. No other part of the conceptual work is as difficult as establishing the detailed technical requirements, including all of the interfaces to people, to machines, and to other software systems. No other part of the work so cripples the resulting system if done wrong. No other part is more difficult to rectify later." In other words, to quote Karl Wiegers (2004), "If you don't get the requirements right, it doesn't matter how well you do anything else."

REQUIREMENTS ENGINEERING PROCESS

Software *requirements engineering* is a disciplined, process-oriented approach to the definition, documentation, and maintenance of software requirements throughout the software development life cycle. Software requirements engineering is made up of two major processes: requirements development and requirements management, as illustrated in Figure 11.1.

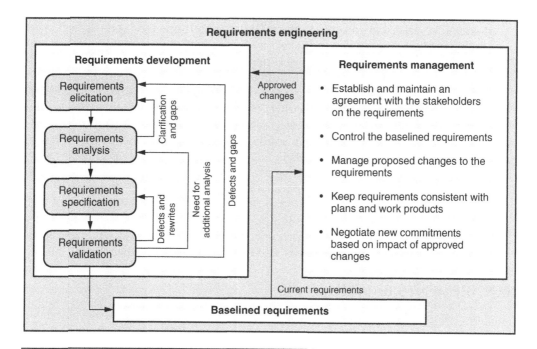

Figure 11.1   Requirements engineering process.

REQUIREMENTS DEVELOPMENT

Requirements development encompasses all of the activities involved in eliciting, analyzing, specifying, and validating the requirements. According to the Software Engineering Institute's (SEI) Capability Maturity Model Integration (CMMI) for Development, "the purpose of requirements development is to produce and analyze customer, product, and product component requirements" (SEI 2006).

Requirements development is an iterative process. Don't expect to go through the steps in the process in a one-shot, linear fashion. For example, the requirements analyst may talk to a stakeholder, then analyze what that stakeholder told them. They may go back to that stakeholder for clarification and then document what they understand as that part of the requirements specification. They may then go on to talk to another stakeholder or hold a joint requirements workshop with several stakeholder representatives. Their analysis may then include building a prototype that they show to a focus group. Based on that information the analyst documents additional requirements in the specification and holds a requirements walk-through to validate that set of requirements. The analyst then moves on to eliciting the requirements for the next feature, and so on.

The *requirements elicitation* step includes all of the activities involved in identifying the requirement's stakeholders, selecting representatives from each stakeholder class, and collecting information to determine the needs of each class of stakeholders. The *requirements analysis* step includes taking stakeholder needs and refining them with further levels of detail. It also includes representing the requirements in various forms including prototypes and models, establishing priorities, analyzing feasibility, looking for gaps that identify missing requirements, and identifying and resolving conflicts between various stakeholder needs. The knowledge gained in the analysis step may necessitate iterations with the elicitation step as clarification is needed, conflicts between requirements are explored, or missing requirements are identified. During the *requirements specification* step, the requirements are documented so that they can be communicated to all the product stakeholders. The last step in the requirements development process is to *validate* the requirements to ensure that they are well written, complete, and will satisfy the stakeholder's needs. Validation may lead to the iteration of other steps in the requirements development process because of identified defects, gaps, additional information or analysis needs, needed clarification, or other issues.

REQUIREMENTS BASELINE

After one or more iterations through the software requirements development process, part or all of the requirements are deemed "good enough" to *baseline* and become the basis for software planning, design, and development. A good saying to remember at this point is "When is *better* the enemy of *good enough*?" The requirements will never be perfect—analysts can always do more and more refinement and gather more and more input (which may or may not actually improve the requirements). At some point, the law of diminishing returns starts to apply, where the additional information is simply not worth the additional effort to obtain it. Requirements baselining is a business decision that should be based on risk assessment. Are the requirements "good enough" to proceed with development—remembering that the developers will obtain valuable information as they implement the software, which can be fed back into requirements updates and enhancements at a future date.

The requirements development process does not assume any specific software development life cycle model. In fact, requirements development may be incremental, as illustrated in Figure 11.2. But whether the project defines all of

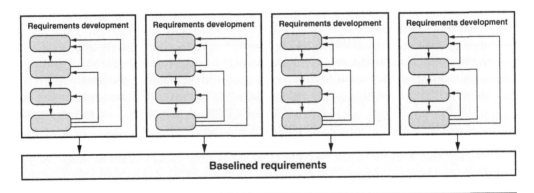

Figure 11.2 Incremental requirements development.

the requirements at once or just part of them, each part must be defined and base-lined before the project can build that part of the software.

REQUIREMENTS MANAGEMENT

Requirements management starts with getting stakeholder buy-in to the base-lined requirements. Requirements management encompasses all of the activities involved in requesting changes to the baselined requirements, performing impact analysis for the requested changes, approving or disapproving those changes, and implementing the approved changes. Requirements management also includes the activities performed to ensure that all work products and project plans are kept consistent and tracking the status of the requirements as the project progresses through the software development process.

1. REQUIREMENTS TYPES

Define and describe various types of requirements, including feature, function, system, quality, security, safety, regulatory, etc. (Understand)

Body of Knowledge III.C.1

Most stakeholders just talk about "the requirements" as if they were all the same thing. However, by recognizing that there are different levels and types of require-ments, as illustrated in Figure 11.3, stakeholders gain a better understanding of what information they need when they are defining the software requirements.

Business Requirements

Business requirements define the business problems to be solved or the busi-ness opportunities to be addressed by the software product. In general, the set of business requirements defines why the software product is being developed. Business requirements are typically stated in terms of the objectives of the cus-tomer or organization requesting the development of the software but may also include objectives of other stakeholders.

Stakeholder Functional Requirements

Stakeholder functional requirements look at the functionality or capability of the soft-ware product from the perspectives of the various stakeholders of that product. These requirements define what the software has to do in order for the users, customers, developers, and other stakeholders to accomplish their objectives (or in the case of "unfriendly" stakeholders like hackers or criminals, to keep them from accomplishing their objectives). Multiple stakeholder-level functional

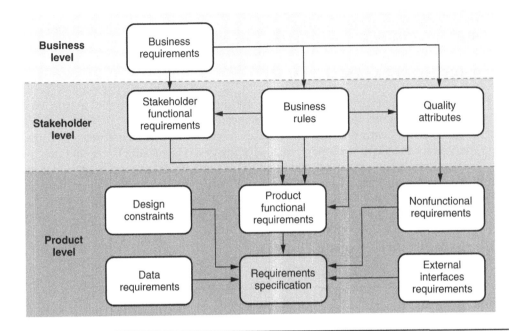

Figure 11.3 Levels and types of requirements.

requirements may be needed in order to fulfill a single business requirement. For example, the business requirement to allow the customer to pay for gas at the pump might translate into multiple stakeholder requirements, including requirements for the customer to be able to:

- Swipe credit, debit, or ATM card

- Enter security personal identification number (PIN)

- Request a receipt at the pump

Product Functional Requirements

The software product's functional requirements (typically just referred to as the functional requirements) define the functionality or capabilities that must be built into the software product to enable users or other stakeholders to accomplish their tasks, thereby satisfying the business requirements. Multiple functional-level requirements may be needed to fulfill a single stakeholder functional requirement. For example, the requirement that the users can swipe their credit, debit, or ATM card might translate into multiple functional requirements, including requirements for the software to:

- Prompt the customer to swipe his or her card using the card reader

- Detect that the card has been swiped

- Determine if the card was incorrectly read and prompt the customer to re-swipe the card if necessary

- Parse the information from the magnetic strip on the card

Business Rules

As opposed to the business requirements, *business rules* are the specific policies, standards, practices, regulations, and guidelines that define how the stakeholders do business (and are therefore considered stakeholder-level requirements). The software product must adhere to these rules in order to function appropriately within the user's domain. Business rules that the pay-at-the-pump software might need to implement include:

- Any laws or regulatory requirements about pumping gas

- Types of credit or debit cards taken (for example, the software may not accept gas station credit cards from competing gas companies)

- Rules about the maximum that can be charged to a credit card (for example, a $75 limit per transaction)

Quality Attributes

Stakeholder-level *quality attributes* are characteristics that define the product's quality from the perspective of the stakeholders. Sometimes called the "ilities" (many but not all of them end in "-ility"), quality attributes include:

- *Usability.* The ease with which a user can operate or learn to operate software

- *Reliability.* The extent to which the software can perform its functions without failure for a specified period of time under specified conditions

- *Availability.* The extent to which the software or a service is available for use when needed

- *Performance.* The levels of performance (for example, capacity, throughput, and response times) required from the software

- *Efficiency.* The extent to which the software can perform its functions while utilizing minimal amounts of computing resources (for example, memory or disk space).

- *Security (integrity).* The probability that an attack of a specific type will be detected, repelled, or handled by the software

- *Safety.* The ability to use the software without adverse impact to individuals, property, the environment, or society

- *Interoperability.* The degree to which the software functions properly and shares resources with other software applications or hardware operating in the same environment

Part III.C.1

- *Accuracy.* The extent to which the software provides precision in calculations and outputs

- *Installability.* The ease with which the software product can be installed on the target platform

- *Flexibility.* The ease with which the software can be modified or customized by the user

- *Robustness (fault tolerance* or *error tolerance).* The extent to which the software can handle invalid inputs or other faults from interfacing entities (for example, hardware, other software applications, the operating system, or data files) without failure

- *Maintainability.* The ease with which the software or one of its components can be modified

- *Reusability.* The extent to which one or more components of a software product can be reused when developing other software products

- *Portability.* The effort required to migrate the software to a different platform or environment

- *Supportability.* The ease with which the technical support staff can isolate and resolve software issues reported by end users

A quality attribute may translate into product functional requirements for the software that specify what functionality must exist to meet a nonfunctional attribute. For example, an ease-of-learning usability requirement might translate into the functional requirement of having the system display pop-up help when the user hovers the cursor over an icon. A quality attribute may also translate into nonfunctional requirements. For example, an ease-of-use usability requirement might translate into nonfunctional requirements for response time to user commands or report requests.

The ISO/IEC 25000:2005 *Software Engineering—Software Product Quality Requirements and Evaluation (SQuaRE)* standard series (transition from the previous ISO/IEC 9126 and 14598 series of standards) provides a reference model and definitions for external and internal quality attributes and quality-in-use attributes. This standards series also provides guidance for specifying requirements, planning, and managing, measuring, and evaluating quality attributes.

Nonfunctional Requirements

Nonfunctional requirements, also called *product attributes,* specify the characteristics that the software must possess in order to meet the quality attributes requirements. For example, a usability requirement might state that the software has to be user-friendly. How does the developer program "user-friendly"; how should it be interpreted from a product perspective? First of all, "user-friendly" for whom? Things that are user-friendly to the novice or infrequent user may drive the power user crazy. Second, there is a difference between ease of learning and ease of use. Examples of "user-friendly" product-level nonfunctional requirements for the pay-at-the-pump system might include:

- All screens and displays at the pump are readable by a person with 20/20 vision from two feet away in bright sunlight (100,000 candelas per square meter)

- Updates to the customizable values in the system require the navigation of no more than three screens per value being updated

- The system responds to all gas purchaser inputs within three seconds with another prompt, message, or indication that processing is occurring

- Less than 0.2 percent of customers with valid credit cards require more than three attempts to be able to swipe a readable (non-damaged) credit card without error

- ≥99 percent of trained gas station managers can perform end-of-month reporting without referring to the user manual or online help

External Interface Requirements

The *external interface requirements* define the requirements for information flow across shared interfaces to hardware, humans, other software applications, the operating system, and file systems outside the boundaries of the software product being developed.

Design Constraints

The design constraints define any restrictions imposed on the choices that the supplier can make when designing and implementing the software. They define "how" to implement the system rather than "what" needs to be implemented. Design constraints might include requirements to use a specific programming language, algorithms, communications protocol, encryption technique, or input/output mechanism (for example, push a button or print an error message to the printer).

Data Requirements

The data requirements define the specific data items or data structures that must be included as part of the software product. For example, the pay-at-the-pump system would have requirements for purchase transaction data, gas price data, gas pump status data, and so on.

System versus Software Requirements

The software may be part of a much larger system that includes other components. In this case, the business- and user-level requirements feed into the product requirements at the system level. IEEE provides a *Guide for Developing System Requirements Specifications* (IEEE 1996). The system architecture then allocates requirements from the set of system requirements downward into the software, hardware, and manual operations components. The software requirements are the requirements that have been allocated to one or more software components of the system.

Requirements Specification

The requirements specification can take many forms. For example, all of the requirements information may be documented in a single *software requirements specification* (SRS) document. On other projects the requirements may be specified in multiple documents. For example:

- Business requirements may be documented in a *business requirements document* (BRD), *marketing requirements document* (MRD), or *project vision and scope document,* or as part of a *concept of operations document* (IEEE provides a *Guide for Information Technology—System Definition—Concept of Operations (ConOps) Document* [IEEE 1998b]).

- Stakeholder requirements may be documented in a set of use cases, user stories, a *user requirements specification* (URS) document, or as part of a concept of operations document.

- The software functional and nonfunctional requirements and other product-level requirements may be documented in a software requirements specification (SRS) (IEEE provides Recommended Practice for Software Requirements Specifications [IEEE 1998c]).

- External interfaces may be included in the SRS or in separate *external interface requirements* documents.

Another way of specifying requirements is to document them in a requirements tool or database. In its simplest form, the requirements specification may simply be a list of "to dos," such as items in a scrum product backlog, elements in a spreadsheet, or documented on sticky notes or index cards displayed on the project's war room wall.

2. REQUIREMENTS ELICITATION

> Describe and use various elicitation methods, including customer needs analysis, use cases, human factors studies, usability prototypes, joint application development (JAD), storyboards, etc. (Apply)
>
> **Body of Knowledge III.C.2**

Requirements elicitation is the data- and information-gathering step in the requirements development process. The first step in requirements elicitation is to define the vision, scope, and limitations for the software product that is being newly developed or updated. The *product vision* defines how the new or updated software product bridges the gap between the current state and the desired future state needed to take advantage of a business opportunity or solve a business problem. The *product scope* defines what will be included in the product, thus defining the boundaries of the product. As requirements analysts elicit and analyze potential business-, stakeholder-, and product-level requirements they should always judge those requirements against the product's scope:

- If they are within scope, the requirements can be included in the product

- If they are out of scope, the requirements should be rejected unless they are so important that the scope of the project should be adjusted to include them

The *product limitations* list documents items that will not be included in the product. It is important to document the scope and limitations because they help establish and maintain stakeholder expectations for the product, and they can also help in dealing with *requirements churn* and *gold-plating* issues.

Once the vision, scope, and limitations are defined, that information is used to identify the software product stakeholders. From this list of all potential product stakeholders, the project needs to determine which stakeholders will participate in the requirements elicitation (and other requirements engineering) activities, how each of those stakeholders will be represented in those activities, and who will represent them. A stakeholder group can be represented by:

- *A stakeholder champion.* One or more champions or representatives of the stakeholder group. For example, if there are multiple testers who will be testing the product, the lead tester might be selected to represent this stakeholder group. The lead tester participates in the requirements engineering activities and is responsible for gathering inputs from other testers and managing communication with them.

- *A sample.* For large stakeholder groups or for groups where direct access is limited for some reason, sampling may be appropriate. In this case it would be necessary to devise a sampling plan for obtaining inputs from a representative set of stakeholders in that particular group. For example, if the company has several thousand employees, it may decide to take a sample set of employees to interview about their needs for the new accounting system.

- *All stakeholders in the group.* If the stakeholder group is small or if it is critical enough to the success of the system, it may be necessary to obtain input from every member of that stakeholder group. For example, if the software product has only one customer or a small set of customers, it might be important to obtain input from each of the customers.

- *Documentation.* Some stakeholder groups will not be contacted directly but may be represented by documentation defining their needs. For example, regulatory standards documentation might be used to represent a regulatory agency stakeholder group.

Direct Two-Way Communication

Probably the most effective way of eliciting requirements data and information is through direct two-way communications (for example, through interviews, focus groups, and facilitated requirements workshops). The major advantage that direct communication with the stakeholders has over many of the other techniques is that it is a two-way communications technique that has a feedback loop that allows the requirements analyst to obtain additional follow-up information and clarify terminology or ambiguities. This feedback can come in the form of a summarization of or questions about what the stakeholder said or in the form of additional information like examples or comments. Feedback can also take the form of nonverbal communications like facial expressions or body language.

Interviews

"One of the most important and most straightforward requirements elicitation techniques is the interview, a simple, direct technique that can be used in virtually every situation" (Leffingwell 2000). Interviews are an excellent mechanism for obtaining detailed information from another person. Prior to the interview, the requirements analyst must decide on the scope of the interview. For a software product of any size, there are often a huge number of topics that could be covered in an interview. If the analyst tries to cover everything all at once, the interviews may be unfocused and the information obtained may be superficial.

Focus Groups

Focus groups can be particularly valuable if the software product has a large and/or very diverse customer/user base. For example, the stakeholder group of gasoline purchasers for the pay-at-the-pump system is very large and diverse. If a stakeholder group doesn't have any obvious candidates for a single stakeholder champion, the requirements analyst might want to consider using one or more focus groups to elicit requirements from this stakeholder type.

Focus groups are small groups of selected stakeholders that represent "typical" stakeholders of the type or types of stakeholders we need input from. Lauesen (2002) recommends that the group include six to 18 people and that the software development staff makes up only one-third of the group. The group should also be fairly homogeneous. For example, the gas purchaser stakeholder group might need to be divided into several homogeneous focus groups that separate family car drivers from drivers of 18-wheelers from fleet drivers (for example taxis, military vehicles).

The focus group stakeholders are brought together in a meeting to discuss one or more aspects of the requirements for the software product. While the members of a focus group typically don't have any decision-making authority, their input into the requirements elicitation process can be valuable. Lauesen (2002) says that "professional product developers carry out several sessions with different people until the issues seem to repeat themselves."

To open the focus group meeting, the topic or theme of the meeting should be presented. It may be beneficial to conduct some sort of icebreaker activities to give the focus group members some time to get to know each other and feel comfortable. The intent is to get the focus group members to interact and discuss the software product. For example, the facilitator might have the focus group discuss what they like about the existing system, or the group could brainstorm a list of bad experiences with a similar product in the same kind of work domain. Another approach is to have the group discuss a future vision for the product, what they wish it would be like. The focus group could also be shown a prototype and asked what they like or dislike about it.

During the focus group session, the goal is to get as many ideas recorded as possible in a short amount of time. The facilitator ensures that everyone's ideas are heard and that ideas are not critiqued, criticized, or rejected during the initial information-gathering session. This can be done directly as part of the focus group meeting or by an observer who is not actively participating in the meeting (for example, someone observing the group through a two-way mirror).

After ideas are gathered, it may be beneficial to have each member of the focus group select their top-priority ideas. For example, ask each participant to make a list of his or her top 10 choices. These lists then become inputs used by the requirements analysis team to help identify product requirements and their priorities.

Facilitated Requirements Workshops

Facilitated requirements workshops bring together cross-functional groups of stakeholders to produce specific software requirements work products. An example of facilitated requirements workshops would be a JAD *(joint application design or joint application development)* workshop used to elicit requirements. By bringing together the appropriate stakeholders, facilitated requirements workshops can help streamline communications and identify and resolve requirements issues between impacted parties. This can reduce the time it takes to elicit the requirements and produce higher-quality requirements work products. These workshops focus on the concepts of collaboration and team-building, which promote a sense of joint ownership of the deliverables and resulting product. Team synergy can also reduce the risk of missing requirements.

A trained, neutral facilitator is used during the workshop to elicit productive interaction from the participants. The facilitator:

- Plans the facilitated requirements workshop session with the workshop leader

- Orchestrates the interactions during the meeting to ensure that everyone is participating and being heard

- Assists in preparing documentation both before and after the meeting

- Expedites follow-up after the session

The workshop team members are stakeholder representatives with decision-making authority and subject matter expertise. These team members are responsible for the content and quality of the requirements deliverable produced during the workshop.

Each workshop should have a recorder who is responsible for keeping a written record of each team meeting. This includes recording decisions and issues and any action items assigned during the session.

Facilitated requirements workshops require a lot of work outside the workshop meetings themselves. The facilitator must prepare for the workshop by working with team members to determine the specific scope and deliverables for the meeting and planning the activities and tools that will be used. The facilitator must custom-design each meeting for the specific team based on the needs of the specific product or deliverables being produced. The workshop typically requires prework on the part of one or more participants. For example, participants may do *brainwriting* of ideas to bring to the meeting or they may create a "straw man" version of a deliverable for the other members to review.

The goal of a facilitated requirements workshop is to create one or more requirements deliverables. For example, a workshop might create a list of business rules, flesh out the details of a set of use cases, or evaluate a prototype. These workshops are an iterative process of discovery and creativity that requires the interaction and participation of all the team members in "serious play." *Serious play* "means playing with models as a means of innovation, invention, and collaboration." It also "means having fun at the meetings as a means of enhancing the group's productivity, energy, and interrelationships" (Gottesdiener 2002).

Document Studies

Sometimes the requirements have already been written down in or can be identified from some other form of documentation. For example, there may already be a detailed specification on how the software must interface with an existing piece of hardware, or a report may already exist that is being created manually and the software just needs to duplicate its contents and layout. As appropriate, requirements elicitation should consider studies of documentation, including:

- Industry standards, laws, and/or regulations

- Product literature (of the development organization or its competition's)

- Process documentation and work instructions from the users

- Change requests, problem or help desk reports

- Lessons learned from prior projects or products

- Reports and other deliverables from the existing system

Other Requirements Elicitation Techniques

Other requirements elicitation techniques include:

- *Observation of work in progress.* This can include site visits where the users are observed performing their actual jobs, or the observation of users in a simulated environment (for example, using a prototype)

- *Questionnaires or surveys.* Sent to stakeholders to obtain their opinions or input, including customer satisfaction surveys and/or marketing surveys

- *Analysis of competitor's products*

- *Reverse engineering existing products*

- *Prototyping*

- *Benchmarking and best practices*

Prototypes

A *prototype* is a demonstration version of the software product that can be used as a straw man to show to the stakeholders to help elicit and analyze requirements and determine if the requirements analyst's understanding of what was heard during the elicitation process was correct. Demonstrating prototypes to various stakeholders can also be used to elicit new information or requirements that might have been missed in the initial discussions and to validate the requirements. Prototypes can be particularly useful if:

- The customers, users, or other stakeholders don't really know or have doubts about what they want

- The developers have doubts about whether or not they understand what the stakeholders are telling them

- The feasibility of the requirement is questionable

Prototypes can be constructed as *throwaway* prototypes or as *evolutionary* prototypes. For throwaway prototypes, development creates it, uses it for requirements elicitation or analysis, and then discards it. Typically, throwaway prototypes are "quick and dirty" development efforts that focus just on the parts of interest of the software product. For example, extra work is not expended on error checking or code comments. On the other hand, evolutionary prototypes are built using a more rigorous development approach. More time is spent creating a prototype that has high enough quality to evolve into a robust, reliable software product.

Prototypes can also be constructed as *horizontal* or *vertical* prototypes. A good analogy for a horizontal prototype, also called a *mock-up*, is the false front scenery on a movie set. Everything looks real, but when the actors walk through the front door of the hotel they aren't walking into an actual lobby, but only through a thin facade propped up by two-by-fours. Horizontal prototypes look and feel like the real system from the outside perspective, but under the surface it's all smoke and mirrors; there isn't much real code backing them up. Horizontal prototypes can be valuable when analyzing the software's user interface or when performing usability evaluations. Vertical prototypes, also called *proofs of concept*, are a single slice through the product with a focus on proving the feasibility of one specific aspect. For example, developers could prototype just the charge card reading and verification process to make sure that timing constraints can be met or that the communication protocols with the credit card clearinghouse are understood.

User Stories

Agile methods use *user stories* to help capture high-level stakeholder requirements. The goal of a story is to capture a stakeholder need in a way that acts as a reminder to have a future discussion about that need. The intent is to defer the work of drilling that need down into implementable requirements until the story is scheduled for actual development—just-in-time requirements development. This eliminates the waste of effort spent elaborating requirements that, for whatever reason, are never implemented (for example, priorities change, customer needs change, or the project gets canceled).

User stories are typically only one or a few sentences long and are written in the language of the stakeholder or business. They are typically created during face-to-face conversations between the developers and the customers of the software. There is no one correct method for capturing user stories. A user story may just be a statement of a need. For example, "A daily transaction summary report is printed every night at midnight." A user story may identify the stakeholder as well as the need. For example, "As a purchaser of gasoline, I can select the type of gas I want to purchase." A user story may also include the justification for the need. For example, "As the owner of the gas station, I want all credit card transactions validated by the credit card clearinghouse in order to minimize my financial exposure from stolen, expired, or over-the-limit cards." User stories may also include other information deemed valuable to act as a reminder of the stakeholder's need and to prompt future discussion.

According to Jeffries (2001), there are three critical aspects of a user story called the three Cs: card, confirmation, and conversation. The "card" is the documentation of the user story and may also include notes from planning, including priority and effort estimates. Acceptance tests should also be written for each user story that provide the criteria for "confirmation" of whether the intent of the user story has been fulfilled. Later, when the story has been selected for implementation, the user story becomes the starting point for additional "conversation" between the developers and the customers to refine and elaborate on the requirements.

Use Cases

A *use case* is a scenario created to describe a thread of usage for the system to be implemented. An entire set of use cases describe how the system will be used and can provide the basis for functional testing. While use cases came out of object-oriented analysis techniques, they can be effectively used for many different types of applications.

The first step in defining use cases is to identify the different actors. *Actors* are entities outside the scope of the system under consideration that interact with that system. The scope of the system under consideration determines who the actors are and are not. For example, if the gas pump is considered part of the system, it is not an actor. However, if the gas pump is considered outside the system under consideration, it would be an actor.

Actors are different than *users*. A user may perform several actor roles when interacting with the system. For example, a single user of a word processing package could have roles including author, reviewer, and editor of a document. Each of these roles would be a separate actor. Actors can also be other hardware devices, other software applications, or systems that interact with the software product. For example, the credit card clearinghouse actor for the pay-at-the-pump product is another software application that the software must interact with to obtain authorization for credit or debit card purchases.

The list of interactions between the actors and the system are then identified. These interactions may be initiated by either the actor or by the software product on behalf of the actor. One mechanism for documenting this list of interactions, and showing their interactions to actors and their interrelationship to each other, is with a *use case diagram,* as illustrated in Figure 11.4. A use case diagram starts with a box that represents the scope or boundaries of the software system. Outside the box are stick figures that represent the various actors that will interact with the product. Each stick figure is labeled with the name of that actor. For example, for the pay-at-the-pump product the actors might be the customer, gas station owner, gas station attendant, and the credit card clearinghouse. The ovals inside the boundary represent the interactions or use cases. Use cases are typically named using a verb and an object (for example, *purchase ticket* or *print a boarding pass* or *add a user*). They may also have additional qualifiers (for example, using adjectives as in *generate monthly tax reports* or other qualifiers such as *purchase gas at pump*).

The arrows in a use case diagram show the interactions between the actor and the use cases. If the arrow goes from the actor to the use case, it indicates that the actor is the primary actor that initiates that use case or that the use case was initiated for (for example, the system might initiate automated nightly reports for the gas station owner). An arrow from a use case to an actor indicates that the actor

Part III.C.2

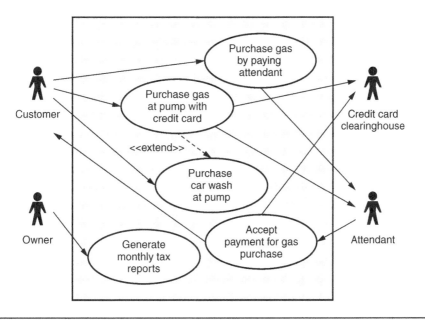

Figure 11.4   Use case diagram—example.

is a secondary actor also involved in the use case. For example, in Figure 11.4, the primary actor for the *purchase gas at pump with credit card* use case is the *customer* who initiates the transaction. Secondary actors that are also involved include the *credit card clearinghouse* and the *attendant*.

Use case diagrams can also indicate the relationships between use cases. An <<extend>> use case adds behavior to the base use case at a specific "extension point." For example, the *purchase gas at pump with credit card* use case can be extended at a specific point with the *purchase car wash at pump* use case. Another relationship between use cases is the <<include>> relationship. An <<include>> use case separates behavior that is similar across multiple use cases into a separate use case in order to remove redundancy and complexity. Of course, the use case diagram in Figure 11.4 has been simplified for illustration purposes and does not show all of the possible actors or use cases. Examples of other use cases might include *purchase gas at pump with debit card, generate weekly reports, change gas price, change tax rates,* and so on.

Use cases are then developed to describe the details of each start-to-finish interaction between the actor and the system. The use cases define:

- *Primary actor.* The actor that initiates the use case.

- *Secondary actors.* Other actors that interact with the use case.

- *Preconditions.* Specific, measurable conditions that must be met before the use case can be initiated (that is, entry criteria).

- *Post-conditions.* Specific, measurable conditions that must be met before the use case is considered complete (that is, exit criteria).

- *Main success scenario.* Also called the *happy path,* the normal or typical sequence that results in a successful interaction with the actor.

- *Alternative variation scenarios.* Other alternate sequences are variations that still result in a successful completion of the task (that is, satisfaction of the post-conditions).

- *Exception variation scenarios.* Other exception sequences are variations that result in an unsuccessful completion of the task (that is, post-conditions are not satisfied).

There are many different ways to document a use case. Table 11.1 illustrates the two-column method where actor actions are documented in one column and system responses are documented in the second column. Again, this example has been simplified. Other alternative scenarios might include purchasing gas with a valid credit card or debit card, entering an incorrect PIN once or twice before entering it correctly, and so on. Other exception scenarios might include the system not being able to communicate with the pump display, the system not being able to print a receipt, the system not being able to read the card's magnetic strip, the customer entering the PIN wrong three times, and so on.

Other methods for documenting use cases include the one-column method where all the steps are listed in a single column, and the use of diagrams where each step is a bubble and arrows show the relationships between the actors and the steps.

Table 11.1   Use case—example.

Use case: Accept payment for gas

Primary actor: Attendant

Secondary actors: Customer, credit card clearinghouse

Preconditions:

• Gas has been successfully pumped

• Customer has arrived at attendant to pay for gas

Post-conditions:

• Payment has been received

• Customer was able to pay for gas with payment type of preference

• Customer received receipt

Main success scenario:

Actor actions	System responses
1. Attendant greets customer and asks which pump was used	
2. Customer identifies pump	
3. Attendant polls system for pump information	4. System reports gallons pumped and total price
5. Attendant confirms price with customer and acknowledges price with system	6. System accepts price and displays price on cash register display
7. Attendant asks if there are other items and customer responds "no"	
8. Attendant asks for payment type and customer pays in cash	
9. Attendant enters cash tendered into cash register	10. System calculates and displays change and prints receipt
11. Attendant provides change and receipt to customer	
12. Attendant ends transaction	13. System saves transaction information and resets pump

Alternative scenarios:

Actor actions	System responses
5a1. Customer identified *wrong pump* and changes pump identification	
5a2. Attendant cancels previous pump	5a3. System resets to "no pump identified"
5a4. Return to step 3	

Continued

Part III.C.2

Table 11.1 *Continued.*

Actor actions	System responses
7a1. Customer *purchases other items*	
7a2. Attendant enters price for each item in cash register	7a3. System accepts price and displays item prices and running total price on cash register
7a4. Return to step 8	

Exception scenarios:

Actor actions	System responses
	4a1. System *can not communicate with pump*
4a2. Attendant manually checks pump display and enters amount into cash register	
4a3. Return to step 7	
8c1. Attendant asks for payment type and customer swipes *invalid credit card type (not accepted type of card)*	8c2. System reads and parses magnetic strip
	8c3. System displays error
8c4. Return to step 8	
8d1. Attendant asks for payment type and customer swipes *invalid credit card (expired, reported stolen, or over limit)* correctly (after one or more tries)	8d2. System reads and parses magnetic strip
	8d3. System establishes communications with credit card clearinghouse and transmits merchant information, credit card information, and transaction amount
8d4. Credit card clearinghouse disapproves transaction	8d5. System displays disapproval
8d6. Return to step 8	

The level of detail used to document the use case depends on the needs of the project. Typically, use cases are documented at a very high level of detail initially and then more details are added as necessary. For example, early in development the use case in Table 11.1 might have just included the following steps (one-column method):

1. Attendant polls pump for gas amount and price

2. Customer pays attendant

3. Attendant provides receipt and change, if any

Other information that should be defined for each use case includes:

- A unique use case identifier and the use case name

- Who created the use case and its creation date

- The use case's modification history (who modified it and the modification dates)

- Use case description

- Use case priority

- Frequency of use

- Related business rules

- Related assumptions

Storyboards

Similarly to the panels in a comic strip, a *storyboard* graphically illustrates who the characters are in a story and describes the order of what happens to those characters and how it happens. For example, Figure 11.5 illustrates a storyboard for the main success scenario from the use case in Table 11.1. Storyboards are mainly used in requirements engineering to describe the human user interfaces. Pictorial sequences can many times be easier for stakeholders to visualize and interpret than written steps. This can aid in understanding and provide a basis for discussion about what needs to happen and how.

Human Factors Studies

Human factors studies consider the ways in which the human users of a software system will interact with that system and its environment. The purpose of doing human factors studies in relationship to software requirements is to ensure that the software system conforms to the abilities and capabilities of its human user. These studies consider ease of use, ease of learning, ergonomics, usage preferences (for example some people prefer to use keyboard entry rather than a mouse,

Figure 11.5   Storyboard–example.

Part III.C.2

or certain screen color combinations may be aesthetically displeasing), education and training levels, physical handicaps, languages, customs, and so on. The
study of human factors can be particularly important where the potential exists
for possible human errors to cause safety concerns, for example, where performing tasks out of sequence might cause unsafe conditions.

3. REQUIREMENTS ANALYSIS

> Identify and use tools such as data flow
> diagrams (DFDs), entity relationship diagrams
> (ERDs), etc., to analyze requirements. (Apply)
>
> **Body of Knowledge III.C.3**

The SEI CMMI for Development states (SEI 2006) that requirements "analysis
occurs recursively at successively more detailed layers of a product's architecture
until sufficient detail is available to enable detailed design, acquisition, and testing of the product to proceed." Utilizing models to aid in the requirements analysis process can be particularly beneficial because models:

- Present a summary view of requirements

- Help decompose business- and user-level requirements into product-level
  requirements

- Aid in communications—"a picture is worth 1000 words"

- Act as a transition between requirements and design

- Aid in the identification of:

  - Requirements defects

  - Missing requirements

  - Non-value-added requirements

Traditional software models including *data flow diagrams, entity relationship diagrams,* and *state transition diagrams and tables* come from structured analysis techniques. These models have been around for decades, but even though they are
older than their object-oriented counterparts, they can still be very useful in analyzing requirements.

Object-oriented techniques bring several additional models to the requirements analysis tool belt. One advantage of these models is that they have been
standardized as part of the Unified Modeling Language (UML) and adopted by
the Object Management Group (OMG), the main standards body for object-
oriented matters (UML 2003). Object-oriented models include the use case diagrams and use cases discussed previously, as well as *class diagrams, sequence
diagrams,* and *activity diagrams.*

Still other requirements analysis models come from outside the software-specific arena. For example:

- *Process flow diagrams* used for defining processes as part of a quality management system can also be used to define processes that are being automated

- *Decision trees*, which will be discussed later as a test design tool, can also be used to analyze system decisions as a basis for requirements analysis

- *Event/response tables* can be used to help analyze error-handling requirements

Data Flow Diagrams

A *data flow diagram* (DFD) is a graphical representation of how data flows through and is transformed by the software system. Figure 11.6 illustrates the Yourdon/DeMarco symbols used in a data flow diagram. In a requirements-type DFD the circles represent a process or set of functions that need to be performed and not specific software components or individual software modules like a circle on design-type DFDs might.

At the highest level, a data flow diagram can be used to define the context of the system where a single circle represents the entire software system and the external entities are represented by rectangles, with arrows depicting the data flows between the system and those external entities.

Data flow diagrams can also be used to decompose and describe the internal workings of the software in progressively more detail. For example, in the DFD illustrated in Figure 11.7, there is a circle that represents the *pump gas and display ongoing gallons and price* process. This circle could be further broken down into a lower-level data flow diagram that describes more detail about the internals of that process, and so on.

Part III.C.3

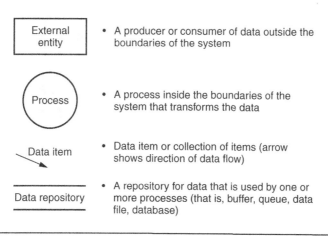

Figure 11.6   Data flow diagram (DFD) symbols.

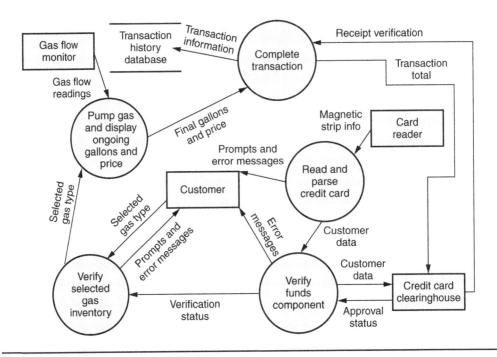

Figure 11.7 Data flow diagram (DFD)—example.

Entity Relationship Diagrams

Entity relationship diagrams (ERDs) graphically represent the relationships between the data objects in the system. The primary components of an ERD include:

- *Data objects*—represented by a labeled rectangle

- *Relationships*—represented by labeled lines connecting the data objects

- *Indicators for cardinality and modality*—represented by symbols or numbers

The example ERD illustrated in Figure 11.8a has five entities (gas station, gas pump, type of gas, transaction, receipt). The labeled lines show the relationships (the gas station contains gas pumps, gas pumps pump different types of gas, gas pumps process transactions, and receipts record transactions).

    Cardinality is the specification of the number of occurrences of one object that can be related to the number of occurrences of another object. As illustrated in Figure 11.8b, the outside set of symbols represents the cardinality with a line symbol indicating a *one* relationship and a "chicken foot" symbol indicating a *many* relationship. Two objects can be related as:

- *One-to-one.* One occurrence of object A can be related to one and only one occurrence of the other object B. For example, each receipt records a single transaction, and each transaction is recorded on a single receipt.

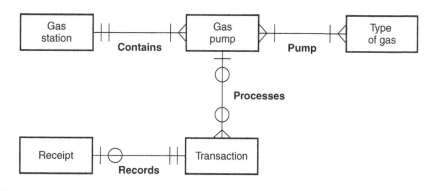

Figure 11.8a   Entity relationship diagram (ERD)–example.

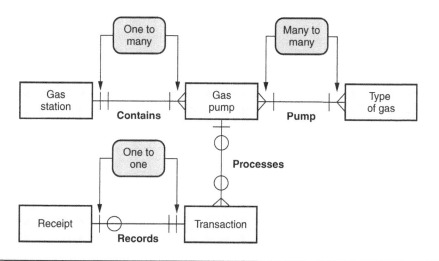

Figure 11.8b   Entity relationship diagram (ERD) cardinality–example.

- *One-to-many.* One occurrence of object A can be related to one or many occurrences of the other object B. For example, a gas station contains one or more gas pumps, but each gas pump is located at only one gas station.

- *Many-to-many.* Each occurrence of object A can be related to one or many occurrences of object B, and each occurrence of object B can be related to one or many occurrences of object A. For example, each gas pump can pump multiple types of gas and each type of gas can be pumped from multiple gas pumps.

As illustrated in Figure 11.8c, the inside set of symbols represents the *modality*. The modality relationship symbol is a circle if the relationship is optional. For example, not every transaction will have a printed receipt. The modality is a straight

Part III.C.3

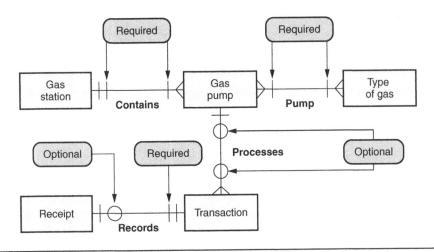

Figure 11.8c   Entity relationship diagram (ERD) modality—example.

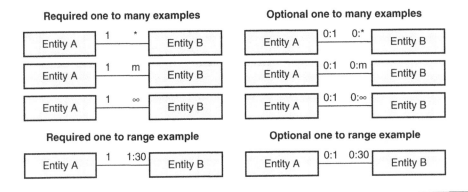

Figure 11.8d   Other cardinality and modality symbols—examples.

line if the relationship is mandatory. For example, every receipt must have an associated transaction.

There are actually many different types of symbols and numbers that can be used to identify the cardinality and modality in an ERD, as illustrated in Figure 11.8d.

State Transition

State transition analysis evaluates the behavior of a system by analyzing its states and the events that cause the system to change states. A state is an observable mode of behavior. For example, a printer could be in either a *wait for print command, printing document, error-jammed,* or *error-empty* state. State transition can either be illustrated using a *state transition diagram,* as illustrated in Figure 11.9, or as *state transition tables,* as illustrated in Table 11.2.

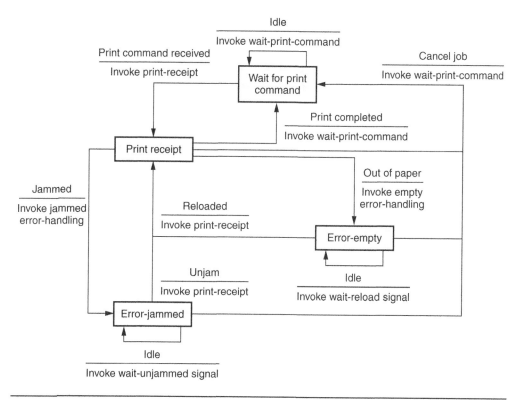

Figure 11.9   State transition diagram graphic—example.

Table 11.2   State transition table—example.

		To state			
		Wait for print command	**Print receipt**	**Error-jammed**	**Error-empty**
From state	**Wait for print command**	Idle	Print command received	—	—
	Print receipt	Print completed or Cancel job	—	Jammed	Out of paper
	Error-jammed	Cancel job	Unjammed	Idle	—
	Error-empty	Cancel job	Reloaded	—	Idle

Class Diagrams

A *class diagram* is an object-oriented model of the static structure of the system that shows the system's classes and their relationships. Classes are the physical or conceptual entities that make up the product, which, as illustrated in the example in Figure 11.10, are drawn in a class diagram as a rectangle with three partitions:

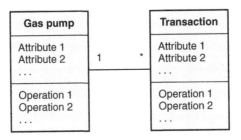

Figure 11.10   Class diagram—example.

- *Name.* Includes the class name that uniquely identifies the class and other general properties of the class. For example, the *gas pump* class or the *transaction* class.

- *Attributes.* A list of the class's properties and data. For example, the gas pump might have a status (idle, in use, out of service) or values like "total gas pumped today."

- *Operations.* A list of operations that the class performs. For example, the gas pump might perform operations like pumping gas, displaying gallons pumped, or printing a receipt.

The lines between the classes in a class diagram show the relationships between the classes. The same cardinality and modality symbols used for ERDs are also used in class diagrams. For example, the *gas pump* class, illustrated in Figure 11.10, has a one-to-many relationship with the *transaction* class.

Sequence Diagrams

A *sequence diagram*, also called an *interaction diagram*, is an object-oriented model that records in detail how objects interact over time to perform a task by describing the sequences of messages that pass between those objects. The example illustrated in Figure 11.11 shows a sequence diagram for validating a credit card.

Activity Diagrams

An *activity diagram* is an object-oriented model that depicts a dynamic, activity-oriented view of the software product's functions and describes the work flow or flow of control through the activity. As illustrated in Figure 11.12, each rounded-corner box represents an action, and arrows show the sequencing of these actions.

Event/Response Table

Event/response tables list the various external events that can occur and define how the software product should respond to those events based on the given state

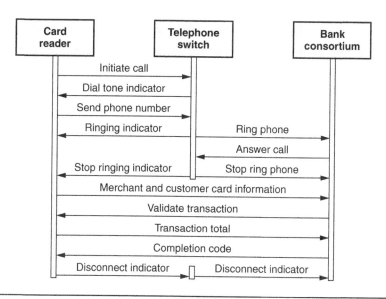

Figure 11.11   Sequence diagram—example.

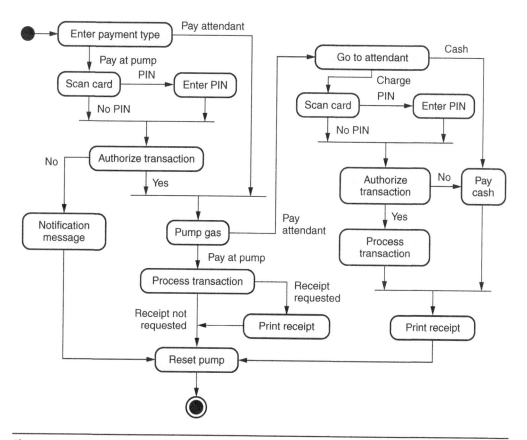

Figure 11.12   Activity diagram—example.

Table 11.3   Event/response table—example.

Event	Pump state	Response
Card inserted into card reader	Pump out of service	N/A
	Idle	Start new transaction—prompt to remove card
	Card already scanned and transaction started—prompting for inputs	Transaction in progress—cancel previous transaction (Y or N) message
	Card being verified with credit card clearinghouse	Transaction in progress—cancel previous transaction (Y or N) message
	Gas being pumped	Error message
	Gas pumping complete—awaiting transaction completion	Error message
Cancel button pressed	Pump out of service	N/A
	Idle	N/A
	Transaction started—prompting for inputs	Cancel transaction and return to idle
	Card being verified with credit card clearinghouse	Cancel transaction (including cancel messages to credit card clearinghouse) and return to idle
	Gas being pumped	Error message
	Gas pumping complete—awaiting transaction completion	Error message
End of day	System active	Process end-of-day reporting
.	.	.
.	.	.
.	.	.

at the time that the events occurred. Events are either initiated by users (actors), including hardware devices like sensors, buttons, and so on, or by time (for example, the end of the day, the elapse of a certain amount of time). An example of a partial event/response table is illustrated in Table 11.3.

Chapter 12

D. Requirements Management

A ccording to the Software Engineering Institute's (SEI) Capability Maturity Model Integration (CMMI) for Development (SEI 2006), "the purpose of requirements management is to manage the requirements of the project's products and product components and to identify inconsistencies between those requirements and the project's plans and work products."

1. PARTICIPANTS

> Identify various participants who have a role in requirements planning, including customers, developers, testers, the quality function, management, etc. (Understand)
>
> **Body of Knowledge III.D.1**

Wiegers (2003) states that, "Nowhere more than in the requirements process do the interests of all the stakeholders in a software or system project intersect." As illustrated in Figure 12.1, there are participants who have a role in requirements activities, including:

- *Customers.* The customers fund the software development effort or acquire the software products in order to meet their business objectives. The requirements define the agreement between the customers and developers about the scope of the software product. The requirements define what is being built. The customer typically has final say and approval over what is included in the requirements and the requirement priorities.

- *Users.* The users, also called the *end users,* directly or indirectly use the software in order to perform their tasks or functions. The software requirements define what the software is that will be delivered to the users. User needs, including usability, must be addressed by the requirements.

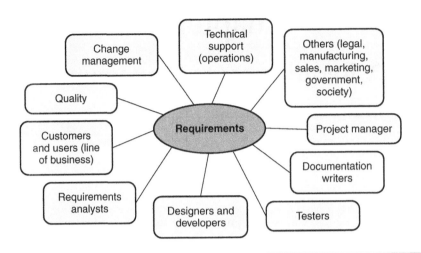

Figure 12.1   Requirements participants.

- *Requirements analysts.* The requirements analysts, also called *business analysts* or *system analysts,* are responsible for eliciting the requirements from the customers, users, and other stakeholders, analyzing the requirements, writing the requirements specification, and communicating the requirements to developers and other stakeholders.

- *Designers and developers.* The designers are responsible for translating the requirements into the software's architectural and detailed designs that specify how the software will be implemented. The developers are responsible for implementing the designs by creating the software products and supporting services. If the software is part of a larger system, hardware designers and developers may also be interested in the software requirements. The needs of the designers and developers, including feasibility, portability, reusability, and maintainability, should be addressed by the requirements.

- *Testers.* The testers use the requirements as a basis for creating test cases, procedures, and scripts that they use to execute the software under specific, known conditions to detect defects and provide confidence that the software performs as specified. The needs of the testers, including testability, should be addressed by the requirements.

- *Quality.* The quality function works to ensure that quality is built into the product throughout the development life cycle and that a quality management system is in place with the capacity and capability necessary to build high-quality software products.

- *Documentation writers.* The documentation writers, also called *technical writers,* are responsible for using the requirements as inputs into the creation of the user documentation including user/operations manuals, help files, installation instructions, release notes, and training materials, as necessary.

- *Project manager.* The project manager is responsible for planning, monitoring, and controlling the project and guiding the software development team to the successful delivery of the software. The software requirements define the size, functionality, performance, and quality of the product being created by the project. It is the project manager's responsibility to ensure a successful project, including delivering the software with its required functionality at the desired performance and quality levels, on time and within budget, while effectively and efficiently using people and other resources.

- *Technical support.* Technical support, also called *operations* or the *help desk,* is responsible for interfacing with the user community to support the software once it has been deployed to the field. Technical support needs should be addressed by the requirements.

- *Change management.* Change management, which may take the form of a product-level *change control board* (CCB), is responsible for:

  - Reviewing proposed changes to the requirements

  - Analyzing their impacts

  - Approving/disapproving changes

  - Ensuring that approved changes are implemented and validated

- *Others.* Depending on the software product and project, there may also be other stakeholders interested in the requirements. Examples of other stakeholders include:

  - Legal or contract management

  - Manufacturing or product release management

  - Sales and marketing

  - Upper management

  - Government or regulator agencies

  - Other product stakeholders

  - Society at large

Not only are there multiple participants involved in software requirements engineering activities, the requirements process doesn't exist in a vacuum. Various organizational and external factors influence these activities, as illustrated in Figure 12.2. The context in which software requirements engineering is performed influences its practices and activities. Therefore, the tools and techniques used in software engineering should be tailored to the needs of the participants, the projects, and the organization.

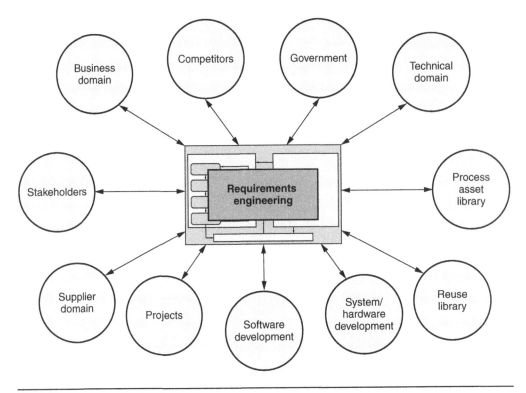

Figure 12.2 Organizational context.

2. REQUIREMENTS EVALUATION

Assess the completeness, consistency, correctness, and testability of requirements, and determine their priority. (Evaluate)

Body of Knowledge III.D.2

Requirements Evaluation

As software requirements are being elicited, analyzed, and specified they should be continuously evaluated and validated to ensure their completeness, consistency, correctness, and testability. This can be done through facilitated requirements workshops, peer reviews, prototypes, and discussions with stakeholders. If the software requirements are not right, it does not matter how well the rest of the project is performed. The project team can do a perfect job of building the wrong product. Requirements development is an iterative process of elicitation, analysis, specification, and validation. At each step along the way, as intermediate

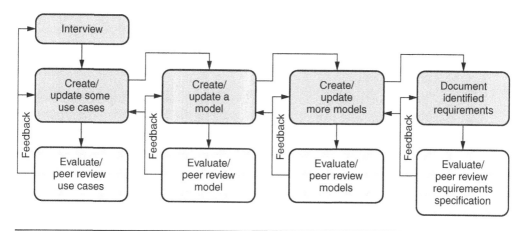

Figure 12.3   Iterative requirements evaluation.

work products are created, those products can be validated as part of the ongoing requirements activities.

For example, as illustrated in Figure 12.3, a requirements analyst may interview a stakeholder, and based on the information obtained one or more use cases may be written. These use cases can then be peer reviewed. This may be a very informal peer review where the requirements analyst asks the interviewee or a colleague to "look them over," or it may be a more formal walk-through as part of a facilitated requirements workshop. This peer review provides feedback into perfecting those use cases and it may also identify the need to ask the interviewee more questions.

Based on the use cases, the requirements analyst may then create a model. This model can be evaluated to provide feedback to update the model or its associated use cases. The requirements analyst might then create additional models or start actually documenting the identified requirements, and additional evaluation sessions or peer reviews can be held. Holding lots of small evaluation sessions or peer reviews during the requirements development process allows the requirements analysts to take small corrective steps as they go. This keeps the requirements analysts from building additional requirements work products based on predecessor products that have defects.

Once the software requirements specification documentation is complete it should be evaluated as a whole to ensure that it is:

- *Complete.* Includes all the functional, nonfunctional, external interfaces, data, and design constraint–type requirements that must be satisfied by the software being developed.

- *Consistent.* Internal conflicts do not exist between requirements that result in the requirements contradicting each other. The requirements also do not conflict with higher-level requirements including business- or stakeholder-level requirements, requirements in external interface specifications or system requirements specifications, or with external standards, regulations, law, or other business rules. Consistent terminology is used to minimize ambiguity:

– A word has the same meaning every time it's used. For example, the word "customer" does not refer to the person buying gas in one requirement and the person acquiring the software in another requirement.

– Two different words aren't used to mean the same thing. For example, the person who drives up and purchases gas is not called the *driver* in one requirement and the *customer* or *purchaser* somewhere else.

- *Modifiable.* Each requirement is stated in only one place and referenced elsewhere so that if changes are needed it is less likely that internal inconsistencies result. To the extent possible, each requirement should be able to be changed without excessive impact on other requirements. For example, all pronouns should be removed from the requirements specifications and replaced with specific nouns. For example, a requirement reads, "The controller board displays an alarm when the metered temperature exceeds 300 degrees and it sends a reset signal to the burner unit." This requirement is later modified to read, "The controller board and operator console display alarms when the metered temperature exceeds 300 degrees and it sends a reset signal to the burner unit." There is now ambiguity as to whether the controller board or operator console sends the reset signal. By replacing the word "it" in the original requirement with its noun "the controller board," the modified requirements would read, "The controller board and operator console display alarms when the metered temperature exceeds 300 degrees and the controller board sends a reset signal to the burner unit" and the ambiguity does not occur.

- *Compliant with the standard.*

In addition to evaluating the software requirements specification documentation as a whole, each individual requirement should also be evaluated to ensure that it is:

- *Clear and unambiguous.* Each requirement statement should have one and only one interpretation. Each requirement should be specified in a coherent, easy-to-understand manner. One trick to identifying ambiguous requirements is to search for words that end in "ly" (for example, quickly, efficiently, completely, user-friendly) and "ize" (for example, optimize, minimize, maximize, standardize). Not every "ly" or "ize" word will result in an ambiguous requirement—but many of them may so they should be evaluated. Other key words such as "flexible," "accommodate," "safe," "fast," "easy," "sufficient," "small," "large," "improve," and "reduce" may also add to ambiguity.

- *Concise.* Each requirement should be stated in short, specific, action-oriented language. Stating requirements in active, not passive, voice can also make them more concise and readable. The requirements analysts need to forget all of the flowery language they learned in college composition class and learn the principles of good engineering writing.

- *Finite.* A requirement should not be stated in an open-ended manner. For example, words such as "all," "always," "every," "usually," "sometimes," and "throughout" should be avoided in requirements statements. Phrases such as "Including but not limited to . . . " should also be avoided.

- *Measurable.* Specific, measurable limits or values should be stated for each requirement as appropriate. Words such as "fast" or "quick" should be replaced with specific times such as "within three seconds" or "in a maximum of not more than 10 nanoseconds."

- *Feasible.* The requirement is able to be implemented using available technologies, techniques, tools, resources, and personnel within the specified cost and schedule constraints.

- *Testable.* There exists a reasonably cost-effective way to determine that the software satisfies the requirement. A requirement is considered testable if an objective and feasible test can be designed to determine whether the software meets the requirement.

- *Traceable.* Each requirement should be traceable back to its source (for example, system-level requirements, standard, business rules, stakeholder needs, enhancement request, and so on). It should also be specified in a manner that allows traceability forward into the design, implementation, and tests.

- *Value-added.* Each requirement is relevant to the defined scope of the product and adds value for at least one of the stakeholders.

One of the main benefits of involving multiple people in a peer review of the requirements specification documents results from the fact that different reviewers have different perspectives of the product and therefore find different types of defects. The reviewers should be selected to maximize this benefit by choosing participants including:

- *Other requirements analysts* because they have the knowledge of the workmanship standards and best practices for the requirements specification. They are also most familiar with the common defects made in requirements work products.

- *The designers and testers* have a strong vested interest in the quality of the requirements because their work depends on the requirements being correct. They are also excellent candidates for looking at issues such as understandability, feasibility, and testability.

- *Customers and users* (or their representatives, including marketing) bring an essential perspective to the requirements inspection. They are also the best candidates to help identify missing requirements or failures to address customer or user needs.

- *Specialists* may also be called on when special expertise can add to the effectiveness of the inspection. Specialists might include experts on efficiency, security, safety, graphical user interfaces, hardware, interfacing product, and so on.

Writing test cases early in the life cycle can also help evaluate the requirements and ensure their quality. Since functional testing only requires knowledge of the requirements and not of the internals of the software product, testers can start writing test cases against the requirements as soon as the requirements are defined. The major advantage to writing the functional test cases early in the life cycle is that writing the test cases helps uncover defects in the requirements. Writing test cases early may result in some rework of the test cases if the requirements change, but the cost of that rework will be more than offset by the savings resulting from finding and fixing more requirements defects earlier.

Prioritizing Requirements

Prioritizing requirements can help the project team:

- Understand what's important to their stakeholders
- Work on the most important requirements first
- Balance project scope against project schedule, cost and staff constraints, and quality goals
- Trade off new high-priority requirements against lower-priority requirements that can be deferred
- Provide the highest possible value at the lowest possible cost
- Deliver the most valuable functionality sooner—saving less-valuable functionality for later releases of the product

During the first pass at requirements prioritization, the requirements can simply be prioritized into three major groups:

- *High.* The high-priority requirements are the requirements that absolutely must be included in the next increment or release of the software product or it will not be considered successful. If a high-priority requirement is not complete, would the project postpone the release of the software product? If the answer is no, then the requirement is not a high priority.

- *Medium.* The medium-priority requirements are the ones the stakeholders would like to have included in the next increment or release of the software product, but these requirements can wait until the following increment or release if necessary. The goal for medium-priority requirements is to get as many of them implemented as possible in the next increment or release.

- *Low.* The low-priority requirements are going to be deferred to a later increment or release. In fact, depending on business objectives, budgets, schedules, and other factors, the project team may never get around to some of these requirements.

During the second pass at requirements prioritization the focus is only on the medium-priority requirements from the first pass. The high-priority requirements definitely must be implemented and the low-priority requirements will not be implemented. There is a possibility that the project will only have the resources to do some of the medium-priority requirements. Therefore, the project team wants to make sure that they implement the most important ones.

To accomplish this, the project team wants to rank the medium-priority requirements. There are several ways to accomplish this, but according to Wiegers (2003), one of the most rigorous is to consider four factors:

- *Benefit.* The first factor considers the benefits that the stakeholder will enjoy if that requirement is present. For example, if the requirement for allowing gas station customers to pay for their gas purchases in cash at the pump is included in the product, then those users will receive the benefit of saving the extra time it takes to go pay the attendant. The gas station owners may also have a competitive advantage if other gas stations don't offer this service and their station gets more business as a result.

- *Penalty.* The second factor considers the penalties that would occur if the requirements were not included. The value here lies in avoiding the penalties by implementing the requirements. There might be legal penalties if a law or regulation was not met by the system, for example, if the system did not handle the taxes on gas purchases correctly. There might also be death, injury, or property damage if the system were unsafe.

- *Cost.* The third factor to consider is the relative cost of implementing one requirement over another. All other factors being equal, less-costly requirements are prioritized higher than more-costly ones.

- *Risk.* The fourth factor to consider is the technical risk of implementing the requirement. Technical risk is the probability that the project team will not be able to get the requirements correctly implemented on the first attempt and incur costs for rework if they don't. All other factors being equal, lower-risk requirements are prioritized higher than higher-risk ones.

These four factors can be used to create a prioritization matrix for the medium-priority requirements, as illustrated in Table 12.1. This example shows a simple weighted prioritization matrix where each requirement is ranked on a scale of one to five in terms of its impact on each of the four factors. Each score is multiplied by the relative weight for that factor, and the sum of the weighted scores for each requirement is used as a ranking.

Part III.D.2

Table 12.1 Requirements prioritization matrix.

	Criteria and weights				
	Benefit (.40)	Penalty (.20)	Cost (.15)	Risk (.25)	Total
Requirement 1	4	2	3	1	2.70
Requirement 2	3	4	1	4	3.15
Requirement 3	1	2	2	2	1.60
Requirement 4	2	3	4	2	2.50

3. REQUIREMENTS CHANGE MANAGEMENT

> Assess the impact that changes to requirements will have on software development processes for all types of life cycle models. (Evaluate)
>
> **Body of Knowledge III.D.3**

Good requirements change management practices identify the requirements specification documents as configuration items. Those configuration items are then placed under formal change control when they are baselined. Defined change control processes should exist where change control boards (CCBs) review proposed requirements changes and perform impact analysis on those proposals. Changes should be traced to all affected work products and to project management plans. If the requested change is approved by the CCB, all those affected work products and the project management plans should be updated accordingly so that they remain consistent with the updated requirements. The updated requirements specifications are then re-baselined. Version control practices track the history of changes to the requirements document baselines. Metrics should also be utilized to track the volatility of the requirements over time.

4. BIDIRECTIONAL TRACEABILITY

> Use various tools and techniques to ensure bidirectional traceability from requirements elicitation and analysis through design and testing. (Apply)
>
> **Body of Knowledge III.D.4**

The ISO/IEC standard, *Systems and Software Engineering—Vocabulary* (ISO/IEC 2009) defines *traceability* as "the degree to which a relationship can be established between two or more products of the development process, especially products having a predecessor–successor or master–subordinate relationship to one another."

Traceability is used to track the relationship between each unique product-level requirement and its source. For example, a product requirement might trace to a business need, a user request, a business rule, an external interface specification, an industry standard or regulation, or to some other source. Traceability is also used to track the relationship between each unique product-level requirement and the work products to which that requirement is allocated. For example, a single product requirement might trace to one or more architectural elements, detailed design elements, objects/classes, code units, tests, user or operational documentation topics, training materials, and/or even to people or manual processes that implement that requirement.

Good traceability practices allow for bidirectional traceability, meaning that the traceability chains can be traced in both the forward and backward directions, as illustrated in Figure 12.4.

Forward traceability looks at:

- Tracing the requirements sources to their resulting product requirement(s) to ensure the completeness of the product requirements specification.

- Tracing each unique product requirement forward into the design, code, tests, documentation, processes, and other work products that implement that requirement. The objective is to ensure that each requirement is implemented in the software products and that each requirement is thoroughly tested.

Forward traceability ensures proper direction of the evolving product (that the project is building the right product) and indicates completeness of the subsequent implementation. For example, if a business rule can't be traced forward to one or more product requirements, then the product requirements specification is incomplete and the resulting product may not meet the needs of the business. If a product requirement can not be traced forward to its associated architectural design elements, then the architectural design is not complete, and so on.

If, on the other hand, there are changes in the business environment (for example, a business rule change or a standard change), then if good forward traceability has been maintained, that change can be traced forward to the associated requirements and all of the work products that are impacted by that change. This greatly reduces the amount of effort required to do a thorough impact analysis when there are changes. It also reduces the risk that any affected work product is forgotten, resulting in an incomplete implementation of the change (a defect).

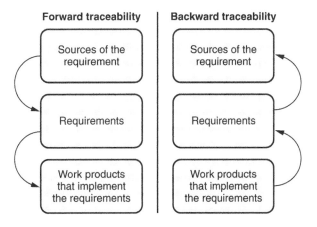

Figure 12.4   Bidirectional (forward and backward) traceability.

Part III.D.4

Backward traceability looks at:

- Tracing each unique work product (for example, design element, object/class, code unit, tests, and user documentation) back to its associated requirement. Backward traceability helps verify that the requirements have been kept current as subsequent work products are built based on those requirements.

- Tracing each requirement back to its source(s) (for example, business/stakeholder needs, regulations and standards).

Backward traceability helps ensure that the evolving product remains on the correct track with regard to the original and/or evolving requirements (that the project is building the product right). The objective is to ensure that the scope of the product is not expanding through the addition of features or functionality not specified in the requirements ("gold-plating"). If there is a change needed in the implementation, or if the developers come up with a creative, new technical solution, that change or solution should be traced backward to the requirements and/or the business needs to ensure that it is within the scope of the desired product. If there is a work product element that doesn't trace back to the requirements, one of two things is true. The first possibility is that there is a missing requirement because the work product element really is needed. In this case, traceability has helped identify the missing requirement and can also be used to evaluate the impacts of adding that requirement to project plans and other work products (forward traceability again). The second possibility is that there is gold-plating going on—something has been added that should not be part of the product. Gold-plating is a high-risk activity because project plans have not allocated time or resources to the work, and the existence of that part of the product may not be well communicated to other project personnel (for example, tester doesn't test it and/or it's not included in user documentation).

Another benefit of backward traceability comes when a defect is identified in one of the work products. For example, if a piece of code has a defect, the traceability matrix can be used to help determine the root cause of that defect. Is it just a code defect or does it trace back to a defect in the design or requirements? If it's a design or requirements defect, what other work products might be impacted by the defect?

Many modern requirements management tools include traceability mechanisms as part of their functionality. These tools support linking between the requirements and their source and subsequent work products.

The classic manual way to perform traceability is by constructing a traceability matrix. As illustrated in Table 12.2, a traceability matrix summarizes in matrix form a trace from original identified stakeholder needs to their associated product requirements and then on to other work product elements. In order to construct a traceability matrix, each requirement, each requirements source, and each work product element must have a unique identifier that can be used as a reference in the matrix. The requirements matrix has the advantage of being a single repository for documenting both forward and backward traceability across all of the work products. While maintaining a manual traceability matrix is a labor-intensive activity, the benefit in higher visibility, reduced impact analysis effort, and reduced risk can make it a value-added activity.

Table 12.2   Traceability matrix–example.

Requirement source	Product requirements	HLD section #	LLD section #	Code unit	UTS case #	STS case #	User manual
Business rule #1	R00120 Credit card types	4.1 Parse magnetic strip	4.1.1 Read card type	Read_Card _Type.c Read_Card _Type.h	UT 4.1.032 UT 4.1.033 UT 4.1.038 UT 4.1.043	ST 120.020 ST 120.022	Section 12
			4.1.2 Verify card type	Ver_Card _Type.c Ver_Card _Type.h Ver_Card _Types. dat	UT 4.2.012 UT 4.2.013 UT 4.2.016 UT 4.2.031 UT 4.2.045	ST 120.035 ST 120.036 ST 120.037 ST 120.038	Section 12
Use case #132 step 6	R00230 Read gas flow	7.2.2 Gas flow meter interface	7.2.2 Read gas flow indicator	Read_Gas _Flow.c	UT 7.2.043 UT 7.2.044	ST 230.002 ST 230.003	Section 21.1.2
	R00231 Calculate gas price	7.3 Calculate gas price	7.3 Calculate gas price	Cal_Gas_ Price.c	UT 7.3.005 UT 7.3.006 UT 7.3.007	ST 231.001 ST 231.002 ST 231.003	Section 21.1.3

Part III.D.4

SRS   R00104 ~~The system~~ shall cancel the transaction if at any time prior to the actual dispensing of gasoline, the cardholder requests cancellation.

SDS

SDS identifier	SRS tag	Component name	Component description	Type	Etc
7.01.032 ◀— R00104		Cancel_ Transaction	Cancel transaction when the customer presses cancel button	Module	

UTS

Test case #	SDS identifier	Test case name	Inputs	Expected results	Etc
23476	7.01.032	Cancel_Before_PIN_Entry			
23477	7.01.032	Cancel_After_Invalid_PIN_Entry			
23478	7.01.032	Cancel_After_Start_Pump_Gas			

Figure 12.5   Trace tagging–example.

A third mechanism for implementing traceability is *trace tagging*. Again, each requirement, each requirement source, and each work product element must have a unique identifier. In trace tagging, however, those identifiers are used as tags in the subsequent work products to identify backward tracing to the predecessor document. As illustrated in Figure 12.5, for example, the *software design specification* (SDS) includes tags that identify the requirements implemented by each uniquely identified design element, and the *unit test specification* (UTS) includes trace tags that trace back to the design elements that each test case verifies. This tagging propagates through the work product set with source code units that include trace tags back to design elements, integration test cases with tags back to architecture elements, and system test cases with trace tags back to requirements, as appropriate, depending on the hierarchy of work products used on the product. Trace tags have the advantage of being part of the work products so a separate matrix isn't maintained. However, while backward tracing is easy with trace tags, forward tracing is very difficult using this mechanism.

All traceability implementation techniques require the commitment of a cross-functional team of participants to create and maintain the linkages between the requirements, their source, and their allocation to subsequent work products. The requirements analyst must initiate requirements traceability and document the original tracing of the product requirements to their source. As system and software architects create the high-level design, those practitioners add their information to the traceability documentation. Developers doing low-level design, code, and unit testing add additional traceability information for the elements they create, as do the integration, system, and alpha, beta, and acceptance testers. For small projects, some of these roles may not exist or may be done by the sample practitioner, which limits the number of different people working with the traceability information. For larger projects, where traceability information comes from many different practitioners, it may be necessary to have someone who coordinates, documents, and ensures periodic audits of the traceability information from all its various sources to ensure completeness and consistency across all traced elements.

Chapter 13

E. Software Analysis, Design, and Development

During the analysis and design activities, there is a change of thinking by the developers from "what needs to be done" to "how it will be done" in the software. Design involves creating the software architecture that defines the software components (subsystems, programs, modules, databases, and other data elements) and the interactions/interfaces between those components. Software requirements can then be allocated to those components. Software analysis and design also include the detailed design of the internal workings and structure of each software component. Development activities then translate the design into the actual software products. This includes source code with comments and documentation (for example, help files, user manuals, operations manuals, installation instructions, and/or version description document or release notes).

1. DESIGN METHODS

> Identify the steps used in software design and their functions, and define and distinguish between software design methods such as object-oriented analysis and design (OOAD), structured analysis and design (SAD), and patterns. (Understand)
>
> **Body of Knowledge III.E.1**

Software design is typically defined from the perspective of either the:

- *Flow of data.* For architectural design, this is the flow of data between the components of the system. For detailed design this is the flow of data internal to each component. Flow of data includes database schema, message definitions, and input and output parameters.

- *Flow of control.* For architectural design, this is the flow of control between components of the system. For detailed design this is the flow of control internal to each component. Flow of control includes execution sequencing, synchronization relationships, critical timing constraints or events, and error handling.

Steps Used in Software Design

For software that is part of a larger system, the first step in software design may be the architectural design of the system. As part of the system architecture, the system-level requirements are allocated to the hardware, software, and manual operations components of the system. The requirements that are allocated to the software may be further refined into software-level requirements. This step may be skipped for software development projects that only include the development of software (and not of systems).

The next major step in software design is to transform the software requirements into the architectural design of the software. The software architectural design specifies the underlying structure of the software and how that structure is partitioned into the various software product components and interactions or interfaces between those software components. Thus, the software architectural design defines the rules for integrating the various software components together into the software products. This step also includes the high-level design for all of the external interfaces between the software components and other components within the system (hardware and human interfaces) and between the software and entities outside the system. As part of this step, verification and validation activities are performed on the architectural design elements.

The final major step in software design is detailed design. The detailed design defines the internals of each software component and refines that design down to individual software modules that can be coded. This includes the detailed design of each database or other data element and the detailed design of the external interfaces. As part of this step, verification and validation activities are performed on the detailed design elements.

The goal is to create high-quality designs that are traceable from both the architectural and detailed levels to their allocated requirements, that are as strongly cohesive as possible, and that are as decoupled as possible. As illustrated in Figure 13.1, *cohesion* is a measure of the extent to which a component in the software design performs a single task or function. *Coupling* is a measure of the interconnectivity between modules in a software structure, as illustrated in Figure 13.2. The more coupled a module is, the larger the impact if that module needs to be changed and the more regression testing needed to ensure that the changes to the coupled module do not adversely impact other unchanged parts of the software.

Structured Analysis and Design (SAD)

According to Yourdon and Constantine (1979), *structured analysis and design* (SAD) is "a collection of guidelines for distinguishing between good designs and bad designs, and a collection of techniques, strategies, and heuristics that generally lead to good design." SAD is a document-based approach to rigorous design, as opposed to the minimal documentation approach of the agile philosophies. SAD techniques include:

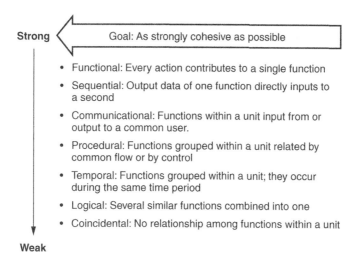

Figure 13.1   Levels of cohesion (based on Yourdon [1979]).

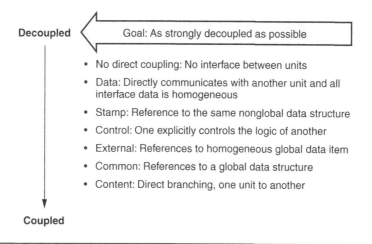

Figure 13.2   Levels of coupling (based on Charette [1986]).

- *Data modeling.* The data elements of the system or software and their relationships are analyzed, modeled, and documented (for example, with entity relationship diagrams).

- *Data flow modeling.* The movement of data around the system/software and the associated data transformations are analyzed, modeled, and documented (for example, with data flow diagrams).

- *Entity behavior modeling.* The events that impact data entities or the sequences of those events are analyzed, modeled, and documented (for example, with control flow diagrams or state diagrams).

Object-Oriented Analysis and Design (OOAD)

The idea behind *object-oriented analysis and design* is to design the software around the elements that are least likely to change over time. For example, 50 years ago gas stations had customers, attendants, owners, gas pumps, and transactions just like they do today. However, think about how the interactions between those entities have changed in those 50 years. In object-oriented analysis and design the *objects* represent specific entities in the software system. Objects are self-contained and have both data associated with them and associated procedures to manipulate the data. There have been lengthy discussions in the industry over what the word "object" really means. An equation for recognizing an object-oriented approach follows:

Objects (encapsulations of attributes and exclusive services; abstractions of entities in the problem space, with some number of instances in the problem space) = Classification + Inheritance + Communication with messages (based on Coad 1990).

In object-oriented analysis and design, objects belong to classes. A class is a category (classification) of objects, or object types, and defines all of the common properties of the different objects that belong to it. *Classes* are the building blocks of object-oriented software. For example, the object *Cathy* belongs to the class of ASQ members, and so does the object *Tom*. Because of this, they share certain attributes (data structures) from that class. For example, they both have a membership number, a membership type, divisions they belong to, and ASQ certifications they hold. They also share procedures (called operations) they can perform. For example, they can pay their dues, join another division, subscribe to an ASQ journal, or recertify. The object *Susan*, who is not a member of ASQ, does not share these attributes or operations.

Inheritance is a relationship between classes that allows the definition of a new class based on the definition of an existing class. For example, if the class *Gasoline* already exists, three new classes can be defined *(Regular, Super, Premium)* to inherit all of the attributes defined for the parent class *Gasoline* without duplicating those attributes in the three new classes. The new classes can also execute all of the operations they inherit from their parent *Gasoline* class.

Developers can also use inheritance to combine common elements from several existing classes to create a new common parent class. For example, common attributes and operations from the two classes *Male* and *Female* can be extracted and placed into a new class, *Person,* thus allowing redundancy to be removed from the software.

Multiple levels of inheritance can exist. For example, the class *Female* inherits attributes and operations from the class *Person,* which inherits from the class *Mammals,* which inherits from the class *Living organisms.* The class *Female* possesses all of the attributes and can perform all of the operations defined in *Person, Mammals,* and *Living organisms.* The class of *Female* also possesses the unique attributes and operations defined within the class *Female.*

The *operations* discussed above are actions that can be applied to an object to obtain a certain effect. Operations fall into several categories:

- *Accessor* operations give information about an object such as the value of some attribute, or general state information. This kind of operation does not change the object on which the operation is being performed.

- *Modifier* operations modify the state of an object by changing one or more attributes to new values.

- *Constructor* operations are used to create a new object, including the initialization of the new instance when it comes into existence.

- *Destructor* operations are used to perform any processing needed just prior to the end of an object's lifetime.

Constructors and destructors are different from accessors and modifiers in that they are invoked implicitly as a result of the birth and death of objects.

A *method* is a piece of software code that implements an operation. While a distinction between operations and methods is not significant for most developers, the distinction is significant to testers. The approach to testing an operation, which is part of a class specification and a way to manipulate an object, is somewhat different from testing a method (McGregor 2001).

Another aspect of object-oriented analysis and design is *polymorphism*. Polymorphism means that the sender of a stimulus (or message) does not need to know the receiving object's class. The receiving object can belong to an arbitrary class. For example, if a person's friend can be either the *Male* class or the *Female* class, polymorphism exists because "friend" is used to refer to either of the two classes. The object that receives the stimulus determines its interpretation. If the receiver's class is known in advance, then polymorphism is not needed, but if the receiver can be of varying classes within limits, then the polymorphism characteristic must specify those limits. An example of this is a method used to draw graphics. If three dimensions are passed in the message, the method *Draw* creates a triangle; if four dimensions are passed, then *Draw* creates a rectangle, five a pentagon, and so on. In this case, there are multiple methods with the same name but they each accept a different number of variables in the method call. Generally, the selection of the variant is determined at run time (dynamic binding) by the compiler, based on, for example, the type or number of arguments passed (Petchiny 1998).

All information in an object-oriented system is stored within its objects. The only way to affect an object (to manipulate its attributes) is when the object is ordered to perform operations. The attributes and operations are encapsulated in the object. Objects support the concept of *information hiding*. That is, they hide their internal structure from their surroundings. *Encapsulation* means that all that is seen of an object is its interface, namely the operations that can be performed on that object. This reduces complexity. Since it is impossible to become involved in the object's internal structure, users can use them only according to their specifications, which define what operations they perform, not how they perform them.

Design Patterns

Pressman (2005) states, " a design pattern describes a design structure that solved a particular design problem within a specific context and amid 'forces' that may have an impact on the manner in which the pattern is applied and used." In software design, there are recurring design-related issues that can be approached using common solutions. For example, an interrupt-driven software architecture could be viewed as a software architecture pattern to solve the issue of event-driven user needs. There are many ways of implementing an interrupt-driven software architecture, but the pattern allows the designer to select an approach based on knowledge from past workable solutions. The classic book *Design Patterns: Elements of Reusable Object-Oriented Software* (Gamma 1994) categorizes design patterns into:

- *Creational patterns.* Patterns related to creating classes and objects. An example of a creational pattern is the *prototype* pattern, which "creates objects by cloning an existing object."

- *Structural patterns.* Patterns related to class and object composition. An example of a structural pattern is the *decorator* pattern, which "dynamically adds/overrides behaviors in an existing method of an object."

- *Behavioral patterns.* Patterns related to communications between objects. An example of a behavioral pattern is the *memento* pattern, which "provides the ability to restore an object to its previous state (undo)" (based on "Design pattern" entry at Wikipedia.com).

2. QUALITY ATTRIBUTES AND DESIGN

> Analyze the impact that quality-related elements (safety, security, reliability, usability, reusability, maintainability, etc.) can have on software design. (Analyze)
>
> **Body of Knowledge III.E.2**

Security

Designing for security involves designing software that resists security attacks, detects those attacks when they happen, and recovers from attacks if they are successful. Design tactics for resisting attacks include:

- Limitations on who can access the system (for example, user authentication and firewalls)

- Limitations on what a user can do once they are in the system (for example, access control privileges and security levels)

- Mechanisms for maintaining data integrity and confidentiality (for example, encryption, handshaking on data communication, and checksums)

- Limitations on exposure (for example, access timeouts and service limitations)

To detect attacks, intrusion detection software must be designed into the system. Recovering from security attacks includes restoration of service, recovering from any damage (for example, backups of critical data and virus analyzers), and maintaining audit trails that aid in the identification of security vulnerabilities.

Reliability

Software reliability problems occur when a defect in the software is encountered during the use of that software in operations, resulting in a software failure. Therefore, good design practices should be used to prevent as many defects as possible from being introduced into software products. For example, one of the major contributors to software reliability issues is high software complexity. Designing software to increase cohesion and make individual software components as decoupled as possible can help increase the reliability of that software. Good verification and validation practices should also be employed to identify and remove as many defects as possible from software products under development before their release into operations.

Software can also be designed to be more robust and fault tolerant, and therefore more reliable. Software components that process inputs and outputs should include appropriate error checking and error handling. Fault-detection mechanisms can include periodic ping/echo or heartbeat tactics. In a *ping/echo tactic,* "one component issues a ping and expects to receive back an echo within a predefined time, from the component under scrutiny" (Bass 2003). In a *heartbeat tactic,* one component periodically sends out a heartbeat signal and another component detects it. If either the ping/echo or heartbeat tactic fails, the nonresponding component is assumed to have a problem. Software designs can also prevent problems from resulting in software failures (reliability issues). For example, if a component is suspected of having a problem, that component can be placed out of service, or if an event or transaction does not occur in the expected time frame, it can be timed-out or retried.

Safety

For safety-critical systems, software design activities typically involve *failure mode effects and criticality analysis* (FMECA) to anticipate ways that the software might fail and the potential effects (possible injury or death of people, damage to property, and/or harm to the environment) and the criticality of those effects. The software is then designed in a manner that attempts to eliminate, minimize, or recover from those failures and/or their resulting effects. Design tactics might include adding redundancy or additional fault tolerance, error handling, or fail-safes to the software design. Increasing decoupling can prevent a failure in one area of the software from cascading into other parts of the software. Safety is closely related to both reliability and security. Since many safety issues involve the inability of the software to function correctly under failure conditions, the more reliable the software, the fewer failure conditions exist. Software can only be safe

Part III.E.2

if it is secure. If someone can break into the software, that person can potentially make the software perform in an unsafe manner.

Usability

Usability involves both ease-of-learning and ease-of-use aspects. For example, for ease of learning the systems should be designed with:

- A consistent, logical user interface
- A vocabulary that is familiar to the typical user
- Visibility into objects, actions, and options
- Adequate help and documentation that is easily searchable

Examples of designing software for ease of use include designs:

- With continuous feedback to the users to keep them informed about what is going on
- Where the order of processing or data entry maps to the order in which tasks are performed by the user
- That minimize the number of keystrokes or pages that the user needs to visit to perform a task or enter data
- With ways to abort, exit, or undo unwanted operations
- With mechanisms that allow users to tailor or customize their interactions with the software
- With error messages that clearly communicate issues, errors, or invalid inputs

Maintainability

Software that is cohesive, decoupled, logically structured, and low in complexity is more maintainable. Consistency of constructs, language, design and coding standards, naming conventions, communication protocols, interfaces, and so on, also adds to the maintainability of the software. Well-written code comments and choosing the right programming language to match the application type are also essential to maintainability.

Reusability

In order to be reusable, the software should be designed to be independent of both the hardware and software operating system. Reusable software designs are cohesive, decoupled, and consistent. In order to reuse a component, the engineers must be able to understand what it does. This requires that the component be clearly documented and that documentation be kept up to date as the component is modified.

3. SOFTWARE REUSE

> Define and distinguish between software reuse, reengineering, and reverse engineering, and describe the impact these practices can have on software quality. (Understand)
>
> **Body of Knowledge III.E.3**

Reuse

Reuse occurs when one or more components of an existing software system or component are reused when developing a new software system or component. Reused software is used "as is" without modification. If even one minor change is made to the component, it is not considered a reused component because a second copy must be maintained separately. Reusability can be applied to any level in the structural hierarchy of the software. Architectural designs, detailed designs, source code modules, and test cases and procedures can all be reused. Dunn (1990) states that "the higher the structural level of the reusable component, the more effectively the concept of reusability has been executed." The reuse of a software component has several benefits including improved quality, reliability, productivity, and cost gains.

Software components that have withstood the test of time, or been improved over time through the removal of latent defects, have obvious advantages with regard to quality. By reusing these components in other systems quality improvements can be realized. However, defects in reused components impact multiple products and therefore multiple customers. Components that are intended for reuse should undergo rigorous testing.

When software components are reused, less time is typically spent creating the plans, designs, code, documents, and data. Therefore, the same level of functionality can be delivered to the user for less effort, improving productivity. Pressman (2005) notes that it appears that 30 percent to 50 percent reuse can result in productivity improvements in the range of 25 percent to 40 percent. However, if the candidate for reuse is not low-complexity, unambiguous, modular, and well documented, it may take considerable time to analyze and understand it in order to be able to reuse it. This can negatively impact potential productivity gains.

The cost benefits of reuse are calculated by subtracting the sum of the costs associated with reuse from the sum of the costs of producing the component from scratch. Pressman (2005) lists the following costs associated with reuse:

- Domain analysis and modeling
- Domain architecture development
- Increased documentation to facilitate reuse

- Support and enhancement of reuse component

- Royalties and licenses for externally acquired components

- Creation or acquisition and operation of a reuse repository

- Training of personnel in design and construction for reuse

In order to make it easy to reuse a source code component, nothing that is changeable should be "hard coded" in the source code. For example, a set of reports is created that output to a printer. These reports include the customer's name in the title. Rather than "hard coding" the customer's name in the source code for each report, the source code reads the name from a file or global variable. This allows the report set to be reused for another customer without major rewrites.

In order to reuse a component, the engineer must be able to access it easily. It must be easier to reuse an existing component than to construct the component from scratch. One mechanism to allow easier access to reuse components is to create a reuse library. Components in the reuse library must be under strict configuration control to prevent unauthorized changes and to ensure the communication of authorized changes to all impacted parties.

Reengineering

Reengineering is the process of starting with a legacy software product and creating a new version of that product by redesigning and/or rebuilding it. The value of reengineering includes the ability to add additional functionality, increased performance and reliability, improved maintainability, and so on. A typical candidate for reengineering is a software product that continues to be useful but that is getting "old" because:

- It breaks too often

- It takes too long to repair

- When it's repaired, something else always seems to break

- It no longer represents the newest technology or can no longer be supported (for example, its software language, operating system, and/or hardware platform are antiquated)

- It can no longer meet updated, modern performance requirements

In reengineering, the existing legacy system often defines the requirements for the new system ("build a system just like the existing one except . . ."). In fact, the legacy system itself may be the only documentation of business processes or rules involved in the automated activities.

Reverse Engineering

In *reverse engineering*, the software requirements, design, and/or interface information is recreated from the source code (or even the object code or executable). Reasons for reverse engineering include:

- The lack of good configuration management practices when the software product was originally developed, resulting in the loss of source code or other needed work products.

- Requirements, design, and/or other documentation were either never created or were not kept up to date and consistent as the software was modified over time.

4. SOFTWARE DEVELOPMENT TOOLS

> Select the appropriate development tools to use for modeling, code analysis, etc., and analyze the impact they can have on requirements management and documentation. (Analyze)
>
> **Body of Knowledge III.E.4**

According to Pressman (2005), "software engineering tools provide automated or semi-automated support for the processes and methods."

Software requirements tools include requirements modeling, prototyping and requirements databases, and traceability tools. These tools are used to aid in the development of the requirements through automation of requirements modeling and prototyping activities and through documentation of the requirements. Software requirements tools can range from a simple template for a requirements document or use case to sophisticated requirements management tools. More-sophisticated requirements tools can be integrated with other tools in the software development platform to provide mechanisms for automated bidirectional traceability of the requirements with predecessor work products.

Software design tools include design optimization and design verification tools. Many of the same tools used in requirements modeling and prototyping can also be used during software design, with additional details being added.

Software implementation tools include tools that are used to translate requirements and design into machine-readable source code and its associated user documentation. These tools include source code editors, interpreters, word processors, and debuggers. Configuration management tools like compilers, assemblers, linkers, loaders, and build scripts are also considered to be development tools.

5. SOFTWARE DEVELOPMENT METHODS

> Define and describe principles such as
> pair programming, extreme programming,
> cleanroom, formal methods, etc., and their
> impact on software quality. (Understand)
>
> **Body of Knowledge III.E.5**

Traditional software development methodologies, also called *plan-driven method-ologies,* focus on defining the "rules" for how the process, people, and technology interact, as illustrated in the triangle on the left in Figure 13.3 from the Software Engineering Institute's (SEI) work developing the Software Capability Maturity Model (CMM) (SEI 1995). In traditional methodologies there may be an emphasis on technology solutions to process issues.

Agile Methods

The triangle on the right in Figure 13.3, though not formally from the agile community, attempts to use a similar structure to show the relationships that seem critical in most agile methods. The primary focus is on communication between the customer, developer, and product because the behavior of the three toward one another matters significantly. Agile methods usually emphasize sociological solutions, rather than technical solutions, to process issues. The agile community believes that "focusing on skills, communication, and community allows the project to be more effective and more agile than focusing on processes." Rather than technology-oriented rules, agile software development uses "light-but-sufficient rules of project behavior" and "human and communication-oriented rules" (Cockburn 2002). The *Agile Manifesto,* illustrated in Figure 13.4, was developed at a meeting in

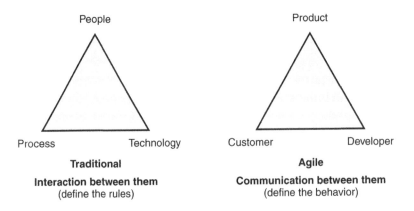

Figure 13.3   Methodology triangles.

Agile Alliance: "We are uncovering better ways of developing software by doing it and helping others do it. Through this work we have come to value:

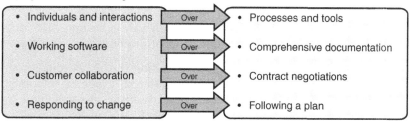

That is, while there is value in the items on the right, we value the items on the left more."

Figure 13.4   Agile manifesto.
Source: www.agilemanifesto.org.

Part III.E.5

Snowbird, Utah, in 2001. This was the first meeting of what later became known as the Agile Alliance. It is important to emphasize the phrase "there is value in the items on the right" since some criticisms of agile methods make it sound like such methods reject process, plans, contracts, and documentation. The word "over" is key. The Manifesto does not say "instead of," which many critics of agile methods seem to imply.

The *Agile Alliance* (www.agilealliance.com) has also defined the following principles to support the Agile Manifesto:

- "Our highest priority is to satisfy the customer through early and continuous delivery of valuable software.

- Welcome changing requirements, even late in development. Agile processes harness change for the customer's competitive advantage.

- Deliver working software frequently, from a couple of weeks to a couple of months, with a preference to the shorter timescale.

- Businesspeople and developers must work together daily throughout the project.

- Build projects around motivated individuals. Give them the environment and support they need, and trust them to get the job done.

- The most efficient and effective method of conveying information to and within a development team is face-to-face conversation.

- Working software is the primary measure of progress.

- Agile processes promote sustainable development. The sponsors, developers, and users should be able to maintain a constant pace indefinitely.

- Continuous attention to technical excellence and good design enhances agility.

- Simplicity—the art of maximizing the amount of work not done—is essential.

- The best architectures, requirements, and designs emerge from self-organizing teams.

- At regular intervals, the team reflects on how to become more effective, then tunes and adjusts its behavior accordingly. "

There are actually many agile methods including scrum, extreme programming (XP), feature-driven development (FDD) and test-driven development (TDD), DSDM (dynamic systems development/design method, also called the framework for business-centered development), Crystal, lean, and others.

Extreme Programming

Because of the many publications on *extreme programming* (XP), including over a dozen books, XP is one of the most widely known of the agile methods. The concept of XP is to take good practices to the extreme. For example, if code inspections are a good thing, XP asks, "how can they be done to the extreme?" Pair programming is the XP practice that evolved to achieve this extreme implementation of code inspections. In order to implement its values and principles into the daily work of software development, XP includes a set of primary and secondary practices. XP primary practices include:

- *Team colocation.* Software should be developed in a workspace large enough for the whole team, including the customers, to work together in a single space.

- *The whole team.* Cross-functional, self-directed teams work together to accomplish their goal when implementing XP projects.

- *Informative workspaces.* XP teams use their workspace to communicate important, active information. At a glance, people should be able to get a feeling of how the project is progressing and be able to identify current or potential problems by simply looking at the information posted around the workspace.

- *Energized work.* XP emphasizes working only as many hours as practitioners can be productive at a sustainable pace, such as eight-hour days, 40-hour weeks, and not coming to work sick. XP also encourages a reasonable amount of playtime at work to rejuvenate individuals and stimulate creativity.

- *Stories.* Developers create the requirements for the system by asking their customers and users to tell stories about who will use the system, how the system will be used, and why. These stories are documented and become the first level of prioritized requirements that are only fleshed out into more detail when those stories are selected for implementation.

- *Quarterly cycle.* On a quarterly cycle, plan to:
  - "Identify bottlenecks—especially those controlled outside the team.
  - Focus on the big picture—where the project fits within the organization.

- Initiate repairs.

- Plan the theme(s) for the quarter.

- Pick a quarter's worth of stories to address those themes"
   (Beck 2005).

- *Weekly cycle.* The team's job is to write test cases and get them running in the next five days. Weekly planning meetings are held to:

   - Review how actual progress matches expected progress.

   - Select customer stories to implement that week.

   - Further redefine the requirements and acceptance criteria for each story as needed.

   - Estimate the duration of the effort needed to implement each story.

   - Divide stories into tasks.

   - Have each team member self-select tasks they accept responsibility for performing.

- *Slack.* Ideally, the team will finish all the committed work in just the amount of time required, but leaving some slack in the weekly schedule allows for making up for any unforeseen events during the weekly cycle.

- *Pair programming.* Pair programming involves two people, one of whom is constantly reviewing what the other is developing. As illustrated in Figure 13.5, pair programming offers a constant exchange of ideas about how the software can work. If one person hits a mental block, the other person can jump in and try something, switching roles. Pair programming helps to ensure that people keep up the steady pace XP advocates through being fully engaged in the work and keeping one another "honest" (consistent about adhering to the project's practices,

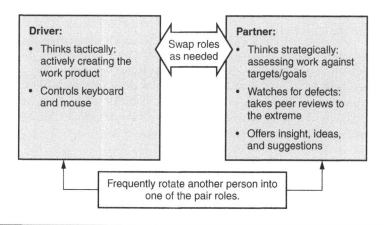

Figure 13.5   Pair programming.

standards, and so on). Martin (2003) notes that pair programming interactions can be "intense." He indicates that people should change partners at least once a day, and that "over the course of an iteration, every member of the team should have worked with every other member of the team and they should have worked on just about everything that was going on in the iteration." By doing this, everyone on the team comes to understand and appreciate one another's work, as well as develop a deep understanding of the software as a whole. This is one way to avoid extraneous documentation since everyone shares in the design knowledge of the project.

- *Test-first programming.* Test-first programming advocates writing the test cases that the code must pass before writing the code. XP also uses the test cases as an aspect of the requirements and design used to implement the code.

- *Incremental design.* Agile methods in general, and specifically XP, do not write what some call *big design up front* (BDUF). That is, the design emerges over time through gradual, persistent effort devoted to reflecting on what already exists in the system and what is needed next.

- *Continuous integration.* XP practices integrate each piece of changed (or new) software code into the system on a continuous basis, creating and testing a new build within a few hours of a code change. This is the opposite end of the spectrum from the traditional waterfall life cycle behavior where all (or most) of the software code is written before integration starts.

- *10-minute build.* To integrate as frequently as desired in an XP project, it must be possible to build the system and run tests very quickly. The goal represented by a 10-minute build is to make this possible.

XP corollary practices include:

- *Team continuity.* High-performance teams should be kept together over time. Taking an effective, high-performance team and breaking it apart is even worse, perhaps, than dividing team members up between different projects.

- *Real customer involvement.* Martin (2003) says that the customer is "the person or group who defines and prioritizes features." The customer needs to be in close contact with the development team (if not actually a member of the team) and take responsibility for the software by participating actively in its definition and validation (writing test cases and possibly even executing test cases).

- *Negotiate scope.* Agile methods usually advocate that the customer gets to define the functionality for the system and the priority for implementing that functionality. The developers get to define the cost and schedule. Together, they agree on what functionality goes into each increment/cycle of development. The XP philosophy says that if something has to "slip" within a given increment, it should be the scope (functionality) rather than manipulating cost, schedule, or quality. Functionality missed because of scope reduction is moved to the next increment.

- *Single code base.* As noted earlier in discussing continuous integration, maintaining a single baseline of code is very desirable. However, branches can occur for a short period of time and then be brought back together through frequent integrations done at least daily.

- *Shared code.* After the team has a sense of collective responsibility, anyone on the team can improve any part of the system at any time (Beck 2005). This requires adoption of teamwide coding standards. "If a change needs to be made, the person who is in the best situation to make it (the developer who sees the immediate need for the change) can make that change" (Astels 2002).

- *Code and tests.* XP's "minimalist" approach to documentation suggests that the code and tests should be the basis for any other documentation, not the reverse. For good or bad, the product is what the software does, so the software code and its tests are the final authority on documenting the product's capabilities.

- *Incremental deployment.* By deploying software incrementally, early in the project and often after that, the project demonstrates tangible and working results on a regular basis. This allows the customer to provide useful feedback just as frequently, so that little time passes between work done and work reflected on. Review of small increments allows for frequent adjustment of project direction and quick identification of defects. Planning for each small increment is also more accurate.

- *Daily deployment.* The XP ideal is to get working software into the hands of customers every day. Except in small cases, this is probably not practical for a wide variety of reasons. However, it is important to realize that the longer software is not being actively used, the more likely development may diverge from what the customer ultimately needs (even if it matches the initial direction the customer thought made sense).

Formal Methods

Formal methods are a set of mathematics-based techniques for the specification, development, and verification of software-intensive systems. Formal methods use the syntax and semantics of a formal specification language (for example, Z or Object Constraint Language [OCL]) to translate the natural language requirements for the software into a more rigorous and formal definition statement. This results in a requirements specification that is more complete, unambiguous, and consistent. Pressman (2005) states that "because formal methods use discrete mathematics as the specification mechanism, logic proofs can be applied to each system function to demonstrate that the specification is correct." However, because formal methods are difficult and require highly trained professionals to implement them, they are typically used only in the development of systems where high integrity is necessary (for example, in mission-critical or safety-critical software systems).

Part III.E.5

Cleanroom

Cleanroom engineering combines the use of formal methods for specifying the software with statistical-based software verification and certification of the software to a reliability level. The focus of cleanroom is defect prevention instead of defect detection and removal. The cleanroom strategy makes use of a specialized version of the incremental software model. Small individual teams develop software increments called *boxes*. A box encapsulates the system (or an aspect of the system) at a specific level of abstraction. Black boxes are used to represent the externally observable behavior of a system. State boxes encapsulate state data and operations. A clear box is used to model the procedural design that is implied by the data and operations of a state box.

Correctness verification is applied once the box structure design is complete. First, the procedural design for a software component is partitioned into a series of sub-functions. To prove the correctness of the subfunctions, exit conditions are defined for each subfunction, and a set of subproofs (proofs of correctness) is applied. If each exit condition is satisfied, the design must be correct.

Once correctness verification is complete, statistical use testing begins. Unlike conventional testing, cleanroom software engineering does not emphasize structural-based unit or integration testing. Instead, the software is tested based on its operational profile by defining a set of usage scenarios, determining the probability of use for each scenario, and then defining random tests that conform to the probabilities. The defect records that result are combined with sampling, component, and certification models to enable mathematical computation of projected reliability for the software component. In other words, software quality is certified in terms of mean time to failure (MTTF).

Chapter 14

F. Maintenance Management

Software maintenance is the process of making changes to software products after they have been delivered to operations or to the user in order to correct defects or improve (optimize or enhance) the product while still preserving its quality and integrity. In other words, the objective of software maintenance is to correct or improve one part of an existing software product without breaking some other part of that product. Maintenance activities and tasks include:

- Process implementation
- Problem and modification analysis
- Modification implementation
- Maintenance review/acceptance
- Migration
- Software retirement

1. MAINTENANCE TYPES

> Describe the characteristics of corrective, adaptive, perfective, and preventive maintenance types. (Understand)
>
> **Body of Knowledge III.F.1**

Corrective Maintenance

Even with the best state-of-the-practice software quality assurance and control techniques, it is likely that the users of the software will encounter at least a few software failures once the software products are delivered to operations. The IEEE *Standard for Software Engineering—Software Life Cycle Processes— Maintenance* (IEEE 2006) defines *corrective maintenance* as "the reactive modification of a software product performed after delivery to correct discovered problems."

213

Corrective maintenance is performed to repair the defects that caused these operational failures.

Adaptive Maintenance

The IEEE (2006) defines *adaptive maintenance* as "modification of a software product, performed after delivery, to keep a software product usable in a changed environment." As time progresses, a software product's operational environment is likely to change. Examples of changes to the external environment in which that software must function include:

- External interface definitions may change (for example, communications, protocols, external data file structures).

- Government regulations or other business rules may change (for example, tax code, reporting requirements).

- Hardware and software that interface with the product may change (for example, operating system reversion, new or updated peripherals or other hardware, new or updated interfacing software applications, additional or modified fields/records in external databases).

Perfective Maintenance

As the software is used, the users, customers, or other external stakeholders may discover additional functions that they would like the software to perform. Marketing or engineering may also come up with new features to add to the software. The ISO/IEC *Systems and Software Engineering—Vocabulary* (ISO/IEC 2009) defines *perfective maintenance* as "improvements in the software's performance or functionality, for example, in response to user suggestions or requests." Perfective maintenance is performed to add new features or functionality to the product (to "perfect" the product). Perfective maintenance is the normal enhancement of successful, working software products over time so that they continue to meet the stakeholders' expanding needs and expectations.

Preventive Maintenance

The IEEE (2006) defines *preventive maintenance* as "modification of a software product after delivery to detect and correct latent faults in the software product before they manifest as failures."

Preventive maintenance is a proactive approach to prevent problems with the software before they occur. For example, additional error handling and fault tolerance might be added to a safety-critical system, or an enhanced encryption methodology might be added to improve software security. Self-diagnostic testing might also be added to the software product.

As software products undergo change over time they can deteriorate, especially if good design techniques were not employed when the software was originally developed. It may be necessary to modify an existing, released software product by refactoring it to eliminate duplication, complexity, or awkward structure, or to reengineer it to make it easier to maintain going forward. This is another type of preventive maintenance.

2. MAINTENANCE STRATEGY

> Describe various factors affecting the strategy for software maintenance, including service-level agreements (SLAs), short- and long-term costs, maintenance releases, product discontinuance, etc., and their impact on software quality. (Understand)
>
> **Body of Knowledge III.F.2**

Process Implementation

Maintenance process implementation includes all of the activities involved in the maintenance part of the quality management system (QMS). This includes establishing and maintaining policies, standards, processes, and work instructions related to software maintenance. This also includes:

- Maintenance planning for each software release and/or product. This planning defines the specifics for implementing the maintenance portion of the QMS for a software release or product. This planning also includes any tailoring or the defining of specific maintenance processes or work instructions needed for that software release or product.

- Transitioning control of the software product from the developers to the maintainers.

- Negotiating service contracts and *service level agreements* (SLAs) with the acquirers of the software.

- Defining and implementing mechanisms for receiving, documenting, and tracking problem reports and enhancement requests to resolution.

- Coordinating with the configuration management processes to manage changes to existing software products and/or product components.

These maintenance process implementation activities should occur early in the software development life cycle, well before the release of the software product into operations. Typically, these activities are part of contract negotiations with the acquirer or are a part of the project planning activities.

An SLA is a formally negotiated agreement between two parties (typically, the maintainer and the acquirer of the software) that defines the agreed-upon level of service to be provided. An SLA defines both the services and measures of service support attributes including availability, performance, responsiveness, timeliness, and completeness of that service. For example, an SLA might include requirements for the availability of help desk services ("technical help desk support is available on a 24/7 basis" or "80 percent of all help desk calls are answered within 30 seconds") or time limits on resolution of problem reports ("95 percent of all major defects are resolved within 30 days"). The SLA may also include service fee agreements, warranties, penalties for violations, escalation procedures, and/or defined responsibilities for both parties.

Problem and Modification Analysis

The maintainers perform problem and modification analysis after the software has been released to operations. It includes all of the activities related to evaluating problems or requested enhancements, determining their impacts, making resolution decisions, and developing solutions to approved changes. For problem reports, the evaluation process may require replication of the problem in order to debug it and identify its root cause and/or the actual software defect(s) involved. Typically, the impact analysis and resolution decision is done through the configuration control process.

Modification Implementation

Once the appropriate authority has approved one or more changes, the maintainer starts the real work of updating the impacted software products or product components to incorporate the change(s). These activities involve all of the software development activities (analysis, design, and implementation) necessary to implement the change(s). This may be as simple as creating a patch or service pact for a corrective release. However, if approved changes are significant enough, their implementation may involve the initiation of a new software development project (for example, evolutionary development).

Maintenance Review and Acceptance

Maintenance review and acceptance includes verification and validation, acceptance, release, and distribution activities of the changed software products. These activities ensure that the changes are correct and that other defects were not interjected into the software when those changes were made. These activities also ensure that the resulting software meets required integrity, quality, and performance levels.

Migration

Migration consists of maintenance processes specific to porting the software and its associated data to another environment (for example, a move to a new hardware platform or new operating system). In addition to many of the maintenance activities described above, migration may also include the development of migration tools, conversion of the software or data, parallel operations in the old and new environments for some period of time, and support for the old environment into the future.

Software Retirement and Product Discontinuance

Software *retirement* is the point when the support of a particular release of the software is terminated or the point when the support of an entire software product is terminated. Issues related to retirement include:

- How long is the software product actively supported?

- How many past releases of the software are actively supported?

- Is retired software removed from its operational environment and, if so, how is this accomplished?

- What mechanisms are used for archiving retired software and its related records?

Agreements about these issues should be included in negotiations between the software developers and acquirers early in the life of the initial software product and renegotiated as necessary with each subsequent software release to manage expectation on both sides.

Part IV

Project Management

Part IV

Chapter 15

A. Planning, Scheduling, and Deployment

A ccording to the Project Management Institute (PMI) (PMI 2008), a *project* is "a temporary endeavor undertaken to create a unique product, service, or result." A project has a specific purpose or goal to be accomplished. That goal is to create a unique outcome in the form of a new or updated product, service, or result.

The fact that a project is temporary means that a project is a set of activities that are performed a single time and not repeated. Projects differ in this respect from the repeated, ongoing operational work of the organization. In fact, the goal of a project is typically to add something new to, change something in, or provide information to ongoing operations. Temporary also means that a project has a definite start and end point, and lasts a specific, finite amount of time. However, temporary does not imply short. Projects may last only a few hours or they may last years. A project ends when its goal has been accomplished. It may also be terminated before the project objectives are met. For example, a project may be terminated if funding is cut, the business needs for the product or service are eliminated, or if it becomes clear that the project will not be able to meet its objectives. Examples of software projects include:

- Development of a new software product

- Addition of new features to an existing software product

- Implementation of a corrective maintenance release for an existing software product

Non-project activities include any ongoing or repetitive activity. These are sometimes referred to as *level of effort* work activities. Examples of non-project activities include:

- Production of monthly reports on field-released software defects

- Ongoing customer support or help desk activities for existing software packages

A software project requires human resources with various skills and other non-human resources to accomplish its objectives. Human resources include analysts, designers, programmers, testers, managers, and specialists (for example, software quality engineers, auditors, configuration management specialists). Nonhuman resources include computers, support software (for example, compilers, test drivers), facilities (for example, office space, test beds), and supplies (for example, paper, CDs). A project is constrained by the limits on the resources available to that project.

Every software project has a customer and/or intended user for its created product, service, or result. The customer may be external to the organization implementing the project (for example, software produced for sale under a contract or to a mass market) or the customer may be internal to the organization (for example, management information systems and internally developed software tools).

As illustrated in Figure 15.1, project management is a system of processes for initiating, planning, executing, tracking and controlling, and closing the project. These project management activities are not one-time events but form a continuous feedback loop that continues throughout the life of the project.

Project initiation includes deciding whether or not to start the project based on needs or a business case analysis:

- Is the project valuable to the organization?

- Is it feasible with current resources and technologies?

- Should the organization proceed with the project?

During project initiation, the initial scope of the project is defined and initial resources are committed to the project. The Project Management Institute (PMI 2008) defines two processes in its project-initiating process group: *develop project charter* and *identify stakeholders*. The major output of the initiation processes is the project charter including the initial scope statement and a list of project stakeholders.

Project planning establishes the strategic and tactical plans for the project, including activities, processes, budgets, staffing, and resources. Replanning also occurs throughout the project as additional information is obtained and fed back as progressive elaboration into the plans.

Part IV.A

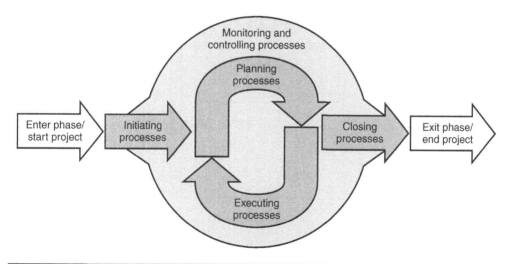

Figure 15.1 Project management processes.
Source: PMI (2008). Reprinted with permission.

Project executing includes the activities and actions required to implement the project's strategic and tactical plans, which are performed in order to meet the project's objectives and create the project's deliverables.

Project monitoring and controlling, also called *tracking and control*, tracks the actual results of the implemented actions and activities against the established plans. These activities also control significant deviation from the expected plans and make any changes required to keep the project in line with its objectives.

Project closure involves shutting down the project when it is completed (or terminated before completion). The Project Management Institute defines two processes in its project-closing process group: *close project* or *phase and close procurements* (PMI 2008).

Not only should these project management processes be performed at the project level, but, as illustrated in Figure 15.2, they should also be repeated as part of each phase of the project. For example, initiation activities may be repeated at the beginning of each phase of the software development life cycle to ensure that the project is still viable and should continue. Planning should be revisited at each phase to add progressive elaboration to the plans based on the information gathered by executing the previous phase. The activities of each phase are then executed and the phase is closed at completion. Throughout this process the activities of the phase are monitored and controlled.

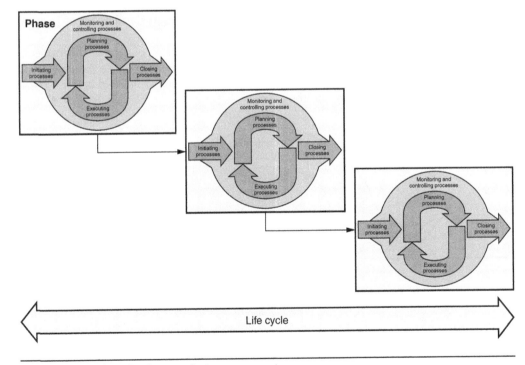

Figure 15.2 Life cycle phase project management processes.
Source: PMI (2008). Reprinted with permission.

Each project has three major drivers: cost, schedule, and scope. As illustrated in Figure 15.3, a good analogy of project management is the juggling of three bowling bowls. Each ball represents one of the three elements. If the project manager and/or team pay too much attention to any one bowling ball, they are likely to drop one of the others and smash the foot of the project. The *cost* driver represents the cost of all the resources that go into the project. The *schedule* driver represents the calendar time it takes to complete the project. The *scope* driver represents the quantity of the work done during the project to produce outputs with the required functionality and quality.

Each project will have a primary driver that is the most important to the project. Cost may be the primary driver on a project with a fixed-price contract. Software that is being built to target a specific market window may have schedule as its primary driver. For example, one company was working on a project where a communication system was being developed for military war games. If the software wasn't delivered on schedule (in time for the military exercise), the government didn't want it and wouldn't pay for it. A project to develop software that impacts the health or safety of people is an example of a project where scope may be the primary driver. All of the required tasks must be performed to ensure that a complete, high-quality product is built. Part of the job of a software project manager is to determine the primary driver and maintain the focus on that driver without losing sight of the other two drivers (dropping the other two bowling balls).

An old project management saying states that a project can fix any two of these elements but not all three. That means that given the project's current capability levels:

- If the project wants to shorten the schedule, they will have to either spend more or reduce the scope of the work being done

- If a larger scope of work is required because of the need for more functionality or a higher level of software quality, the project will take longer and/or cost more

- If cost reductions are necessary, the schedule and/or the scope will be impacted

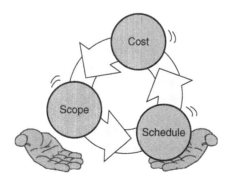

Figure 15.3   Cost/schedule/scope trilogy.

The good news is that empirical evidence from the software industry shows that improving process maturity and implementing effective and efficient quality management systems allows a win–win–win across this trilogy—software projects can create increased scope to build in more functionality with higher quality in less time at a reduced cost.

A project is considered successful if the project objectives are completed on schedule, within budget, at the desired quality and performance level without reducing the scope of the project while effectively and efficiently utilizing people and other project resources. The goal of project planning and deployment is to plan for and execute a successful project.

1. PROJECT PLANNING

> Use forecasts, resources, schedules, task and cost estimates, etc., to develop project plans.
> (Apply)
>
> **Body of Knowledge IV.A.1**

Project planning is one of the process areas of the Software Engineering Institute's (SEI) Capability Maturity Model Integration (CMMI) for Development (SEI 2006). The CMMI for Development defines the following goals for software project planning:

- "Estimates of project planning parameters are established and maintained

- A project plan is established and maintained as the basis for managing the project

- Commitments to the project plan are established and maintained"

As illustrated in Figure 15.4, project planning provides the road map (project plan) for the project journey. It defines the reason for the trip (mission statement), the destination (project objectives), the vehicle (methods), the people taking the trip (staff and other stakeholders), the expected cost of the trip (budget), and the stops along the way (milestones).

Performing project planning includes all of the activities necessary to select the appropriate life cycle and processes, define the various subsidiary plans, create estimates, the work breakdown structure (WBS), and activity network, and integrate all of that into the overall software project plans for the project. As illustrated in Figure 15.5, the inputs into project planning include the project charter, environmental factors, and organizational process assets.

The outputs of project planning are the software project plans. The *Standard for Software Project Management Plans* (IEEE 1998) provides an example outline and

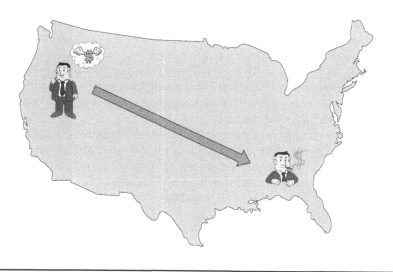

Figure 15.4   Project planning is the road map for the project journey.

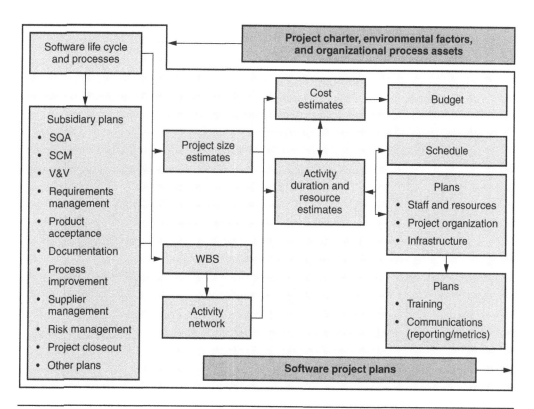

Figure 15.5   Project planning.

guidance for documentation of the project plans. IEEE also has standards that provide outlines and guidance for many of the subsidiary plans. These subsidiary plans (for example, software quality assurance [SQA] plans, verification and validation [V&V] plans, software configuration management [SCM] plans, risk management plans) may be incorporated as sections into a single project plan document or they may be separate stand-alone documents that are referenced by this primary project plan document.

Planning is an iterative process. As illustrated in Figure 15.6, generic tasks can be planned in advance, but many tasks can not be planned to any level of detail until predecessor activities are completed. During the early phases of a project the project team must usually settle for high-level general plans. As the project, progresses, more and more detail can be added to these plans. For example, during the initial planning phase there may be an estimate that five programmers will be needed to code, inspect, and unit test 60 modules over a period of four months. By the end of the architectural design phase, the project may have identified:

- The specific 57 modules to be coded, inspected, and unit tested

- The order in which they will be implemented

- A detailed schedule for that implementation over a 17.5-week period

- Specific assignments for five programmers responsible to do the coding

Planning a project requires the integration of many different process activities. Figure 15.7 illustrates the various processes in the Project Management Institute's planning process group and how they interact and are integrated into developing the project management plan. The numbers preceding each process name indicate the section in the Project Management Body of Knowledge Guide (PMBOK) (PMI 2008) that describes that process.

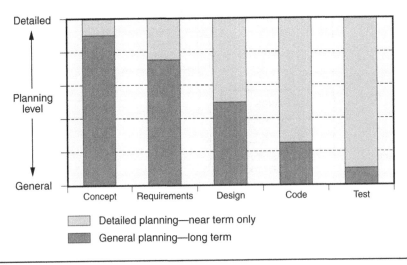

Figure 15.6   Long-term versus near-term planning.

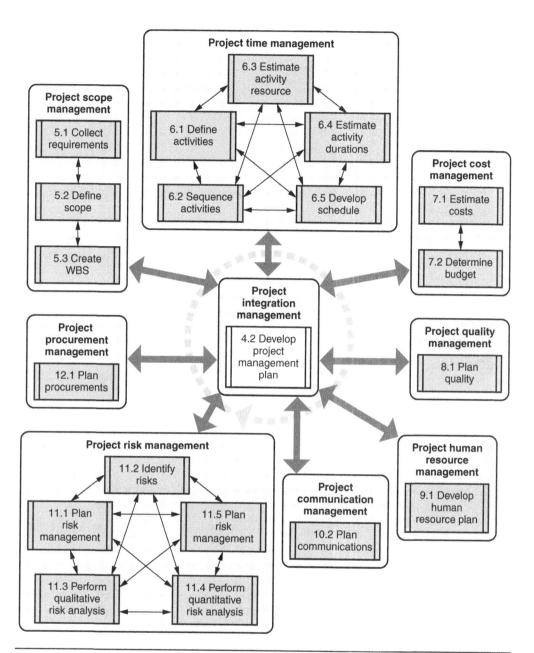

Figure 15.7 PMI project planning process group.
Source: PMI (2008). Reprinted with permission.

Project Charter

The *project charter* is the document that formally authorizes the project and is created during project initiation. The project charter includes:

- A justification for the project
- The initial scope statement of the business needs and project objectives
- A definition of the products, services, or results that are expected as the outcome of the project
- A list of the project stakeholders

Environmental Factors and Process Assets

Environmental factors include all of the elements that surround the project, including items such as:

- Organizational culture
- Infrastructure (for example, existing office space, computer equipment, and labs)
- Tools (for example, software development tools, project management tools, testing tools, configuration management tools)
- Experience and training levels of the staff assigned to the project

Organizational process assets are the artifacts considered "useful to those who are defining, implementing, and managing processes in the organization" (SEI 2006). These process assets represent organizational learning and knowledge, which can be tailored to meet the needs of each program or project. These process assets may include:

- The organization's quality management system (for example, policies, standard processes, standard work instructions)
- Definitions of the software life cycles approved for use within the organization
- Guidelines and criteria for tailoring the organization's set of standard processes
- Metrics repository including historic data and metrics for previous projects, processes, and work products
- Historic information (for example, plans, work products, and lessons learned from previous projects)

Software Development Life Cycle and Processes

The project planning process includes the selection and/or defining of the software life cycle that will be used for the project. Planning also includes selecting, defining, and/or tailoring the software processes and work instructions that will be used during the project.

Planning must also select and specify the methods, tools, and techniques that will be used on the project. These include development methodologies, programming languages, and other tools, techniques, or workmanship standards (for example, coding or documentation standards) used to specify, design, build, test, integrate, document, deliver, modify, and maintain the project's work product and deliverables.

Subsidiary Plans

The project planning process includes working with the appropriate stakeholders within the organization to develop the subsidiary plans. Many of these plans are discussed elsewhere in this book:

- *Software quality assurance* (SQA) *plan* specifies the plans, tools, techniques, schedules, and responsibilities for assuring that the required quality levels are met for the software processes and work.

- *Software configuration management* (SCM) *plan* specifies the plans, methods, techniques, procedures, and tools for configuration identification, control, status accounting, and auditing, and for release management.

- *Verification and validation* (V&V) *plan* specifies the scope, tools, techniques, schedules, and responsibilities for the verification and validation activities of the project.

- *Requirements management plan* specifies plans, tools, techniques, schedules, and responsibilities for measuring, reporting, and controlling change to the product requirements.

- *Product acceptance plan* specifies the plans for obtaining the customer's approval of the external product deliverables, including the objective criteria for accepting each deliverable.

- *Documentation plan* specifies the list of documents to be prepared and the tools, techniques, activities, schedules, and responsibilities for preparing, reviewing, baselining, and distributing those documents.

- *Process improvement plan* specifies process improvement activities, including periodically assessing the project, determining areas for improvement, and implementing those improvements, and any piloting of organizational-level process improvement that will be done as part of the project.

- *Supplier management plan* specifies the selection criteria for any suppliers and a tailored management plan for managing each supplier that will contribute outsourced work products to the project.

- *Risk management plan* specifies the methods, techniques, and tools for identifying, analyzing, planning mitigations, tracking, and controlling project-related risks.

- *Project closure plan* specifies the activities for the orderly closure of the project. For example, project closure activities include delivering the project's products into operations and transferring their ownership from development to maintenance and technical support, archiving project files

Part IV.A.1

and quality records, transitioning people and other project resources to future projects, closing down project charge numbers with accounting/finance, and conducting post-project reviews.

- Other plans include any special plans needed for the project. For example, projects that are producing safety-critical software might need safety plans, or projects where security is a major concern might have separate security plans.

Staff and Resource Plans

Staffing plans specify the number of staff required by skill levels, when they are needed, and source (for example, internal transfer, new hire, contracted). Resource plans specify the number of other resources required by type, when they are needed, and source (for example, internal transfer, purchased, rented). Challenges that the project manager faces when allocating staff and other resources to a project include:

- Lack of sufficient resources for the optimum schedule.

- Allocation/leveling of multiple resource types: for example, software requires highly skilled people, and a project may involve many different specialists (for example, analysts, designers, coders, testers, technical writers, quality specialist). If one specialist has slack time it doesn't mean they can be used to cover the overload in another specialty. The same is true with other resources; having an extra computer doesn't necessarily mean that it has the correct configuration to use it as a test bed.

- Allocation and/or leveling of resources across multiple projects.

- Productive work time is not eight hours per day because team members spend time on overhead (for example, staff meetings, e-mail, status reports, phone calls) and on supporting other projects or product maintenance.

- A person working on more than one task at a time (multitasking) can involve extra effort because of switching back and forth between tasks. This can also be true for resources that are being used on more than one project or activity. For example, the software, database, and tool set on a test bed might have to be reloaded each time a switch is made.

- More than one person working on the same task can involve extra effort because of additional time required to communicate.

Project Organization Plans

Project plans should include a description of the internal project team organization and structure including internal interfaces (for example, lines of authority, responsibility, and communication) within software development and supporting organizations. This description typically includes a project organizational chart.

The project team members may also need to interact with other external stakeholders during the project. Examples of these external stakeholders include the parent organization, customer/user organizations, subcontracting organizations, marketing, legal, customer service, other projects, and training. The project plan should describe these interfaces and define project team members as the liaisons to those external stakeholders. For example, the project doesn't want 30 different team members all calling the same customer with requirements questions. In this case a requirements analyst would be assigned as the liaison to that external customer for requirements issues, and other project team members would take their questions to that analyst. The requirements analyst may already know the answer, which keeps the customer from being annoyed with redundant questions. Even if they don't know the answer, they probably have established communications channels to that customer to make obtaining the needed answer easier. The project manager might also be assigned to that same external customer for issues related to project budgets, schedule, or status reporting.

The project organization section of the project plan also defines the roles and responsibilities of the project team members. In Chapter 6, when process definition was discussed, generic roles were assigned to the various process activities. This section is where actual team members are mapped to those generic roles. For example, the system test process definition might include roles for test manager, tester, test bed coordinator, configuration manager, and developer. For a very large project, George might be the test manager with 50 individuals assigned as testers, the test bed coordinators may be Tom and Cindy, the configuration managers are Alice, Katie, and Brian, and 100 other individuals are assigned to the developer role. On a tiny project, Simon may be assigned the test manager, tester, and test bed coordinator roles while Ajit is assigned to the developer and configuration manager roles. This allows the process documentation to remain very generic while minimizing the amount of tailoring that needs to be done on the project.

Infrastructure Plans

The project's infrastructure refers to the technical structures that support the project (rather than the actual non-resources used on the project). The infrastructure plan specifies the plans for developing and maintaining this technical structure. Infrastructure examples include:

- Office space, conference rooms, break rooms, cafeterias, and restrooms, and their associated building maintenance, janitorial services, and so on

- Computer networks and their associated hardware, operating system, software, IT support, and so on

- Telephone systems

- Administrative support including secretarial, legal, human resources, and so on

Training Plans

Training plans specify the training needed to ensure that necessary skill levels required by the project are available, and the schedules, tools, methods, and techniques for obtaining that training.

Communication Plans

The communication plans define the information needs of the various project stakeholders and the communication methods and techniques that will be used to fill those needs, including descriptions, responsibilities, and schedules for project review meetings and selected metrics.

Project Estimation and Forecasting

The project plan should include specification of the methods, tools, and techniques used to estimate, reestimate, and forecast the project elements. These project elements include estimates of the project's size, effort, costs, and calendar time (schedule). They also include forecasts of staffing needs, skill levels, productivity and availability, resource needs and availability, and project risks and opportunities. As illustrated in Figure 15.8, these estimates are interrelated. The size of the project is estimated and the WBS is defined. Depending on the methods used, the size estimate and/or the WBS are used as a basis for estimating project effort and cost. Effort and cost are then allocated to the activities in the WBS and used (along with the activity network) to create the calendar-time estimates and staffing/resource forecasts. To do this, trade-offs are evaluated and choices are made based on the cost/schedule/scope trilogy. The allocation of effort and/or cost estimates across the work to be done (as defined in the WBS) also creates the necessary basis for performing *earned value management* analysis during project tracking.

Estimates for effort, cost, and calendar time, forecasts for staffing and resources, and the WBS all then become inputs into forecasting risks and opportunities.

One of the fundamental project estimations is the size of the software and other artifacts being produced by the project. These size estimates are often used as inputs to help estimate the effort and cost of the project. Size metrics include function points, lines of code, weighted requirements counts, story points, and so on.

Effort is the amount of engineering work time (hours, days, months) it will take the people projected to be assigned to the project to complete that project (or one of its activities) working at their normal work rate. For example, if an activity is estimated at 40 hours of effort and it is assigned to one person working full time, that activity should be finished in approximately one 40-hour workweek.

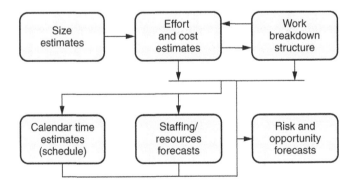

Figure 15.8   Project estimates and forecasts.

Work rates can vary depending on the work environment and other factors. In an eight-hour workday, getting 80 percent (about 6.5 hours) on-task work from an individual contributor may be optimistic for many organizations. Where does the rest of the time go? It goes to phone calls, e-mails, bathroom breaks, conversations, sick time, interruptions, time spent putting one task away and getting up to speed on the next one, and so on.

Calendar time is the actual duration (hours, days, months) that it will take to complete the project (or one of its activities) from start to finish. Calendar time is typically a function of effort and staff/resource loading, so trade-offs can be made between calendar time and staffing/resource estimates. For example, if the activity with the estimate of 40 hours of effort discussed above is assigned to a person who can only work on it half time, that 40 hours of effort may take a little over two weeks to accomplish. On the other hand, if two people are assigned to that activity full time, it may take a little over one-half week of calendar time. Of course, that assumes that more than one person working on the activity can shorten its calendar time. As the old adage goes, assigning nine women to the task of having a baby will not result in producing a baby in one month rather than nine months.

Cost is the amount of money it will take to complete the project. Examples of costs for the project include direct labor and overhead, travel, capital equipment, and other expenses (for example, supplies, rents, and subcontractor costs).

Critical computer resources should also be forecast for the project. Computer resources may be forecast for the development platform, the test platforms, or the target platform. Examples of critical computer resources include memory capacity, disk space, processor usage, and communications capacity.

There are two basic classes of estimation methods, expert judgment methods and model-based estimation methods. Since each estimation technique has its own strengths and weaknesses, experts recommend the use of multiple estimation techniques. The resulting estimates are then compared and differences are evaluated to determine the final estimates that will be used for the project.

Estimates are not a one-time activity. The project should plan to reestimate as additional information is obtained (for example, at the completion of requirements, high-level design, and detailed design activities). Regular review of the project's progress, assumptions, and product requirements should be done to detect changes and violations of the assumptions underlying the estimates. If variances between the actuals and estimates become too large, it may also signal the need to reestimate.

Expert-Judgment Estimation Techniques

Expert-judgment techniques are manual methods where individuals or teams make experience-based estimations and/or forecasts. Expert-judgment techniques typically start with the WBS and estimate effort for each activity. These estimates are then rolled up for an overall project-level effort estimate. Expert-judgment techniques include *Delphi, wideband Delphi, planning poker,* and other team techniques.

Delphi technique steps:

- *Step 1.* Coordinator presents each expert with project specifications and other relevant information.

Part IV.A.1

- *Step 2.* Several experts, in isolation from one another, use their personal experience and judgment to estimate the cost, size, or effort for each activity in the WBS.

- *Step 3.* The coordinator collects the estimates from each expert and prepares a summary of the experts' responses and their rationales.

- *Step 4.* Each expert receives this composite feedback and is asked to make new predictions based on that feedback.

- *Step 5.* Repeat steps 1 through 4 until consensus is reached that the estimates are close enough to use their average as the estimate.

Wideband Delphi is a variation of the Delphi technique (Futrell 2002). The primary difference is that the wideband Delphi technique includes estimation team meetings where the experts discuss their current estimates and the reasons for them, considering them in the context of other estimates. These meetings typically reduce the time it takes to come to consensus.

Planning poker is an agile estimation technique where all of the members of the agile development team participate. Since agile teams are kept small, they will typically not exceed 10 people. Each participant is given a deck of cards where each card has a single valid estimate written on it (for example, the cards may list a Fibonacci sequence: 1, 2, 3, 5, 8, 13, 21, 34, 55, 89). For each user story being estimated, the facilitator presents a description of the story, the team discusses the story, and the product owner answers questions. At the end of the discussion, each team member selects a card from the deck that represents his or her relative estimate for that story. All cards are then simultaneously turned over to reveal the individual estimates. If the estimates vary, the team members with the highest and lowest estimates explain their estimates and the reasons behind them. Other group members can also join this discussion, and again the product owner answers questions; however, the facilitator actively works to minimize the time frame of the discussion. Each team member then re-selects a card that represents their new estimate for the story based on this additional discussion, and those cards are again simultaneously revealed. This process of discussion and reestimation is repeated until the estimates converge enough to obtain consensus on an estimate for the story. Throughout this estimation process the facilitator records information from the discussion that might be helpful when the story is implemented and tested in the future.

Other expert team techniques can also be used. For example, a panel of experts is convened, and each activity from the WBS is discussed. Based on this discussion and their own expert judgment, these experts estimate the effort for each task. Mathematical averages are taken of the individual estimates to represent the team's estimate. This process is iterated until consensus is reached that the average is acceptable as an estimate.

Another variation on the expert-judgment method is to use the *program evaluation and review technique* (PERT) method where three estimates are made for each activity in the WBS instead of one, including:

- a = most optimistic estimate

- m = most likely estimate

- b = most pessimistic estimate

As illustrated in Figure 15.9, these three estimates are used to define a beta probability distribution for the estimate, and the final estimate (e) used for each work package is the expected value based on the estimates, which are calculated as $e = (a + 4m + b)/6$ with a standard deviation $\sigma = (b - a)/6$. Today the PERT method is typically replaced with more modern models where these same three estimates are fed into project estimation software that uses Monte Carlo estimation techniques to sample values all along the curve to produce the final estimate.

The strengths of the expert-judgment techniques include the fact that experts often understand differences between past experiences and the new techniques that will be used in the project being estimated. Experts can also factor in special characteristics of the project such as personnel issues or political considerations. For example, the team for this project has extensive experience building similar software, which will reduce the time needed for design and coding. Another example might be a project for a customer that has been historically difficult to work with and therefore will require additional time to perform the requirements activities.

The weaknesses of the expert-judgment techniques include the fact that the technique is no better than the expertise and objectivity of the experts. If the experts are lousy estimators, the result will be lousy estimates. The experts may also be biased by a desire to please or a desire to win the project. Finally, software managers and engineers tend to typically be very optimistic in their estimates. For example, they may include time to code, peer review, and unit test a module in their effort estimations but include no time in their estimates for rework or re–peer review or testing—because, of course, the code will be written perfectly the first time.

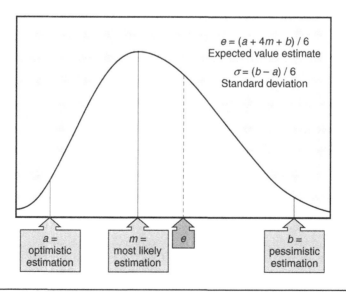

Figure 15.9   Program evaluation and review technique (PERT) method.

Model-Based Estimation Techniques

A second major type of estimation methods involves models (mathematical formulas) used to calculate the estimates for the project. These models typically start with an estimation of the software's size (for example, lines of code or function points) and any other inputs related to the characteristics of the project. These models are based on historic data from the industry, and many of them can be tailored using actual data from the organization's own past projects.

The strengths of the model-based estimating techniques include the fact that mathematical models eliminate most of the biases found in expert-judgment techniques, and automated tools exist to support most models. Weaknesses of these techniques include:

- The fact that skilled individuals are required to count function points, and these individuals may not be available in some organizations

- It may be difficult (if not impossible) to accurately estimate lines of code early in the project.

- Using the models with the default historic industry data may not match with the characteristics of the project being estimated, but tuning them to match the organization's or project's actual characteristics may require historic metrics data from similar projects. Many lower-maturity organizations simply do not have this type of historic data.

The *constructive cost model—version 2* (COCOMO II) (Boehm 2000) is an updated version of the classic COCOMO model documented by Barry Boehm in *Software Engineering Economics* (Boehm 1981). COCOMO II offers estimating capability at three levels of granularity, capturing three stages of software development activity, and providing three levels of model precision: prototyping, early design, and post-architecture:

- *Prototyping.* Input sized in object points.

- *Early design.* Input sized in function points or lines of code, with seven cost drivers (effort multipliers). Effort (person-months) = A × Size × (ΠEM_i), where ΠEM_i is equal to the values of the seven cost drivers multiplied together.

- *Post-architecture.* Input sized in function points or lines of code, with 17 cost drivers (effort multipliers). Effort (person-months) = A × (Size)^B × (ΠEM_i), where ΠEM_i is equal to the values of the 17 cost drivers multiplied together. "A" is a constant, which the University of Sothern California (USC), Center for Systems and Software Engineering COCOMO II tool currently calibrates at 2.45 (USC 1999). The COCOMO II model uses an exponential factor B to account for the diseconomies of scale encountered by software projects based on five scale factors, each of which is scored on a scale of 0 to 5 ("Cost Models for Future Software Life Cycle Processes: COCOMO 2.0" in Thayer 1997). "B" in this equation is equal to $1.01 + 0.01 \times \Sigma W_i$, where ΣW_i is the sum of the weighted scale factors (see Table 15.1).

Table 15.1 Weighted scale factors for the COCOMO II model.

Scale factor (W_i)	Very low (5)	Low (4)	Nominal (3)	High (2)	Very high (1)	Extra high (0)
Precedentedness	Thoroughly unprecedented	Largely unprecedented	Somewhat unprecedented	Generally familiar	Largely familiar	Thoroughly familiar
Development flexibility	Rigorous	Occasional relaxation	Some relaxation	General conformity	Some conformity	General goals
Architecture/ risk resolution	Little (20%)	Some (40%)	Often (60%)	Generally (75%)	Mostly (90%)	Full (100%)
Team cohesion	Very difficult interactions	Some difficult interactions	Basically cooperative	Largely cooperative	Highly cooperative	Seamless interactions
Process maturity	5 minus weighted average of "Yes" answers on CMMI for Development Maturity Questionnaire					

Source: "Cost Models for Future Software Life Cycle Processes: COCOMO 2.0" in Thayer (1997).

Table 15.2 Cost drivers for COCOMO II model.

	Early design cost drivers	Counterpart combined post-architecture cost drivers
Product factors	RCPX	RELY, DATA, CPLX, DOCU
	RUSE	RUSE
Platform factors	PDIF	TIME, STOR, PVOL
Personnel factors	PERS	ACAP, PCAP, PCON
	PREX	AEXP, PEXP, LTEX
Project factors	FCIL	TOOL, SITE
	SCED	SCED

Source: "Cost Models for Future Software Life Cycle Processes: COCOMO 2.0" in Thayer (1997).

An effort multiplier (EM) is scored for each of the cost drivers (see Table 15.2).

"COCOMO II continues the COCOMO and Ada COCOMO practice of using a set of effort multipliers (EM) to adjust the nominal person-month obtained from the project's size and exponent drivers" ("Cost Models for Future Software Life Cycle Processes: COCOMO 2.0" in Thayer 1997). The COCOMO II effort multiplier cost drivers include:

- Product factors:

    – RCPX—Product reliability and complexity (combines RELY, DATA, CPLX, DOCU)

    – RELY—Required software reliability (from slight inconvenience to risk of human life)

    – DATA—Database size

    – CPLX—Product complexity

    – DOCU—Documentation match to life cycle needs

    – RUSE—Required reusability (from none to across multiple product lines)

- Platform factors (refers to the target-machine complex of hardware and infrastructure software):

    – PDIF—Platform difficulty (combines TIME, STOR, PVOL)

    – TIME—Execution time constraints

    – STOR—Main storage constraints

    – PVOL—Platform volatility

- Personnel factors:

    – PERS—Personnel capability (combines ACAP, PCAP, PCON)

– PREX—Personnel experience (combines AEXP, PEXP, LTEX)

– ACAP—Analyst capability

– PCAP—Programmer capability

– PCON—Personnel continuity

– AEXP—Applications experience

– PEXP—Platform experience

– LTEX—Language and tool experience

• Project factors:

– FCIL—Facilities (combines TOOL, SITE).

– TOOL—Use of software tools.

– SITE—Multisite development considers two factors: site colocation (from fully colocated to international distribution) and communication support (from surface mail and some phone access to full interactive media).

– SCED—Required development schedule.

Another software estimation model is the *software life cycle management* (SLIM) model developed by Putnam (2003) used to estimate effort, time, and cost. As illustrated in Figure 15.10, the SLIM model is based on the equations for the Rayleigh curve for the project, which is the sum of the separate curves for design and code, test and validation, maintenance, and management. The area under each Rayleigh curve corresponds to cumulative effort for that activity. These curves for the individual activities are then added together to obtain a Rayleigh curve that represents

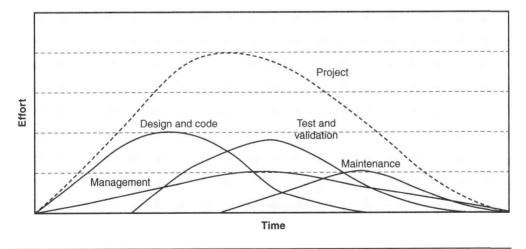

Figure 15.10   Rayleigh staffing curve.

the total effort for the project. The project curve does not include a requirements specification phase in the model. The SLIM model includes empirical results from 50 U.S. Army projects. Two central indicators used by the SLIM model are the productivity index and a manpower-buildup index. According to Kan (2003), the productivity index is a "big picture measure of the total development capability of the organization." The manpower-buildup index is the rate at which the total number of staff assigned to the project is growing.

Budget

Initial *budgets* specify the plans for allocating the cost of the project across its various budget categories. During the execution of the project, actual costs for each category can be tracked against the budget to provide insight into when and how the project is spending its monetary resources. Examples of budget categories include:

- *Labor costs—staff and contractors* (engineering, management, support, administrative):
  - Wages, salaries, and benefits
  - Travel and relocation
  - Training (conferences, tuition, course fees)
- *Capital costs:*
  - Computers and peripherals (host, test, and target computers)
  - Networks
  - Software engineering environment (tools, processes)
  - Physical facilities (office space and equipment, labs)
- *Other costs:*
  - Subcontract/supplier cost
  - Supplies and materials
  - Rents

2. PROJECT SCHEDULING

> Use PERT charts, critical path method (CPM), work breakdown structure (WBS), Scrum, burn-down charts, and other tools to schedule and monitor projects. (Apply)
>
> **Body of Knowledge IV.A.2**

Work Breakdown Structure

A *work breakdown structure* (WBS) is a hierarchical decomposition of the project into subprojects, tasks, and subtasks. The goal is to break the project work down into manageable elements called *activities* that can be easily estimated, budgeted, scheduled, tracked, and controlled. The WBS becomes the basis for the effort, cost, and schedule estimates of the project. Just remember, "if an activity is not in our WBS, we will have to do it in zero time and for free" (Ould 1990). In other words, any activity that is not specified in the WBS will not be allocated effort, budget, staff, or resources. The benefits of creating a WBS include:

- Ensuring that all work activities are identified and understood

- Helping to determine estimates and schedules for the project

- Modularizing the project into manageable pieces that can be tracked and controlled

- Helping quantify people and skills needed

- Aiding in the communication of the work that needs to be accomplished

- Providing useful information for analyzing impacts of proposed changes

There are no hard and fast rules for how far to break the project down into activities when creating a WBS. The larger in size or more complex a project is, the more likely that it will require more breadth (substructures) and depth (levels) in the WBS. Projects that include suppliers or that span multiple organizational entities may require additional breadth and depth. The WBS should be broken down as far as possible based on the current information, but only as far as necessary for understanding. This balancing between providing enough visibility without micromanaging the project requires the application of good engineering judgment. Activities in the WBS should have a cohesive time frame (no gaps for other activities) and should include only related work items. Each activity should produce one or more work products, and most of the steps should be the responsibility of the same team members. For example, the activity for coding module X might include the actual coding, peer review, and unit testing of that module. The author of the code is responsible for all of these processes, even though other individuals might be involved in the peer review. A good rule of thumb is that an activity typically has a time frame of one to two people for one percent to two percent of total project time (about one to two weeks on a one- to two-year-long project).

As illustrated in the example in Figure 15.11, one method used to represent a work breakdown structure is a tree-structure graph. The top level of the tree-structure graph always contains a single item (the product being produced or the project being implemented). The second level contains the major components of that top-level item. The third level includes subcomponents of the second-level items. The fourth level includes subcomponents of the third-level items, and so on down the tree. An indented list can also be used to represent a WBS. This is the way that the WBS is documented in most project management tools.

There are two basic types of WBS, the product type and the process type. Figure 15.11 illustrates an example of a product-type WBS, which partitions the

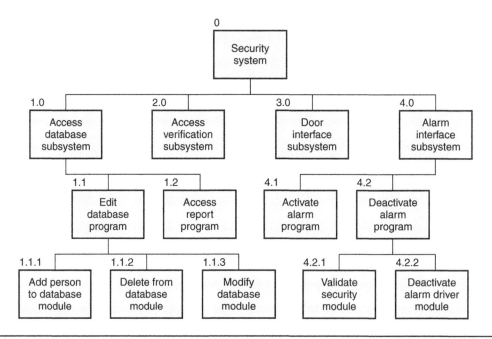

Figure 15.11 Product-type work breakdown structure–example.

project by breaking down the project's product, service, or result into smaller and smaller parts. At its lowest levels, the product is broken down into the activities that produce the individual component of the project's deliverables.

Figure 15.12 illustrates an example of a process-type WBS, which partitions the project into smaller and smaller processes. At its lowest levels, the process is broken down into individual activities. Utilizing a process-type WBS for software has the following advantages for software projects:

- Allows standardization of WBS templates that can be tailored to each project—rather than starting from scratch with each new product

- Does not require locking in the project architecture early in the planning process

- Facilitates comparison between projects

- Provides a mechanism for defining tasks not directly linked to the creation of product components (project planning, software quality assurance, software configuration management)

Of course, the two main WBS types can be combined into a hybrid WBS, as illustrated by the example in Figure 15.13. Advantages of the hybrid-type WBS include all of the advantages of the process-type WBS, plus it links product components directly to the processes that create them. Using a hybrid-type WBS allows the project to start from a process-oriented work plan and then progressive elaboration that plan with additional detail once the software architectural information is available.

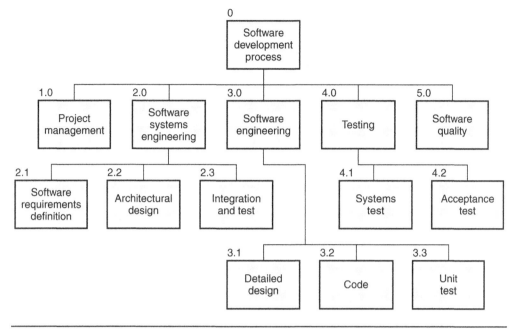

Figure 15.12   Process-type work breakdown structure—example.

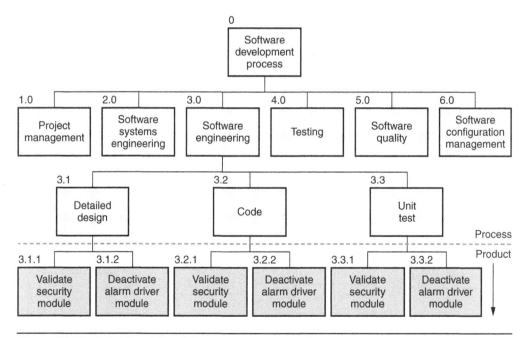

Figure 15.13   Hybrid work breakdown structure—example.

Part IV.A.2

Activity Networks

Activities are the lowest-level leaves of the WBS. When those activities are diagrammed together with their predecessor/successor relationships, an *activity network* is formed. Activity networks can be represented in two ways. Figure 15.14 illustrates an example of an "activity on the line" network where the lines represent the activities and the nodes represent events. An event is the beginning or ending point (in time) of an activity. In this example, activity A starts at event 1 and ends by event 2, activity C starts at event 2 and ends by event 3, while activity B also starts at event 1 but ends by event 3. The reason for using "by event 3" is because if the duration of activity A plus activity C is longer than the duration of activity B, then activity B is said to have "slack" and can actually finish sooner but must finish before event 3, which starts activities E and G. Of course the opposite is true: if the duration of activity A plus activity C is shorter than the duration of activity B, then activities A plus C have "slack."

Figure 15.15 illustrates an example of an "activity on the node" network where the nodes represent the activities and the lines simply represent their predecessor/successor relationships. Both Figure 15.14 and Figure 15.15 are examples of activity networks for an identical set of activities.

Figure 15.16 illustrates the four different possible activity network relationships using activity on the node–type diagrams:

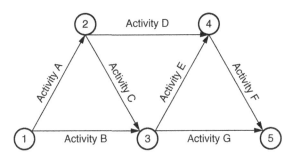

Figure 15.14   Activity on the line network–example.

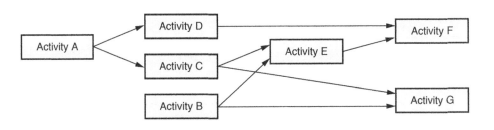

Figure 15.15   Activity on the node network–example.

- In a *finish-to-start relationship*, the first activity A must finish before the second activity B can start. A lag time may also be specified in this relationship, in this example a lag time of five days. An example of this type of relationship might be that the design review (activity B) is held five days after the design document is completed and distributed (activity A) in order to give participants time to prepare.

- In a *start-to-start relationship*, the first activity C must be started before the second activity D can start. Again, a lag time may be specified (10 days in this example). An example of this type of relationship might be that the writing of the user manual (activity D) can start 10 days after the start of detailed design (activity C) to allow enough of the design to be defined so enough information is available to start the user manual.

- In a *finish-to-finish relationship*, the first activity E must be finished before the second activity F can finish. Again, a lag time may be specified (four days in this example). An example of this type of relationship might be that integration test (activity F) can run concurrently with coding and unit test (activity E), but integration test will not be completed until four days after the last module has passed unit test.

- In a *start-to-finish relationship*, the finish of the second activity H must lag the start of the first activity G by the specified lag time (15 days in this example). There are not many practical examples of this type of relationship, and many project management tools do not even support it, but it is a possible relationship.

A common mistake that should be avoided when diagramming activity networks is diagramming activities in sequence when they could be done in parallel. This is typically done based on known people or resource dependencies. However, the activity network should only include natural dependencies based on logical flow of the activities; staff/resource dependencies are handled later. Another common mistake is where an activity is shown as dependent on total completion of another activity but it is actually only dependent on completion of part of that other activity.

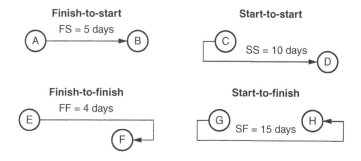

Figure 15.16   Types of activity network relationships.

Part IV.A.2

Critical Path Method

The *critical path method* (CPM) utilizes the predecessor/successor relationship in the activity network and the estimated duration for those activities to determine the project's total duration (calendar time). The critical path is the longest path through the activity network, which defines the shortest amount of time in which the project can be completed. A critical activity is any activity in the activity network that must be completed by a certain time (event) and has no slack time. A critical activity is always on the critical path.

The first step in the critical path method is to set the duration of each activity in the network to the effort estimate for that activity. Available staff and resources are then allocated across the activities and resource leveling is done. Resource leveling examines the resource allocation, looking for areas where the use of staff or other resources is unbalanced or over-allocated and resolves any identified issues. Resource leveling requires trade-offs in the cost/schedule/scope trilogy. This step establishes the initial duration for each activity in the network, based on activity predecessor/successor relationships, efforts estimates, and staff/resource allocations.

The longest path (critical path) through the activity network is then determined. To illustrate this step in the critical path method, consider the "activity on the line" network example in Figure 15.17 and assume that the numbers on each line specify the estimated effort in days of the associated activity (for example, the activity from event 1 to event 2 has a duration of 12 days). The duration of each path is then calculated by adding together the effort estimates for each activity on that path. In this example:

- The duration for the path through events 1-2-5-6-8 = 12 + 10 + 5 + 10 = 37
- The duration for the path through events 1-2-5-8 = 12 + 10 + 11 = 33
- The duration for the path through events 1-5-6-8 = 18 + 5 + 10 = 33

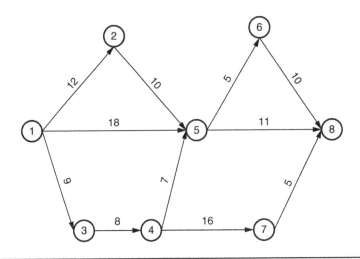

Figure 15.17   Critical path analysis—example.

- The duration for the path through events 1-5-8 = 18 + 11 = 29

- The duration for the path through events 1-3-4-5-6-8 = 9 + 8 + 7 + 5 + 10 = 39

- The duration for the path through events 1-3-4-5-8 = 9 + 8 + 7 + 11 = 35

- The duration for the path through events 1-3-4-7-8 = 9 + 8 + 16 + 5 = 38

Therefore, the longest path through the network is 39 days, so the path through events 1-3-4-5-6-8 is the critical path.

To continue this example, assume that the customer needs the product being produced by this project in 35 days. Since the original critical path method analysis calculated a critical path of 39 days, the project must find a way to shorten one or more tasks on the critical path. There are four ways to shorten the duration of a task based on making trade-off choices based on the cost/schedule/scope trilogy.

First, the human resources for the task can be changed, either by adding more people or assigning more efficient or experienced people to the task. Each task was originally estimated based on the assumed skill level of the type of person that would be assigned to the task. For example, if the task that starts at event 5 and ends at event 6 was originally assigned to a junior-level engineer, a choice could be made to assign a senior-level engineer to that task and reestimate that task to take four days. The project manager might also decide to assign two people to the task that starts at event 6 and ends at event 8, which would result in it being reestimated to take six days instead of 10. The duration for the path through events 1-3-4-5-6-8 would then be reduced to 9 + 8 + 7 + 4 + 6 = 34 days.

Unfortunately, while the original critical path has now been reduced to less than the 35-day goal, it doesn't completely solve the problem. The path through events 1-3-4-7-8, which has the duration of 38 days, now becomes the new critical path for the project. Now that path has to be shortened to less than 35 days, and so on, until all paths through the program are less than 35 days long.

One note of caution: the project may be tempted to change the human resources by planning overtime into the project schedule. This is never a good idea. People can only work so many productive hours a day, and if overtime is scheduled into the project, people tend to burn out or make more mistakes because they are tired, both of which can have negative impacts on the project schedule in the long run. Also, if people are already working overtime, they have nothing left to give when additional effort is needed for corrective actions to bring a project back under control.

A second way to shorten the duration of a task is to reduce the objectives or specifications. In other words, don't do all of the work initially planned. One method for doing this is to prioritize the requirements and shift one or more of the lowest-level requirements into a future incremental release or simply remove them from the scope. Another method is to reduce the activities or processes. For example, hold fewer meetings or decide to run fewer test cases (or cycles of testing) than originally planned. A caution here is that not performing certain activities may result in the reduction of the quality of the product. This is a serious concern if it creates a risk that the product may no longer meet its required quality levels.

A third way to shorten the duration of a task is to change the materials or technical resources being used for that task. Sometimes resources other than human resources are the constraining factor on a task. In this case adding more resources may help. For example, if test beds are a constraining resource, making additional test bed resources available to the project could reduce task duration.

A fourth way to shorten the duration of a task is to change the processes or methods of working. Process improvements specifically targeted at cycle time reductions can impact the duration of tasks that use those processes. The word of caution here is to remember the learning curve. Making changes to the processes may actually negatively impact the cycle time for some period of time.

When performing critical path analysis, if the project has more than one critical path, it increases the risk of the project slipping its schedule. Therefore, tasks on selected multiple critical paths should be manipulated until only one critical path exists. Rules of thumb for selecting which of the multiple critical paths to reduce include selecting the path with:

- Largest number of activities

- Least-skilled personnel

- Greatest technical risk or where there is questionable feasibility

- Risk factors that are outside the control of the project team

- Activities that would have the greatest cost impact if they slipped

- Tasks that are new (no historical information used to estimate)

- Tasks that have historically been problems

- Risky activities with no contingency (backup) plans

- Tasks that are the most difficult

Scrum

The term "scrum" originally derives from a strategy in the game of rugby where it denotes "getting an out-of-play ball back into the game" with teamwork (Schwaber 2002). *Scrum* is an agile methodology that focuses primarily on project planning and monitoring aspects of software development rather than on technical implementation techniques. In fact, many organizations use both scrum and extreme programming (XP) together since they complement one another well.

The scrum defines specific roles with defined responsibilities. The *product owner* represents the project stakeholder and acquires initial and ongoing funding for the project. The product owner manages, controls, and makes the product backlog visible so that each of the iterations address the most valuable requirements remaining in the product backlog. The product owner also helps prioritize and estimate features in the product backlog.

The *scrum master* is a new management role introduced by scrum. The scrum master is responsible for ensuring that the project is conducted according to the practices, values, and rules of scrum, and that it progresses as planned. The scrum master interacts with the *scrum team* as well as with the product owner during the project to define the items from the product backlog that constitute each sprint backlog. The scrum master is also responsible for acquiring needed resources, removing impediments, teaching project participants about scrum, and helping change the process to keep the team working as productively as possible. The scrum master runs the daily scrum meetings and validates decisions made with the product owner. The scrum master, along with the product owner, tracks progress and team velocity (the team's overall ability to deliver work) during each sprint. The scrum master also facilitates the sprint planning meetings, sprint review meetings, and sprint retrospective meetings.

The *scrum team* is a self-managing and self-organizing team that has the authority to decide on the necessary actions to achieve the goals of each sprint. For example, besides the activities that the scrum team is involved in during the iteration, they are also involved in estimating effort, creating the sprint backlog, reviewing the product backlog list, and suggesting impediments to remove from the project. The ideal scrum team size is from five to nine members. If there is a need for more people, scrum suggests forming multiple teams. In such a case, using a "scrum of scrums" (a daily scrum meeting made up of representatives from each of the scrum teams) allows scaling up.

Management is in charge of final decision making and establishes the charters, standards, and conventions the project must follow. Management also participates in the setting of goals, objectives, and requirements for the project. For example, management is involved in selecting the product owner, gauging the progress, and reducing the product backlog.

The customer participates in the tasks related to product backlog items for the system being developed or enhanced. The customer receives the delivered software iterations and provides feedback to the scrum team. The customer is also involved in selecting the product owner.

As illustrated in Figure 15.18, the scrum process starts with a vision, including anticipated return on investment (ROI), releases, and milestones. The initial *product backlog* contains a list of prioritized product requirements (for example, user stories or features). Over time, additional requirements emerge and are prioritized and added to the product backlog.

Each *sprint* starts with a *sprint planning meeting* organized by the scrum master. This meeting is actually two meetings back to back. During the first part of the sprint planning meeting the scrum team and scrum master meet with the product owner to:

- Identify a sprint "goal," which is a short description of the overall work to be achieved during the sprint that helps "focus" the effort and tie it together conceptually

- Prioritize the items left in the product backlog based on any new information or on new items added or returned to the product backlog

- Obtain answers from the product owner to any questions the scrum team has about the items in the product backlog, including questions on the content, purpose, meaning, and intention

- Select as many items from the product backlog as they believe the scrum team can turn into a completed increment of deliverable product functionality by the end of the sprint

Part IV.A.2

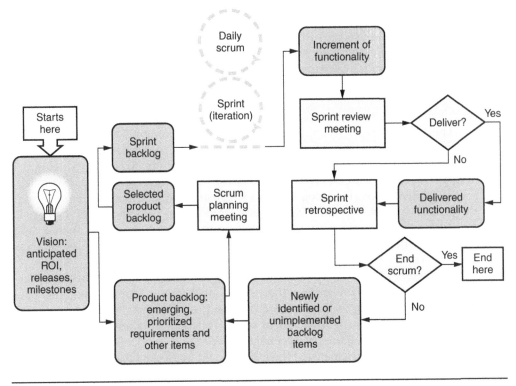

Figure 15.18   Scrum process.

- The scrum team commits to the product owner that it will do its best to deliver these selected items

During the second part of the sprint planning meeting the scrum team and scrum master plan the sprint activities by:

- Translating each selected product backlog item into one or more *sprint backlog* tasks. For example, if the backlog item is a story, tasks might include writing test cases, developing one or more pieces of code, developing an additional database record, and executing the tests.

- Adding additional tasks to the sprint backlog as needed to conduct the sprint.

Unlike the product backlog, the *sprint backlog,* also called the *release backlog,* is stable until the sprint is completed. During the sprint, management can add or change items in the product backlog (not in the sprint backlog). Management leaves the scrum team alone during a sprint.

It is said, "The product owner prioritizes but the scrum team sequences" (Schwaber 2007). That is, the product owner identifies the importance of product backlog items, but the scrum team, using its understanding of the team's historic velocity, picks the items for the sprint backlog. It is assumed that the top item(s) will always be selected, but due to technical concerns, effort required, and so on, the team may skip some items to address lower-priority ones. When lower-priority items are selected, the reason(s) for this should be explained to the product owner since the owner bears the ultimate "risk" for the product.

Scrum uses a short (for example, 30-day or 14-day) incremental development cycle (sprint)—to address the selected sprint backlog items—within which the scrum team holds brief daily meetings (scrums). At the end of each sprint, the scrum team delivers the new functionality developed during the sprint. This delivery process includes holding a *sprint review* with the customer and any interested stakeholders to help determine what to do next. A *sprint retrospective* is held where the scrum master and scrum team address needed process improvements for the next sprint. The major output of each sprint is a "potentially shippable product increment" (Schwaber 2007), which is working software of high quality. However, the working software may not have all the functionality desired to actually ship, but could be shipped. At the end of a sprint, new requirements may be identified based on customer feedback or other stakeholder needs. In addition, there may be incomplete sprint backlog items from the sprint that just ended. These requirements are prioritized and added into the product backlog. The next sprint planning meeting is then held to start the cycle again, repeating the cycle until all features are implemented or the customer decides to teminate the project.

Agile Project Metrics

One of the primary practices of XP is the *informative workspace*, which uses the workspace to communicate important, active information. For example, story cards (sorted by "done," "to be done this week," "to be done this release") or big, visible charts for tracking progress over time of important issues might be posted on the wall. Beck (2005) says, "An interested observer should be able to walk into the team space and get a general idea of how the project is going in 15 seconds. He should be able to get more information about real or potential problems by looking more closely."

Another agile methodology called *crystal* has a strategy called *information radiators*. Information radiators are forms of (displayed) project documentation used or placed in areas where people can easily see them. Examples of information radiators include posting:

- Flip-chart pages from facilitated sessions

- Index cards or sticky notes with documented user stories

- Butcher paper depicting project timelines and milestones

- Photographs of or printouts from whiteboard results from informal discussions

- Computer-generated domain models, graphs, or other outputs printed to plotters that produce large-size images

Information radiators show status such as the:

- Current iteration's work set (use cases or stories)
- Current work assignments
- Number of tests written (or passed)
- Number of use cases (or stories) delivered
- Status of key servers (up, down, or in maintenance)
- Core of the domain model
- Results of the last reflection workshop (Cockburn 2005)

Crystal has a strategy called *burn charts*. Burn charts are intended to be posted in a visible location—as part of the information radiator—and should show how the project's estimations (predictions) compare to its actual accomplishments. Figure 15.19 shows a *burn-up chart* example, and Figure 15.20 shows a *burn-down chart* example.

A burn-up chart starts with zero and tracks progress by graphing the number of items completed up to the ceiling (goal). This ceiling line can move up or down if the goal changes. A burn-down chart starts with the total number of items that need to be done and tracks progress by graphing the number of items left to do down to the baseline. The baseline would typically be "zero items left to do," but the baseline can move up or down if the goal changes. For example, if there were originally 100 test cases to execute, the burn-down chart would start at 100 and track down to zero. However, if 10 more test cases were added later, the baseline would drop to negative 10.

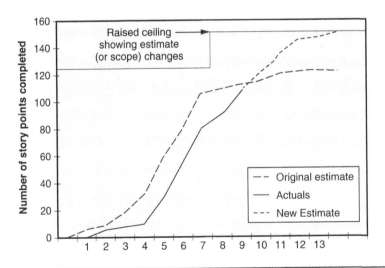

Figure 15.19   Burn-up chart—example.

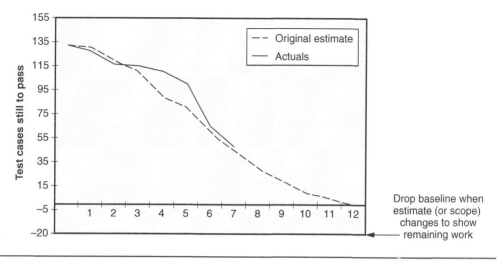

Figure 15.20   Burn-down chart—example.

3. PROJECT DEPLOYMENT

> Use various tools, including milestones,
> objectives achieved, task duration, etc., to set
> goals and deploy the project. (Apply)
>
> **Body of Knowledge IV.A.3**

Project deployment involves the actual execution of the project activities, including:

- Working toward achieving the project's objectives and milestones
- Implementing processes, methods, and standards
- Executing the planned actions and activities specified in the WBS
- Creating, controlling, verifying, and validating deliverables
- Expending effort and spending money
- Communicating with stakeholders and managing their expectations
- Staffing, training, and managing people
- Obtaining and using materials, equipment, facilities, and other resources
- Implementing risk plans and managing risks
- Selecting and managing suppliers

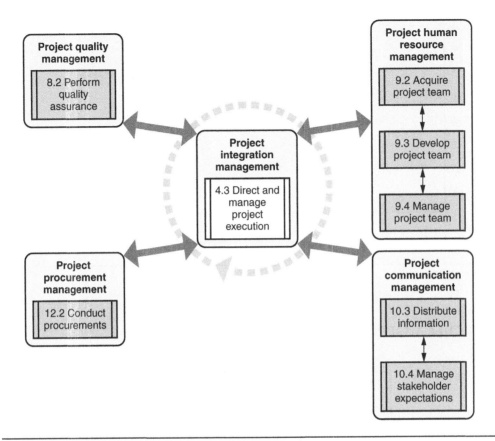

Figure 15.21 PMI executing process group.
Source: PMI (2008). Reprinted with permission.

Figure 15.21 illustrates the various processes in the Project Management Institute's executing process group and how they interact and are integrated into directing and managing the project's execution. The numbers preceding each process name indicate the section in the Project Management Body of Knowledge Guide (PMBOK) (PMI 2008) that describes that process.

Project Objectives

Project objectives define the specifics of what success looks like for the project—what exactly the project is trying to accomplish from a business-level perspective. Each project objective should:

- Be specific
- Be measurable
- Be verifiable—so the project team knows when they have achieved it
- Align with higher-level organizational objectives
- Be stated in terms of deliverable items

- Be understandable—stated in a way that other people will know what the project is trying to achieve

- Include a time limit

- Be attainable

There may be many different types of objectives for the project. Examples of project objectives include:

- *Business objectives:*

  – Capture a market share of X percent within Y months

  – Achieve an X percent increase in profitability or return on investment within Y months

- *Cost objectives:*

  – Complete the project under a cost of $\$X$

  – Reduce the cost of ownership of the new ABC system over X months (or years) by Y percent

- *Schedule, milestone, or cycle time objectives:*

  – Deliver the project or complete a major milestone by X date

  – Achieve an X percent reduction in the cycle time for producing work product X or for performing activity Y

- *Product technical objectives:*

  – Add ABC new functionality to an existing product

  – Increase the software's capacity so that it can handle X number of transactions in an hour

- *Product quality and reliability objectives:*

  – Keep the total postrelease software outage levels below X minutes per site per year

  – Reduce customer-reported defects by X percent below prior product releases

- *Organizational or personnel objectives:* train X additional software engineers in UML techniques

- *Contract and procurement objectives:* qualify a new XYZ tool supplier

- *Management system objectives:* pilot the new process improvement ABC

Throughout the deployment of the project, the project manager and project team members should align strategies and tactics with and focus project work efforts on identified project objectives to ensure that progress continues to be made toward their achievement. Once a project objective has been achieved, effort and other resources from the implementation of that objective can be refocused on other project objectives.

Part IV.A.3

Project Communications

Effective communication with the project team and other stakeholders is essential to ensure project success. Examples of checklist items that could be used to monitor the effectiveness of communications with the project team and support staff include:

- The project objectives have been communicated, and project team and support staff members understand how their efforts contribute to accomplishing those objectives

- Project risks have been identified and communicated

- The people who will implement the project plans participated in their creation

- Project team and support staff members have access to up-to-date project plan documentation

- The project plan has been reviewed and committed to by project team and support staff members

- Project team members have been colocated to facilitate communications or, where this is not possible, a mechanism is in place for virtual colocation

- Agreement exists that engineering and support staff managers inform project managers before reassigning project personnel to other non-project work

- Roles and responsibilities of each project team and support staff member have been clearly defined and communicated

- Project team meetings are scheduled on a regular basis to review progress

- Transfer or termination of team members is coordinated with his or her replacement, or written instructions are left for successor

- Where cross-functional activities are required to complete tasks, frequent coordination meetings are held to keep everyone informed

- Project team and support staff members are encouraged to provide early warnings of project risks and problems

- Consensus decisions are made when appropriate

- People are kept informed of decisions or changes that impact their work

- Upper management is aware of the project's status

- Managers interact routinely with project team and support staff members to provide assistance, listen to their problems, help solve problems, and understand the status of the project firsthand

- Metrics used to track the project are made available to project team and support staff members

Examples of checklist items that could be used to monitor the effectiveness of communications with external stakeholders include:

- The "real" project stakeholders or models of the "real" stakeholders have been identified and consulted in order to define project requirements.

- The project objectives have been communicated to all external stakeholders.

- The customer and other external stakeholders are involved in and aware of project status.

- Changes are understood and agreed to by all impacted external stakeholders.

- Senior management reviews all commitment changes and new software project commitments made to individuals and groups external to the organization, as appropriate, when changes occur.

- Where external stakeholders are involved in activities that are required to complete tasks, frequent coordination meetings are held to keep everyone informed.

- External stakeholders are provided early warning of risks and problems that may impact them.

- Suppliers' representatives were included in project planning and have committed to schedules, milestones, deliverables, and quality level requirements that affect them.

- Progress and problems of the suppliers are tracked and communicated.

- Project status meetings are held periodically with the suppliers (these may be part of the overall project tracking meetings).

Chapter 16

B. Tracking and Controlling

Tracking the project involves all of the activities required to monitor and review the project's ongoing activities, performance, and progress against the project plans and project performance baselines to identify any significant problems, issues, and/or risks. There are two primary methods for project tracking: reviews and metrics. Tracking activities include:

- Measuring progress against project objectives

- Assessing adherence to methods and standards

- Evaluating actions and activities status against project plans

- Monitoring requirements volatility and product quality

- Measuring effort and cost actuals against schedule and budgets

- Monitoring the utilization of materials, equipment, facilities, and people

- Tracking the status of risks and risk-handling activities

- Monitoring supplier performance against contracts, plans, and requirements

Controlling the project involves all of the activities required to evaluate identified issues and problems in order to determine the appropriate corrective actions, to identify preventive actions in anticipation of possible problems (risks), and to manage those corrective and preventive actions to closure. Control activities include:

- Realigning with project and organizational objectives

- Improving methods and standards

- Modifying or controlling actions and activities

- Controlling requirements volatility and product quality

- Controlling costs and schedules or replanning them

- Controlling the utilization of materials, equipment, facilities, and people

- Controlling risks

- Coordinating with suppliers on any necessary corrective and preventive actions

Continuous tracking and controlling activities provide the project team and management with visibility into the health of the project and early identification of any problems or risks that require investigation and/or action. Project tracking and control are used to identify differences between the plans and estimates of what should happen and what is actually happening as the project progresses. So why are actuals different than plans and estimates? Because of:

- *Bad estimates.* The software industry is notoriously bad about underestimating costs, effort, and schedules.

- *Forgotten tasks.* Necessary activities are not included in the work breakdown structure and therefore not considered in the estimates. For example, if a six-month-long project has weekly project team meetings that last one hour with 20 people in attendance, that is 26 meetings × 20 people × 1 hour = 520 hours of effort, not including the time people spend preparing for these meetings. If the effort and schedule estimations don't include these meetings, the project is 520 hours behind before it starts.

- *Poorly executed tasks.* Tasks that require more rework and/or testing than estimated. For example, if a poor-quality product reaches system test, more cycles of defect correction and regression testing may be required than were planned.

- *Natural and human disasters.* Fires, floods, snowstorms, illness, death, and other disasters may impact people's ability to even get to work in order to make progress on the project. These disasters can be positive as well as negative. For example, the lead architect on a project was getting married. He was useless for about six weeks prior to the wedding. In fact, all he wanted to do was sit and talk about the wedding with other team members, which impacted their ability to make progress as well. What was particularly amusing was that his future wife also worked on the project and she was extremely productive because she wanted all of her work done before the wedding.

- *Change.* There is an old military saying that "no battle plan ever survived the encounter with the actual enemy." Well, "no project plan ever survived the encounter with the actual project" either. Why? Because things change! Objectives change, requirements change, technology changes, people leave the project and new people come onboard, the economy changes, and the marketplace changes (for example, an organization's competitors may announce a product, and the project may need to change to address this new competitive threat).

Since what actually happens on the project is different than what is planned, when are controlling actions necessary? The answer to this question goes back to the definition of project success. If the variance between actuals and plans is large enough to negatively impact the project's ability to deliver the product on time, within budget, with all of the required functionality, at the needed quality and performance levels, while effectively and efficiently utilizing people and other resources, then corrective action is needed. In other words, if the variance is significant enough to cause the project to fail on any one or more of the five project success factors (that is, on schedule, on budget, producing a product with all required scope, at the required quality and performance levels, while effectively and efficiently utilizing people and other resources), controlling actions should be considered.

Remember the project plan that created the nice straight road map to the project's destination? Then reality happens, as illustrated in Figure 16.1. Because what actually happens on a project is different than what was estimated, flexibility is the key. Project plans have to be living documents that are designed to change as reality happens. Project tracking is the information system that provides the project team and management with the facts and information needed to make informed decisions about what needs to be changed. Project control provides the mechanisms to make those changes in an organized, intelligent manner, communicate them to the project stakeholders, and track them to closure.

Tracking and controlling a project requires the integration of many different process activities. Figure 16.2 illustrates the various processes in the Project Management Institute's monitoring and controlling process group and how they interact and are integrated. The numbers preceding each process name indicate the section in the Project Management Body of Knowledge Guide (PMBOK) (PMI 2008) that describes that process.

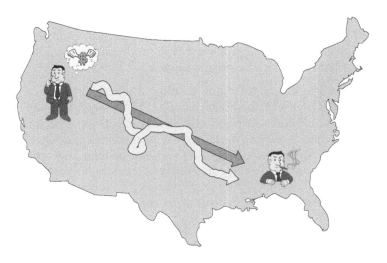

Figure 16.1 Actual project journey.

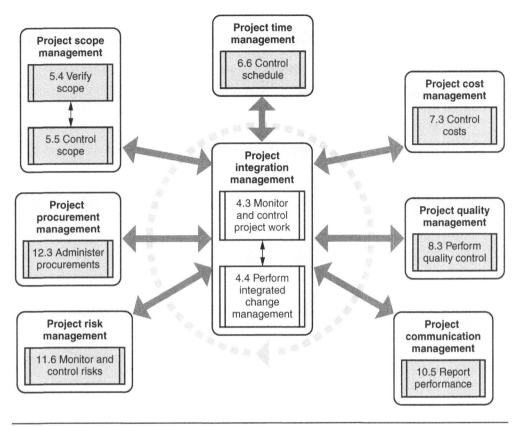

Figure 16.2   PMI monitoring and controlling process group.
Source: PMI (2008). Reprinted with permission.

1. PHASE TRANSITION CONTROL

Use phase transition control tools and techniques such as entry/exit criteria, quality gates, Gantt charts, integrated master schedules, etc. (Apply)

Body of Knowledge IV.B.1

As a project transitions from one phase to another (or from one process or activity to another), checkpoints can be added to ensure that the project remains in control. Tools and techniques including entry/exit criteria, quality gates, Gantt charts, integrated master schedules, and budgets can be used to monitor progress at these checkpoints. If the project is not on track, corrective actions should be implemented and tracked to closure before the phase transition is considered complete.

Entry/Exit Criteria

Entry and exit criteria are the specific, measurable conditions that must be met before a phase, process, or activity can be started or completed. These criteria can include:

- Work products that must be completed, approved, and/or placed under configuration control

- Tasks and/or verification steps that must be satisfactorily completed

- Specific measured values that must be obtained

- Staff with appropriate levels of expertise that must be available to perform the process

- Other resources that must be available and/or ready for use during the process

During the actual execution of each phase, process, or activity implemented as part of the project, the entry and exit criteria should be verified. If entry criteria are not met, corrective actions should be implemented and tracked to closure before that phase, process, or activity is started. If exit criteria are not met, corrective actions should be implemented and tracked to closure before that phase, process, or activity is considered complete. Of course, business decisions can always be made to override the entry and exit criteria. However, any exceptions should be handled through formal deviation (if the exception is temporary) or waiver (if the exception is permanent) processes with the appropriate approvals.

As discussed in Chapter 2, the entry and exit criteria for a process are documented as part of the definition of each process. However, the project plans may tailor these criteria to match the specific needs of the project. The project plan may also define specific values for entry or exit criteria as required by the project. For example, the standard system-test process might define one of its exit criteria as, "The number of non-closed defects do not exceed the limits specified in the project plans." For a specific project, the project plans (quality or verification and validation plans) might then define the required values for this criterion as:

- No non-closed critical-severity defect can exist

- No more than 10 non-closed major defects can exist, all of which must have work-arounds approved by the customer

- No more than 25 non-closed minor defects can exist

Quality Gates

A *quality gate* is a checkpoint or review that a work product must pass through in order to be acquired (baselined and placed under formal change control) or to transition to the next project phase, process, or activity. The project's configuration management plans should define the acquisition point quality gates for each configuration item. The project's quality plans should define additional quality gates used throughout the project and the required acceptance criteria for each product passing through each quality gate. If the acceptance criteria for a given configuration item are not met at a quality gate, corrective actions should be implemented and tracked to closure before that product is considered to have transitioned through that quality gate. Again, exceptions can be handled through formal deviation or waiver processes with the appropriate approvals.

When the person responsible for a project activity indicates that they are done with that activity, if that activity's work product(s) have a defined quality gate, a different person or team of people then conducts the checkpoint or review activities. The intent of the quality gate is to ensure that the work product meets its requirements and workmanship standards before it becomes the basis for future work. Quality gates might be as simple as the team lead checking that a module of code meets the coding standard before it is baselined or as complex as a formal phase-end review as discussed below. Peer reviews, product audits, and tests can also act as quality gates. For example, once the peer review team has reviewed and accepted the system test report it is considered to have passed its quality gate.

Gantt Charts

A commonly used project management tool is the Gantt chart. A *Gantt chart* is a bar diagram that shows the schedule and duration for each task and highlights milestones in the schedule. Milestones on a Gantt chart are typically depicted as diamonds. As illustrated in Figure 16.3, a scheduling Gantt chart shows the schedule for each task with a bar that starts when the task is scheduled to start and ends when the task is scheduled to end.

Once the schedule is baselined, a second set of bars is added to the Gantt chart to represent the actual schedule. As illustrated in Figure 16.4, a tracking Gantt chart shows the light gray planning bars from the baselined schedule and a second set of bars for the actuals. For example, the black tracking bar for task A shows that it started late (the tracking bar starts to the right of the planning bar) and ended late (the tracking bar stops to the right of the planning bar) but had the

Task name	Week 1					Week 2					Week 3					Week 4					Week 5				
	M	T	W	T	F	M	T	W	T	F	M	T	W	T	F	M	T	W	T	F	M	T	W	T	F
Task A																									
Task B																									
Task C																									
Task D																									
Task E																									
Task F																									
Task G																									
Milestone A																									

Figure 16.3 Scheduling Gantt chart—example.

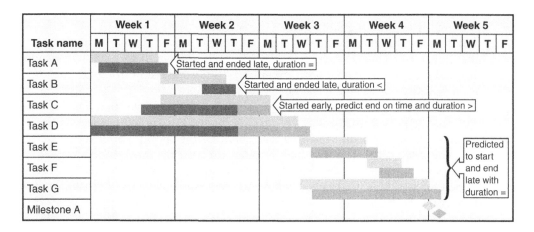

Figure 16.4   Tracking Gantt chart—example.

same duration (the tracking and planning bars are the same length). Task B started and ended late but had a shorter duration than planned (the tracking bar is shorter than the planning bar). The split tracking bar for tasks C and D shows that these tasks are only partly complete. The black part of the tracking bar shows when the tasks actually started and their duration to date. The dark gray part of the tracking bar shows the predicted duration of the part of the task yet to be completed and its predicted completion point. Based on this example, task C started early, is about three-quarters complete, and is predicted to end on time. Task D started on time, is about two-thirds complete, and is predicted to end late. The dark gray tracking bars for tasks E through G show that they have not yet started but are predicted to start and end late and have the same duration as originally planned.

Finally, based on the current status, milestone A is predicted to occur later than originally scheduled.

If the difference between planned and tracked activity status is considered significant, corrective actions should be implemented and tracked to closure. Again, exceptions can be handled through formal deviation or waiver processes with the appropriate approvals.

Integrated Master Schedules

Gantt charts show the detailed status of the individual activities from the project's work breakdown structure. However, on large or complex projects with hundreds of individual activities, it is easy to get lost in these details. It may be beneficial to break these large or complex projects down into subprojects, each with their own Gantt charts. An *integrated master schedule* can then be used to summarize the status of the lower-level subprojects into a higher-level project view.

Another use for integrated master schedules is for programs where multiple projects are being coordinated together. In this case, the integrated master schedule is used to provide a combined view of the high-level interrelationships and dependencies between the projects.

A final use for integrated master schedules is when rapid application development (RAD) or incremental development is being used to develop software. In this case, each increment has its own detailed schedule, and the integrated master schedule is used to provide visibility into the interrelationships and dependencies between the increments.

If the difference between the planned and tracked schedule is considered significant, corrective actions should be implemented and tracked to closure. Exceptions can be handled through formal deviation or waiver processes with the appropriate approvals.

Budgets

Just as Gantt charts and integrated master schedules are tools for tracking project activities and schedules, *budgets* are tools for tracking project costs and expenditures. The initial planning budget allocates the estimated project costs into cost categories and subcategories. Once the planning budget is baselined, actual costs to date are tracked against each budget category and subcategory. Budget reports can be generated and checked at phase (or process or activity) transition points or at other times (for example, as part of the input into project reviews). If actual costs deviate significantly from planned costs, corrective actions should be implemented and tracked to closure. Exceptions can be handled through formal deviation or waiver processes with the appropriate approvals.

Project Corrective Action

When a major project issue is identified, (for example, the deviation from baselined budgets, baselined schedules, or required quality levels is considered significant) then corrective actions should be identified, implemented, and tracked to closure. When identifying project corrective actions, there are basically two major choices. The first is to return to the plan, that is, to take corrective action that realigns project actuals with the plan and continue with the implementation of the current plan. The second choice is to replan, make the appropriate adjustments to the project plans, and create a new baselined plan. The first choice should always be to return to plan because a project does not occur in a vacuum. For example, customers and users may have made plans or commitments based on the current plan, or other projects may be dependent on this project releasing people or other resources on schedule, and the success of those other projects may be impacted if those people or resources are not available.

The first step in the project corrective action process is to identify the root cause of the issue or variance. Alternate approaches to correcting that root cause should then be considered. A trade-off discussion should be performed to identify and analyze the risks, impacts, and costs/benefits for each approach. It is usually valuable to involve stakeholders affected by the issue in these discussions to obtain a broad perspective on the problem and the risks and impacts of its potential solutions. Based on these discussions, the appropriate alternative solution is selected. If a return-to-plan approach is selected, an action plan should be created that includes:

- Defining specific actions to be taken

- Assigning a person responsible for ensuring that each action is performed

- Estimating effort for each action

- Determining due dates for the completion of each action

- Selecting mechanisms or measures to determine if the desired effect is achieved

If a replan approach is taken, any and all of the project plans may need to be adjusted, including:

- Adjusting the activities (add, change, or delete activities)

- Changing activity duration estimates and schedules

- Changing staff and resource-acquisition plans and/or assignments

- Changing cost estimates and the budget

- Changing the project scope or product requirements

The changed project plans or corrective action plan should be communicated to all affected stakeholders, and their commitment to the plan(s) should be obtained. If replanning is required, and the changes result in the critical path extending past the due date, this activity may include negotiating changes to contracts with the customer and/or suppliers.

When replanning is selected, not only should baselines be created for the new plans, but the original baselines should also be retained. This provides project retrospectives, post-project reviews, and other quality engineering efforts (for example, studies of the accuracy of the project estimation as part of process improvement) a broader, more factual information base for analysis.

If the replan option is selected, corrective action implementation simply means the project continues based on the updated plans. If the return-to-plan option is selected, the implementation step includes:

- Implementing each planned corrective action

- Tracking each corrective action to closure

- Ensuring that corrective action activities are being performed and that their outcomes have the desired impact on the project:

  - Ensuring that the corrective action plan is staying on schedule

  - Monitoring staff and resource estimates against actuals

  - Monitoring cost estimates against actuals

  - If significant problems are identified, repeating the analysis step

2. TRACKING METHODS

> Calculate project-related costs, including earned value, deliverables, productivity, etc., and track the results against project baselines. (Apply)
>
> **Body of Knowledge IV.B.2**

Tracking Earned Value

According to the Project Management Institute (PMI) (PMI 2005), "*Earned value management* (EVM) has proven itself to be one of the most effective performance measurements and feedback tools for managing projects." While many metrics exist that show the details of the project status, earned value metrics provide management with summary-level project metrics that provide insight into the overall performance of the project against its schedule and budget.

The steps involved in performing earned value tracking include:

1. Determining the critical resources to be tracked. Typically, earned value is calculated in dollars and effort (for example, staff-months or engineering-hours).

2. Allocating the resource budget to individual tasks in the work breakdown structure.

3. Calculating the planned value, earned value, and actual value metrics.

4. Analyzing the earned value metric compared to the other metrics to date:

   - If earned value < actual value, then the project is over budget.

   - If earned value < planned value, then the project is behind schedule.

The planned value indicates how far along the work is supposed to be at any given time compared to the baselined plan. The earned value indicates the actual amount of work that has been accomplished at any given time based on the associated baselined plan of budgeted resources. The actual value reflects the amount of resources expended to accomplish the amount of work that has been accomplished at any given time. The basic earned value metrics include:

- Planned value (PV) = the budgeted cost of work scheduled (BCWS)

- Earned value (EV) = the budgeted cost of work performed (BCWP)

- Actual value (AV) = the actual cost of work performed (ACWP)

- Cost variance = BCWP – ACWP

- Cost performance index (CPI) = BCWP/ACWP

- Schedule variance = BCWP – BCWS

- Schedule performance index (SPI) = BCWP/BCWS

There are two basic ways of calculating work performed. The first, and simplest, is to earn back the value only when the task is complete. The second is to earn back a portion of the value based on the percentage of the task that is completed. For example, if a task is scheduled to take 20 days and it is 50 percent done, then the budgeted cost of work performed would be 10 days, which can be compared to the actual number of days spent performing the task to date. This second method is more complex because it requires intermediate reporting of progress to date and cost to date on uncompleted tasks. Another issue with using the second method for software is that tasks may be reported as 90 percent complete for the last 90 percent of the time spent performing them. For most software projects, earned value metrics are calculated using only work completed.

Table 16.1 includes an example of a small five-task project that illustrates the calculation of the earned value metrics. The planned value is equal to the budgeted costs for the tasks scheduled to be completed by now. Since tasks A, B, and C were scheduled to be completed, BCWS = 3 + 12 + 9 = 24 days. The earned value is equal to the budgeted costs for the tasks actually completed. Since tasks A, C, and E are completed, BCWP = 3 + 9 + 8 = 20 days. The actual value is equal to the actual costs for the tasks actually completed. Since tasks A, C, and E are completed, ACWP = 4 + 9 + 6 = 19 days.

A positive cost variance indicates a cost underbudget condition. In this case, the cost variance = BCWP – ACWP = 20 days – 19 days = 1 day to complete the work that has been completed. In other words, 20 days were budgeted to do the work that it only took 19 days to do, or the project is one day under budget. The cost performance index (CPI) = BCWP/ACWP = 20/19 = 105%, or the project is getting 1.05 hours of work for every hour budgeted. A negative schedule variance indicates a behind-schedule condition. In this case, the schedule variance = BCWP – BCWS = 20 days – 24 days = –4 days to complete the work that was scheduled to be completed. In other words, 24 days of work should have been done by now and only 20 days of work has been accomplished, or the project is four days

Table 16.1 Earned value—example.

	Task A	Task B	Task C	Task D	Task E
Status	Done	Started	Done	Not started	Done
Schedule	Done	Done	Done	Not done	Not done
Budget	3 days	12 days	9 days	5 days	8 days
Actual	4 days	2 days	9 days	—	6 days

Table 16.2   Interpreting earned value.

Relationships	Interpretation
ACWP = BCWP = BCWS	No variance—everything is going according to plan
(BCWS = ACWP) < BCWP ACWP < BCWS < BCWP BCWS < ACWP < BCWP	Work is *ahead of schedule,* and costs are *under budget* for work that has been accomplished. Looks good but may lead to missed opportunities.
BCWS < (ACWP = BCWP)	Work is *ahead of schedule,* and costs are being maintained for work that has been accomplished
ACWP < (BCWS = BCWP)	Work is on schedule, and costs are *under budget* for work that has been accomplished
(ACWP = BCWP) < BCWS	Work is *behind schedule,* but costs are being maintained for work that has been accomplished
(BCWS = BCWP) < ACWP	Work is on schedule, but costs are *over budget* for work that has been accomplished
BCWS < BCWP < ACWP	Work is *ahead of schedule,* but costs are *over budget* for work that has been accomplished
ACWP < BCWP < BCWS	Work is *behind schedule,* but costs are *under budget* for work that has been accomplished
BCWP < (BCWS = ACWP) BCWP < BCWS < ACWP BCWP < ACWP < BCWS	Work is *behind schedule,* and costs are *over budget* for work that has been accomplished

behind schedule. The schedule performance index (CPI) = BCWP/BCWS = 20/24 = 83%, or the project is only getting .83 hours of scheduled work done for every hour worked.

The current values of the earned value metrics provide a snapshot of the current project status. Table 16.2 includes information that can be used to interpret the earned value metrics.

Trending the earned value metrics over time can provide even more valuable insight into the project. As illustrated in Figure 16.5, the planned value (BCWS) can be plotted out to the end of the project based on the current schedule. The earned value (BCWP) and actual value (ACWP) can then be plotted over time. Remember that the cost variance = BCWP – ACWP. As can be seen on this graph, not only is this project over budget and behind schedule at this time, but the trends also show that things are getting worse (the variances are increasing) as the project progresses. The earned value and actual value curves can also be extrapolated to determine when the project will be done and how much it will cost based on current trends.

If the cost or schedule variance is considered significant, corrective actions should be implemented and tracked to closure. Exceptions can be handled through formal deviation or waiver processes with the appropriate approvals.

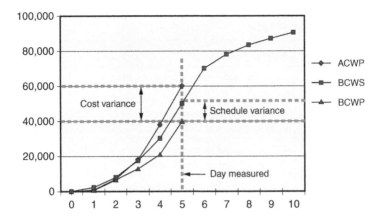

Figure 16.5 Interpreting earned value.

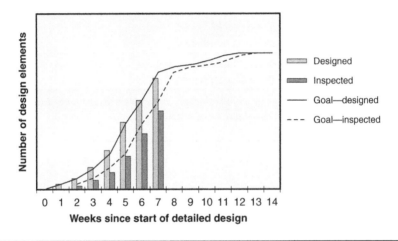

Figure 16.6 Design deliverable status–example.

Tracking Deliverables

The ultimate goal of any project is to create releasable deliverables. Therefore, tracking the creation and verification of these deliverables against the baselined plans provides valuable information on the health of the project. Deliverables metrics help keep the product component of the project management trilogy of cost, schedule, and product visible to the project team and management.

The design deliverable status metric illustrated in Figure 16.6 can be used to track and control the number of design elements (modules, classes, data elements) from the architectural design that have completed detailed design and the number of detailed designs for those design elements that have been inspected against the planned goals needed in order to keep the detailed design process on schedule. This type of graph can also provide a summary view that can get lost in the details of a Gantt chart. For example, in this graph it is easy to see that while

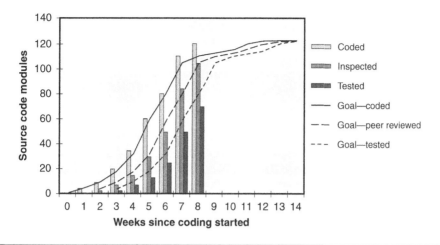

Figure 16.7   Code deliverable status–example.

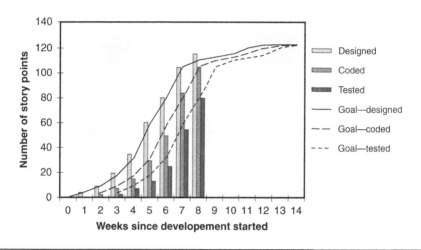

Figure 16.8   Story point deliverable status–example.

creating the detailed designs is on schedule, getting them peer reviewed is currently behind schedule.

As illustrated in Figure 16.7, similar graphs can be created for code deliverable status metrics that track the status of writing, peer reviewing, and unit testing code against the schedule to keep the code and unit test process on schedule. In this example, the project is ahead of schedule in getting source code modules coded, on schedule for peer reviewing them, but falling behind the goal for getting the code unit tested.

As illustrated in Figure 16.8, similar metrics can be developed to track the status of whatever is viewed as a deliverable. In this example, the graph tracks story points as the deliverable. It looks at the schedule progress of the story points as they are designed, coded, and tested.

Depending on the project, it might also be useful to track the completion status of other possible deliverables, including documentation, training materials, features, functions, product requirements, or use cases (or use case steps). Each project should decide what deliverables are appropriate to track for that project.

Tracking Productivity

Productivity is typically measured in terms of the amount of work product produced per staff effort. As illustrated in Table 16.3, different metrics can be used depending on the type of work.

From a project tracking and control perspective, an assumed productivity level is used when estimating project effort and schedule values. The project risk is that the productivity level will be significantly less than this assumed value. Therefore, as illustrated by the example in Figure 16.9, a metric can be used to track the variance between planned and actual productivity levels if this is considered a high-priority risk for the project.

Table 16.3   Productivity metric–examples.

Type of work	Productivity metric
Eliciting, analyzing, and specifying requirements	Number of requirements/effort
Writing user documentation	Number of pages/effort
Developing software component	Function points/effort LOC/effort
Testing	Test cases executed/effort Test cases passed/effort Defects found/effort

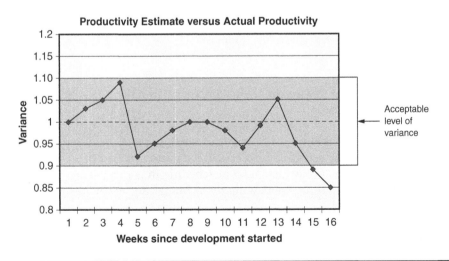

Figure 16.9   Productivity metric–example.

Tracking Resources and Staffing

Resource utilization metrics are used to track and control the utilization of various resources during the implementation of the software project in order to ensure that adequate resources exist to meet schedules and to monitor resource overruns that may affect the budget. Examples of these metrics might include:

- Number of personnel assigned to the project (actuals versus planned)
- Number of staff hours expended on the project (actuals versus planned)
- Number of test bed hours (available/utilized versus planned)
- Number of square feet of office space (available/utilized versus planned)
- Number of dollars spent (actuals versus planned)

As illustrated in the example resource utilization metric in Figure 16.10, the actual resource utilization (solid line) can be tracked against the predicted resource utilization from the initial plan (dotted line). The planned resource utilization should be updated based on what is actually occurring on the project. This new current plan (dashed line) can also be included in the metric.

A complementary metric to tracking the number of people or staff hours available to the project is the tracking of *staff turnover*. Because of the learning curve, even if an experienced engineer can be replaced immediately, there will be an impact to productivity until the replacement is up to speed on the processes and work products.

In the example metric illustrated in Figure 16.11, a threshold has been set so that the metric can be used as a risk trigger. In this example the project manager planned the project effort and schedule based on historic turnover rate for similar projects. By tracking against that threshold, contingency plans can be implemented if the turnover rate exceeds 15 percent.

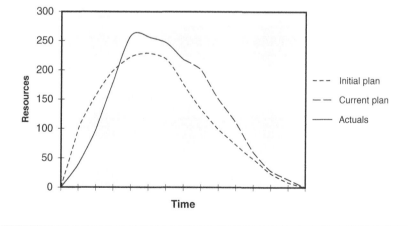

Figure 16.10 Resource utilization metric—example.

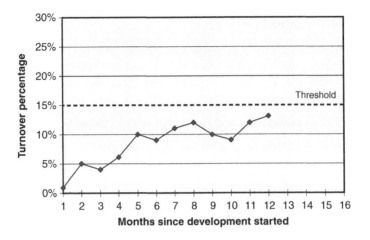

Figure 16.11 Staff turnover metric—example.

Selecting Project Metrics

Chapter 19 describes a sampling of other product and process metrics, and cost-of-quality metrics are discussed in Chapter 7. Any or all of these metrics may be useful to the project team and management in estimating, tracking, and controlling their project. As part of project planning, each project should use the goal/question/metric paradigm, as discussed in Chapter 19, or a similar process to select which metrics will be collected and tracked based on the goals and information needs of that project.

3. PROJECT REVIEWS

> Use various types of project reviews such as phase-end, management, and retrospectives or post-project reviews to assess project performance and status, to review issues and risks, and to discover and capture lessons learned from the project. (Apply)
>
> **Body of Knowledge IV.B.3**

Project reviews bring project stakeholders together to discuss the project and exchange information. The purposes of holding these project reviews are to:

- Determine if the overall status of the project work to date is acceptable

- Appraise the progress and performance of what is actually being accomplished on the project compared to the plans

- Provide a basis for management and engineering decisions on how to proceed

- Identify potential problems (risks) and deal with them before they negatively impact project success

- Ensure that necessary corrective action plans to control the project are put in place before unrecoverable harm is done to the project, and track those plans to closure

- Provide and receive basic project status and communications

Phase Gate Reviews

Phase gate reviews, also called *phase-end, phase transition,* or *major milestone* reviews, are event-driven reviews that are held at major milestones in the project. The purpose of these reviews is to act as a quality gate or checkpoint to ensure that all required activities have been completed satisfactorily and that all work products have achieved the quality levels required to move into the next major phase or activity of the project. Examples of these reviews include:

- Software requirements review

- Architectural design review

- Detailed design reviews

- Test readiness reviews

- Ready-to-ship review

The *requirements review* is held at the transition from the requirements activities (phase) to the architectural design activities (phase). Examples of typical milestone-specific work products reviewed at this meeting include:

- Satisfactory completion of the software requirements specification

- Results of software requirements specification peer reviews

- Traceability of software requirements to their source (for example, system requirements, use cases, business rules, standards, or regulations)

The *architectural design review,* also called the *preliminary* or *high-level design review,* is held at the transition from the architectural design activities (phase) to the detailed design activities (phase). Examples of typical milestone-specific work products reviewed include:

- Satisfactory completion of the software architecture specification

- Satisfactory completion of any external interface specifications

- Traceability of software architectural design elements to software requirements

- Results of software architecture and external interface specification peer reviews

The *detailed design review,* also called the *critical design review,* is held at the transition from the detailed design activities (phase) to implementation activities (code and unit test phase). There may be multiple detailed design reviews, one for each of the major design elements. Examples of typical milestone-specific work products reviewed include:

- Satisfactory completion of the detailed software design

- Traceability of detailed design elements to software architectural design elements

- Satisfactory completion of software test plans and test cases

- Satisfactory completion of system test plans and test cases

- Satisfactory completion of acceptance test plans and test cases

- Peer review results (detailed design, test plans, test cases)

Test readiness reviews are held at the beginning of the major test cycles (for example, integration test, software test, system test, acceptance test, beta test). Examples of typical milestone-specific work products reviewed at an integration test readiness review include:

- Traceability of integration test cases to software design elements

- Results of peer reviews (code and integration test case and plans)

- Unit test results, including execution and pass/fail status of unit-test cases

- Unresolved defect reports

Examples of typical milestone-specific work products reviewed at a software/system test readiness review include:

- Traceability of software/system test cases to software requirements

- Integration test results, including execution and pass/fail status of integration test cases

- User documentation (user's manual and other user-deliverable documentation, including the installation instructions) and peer review results

- Unresolved defect reports

The *ready-to-ship reviews,* also called *ready-to-release reviews,* are held at the transition from the final test cycle to release (deployment) of the completed software or system. Examples of typical milestone-specific work products reviewed include:

- Software/system, acceptance, and/or beta test results, including execution and pass/fail status of test cases

- Satisfactory completion of the final user manual and other user-deliverable documentation, including the installation instructions (with any corrections to defects found in testing cycles)

- Unresolved defect reports

For scrum projects, a close equivalent to the ready-to-ship reviews is the *sprint review meeting*. On the last day of the sprint, the scrum master facilitates the sprint review meeting where the scrum team presents the working product increment to the product owner, management, customers, and other stakeholders. This informal meeting is limited to no more than four hours in duration. The scrum team presents the functionality developed during the sprint to the other attendees for delivery, assessment, and acceptance of the product increment. The attendees collaboratively decide what to do next. Choices include determining whether:

- To implement the current functionality in production

- New functionality needs to be added to the product backlog

- Functionality that was planned for the sprint but not delivered as expected should go back into the product backlog

- To continue the project by holding the next sprint planning meeting or to terminate the project

Project Team Reviews

Project team reviews are held periodically throughout the project based on its size, complexity, and risk (for example, daily, weekly, or monthly). The project manager usually runs these meetings. Attendance at these meetings typically includes project team members (or representatives of each subteam for large projects), project support personnel assigned to the project (for example, configuration management, quality assurance, and verification and validation team members), and representatives from other stakeholder groups (for example, marketing, hardware engineering, technical publications). Depending on the project, external stakeholders (for example, customers and suppliers) may also attend these meetings.

Project team reviews are held to monitor the current status and results of the project against the project's documented estimates, plans, commitments, and requirements and to identify project issues in a timely manner so that effective control actions can be taken. A sample agenda for a project team meeting might include:

- Project accomplishments for the reporting period

- Changes to the project objectives or business climate, if any

- Current project status:

  - Upcoming tasks and milestones

  - Late activities—why they are late, what the impact is, what recovery plan and help are needed

  - Dependencies between groups

  - Staffing and other resource availability

  - Technical status: functionality and quality

Part IV.B.3

    – Cost or budget status

    – Current risk activities and new/closed risks

    – Current corrective action status

- Issues, conflicts, or problems

- Review of assigned action items

On scrum projects, the team conducts daily meetings, called *scrums*. Schwaber (2002) states that the primary purpose of the scrum is to have each team member answer three questions:

- "What have you done since the last scrum?"

- "What will you do between now and the next scrum?"

- "What got in your way of doing the work?"

Scrums help the team keep continuous track of the progress of the scrum team, plan ongoing activities, and discuss and control problems and other issues including deficiencies or impediments in the software development process or engineering practices. Scrums are short, stand-up meetings (people literally stand up—no sitting in chairs allowed) of no more than 15 minutes in duration. The scrum master follows up outside the scrum as needed with the appropriate individuals to handle any identified issues or actions. The scrum master and scrum team actively participate in the scrums. Other individuals may attend the scrum for informational purposes but do not actively participate.

Management Reviews

Management review meetings are also held periodically throughout the project based on its size, complexity, and risk but usually less often than project team meetings (for example, monthly or quarterly). Attendees at these meetings include senior management, project managers (several projects may be discussed in these meetings, especially if those projects are being coordinated as a program), project team representatives, management from project support groups, and management from other stakeholder groups affected by the project (for example, marketing, hardware engineering, technical publications). Depending on the project, external stakeholders (for example, customers and suppliers) may also attend these meetings.

    Management review meetings are held to provide management awareness of and visibility into software project activities. A sample agenda for a management meeting might include:

- Technical (functionality and quality), cost/budget, staffing, and schedule performance summaries (typically presented at the major feature or major milestone level)

- Changes to the project objective or business climate, if any

- Review of high-priority software project risks

- Issues, conflicts, or problems not resolved at lower levels

- Review of assigned action items

Post-Project Reviews and Retrospectives

Post-project reviews, also called *post-mortems* or *retrospectives,* are meetings held at or near the end of the project to provide a mechanism for learning from the project experiences, both good and bad, and feed those lessons back into future projects. These reviews examine what went well on the project and determine the best ways to repeat these successes on future projects. These reviews also examine what went wrong and determine the best ways to keep those problems from happening again in the future. Post-project reviews should be held whether or not the project was successful. In fact, in some cases more may be learned from a failed project than a successful one—like how not to even start one of these projects again.

At least one representative from each major group or team involved in or affected by the project should be invited to participate in the post-project review. Norm Kerth (2001) expands this by recommending that everyone on the project team should participate. Managers are typically omitted from participation because they may inhibit the candidness of the review team or the free flow of ideas. Management can hold a separate post-project management review if it is seen as value added.

Each participant should prepare for the review by completing a post-project review form. Forms are designed as checklists to help guide participants through thinking about project successes and problems and about suggestions for future improvements. Forms can be generalized, or different forms can be customized to specific areas (for example, project planning, software design, coding, and system test). Forms should be tailored to meet needs and characteristics of the specific project. Participants should focus on their personal areas of expertise and work assignments for the project being evaluated.

The review meeting atmosphere must encourage full participation and open sharing of views and ideas. During the meeting, questions should be encouraged and different views should be expected and encouraged. Having a good facilitator for the meeting can help keep it focused on the project's processes and products and not on people. The focus should also be on lessons learned and not on laying blame.

The review meeting includes the creation of a list of what went right on the project, with participants presenting their ideas from the preprepared review forms and adding new thoughts based on actively listening to the ideas of other participants. It may be helpful to order this discussion in general life cycle order. The team can then prioritize the "what went right" list by the benefit to the project through the use of multivoting or other nominal group techniques. This activity is then repeated by creating a "what went wrong" list prioritized by negative impact on the project. Always do the positives first, because once people start talking about the negatives, it is hard to get them thinking positively again.

After these lists are created, the team selects high-priority items from the lists that need to be addressed. They develop a proposal to management on lessons learned and recommendations on how best to incorporate those lessons into future project activities. For example, additional training might be recommended to implement one lesson, or updates to the quality management system (for example, to processes, templates, or checklists) might be recommended to implement other lessons learned.

The results and recommendations from the post-project review meeting are then presented to management. Management must commit to the recommendations for change and provide time, people, and resources to implement those changes. The lessons learned must be propagated into improvements on future projects for the post-project review meeting to be truly effective.

Scrum projects also hold retrospectives. After the completion of the sprint and before the next sprint planning meeting, the scrum master facilitates the sprint retrospective meeting with the scrum team. The intent of the *sprint retrospective meeting* is to identify lessons learned from the completed sprint and determine process improvement actions to improve future sprints. This informal meeting is limited to no more than three hours in duration. During this retrospective, the scrum team reviews what went well with the sprint so that positive lessons learned can be repeated in future sprints. They also review what did not work well on the sprint and determine process improvement actions that they need to add to the product backlog to correct those issues in future sprints.

While these post-project reviews and retrospectives help future projects, industry experts (for example, Rothman[2007] and Derby [2006]) recommend that interim retrospectives be used throughout the project to feed lessons learned back into improvements as the project progresses. That way the project benefits directly from those lessons. Improvement comes from learning about the causes of problems (or potential ones) and finding a solution to correct (or avoid) those problems. The extreme programming (XP) principle called *reflection* asks the team to continuously consider what they are doing and why. This provides input and feedback that allows immediate reuse of good ideas and quick elimination of problems. "Good teams don't just do their work, they think about how they are working and why they are working. Don't try to hide mistakes—expose them and learn from them. Learning is action reflected" (Beck 2005).

4. PROGRAM REVIEWS

> Define and describe various methods
> for reviewing and assessing programs
> in terms of their performance, technical
> accomplishments, resource utilization, etc.
> (Understand)
>
> **Body of Knowledge IV.B.4**

The PMI (2008) defines a *program* as "a group of related projects managed in a coordinated way to obtain benefits and control not available from managing them individually." Tracking and controlling a program involves gathering and consolidating status information from the individual projects being managed as parts of that program.

Program review meetings are held periodically throughout the program based on its size, complexity, and risk. The program manager or a representative from the program management office typically runs these meetings. Attendees at these meetings include the project managers of the various projects that are part of the program. In addition, team representatives from various projects, management from program support groups, and management from other stakeholder groups affected by the program (for example, marketing, hardware engineering, technical publications, suppliers, and customers) may also be in attendance. This may include acquisition project managers, supplier project managers, and other individuals from supplier-run projects as well, if the program includes acquisition projects. Supplier personnel may only be invited to attend portions of the project review if confidential information or trade secrets are being discussed.

Program review meetings are held to track and control the coordinated program activities. These meetings examine aggregated program performance information from the cost, schedule, technical, resource, staffing, scope, risk, and supplier management information from the individual project and non-project activities. A sample agenda for a program review meeting might include:

- Program accomplishments for the reporting period

- Changes to the program objectives or business climate, if any

- Current program status:

  - Schedule and milestone status from individual projects and non-project-related program activities

  - Late activities—why they are late, what the impact is, what recovery plan and help are needed

  - Dependencies between projects and groups

  - Staffing and other resource availability

  - Technical status: functionality and quality

  - Cost or budget status

  - Program risks and current risk-handling activities

  - Current corrective action status

- Issues, conflicts, or problems that can not be handled at the individual project level

- Review of assigned action items

Chapter 17

C. Risk Management

There are many risks involved in creating high-quality software on time and within budget. With ever-increasing software complexity and increasing demand for bigger, better, and faster product, the software industry is a high-risk business. When teams don't manage risk, they leave projects vulnerable to factors that can cause major rework, major cost or schedule overruns, or complete project failure. Adopting software risk management processes is a step that can help effectively manage software development and maintenance initiatives. However, in order for it to be worthwhile to take on these risks, the organization must be compensated, with a perceived opportunity to obtain a reward. The greater the risk, the greater the opportunity must be to make it worthwhile to take the chance. In software development the possibility of reward is high, but so is the potential for disaster. Risk exists whether it is acknowledged or not. People can stick their heads in the sand and ignore the risks, but this can lead to unpleasant surprises when some of those risks turn into actual problems. The need for software risk management is illustrated in Gilb's risk principle: "If you don't actively attack the risks, they will actively attack you" (Gilb 1988). In order to successfully manage a software project and reap the rewards, software practitioners must learn to identify, analyze, and control these risks.

In the software industry the future seems to be coming at us at an ever-increasing rate. Effective software managers and practitioners proactively think about all the possibilities that the future may bring, but those possibilities have uncertain outcomes. These possibilities are called *opportunities* (the Project Management Institute [2008] refers to them as *"positive risks"*) if positive outcomes are expected. For example, an opportunity exists to successfully complete a software project and make a substantial profit, or an opportunity exists to introduce a new product into the marketplace first and capture the lion's share of the market. These possibilities are called *risks* (or *negative risks* [PMI 2008]) if negative outcomes are expected. For example, the risk exists of not successfully completing that same software project and losing the investment, or the risk exists of the competition beating an organization to the marketplace with a new product and that organization losing market share. To quote Tom DeMarco, "Moving aggressively after opportunity means running toward rather than away from risk" (Hall 1998).

As illustrated in Figure 17.1, good risk management practices are a balancing act between the risk and the opportunity. While this chapter focuses on negative risk management, the associated opportunity also needs to be identified and managed. Not paying attention to opportunities and balancing opportu-

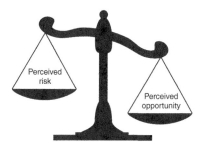

• Probability of problem	• Probability of reward
• Loss associated with the problem	• Benefit associated with the reward

Figure 17.1   Risk/opportunity balance.

nity management along with risk management can lead to the loss of important opportunities.

Different people and different organizations have different risk tolerance levels. A person or organization's risk tolerance influences their perceived risk/opportunity balance point. For risk-takers the sheer pleasure of taking the risk adds weight to the opportunity side of the risk/opportunity balance. Risk-takers are more willing to take a risk even if the financial, economic, material, or other gains are less than the loss associated with the potential problem. Risk-avoiders are averse to taking risks, and the mere presence of the risk adds weight to the risk side of the risk/opportunity balance. Risk-avoiders need additional financial, economic, material, or other incentives to take on the risk. People or organizations that are risk-neutral look for at least a balance between the risks and opportunities. They have no emotional investment in either avoiding or taking the risk.

So, what are risks? IEEE (2006a) defines a *risk* as "the likelihood of an event, hazard, threat, or situation occurring and its undesirable consequences." A risk is simply the possibility of a problem occurring some time in the future. "Risk, like status, is relative to a specific goal. Whereas status is a measure of progress toward a goal, risk is a measure of the probability and consequences of not achieving the goal" (Hall 1998). For example, every time a person crosses the street, that person runs the risk of being hit by a car. As illustrated in Figure 17.2, a risk starts when the commitment associated with that risk is made; the risk of getting hit by a car in the street does not exist until the person steps into the street. Of course there is the risk of getting hit by a car while standing on the sidewalk, but that is an entirely different risk. A project doesn't have the risks of Acme delivering a low-reliability software component or of Acme being late in delivering that software component until the project selects Acme as its subcontractor for that component. If the project chooses to build the software component in-house, a different set of risks exists. A risk ends when one of two things happens:

1. Bang!! The person gets hit in the middle of the street by a car. The problem actually occurs. It is now a problem and is no longer a risk.

2. The person safely steps onto the sidewalk on the other side of the street. The risk disappears since there is no longer the possibility of a future problem because the goal has been obtained.

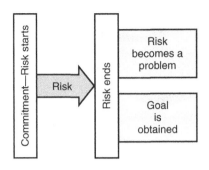

Figure 17.2 Risk duration.

Table 17.1 Project management versus risk management.

Project management	Risk management
Designed to address general or generic risks	Designed to focus on risks unique to each project
Looks at the big picture and plans for details	Looks at potential problems and plans for contingencies
Plans what should happen and looks for ways to make it happen	Evaluates what could happen and looks for ways to minimize the damage
Plans for success	Plans to manage and mitigate potential causes of failure

Acme either delivers a high-quality product component on time (goal is reached) or they don't (problem occurs). Before it turns into an actual problem, "a risk is just an abstraction. It's something that may affect your project, but it also may not. There is a possibility that ignoring it will not come back to bite you" (DeMarco 2003). If a person ignores the risk and runs into the street without looking, there can be dire consequences. There may not be a problem every time—in fact that person may get away with it over and over again. But then it only takes one instance of the problem occurring for disaster to happen.

There are basic day-to-day risks that are generic to almost all software projects. For example, there will always be some level of requirements change or staff turnover risk on every project. These types of basic risks are addressed by good project management techniques. For example, an experienced project manager considers average requirements change and staff turnover levels when doing estimations for project scheduling, costs, and staffing. Risk management deals with the large, unique risks for the project that have the potential of impacting project success. For example, risk management deals with the risk that there will be more requirements change or staff turnover than planned for, or that one of the critical staff members will leave the project. In good risk management practices the "emphasis is shifted from crisis management to anticipatory management" (Down 1994). Table 17.1 shows several ways in which risk management differs from project management:

1. RISK MANAGEMENT METHODS

> Use risk management techniques (assess, prevent, mitigate, transfer) to evaluate project risks. (Evaluate)
>
> **Body of Knowledge IV.C.1**

Risk Management Process

Software Engineering Institute's (SEI) Capability Maturity Model Integration (CMMI) for Development has a risk management process area and states that its purpose "is to identify potential problems before they occur so that risk-handling activities can be planned and invoked as needed across the life of the product or project to mitigate adverse impacts on achieving objectives" (SEI 2006). Risks should be taken into consideration when estimates are made of the initial project effort, schedule, and budget. Risk management is an ongoing process that is implemented as part of the initial project planning activities. Risk management must also be an ongoing part of managing any software development project. It is designed to be a continuous feedback loop where additional information, including risk status and project status, are utilized to refine the project's risk list and risk management plans.

The *risk management process* is illustrated in Figure 17.3. This process starts with the identification of a list of potential risks. Each of these risks is then analyzed and prioritized. A risk management plan is created to identify risk mitigation actions for high-priority risks. These plans can identify *risk-handling* options, also called *risk response strategies,* to avoid the risk, to learn more about the risks, to transfer the risk, or to take mitigation actions that will reduce the probability of the risk occurring and/or reduce the impact if the risk turns into a problem. These

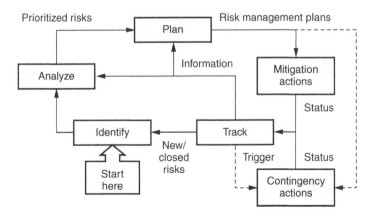

Figure 17.3   Risk management process.

plans can also include contingency actions that will be taken only if the associated risk triggers indicate that the risk is turning into a problem or the problem actually occurs. The mitigation part of the plan is then implemented and the planned risk-reduction actions are taken. The tracking step involves monitoring the status of known risks as well as the results of risk-reduction actions and other project activities. If a trigger indicates that is risk is turning into a problem, the corresponding contingency plans are implemented. As new status reports and information are obtained, additional risk analysis is done and/or the risk management plans are updated accordingly. Tracking may also result in the addition of newly identified risks or in the closure of known risks.

The risk management process is an ongoing part of managing the software development and maintenance projects. In fact, DeMarco and Lister (DeMarco 2003) call risk management "project management for adults." Small children run into the street after the ball, but as they grow up they learn to look both ways first. Risk management is designed to be a continuous feedback loop where additional information and risk status are utilized to refine the project's risk list and risk management plans.

Risk Identification

During the first step in the software risk management process, the project team risks are identified and added to the list of known risks. *Risk identification* requires a fear-free environment where risks can be identified and discussed openly. The output of this step is a list of project-specific risks that have the potential of compromising the project's success. The project team should be as thorough as possible on the first round of risk identification but not obsessive. It's probably impossible to identify all of the project risks on the initial pass through the risk management process. The team just doesn't have enough information yet. There are technical requirements yet to elicit, staffing issues yet to decide, design decisions yet to be made, and all kinds of commitments yet to be made. The risk identification step will need to be revisited repeatedly throughout the project as more information is obtained from project execution, tracking, and control.

There are many techniques for identifying risks, including interviewing, reporting, decomposition, critical path analysis, assumption analysis, and utilization of risk taxonomies.

The first technique is interviewing or brainstorming with project personnel, customers, users, and suppliers. Since stakeholders at different levels inside and outside the development organization have different perspectives on the project, one goal of risk identification is to involve a variety of stakeholders in the risk process in order to obtain a broader, more complete perspective of the project's risks. Using open-ended questions such as the following can help identify potential areas of risk:

- What problems do you see in the future for this project?

- Are there areas of this project that you feel are poorly defined?

- What interface issues still need to be defined?

- What requirements exist that the team isn't sure how to implement?

- What concerns does the team have about their ability to meet the required quality levels? Performance levels? Reliability levels? Security levels? Safety levels?

- What tools or techniques might this project require that it doesn't have?

- What new or improved technologies does this project require? Does the project team have the expertise to implement those technologies?

- What difficulties do you see in working with this customer? Subcontractor? Partner?

Another risk identification technique is voluntary reporting, where any individual who identifies a risk is encouraged to bring that risk to management's attention. This requires the complete elimination of the "shoot the messenger" syndrome. It avoids the temptation to assign risk-reduction actions to the person who identified the risk. Risks can also be identified through required reporting mechanisms such as status reports or project reviews.

A third risk identification technique is decomposition. As the product is being decomposed during the requirements and design activities, another opportunity exists for risk identifications. Every TBD ("to be done/determined") is a potential risk. As Ould (1990) states, "The most important thing about planning is writing down what you *don't know*, because what you don't know is what you must find out." Feasibility or lack of stability in areas of the requirements or design can signal areas of risk. A requirement or design element may also be risky if it requires the use of new and/or innovative technologies, techniques, languages, and/or hardware. However, even if the technologies, techniques, languages, and/or hardware have been around in the industry for a while, there still may be a risk if this is the first time this organization has attempted to utilize them. For example, Java has been around for a while, but if this is the first time this organization has used Java on a project, there may be risks because of lack of expertise that might affect the quality of the end product or impact the schedule because of a learning curve. Remember, a risk starts when a commitment is made. As the software requirements are being defined (or being allocated from the system-level requirements), the project is committing to what is going to be developed. As the software is being designed, the project is committing to choices about how the software is going to be developed. As the project makes these commitments, the team needs to keep asking themselves "What risks are associated with the commitment to meet this requirement or implement this design element?" in order to help identify the associated risks.

Decomposition can also come in the form of work breakdown structures during project planning, which can also help identify areas of uncertainty for specific subprojects, tasks, or activities that may need to be recorded as risks. Are there any feasibility, staffing, training, or resource issues associated with each identified activity?

A fourth risk identification technique is for the project team to remain on the alert to identify risks as critical path analysis is performed on the project schedule.

Part IV.C.1

Any possibility of schedule slippage on the critical path must be considered a risk because it directly impacts the ability to meet schedule.

A fifth risk identification technique is the analysis of process, product, or planning assumptions. Example assumptions might include the assumption that hardware will be available by the system test date or that three additional experienced C++ programmers will be hired by the time coding starts. If these assumptions prove to be false, what potential problems might occur? In other words, what are the risks associated with each assumption? If there are not any risks associated with an assumption, then it may not be a real assumption.

The final risk identification technique is to use a risk taxonomy. If any experienced software person on the project is asked "What will go wrong on this project?" they will be able to answer with uncanny accuracy. Why? Because they know what went wrong on the last project and the one before that and the one before that. The problems from previous projects are some of the best indicators of the risks on new or current projects. This is why risk taxonomies are such a great tool. Risk taxonomies are lists of problems that have occurred on other projects and can be used as checklists to help ensure that all potential risks have been considered. Risk taxonomies can also be used during the interview process to help develop interview questions. Examples of risk taxonomies include:

- Software Engineering Institute's Taxonomy-Based Risk Identification report, which covers 13 major risk areas with about 200 questions (SEI 1993)

- Capers Jones's entire book, *Assessment and Control of Software Risks*, which could be viewed as a risk taxonomy (Jones 1994)

- Steve McConnell's book, *Rapid Development: Taming Wild Software Schedules*, which also includes an extensive list of what he labels as "potential schedule risks" (McConnell 1996)

When an organization is just starting their risk management efforts, they can start with taxonomies such as these from the literature. These industry taxonomies should then be evolved and tailored over time to match the actual problem types encountered by the organization. One last word of caution: when using risk taxonomies, a delicate balance must be maintained between making sure that known issues are handled and focusing so much on the items from the list that new and novel risks are missed.

Once a risk is identified it should be communicated to everyone who needs to know about it. This includes management, people who could be affected if the risk became a problem, people who will analyze the risk, and people who will take action to mitigate the risk. It may also need to be communicated to customers, suppliers, or vendors. According to Hall (1998), "communication of identified risks is best when it is both verbal and written."

Verbal communications allow discussion of the risk that can help clarify the understanding of the risk. The listener has a chance to ask questions and interact with the person communicating the risk. This two-way interaction may result in additional information about the risk, its sources, and its consequences.

Written communications result in historical records that can be referred to in the future. Everyone who received the written communication has identical information about the risk. Written communications can also allow for easy dissemination of the risk information if the people who need the information are in multiple locations. The creation of an online risk database may provide a consistent and easily accessed mechanism for providing written risk information.

A written *risk statement* consists of the risk condition and its potential consequences for the project. The *condition* is a brief statement of the potential problem that "describes the key circumstances, situation, and so on, causing concern, doubt, anxiety, or uncertainty" (Dorofee 1996). The *consequence* is a brief statement that describes immediate loss or negative outcome if the condition turns into an actual problem for the project.

Figure 17.4 includes two example risk statements. In example 1, a software quality engineer (SQE) reviewed the subcontractor portion of the project plan and performed an assumption analysis. The SQE noticed that the project was assuming that Acme would deliver software of the required reliability and that no provisions had been made in the schedule to deal with major defects found in the XYZ controller.

For example 1 the risk statement (highlighted in gray) would be: *Acme may not deliver the subcontracted XYZ controller component with the required software reliability and, as a result, we will spend additional effort with Acme on defect resolution and regression testing.*

For example 2, during the requirements inspection process, the inspection team noticed a TDB in the interface specification requirements for the notification controller. This controller is an external piece of equipment that the system must interface with to send delinquent notices as part of the billing system. For example 2 the risk statement would be: *The interface specification to the notification controller may not be defined before the scheduled time to design its driver and, as a result, the schedule will slip for designing the notification driver.* Note that in these examples,

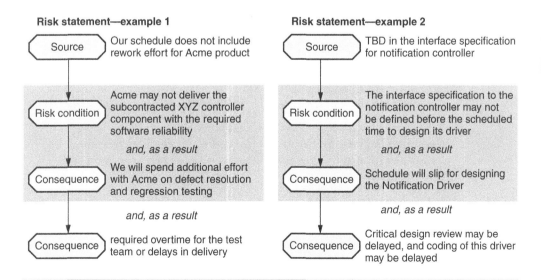

Figure 17.4   Risk statement—examples.

the source of the risk is not part of the risk statement and neither are any subsequent consequences to the initial consequences.

Types of Software Risks

Software development and maintenance may encounter various types of risks. Note that this list of risks by type could be used as a high-level risk taxonomy. Types of risks include:

- *Technical risks.* Examples include potential problems with:
  - Incomplete or ambiguous requirements or design
  - Excessive constraints
  - Large size or complexity
  - New languages, tools, or platforms
  - New or changing methods, standards, or processes
  - Dependencies on organizations outside the direct control of the project team

  Technical risks also include risks related to the operations of the product in the field, including potential problems related to reliability, functionality, safety, or security.

- *Management risks.* Examples include lack of planning, lack of management experience and training, incomplete or inadequate planning, communications problems, organizational issues, issues with customer or supplier relations, lack of authority, and control problems.

- *Financial risks.* Include cash flow, capital and budgetary issues, and return-on-investment constraints.

- *Contractual and legal risks.* Examples include changing requirements, market-driven schedules, government regulation, and product warranty issues.

- *Personnel risks.* Examples include staffing lags, experience and training problems, ethical and moral issues, staff conflicts, and productivity issues.

- *Other resource risks.* Examples include unavailability or late delivery of equipment and supplies, inadequate tools, inadequate facilities, distributed locations, unavailability of computer resources, and slow response times.

Risk Analysis

The primary goal of the *risk analysis* step of the risk management process is to analyze the identified list of risks and prioritize those risks for further planning and action. During the risk analysis step, each risk is assessed to determine its context, estimated probability, estimated loss, and time frame.

A risk's context includes the events, conditions, constraints, assumptions, circumstances, contributing factors, project interrelationships, and related issues that can lead to the potential for a problem. The risk's context provides all of the additional information that surrounds and affects the risk and helps determine its probability and potential loss. Documenting the risk's context can be especially useful after time has passed and a risk is being reevaluated. Gaps between the original documented context and the current situation can help the project staff better understand how or if the risk has changed.

An estimated *risk probability* is the likelihood that the risk will turn into a problem. The *risk loss* is the estimated impact or consequences to the project if the risk does turn into a problem. Losses can come in the form of additional costs (dollars or effort), required changes to the schedule, or technical effects on the product being produced (for example, its functionality, performance, or quality). Losses can also result from other types of impacts. For example, the organization could lose corporate goodwill, market share, or employee satisfaction. Not only should each risk be assessed individually, but the interrelationships between risks must also be assessed to determine if compounding risk conditions exist that magnify losses.

A risk's significant time frames are when the risk needs to be addressed and when the risk may turn into a problem. A risk associated with time frames in the near future may have higher priority than similar risks associated with later time frames, even if it has a lower risk exposure.

The level of formal risk assessment needed for a project can range from the simple qualitative assignment of each risk to a category (for example, high, medium, or low) to the use of complex quantitative mathematical modeling (for example, Monte Carlo modeling). The project manager and/or project team should use the simplest method available that allows them to make reliable risk-planning decisions. Different risks may be assessed at different levels of formality. For example, a high-impact risk with a high probability may require very formal and detailed analysis to determine the appropriate mitigation plans. However, knowing that a risk is unlikely to turn into a problem and that it will have very little impact if it does may be all the team needs to know about that risk.

Boehm (1989) defines a risk exposure equation to help quantitatively establish risk priorities. Risk exposure measures the impact of a risk in terms of its expected value. *Risk exposure* (RE) is defined as the probability of an undesired outcome (the problem actually occurs) times the expected loss (cost of the impact or consequences) if that outcome occurs.

$$RE = \text{Probability (UO)} \times \text{Loss (UO), where UO} = \text{Unexpected outcome}$$

For example, if a risk is estimated to have a 10 percent chance of turning into a problem with an estimated impact of $100,000, then the risk exposure for that risk is 10% × $100,000 = $10,000. Comparing the risk exposure measurement for various risks can help identify those risks with the greatest probable negative impact to the project and thus help establish which risks are candidates for further action.

The analysis step in the risk management process is used to prioritize the list of risks. Risks can be prioritized using just their risk exposures or by using a combination of their risk exposures and time frames. When risks need to be prioritized on multiple criteria (risk exposures), a prioritization matrix can be used such as the one in Table 17.2. In this example, a risk exposure score of 1 to 5 (5 being the highest) is used, as illustrated in Table 17.3.

Since resource limitations rarely allow the consideration of all risks, the prioritized list of risks is used to identify the top risks for risk mitigation planning and action. Other risks may simply have tracking mechanisms put in place to monitor them closely. At the lowest priorities, other risks are simply documented for possible future consideration. This prioritized list of risks should be reviewed periodically. Based on changing conditions, additional information, the identification of new risk items, or simply timing, the list of prioritized risks may require periodic updates.

Table 17.2 Risk exposure prioritization matrix—example.

| | Criteria and weights | | | | |
	Technical exposure (.25)	Cost exposure (.15)	Schedule exposure (.20)	Customer satisfaction (.40)	Total
Risk 1	1	3	2	4	2.7
Risk 2	4	1	4	3	3.15
Risk 3	2	2	2	1	1.6
Risk 4	2	4	3	2	2.5

Table 17.3 Risk exposure scores—example.

Exposure score	Technical	Schedule	Cost	Customer satisfaction
5	Unusable system	> 18 months slip	>10% project budget	Will replace purchased product with competitor's product
4	Unusable function or subsystem	12 to 18 months slip	7% to 10% project budget	Unwilling to purchase
3	Major impact to functionality, performance, or quality	6 to 12 months slip	5% to 7% project budget	Willing to purchase for limited use
2	Minor impact to functionality, performance, or quality	3 to 6 months slip	1% to 5% project budget	Willing to purchase and use but will result in complaints
1	Minimal or no impact	< 3 months slip	< 1%	Willing to purchase and use but may not recommend

Risk Management Planning

During the planning step of the software risk management process, the appropriate risk-handling techniques are selected and alternative risk-handling actions are evaluated. Whatever handling options are selected, the associated actions should be planned in advance to proactively manage the project's risks rather than waiting for problems and reacting in a firefighting mode. The resulting risk management plans should then be incorporated into the project plans with assigned staff and resources.

Taking the prioritized risk list as input, plans are developed for the handling actions chosen for each risk. As illustrated in Figure 17.5, specific questions can be asked to help focus the type of planning required.

Do we know enough? If the answer is no, plans can be made to "buy" additional information through mechanisms such as prototyping, modeling, simulation, or conducting additional research. Once the additional information has been obtained, the planning step should be revisited. Based on the results of these activities and the information obtained, it may also be appropriate to repeat the risk analysis step for the risk, resulting in changes to its priority. Table 17.4 illustrates examples of obtaining additional information actions for the example risk statements from Figure 17.5.

Is it too big a risk? If the risk is too big to be willing to accept, the risk can be avoided by changing the project strategies and tactics to choose a less risky alternate or to decide not to do the project at all. Things to remember about avoiding risks include:

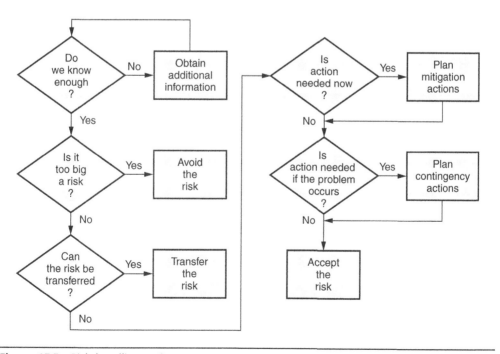

Figure 17.5   Risk-handling options.

- Avoiding risks may also mean avoiding opportunities

- Not all risks can be avoided

- Avoiding a risk in one part of the project may create larger risks in other parts of the project

Once the risk has been successfully avoided, it can be closed. Table 17.5 illustrates examples of risk-avoidance actions for the example risk statements from Figure 17.5.

Can the risk be transferred? If it is not the project's risk or if it is economically feasible to pay someone else to assume all or part of the risk, a plan can be developed

Table 17.4 Obtaining additional information action–examples.

Risk	Obtain additional information
Acme may not deliver the subcontracted XYZ controller component with the required software reliability level, and as a result the project will spend additional effort working on defect resolution issues with Acme and doing regression testing	• Perform a capability assessment of Acme • Ask for references from past customers and check on the reliability of previous Acme products
The interface specification to the notification controller may not be defined before the scheduled time to design its driver, and as a result the schedule will slip for designing the notification driver	• Establish communications link with device provider to obtain early design specification for the device • Research interface specs for prior releases of the same controller or for other control devices by same provider

Table 17.5 Risk avoidance action–examples.

Risk	Risk avoidance actions
Acme may not deliver the subcontracted XYZ controller component with the required software reliability level, and as a result the project will spend additional effort working on defect resolution issues with Acme and doing regression testing	• Develop all software in-house • Switch to a subcontractor with a proven reliability track record even though they are more expensive
The interface specification to the notification controller may not be defined before the scheduled time to design its driver, and as a result the schedule will slip for designing the notification driver	• Negotiate with the customer to move the implementation of this control device into a future software release • Replace the selected control device with an older device that has a well-defined interface

to transfer the risk to another organization (for example, buying insurance). Once the risk has been successfully transferred, that risk can be closed because it is no longer a project risk. In some cases the project may want to set up a monitoring mechanism to make sure that the people who assumed the risk are appropriately handling it. Transferring the risk to another party may also create other risks that need to be identified, analyzed, and managed. It should be remembered that transferring the risk doesn't eliminate it; it simply shifts responsibility and potentially changes the risk's exposure (probability it will turn into a problem or impact to the project if it does). Table 17.6 illustrates examples of risk-transfer actions for the example risk statements from Figure 17.5.

Is action needed now? Sometimes the risk can not be avoided but it is still too big a risk to just accept. If the project decides to attack the risk directly, they typically start with creating a list of possible *risk mitigation actions*, also called *risk containment actions*, which can be taken to reduce the risk. Two approaches to risk mitigation plan actions should be considered:

- Actions that reduce the likelihood that the risk will occur

- Actions that reduce the impact of the risk should it occur

Table 17.7 illustrates examples of risk mitigation plans for the example risk statements from Figure 17.5.

From the list of possible risk mitigation actions, the project team selects those that are actually going to be implemented. When considering which risk reduction activities to select, a cost/benefit analysis must be performed. Boehm (1989) defines the *risk reduction leverage* (RRL) equation to help quantitatively establish the cost/benefit of implementing a risk reduction action. RRL measures the return on investment of the available risk reduction techniques based on expected values. RRL is defined as the difference between the *risk exposure* (RE) before and after the reduction activity divided by the cost of that activity.

$$RRL = (RE_{Before} - RE_{After})/\text{Risk reduction cost}$$

Table 17.6 Risk-transfer action—examples.

Risk	Risk transfer actions
Acme may not deliver the subcontracted XYZ controller component with the required software reliability level, and as a result the project will spend additional effort working on defect resolution issues with Acme and doing regression testing	• Transfer the risk to the subcontractor by building penalties into the contract for delivered software that does not have the required reliability to compensate for the potential loss
The interface specification to the notification controller may not be defined before the scheduled time to design its driver, and as a result the schedule will slip for designing the notification driver	• Transfer the risk to the customer by building late-delivery alternatives into the contract if the customer does not supply the specification by its due date

Table 17.7 Risk mitigation plans—examples.

Risk	Risk mitigation plans
Acme may not deliver the subcontracted XYZ controller component with the required software reliability level, and as a result the project will spend additional effort working on defect resolution issues with Acme and doing regression testing	• Assign a project engineer to participate in the requirements and design inspection and to conduct alpha testing at the subcontractor's site • Require defect data reports from the subcontractor on a weekly basis during integration and system test
The interface specification to the notification controller may not be defined before the scheduled time to design its driver, and as a result the schedule will slip for designing the notification driver	• Assign a senior software engineer who has experience with similar control devices to the design task • Move the design task later in the schedule and increase its effort estimate

Table 17.8 Risk reduction leverage—example.

Risk #		Probability$_{Before}$	Loss$_{Before}$		RE$_{Before}$	
143		25%	$300K		$75K	
Alternative	Probability$_{After}$	Loss$_{After}$	RE$_{After}$	Cost	RRL	
1	4%	$300K	$12K	$150K	0.4	
2	25%	$180K	$45K	$20K	1.5	
3	20%	$300K	$60K	$2K	7.5	

If the RRL is less than one, it means that the cost of the risk reduction activity outweighs the probable gain from implementing the action. Table 17.8 illustrates an example of RRL for three alternative risk reduction actions. In this example, the original risk exposure after the risk analysis was determined to be 25% × $300K = $75K. The project team determined that they could not accept risks over $50K so this risk needed a mitigation plan. Team members came up with three alternatives. The team estimated that alternative 1 will reduce the risk's probability to four percent so its new risk exposure is 4% × $300K = $12K. The expected value of the benefit is then $75K – $12K = $63K. Since alternative 1 is estimated to cost $150K, the RRL = $63K/$150K = 0.4. This alternative is then rejected because it will cost over twice as much to implement as its expected value savings. Alternative 2 has an RRL of ($75K – $45)/$20K = 1.5 and alternative 3 has an RRL of ($75K – $60K)/$2K = 7.5. At first glance, alternative 3 has a greater expected benefit-to-cost ratio at 7.5. However, remember that the project determined that they couldn't accept risks over $50K, and this alternative only reduced the risk to

$60K. Therefore, if only one alternative can be selected, alternative 2 is the correct choice (but the best choice may be to combine alternatives 2 and 3 if possible).

Mitigation plans are considered effective if the risk exposure has been reduced to a level where the project can live with the possible impact if the risk turns into a problem.

Is action needed if the problem occurs? If risk mitigation actions are not taken or if those actions reduce but do not eliminate the risk, it may be appropriate to develop risk contingency plans. *Contingency plans* are plans that are implemented only if the risk actually turns into a problem. One or more risk triggers should be established for each risk with a contingency plan. A trigger is a time or event in the future that acts as an early warning system that the risk is turning into a problem. For example, if there is a risk that outsourced software will not be delivered on schedule, the trigger could be whether the critical design review was held on schedule. A trigger can also be a relative variance or threshold metric. For example, if the risk is the availability of key personnel for the coding phase, the trigger could be a relative variance of more than 10 percent between actual and planned staffing levels. There are trade-offs in utilizing triggers in risk management. The trigger needs to be set as early as possible in order to ensure that there is plenty of time to implement risk contingency actions. It also needs to be set as late as possible because the longer the project waits, the more information they have to make a correct decision and not implement unnecessary actions. Table 17.9 illustrates examples of risk contingency plans for the example risk statements from Figure 17.5.

A project is never able to remove all risk—software is a risky business. A project will therefore typically choose to accept many of its identified risks. The key difference is that a conscious choice has been made from a position of information and analysis rather than an unconscious choice. Even if the project accepts a risk, they may want to put one or more risk triggers in place to warn them that the risk is turning into a problem. Risks that are assigned these triggers can then be set at a "monitor only" priority until the trigger occurs. At that time, the risk analysis step can be repeated to determine if risk reduction action is needed.

Risk management plans should be integrated back into the overall project plans as appropriate. This integration should include schedules, budgets, staffing, and resource allocation, and other planning for the risk actions that will be taken. It should also include buffers to reserve time, budget, staff, and other resources to handle those risks that do turn into problems. It should be noted that some risk-handling actions might be small enough that they can be implemented with action item lists and do not need to be incorporated into the overall project plans.

Taking Action

During the "taking action" step, the assigned individuals implement the risk-handling plans. Additional information is obtained, actions are taken to avoid or transfer the risks, and planned risk mitigation actions are executed. If risk triggers are activated, analysis is performed and contingency actions are implemented as appropriate. Note that with some luck and good risk-handling plans, many of a project's contingency plans may never be implemented. Contingency plans are only implemented if the risks turn into problems.

Table 17.9　Risk contingency plan—examples.

Risk	Risk contingency plans
Acme may not deliver the subcontracted XYZ controller component with the required software reliability level, and as a result the project will spend additional effort working on defect resolution issues with Acme and doing regression testing	• Risk assumption: this is the best subcontractor for the job, and the team will trust them to deliver reliable software • Early trigger (reassessment of risk indicated): completion of critical design review (CDR) later than June 1 • Contingency plan trigger: more than two critical and 25 major defects detected during third pass of system test • Contingency plan: assign an engineer to liaison with the subcontractor on defect resolution, and implement the regression test plan for maintenance releases from the subcontractor
The interface specification to the notification controller may not be defined before the scheduled time to design its driver, and as a result the schedule will slip for designing the notification driver	• Risk assumption: this new technology will greatly improve the usability of the system • Early trigger (reassessment of risk indicated): interface definition not received by start of preliminary design review (PDR) • Contingency plan trigger: interface definition not received by start of CDR • Contingency plan: hold CDR with a "to be done" and hold a second CDR for just the subsystem that uses the device

Risk Tracking

The project team must track the results and impacts of the risk-handling plan implementation. The tracking step involves gathering data, compiling that data into information, and then reporting and analyzing that information. This includes measuring identified risks and monitoring triggers, as well as measuring the impacts of risk reduction activities. The results of the tracking can be:

• Identification of new risks that need to be added to the risk list

• Validation of known risk resolutions so risks can be removed from the risk list because they are no longer a threat to project success

• Information that dictates additional planning requirements

• Implementation of contingency plan

There are two primary mechanisms for tracking risks. The first is review of the items on the risk list and their status by project staff and management. The second is through the use of metrics.

Many of the reviews typically used to manage software projects can also be used to track risks. For example, tracking activities can be included in project team meetings, senior management meetings, and milestone and phase-gate review meetings. At the beginning of a process, the entry criteria should be evaluated to determine if the process is truly ready to start. As part of that review, risks associated with the process and its tasks and products could also be evaluated. At the end of a process, the exit criteria should be evaluated to determine if the process is truly complete. This provides another opportunity to review the risks associated with that process and its tasks and products.

Many of the software metrics typically used to manage software projects can also be used to track risks. For example, Gantt charts, earned value measures, and budget and resource metrics can help identify and track risks involving variances between plans and actual performance. Requirements churn, defect identification rates, and defect backlogs can be used to track other risks, including rework risks, risks to the quality of the delivered product, and even schedule risks.

2. SOFTWARE SECURITY RISKS

> Evaluate risks specific to software security, including deliberate attacks (hacking, sabotage, etc.), inherent defects that allow unauthorized access to data, and other security breaches, and determine appropriate responses to minimize their impact.
> (Evaluate)
>
> **Body of Knowledge IV.C.2**

Software increasingly controls or enables not just the digital infrastructure but the physical one as well. Everything from transportation systems (airplanes, trains, and subways) to financial institutions, hospitals, delivery systems (postal, shipping, and pipeline), telecommunications, and e-commerce are now heavily controlled or run by software systems. Because of this increased dependence on software, the security of that software is an increasing concern. The news is full of reports on stolen credit card information, identity thefts, virus attacks, and other software security–related issues.

Software security focuses on the probability that an attack on the software will be detected, prevented, or recovered from. Examples of security attacks include attempts to:

- *Gain unauthorized access to the software.* For example, accessing the software through a back door, or through spoofing, hacking, or tunneling

- *Compromise the software's integrity, availability, or confidentiality.* For example, through viruses, worms, denial-of-service attacks

- *Inappropriately collect, falsify, or destroy data.* For example, unauthorized or inadvertent disclosure of confidential information, breaching data encryption, or contamination

Security attacks can come from the outside from hackers, stolen identification or password, or other people trying to take advantage of security vulnerabilities in the software. Security attacks can also come from the inside through acts of sabotage, malicious code (for example time bombs, logic bombs, or Trojan horses), or back doors created by software practitioners. Software security focuses on four main objectives:

- Maintaining access control (passwords, firewalls, multilevel privileges)

- Preserving the integrity of the software and its data

- Providing backup and/or recovery if security mechanisms should fail, resulting in corruption of the software or data

- Providing an audit trail of documented records of the software's access and use in order to provide the information needed for accountability

So where do software security vulnerabilities come from? While some of them are intentional (malicious) in nature, such as malicious code, many of them are accidental in nature, caused by security holes. A *security hole* is an unintended function, mode, or state caused by design flaws or coding bugs (one or more defects), that an attacker can exploit to result in a security breach.

In software where security is important, security validation activities need to be incorporated into every stage of the software development life cycle. Therefore, security threat analysis should be performed as part of each level of peer review and testing. For example, appropriate security-focused test cases should be developed based on that analysis for each level of testing. Security risks can be found anywhere in the software. However, code that deals with the outside world and code that has anything to do with internal/external privileges are naturally more vulnerable. Therefore, when performing security threat analysis, particular attention needs to be paid to any part of the software or system that:

- Operates with special privileges

- Performs authentication, including verification of the digital identity of the sender (a sender can be a person, computer, or program) of a communication

- Provides easy access to user data or facilities (such as network server or relational database management systems)

- Includes certain language constructs in programming languages that have been identified as vulnerabilities because multiple software faults have had their root causes traced to the use of those constructs

- Stores, transmits, or backs up any confidential data or information

- Provides entry points into the system, because these are the locations where outside input is parsed, processed, or interpreted (for example, Web forms, network sockets, and media players, as the attacker can craft bad inputs, malformed network packets, or malformed digital media in an attempt to breach security)

According to the Open Web Application Security Project (OWASP 2009), proven security principles for software applications include:

- *Applying defense in depth through the use of multilayered security mechanisms.* For example, if an attack breaches one level of security, another level of security might still be successful in identifying and repelling that attack.

- *Defining a positive security model that identifies what is allowed and rejects everything else.* For example, with an input filter screen for the valid characters rather than attempting to screen for invalid characters (some of the invalids might be missed and cause security vulnerabilities).

- *Failing securely when handling errors or failures.* For example, any failures encountered during an authorization operation should result in an "unauthorized" return code.

- *Executing each operation with the lowest level of privileges required.* For example, if a function only needs to read information from a database, then open that database file with read-only privileges.

- *Not depending on obscurity or secrecy when implementing security.*

- *Keeping the security simple.* The more complex the software, the greater the opportunity for security issues and the more difficult it is to verify the security.

- *Detecting intrusions requires a log (audit trail) of security-relevant events, regular monitoring of that log, and proper responses to detected intrusions.* Without proper intrusion detection, the attacker is given unlimited time to perfect or take advantage of their attack.

- *Not trusting the infrastructure or external services.* If it comes from outside the software, perform error and security checking.

- *Establishing security defaults that emphasize security.* If necessary, allow the software's users to tailor the software to reduce the security levels, but default to the highest-level security requirements. For example, the default might be to log the user out after five minutes of keyboard inactivity, but allow the user to customize this delay to a longer interval.

3. SAFETY AND HAZARD ANALYSIS

Evaluate safety risks and hazards related to software development and implementation and determine appropriate steps to minimize their impact. (Evaluate)

Body of Knowledge IV.C.3

Part IV.C.3

Safety-critical software is software that can result in an accident if it:

- *Inadvertently responds to stimuli.* For example, a fire detection system that might turn on the sprinkler in response to a false alarm

- *Fails to respond when required.* For example, a 911 phone system that fails to connect an incoming call to the police operator

- *Responds out-of-sequence.* For example, an energy management system that turned on the blower fans before opening the vents, causing damage to the air-handling units

- *Responds in combination with other responses.* For example, software that monitors dispensing pain medications that could potentially cause an overdose if the button is pressed too often

Safety-critical software is also software that is intended to mitigate or recover from the results of an accident. The IEEE *Standard for Software Safety Plans* (IEEE 1994) defines an accident as "an unplanned event or series of events that result in death, injury, illness, environmental damage, or damage to or loss of equipment or property."

Software safety program activities include:

- Defining safety requirements and acceptable risks

- Documenting software safety plans

- Designing and implementing safety-critical portions of the software

- Performing software safety analysis

- Testing safety-critical features

- Auditing the safety plan's implementation

- Training personnel in methods, tools, and techniques for developing safe software

- Ensuring that adequate safety records are kept

In *failure mode effects and criticality analysis* (FMECA) the software or a component of the software is analyzed in an attempt to determine all the possible ways that it could fail. Each potential failure is then analyzed to estimate its effects on the safety of the system. The criticality of those effects is then assigned and used to prioritize the effects. As a result of this analysis, plans are made and actions are taken to either reduce the probability of the failure occurring or to minimize the effects if the failure does occur. Examples of these plans might include:

- *Changing the design.* For example, additional error-handling, fault tolerance, or fail-safes could be designed into the software, or redundancy could be built into the system

- *Additional or more rigorous testing to specifically test for failure conditions.*

Some systems are inherently hazardous. For example, a missile guidance system is intended to direct missiles to destroy property or cause bodily harm. Fire sprinkler systems are intended to douse everything with water to put out a fire, which will always result in some property damage. For these systems, hazard analysis focuses on the inadvertent or unintended occurrence of these hazards (for example, a missile being fired inadvertently or without proper authorization, or sprinkler systems going off when there is no fire).

Security is directly related to safety. If the software is not secure it can not be safe because someone intending to cause an accident could breach the software's security and intentionally cause it to be unsafe.

Part IV.C.3

Part V
Software Metrics and Analysis

Software metrics and analysis provide the data and information that allows an organization's quality management system to be based on a solid foundation of facts. The objective is to drive continual improvement in all quality parameters through a goal-oriented measurement and analysis system.

Software metrics programs should be designed to provide the specific information necessary to manage software projects and improve software engineering processes, products, and services. The foundation of this approach is aimed at making practitioners ask not "what should I measure?" but "why am I measuring?" Or "what business needs does the organization wish its measurement initiative to address?" (Goodman 1993).

Measuring is a powerful way to track progress toward project goals. As Grady (1992) states, "Without such measures for managing software, it is difficult for any organization to understand whether it is successful, and it is difficult to resist frequent changes of strategy."

Part V

Chapter 18

A. Metrics and Measurement Theory

According to Humphrey (1989), there are four major roles (reasons) for collecting data and implementing software metrics:

- *To understand.* Metrics can be gathered to learn about software processes, products, and services, and their capabilities. The resulting information can be used to:

  - Establish baselines, standards, and goals

  - Derive models of the software processes

  - Examine relationships between process parameters

  - Target process, product, and service improvement efforts

  - Better estimate project effort, costs, and schedules

- *To evaluate.* Metrics can be examined and analyzed as part of the decision-making process to study products, processes, or services in order to establish baselines, to perform cost/benefit analysis, and to determine if established standards, goals, and entry/exit/acceptance criteria are being met.

- *To control.* Metrics can be used to control projects, resources, processes, products, and services by providing triggers (red flags) based on variances, thresholds, control limits, or standards and/or performance requirements.

- *To predict.* Metrics can be used to predict the values of attributes in the future (for example, budgets, schedules, staffing, resources, risks, quality, and reliability).

Effective software metrics provide objective data and information necessary to help an organization, its management, its teams, and individuals:

- Make day-to-day decisions

- Identify project issues

- Correct existing problems

- Identify, analyze, and manage risks

- Evaluate performance and capability levels

- Assess the impact of changes

- Accurately estimate and track effort, costs, and schedules

The bottom line is that effective metrics help improve software products, processes, and services.

1. TERMINOLOGY

Define and describe metrics and measurement terms including reliability, internal and external validity, explicit and derived measures, etc. (Understand)

Body of Knowledge V.A.1

Metrics Defined

The term *metrics* means different things to different people. When someone buys a book or picks up an article on software metrics, the topic can vary from project cost and effort prediction and modeling to defect tracking and root cause analysis, a specific test coverage metric, computer performance modeling, or even the application of statistical process control charts to software.

Goodman (1993) defines software metrics as, "The continuous application of measurement-based techniques to the software development process and its products to supply meaningful and timely management information, together with the use of those techniques to improve that process and its products."

As illustrated in Figure 18.1, Goodman's definition can be expanded to include software services. Examples of software services include responding with fixes to

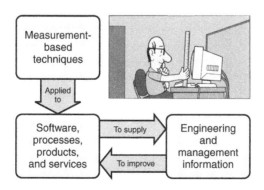

Figure 18.1   Metrics defined.

customer-reported problems, training courses provided for the software, installing the software, or providing the customer with technical assistance. Goodman's definition can be expanded to include engineering as well as management information. In fact, measurement is one of the key required elements to move the software discipline from a craft to an engineering discipline.

Software metrics are standardized ways of measuring the attributes of software processes, products, and services in order to provide the information needed to improve those processes, products, and services. The same metrics can then be used to monitor the impacts of those improvements, thus providing the feedback loop required for continual improvement.

Measurement Defined

The use of *measurement* is common. People use measurements in everyday life to weigh themselves in the morning or when they glance at the clock or at the odometer in their car. Measurements are used extensively in most areas of production and manufacturing to estimate costs, calibrate equipment, and monitor inventories. Science and engineering disciplines depend on the rigor that measurements provide. What does measurement really mean?

According to Fenton (1997), "*measurement* is the process by which numbers or symbols are assigned to attributes of entities in the real world in such a way as to describe them according to clearly defined rules." Entities are nouns, for example, a person, place, thing, event, or time period. An attribute is a feature or property of an entity.

To measure, the *entity* being measured must first be determined. For example, a car could be selected as the entity. Once the entity is selected, the attributes of that entity that need to be described must be chosen. According to IEEE (1998d), an *attribute* is a measurable physical or abstract property of an entity. Attributes for a car include its speed, its fuel efficiency, and the air pressure in its tires. Entities have two types of attributes:

- *Internal attributes* can be measured in terms of the entity itself. Using a person as an example, internal attributes include height, weight, and sex.

- *External attributes* of an entity can only be measured in reference to that entity's environment. For example, a person's productivity may vary based on how quiet the work area is or whether they have the right tools for the job. A person's experience level varies based on the job they are asked to do (10 years of experience on a UNIX platform and two years of experience with C++). Table 18.1 illustrates examples of internal and external attributes that might be measured for a code inspection (entity).

Finally, a *mapping system*, also called the *measurement method* or *counting criteria*, must be defined and accepted. It is meaningless to say that the car's speed is 65 or its tire pressure is 32 unless people know that they are talking about miles per hour or pounds per square inch. So what is a mapping system?

In ancient times there were no real standard measurements. This caused havoc with commerce. Was it better to buy cloth from merchant A or merchant B? What were their prices per length? In England they solved this problem by

Table 18.1   Internal and external attributes of a code inspection.

Internal attribute examples	External attribute examples
• Preparation time or rate	• Level of adherence to the inspection process
• Inspection time or rate	• Effectiveness of the inspection
• Number of participants in inspection	• Efficiency in the inspection
• Lines of code inspected	• Synergy of the inspection team
• Number of defects found	

standardizing the "yard" as the distance between King Henry I's nose and his fingertips. The "inch" was the distance between the first and second knuckle of the king's finger and the "foot" was literally the length of his foot.

To a certain extent, the software industry is still in those ancient times. As software practitioners try to implement software metrics, they quickly discover that very few standardized mapping systems exist for their measurements. Even for a seemingly simple metric such as the severity of a software defect, no standard mapping system has been widely accepted. Examples from different organizations include:

- Outage, service-affecting, non-service-affecting

- Critical, major, minor

- C1, C2, S1, S2, NS

- 1, 2, 3, 4 (with some organizations using 1 as the highest severity and other organizations using 1 as the lowest)

An important element of a successful metrics program is the selection, definition, and consistent use of mapping systems for selected metrics. The software industry as a whole may not be able to solve this problem, but each organization must solve it to have a successful metrics program.

Reliability and Validity

Metric reliability is a function of consistency or repeatability of the measure. A metric is *reliable* if different people (or the same person multiple times) can use that metric over and over to measure an identical entity and obtain the same results each time. For example, if two people count the number of lines of code in a source code module, they would both have the same, consistent count (within an acceptable level of variation). Or, if one person measured the cyclomatic complexity of a detailed design element today and then measured the same design element tomorrow, that person would get the same, consistent measure (within an acceptable level of variation).

A metric is *valid* if it accurately measures what it is expected to measure, that is, it captures the real value of the attribute it is intended to describe. IEEE (1998d) describes validity in terms of the following criteria:

- *Correlation.* Whether there is a sufficiently strong linear association between the attribute being measured and the metric

- *Tracking.* Whether a metric is capable of tracking changes in attributes over the life cycle

- *Consistency.* Whether the metric can accurately rank, by attribute, a set of products or processes

- *Predictability.* Whether the metric is capable of predicting an attribute with the required accuracy

- *Discriminative power.* Whether the metric is capable of separating a set of high-quality software components from a set of low-quality software components

This definition of validity actually refers to the *internal validity* of the metric or its validity in a narrow sense—does it measure the actual attribute? *External validity,* also called *predictive validity,* refers to the ability to generalize or transfer the metric results to other populations or conditions. For a metric to be externally valid, it must be internally valid. It must also be able to be used as part of a prediction system, estimation process, or planning model. For example, can the mean time to fix a defect that is measured for one project be generalized to predict the mean time to fix for other projects? If so, then the mean-time-to-fix metric is considered externally valid. External validity is verified empirically through comparison of the predicted results to the subsequently observed actual results.

A metric that is reliable but not valid can be consistently measured, but that measurement does not reflect the actual attribute. An example of a metric that is reliable but not valid is using cyclomatic complexity as a reliability metric. Cyclomatic complexity can be consistently measured because it is well defined and has a consistent mapping system. However, it is internally invalid as a reliability metric because it is a measure of complexity, not of reliability. A metric is internally valid but not reliable if it measures what it is supposed to measure but can not be measured consistently. For example, if criteria are not clearly defined on how to assign the numbers 1 through 4 to the severity of a reported problem, the severity metric may be valid but not reliable. For example, if two different people assign severities to the same problem, one person might assign it a severity of 2 while the other person assigns it a severity of 3. As illustrated in Figure 18.2, the goal is to have metrics that are both reliable and internally valid. In fact, IEEE (1998d) actually includes reliability as one of the criteria for validity. For predictive-type metrics, external validity is also required.

To have metrics that are both reliable and valid, there must be agreement on standard definitions for the entity and its attributes that are being measured. Software practitioners may use different terms to mean the same thing. For example, the terms *defect report, problem report, incident report, fault report,* or *customer call report* may be used by various organizations or teams for the same item. But unfortunately, they may also refer to different items. One organization may use "customer call reports" for a customer complaint and "problem reports" as the description of a problem in the software. Their customer may use "problem reports" for the

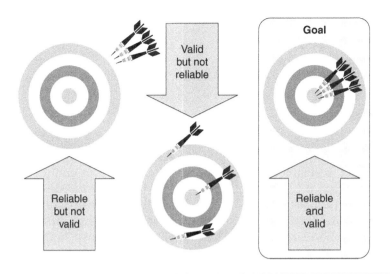

Figure 18.2   Reliability and validity.

initial complaint and "defect reports" for the problem in the software. Different interpretations of terminology can be a major barrier to correct interpretation and understanding of metrics.

For example, a metric was created to report the "trend of open software problems" for a software development manager. The manager was very pleased with the report because she could quickly pull information that had previously been difficult to get from the antiquated problem-tracking tool. One day the manager brought this report to a product review meeting so she could discuss the progress her team had made in resolving the problem backlog. The trend showed a significant decrease from over 50 open problems six weeks ago to only three open problems currently. When she put the graph up on the overhead, the customer service manager exploded. "What's going on here? Those numbers are completely wrong! I know for a fact that my customers are calling me every day to complain about the over 20 *open* field problems!" The problem wasn't with the numbers, but with the interpretation of the word "open." To the software development manager, the problem was no longer open when they had fixed it, checked the source into the configuration management library, and handed it off for system testing. But to the customer service manager, the problem was still open until his customers in the field had their fix.

As the above examples illustrate, the software industry has very few standardized definitions for software entities and their attributes. Everyone has an opinion, and the debate will probably continue for many years. An organization's metrics program can not wait that long. The suggested approach is to adopt standard definitions within an organization and then apply them consistently. Glossaries such as the ISO/IEC *Systems and Software Engineering—Vocabulary* (ISO/IEC 2009) or the glossary in this text can be used as a starting point. An organization can then pick and choose the definitions that match with their objectives or use them as a

Part V.A.1

basis for tailoring their own definitions. It can also be extremely beneficial to include these standard definitions as an appendix to each metrics report (or definition pop-up to online reports) so that everyone who receives the report understands what definitions are being used.

Explicit Measures

Explicit measures, also called *base measures, metrics primitives,* or *direct metrics,* are measured directly. The Software Engineering Institute (SEI 2006) defines a base measure as "a distinct property or characteristic of an entity and the method for quantifying it." For example, explicit measures for a code inspection would include the number of lines of code inspected (loc_insp), the number of engineering hours spent preparing for the inspection (prep_hrs), the number of engineering hours spent in the inspection meeting (insp_hrs), and the number of defects (defects) identified during the inspection.

For explicit measures, the mapping system, also called the measurement method, used to collect the data for each measure must be defined. Some mapping systems are established by using standardized units of measure (for example, dollars, hours, days). Other mapping systems define the counting criteria used to determine what does and does not get counted when performing the measurement. For example, if the metric is the "problem report arrival rate per month," the counting criteria could simply count all of the problem reports in the problem-reporting database that had an open date during each month. However, if the measure was "defect counts" instead, the counting criteria might exclude all the problem reports in the database that didn't result from a product defect (for example, those defined as "works as designed," "operator error," or "withdrawn").

Some counting criteria are very complex. The counting criteria for measuring function points is an example. Another example is the criteria for counting effort on a project. First, the units of effort might be defined in terms of staff hours, months, or years, depending on the size of the project. Other counting criteria decisions include:

- *Whose time counts?* Does the systems analyst's time count? Does the programmer's or engineer's time count? How about the project manager? The program manager? Upper management? The lawyer? The auditor?

- *When does the project start or end?* Does the time spent doing the cost/benefit analysis count? Does the time releasing, replicating, delivering, and installing the product in operations count?

- *What activities count?* If the programmer's time counts, does the time they are coding count? How about the time they spend fixing problems on a previous release? Or the time they spend in training?

- *Does overtime (paid or unpaid) count?*

Of course, many organizations solve this problem by simply stating that if the time is charged to the project account number, then it counts. But they still have to have counting criteria established that define the rules for how to charge to those account numbers.

Having a clearly defined and communicated mapping system helps everyone interpret the measures the same way. The metrics mapping system and, if applicable, data needed based on the associated counting criteria also define the first level of data that needs to be collected in order to implement the metric.

Derived Measures

According to the SEI (2006), a *derived measure*, also called *complex metrics*, is "data resulting from the mathematical function of two or more base measures" (the mathematical combinations of explicit measures or other derived metrics). For a code inspection, examples of derived metrics would include:

- *Preparation rate,* which is the number of lines of code inspected divided by the hours spent preparing for the inspections (loc_insp/insp_hrs)

- *Defect detection rate,* which is the number of defects found during the inspection divided by the sum of the hours spent preparing for the inspections and the hours spent inspecting the work product (defects/ [prep_hrs + insp_hrs])

Most measurement functions include an element of simplification. When creating a function, an organization needs to be pragmatic. If they try to include all of the elements that affect the attribute or characterize the entity, their functions can become so complicated that the metric is useless. Being pragmatic means not trying to create the perfect function. Pick the aspects that are the most important.

The ideal measurement function is simple enough to be easy to use and at the same time provide enough information to help people in the organization make better, more informed decisions. Remember that the function can always be modified in the future to include additional levels of detail as the organization gets closer to its goal. The people designing a function should ask themselves:

- Does the measurement provide more information than is available now?

- Is that information of practical benefit?

- Does it tell the individuals performing the measure what they want to know?

Measurement functions should be selected and tailored to the organization's information needs. As illustrated in Figure 18.3, to demonstrate the selection of a tailored function, consider a metric for the duration of unplanned system outages.

- If a software system installed at a single site that is running 24/7 is being measured, a simple function such as the sum of all of the minutes of outage for the calendar month may be sufficient.

- If the software system is installed at a single site that runs a varying number of operational hours each month, or if different software releases

> **Metric: Duration of unplanned outages**
> - Total minutes of outage: Σ (minutes of outage this month)
> - Minutes of outage per 1000 operation hours:
> $$\frac{\Sigma \text{ (minutes of outage this month this release)}}{\Sigma \text{ (minutes of operation this month this release)}} \times 6000$$
> - Minutes of outage per site per year:
> $$\frac{\Sigma \text{ (minutes of outage this month this release)}}{\text{number of sites this month this release}} \times 12$$

Figure 18.3   Metric function–examples.

are installed on a varying number of sites each month, this might lead to the selection of a function such as "minutes of outage per 1000 operation hours per release."

- If the focus is on the impact to the customers, this might lead to the selection of a function such as "minutes of outage per site per year."

2. BASIC MEASUREMENT THEORY AND STATISTICS

> Define the central limit theorem, and describe and use mean, median, mode, standard deviation, variance, and range. Apply appropriate measurement scales (nominal, ordinal, ratio, interval) in various situations. (Apply)
>
> **Body of Knowledge V.A.2**

Central Limit Theorem

The *central limit theorem* states that, "Irrespective of the shape of the distribution of the population or universe, the distribution of average values of samples drawn from that universe will tend toward a normal distribution as the sample size grows without bound." Why is this important? Because the basic statistical process control chart concept is based on the population having a normal distribution. If the population of data from a process has a normal distribution, then individual data items can be plotted on the control chart. Based on the central limit theorem, for populations of data from a process that does not have a normal distribution, samples can be taken and the mean of those sampled values can be plotted on the control chart. Without the central limit theorem, there would have to be a separate statistical model developed to create control charts for every nonnormal distribution encountered in practice.

Mean, Median, and Mode

The mean, median, and mode are three mechanisms for defining the central tendency of a set of data.

The *mean* is the arithmetic average of the numbers in the data set. The mean is "used for symmetric or near-symmetric distributions or for distributions that lack a clear, dominant single peak" (Juran 1999). The mean is calculated by summing the data values and dividing by the number of data items. For example, if the data items were 3, 5, 10, 15, 19, 21, 25, the mean would be (3 + 5 + 10 + 15 + 19 + 21 + 25) / 7 = 14

The *median* is the middle value when the numbers are arranged according to size. The median is "used for reducing the effects of extreme values or for data that can be ranked but are not economically measurable (shades of color, visual appearance, odors)" (Juran 1999). For example, if the data items were 3, 5, 10, 15, 19, 21, 102, the mean would be (3 + 5 + 10 + 15 + 19 + 21 + 102) / 7 = 25, but the median would be 15. If there is an even number of items in the data set, then the median is typically calculated by adding the two middle values and dividing by two. For example, if the data items were 3, 5, 10, 15, 19, 21, 46, 102, the middle two items are 15 and 19, so the median would be calculated by (15 + 19) / 2 = 17.

The *mode* is the value that occurs most often in the data. The mode is "used for severely skewed distributions, describing irregular situations where two peaks are found, or for eliminating the effects of extreme values" (Juran 1999). For example, if the data items were, 1, 1, 1, 1, 1, 3, 3, 5, 10, 21, 96:

- The mean would be (1 + 1 + 1 + 1 + 1 + 3 + 3 + 5 + 10 + 21 + 96) / 11 = 13

- The median would be 3

- The mode would be 1

Range, Standard Deviation, and Variance

The range, standard deviation, and variance are three mechanisms for defining the amount of variation in a data set.

The *range* is simply the difference between the maximum and minimum data values in the data set. For example, if the data items were 3, 5, 10, 15, 19, 21, 25, the range would be equal to 25 − 3 = 22.

The *standard deviation* is typically represented by sigma (σ). The larger the standard deviation, the more variation there is in the data. The standard deviation is calculated as:

$$\sigma = \sqrt{\frac{\Sigma(X - \bar{X})^2}{n-1}} \text{ or } \sigma = \sqrt{\frac{n\Sigma(X^2) - (\Sigma X)^2}{n(n-1)}}$$

where:

σ = standard deviation

X = observed values (data items in the data set)

$\bar{X}$ = arithmetic mean of the observed values

n = number of observations

For example, if the data items sampled from a normal distribution were 3, 5, 10, 15, 19, 21, 25, the standard deviation would be equal to:

$$\sqrt{\frac{7\left(3^2+5^2+10^2+15^2+19^2+21^2+25^2\right)-\left(3+5+10+15+19+21+25\right)^2}{7\left(7-1\right)}}$$

$$=\sqrt{\frac{7\left(9+25+100+225+361+441+625\right)-\left(98\right)^2}{42}}$$

$$=\sqrt{\frac{7\left(1786\right)-9604}{42}}$$

$$=\sqrt{69}$$

$$\approx 8.3066$$

Figure 18.4 illustrates the percentage of data items under a normal distribution curve at plus and minus various standard deviations. For example, at ±1 standard deviation, 68.26 percent of all data items in a normal distribution fall under the curve. At ±3 standard deviations, 99.73 percent of all data items in a normal distribution fall under the curve.

The *variance* for a normal distribution is the square of the standard deviation, which in the case of these data items would equal 69.

Nominal Scale Measurements

The *nominal scale* is the simplest form of measurement. In nominal scale measurements, items are assigned to a classification (one-to-one mapping), where that classification categorizes the attribute of the entity. Examples of nominal scale measurements include:

- Development method (waterfall, V, spiral, other)

- Root cause (logic error, data initialization error, data definition error, other)

- Document author (Linda, Bob, Susan, Tom, other)

The categories in a nominal scale measurement must be jointly exhaustive and cover all possibilities. This means that every measurement can be assigned into

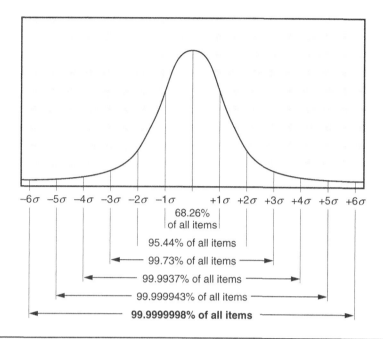

Figure 18.4   Area under the normal curve.

a classification. This is why many nominal scale measures include a category of "other," so everything fits somewhere. The categories must also be mutually exclusive (one and only one). If an attribute is classified in one category, it can not be classified in any of the other categories.

The nominal scale does not make any assumptions about order or sequence. The only math that can be done on nominal scale measures is to count the number of items in each category and look at their distributions. For example, even though numbers are used as symbols for the customer satisfaction nominal scale metric above, this does not mean that it is appropriate to calculate an average (mean) satisfaction score. Therefore, a useful central tendency statistic for nominal scale metrics is the mode (highest-frequency category).

Ordinal Scale Measurement

The *ordinal scale* classifies the attribute of the entity by order. However, there are no assumptions made about the magnitude of the differences between categories (a defect with a critical severity is not twice as bad as one with a major severity). Examples of ordinal scale measurements include:

- Defect severity (critical, major, minor)
- Requirement priority (high, medium, or low)

Part V.A.2

- SEI CMM level (1 = initial, 2 = repeatable, 3 = defined, 4 = managed, 5 = optimized)

- Process effectiveness (1 = very ineffective, 2 = moderately ineffective, 3 = nominally effective, 4 = moderately effective, 5 = very effective)

Since there is order, the transitive property is valid for ordinal scale measures (if critical > major and major > minor, then critical > minor). However, without an assumption of magnitude, mathematical operations of addition, subtraction, multiplication, and division can not be used on ordinal scale measurement values. Either the mode or the median can be used as the central tendency statistic for ordinal scale metrics.

Interval Scale Measurement

For *interval scale* measurements, the exact distance between the scales is known. This allows the mathematical operations of addition and subtraction to be applied to interval scale measurement values. However, there is no absolute or nonarbitrary zero point in the interval scale, so multiplication and division do not apply. The classic example of an interval scale measure is calendar time. For example, it is valid to say, "May 1st plus 10 days is May 11th," but saying "May 1st times May 11th" is invalid. Interval scale measurements require well-established units of measure that can be agreed upon by everyone using the measurement. Either the mode or the median can be used as the central tendency statistic for interval scale metrics.

Ratio Scale Measurement

Ratio scale is the highest-level form of measurement. In the ratio scale, not only is the exact distance between the scales known, but there is an absolute or nonarbitrary zero point. All mathematical operations can be applied to ratio scale measurement values, including multiplication and division. Examples of ratio scale measurement include:

- Defect counts

- Defect density (defects per size)

- Minutes of outage

- Hours of effort

- Cycle times

- Rates (for example arrival rates and fix rates)

Note that since derived measures are mathematical combinations of two or more explicit measures or other derived measures, those explicit and derived measures must at a minimum be interval scale measurements (if only addition and subtraction are used in the measurement function) and they are typically ratio scale measurements. The mode, median, or mean (arithmetic average) can be used as the central tendency statistic for ratio scale metrics.

3. PSYCHOLOGY OF METRICS

> Describe how metrics and measuring affect
> the people whose work is being measured
> and how people affect the ways in which
> metrics are used and data are gathered.
> (Understand)
>
> **Body of Knowledge V.A.3**

Metrics and Measuring Affect People

Measurements affect people, and people affect measures. For example, think about the fact that most people study harder if there is going to be a test than they might just because they were taking a class or had a desire to learn something new. This is known as the *Hawthorne effect*. The Hawthorne effect was first noticed in the Hawthorne Works plant where production processes were being studied to determine the impact of various conditions (for example, lighting levels and rest breaks) on productivity. However, each change in these conditions resulted in overall increases in productivity, including the return to the original conditions. It was concluded that productivity increased not as a consequence of actual changes in working conditions but because of the simple act of measurement, which gave attention (demonstrated interest by management) to values being measured and therefore caused the workers to endeavor to make those measurements improve.

Whether a metric is ultimately useful to an organization or not depends on the attitudes of the people involved. Therefore, the organization must consider these human factors when selecting metrics and implementing their metrics program.

People Affect Metrics and Measuring

The simple act of measuring affects the behavior of the individuals who are performing the processes and producing the products and services being measured. When something is being measured it is automatically assumed to have importance. People want to look good; therefore they want the measures to look good. They will modify their behavior to focus on the areas being measured.

People also affect measures by changing their data collection behaviors by:

- Being more careful, accurate, or complete when collecting data or not

- Correcting data inaccuracies and updating incomplete data or not

- Utilizing the measurements in appropriate or inappropriate ways

- Attempting to "beat" the metric or measurement

When implementing a metric, the people doing that implementation must always decide what behaviors they want to encourage. Then take a long look at what other behaviors might result from the use or misuse of the metric. For example, a team implemented a metric to monitor an initiative aimed at reducing the number of unfixed problem reports each development team had in their backlog. The desired behavior was for managers to dedicate resources to this initiative and for engineers to actively work to correct the problems and thus remove them from the backlog. However, on the negative side, some people tried to beat the metrics by:

- Not recording new problems (going back to the "paper napkin" or e-mail reporting mechanism), which caused a few problems to slip through the cracks and be forgotten.

- "Pencil whipping" existing problems by closing them as "can not duplicate" or "works as designed."

- One manager got very creative; he determined that the metrics were only extracting data and counting software problems on the last day of the month. Just before he went home that evening the manager transferred all of his group's problems over to his buddy in hardware so his numbers looked great for the senior management meeting.

To quote an unknown source, "Don't underestimate the intelligence of your engineers. For any one metric you can come up with, they will find at least two ways to beat it." While the goal was to appropriately close out problems and improve product quality by decreasing the product defect backlog, the organization also didn't want to have to rediscover "known" problems later in operations because they had been forgotten or inappropriately closed.

Metric and Measurement Do's and Don'ts

There are ways to minimize the negative impacts of implementing software metrics. The following is a list of do's and don'ts that can help increase the probability of implementing a successful metrics program. To minimize negative impacts:

- *Don't measure individuals.* The state of the art of software metrics is just not up to this yet and may never be. Individual productivity measures are the classic example of this mistake. Managers typically give their best and brightest people the hardest work and then expect them to mentor others in the group. If productivity is then measured in product produced per hour (the typical productivity metric), these people may concentrate on their own work to the detriment of the team and the project. They may also come up with creative ways of increasing their output (for example if productivity is measured in lines of code per hour, the coder may program the same function using many more extra lines of code then they normally would just to appear more productive).

- *Don't use metrics as a stick.* Never use metrics as a "stick" to beat up people or teams. The first time a metric is used against an individual or a group is probably the last time unbiased data will be collected.

- *Don't ignore the data.* A sure way to kill a metrics program is for management to ignore the data when making decisions. "Support your people when their reports are backed by data useful to the organization" (Grady 1992). If the goals management establishes and communicates don't agree with management's actions, then the individual contributors will perform based on management behavior, not their stated goals.

- *Don't use only one metric.* Software development, operations, and maintenance are complex and multifaceted. A metrics program must reflect that complexity. A balance must be maintained between cost, product quality and functionality, and schedule attributes to meet all of the customer's needs. Focusing on any single metric can cause the attribute being measured to improve at the expense of the other attributes, resulting in an anorexic software process. It is also much harder to beat a set of metrics than it is to beat a single metric.

- *Do align metrics with goals.* To have a metrics program that meets the organization's information needs, metrics must be selected that align with the organization's goals and provide information about whether the organization is moving toward its goals or obtaining its goals. If what gets measured gets done, then the measurements must align with and support the goals.

- *Do focus the metrics on processes, products, and services.* Products, processes, and services are what the organization wants to improve. Management needs to continually reinforce this through both words and deeds. This can be a fine line. Everyone knows that George wrote that error-prone module. But is the metric being used appropriately to focus on reengineering opportunities or risk-based peer reviews or testing, or it is being used inappropriately to beat up George?

- *Do provide feedback to the data providers.* Providing regular feedback to the team about the data they help collect has several benefits. First, when the team sees that the data are actually being used and are useful, they are more likely to consider data collection important and improve their data collection behaviors. Feedback helps maintain the focus on data collection. Second, if data collectors are kept informed about the specifics of data usage, they are less likely to become suspicious that the data may be being used against them. Third, by involving data collectors in data analysis and process improvement efforts, the organization benefits from their unique knowledge and experience. Finally, feedback on data collection problems and data integrity issues helps educate team members responsible for data collection, which can result in more accurate, consistent, and timely data.

- *Do obtain buy-in for the metrics.* To have buy-in to both the goals and the metrics in a measurement program, team members need to have a feeling of ownership. Participating in the definition of the metrics will enhance this feeling of ownership. In addition, the people who work with a process, product, or service on a daily basis will have intimate knowledge of that process, product, or service. This knowledge gives them a valuable perspective on how it can best be measured to ensure accuracy and validity and how to best interpret the measured result to maximize usefulness.

Other Human Factors

A famous quote usually attributed to Mark Twain talks about the three kinds of lies—"lies, damn lies, and statistics." Marketers use statistical tricks all the time to help sell their products. When an organization puts its metrics program together, it needs to be aware of these issues and make conscious decisions on how to display the metrics for maximum usefulness and minimum "deviousness." If engineers and managers catch the metrics producer playing a marketing-type trick to make the metrics look good, they will stop believing the metrics.

Different colors also have physiological impacts (for example, in the United States green is *go*, red is *stop*, yellow is *caution*). Care should be taken when using color in metrics charts. In fact, recommended practice is to stay with shades of gray (or a single color like a shade of blue) or patterns to distinguish differences rather than using different colors. This is especially true when there is a chance the report will be printed (or copied) in black and white where information can be lost from the report if different colors translate into the same shade of gray.

Chapter 19

B. Process and Product Measurement

With all of the possible software entities and attributes, it is easy to see that there is a huge number of possible metrics that could be implemented. So how does an organization or team decide which metrics to use? The first step is to identify the customer. The customer of the metrics is the person (or team) who will be making decisions or taking action based on the metrics. The customer is the person who needs the information supplied by the metrics.

If a metric does not have a customer—someone who will make a decision based on that metric (even if the decision is "everything is fine—no action is necessary")—then stop producing that metric. Remember that collecting data and generating metrics is expensive, and if the metrics are not being used, it is a waste of people's time and the organization's money.

There are many different types of customers for a metrics program. This adds complexity because each customer may have different information requirements. It should be remembered that metrics don't solve problems—people solve problems. Metrics can only provide information so that those people can make informed decisions based on facts rather than "gut feelings." Customers of metrics may include:

- *Functional managers* who are interested in applying greater control to the software development process, reducing risk, and maximizing return on investment.

- *Project managers* who are interested in being able to accurately predict and control project size, effort, resources, budgets, and schedules. They are also interested in controlling the projects they are in charge of and communicating facts to management.

- *Individual software practitioners* who are interested in making informed decisions about their work and work products. They will also be responsible for generating and collecting a significant amount of the data required for the metrics program.

- *Specialists* are the individuals performing specialized functions (marketing, software quality assurance, process engineering, configuration management, audits and assessments, customer technical assistance). They are interested in quantitative information on which they can base their decisions, findings, and recommendations.

- *Customers and users* are interested in on-time delivery of high-quality, useful software products and in reducing the overall cost of ownership.

Basili and his colleagues defined a *goal/question/metric* paradigm, which provides an excellent mechanism for defining a goal-based measurement program (Grady 1992). The goal/question/metric paradigm is illustrated in Figure 19.1.

The first step to implementing the goal/question/metric paradigm is to select one or more measurable goals for the customer of the metrics. At the organizational level, these are typically high-level strategic goals, for example, being the low-cost provider, maintaining a high level of customer satisfaction, or meeting projected revenue or profit margin target. At the project level, the goals typically emphasize project management and control issues or project-level requirements and objectives. These goals typically reflect the project success factors such as on-time delivery, finishing the project within budget, delivering software with the required level of quality or performance, or effectively and efficiently utilizing people and other resources. At the specific task level, goals emphasize task success factors. Many times these are expressed in terms of satisfying the entry and exit criteria for the task.

The second step is to determine the questions that need to be answered in order to determine whether each goal is being met or if progress is being made in the right direction. For example, if the goal is to maintain a high level of customer satisfaction, questions might include:

- What is our current level of customer satisfaction?
- What attributes of our products and services are most important to our customers?
- How do we compare with our competition?
- How do problems with our software affect our customers?

Finally, metrics are selected that provide the information needed to answer each question. When selecting metrics, be practical, realistic, and pragmatic. Metrics customers are turned off by metrics that they see as too theoretical. They need

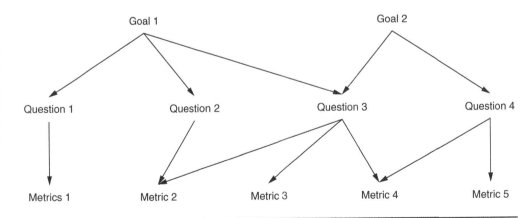

Figure 19.1   Goal/question/metric paradigm.

information that they can interpret and utilize easily. Avoid the "ivory tower" perspective that is completely removed from the existing software engineering environment (currently available data, processes being used, tools). Customers will also be turned off by metrics that require a great deal of work to collect new or additional data. Start with what is possible within the current process. Once a few successes are achieved, the metrics customers will be open to more radical ideas—and may even come up with a few metrics ideas of their own.

Again, with all of the possible software entities and attributes, it is easy to see that there is a huge number of possible metrics that could be implemented. This chapter only touches on a few of those metrics as examples of the types of metrics used in the software industry. The recommended method is to use the goal/question/ metric paradigm or some other mechanism for selecting appropriate metrics that meet the information needs of an organization and its teams, managers, and engineers. It should also be noted that these information needs will change over time. The metrics that are needed during requirements activities will be different than the metrics needed during testing or once the software is being used in operations. Some metrics are collected and reported on a periodic basis (daily, weekly, monthly), others are needed on an event-driven basis (when an activity or phase is started or stopped), and others are used only once (during a specific study or investigation). The Software Engineering Institute's (SEI) Capability Maturity Module Integration (CMMI) for Development (SEI 2006) Measurement and Analysis process area provides a road map for developing and sustaining a measurement capability that is used to support management information needs.

1. SOFTWARE METRICS

> Use metrics to assess various software attributes such as size, complexity, number of defects, the amount of test coverage needed, requirements volatility, and overall system performance. (Apply)
>
> **Body of Knowledge V.B.1**

Software product entities are the outputs of software development, operations, and maintenance processes. These include all the artifacts, deliverables, or documents that are produced. Examples of software product entities include:

- Requirements documentation
- Software design specifications (entity diagrams, data flow diagrams)
- Code (source, object, and executable)
- Test plans, scripts, specifications, cases, and test reports
- Project plans, budgets, schedules, and status reports

- Customer call reports and problem reports

- Quality records and metrics

Examples of internal attributes associated with software products include size, complexity, number of defects, test coverage, and volatility. Examples of external attributes associated with software products include reliability, availability, performance, and maintainability.

Size—Lines of Code

Lines of code (LOC) counts are one of the most used and most often misused of all the software metrics. Some estimation methods are based on KLOC (thousands of lines of code). The LOC metric may also be used in other derived metrics to normalize the measures so releases, projects, or products of different sizes can be compared (for example, defect density or productivity). The problems, variations, and anomalies of using lines of code are well documented (Jones 1986). Some of these include:

- Problems in counting LOC for systems using multiple languages

- Difficulty in estimating LOC early in the software life cycle

- Productivity paradox—if productivity is measured in LOC per staff month, productivity appears to drop when higher-level languages are used even though higher-level languages are inherently more productive

No industry-accepted standards exist for counting LOC. Therefore, it is critical that specific criteria for counting LOC be adopted for the organization.

- Are physical or logical lines of code counted?

- Are comments, data definitions, or job control language counted?

- Are macros expanded before counting? Are macros counted only once?

- How are products that include different languages counted?

- Are only new and changed lines or all lines of code counted?

The Software Engineering Institute (SEI) has created a technical report specifically to present guidelines for defining, recording, and reporting software size in terms of physical and logical source statements (CMU/SEI 1992). This report includes check sheets for documenting criteria selected for inclusion or exclusion in LOC counting for both physical and logical LOC.

Size—Function Points

Function points is a size metric defined by Albrecht that is intended to measure the size of the software without considering the language it is written in. The first step in measuring function points is to decide what to count (total number of function points or just new or changed function points). Function points are counted based on adding the weighted counts for each of the five function types illustrated in Figure 19.2 (Putman 1992).

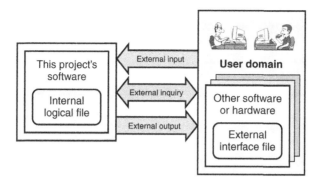

Figure 19.2 Function points.

- *External input* is the weighted count of the number of unique data or control input types that cross the external boundary of the application system and cause processing to happen within it.

- *External output* is the weighted count of the number of unique data or control output types that leave the application system, crossing the boundary to the external world and going to any external application or element.

- *External inquiry* is the weighted count of the number of unique input/ output combinations for which an input causes and generates an immediate output.

- *Internal logical file* is the weighted count of the number of logical groupings of data and control information that are to be stored within the system.

- *External interface file* is the weighted count of the number of unique files or databases that are shared among or between separate applications.

In order to determine whether a function is internal or external to the application, the boundaries of that application must be defined. This is step 2 in the function point counting procedure. Step 3 is to count the raw function point counts. Within each function type, the counts are weighted based on complexity and contribution factors. Raw function point counts have clearly defined counting criteria as established by the International Function Point Users Group (IFPUG).

Step 4 in the function point counting procedure is to calculate the *value adjustment factor*. There are 14 adjustment factors defined by IFPUG and each is measured on a scale of zero to five degrees of influence. These adjustment factors include:

1. Data communications

2. Distributed data or processing

3. Performance objectives

4. Heavily used configuration

Part V.B.1

5. Transaction rate

6. Online data entry

7. End user efficiency

8. Online update

9. Complex processing

10. Reusability

11. Conversion and installation ease

12. Operational ease

13. Multiple site use

14. Facilitate change

Step 5 in the function point counting procedure is to adjust the function point count. To do this, the sum of all 14 degrees of influence is multiplied by .01 and added to .65. This results in a value adjustment factor from 65 percent to 135 percent (SPR 1995).

For example, if the sum of the degrees of influence is 42 and the raw function point count is 450, then the adjusted function point count is calculated as:

$$VAF = .65 + (.01 \times 42) = 1.07 \text{ or } 107\%$$
$$\text{Adjusted function point count} = 450 \times 107\% = 482$$

As with lines of code, function points are used as the input into many project estimation tools and may also be used in derived metrics to normalize those metrics so that releases, projects, or products of different sizes can be compared (for example, defect density or productivity).

Other Size Metrics

There are many other metrics that may be used to measure the size of different software products. In object-oriented development, size may be measured in terms of the number of objects, classes, or methods. Requirements size may be measured in terms of the count of unique requirements, or weights may be included in the counts (for example, large requirements might be counted as 5, medium requirements as 3, and small requirements as 1). Design size may be measured in terms of the number of design elements (configuration items, subsystems, or modules). Documentation is typically sized in terms of the number of pages or words, but for graphics-rich documents, counts of the number of tables, figures, charts, and graphs may also be valuable as size metrics. The testing effort is often sized in terms of the number of test cases or weighted test cases (for example, large test cases might be counted as 5, medium test cases as 3, and small test cases as 1).

Cyclomatic Complexity

McCabe's *cyclomatic complexity* is a measure of the number of linearly independent paths through a module or detailed design element. Cyclomatic complexity can

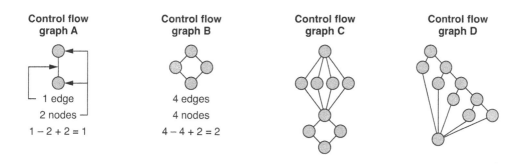

Figure 19.3 Cyclomatic complexity—examples.

therefore be used in structural testing to determine the minimum number of path tests that must be executed for complete coverage.

Cyclomatic complexity is calculated from a control flow graph by subtracting the number of nodes from the number of edges and adding two times the number of unconnected parts of the graph (edges − nodes + 2p). In well-structured code, with one entry point and one exit point, there is only a single part to the graph so p is 1.

As illustrated in Figure 19.3, straight-line code (control flow graph A) has one edge and two nodes and one part to the graph, so its cyclomatic complexity is 1 − 2 + 2 × 1 = 1. Control flow graph B is a basic if–then–else structure and has four edges and four nodes, so its cyclomatic complexity is 4 − 4 + 2 × 1 = 2. Control flow graph C is a case statement structure followed by an if–then–else structure. Graph C has 12 edges and nine nodes, so its cyclomatic complexity is 12 − 9 + 2 × 1 = 5. Another way of measuring the cyclomatic complexity for well-structured software (no two edges cross each other in the control flow graph, and there is one part to the graph) is to count the number of regions in the graph. For example, control flow graph C divides the space into five regions, four enclosed regions, and one for the outside, so its cyclomatic complexity is again 5. Graph A has a single region and a cyclomatic complexity of 1; graph B has two regions and a Cyclomatic complexity of 2. Control flow graph D is a repeated if–then–else structure and has 13 edges and 10 nodes, so its cyclomatic complexity is 13 − 10 + 2 × 1 = 5 (note that it also has five regions). Static analysis tools exist for drawing control flow graphs and/or calculating cyclomatic complexity from source code.

Structural Complexity

While cyclomatic complexity is looking at the internal complexity of an individual design element or source code module, structural complexity is looking at the complexity of the interactions between the modules in a calling structure (or in the case of object-oriented development, between the classes in an inheritance tree). Figure 19.4 illustrates four structural complexity metrics. The depth and width metrics focus on the complexity of the entire structure. The fan-in and fan-out metrics focus on the individual elements within that structure.

The *depth* metric is the count of the number of levels of control in the overall structure. Depth can be measured for an individual branch in the structure. For

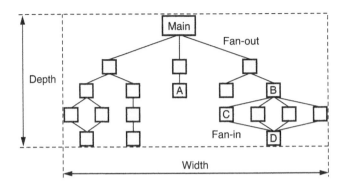

Figure 19.4 Structural complexity—examples.

example, the branch that starts with the element labeled "Main" and goes to the element labeled "A" in Figure 19.4 has a depth of three. Each of the four branches that starts with the element labeled "Main" and go to the element labeled "D" has a depth of five. The depth for the entire structure is measured by taking the maximum depth of the individual branches. For example, the structure in Figure 19.4 has a depth of five.

The *width* metric is the count of the span of control in the overall software system. Width can be measured for an individual level in the structure. For example, the level that includes the element labeled "Main" in Figure 19.4 has a width of one. The level that includes the elements labeled "A" and "B" has a width of five. The level that includes the element labeled "C" has a width of seven. The width for the entire structure is measured by taking the maximum width of the individual levels. For example, the structure in Figure 19.4 has a width of seven.

Depth and width metrics can help provide information for making decisions about the integration and integration testing of the product and the amount of effort required.

Fan-out is a measure of the number of modules that are directly called by another module (or that inherit from a class). For example, the fan-out of module Main in Figure 19.4 is three. The fan-out of module A is zero, the fan-out of module B is four, and the fan-out of module C is one.

Fan-in is the count of the number of modules that directly call a module (or that the class inherits from). For example, the fan-in of module A in Figure 19.4 is one, the fan-in of module D is four, and the fan-in of module Main is zero.

Fan-in and fan-out metrics can also help provide information for making decisions about the integration and integration testing of the product. These metrics can also be useful in evaluating the impact of a change and the amount of regression testing needed after the implementation of a change.

Defect Density

Defect density is a measure of the total known defects divided by the size of the software entity being measured (Number of known defects / Size). The number of known defects is the count of total defects identified against a particular software entity during a particular time period. Examples include:

- Defects to date since the creation of the module

- Defects found in a work product during an inspection

- Defects to date since the shipment of a release to the customer

For defect density, size is used as a normalizer to allow comparisons between different software entities (for example, modules, releases, products) of different sizes. To demonstrate the calculation of defect density, Table 19.1 illustrates the size of the three major subsystems that make up the ABC software system and the number of prerelease and post-release defects discovered in each subsystem.

Post-release defect density in defects per KLOC would be calculated as follows:

$$\text{Size of ABC} = 3432 + 2478 + 6912 = 12,822 \text{ LOC}$$

$$\text{Post-release defects} = 5 + 12 + 23 = 40 \text{ defects}$$

$$\text{Defect density} = 40 \text{ defects} / 12,822 \text{ LOC}$$
$$= .00312 \text{ defects per LOC}$$
$$= 3.12 \text{ defects per KLOC}$$

Defect density is used to compare the relative number of defects in various software components. This helps identify candidates for additional inspection or testing or for possible reengineering or replacement. Identifying defect-prone components allows the concentration of limited resources into areas with the highest potential return on the investment. Typically this is done using a Pareto diagram. Figure 20.2 illustrates a typical example for defect density when it is being utilized in this manner.

Another use for defect density is to compare subsequent releases of a product to track the impact of defect reduction and quality improvement activities. Normalizing defect arrival rates by size allows releases of varying size to be compared. Differences between products or product lines can also be compared in this manner. Figure 19.5 illustrates a typical reporting format for defect density when it is being utilized in this manner.

Table 19.1   Defect density example inputs.

Subsystem	Size	Prerelease defects	Post-release defects
A	3432 LOC	64	5
B	2478 LOC	32	12
C	6912 LOC	102	23

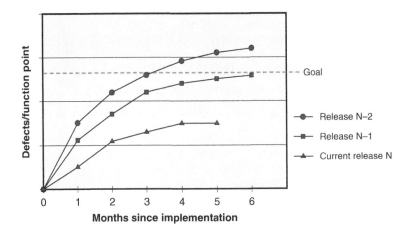

Figure 19.5   Post-release defect density–example.

Arrival Rates

Arrival rates graph the trends over time of problems newly opened against the product. Note that this metric looks at problems, not defects. Testers, customers, technical support personnel, or other originators report problems because they think there is something wrong with the software. The software developers must then debug the software to determine if there is actually a defect. In some cases the problem report may be closed after this analysis as "operator error," "works as designed," "can not duplicate," or some other non-defect-related disposition.

Prior to release, the objective of evaluating the arrival rate trends is to determine if the product is stable or moving toward stability. As illustrated in Figure 19.6, when testing is first gearing up, arrival rates may be low. During the middle of testing, arrival rates are typically higher with some level of variation. However, as shown for product A, the goal is for the arrival rates to trend downward toward zero or stabilize at very low levels (the time between failures should be far apart) prior to the completion of testing and release of the software. By stacking the arrival rates by severity, additional information can be analyzed. For example, it is one thing to have a few minor problems still being found near the end of testing, but if critical problems are still being found, it might be appropriate to continue testing. Product B in Figure 19.6 does not exhibit this stabilization and therefore indicates that continued testing is appropriate. However, arrival rate trends by themselves are not sufficient to signal the end of testing. The easiest way to make this metric "look good" is to simply slow the level of effort being expended on testing. Arrival rates should be evaluated in conjunction with other metrics when evaluating test sufficiency.

Post-release arrival rate trends can also be evaluated. In this case the goal is to determine the effectiveness of the defect detection and removal processes and process improvement initiatives. For example, as illustrated in Figure 19.5, post-release defect arrival rates can be normalized by release size to compare them over subsequent releases. Note that this metric must wait until after the problem report has been debugged, and counts only defects.

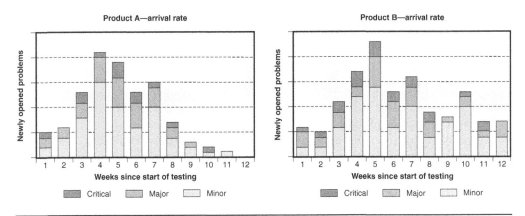

Figure 19.6   Problem report arrival rate–examples.

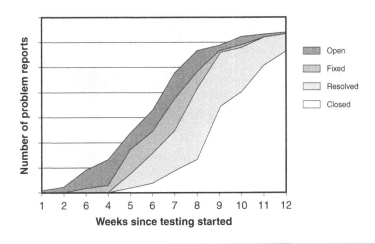

Figure 19.7   Cumulative problem reports by status–example.

Problem Report Backlogs

Arrival rates only track the number of problems being identified in the software. Those problems must also be debugged and defects corrected before the software is ready for release. Therefore, tracking the backlog of unclosed problems over time provides additional information. The cumulative problem reports by status metric illustrated in Figure 19.7 combines arrival rate information with problem report backlog information. In this example, four problem report statuses are used:

- *Open.* The problem has not been debugged and corrected (or closed as not needing correction) by development.

- *Fixed.* Development has corrected the defect and that correction is awaiting integration testing.

- *Resolved.* The correction passed integration testing and is awaiting system testing.

- *Closed.* The correction passed system testing, or the problem was closed because it was not a defect.

The objectives for this metric, as testing nears completion, is for the arrival rate trend (the shape of the cumulative curve) to flatten—indicating that the software has stabilized—and for all of the known problems to have a status of closed.

Amount of Test Coverage Needed

There are a number of metrics that can help predict the amount of *test coverage* needed. For example, for unit-level structural tests, coverage metrics might include:

- *Number of units.* At its simplest, coverage is measured to ensure that all source code modules are unit tested.

- *Number of lines of code.* Coverage is measured to ensure that all statements are tested.

- *Cyclomatic complexity.* Coverage is measured to ensure that all logically independent paths are tested.

- *Number of decisions.* Coverage is measured to ensure that all choices out of each decision are tested.

- *Number of conditions.* Coverage is measured to ensure that all conditions used as a basis for all decisions are tested.

For integration testing, coverage metrics might include:

- *Fan-in and fan-out.* During integration testing, coverage is measured to ensure that all interfaces are tested.

- *Integration complexity.* Coverage is measured to ensure that all paths through the calling tree are tested.

For functional (black box) testing, coverage metrics might include the number of requirements and the historic number of test cases per requirement. By multiplying these two metrics (Number of requirements × Historic number of test cases per requirement), the number of functional test cases for the project can be estimated. A forward-traceability metric can be used to track test case coverage during test design. For example, dividing the number of functional requirements that trace forward to test cases by the total number of functional requirements provides an estimate of the completeness of functional test case coverage. A graph such as the one depicted in Figure 19.8 can then be used to track the completeness of test coverage against the number of planned test cases during test execution.

Requirements Volatility

Requirements volatility, also called *requirements churn* or *scope creep*, is a measure of the amount of change to the requirements once they are baselined. Jones (2008)

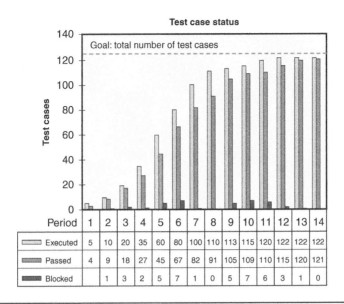

Figure 19.8   Amount of test coverage needed—example.

reports that in the United States, requirements volatility averages range from 0.5 percent monthly for end user software, to 1.0 percent monthly for management information systems and outsourced software, to 2.0 percent monthly for systems and military software, to 3.5 percent monthly for commercial software, to 5.0 percent monthly for Web software, through 10.0 percent monthly for agile projects. Jones notes, however, that the "high rate of creeping requirements for agile projects is actually a deliberate part of the agile method."

It is not a question of "if the requirements will change" during a project but "how much will the requirements change." Since requirements change is inevitable it must be managed, and to appropriately manage requirements volatility it must be measured. Figure 19.9 is an example of a graph that tracks changes to requirements over time. The line on this graph reports the current requirements size (number of requirements). The data table includes details about the number of requirements added, deleted, and modified. This detail is necessary to understand the true requirements volatility. For example, if five requirements are modified, two new requirements are added, and two other requirements are deleted, the number of requirements remains unchanged even though a significant amount of change has occurred.

Another example of a requirements volatility metric is illustrated in Figure 19.10. Instead of tracking the number of changes, this graph looks at the percentage of baselined requirements that have changed over time. A good project manager understands that the requirements will change and takes that into consideration when planning project schedules, budgets, and resource needs. The risk isn't that requirements will change—that is a given. The risk is that more requirements change will occur than the project manager estimated when planning the project. In this example, the project manager estimated 10 percent requirements volatility and then tracked the actual volatility to that threshold. In this example,

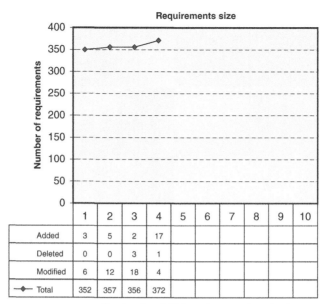

Figure 19.9 captioned below with table:

	1	2	3	4	5	6	7	8	9	10
Added	3	5	2	17						
Deleted	0	0	3	1						
Modified	6	12	18	4						
Total	352	357	356	372						

Months since initial requirements baselined

Figure 19.9   Changes to requirements size–example.

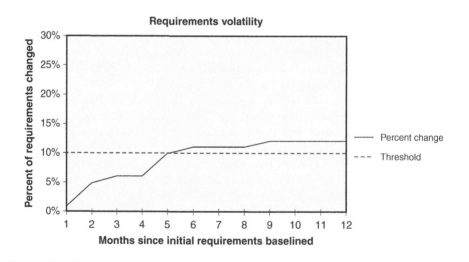

Figure 19.10   Requirements volatility–example.

the number of changed requirements is the cumulative count of all requirements added, deleted, or modified after the initial requirements are baselined and before the time of data extraction. If the same requirement is changed more than once, the number of changed requirements is incremented once for each change. These metrics acts as triggers for contingency plans based on this risk.

A metric related to requirements volatility is *function point churn,* which is the ratio of the function point changes to total number of function points baselined. Function point churn is used to identify the significance of changes in the project's scope based on function points.

Reliability

The ISO/IEC *Systems and Software Engineering—Vocabulary* (ISO/IEC 2009) defines reliability as "the ability of a system or component to perform its required functions under stated conditions for a specified period of time." The actual reliability of a software product is typically measured in terms of the number of defects in a specific time interval (for example, the number of failures per month) or the time between failures (mean time to failure). Software reliability models are utilized to predict the future reliability or the latent defect count of the software. There are two types of reliability models: static and dynamic.

Static reliability models use other project or software product attributes (for example, size, complexity, programmer capability) to predict the defect rate or number of defects. Typically, information from previous products and projects is used in these models, and the current project or product is viewed as an additional data point in the same population.

Dynamic reliability models are based on collecting multiple data points from the current product or project. Some dynamic models look at defects gathered over the entire life cycle, while other models concentrate on defects found during the formal testing phases at the end of the life cycle. Examples of dynamic reliability models include:

- Rayleigh model

- Jelinski-Moranda (J-M) model

- Littlewood (LW) models

- Goel-Okumoto (G-O) imperfect debugging model

- Goel-Okumoto nonhomogeneous Poisson process (NHPP) model

- Musa-Okumoto (M-O) logarithmic Poisson execution time model

- Delayed S and inflection S models

Appropriately implementing a software reliability model requires an understanding of the assumptions underlying that model. For instance, the J-M model's five assumptions are:

- There are N unknown software faults at the start of testing.

- Failures occur randomly, and times between failures are independent.

- All faults contribute equally to cause a failure.

- Fix time is negligible.

- Fix is perfect for each failure; there are no new faults introduced during correction (Kan 2003).

Various other models are attempts to overcome the restrictions imposed by the assumptions of the J-M model. When selecting a model, consideration must be given to the likelihood that the model's assumptions will be met by the project's software environment.

Availability

Availability is a quality attribute that describes the extent to which the software or a service is available for use when needed. Availability is closely related to reliability because unreliable software that fails frequently is typically unavailable for use because of those failures. Availability is also dependent on the ability to restore the software product to a working state. Therefore, availability is also closely related to maintainability in cases where a software defect caused the failure and that defect must be corrected before the operations can continue.

In the example of an availability metric illustrated in Figure 19.11, post-release availability is calculated each month by subtracting from 1 the sum of all of the minutes of outage that month divided by the sum of all the minutes of operations that month and multiplying by 100 percent. Tracking availability helps relate software failures and reliability issues to their impact on the user community.

System Performance

System performance metrics are used to evaluate a number of execution characteristics of the software. These can be measured during testing to evaluate the future performance of the product or during actual execution. Examples of performance metrics include:

- *Throughput.* A measure of the amount of work performed by a software system over a period of time (for example, transactions per hour or jobs per day).

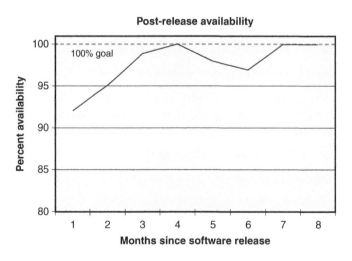

Figure 19.11   Availability–example.

- *Response time.* A measure of how quickly the software reacts to a given input or how quickly the software performs a function or activity.

- *Resource utilization.* A measure of the average or maximum amount of a given resource (for example, memory, disk space, bandwidth) used by the software to perform a function or activity.

- *Accuracy.* A measure of the level of precision, correctness, and/or freedom from error in the calculations and outputs of the software.

- *Capacity.* A measure of the maximum number of activities, actions, or events that can be concurrently handled by the software or system.

Maintainability

The ISO/IEC *Systems and Software Engineering—Vocabulary* (ISO/IEC 2009) defines maintainability as "The ease with which a software system or component can be modified to change or add capabilities, correct faults or defects, improve performance or other attributes, or adapt to a changed environment." Again, several metrics can be used to measure maintainability. Examples include *mean time to change* the software when an enhancement request is received or *mean time to fix* the software when a defect is detected. Another maintenance metric looks at the number of function points a maintenance programmer can support in a year.

2. PROCESS METRICS

> Measure the effectiveness and efficiency of software using functional verification tests (FVT), cost, yield, customer impact, defect detection, defect containment, total defect containment effectiveness (TDCE), defect removal efficiency (DRE), process capability and efficiency, etc. (Apply)
>
> **Body of Knowledge V.B.2**

Process entities include software-related activities and events. Process entities can be major activities, such as the entire software development process from requirements through delivery to operations, or small individual activities such as the inspection of a single piece of a document. Process entities can also be time intervals, which may not necessarily correspond to specific activities. Examples of time intervals include the month of January or the first six months of operations after delivery.

Examples of internal attributes associated with process entities include cycle time, effort, and the number of incidents that occurred during that process (for example, the number of defects found, the number of pages inspected, the number of tasks completed). Examples of external attributes associated with process entities include controllability, efficiency, effectiveness, stability, and capability.

Cost

The *cost* of a process is typically measured as either the amount of money spent or the amount of effort expended to implement an occurrence of that process, for example, the number of U.S. dollars spent (money) for conducting an audit or the number of engineering hours (effort) expended preparing and conducting a peer review. Collecting metrics on average cost of a process and cost distributions over multiple implementations of that process can help identify areas of inefficiencies and low productivity that provide opportunities for improvement to that process. After those improvements are implemented, the same cost metrics can be used to measure the impacts of the improvements on process costs in order to evaluate the success of the improvement initiatives.

Cost metrics are used to estimate the costs of a project and project activities as part of project planning and to track actual costs against budgeted estimates as part of project tracking. The collection and evaluation of process cost metrics can help an organization understand where, when, and how they spend money and effort on their projects. This understanding can help improve the cost estimation models for predicting costs on future projects.

First-Pass Yield

First-pass yield evaluates the effectiveness of an organization's defect prevention techniques. First-pass yield looks at the percentage of products that do not require rework after the completion of a process. First-pass yield is calculated as a percentage of the number of items not requiring rework because of defects after the completion of the process, divided by the total number of items produced by that process. For example, if the coding process resulted in the creation and baselining of 200 source code units, and 35 of those units were later reworked because defects were found in those 35 units, then the first-pass yield for the coding process is ([200 – 35] / 200) × 100% = 82.5%. As another example, if 345 requirements are documented and baselined as part of the requirements development process, and 69 of those requirements were modified after baselining because of defects, then the first-pass yield of requirements development is ([345 – 69] / 345) × 100% ≈ 80%.

Cycle Time

Cycle time is a measurement of the amount of calendar time it takes to perform a process from start to completion. Knowing the cycle times for the processes in an organization's software development life cycle allows better estimates to be done for schedules and required resources. It also enables the organization to monitor the impacts of process improvement activities on the cycle time for those processes. Cycle time can be measured as either static or dynamic cycle time.

Static cycle time looks at the average actual time it takes to perform the process. Cycle time helps answer questions such as "how long on average does it take to code a software unit, to correct a software defect, or to execute a test case?" For example, if four source code units were programmed this week and they took five days, 10 days, seven days, and eight days, respectively, to program, the static cycle time = (5 + 10 + 7 + 8) / 4 = 7.5 days per unit.

Dynamic cycle time is calculated by dividing the number of items in progress (items that have only partially completed the process) by one-half of the number of new starts plus new completions during the period. For example, if 52 source code units were started this month, 68 source code units were completed this month, and 16 source code units were in progress at the end of the month, the dynamic cycle time = (16 / [(52 + 68) / 2]) × 23 days (the number of working days this month to convert months to days) ≈ 6.1 days per unit.

Customer Impact—Customer Satisfaction

Customer satisfaction is an essential element to staying in business in this modern world of global competition. An organization must satisfy and even delight its customers with the value of its software products and services to gain their loyalty and repeat business. So how satisfied are an organization's customers? The best ways to find out is to ask them using customer satisfaction surveys. Several metrics can result from the data collected during these surveys. These metrics can provide management with the information they need to determine their customer's level of satisfaction with their software products and with the services associated with those products. Software engineers and other members of the technical staff can use these metrics to identify opportunities for ongoing process improvements and to monitor the impact of those improvements.

Figure 19.12 illustrates an example of a metrics report that summarizes the customer satisfaction survey results and indicates the current customer satisfaction level. For each quality attribute polled on the survey, the average satisfaction and importance values are plotted as a numbered bubble on an *x–y* graph. It should be remembered that to make calculation of average satisfaction level valid, a ratio scale measure should be used (for example, a range of zero to five, with five being

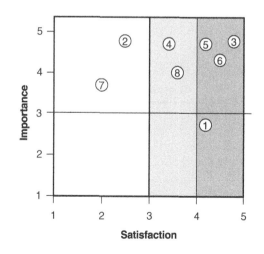

Customer satisfaction survey results

1. Installation
2. Initial software reliability
3. Long-term reliability
4. Usability of software
5. Functionality of software
6. Technical support
7. Documentation
8. Training

Figure 19.12   Customer satisfaction summary report—example.

Part V.B.2

very satisfied). If an ordinal scale metric is used, the median should be used as the measure of central tendency. The darker shaded area on this graph indicates the long-term goal of having an average satisfaction score of better than 4 for all quality attributes. The lighter shaded area indicates a shorter-term goal of having an average satisfaction score better than 3. From this summary report it is possible to quickly identify "initial software reliability" (bubble 2) and "documentation" (bubble 7) as primary opportunities to improve customer satisfaction. By polling importance as well as satisfaction level in the survey, the person analyzing this metric can see that even though documentation has a poorer satisfaction level, initial software reliability is much more important to the customers and therefore should probably be given a higher priority.

Figure 19.13 illustrates an example of a metrics report that shows the distribution of satisfaction scores for three questions. Graphs where the scores are tightly clustered around the mean (question A) indicate a high level of agreement among the customers on their satisfaction level. Distributions that are widely spread (question B), and particularly bimodal distributions (question C), are candidates for further detail analysis.

Another way to summarize the results of a satisfaction survey is to look at trends over time. Figure 19.14 illustrates an example of a metrics report that trends the initial software reliability based on quarterly surveys conducted over a period of 18 months. Again, the dark and light shaded areas on this graph indicate the long- and short-term satisfaction level goals. One note of caution is that to trend the results over time the survey must remain unchanged in the area being trended. Any rewording of the questions on the survey can have major impacts on the

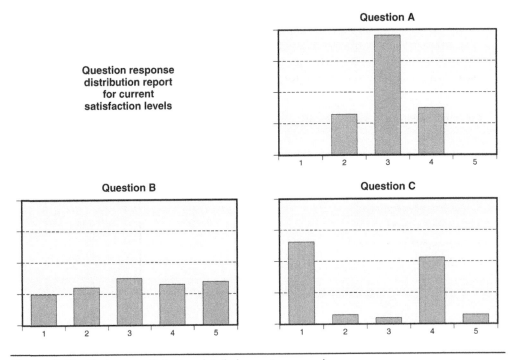

Figure 19.13   Customer satisfaction detailed reports—example.

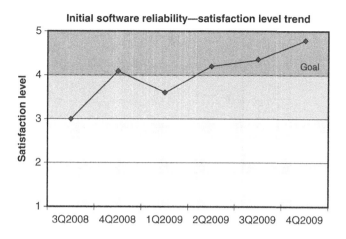

Figure 19.14   Customer satisfaction trending report–example.

survey results. Therefore, historic responses from before wording changes should not be used in future trends.

The primary purpose of trend analysis is to determine if the improvements made to the products, services, or processes had an impact on the satisfaction level of the customers. It should be remembered, however, that satisfaction is a lagging indicator (it only provides information about what has already occurred). Customers have long memories; the dismal initial quality of a software version three releases back may still impact their perception of the product even if the last two versions have been superior.

Customer satisfaction is a subjective measure. It is a measure of perception, not reality, although when it comes to a happy customer, perception is more important than reality. One phenomenon that often occurs is that as the quality of software improves, the expectations of the customers also increase. The customers continue to demand bigger, better, faster software. This can result in a flat trend even though quality is continuously improving. Worse still, it can cause a declining graph because improvements to quality are not keeping up with the increases in the customer's expectations. Even though this impact can be discouraging, it is valuable information that the organization needs to know in the very competitive world of software.

Customer Impact—Responsiveness to Problem Reports

When a customer has a problem with software, the developer must respond quickly to resolve and close the reported problem. For example, service level agreements may define problem report response time goals based on the severity of the incident (for example, critical problems within 24 hours, major problems within 30 days, and minor problems within 120 days). The graph in Figure 19.15 illustrates an example of a metric to track actual performance against these service level agreements. This graph trends the percentage of problem reports closed within the service level agreement time frames each month. This metric is a lagging indicator, a view of the past. Using lagging indicator metrics is like painting

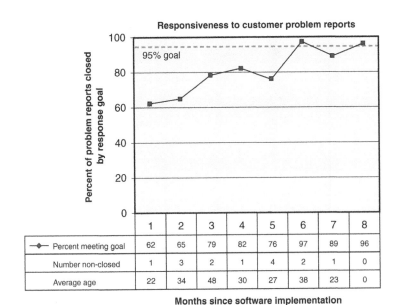

Figure 19.15   Responsiveness to customer problems–example.

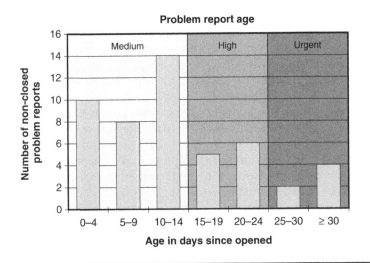

Figure 19.16   Defect backlog aging–example.

the front windshield of a car black and monitoring the quality of the driving by counting the dead bodies that can be seen in the rearview mirror. If an organization waits until the problem report is closed before tracking this response-time metric, they can not take proactive action to control their responsiveness.

The graph in Figure 19.16 shows all non-closed, major problem reports distributed by their age since they were opened. Analysis of this graph can quickly identify problem areas, including problem reports that are past their service level agreement goal and reports approaching their goal. This information allows a proactive approach to controlling responsiveness to customer-reported problems. This metric is a leading indicator because it helps proactively identify issues. Similar graphs can also be created for minor problems (since critical problems must be corrected within 24 hours it is probably not cost-effective to track them with this metric).

Defect Detection

One way to measure the effectiveness of a defect detection process is to measure the number of *escapes* from that process. An analogy for escapes is to think of each defect detection process as a screen door that is catching bugs. Escapes are the bugs that make it through the screen door and get farther into the house. A person can not determine how effective the screen door is by looking at the bugs it caught; that person must go inside and count the number of bugs that got past the screen door.

In software there is no way of counting how many defects actually escaped a defect detection technique. The types of defects detected by subsequent defect detection techniques can be examined to approximate the number of actual escapes. For example, as illustrated in Figure 19.17a, at the end of the first defect detection technique (requirement defect detection—typically a requirement peer review) there are no known escapes.

However, as illustrated in Figure 19.17b, after analyzing the defects found by the second design defect detection technique, there are not only design-type defects (seven dark gray bugs) but also requirement-type defects (three light gray bugs), so three requirement escapes have been identified.

As illustrated in Figure 19.17c, after analyzing the defects found by the third coding defect detection technique, there are not only coding-type defects (seven black bugs) but also requirement-type defects (one light gray bug) and design-type

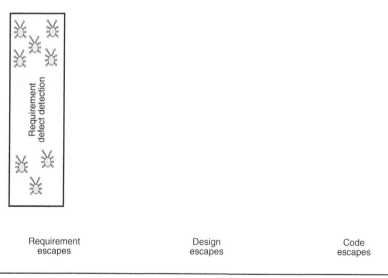

Part V.B.2

Figure 19.17a   Measuring escapes—requirements example.

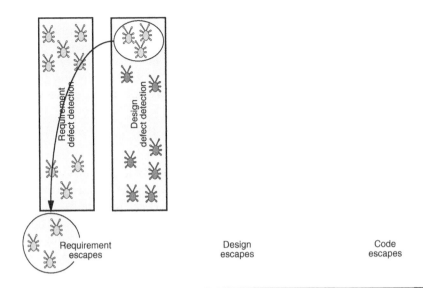

Figure 19.17b   Measuring escapes–design example.

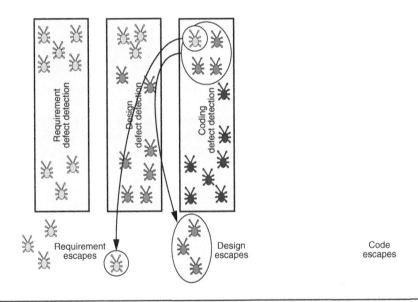

Figure 19.17c   Measuring escapes–coding example.

defects (three dark gray bugs). So four requirement escapes and three design escapes have now been identified.

As illustrated in Figure 19.17d, everything found in the testing defect detection technique is an escape because no new defects are introduced through the testing process (new defects introduced during testing are the result of requirement, design, or code rework efforts). Analysis of defects found in testing shows requirement-type defects (two light gray bugs), design-type defects (five dark

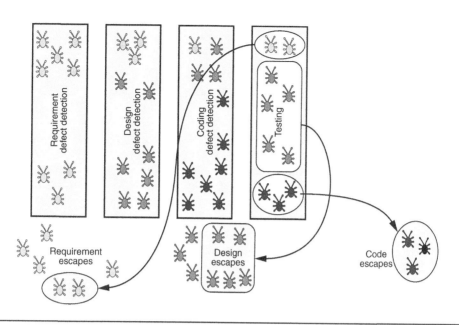

Figure 19.17d   Measuring escapes—testing example.

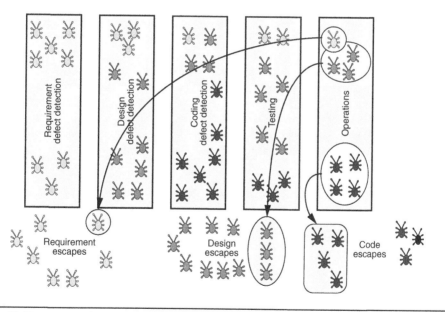

Figure 19.17e   Measuring escapes—operations example.

gray bugs) and coding-type defects (three black bugs). There are now six requirement escapes, eight design escapes, and three coding escapes.

Finally, as illustrated in Figure 19.17e, everything found in operations is also an escape. Analysis of defects found in operations shows requirement-type defects (one light gray bug), design-type defects (three dark gray bugs), and coding-type defects (four black bugs). There are now a total of seven requirement escapes, 11 design escapes, and seven coding escapes. Of course these counts will continue to change if additional defects are identified in operations.

Defect Containment and Total Defect Containment Effectiveness (TDCE)

Defect containment looks at the effectiveness of defect detection techniques to keep defects from escaping into later phases or into operations. *Phase containment effectiveness* metrics show the effectiveness of defect detection techniques in identifying defects in the same phase as they were introduced. Many studies have been done that demonstrate that defects that are not detected until later in the software development life cycle are much more costly to correct. By understanding which processes are allowing phase escapes, organizations can better target their defect detection improvement efforts. Phase containment is calculated by:

$$\frac{\text{Number of defects found that were introduced in the phase}}{\text{Total defects introduced during the phase (including those found later)}} \times 100\%$$

Figure 19.18 illustrates an example of calculating phase containment. For the requirements phase, 15 requirement-type defects were found and fixed during that phase, and 10 requirement-type defects were found in later phases for a total of 25 requirement-type defects. The requirements phase containment is 15 / 25 = 60%. For the design phase, 29 design-type defects were found and fixed during that phase, and 12 design-type defects were found in later phases for a total of 41 design-type defects. The design phase containment is 29 / 41 ≈ 71%. To continue this example, for the code phase, 86 code-type defects were found and fixed during that phase, and 26 code-type defects were found in later phases for a total of 112 code-type defects. The code phase containment is 86 / 112 ≈ 77%. Since the requirements phase containment percentage is the lowest, the requirements phase would be considered as a target for process improvement.

Phase detected	Phase detected defect was introduced		
	Requirements	Design	Code
Requirements	(15)		
Design	5	29	
Code	1	7	86
Test	3	3	19
Field	1	2	7
Total	(25)	41	112

Requirements: (15)/(25) = 60%

Design: 29 / 41 ≈ 71%

Code: __ / __ = __%

Prerelease: __ / __ = __%

Figure 19.18 Defect containment effectiveness—example.

While this example shows the phase containment metrics being calculated after the software has been in operations for some period of time—in real use— phase metrics should be calculated after each phase. At the end of the requirements phase, the requirement phase containment is 15/15 = 100%. At the end of the design phase, requirement phase containment is 15/20 = 75%. These ongoing calculations can be compared with average values baselined from other projects to determine if corrective action is necessary at any time. For example, if instead of five requirement-type defects being found in the design phase, assume that 30 requirement-type defects were found. In this case, the requirements phase containment would be calculated as 25/55 ≈ 45%. This much lower value might indicate that corrective action in terms of additional requirements defect detection activities should be performed before proceeding into the code phase.

The *total defect containment effectiveness* (TDCE) metric shows the effectiveness of defect detection techniques in identifying defects before the product is released into operation. TDCE is calculated as:

$$\frac{\text{Number of defects found prior to release}}{\text{Total defects found (including those found after release)}} \times 100\%$$

For the example in Figure 19.18, 24 requirement-type defects, 39 design-type defects, and 105 code-type defects, for a total of (24 + 39 + 105) = 168 defects, were found prior to release. Total defects found (including those found after release) is (25 + 41 + 112) = 178. TDCE for this example is 168/178 ≈ 94%. The TDCE for this project could then be compared with the TDCE for previous projects to determine if it is at an appropriate level. If process improvements have been implemented, this comparison can be used to determine if the improvements had a positive impact on the TDCE metric value.

Defect Removal Efficiency

Defect removal efficiency (DRE), also called *defect detection efficiency* or *defect detection effectiveness,* is a measure of the percentage of all defects in the software that were found and removed when a detection/rework process was executed. Unlike phase containment, this metric can be calculated for each defect detection technique (instead of by phase). For example, if both code reviews and unit testing were done in the coding phase, each technique would have its own DRE percentage. DRE also includes all defects that could have been found by that technique, not just the ones introduced during that phase. DRE is calculated by:

$$\frac{\text{Number of defects found and removed by the activity}}{\text{Total number of defects present at the activity}} \times 100\%$$

Figure 19.19a illustrates an example of the calculation of DRE. Note that the DRE for the requirements review process is 15/25 = 60%. Since this is the first defect detection/removal process and the only types of defects available to find are requirement-type defects, then the phase containment and DRE numbers are the same. However, in the design review processes, not only can design-type defects be found, but the defects that escaped from the requirements review can also be found. As illustrated in Figure 19.19a, there were five requirement-type defects and 29 design-type defects found during the design review. However, an additional five requirement-type defects and 12 design-type defects escaped and were found later. The DRE for the design review is $(5 + 29) / (5 + 29 + 5 + 12) \approx 67\%$.

As illustrated in Figure 19.19b, the DRE for the code review is approximately equal to $(1 + 3 + 54) / (1 + 3 + 54 + 4 + 9 + 58) \approx 45\%$. To complete this example, the DRE for:

- Unit testing $= (0 + 4 + 32) / (0 + 4 + 32 + 4 + 5 + 26) \approx 51\%$

- Integration testing $= (1 + 3 + 13) / (1 + 3 + 13 + 3 + 2 + 13) \approx 49\%$

- System testing $= (2 + 0 + 6) / (2 + 0 + 6 + 1 + 2 + 7) \approx 44\%$

Detection technique	Phase detected defect was introduced		
	Requirements	Design	Code
Requirements review	15		
Design review	5	29	
Code review	1	3	54
Unit testing	0	4	32
Integration testing	1	3	13
System testing	2	0	6
Operations	1	2	7
Total	25	41	112

Design review: $(5 + 29) / (5 + 29 + 5 + 12) = 34 / 51 \approx 67\%$

Figure 19.19a   Defect removal efficiency–design review example.

Detection technique	Phase detected defect was introduced		
	Requirements	Design	Code
Requirements review	15		
Design review	5	29	
Code review	1	3	54
Unit testing	0	4	32
Integration testing	1	3	13
System testing	2	0	6
Operations	1	2	7
Total	25	41	112

Code review: $((1 + 3 + 54)) / ((1 + 3 + 54 + 4 + 9 + 58)) = 58 / 129 \approx 45\%$

Figure 19.19b   Defect removal efficiency–code review example.

Part V.B.2

Note that of the peer reviews, the coding peer review had the lowest DRE in this example at 45 percent. Of the testing activities, system testing had the lowest DRE. Therefore, these two activities would be candidates for process improvement.

As with phase containment effectiveness, while these examples show the defect removal efficiency metrics being calculated after the software has been in operations for some period of time, in real use these metrics should be calculated after each major defect detection/removal process and compared with baselined values to identify potential issues that need corrective action.

Process Capability

When measuring process capability, the software industry offers guidance in the form of the CMMI for Development Continuous Representation (SEI 2006) and the ISO/IEC 15504 set of standards. Based on these documents, each process area is assigned a capability level from zero to five based on whether the implementation of that process within the organization meets defined good practice criteria.

Many of the metrics already discussed can be used to understand the process capabilities of each individual process, help an organization recognize the amount of variation in its processes, and act as predictors of future process performance. Examples include first-pass yield, phase containment, defect detection efficiency, cycle time, productivity, cost, and defect density of the product being produced.

3. METRICS REPORTING TOOLS

Use various metric representation tools, including dashboards, stoplight charts, etc., to report results efficiently. (Apply)

Body of Knowledge V.B.3

Charts and Graphs

As the old saying goes, "A picture is worth a thousand words." Metrics are no exception. In fact, many people will look at the picture and ignore the words. So what should the metric look like? Is the metric included in a table with other metrics values for the period? Is it added as the latest value in a trend chart that tracks values for the metric over multiple periods? Would a bar, line, or area graph be the best way to display the trend? Should there be thresholds, goals, or control limits? The answers to these and other questions are part of designing a good metrics report. When selecting the graph or chart for the metric, consideration should always be given to the "message" of the metric. The selected format should make the intended message easy to identify and interpret. Different types of charts and graphs are better at communicating different messages.

Data tables, as illustrated in Figure 19.20, provide a mechanism to display large amounts of detail in a small area. Data tables are compact and well structured.

	Open	Fixed	Resolved
Jan	23	13	3
Feb	27	24	11
Mar	18	26	15
Apr	12	18	27

Figure 19.20   Data table—example.

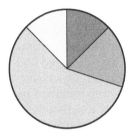

Figure 19.21   Pie chart—example.

However, tables show only the values that the user must compare and evaluate, they do not provide a summary view or easily show trends. Graphs and charts are usually easier for the user to interpret than columns of numbers. Where specific detail is needed, consider adding a data table to the graph or chart.

Pie charts, as illustrated in Figure 19.21, are used to show the size of each part as a percentage of the whole. Multiple pie charts can be used to represent multiple groups. Sometimes one or more slices of the pie are separated from the whole for emphasis. However, pie charts only show individual values and not trends over time. Showing more than five or six slices in a pie chart makes the chart busy and difficult to interpret (a simple bar chart might be a better choice).

Line graphs are typically used to show changes or trends over time. An example of a line graph is illustrated in Figure 19.22. Line graphs are also used to report nondiscrete variables. Each line on the graph is typically independent of the other lines. Care should be taken to ensure that there are not so many lines on a single graph that the message becomes muddled. If this is the case, consider using multiple line charts, each with a clear individual message.

Bar charts are a simple way to show the relationships between numbers, ratios, or proportions. A simple bar chart, such as the example in Figure 19.23, includes one quantitative or discrete variable. Pareto charts and histograms are typically presented using a simple bar chart.

As illustrated in Figure 19.24, bar charts can be displayed horizontally as well as vertically. Experimentation can be used to determine which type emphasizes the message better.

Grouped bar charts, as illustrated in Figure 19.25, show the comparison of two or more categories, for example, the differences between the values of a variable

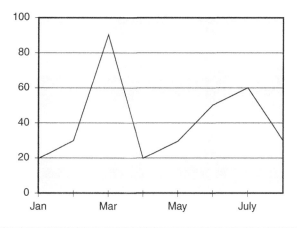

Figure 19.22   Line graph–example.

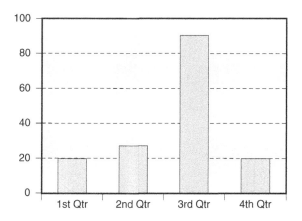

Figure 19.23   Simple bar chart–example.

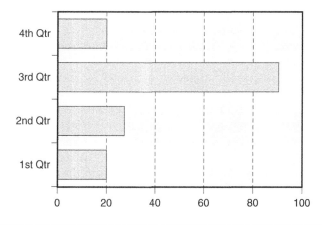

Figure 19.24   Horizontal bar chart–example.

Part V.B.3

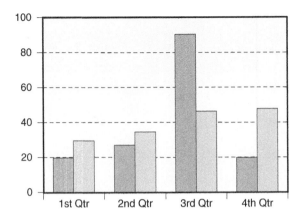

Figure 19.25   Grouped bar chart—example.

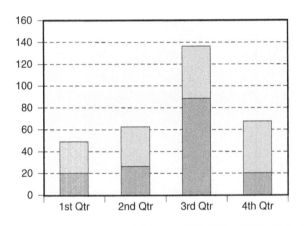

Figure 19.26   Stacked bar chart—example.

for project A and the same variable for project B as they compare over time. Showing more than three categories makes the grouped bar chart busy and difficult to read.

Stacked bar charts, as illustrated in Figure 19.26, show how a total breaks into categories, for example, how the total incident arrival rate for a period is distributed by severity. The height of the intermediate bars corresponds to the frequency for that category.

The choice between grouped or stacked bar charts is determined by what message needs to be emphasized. For example, the data shown in Figures 19.25 and 19.26 are identical, but the messages shown in the graphs are very different. If the chart needs to emphasize the differences between the categories, a grouped bar chart should be chosen. If the chart needs to emphasize the differences between the totals, a stacked bar chart is easier to interpret.

Area graphs, as illustrated in Figure 19.27, are also used to show trends over time. Unlike the line graph, however, the lines within an area graph are dependent because those lines divide the total area into parts (similar to a stacked bar chart). An area graph is more effective than a line chart when the graph needs to emphasize both the trends and the size of or relationship between the areas.

Box charts, also called *box-and-whisker-diagrams*, as illustrated in Figure 19.28, compress a set of data into each box and show its variance. Box charts can be used to show both the differences within a group of data and between groups of data. The various components of a box chart are illustrated in Figure 19.29. Around 50 percent of all data values are between the lower and upper quartiles. About 25 percent of all data values are lower than the lower quartile, and about 25 percent are higher than the upper quartile. The median is the middle data value.

Different colors have physiological impacts (for example, green is *go*, red is *stop*, yellow is *caution*). Care should be taken when using color in metrics graphs and charts.

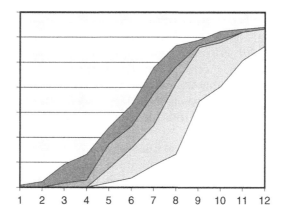

Figure 19.27   Area graph–example.

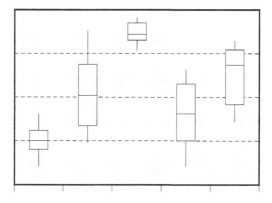

Figure 19.28   Box chart–example.

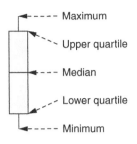

Figure 19.29   Box chart components.

Stoplight Charts

According to the ISO/IEC 15939 *Software Engineering—Software Measurement Process* standard (ISO/IEC 2002), decision criteria are the "thresholds, targets, or patterns used to determine the need for action or further investigation or to describe the level of confidence in a given result." In other words, decision criteria provide guidance that will help the users of the metric interpret the metric results. One way of doing this is to create a *stoplight chart* that provides a red/yellow/green signal to the user of the metric. A red signal indicates that the metric result needs immediate action or further investigation. A yellow signal indicates that the metric result doesn't need immediate attention but is in a cautionary state and should be monitored. A green signal indicates that no action or investigation is needed at this time.

Figure 19.30 illustrates several types of stoplight charts. In the chart on the left, the red/yellow/green signals are built into the chart as colored areas in the background (one place where color is appropriate when displaying a metric). Since this book is not in color, the regions on this graph are labeled with the stoplight colors. The table in the upper right of Figure 19.30 simply lists the metrics and their current stoplight colors. This type of summary table can include hyperlinks to the detailed metrics behind each reported stoplight status. A third example is simply a visual stoplight indicator for the metric, as illustrated in the lower right of Figure 19.30.

Dashboards

The concept of a metrics dashboard is analogous to a dashboard in a car. All of the key information about the status of the car can be identified quickly by looking at the set of metrics on the dashboard, including fuel levels, speeds, engine temperature, and alarm lights for controlled items such as oil pressure and other maintenance items, doors that are ajar, or seat belts that are not fastened.

In some cases it takes multiple metrics to get a complete picture of the status of a process, product, or service. A metrics *dashboard* accumulates all of the key metrics and allows the user to see in a single collection the relevant information about the subject of that dashboard. For example, a software project dashboard might include information about schedule, budget, product functionality, product quality, and effective and efficient utilization of project staff and other resources.

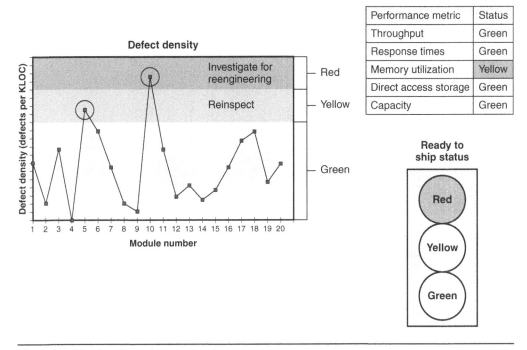

Figure 19.30   Stoplight chart—examples.

Figure 19.31 shows another example of a dashboard, which reports the status of the system testing process. This dashboard includes graphs and charts showing:

- Test effort variances

- Test case status

- Cumulative defects by status (three graphs, one for each severity)

- Performance metrics stoplights

- Arrival rates by severity

Kiviat Chart

Another way to show a summary view of a set of metrics is to use a *Kiviat chart*, also called a *polar chart, radar chart,* or *spider chart.* In a Kiviat chart, each "spoke" represents a metric with the metric's value plotted on that spoke. An outer circle (or pattern) on a Kiviat chart can be used as the objective or threshold, or inner and outer circles (or patterns) can be used to depict valid ranges. Alternately, the Kiviat chart can be combined with a stoplight chart by adding red/yellow/green bands to the chart.

Figure 19.32 illustrates an example of a Kiviat chart that summarizes the customer satisfaction scores shown previously in Figure 19.12. From this chart, it is fairly easy to identify "documentation" as the area that is farthest away from the

Part V.B.3

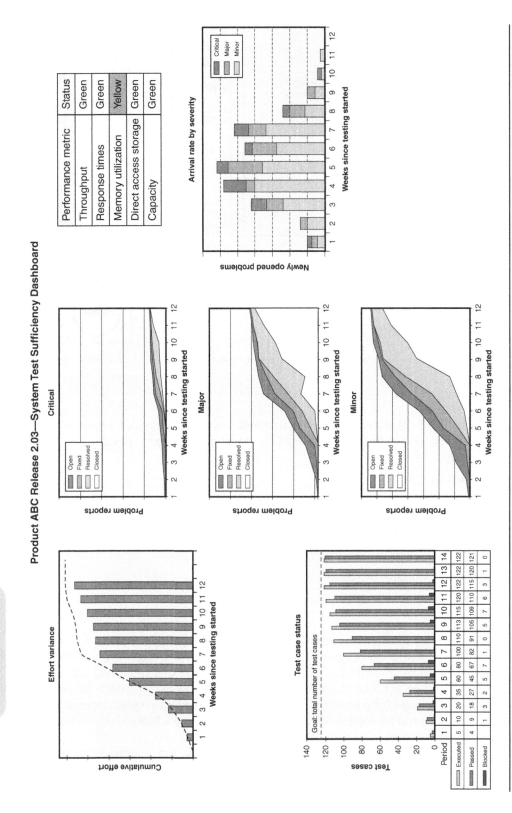

Figure 19.31   Dashboard—example.

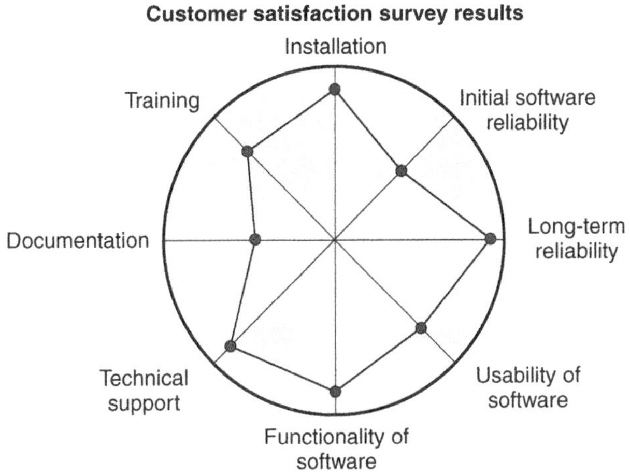

Figure 19.32 Kiviat chart—example.

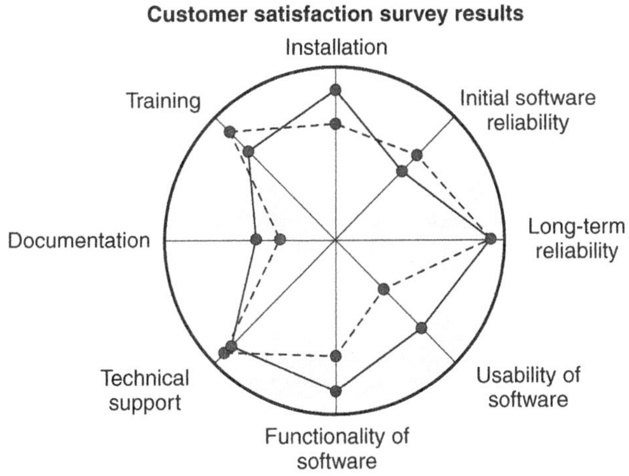

Figure 19.33 Kiviat chart comparison—example.

outer circle goal of having a 5 as a satisfaction score. Therefore, documentation presents the best opportunity for process improvement according to this chart.

A Kiviat chart can also be used to compare several different items (for example, projects, products, or processes) across several parameters against the ideal by plotting additional sets of points. For example, Figure 19.33 illustrates the comparison of customer satisfaction results for two different products.

Part V.B.3

Chapter 20

C. Analytical Techniques

Software quality engineers (SQEs) need a variety of analytical tools in their software quality tool belt so that they can pull out the correct tool for the correct job. The SQE needs to know when and how to use different sampling techniques in order to effectively use sampling during product and project management, audits, testing, and product acceptance.

The SQE should be able to analyze the integrity of the data used to provide metrics and other information products. They should be able to analyze the metrics design and implementation processes and the data collection and analysis processes to evaluate the quality, accuracy, completeness, and timeliness of the data and metrics.

The SQE must be familiar with and know how to utilize classic quality tools including flowcharts, Pareto charts, cause-and-effect diagrams, check sheets, scatter diagrams, run charts, histograms, and control charts. The SQE must also be familiar with and know how to utilize basic problem-solving tools, including affinity diagrams, tree diagrams, matrix diagrams, interrelationship digraphs, prioritization matrices, activity network diagrams, and root cause analysis in order to help teams and projects identify and solve potential quality issues and implement improvements to software products, processes, and services.

1. SAMPLING

> Define and distinguish between sampling methods (e.g., random, stratified, cluster) as used in auditing, testing, product acceptance, etc. (Understand)
>
> **Body of Knowledge V.C.1**

When the set of all possible items in a population is very large it may be too costly or time-consuming to do a comprehensive analysis of all of the items. For example, during an audit, there is just not enough time or resources to talk to every auditee, witness every process step, or look at every quality record. If the customer base is large, it may be too costly to survey all the customers to determine their satisfaction level. Evaluating or estimating attributes or characteristics of the entire system, process, product, or project through a representative sample can be more efficient while still providing the required information. To legitimately be able to use a sample to extrapolate the results to the whole population requires the use of one of four statistical sampling methods.

Random Sampling

The first statistical sampling method is simple *random sampling*. In this method, each item in the population has the same probability of being selected as part of the sample as any other item. For example, a tester could randomly select five inputs to a test case from the population of all possible valid inputs within a range of 1 through 100 to use during test execution. To do this the tester could use a random number generator or simply put each number from 1 through 100 on a slip of paper in a hat, mixing them up and drawing out five numbers. Random sampling can be done with or without replacement. If it is done without replacement, an item is not returned to the population after it is selected and thus can only occur once in the sample.

Systematic Sampling

Systematic sampling is another statistical sampling method. In this method, every nth element from the list is selected as a sample, starting with a sample element n randomly selected from the first k elements. For example, if the population has 1000 elements and a sample size of 100 is needed, then k would be $1000/100 = 10$. If number 7 is randomly selected from the first 10 elements on the list, the sample would continue down the list, selecting the seventh element from each group of 10 elements. Care must be taken when using systematic sampling to ensure that the original population list has not been ordered in a way that introduced any nonrandom factors into the sampling. An example of systematic sampling would be if the auditor of an acceptance test process selected the 14th acceptance test case out of the first 20 test cases in a random list of all acceptance test cases to retest during the audit process. The auditor would then keep adding 20 and select the 34th test case, 54th test case, 74th test case, and so on, to retest until the end of the list is reached.

Stratified Sampling

The statistical sampling method called *stratified sampling* is used when representatives from each subgroup within the population need to be represented in the sample. The first step in stratified sampling is to divide the population into subgroups (strata) based on mutually exclusive criteria. Random or systematic samples are then taken from each subgroup. The sampling fraction for each subgroup may be taken in the same proportion the subgroup has in the population. For example, the person conducting a customer satisfaction survey selects random customers from each customer type in proportion to the number of customers of that type in the population. That is, if 40 samples are to be selected, and 10 percent of the customers are managers, 60 percent are users, 25 percent are operators, and five percent are database administrators, then four managers, 24 users, 10 operators, and two administrators would be randomly selected. Stratified sampling can also sample an equal number of items from each subgroup. For example, a development lead randomly selected three modules out of each programming language used to examine against the coding standard.

Cluster Sampling

The fourth statistical sampling method is *cluster sampling*, also called *block sampling*. In cluster sampling, the population that is being sampled is divided into groups called *clusters*. Instead of these subgroups being homogeneous based on a selected criterion as in stratified sampling, a cluster is as heterogeneous as possible to match the population. A random sample is then taken from within one or more selected clusters. For example, if an organization has 30 small projects currently under development, an auditor looking for compliance to the coding standard might use cluster sampling to randomly select four of those projects as representatives for the audit and then randomly sample code modules for auditing from just those four projects. Cluster sampling can tell us a lot about that particular cluster, but unless the clusters are selected randomly and a lot of clusters are sampled, generalizations can not always be made about the entire population. For example, random sampling from all the source code modules written during the previous week, or all the modules in a particular subsystem, or all modules written in a particular language may cause biases to enter the sample that would not allow statistically valid generalization.

Haphazard Sampling

There are also other types of sampling that, while nonstatistical (information about the entire population can not be extrapolated from the sample), may still provide useful information. In *haphazard sampling*, samples are selected based on convenience but preferably should still be chosen as randomly as possible. For example, the auditor may ask to see a list of all of the source code modules and then closes his eyes and points at the list to select a module to audit. Or the auditor could grab one of the listing binders off the shelf, flip through it, and randomly stop on a module to audit. Haphazard sampling is typically quicker and uses smaller sample sizes than other sampling techniques. The main disadvantage of haphazard sampling is that since it is not statistically based, generalizations about the total population should be made with extreme caution.

Judgmental Sampling

Another nonstatistical sampling method is *judgmental sampling*. In judgmental sampling, the person doing the sample uses his/her knowledge or experience to select the items to be sampled. For example, based on experience an auditor may know which types of items are more apt to have nonconformances or which types of items have had problems in the past or which items are a higher risk to the organization. In another example, the acceptance tester might select test cases that exercise the most complex features, mission-critical functions, or most used sections of the software.

2. DATA COLLECTION AND INTEGRITY

> Describe the importance of data integrity from planning through collection and analysis, and apply various techniques to ensure its quality, accuracy, completeness, and timeliness. (Apply)
>
> **Body of Knowledge V.C.2**

If the right data items are not collected, then the objectives of the measurement program can not be accomplished. Data analysis is pointless without good data. Therefore, establishing a good data collection plan is the cornerstone of any successful metrics program. The data collection plans may be part of standardized metrics definitions at the organizational level, or included in or tailored to project plans or subplans (for example, measurement plans, communication plans, quality assurance plans). A data collection plan should include who is responsible for collection and/or validation of the data, how the data should be collected (for example, measurement units used, environmental conditions), when the data is collected, and where and how the data is stored. Data collection plans may also include information about archiving or retiring data.

Who Should Collect the Data?

Deciding who should collect the data is an important part of ensuring that good data is collected. In most cases the best choice is the "owner" of the data. The data owner is the person with direct access to the source of the data and in many cases is actually responsible for generating the data. Table 20.1 includes a list of example data owners and the types of data that they own. For example, when a user calls in to the help desk, the help desk staff has direct access to the problem identification data that is being reported by the user and collects that data into a customer call report database. On the other hand, in some cases the users themselves have access to a problem-reporting database. In that case the users are the owners of the problem-identification data and collect that data.

The benefits of having the data owner collect the data include:

- Data owners can collect the data as it is being generated, which helps increase accuracy and completeness.

- Data owners are more likely to detect anomalies in the data as it is being collected, which helps increase accuracy.

Table 20.1   Data ownership—examples.

Data owner	Examples of data owned
Management	• Schedule
	• Budget
Software developers	• Time spent per task
	• Inspection data, including defects found
	• Root cause of defects
Testers	• Test cases planned/executed/passed
	• Problem identification data
	• Test coverage
Configuration management	• Defects corrected per build
	• Modules changed per build
Users	• Problem-identification data
	• Operational hours

  • Having data owners collecting the data helps to eliminate the human error of duplicate recording (once by data recorder and again by data entry clerk), which helps increase accuracy.

Once the people who need to gather the data are identified, they must agree to do the work. They must be convinced of the importance and usefulness of collecting the data. Management has to support the program by giving the data owners the time and resources required to perform data collection activities. To quote Watts Humphrey (1989), "The actual work of collecting data is tedious and must generally be done by software professionals who are busy with other tasks. Unless they and their immediate managers are convinced that the data is important, they either won't gather it or will not be very careful when they do."

So what can the metrics providers do to help ensure that the data owners collect good data? First, the metrics providers can design metrics that are as objective and unambiguous as possible. A data item is objective if it is collected the same way each time. Subjective data can also be valuable; for example, customer satisfaction metrics are typically subjective. However, the goal is to make the data as objective as possible. A data item is unambiguous if two different people collecting the same measure for the same item will collect the same data. This requires standardized definitions and well-defined measurement methods.

Second, the metrics provider can design the metrics and establish data collection mechanisms that are as unobtrusive and convenient as possible. Data collection must be an integral part of the software development process and not some outside step that detracts from the "real work." Data collection must be simple enough not to disrupt the working patterns of the individual collecting the data any more than absolutely necessary. In some cases this means automating all or part of the data collection. For example, having a pull-down pick list is much more convenient than making the data owner type in "critical," "major," or "minor" (and it can also contribute to more accurate data by eliminating misspellings or abbreviations). As another example, don't make the data owner type in the current date. The computer knows the date—have the computer default that data item.

Third, the data owners must be trained in how to collect the data so that they understand what to do and when to do it. For simple collection mechanisms, training can be short (≤ one hour). Hands-on, interactive training, where the group works with actual data collection examples, can many times provide the best results. Without this training, hours of support staff time can be wasted answering the same questions over and over again. An additional benefit of training is promoting a common understanding about when and how to collect the data. This reduces the risk of invalid and inconsistent data being collected.

Fourth, the metrics providers must feed the metrics information back to the data owners so that they can see that the data items are used and not just dropped into a black hole. Better yet, the metrics providers can use the data to create metrics that are directly useful to the data owners. There must also be people assigned to support the data collection effort so that the data collectors can get their questions answered, and issues related to data and data collection problems are handled.

How Should the Data Be Collected?

The answer is automate, automate, automate, automate:

- Automate data collection and validation
- Automate the databases
- Automate data extraction
- Automate metrics reporting and delivery

There is widespread agreement that as much of the data-gathering process as possible should be automated. At a minimum, standardized forms should be used for data collection, but the data from these forms must at some point be entered into a metrics database if it is to have any long-term usefulness. Information that stays on forms can quickly get buried in file drawers, never to see the light of day again. In order for data to be useful and used, easy access to the data is required. The people who need the data have to be able to get to it easily. The easier the data items are to access, the easier it is to generate timely metrics reports.

Dumping raw data and hand-tallying or calculating measurements is another way to introduce human error into the measured values. Even if the data are recorded in a simple spreadsheet, automatic sorting, extracting, and calculations are available and should be used. They also increase the speed of producing the metrics and therefore can help increase timeliness.

Automating metrics reporting and delivery eliminates hours spent standing in front of copy machines. It also increases usability because the metrics are available on the computer instead of buried in a pile of papers on a desk. Remember, metrics are expensive. Automation can reduce the expense while making the metrics available in a timely manner.

Part V.C.2

Quality Data and Measurement Error

In order to have high-quality data, the measurements taken need to be as free from error as possible. A *measurement error* occurs when the measured value or data item collected (the assigned number or symbol) differs from the actual value that would be mapped to the attribute of the entity in a perfect world. For example, a person might be measured as 6 foot 2 inches tall, while in reality that person might be 6 foot 2.1385632 inches tall. The .1385632 inches is the measurement error. According to Arthur (1985), measurement error can happen for a number of reasons, including:

- *Imperfect definition of what is being measured.* For example, if asked to measure how "big" the person is, the data owner might measure the person's height when the individual requesting the measurement actually wanted to know that person's weight.

- *Imperfect understanding of how to convert what is being measured into the measurement signal (data).* For example, if a three-year-old is asked to measure a person's height, there might be an error because they don't understand how to even take that measurement.

- *Failure to establish the correct conditions for taking the measurement.* Should the person be measured with or without shoes? How should the data owner deal with a full head of hair piled up above the scalp?

- *Human error.* Then there is error simply because people make mistakes. For example, the data owner might have misread a 3 as a 2, or might have incorrectly converted the 75 inches they measured into 6 foot 2 inches instead of 6 foot 3 inches.

- *Defective or deficient measurement instruments.* The tool used to take the measurement might also be defective in some way. For example, a tape measure might be old and all stretched out of shape.

Data Accuracy

What if data is inaccurate? Can inaccurate data be accepted and used anyway? Actually there are two reasons why the answer may be yes. First, the data may be accurate enough to meet the required objectives. Go back to the time sheet example. When reconstructing the data, the engineer may overstate one project by a few hours one week and understate it the next. The result is a fairly good approximation of total time spent over the life of the project. When estimating time requirements for future projects, the time card data is usually adequate enough for its intended use.

The second reason for reporting inaccurate data is to make it accurate. For example, a metrics analyst created metrics reports to show the trend over time for non-closed problems. However, the project managers complained that the reports were inaccurate. They said that many of the problems were actually closed, but the database had not been updated. However, upper management utilized these reports to continue the focus on reducing the backlog of uncorrected problems. This provided the leverage needed to update the data and increase its accuracy.

If metrics providers wait for 100 percent data accuracy, they may never produce any metrics. Remember—good enough is good enough. On the other hand, metrics providers and users need to be aware of data inaccuracies and consider those inaccuracies when determining how reliable and valid the metrics are. This awareness can help determine the level of confidence that can be placed in the measurement results.

Data Completeness

What if the data are incomplete? Again there are similar circumstances where the metrics provider can still use the data. In the time sheet example, the data might be considered incomplete because it does not include overtime. In this case, the metrics provider can change the metrics algorithm for estimating the next project to take this into consideration. If they know engineers are working about 10 hours a week unpaid overtime, they can use a 1.25 multiplication factor in the model to estimate total engineering effort for the next project.

The reporting of incomplete data can be used to make the data more complete. When one company first started reporting code review metrics, the initial reports indicated that only a small percent of the code was being reviewed. Actually, a much higher percent was reviewed, but data were not being recorded in the database. By reporting incomplete data, emphasis was placed on recording accurate and complete data. This is especially true when projects recording data use that data to demonstrate both cost and time savings to upper management.

However, as with accuracy, metrics providers and users need to be aware of data incompleteness as a consideration when determining how reliable and valid the metrics are so they can determine the level of confidence that can be placed in the measurement results.

Data Timeliness

Data collection and reporting must be timely. For example, if a supplier is trying to make a decision on whether or not to ship a software product, having defect status data from last week is of little value.

Two times need to be considered when talking about timeliness and data collection:

1. *Data collection time.* Are the data being collected in a timely manner? The longer the time period between the time an event happens and the time when the data about that event are collected, the less integrity the data probably has. For example, if an engineer records the time spent on each task as that engineer is working on those tasks, the effort data is typically much more accurate than it would be if the engineer waits until the end of the week to complete the data on a time sheet.

2. *Data availability time.* Is the collected data being made available in a timely manner? If there is a large gap of time between when the data are collected and when they are available in the metrics database, the integrity of the reported metrics can be impacted. For example, even if

inspection data is collected on forms during the actual inspection, those forms may sit for some period of time before the data are entered into the inspection database.

There are also two times to consider when talking about timeliness and data reporting:

1. *Data extraction time.* Looks at the timeliness of extracting the data from the metrics database. This timing may be an issue in information warehouse environments where data are extracted from production systems on a periodic basis and made available for metrics reporting. For example, data extracted the previous midnight might be considered untimely for an immediate ship/no ship decision while being perfectly timely for monthly summary reports.

2. *Data reporting time.* Looks at the timeliness of report generation and distribution from the extracted data. This timing may especially be an issue if the metrics are hand-calculated and distributed in hard copy.

The timing of data synchronization is also important. If the data for a metrics report are pulled while data is being input or refreshed it could result in part of the data extraction being old data that are out of sync with another part of the extraction that reflects newer data. Data synchronization may also be a problem if data collection, availability, or extraction times vary for different data sets used in the same metrics report. If these data time frames are not synchronized for the measurements being analyzed, that analysis will be severely limited or even completely defective/erroneous.

3. QUALITY ANALYSIS TOOLS

Describe and use classic quality tools (flowcharts, Pareto charts, cause-and-effect diagrams, control charts, histograms, etc.) and problem-solving tools (affinity and tree diagrams, matrix and activity network diagrams, root cause analysis, etc.) in a variety of situations. (Apply)

Body of Knowledge V.C.3

Flowcharts

Flowcharts are used to graphically represent the inputs, actions, decision points, and outputs of a process. Historically, flowcharts were used in software design to map out the functions performed by a module (detailed design). While flowcharts have typically been replaced with more modern design-modeling tools, they are still used extensively in process definition to map the process. Flowcharting a process is a good starting point to help a team come to a common understand-

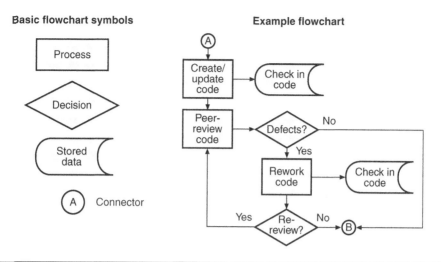

Figure 20.1   Basic flowchart symbols and flowchart—examples..

ing of the current process. As a quality analysis tool, flowcharts can help identify bottlenecks or problem areas (for example, missing steps, unnecessary loops,
redundant steps) in a process. Flowcharts can help a team come to consensus on
the steps in a standard process and explore where tailoring to special projects is
needed. Flowcharts can also act as a training aid to help trainees visualize how the
individual steps in a process interact.

While there are many different flowchart symbols, Figure 20.1 illustrates a
few of the basic symbols and shows an example flowchart.

Pareto Charts

Pareto analysis is the process of ranking problems or categories based on their frequency of occurrence or the size of their impact in order to determine which of
many possible opportunities to pursue first because they have the greatest potential for improvement. Pareto analysis is based on the *Pareto principle*: 80 percent of
the variation in a process comes from about 20 percent of the sources. The intent
is to identify the "critical few" that need the most attention among the "insignificant many."

A *Pareto chart* is a bar chart where the height of each bar indicates the frequency or impact of problems or categories. For example, as illustrated in Figure
20.2, a Pareto chart can be used to identify defect-prone modules that need more
testing or that are candidates for reengineering.

To construct a Pareto chart:

1. *Determine the problems or categories for the chart.* For example, a team
   might decide to examine the number of defects identified in each
   module. Other examples might include problems by root cause, by
   phase introduced, or by reporting customer.

2. *Determine a unit of measure such as frequency or cost.* For example, the
   number of defects in each module. Other examples might be defects per
   KLOC (or function point) in each module or the cost (dollars or effort)
   of fixing defects in each module.

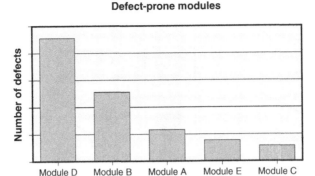

Figure 20.2   Pareto chart—example.

3. *Select a time interval for analysis.* For example, the team could look at all defects reported in the last six months.

4. *Gather the data and rank-order the problems or categories from the largest total occurrences to the smallest* and create a bar chart where the bars are arranged in descending order of height from left to right. In the example in Figure 20.2, module D has the highest number of defects and module C has the lowest.

Cause-and-Effect Diagrams

Improving quality involves taking action on the root causes of a problem or the causes of variation in a process. "With most practical applications, the number of possible causes for any given problem can be huge. Dr. Kaoru Ishikawa developed a simple method of graphically displaying the causes of any given quality problem" (Pyzdek 2001). In a *cause-and-effect diagram*, also referred to as an *Ishikawa diagram* or *fishbone diagram*, the problem (or effect) is put at the "head" of the fish. The major fish bones are typically major drivers such as management, people, environment, methods, measurements, and materials. From these major drivers, specific drivers that are causing the problem are listed. The example cause-and-effect diagram illustrated in Figure 20.3 only shows a single level of causes off the major drivers, but sublevels and sub-sublevels can also be added as additional branches off each of these branches.

A variation on the cause-and-effect diagram is the *process-type cause-and-effect diagram*. As illustrated in Figure 20.4, in a process-type cause-and-effect diagram the causes of the problem related to each step in a process are investigated. For example, if the analysis team is looking at the problem of unreliable software, they might look at the major steps in the software development process (for example, requirements, design, code, integration test, system test) and analyze any causes related to each of those process steps. If the problem is that too many defects are escaping from the detailed design inspection, the team could look at the major steps in the inspection process (for example, overview, preparation, inspection meeting, and follow-up) and the causes related to each of those process steps.

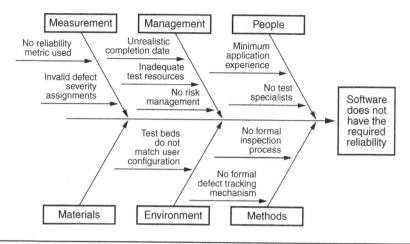

Figure 20.3 Cause-and-effect diagram—example.

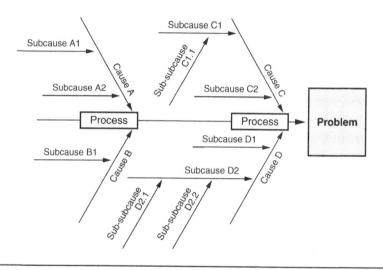

Figure 20.4 Process-type cause-and-effect diagram—example.

Cause-and-effect diagrams are not only useful in the analysis of actual problems, they can be used to analyze potential problems and their potential causes. For example, in risk analysis or hazard analysis, the potential problem (risk or hazard) is placed at the head of the fish, and potential drivers that might cause the risk or hazard to turn into an actual problem are documented as the branches of the diagram.

Check Sheets

Check sheets are tools used in data collection. In their simplest form, check sheets make the data collection process easier by providing prewritten descriptions of categories or events that should be counted either from historic data or as events

Requirements defect root cause	Frequency
Missing requirement	⊮⊬ ‖‖
Ambiguous requirement	⊮⊬ ⊮⊬ ‖
Incomplete requirement	⊮⊬ ‖
Incorrect requirement	⊮⊬ ‖‖‖
Contradictory requirement	‖‖‖
Change to requirements not communicated	‖‖‖‖

Figure 20.5   Check sheet–example.

occur in the future. For example, the potential causes identified in a cause-and-effect diagram could be used on a check sheet to collect the number of actual occurrences of each identified cause during the next three weeks. While check sheets can take on several forms, they typically use X's or tally marks to count the number of occurrences. Figure 20.5 illustrates a check sheet used to collect data on the root cause of requirements-type defects. Check sheets serve as reminders that direct the data collector to items of interest and importance. The data collected on a check sheet can also be used as input into creating a Pareto chart or a histogram.

Scatter Diagrams

A *scatter diagram* is an *x–y* plot of one variable versus another that is used to determine if there is any potential relationship between two variables. One variable, called the *independent variable*, is typically plotted on the *x*-axis. The second variable, called the *dependent variable*, is typically plotted on the *y*-axis. Scatter diagrams are used to investigate whether changes to the independent variable are correlated to changes in the dependent variable. Scatter diagrams can help answer questions such as:

- Does the cyclomatic complexity of a module impact the number of defects in that module?
- Does reuse cause productivity to increase?
- Is there a relationship between the number of defects found during testing and the number of defects that will be found post-release?
- As the experience level of the programmer increases, does the number of defects in their code decrease?

As illustrated in Figure 20.6, there is a *positive correlation* between the independent and dependent variables if the dependent variable increases as the independent variable increases. There is a *negative correlation* between the two variables if the dependent variable decreases as the independent variable increases. The more tightly the data points are clustered, the stronger the correlation between

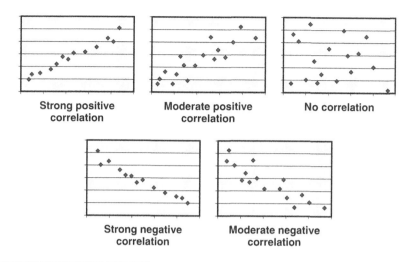

Figure 20.6 Scatter diagram—examples.

the two variables. If the data points on the scatter diagram are randomly scattered, then *no correlation* exists between the two variables.

When interpreting a scatter diagram, it should be noted that correlation does not necessarily imply causation. Other interpretation considerations include:

- Ensuring that enough data has been collected to indicate a trend (typically at least 20 data points)

- Ensuring that the independent variable in the data set varies over a large enough range to determine correlation

- Being careful not to use the information to predict (extrapolate) the dependent variable values using independent variable values that lie outside the study's range

Run Chart

Run charts are plots of data arranged in time sequence. Many factors can affect an attribute (of a process, product, or service) over time. Run charts can make it easier to see what is happening to that attribute and detect trends, shifts, or patterns. Run charts can be used to monitor and detect these shifts in an attribute after a process or product improvement activity has been conducted to monitor the impact of that improvement. For example, the run chart in Figure 20.7 could be used to monitor the impacts on system availability as improvements are made to network resources over time. Analysis of a run chart can also suggest possible areas where further investigation is needed to determine cause before any conclusions can be reached. Patterns to watch for when analyzing run charts include:

- Repeating patterns
- Sudden shifts or stepwise jumps

Part V.C.3

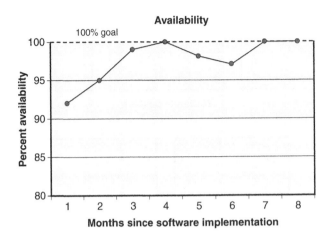

Figure 20.7   Run chart–example.

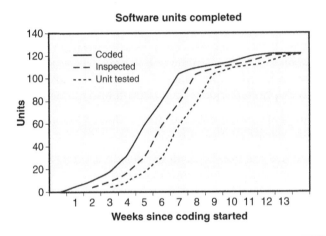

Figure 20.8   S-curve run chart–example.

- Outlying data points
- Upward or downward trends

Another type of run chart that is frequently used in software is the *S-curve run chart*, which tracks the cumulative progress of a parameter over time. Examples of S-curve run charts for software include:

- Completion of the design of software components over time or of design reviews
- Completion of coding, inspection, or unit testing of software units, as illustrated in Figure 20.8
- Completion of writing or execution of test cases
- The arrival of problem reports during testing (or post-release)

Many times these S-curve run charts are compared to predicted values (engineering effort expended versus predicted, or dollars spent versus predicted) or against historic data (release to release defect density) so that the analysis can be placed into the proper context.

Histograms

A *histogram* is a bar chart that shows the frequency counts for a set (or sample) of data. Histograms are created by:

- Selecting the characteristics or ranges that will be used to sort the data and listing them on one axis (typically the x-axis)

- Counting the number of occurrences in the data set for each characteristic or range

- Graphing a bar on the chart for each characteristic or range where the height of the bar represents the frequency (number of elements from the data set) with that characteristic or in that range

According to Kan (2003), "In a histogram, the frequency bars are shown by order of the X variable, whereas in a Pareto diagram the frequency bars are shown by order of the frequency counts." For this reason, histograms are not valid for nominal-scale metrics because there is no order. Other experts question their validity for ordinal-scale metrics as well because there is no assumption made about the magnitude of the differences, and therefore the "shape" of the curve may not be meaningful. Examples of software histograms include:

- Distribution of problem report arrival rates (see Figure 20.9)

- Distribution of problem report backlog by age (see Figure 20.9)

- Distribution of the experience level of the staff

- Distribution of defects by severity (note that this is an ordinal-scale metric)

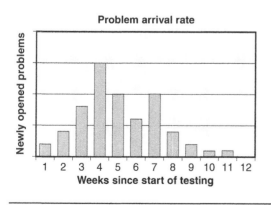
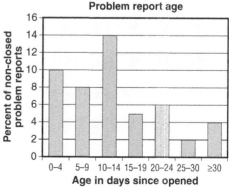

Figure 20.9   Histogram—examples.

- Distribution of customer satisfaction responses by satisfaction level (note that this is an ordinal-scale metric)

Control Charts

The purpose of a *control chart* is to control one of the attributes of a process over time by identifying improbable patterns that may indicate that the process is out of control. As illustrated in Figure 20.10, classic control charts have a centerline (CL), upper control limit (UCL), and lower control limit (LCL). These are calculated using statistical techniques and based on data collected while the process is actually running and considered under control.

The centerline is typically the observed process average (mean), but other measures of central tendency such as the median can be used. The upper and lower control limits are based on the variation of the process. For classic control charts, these control limits are set at ±3 sigma (standard deviations) from the centerline. If the lower control limit falls below zero and negative numbers are not valid for the attribute, the lower control limit is set to zero. The zones on a classic control chart are areas bracketed by ±1 sigma (zone A), ±2 sigma (zone B), and ±3 sigma (zone C).

There are different types of control charts. These types are based on the type of data collected (variable data versus attribute data) and how those data are collected and combined.

After the initial control chart is created, data continues to be collected and added to the chart as the process is implemented over time. These ongoing control chart data are analyzed by looking for occurrences of one of five statistically improbable patterns that are clues that the process may be unstable. As illustrated in Figure 20.11, these five patterns include:

1. Any single data point that is outside of zone C (more than three standard deviations from the centerline)

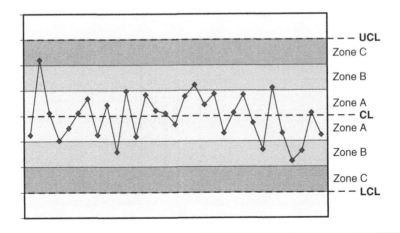

Figure 20.10   Creating a control chart—example.

2. Any two out of three data points in a sequence beyond zone B (more than two standard deviations from the centerline)

3. Any four out of five data points in a sequence beyond zone A (more than one standard deviation from the centerline)

4. Any eight successive points on the same side of the centerline

5. Any eight successive points in a trend (all up or all down)

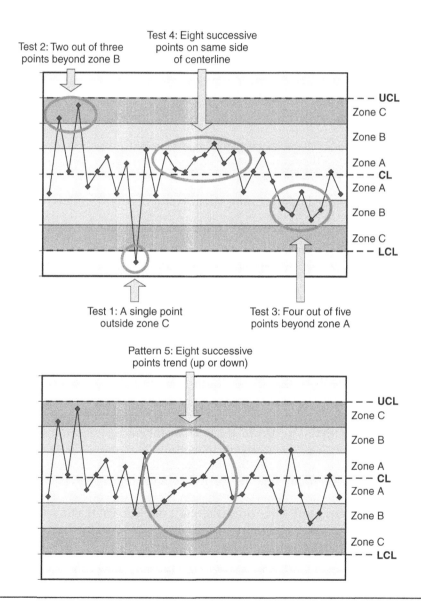

Figure 20.11 Statistically improbable patterns—examples.

When one of these patterns is identified, it only indicates that something improbable has happened that should be investigated. For example, observing eight successive points on the same side of the centerline is similar to flipping a coin eight times and having it come up heads each time. Can it happen? Yes, but it is highly unlikely enough that the coin should be examined for anomalies. If after investigation it is determined that the observed pattern is just part of the normal variation in the process, it is part of what is called common cause variation. *Common cause variation* is simply part of the expected variation in the process due to typical causes including influences from people, machinery, environmental factors, materials, measurements, or methods. However, if after investigation the pattern can be attributed to one or more special factors outside the normal expected variation in the process it is called *special cause* (or *assignable cause*) *variation*. When special cause variation occurs, the process is considered out of control, and corrective action should be implemented to eliminate the special causes.

Affinity Diagrams

An *affinity diagram* is used to organize a large number of ideas (or data items) into categories so that they can be reviewed and/or analyzed. For example, an affinity diagram could be used to organize:

- Outputs of a brainstorming session into useful categories

- Customer quality requirements into quality attribute categories

- Customer survey comments or customer complaints

- Audit observations into evidence categories to support findings

- Defect root cause data to create a root cause taxonomy

The steps in constructing an affinity diagram include:

1. Writing each idea (or data item) to be sorted on a card or piece of paper (sticky note or 3×5 card) and placing them randomly on the wall or on a flip chart where the entire team can get access to them.

2. The team works in silence, with each team member moving the items around and collecting similar items into related groups (categories). By doing this in silence, the team members are not influencing each other's ideas, and everyone must think for themselves. Silence also helps keep people in their right brain, enhancing creativity and pattern recognition (the left side of the brain tends to be more linear and language oriented). If an item is being moved back and forth between groups, consider making a duplicate of that item and putting it in both groups. Some items may stand by themselves as one-item groups.

3. For organizing ideas from a brainstorming, new items can also be added to the sets of ideas during the generation of the affinity diagram. If, for example, a team member notices something missing once a

category is taking shape, they can create a new item and add it to that category. Additional details may also be added to existing items.

4. Once everything is sorted into groups, the team should consider whether large clusters need to be broken down into subgroups

5. After a few minutes have elapsed without additional changes, the team breaks the silence and starts a discussion of the final configuration. At this time, a short label (one to five words in length) should be assigned to each category to describe that category.

The team finishes by reviewing the resulting affinity diagram and deciding what to do with the results.

Figure 20.12 illustrates an example where the affinity diagram technique was used to organize the ideas from a brainstorming session on "How can the peer review process be improved?" into categories.

Tree Diagrams

The purpose of a *tree diagram* is to break down or stratify ideas into progressively more detail. A tree diagram can help organize information or make the underlying complexities of the ideas more visible. Examples of tree diagrams include:

- Project work breakdown structures (see Figures 15.10, 15.11, and 15.12, pages 239, 242, and 243 for examples)

- Directory structures for files on a disk

- Root cause taxonomies (see Figure 20.13 for an example of one section of a software defect root cause taxonomy tree diagram)

- Risk taxonomies

- Cause-and-effect diagrams (see Figures 20.3 and 20.4 for examples)

- Decision trees (see Figure 22.12, page 419, for an example)

Matrix Diagrams

The purpose of a *matrix diagram* is to analyze the relationships between two or more sets of data. Matrix diagrams can be used to systematically analyze the correlation between two or more data sets and the strength of that correlation. Figure 20.14 illustrates an example of a matrix diagram where the rows represent the defect root causes and the columns represent the defect-detection technique. Each cell contains the number of defects found using each detection technique for that root cause. This example matrix diagram could be used to analyze whether certain defect-detection techniques are better at finding certain types of defects. In other matrix diagrams, the cells might contain a relationship indicator (for example, 5 = high importance to 1 = low importance with zero indicating no relationship). In the case of an assignment matrix diagram, the rows might be project roles and the columns might indicate work products or activities with the cells indicating

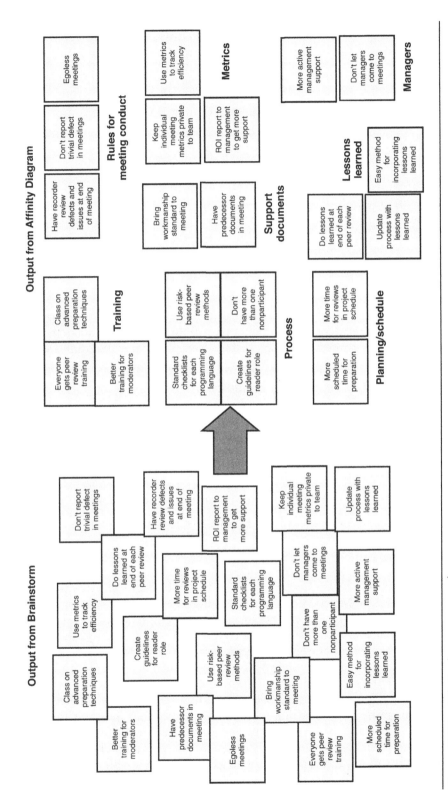

Figure 20.12   Affinity diagram—example.

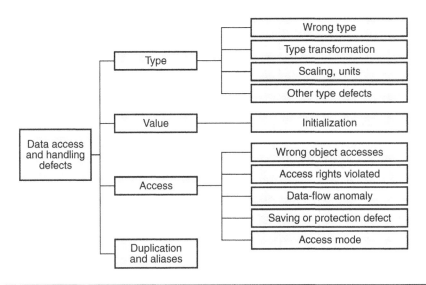

Figure 20.13   Tree diagram—example.

	Detection technique					
Root cause	Requirements inspection	Design inspection	Code inspection	Unit test	Integration test	System test
Requirements defects	20	5	1		2	6
Functionality implementation defects		15	5	2	2	25
Structural/control flow defects		20	15	6	5	1
Processing defects		4	18	12	4	5
Data defects		2	20	13	5	2
Internal interface defects		21	7	1	15	3
External interface defects	6	2	1	0	2	12

Figure 20.14   Matrix diagram—example.

responsibilities (for example, P = primary responsibility, M = team member, R = reviewer, A = approval authority).

Interrelationship Digraph

The purpose of an *interrelationship digraph* is to organize ideas and define the ways those ideas influence each other. Like an affinity diagram, the ideas that are used as inputs into the interrelationship digraph can come from many sources, including

Part V.C.3

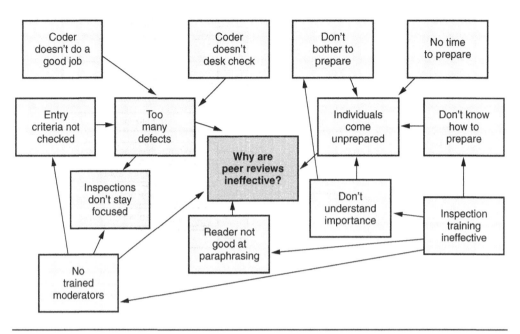

Figure 20.15   Interrelationship digraph—example.

brainstorming, surveys, reported defects, and so on. Using this tool, the team organizes the ideas and defines their influences by drawing arrows between the ideas,
as illustrated in Figure 20.15. For example, in this interrelationship digraph the
arrows drawn from the "Inspection training ineffective" idea to the "Don't know
how to prepare" idea show a causal relationship (ineffective inspection training is
a cause of reviewers not knowing how to prepare). Interrelationship digraphs can
help identify the prime cause or contributing item (the item with the most arrows
leaving it) and the prime outcome (the item with the most arrows arriving). This
enables the team to focus on the most important relationships first.

Activity Networks

The purpose of an activity network is to show the order in which activities must
occur and any successor/predecessor relationships. Activity networks are discussed in Chapter 15.

Root Cause Analysis

The primary objective of root cause analysis is to identify the actual cause of a
problem, nonconformance, or other issue so the true cause can be corrected. Doing
a thorough root cause analysis prevents the band-aid effect of correcting just the
symptoms without really correcting the underlying cause, which does not prevent future reoccurrences of the same or a related issue in the future. Root cause
analysis provides opportunities to identify specific ways of improving software

products, processes, and services through correcting actual problems rather than just their symptoms.

There are many different facets to analyzing the root cause of defects in software products and processes. Analyzing when and in what processes defects were introduced into the software products can help focus corrective and preventive actions on the process that will have the greatest opportunity to prevent similar defects in the future. For example, if analysis shows that 55 percent of an organization's defects were introduced during requirements elicitation, efforts should focus on those actions that will improve the elicitation process. Further analysis can be done on the type of defect being introduced within that phase or process (for example, ambiguous requirement, missing requirement, missing stakeholder, incorrect requirement), which can help further focus improvement opportunities. For example, if analysis shows that requirement ambiguity is a major issue, standardized requirement statement templates or additional training might be provided to help requirements analysts specify better, less ambiguous requirements.

Analyzing defect types, combined with knowing when the defect was detected, identifies opportunities to improve the defect-detection processes. By identifying processes that failed to detect the defect, earlier detection rates can be improved by updating methods to look for a specific type of defect. For example, if analysis shows that a large percentage of ambiguous requirements are not being found during requirements peer reviews, items can be added to the requirements peer review checklist to look for ambiguity, or peer reviewers can receive training to help them better detect that type of defect.

Analyzing defect-prone software components helps identify components where software reengineering can benefit the overall reliability of the product or where risks exist that require additional attention during peer reviews or testing. Analyzing similar software components can identify components that also have a high potential for similar defects. If the mistake was made in one part of the product, it may be repeated in a similar product component. Analyzing similar processes can identify processes that have a high potential for benefiting from similar improvements.

Finally, analyzing process problems identified during assessments, audits, or lessons-learned sessions and addressing their root causes can have a long-term impact on both process effectiveness and efficiency and thereby on product quality through prevention of defect introduction.

This book has already discussed several metrics and tools for root cause analysis. Defect density can be used to identify defect-prone components, and this chapter talked about using Pareto charts for the same purpose (see Figure 20.2). The analysis of escape, phase containment, and defect-detection efficiency metrics can also be used to identify ineffective detection processes. Check sheets (see Figure 20.5) or matrix diagrams (see Figure 20.14) are useful in conjunction with defect taxonomies (see Figure 20.13) to analyze root causes by defect types. Flowcharts (see Figure 20.1) can be used to identify process inefficiencies, bottlenecks, or other problems. Cause-and-effect diagrams (see Figures 20.3 and 20.4) can be used to explore potential root causes.

Another tool for getting to the root cause is called the *five whys* method. In this method, the question "why?" is repeatedly asked and answered (typically this can take five whys or maybe even more) until the root cause is identified. For example, if a problem exists because the interface specification to the notification controller was not defined before the scheduled time to design its driver, the individuals performing root cause analysis might ask the following five whys:

1. Why? Because the customer has not sent us the specification

2. Why? Because the customer did not have the specification

3. Why? Because the controller supplier has not provided the specification to the customer

4. Why? Because the customer has not purchased the controller

5. Why? Because the customer is waiting for a new product release that has the needed new features

The five whys method is very useful in a team setting to encourage team members to identify and discuss the chain of symptoms and their causes to drill down to the initial, underlying root cause of a problem so that it can be addressed with corrective action resulting in a permanent long-term solution.

Part VI

Software Verification and Validation (V&V)

Chapter 21

A. Theory (of V&V)

According to ISO/IEC *Systems and Software Engineering—Vocabulary* (ISO/IEC 2009), *verification* is "the process of evaluating a system or component to determine whether the products of a given development phase satisfy the conditions imposed at the start of that phase." Verification is concerned with the process of evaluating the software to ensure that it meets its specified product requirements and adheres to the appropriate standards, practices, and conventions. Verification also looks one phase back. For example, code is verified against the detailed design and the detailed design against the architectural design. The Software Engineering Institute's (SEI) Capability Maturity Model Integration (CMMI) for Development (SEI 2006) defines a verification process area. This process area states that the purpose for verification "is to ensure that selected work products meet their specified requirements." In other words, "Is the software being built right?"

Validation is the "confirmation, through the provision of objective evidence, that the requirements for a specific intended use or application have been fulfilled" (ISO/IEC 2009). Validation is concerned with the process of evaluating the software to ensure that it meets its intended objectives and matches the user's actual needs. The SEI's CMMI for Development defines a validation process area. This process states that the purpose for validation "is to demonstrate that a product or product component fulfills its intended use when placed in its intended environment." In other words, "Is the right software being built?" These definitions of verification and validation are illustrated in Figure 21.1.

The real strength of verification and validation (V&V) is their combined employment of a variety of different techniques to ensure that the software systems and its intermediate components are high-quality, comply with the specified requirements, and will be fit for use when delivered. V&V activities occur throughout the software life cycle and are an integral part of software development, operations, and maintenance.

Not only do V&V activities provide objective evidence that quality has been built into the software, they also identify areas where the software lacks quality, that is, where defects exist. As illustrated in Figure 21.2, every organization has formal and/or informal processes that they implement to produce their software products. These software products can include both the final products that are used by the customers (for example, executable software, user manuals) and interim products that are used internally to the organization (for example, requirements, designs, source/object code, test cases). V&V methods are used

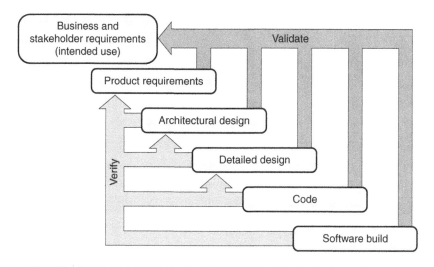

Figure 21.1   Verification and validation.

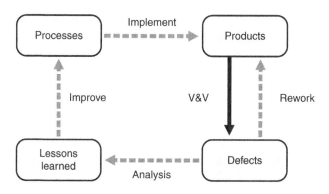

Figure 21.2   V&V techniques identify defects.

to identify defects in those products. These defects are then eliminated through rework, which has an immediate effect on the quality of the work products produced. Thus, V&V activities provide the mechanisms for early defect discovery, minimizing operational changes due to escaped defects. The defects found with V&V methods should also be analyzed to determine their root cause. The lessons learned from this analysis can be used to improve the processes used to create future products and therefore prevent future defects, thus having an impact on the quality of future products produced.

The data recorded during the V&V activities can also be used for making better management decisions about issues such as:

- Whether the current quality level of the software is adequate

- What risks are involved in releasing the software in its current state

- Whether additional V&V activities are cost-effective

- What the staff, resource, schedule, and budget estimates for future V&V efforts should be

1. V&V METHODS

Select and use V&V methods, including static analysis, structural analysis, mathematical proof, simulation, etc., and analyze which tasks should be iterated as a result of modifications. (Analyze)

Body of Knowledge VI.A.1

Static Analysis

Static analysis methods perform V&V by evaluating a software work product to assess its quality and identify defects without actually executing that work product. Analysis, reviews, and mathematical proofs are all forms of static analysis.

Analysis can be performed using tools (for example, spell checkers, grammar checkers, compilers, and code analyzers). Individuals or teams can also perform analysis activities through in-depth assessments of the requirements or of other software products. For example, Chapter 11 included a discussion of various models that can be useful in analyzing the software requirements for completeness, consistency, and correctness. Other forms of analysis might include hazard analysis, security analysis, or risk analysis used to help identify and mitigate issues, and requirements allocation and traceability analysis used to ensure that the software (or system) requirements were implemented completely and accurately.

Static analysis techniques include various forms of product and process reviews to evaluate the completeness, correctness, consistency, and accuracy of the software products and the processes that created them. These reviews include entry/exit criteria reviews and quality gates used to ensure that the products of a process or major activity (phase) are of high enough quality to transition to the next activity. Peer reviews can be used for engineering analysis and as defect-detection mechanisms where peers of the software work product's author examine the product, evaluate its quality, and identify defects. Examples of peer review techniques include desk checks, walk-throughs, and inspections. Other forms of managerial and technical reviews can also be used to assess and evaluate software products and processes.

Mathematical proofs, also called *proof of correctness,* are "a formal technique used to prove mathematically that a computer program satisfies its specified requirements" (ISO/IEC 2009). Mathematical proofs use mathematical logic to deduce that the logic of the design or code is correct. Mathematical proofs are also a type of static analysis technique.

Dynamic Analysis

Dynamic analysis includes methods of performing V&V by evaluating a software component or product by executing it and comparing the actual results to expected results. Testing and simulations are forms of dynamic analysis.

Piloting is another type of dynamic analysis technique. For software deliverables such as training and help desk support, piloting can be a useful dynamic analysis technique. For example, a set of typical software issues or problem areas could be compiled during system test execution and used to create a set of "typical" problem scenarios used to pilot the help desk. The testers could call the help desk, describe one of the scenarios, and evaluate whether the help desk personnel could adequately handle the call.

Product Audits

Product audits throughout the life cycle can evaluate the product against the requirements and against required standards (coding standards, naming conventions, required document formats). Physical and functional configuration audits are also used as a final check for defects before the product is transitioned into production. Product audits usually use static analysis techniques but they can also use dynamic analysis techniques, for example, if the auditor selects a sampling of test cases to execute as part of the audit.

V&V Task Iteration

Whenever a change is made to a software work product that has already undergone one or more V&V activities, analysis should be done to examine the change and determine the depth and breadth of the effects that change could have on the software. This analysis helps determine how many already executed V&V activities will need to be re-executed (iterated). For example, if a design specification has been changed after it has been peer reviewed, a determination must be made about whether or not the change is extensive enough to make it value-added to conduct another peer review. If a source code module is changed during the system testing processes, should that module be re–peer reviewed, and how many of the already executed unit, integration, and systems test cases should be re-executed? Once software development has moved past unit testing activities, regression test analysis is used to determine the amount of retesting that is necessary.

V&V task iteration is always based on risk and the concept of *V&V sufficiency*. As illustrated in Figure 21.3, V&V sufficiency analysis must balance the risk that the software still has undiscovered defects and the potential loss associated with those defects against the cost of performing additional V&V activities and the benefits of additional V&V activities. Just because the software was changed doesn't mean new defects were introduced or that those defects will cause future failures. For example, if a defect is in part of the code that is never used, it will probably not cause a failure. Just because V&V tasks were iterated doesn't mean that any new or additional defects will be found.

Task iteration analysis should also be based on the quality and integrity needs of the product or product component. For example, software work products that

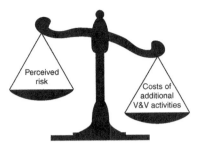

- Probability of undiscovered defects
- Loss associated with the defects
- Cost of continued V&V activities
- Benefits of additional V&V activities

Figure 21.3   Verification and validation sufficiency.

are mission-critical, safety- or security-related, have been defect-prone in the past, and/or are part of the most used functionality are all typically candidates for more V&V task iteration than those that are not.

Metrics can be used so that these trade-off decisions can be made based on facts and information rather than "gut feelings." For example, metrics information can be used to tailor the V&V plans based on data collected on previous products or projects, on the estimated defect counts for various work products, and on an analysis of how applying the various techniques can yield the best results given the constraints at hand. As the project progresses, metrics information can also be used to refine the V&V plans using actual results to date.

2. SOFTWARE PRODUCT EVALUATION

> Use various evaluation methods on documentation, source code, test results, etc., to determine whether user needs and project objectives have been satisfied.
> (Analyze)
>
> **Body of Knowledge VI.A.2**

Common V&V methods used to evaluate documentation include the use of static analysis tools (for example spell checkers and grammar checkers), analysis, peer reviews, and other types of reviews. For some documents, tests may be performed to evaluate those documents. For example, during system testing the testers may evaluate the user manual by performing tests that follow the instructions in the manual in order to ensure that the documentation matches what actually happens when the software is executed. Testers may also use test cases to evaluate the installation instructions and other user-deliverable documentation.

Common V&V techniques used to evaluate source code include the use of static analysis tools (for example compilers, more-sophisticated code analyzer's tools). Other static analysis techniques used for code are pair programming, peer reviews, and other types of technical reviews. From a dynamic analysis perspective, the source code is tested directly during unit testing, and once the code is integrated into a software build, other levels of testing, including integration, system, alpha, beta, and acceptance testing, are used to evaluate the software against its requirements and the user needs.

Common V&V techniques used for requirements are discussed in other chapters of this book, including analysis, peer reviews, testing, and functional configuration audits.

Risk-Based V&V

Risk-based V&V focuses on the identification of software items (work products, product components, or features/functions) with the highest risk exposure. The risk exposure is calculated based on probability and impact. In risk-based V&V, probability is the estimated likelihood that yet undiscovered, important defects will exist in the software item after the completion of a V&V activity. Multiple factors or probability indicators may contribute to a software item having a higher or lower risk probability. These probability indicators may vary from project to project or from environment to environment. Therefore, each organization or project should determine and maintain a list of probability indicators to consider when assigning risk probabilities to its software items. Figure 21.4 illustrates examples of probability indicators, including:

- The more churn there has been in the requirements allocated to the software item, the more likely it is that there are defects in that item.

- Software items that have had a history of defects in the past are more likely to have additional defects.

- Larger and/or more-complex software items are more likely to have defects than smaller and/or simpler software items.

- The higher the constraints on the quality attribute (for example, reliability, performance, safety, security, maintainability), the more likely it is that there are related defects in the software item.

- The more used an item in the software is, the more likely it is that users will encounter any defects that might exist in that part of the software.

- Novice software developers with less knowledge and skill tend to make more mistakes than experienced developers, resulting in more defects in their work products.

- If the developer is very familiar with the programming language, tool set, and business domain, they are less likely to make mistakes than if they are working with new or leading-edge technology.

- Higher-maturity processes are more likely to help prevent defects from getting into the work products.

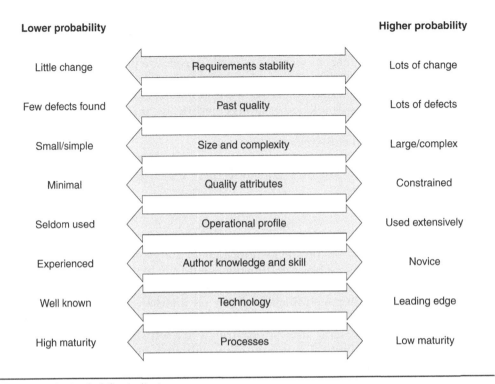

Figure 21.4 Probability indicators.

Risk-based V&V also analyzes risk impact, which is the estimated cost of the result or consequence if one or more undiscovered defects escape detection during the V&V activity. Again, multiple and varying factors or impact indicators may contribute to a software item having a higher or lower risk impact. Each organization or project should determine and maintain a list of impact indicators to consider when assigning risk impacts to its work products. Examples of impact indicators include:

- Schedule and effort impacts
- Development and testing costs
- Internal and external failure costs
- Corrective action costs
- High maintenance costs
- Customer dissatisfaction or negative publicity
- Lost market opportunities
- Litigation, warranty costs, or penalties
- Noncompliance with regulatory requirements

The IEEE *Standard for Software Verification and Validation* (IEEE 2004) uses the assignment of an integrity level (instead of a risk exposure as discussed above) to determine the required set of V&V activities and their associated level of rigor. "Software integrity levels are a range of values that represent software complexity, criticality, risk, safety level, security level, desired performance, reliability, or other project-unique characteristics that define the importance of the software to the user and acquirer" (IEEE 2004). However, this IEEE standard leaves the characteristic used to determine the selected integrity scheme up to the needs of the project and includes a description of an example scheme based on risk in an appendix.

V&V Plans

Each project documents its V&V strategies and tactics in their V&V plans. These V&V plans may be included in a separate document or be included as a section in another planning document (for example, the project plans or quality assurance plans). IEEE *Guide for Software Verification and Validation Plans* (IEEE 1998a) provides specific guidance about planning and documenting V&V plans. Like other planning documents, the V&V plans should include information about the project's organizational structure, schedule, budget, roles and responsibilities, resources, tools, techniques, and methodologies related to the V&V activities. The V&V plans define the risk-based V&V activities that are planned for each phase of the software development life cycle to evaluate the work products produced or changed during those phases. The V&V plans should included plans for ongoing status reporting on identified problems and V&V activities and for V&V summary reports required at major milestones. The plans should also define V&V administrative procedures including:

- Processes for reporting identified problems and tracking them to resolution

- Policies for V&V task iteration

- Policies for obtaining deviation or waivers

- Processes for controlling V&V-related configuration items

- V&V standards, practices, and conventions that are being used on a project, including those adopted or tailored from the organizational level and any that are project-specific

Chapter 22

B. Test Planning and Design

T*esting* is a dynamic analysis verification and validation (V&V) method. ISO/ IEC *Systems and Software Engineering—Vocabulary* (ISO/IEC 2009) defines testing as "the process of operating a system or component under specified conditions, observing or recording the results, and making an evaluation of some aspect of the system or component."

One of the objectives of testing is to find yet undiscovered, relevant defects in the software. Relevant defects are defects that will negatively impact the customer. Both software developers and software testers are responsible for the quality of the delivered software. It has to be a team effort. The job of a software developer is to prevent defects in the product and to build quality into the software products. As the software moves into testing, however, a mental shift must occur. While software developers make the software work, testers do everything they can to find all the ways that they can "break" the software. A tester is successful every time they uncover a yet undiscovered, relevant defect because one less defect will make its way to the user of the software and impact the user's satisfaction with that product (assuming of course that the uncovered defect is actually corrected).

Given that testing, like all other development activities, has a limited amount of resources (time, people, equipment), the goal of the tester is to select a set of test cases that are most likely to uncover as many different relevant defects as possible within those three constraints. Therefore, the tester is part detective, hunting for clues as to how the software might fail. The tester is also part amateur psychologist trying to look into the mind of the programmer to figure out what kinds of errors they might have made in the code, and into the minds of the users to figure out how they might use the software inappropriately or in ways not accounted for.

Testing requires the execution of a software system or one of its components. Therefore, test execution can not be performed until executable software exists. With the exception of prototypes and simulations, this means that most test execution starts during or after the coding phase of the software development life cycle. The "V" software development life cycle model illustrates the relationships between software products produced in the early life cycle phases and the later test execution phases. The example of the V software life cycle model shown in Figure 22.1 includes five test execution phases: unit test, integration test, subsystem test, system test, and acceptance test. The number of actual test execution phases in the life cycle selected by an organization should be tailored to the needs of that organization.

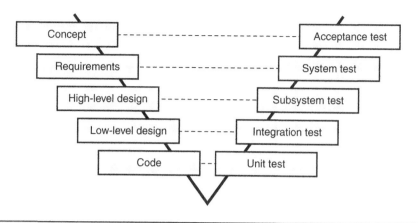

Figure 22.1   When testing happens in the life cycle.

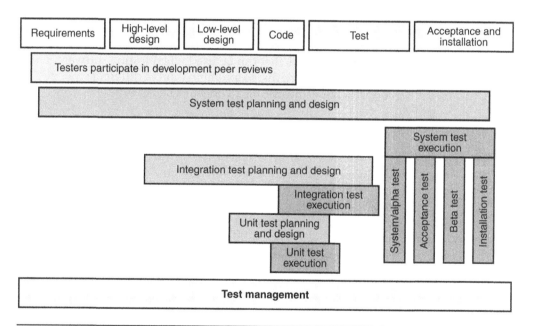

Figure 22.2   Test activities throughout the life cycle.

While test execution can not start until these later phases, test planning and design should be done as early as possible in the life cycle, as illustrated in Figure 22.2. In fact, test planning and design can start as soon as the software requirements are identified. Simply designing test cases (even without actually executing them) can help identify defects in the software work products, and the earlier those defects are discovered, the less expensive they will be to correct. Testers are also excellent candidates for participating in peer reviews. This can be especially true if the work product being reviewed will provide the basis for the test design.

For example, a tester who will write test cases to validate the requirements could participate in the peer review of the requirements specification, and the integration tester could participate in the peer review of the architectural design. Finally, the testing effort must be managed throughout the software life cycle.

1. TEST STRATEGIES

Select and analyze test strategies (test-driven design, good-enough, risk-based, time-box, top-down, bottom-up, black-box, white-box, simulation, automation, etc.) for various situations. (Analyze)

Body of Knowledge VI.B.1

There are many different strategies that can be used when testing software. Each of these strategies has its own strengths, so a combination of different strategies is typically the best approach for uncovering a variety of defect types.

White-Box Testing

White-box testing, also known as *structural, clear-box,* or *glass-box testing,* is testing that is based on the internal structure of the software and looks for issues in the framework, construction, or logic of the software. White-box testing is typically performed starting at the unit level and may also be performed as units are combined into components. White-box testing explores the internals of each unit or component in detail.

White-box testing can find certain types of control or logic-flow defects that are all but invisible during black-box testing. It is also much easier to thoroughly investigate a suspicious unit or component when the tester can clearly see into its internal structure. Early structural testing allows the tester to more easily trace defects back to their origin by isolating them to individual units or paths. Other strengths of white-box testing include the ability to look at:

- *Coverage.* When the testers can see into the unit or component's internal structure, they can devise tests that will cover areas of the code that may not be touched by black-box testing.

- *Flow.* When the testers can see into the unit or component's internal structure, they can determine what the software is supposed to do next as a function of its current state. The testers can use a debugger or other tool to run the software in order to track the sequence in which lines of code are executed and determine the values of key variables at specific points during the execution.

- *Data integrity.* When the testers know which parts of the software modify (or should modify) a given item of data, they can determine the value a selected data item should have at a given point in the software, compare that value with the value the variable actually has, and report any defects. The white-box testers can also detect data manipulation by inappropriate units or components.

- *Boundaries.* Using structural techniques, the tester can see internal boundaries in the code that are completely invisible to the functional tester. For example, if an input condition specifies a range bounded by values x and y, test cases should be designed with values x and y and values just above y and just below x.

- *Algorithms.* Using structural techniques, the testers can check for common ways that miscalculations are made.

Gray-Box Testing

When larger numbers of units or components are integrated together, it usually becomes unwieldy to perform pure white-box testing. In any complex system there are just too many possible paths through the software. As illustrated in Figure 22.3, at some point testing typically progresses into various levels (shades) of *gray-box testing* (a blending of the white-box and black-box testing strategies). Units or components are integrated into programs, programs into subsystems, and subsystems into the software system (note that the number of levels of integration can vary based on the needs of the project). At the lowest level of gray-box testing, the individual units or components are treated as gray boxes, where the tester peeks into the internals of each unit or component just enough to determine how they interact and interface with each other but ignores the rest of the internal details. At each subsequent level of integration, the individual programs/subsystems

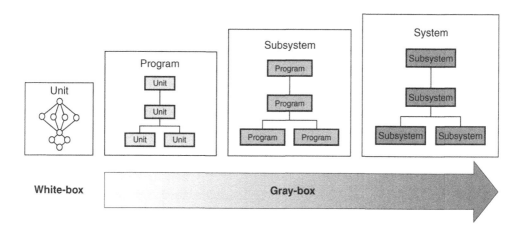

Figure 22.3   White-box → gray-box testing.

are treated as gray boxes where the tester peeks into their internals just enough to determine how those programs or subsystems interact and interface.

There are two basic strategies for doing gray-box testing as the software units are integrated into various levels of components, programs, subsystems, and the completely integrated software system. The first strategy, called *top-down,* is illustrated in Figure 22.4 at the unit to component integration level. The top-down strategy tests one or more of the highest-level software items (units, components, program, subsystems) in the tree, using stubs for lower-level called software items that have not yet been integrated (or developed). These stubs simulate the required actions of those lower-level software items. The lower-level software items and their stubs are then integrated, one or more at a time, replacing these stubs. Testing focuses on the interfaces of the newly integrated software items as they are added, and their interactions with other already integrated software. The top-down strategy should be chosen when:

- Control flow structures are critical or suspected of being defect-prone

- Critical or high-risk software items are near the top of the structure (the items that are integrated earlier will be exercised more extensively during testing)

- Top-level software items contain menus or other important external interface elements

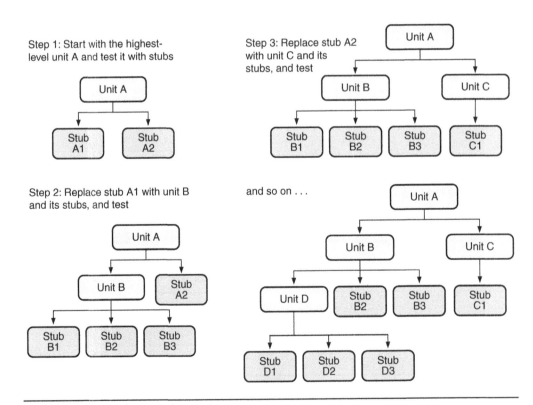

Figure 22.4   Top-down testing strategy.

- There is more fan-out than there is fan-in in the software structure being integrated

- A skeletal version would be beneficial for demonstration

- It will take less effort to create stubs than drivers

The second integration strategy is called *bottom-up,* as illustrated in Figure 22.5. This strategy tests one or more of the lowest-level software items in the tree using drivers for higher-level calling software items that have not yet been integrated (or developed). These drivers simulate the required actions of those higher-level software items. The higher-level software items and their drivers are then integrated one or more at a time, replacing these drivers. Testing again focuses on the interfaces to the newly integrated software items as they are added, and their interactions with other already integrated software items. The bottom-up strategy should be chosen when:

- Critical or high-risk software items are near the bottom of the structure

- Bottom-level software items contain menus or other important external interface elements

- There is more fan-in than there is fan-out in the software structure being integrated

- It will take less effort to create drivers than stubs

Selection of an integration testing strategy depends on software characteristics, and sometimes project schedule. Different approaches can also be used for different

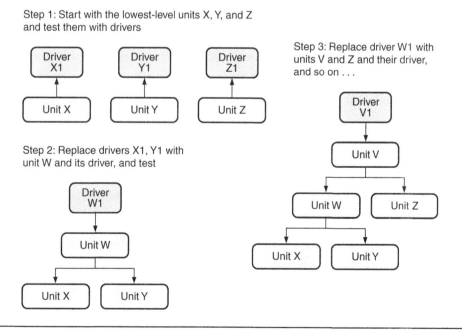

Figure 22.5   Bottom–up testing strategy.

parts of the software. For example, some parts of the software can be integrated using a bottom-up strategy, and other parts using a top-down strategy. The resulting software items could then be integrated using a top-down strategy.

Black-Box Testing

Black-box testing, also known as *data-driven, input/output-driven,* or *functional* testing, ignores the internal structure of the software and tests the behavior of the software from the perspective of the users. As illustrated in Figure 22.6, black-box testing is focused on inputting values into the software under known conditions and states and evaluating the resulting outputs from the software against expected values while treating the software itself as a black box. The software is treated as a black box, where its internal structure is not considered when designing and executing the tests. This helps maintain an external focus on the software requirements and user needs.

Since black-box testing does not require an intimate knowledge of the software's internal structure, individuals other than the developers of the source code can perform it. This allows a second set of eyes to evaluate the software. Developers have a natural bias and will test the software based on the same set of assumptions they used to create that software. Independent testing allows for more objectivity and a different perspective that can result in more defects being identified. Developers are also focused on making the software work. It is easier for an independent tester to focus on how to "break" the software.

The entire assembled software system is often too large and complex to test using pure white-box testing strategies. Black-box testing can be used to test the entire system as well as its smaller individual units and components, as illustrated in Figure 22.6. Another strength of black-box testing includes the ability to find defects that are very difficult or impossible to identify using structural testing. For example:

- Timing related issues and race conditions

- Unanticipated error conditions and interoperability issues that may be initiated by another interfacing software application or hardware component

- Inconsistencies in how the user interfaces with the system

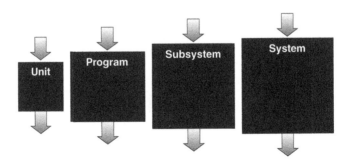

Figure 22.6 Black-box testing.

- Inconsistencies between different displays and reports

- Issues related to how the software tolerates real-time functioning and multiple tasking, including high levels or volumes of environmental load or stress

In fact, many of the strengths of black-box testing are weaknesses of white-box testing, and many of the strengths of white-box testing are weaknesses of black-box testing. Therefore, the best strategy is usually a balancing of both approaches.

Test-Driven Design

Test-driven design (TDD), also called *test-driven development,* is actually an iterative software development methodology. As discussed in Chapter 9, TDD implements software functionality based on writing the test cases that the code must pass. Those test cases become the requirements and design documentation used as the basis for implementing the code. Those test cases are then run often to verify that changes have not broken any existing capability (regression testing). While TDD obviously has a testing component, it is in no way limited to being a testing technique. TDD addresses the entire software development process.

Risk-Based Testing, Time-Box Testing, and Good-Enough Software

According to Myers (2004), "it is impractical, often impossible, to find all the errors in a program." One reason for this is that exhaustive testing is impossible. For example, consider the black-box testing of a function that accepts a positive integer as one of its inputs. How many possible test cases are there? To exhaustively test this single input there are literally an infinite number of possible test cases. First, there are an infinite number of positive integers to test. There is always the possibility that inputting the number 3,256,319 will cause some strange and wonderful anomaly to happen. Then there are also an infinite number of invalid inputs that could be tested, including negative numbers and non-numbers (character strings including one or more alpha or other nonnumeric characters). Since exhaustive testing is impossible, then all testing in the real world is based on sampling. Answering the question "How much sampling is needed?" leads to the concepts of risk-based testing and good-enough software.

Risk-based testing focuses on identifying software items (for example, work products, product components, features, functions) with the highest risk. Limited testing resources are then proportionally distributed to spend more resources testing higher-risk areas and fewer resources testing lower-risk items. Risk-based testing also embraces the "law of diminishing returns": At the start of testing a large number of defects are discovered with little effort. As testing proceeds, discovering subsequent issues requires more and more effort. At some point, the return on investment in discovering those last few defects is outweighed by the cost of additional testing.

In project management, a *time box* is a fixed amount of calendar time allocated to complete a given task like testing. In *time-box testing*, the calendar time for testing is fixed, and the scope of the testing effort must be adjusted to fit inside that time box. This can be accomplished by prioritizing test activities and tests based on risk and benefit and then executing the activities and/or tests in priority order. If time runs out before all of the activities and tests are accomplished, at least the lowest-priority ones are left unfinished.

The concept of *good-enough software* recognizes the fact that not all software applications are created equal. For example, word processing software does not require the same level of integrity as banking software, and banking software doesn't require the same level of integrity as biomedical software that is controlling someone's pacemaker. Doing good-enough software analysis has to do with making conscious, logical decisions about the trade-offs between the level of quality and integrity that the stakeholders need in the software and the basic economic fact that increasing software quality and integrity typically costs more and takes longer. This is not meant to discount the impacts of long-term continual improvement initiatives—but right now, on today's project, with current skills and capabilities, this is reality. Hard business decisions need to be made about how much testing (and other V&V activities) a project can afford and what the stakeholders are really willing to pay for it.

Simulation

The test environment often can not duplicate the real-world environment where the software will actually be executed. For example, in the test bed, the tests performing capacity testing for a telecommunications switch do not have access to 10,000 people all calling in to the switch at once. One way of solving this gap is to create a *simulator* that imitates the real world by mimicking those 10,000 people. An example of when simulators might be needed is when other interfacing software applications or hardware are being developed in parallel with the software being tested and are not ready for use, or for some other reason are not available for use during testing. Remember, a simulator only mimics the other software and hardware in the real-world environment.

Strategic decisions need to be made about when it is appropriate to spend testing resources creating simulators and utilizing simulation. These are again risk-based decisions because:

- Resources spent creating the simulators are not spent testing other parts of the software.

- Simulators are not the real environment; if incorrect choices are made in creating the simulators, defects may still escape testing, or issues that would never have become actual defects may be reported, and unnecessary or incorrect changes could be made.

Test Automation

Test automation is the use of software to automate the activities of test design, test execution, and the capturing and analysis of test results. Strategic decisions here involve how much of the testing to automate, which tests or test activities to automate, which automation tools to purchase, and how to apply limited resources to the automation effort. Automated tests can typically be run much more quickly and therefore more often than manual tests, providing increased visibility into the quality of the software at any given time. This can be particularly beneficial during regression testing. Automation can also eliminate human error when comparing large amounts of output data with expected results. As a trade-off, however, test automation requires an initial investment in tools and resources to create the automation and a long-term investment to maintain the automated test suites as the software changes over time. Automation also requires a different skill set than testing.

2. TEST PLANS

> Develop and evaluate test plans and procedures, including system, acceptance, validation, etc., to determine whether project objectives are being met. (Create)
>
> **Body of Knowledge VI.B.2**

Test planning starts with the overall V&V planning where decisions are made about the levels of testing that will be done, the testing objectives, strategies, and approaches that will be used at each level, testing staff and other resource allocation, and what V&V activities will be used to evaluate the implementation of each requirement.

For each of the major testing levels (for example, system testing, acceptance testing, beta testing), additional test plans may be created to refine the approach and define additional details for that level. Each test plan defines the specific strategies and tactics that will be used to ensure that project objectives associated with that level of testing are being met, and that the requirements that are to be verified and/or validated at that level (as allocated by the V&V plan) are adequately tested. Each test plan may be a separate document or it can be incorporated as part of a single V&V plan or SQA plan, or even be sections in the overall project plan.

The test plan process includes developing the test plan and reviewing and approving that plan.

According to IEEE *Standard for Software Test Documentation* (IEEE 2008b), a *test plan* should include:

- *The items to be tested.* A list of the software configuration units, components, or items that will be tested under the plan.

- *The features that will and will not be tested.* For example, if the project is adding additional features to an existing product, risk-based analysis is used to determine which existing features are not impacted by the changes and therefore do not need to be retested. Based on risk, this section may also include the depth and rigor of testing required for each feature or function within that feature, and establish priorities for testing.

- *The test approaches and methods that will be used for the testing level.* This includes the identification of policies, approaches, and manual and automated testing methods that will be used for:

  - Functional, user scenario, and/or operational profile testing

  - Testing quality and product attribute requirements (for example, usability, performance, environmental load/volume/stress, safety, security, interoperability, conversion, installability, internationalization)

  - External interface and environmental configuration testing

  - Data and database testing

  - Testing user documentation (for example, user manuals, operator manuals, marketing materials, installation instructions)

  - Regression testing

  This may include additional details in the system test matrix that defined the exact approaches and methods to use for each requirement being tested at the stated level of testing.

  In addition, this section defines approaches and methods for:

  - Problem reporting and resolution

  - Issues reporting and resolution

  - Configuration management of test deliverables and testing tools

  - Test status reporting, including reviews and metrics

- *Item pass/fail criteria.* Specific, measurable criteria for determining if the item under test has successfully passed the cycle of tests that are typically used as exit criteria for the testing cycle. Examples might include the allowable:

  - Test coverage requirements

  - Number of non-closed problem reports by severity, and requirements for work-arounds

  - Arrival rates of new problems

  - Number of unexecuted or unpassed test cases

  - Variance between planned and actual testing effort

- *Suspension criteria.* Specific, measurable criteria that when met indicate that the testing activities should be stopped until the resumption criteria are met. For example, if a certain number of critical defects are discovered or if a certain percentage of test cases are blocked, it may no longer be considered cost-effective to continue the testing effort until development corrects the software.

- *Resumption requirements.* Specific, measurable criteria that when met indicate that the testing activities should be restarted. For example, a new build is received from development with corrections to most of the critical defects or defects that are blocking test case execution.

- *Test deliverables.* The list of outputs from this cycle of testing, including:
  - Test plans
  - Test designs, including test cases, procedures, and scripts
  - Problem reports (change requests)
  - Status reports and metrics
  - Test logs
  - Interim and final test summary reports

- *Testing tasks with assigned responsibilities, resources, and schedules.* This includes the work breakdown structure, schedule, and allocated staffing and other resources for this level of testing. This information may be kept as part of the project information in a project management tool as pointed to from the test plan.

- *Environmental needs.* This section defines:
  - Test bed requirements including the physical setup, technologies, and tools
  - Mechanisms for validating the test bed setup
  - Methods for requesting updates or changes to the test bed configuration during testing
  - Allocation and schedules of test bed resources

- *Staffing plans and training needs for test personnel.* Testing personnel may include test managers, test designers, test automation specialists, testers (people to perform manual and exploratory testing), test bed coordinators, and support staff. Skill gap analysis should be performed to ensure that the testing personnel have the requisite knowledge and skills, and training plans need to define how identified gaps will be filled.

- *Risk management plans for risks associated with this level of testing.*

A test design specification is a further refinement of a test plan and is only needed if the complexity of the system is high or there is a need for additional levels of information. According to IEEE (IEEE 2008b), a test design specification is an optional document that defines the features to be tested, the approach refinements, test identification, and feature pass/fail criteria.

3. TEST DESIGNS

> Select and evaluate various test designs, including fault insertion, fault-error handling, equivalence class partitioning, boundary value, etc. (Evaluate)
>
> **Body of Knowledge VI.B.3**

Test design activities include performing requirements analysis to determine the approach needed to evaluate the implementation of each requirement. Test design includes performing risk, criticality, and hazard analysis to determine how extensively to test each requirement. Based on this analysis, tests are then designed, documented, and verified. Test design also includes performing traceability analysis to ensure the completeness of the set of tests. Finally, test design activities may include the automation of tests that will be repetitively executed.

There are techniques the tester can use during test design to systematically minimize the number of tests while maximizing the probability of finding undiscovered relevant defects.

Equivalence Class Partitioning

Equivalence class partitioning is a testing technique that takes a set of inputs and/or outputs and divides them into valid and invalid sets of data that are expected to be treated in the same way by the software. This allows the tester to systematically sample from each equivalence class during testing using a minimum set of tests while still achieving coverage. The assumption is that if one sampled value from an equivalence class uncovers a defect, then any other sample from the same equivalence class would probably catch the same defect. If the sampled value doesn't catch a defect, other samples probably wouldn't catch it either. Rules of thumb when selecting equivalence classes include:

- If the input/output is a continuous range (for example, from 1 to 100), there is one valid input class (number from 1 to 100) and two invalid classes (number less than 1 and numbers greater than 100).

- If the input/output condition is a "must be" (for example, the first character must be a numeric character), there is one valid input class (inputs where the first character is a numeric) and one invalid class (inputs where the first character is not a numeric).

- If the input/output condition specifies a set of valid input values (for example, the jobs of programmer, analyst, tester, QA, and manager), then each valid input is its own equivalence class (in this example there are five valid classes) and there is one invalid class (everything that is not in the list of valid inputs).

- If the input/output condition is a specific number of values (for example one to six inspectors can be listed for a formal inspection), there is one valid equivalence class (having one to six inspectors) and two invalid classes (zero and more than six inspectors).

When sampling representatives from an equivalence class, testers should pick the values that they think are most likely to make the software fail.

Boundary Value

Boundary value analysis explores the values on or around the boundaries of the equivalence classes for each input or output. This technique will help identify an error where the programmer uses $<$ instead of $\leq$, uses $>$ instead of $\geq$, or forgets or mishandles the boundary in some other way. In boundary value testing, tests are created to test values at the boundaries, the minimum value, and the maximum value, and values just below the minimum and just above the maximum. For example, for the inputs in the range of 1 to 100, boundary value tests would include the inputs of 0, 1, 100, and 101.

Another example of boundaries would be to consider an input dialog box as illustrated in Figure 22.7. Assuming that the box displays up to 25 characters and that it is a scrolling box that actually allows an input string of up to 255 characters, boundary value testing would test the null input, a single character, 25 characters, 26 characters, 255 characters, and 256 characters. There may also be invisible boundaries for this input, for example, the input buffer size used by the operating system that the tester might want to explore. Other boundaries to consider include:

- *Zero.* The boundary between positive and negative numbers

- *Null.* The boundary between having an input and not having an input

- *Hard copy output sizes.* Characters per line or lines per page on outputs to a printer (remember, paper sizes can vary in different countries)

- *Screen output sizes.* Screen width, length, and pixels

- *Hardware device outputs.* Communication packet sizes or block sizes used in storing data on media

- *Lists.* First item and last item in each list

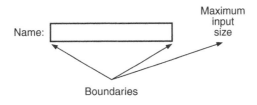

Figure 22.7   Input field boundary—example.

Fault Insertion

Fault insertion, also called *fault seeding*, is a mechanism for estimating the number of undetected defects that escaped from a testing process. Fault insertion literally intentionally inserts known defects into the software. The software is then tested and the defects that are found are analyzed to determine if they are part of the intentionally inserted, known defects or if they are new, unknown defects. The number of unfound unknown defects is then estimated. For example, assume 100 known defects were inserted into the software prior to system test. The software is tested and 72 of the inserted defects were found and 165 other defects were found. That means that 28 (100 minus 72) of the inserted (known) defects were not found during system test. The number of unfound unknown defects (UUD) can be estimated:

$$165 / 72 = UUD / 28 \text{ or } (165 / 72) \times 28 = UUD$$
$$\text{Since } 165 / 72 \approx 2.29$$
$$2.29 \times 28 \approx UUD \text{ so } UUD \approx 64 \text{ defects}$$

This technique assumes that the known defects are being found at the same rate as the unknown defects. Care must be taken to "seed" the software with a representative set of defects for this assumption to hold true. Care must also be taken to remove all of the known defects so that new defects are not introduced by mistake. After this removal, regression testing should be performed.

Fault-Error Handling

Testing techniques that examine *exception handling*, also called *fault-error handling*, look at how well the software handles errors, invalid conditions, invalid or out-of-sequence inputs, and invalid data.

Testing should check to ensure that exception handling is triggered whenever an exception occurs. Exception handlers should allow graceful software recovery or shutdown if necessary. They should prevent abandonment of control to the operating system (obscure crashes). Testing should also check that any reserved system resources (for example buffers or allocated memory) are appropriately released by creating tests that produce multiple exceptions to see how the software handles these repeated exception conditions.

One technique for selecting fault-error handling tests is called error guessing. The main idea behind error guessing is to "attack" the software with inputs that expose potential programmer mistakes or represent the kinds of invalid inputs that the software would receive if user or hardware mistakes occurred. It is hard to specifically describe this technique since it is largely intuitive and experience based. The main process is given the specific software to brainstorm probable types of faults or errors that might occur. For example:

- *What mistakes do programmers make?*

  - < versus ≤ or > versus ≥ (boundary value testing)

  - Not appropriately handling zero, negative numbers, or null inputs

- Failure to initialize data or variables

- Zero times through the loop, once through the loop

- Incorrect logic or control flow

- Not releasing resources or not reinitializing variables

- *What mistakes do users make?*

  - Creative invalids (alpha versus numeric, alt versus shift, left versus right mouse clicks)

  - Invalid combinations (State = TX but NY zip code)

  - Invalid processes (attempting to delete a customer record from the database before it is added)

  - Incorrect usage (hint: look at problem reports from the field that were operator errors)

- *What errors do machines make?*

  - Defective boards (hint: collect them as they are returned from the field)

  - Bad or corrupted data

  - Interrupted or incomplete communications

  - Limited, unavailable, or busy resources

  - Damaged media (no media in drive or corrupted block or sector on media)

  - Race conditions and other timing issues

Cause–Effect Graphing

Cause–effect graphing (CEG) is a model used to help design productive test cases by using a simplified digital-logic circuit (combinatorial logic network) graph. It's origin is in hardware engineering but it has been adapted for use in software. The CEG technique takes into consideration the combinations of causes that result in effecting the system's behavior. The commonly used process for CEG can be described in six steps.

Step 1: In the first step, the functional requirements are decomposed and analyzed. To do this, the functional requirements are partitioned into logical groupings, for example, commands, actions, and menu options. Each logical grouping is then further analyzed and decomposed into a list of detailed functions, subfunctions, and so forth.

Step 2: In the second step the causes and effects are identified. The first part of step 2 is to identify the causes and assign each cause a unique identifier. A cause can also be referred to as an input, as a distinct input condition, or as an equivalence class of input conditions. Examining the specification, or other similar artifact, word-by-word and underlining words or phrases that describe inputs helps to identify the causes. An input (cause) is an event that is generated outside an application that the application must react to in some fashion. Examples of inputs include hardware events (for example, keystrokes, pushed buttons, mouse clicks, sensor activations), API calls, return codes, and so forth.

The second part of step 2 is to identify the effects or system transformations and assign each effect a unique identifier. An effect can also be referred to as an output action, as a distinct output condition, as an equivalence class of output conditions, or as an output such as a confirmation message or error message. Examples of output include a message printed on the screen, a string sent to a database, a command sent to the hardware, a request to the operating system, and so forth. System transformations such as file or database record updates are considered effects as well. As with causes, examining the specification, or other similar artifact, word-by-word and underlining words or phrases that describe outputs or system transformations helps to identify the effects.

For example, Table 22.1 list the causes and effects for the following example set of requirements for calculating car insurance premiums:

- R101 For females less than 65 years of age, the premium is $500

- R102 For males less than 25 years of age, the premium is $3000

- R103 For males between 25 and 64 years of age, the premium is $1000

- R104 For anyone 65 years of age or more, the premium is $1500

Listing the causes and effect can help identify the completeness of the requirements and identify possible problem areas. For example, these requirements do not list a minimum or maximum age or what should happen if an entry other then "male" or "female" is entered into the sex field. The tester can use these potential problem areas to design test cases to ensure that the software either does not allow the entry of invalid values or responds appropriately with invalid input error messages. Of course, the tester should also ask the requirements analyst about these issues when they are identified so that potential problems can be corrected as soon as possible in the product life cycle.

Table 22.1   Causes and effects—example.

Causes (input conditions)	Effects (output conditions)
1. Sex is male	a. Premium is $1000
2. Sex is female	b. Premium is $3000
3. Age is < 25	c. Premium is $1500
4. Age is ≥ 25 and < 65	d. Premium is $500
5. Age is ≥ 65	e. Invalid input error message
6. Sex is not male or female	
7. Age is < ?	
8. Age is > ?	

Step 3: In the third step, cause–effect graphs are created. The semantic content of the specification is analyzed and transformed into Boolean graphs linking the causes and effects. These are the cause–effect graphs. Semantics, in this step's instructions, reflect the meaning of the programs or functions. This meaning is discerned from the specification and transformed into a Boolean graph that maps the causes to the resulting effects. It is easier to derive the Boolean function for each effect from their separate CEGs. Table 22.2 illustrates the individual cause–effect graphs from the example list of requirements.

Table 22.2   Cause–effect graphs–example.

CEG	Interpretation
CEG #1:	Causes: 1. Sex is male and ( ) 4. Age is ≥ 25 and < 65 Effect: a: Premium is $1000
CEG #2:	Causes: 1. Sex is male and ( ) 3. Age is < 25 Effect: b: Premium is $3000

CEG #3:	Causes: 1. Sex is male
	and ( )
	      5. Age is ≥ 65
	or ( )
	      2. Sex is female
	and ( )
	      5. Age is ≥ 65
	Effect: c: Premium is $1500

CEG #4:	Causes: 2. Sex is female
	and ( )
	      3. Age is < 25
	or ( )
	      2. Sex is female
	and ( )
	      4. Age is ≥ 25 and < 65
	Effect: d: Premium is $500

CEG #5:	Causes: 6. Sex is not male or female
	or ( )
	      7. Age is < ?
	or ( )
	      8. Age is > ?
	Effect: e: Invalid input error message

Step 4: In the fourth step the graphs are annotated with constraints describing combinations of causes and/or effects that are impossible because of syntactic or environmental constraints or considerations. For example, for the purpose of calculating the insurance premium in the above example, a person can not be both a "male" and a "female" simultaneously, as illustrated in Figure 22.8.

To show this, the CEG is annotated, as appropriate, with the constraint symbols shown in Table 22.3.

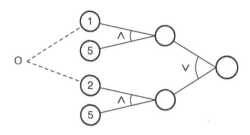

Figure 22.8   Cause-and-effect graph with constraints—example.

Table 22.3   Cause–effect graph constraint symbols—example (based on Myers [2004]).

Constraint symbol	Definition
E	The "E" (exclusive) constraint states that both causes *a* and *b* can not be true simultaneously.
I	The "I" (inclusive [at least one]) constraint states that at least one of the causes *a*, *b*, and *c* must always be true (*a*, *b*, and *c* can not be false simultaneously).
O	The "O" (one and only one) constraint states that one and only one of the causes *a* and *b* can be true.
R	The "R" (requires) constraint states that for cause *a* to be true, then cause *b* must be true. In other words, it is impossible for cause *a* to be true and cause *b* to be false.
M	The "M" (mask) constraint states that if effect *x* is true, effect *y* is forced to be false. (Note that the mask constraint relates to the effects and not the causes like the other constraints.)

Step 5: In the fifth step state conditions in the graphs are methodically traced and converted into a limited-entry decision table. The ones (1) in the limited-entry decision table column indicate that the cause (or effect) is true in the CEG and zeros (0) indicate that it is false. Table 22.4 illustrates the limited-entry decision table created by converting the CEG from the "calculating car insurance premiums" example. For example, the CEG #1 from step 3 converts into test case column 1 in Table 22.4. From CEG #1, causes 1 and 3 being true result in effect *b* being true.

Some CEGs may result in more than one test case being created. For example, because of the one and only one constraint in the annotated CGE #3 from step 4, this CEG results in test cases 3 and 4 in Table 22.4.

Step 6: In the sixth step the columns in the decision table are converted into test cases, as illustrated in Table 22.5. It should be noted that the example used above to illustrate the basic steps of CEG was kept very simple. An astute software developer could probably jump right to this set of test cases from the requirements without using the CEG method. However, for large, complex systems with multiple causes (inputs) and effects (outputs or transformations) this method is a systematic way to analyze them to create test cases. If CEG is performed early in the project, it can help in developing and verifying the completeness of the specification.

Table 22.4   Limited-entry decision table–example.

Control flow graph (CEG #)	2	1	3		4		5		
Test case	**1**	**2**	**3**	**4**	**5**	**6**	**7**	**8**	**9**
Causes:									
1. (Sex = male)	1	1	1	0	0	0	0	1	0
2. (Sex = female)	0	0	0	1	1	1	0	0	1
3. (Age < 25)	1	0	0	0	1	0	0	0	0
4. (Age ≥ 25 and < 65)	0	1	0	0	0	1	1	0	0
5. (Age ≥ 65)	0	0	1	1	0	0	0	0	0
6. (Sex not male or female)	0	0	0	0	0	0	1	0	0
7. (Age < ?)	0	0	0	0	0	0	0	1	0
8. (Age > ?)	0	0	0	0	0	0	0	0	1
Effects:									
a. (Premium is $1000)	0	1	0	0	0	0	0	0	0
b. (Premium is $3000)	1	0	0	0	0	0	0	0	0
c. (Premium is $1500)	0	0	1	1	0	0	0	0	0
d. (Premium is $500)	0	0	0	0	1	1	0	0	0
e. (Invalid input error message)	0	0	0	0	0	0	1	1	1

Table 22.5   Test cases from cause–effect graphing–example.

| Test case # | Input (causes) | | Expected output (effects) |
	Sex	Age	Premium
1	Male	< 25	$3000
2	Male	≥ 25 and < 65	$1000
3	Male	≥ 65	$1500
4	Female	≥ 65	$1500
5	Female	< 25	$500
6	Female	≥ 25 and < 65	$500
7	Other	≥ 25 and < 65	Invalid input
8	Male	< ?	Invalid input
9	Female	> ?	Invalid input

4. SOFTWARE TESTS

Identify and use various tests, including unit, functional, performance, integration, regression, usability, acceptance, certification, environmental load, stress, worst-case, perfective, exploratory, system, etc. (Apply)

Body of Knowledge VI.B.4

Levels of Testing

There are various levels of software testing that can be done, as illustrated in Figure 22.9. At the lowest level, the individual units that make up the software product are tested separately. A unit is the smallest software element that can be separately compiled. The programmer of a unit usually performs *unit testing*. One of the advantages of unit testing is fault isolation. Any problems that are found are isolated to the individual unit being tested. Unit testing is typically the earliest level of testing and therefore identifies defects earlier, when they are less expensive to fix than if they were found during later levels of testing. At the unit level it is also easier to ensure that every line of code or every branch through the unit is tested. An analogy for unit testing is to make sure that the individual bricks are good before the workers start building the wall out of them.

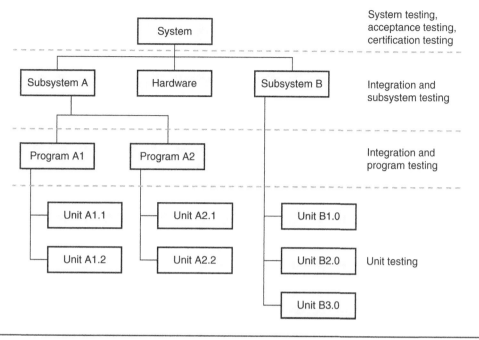

Figure 22.9   Levels of testing.

During integration, aggregating two or more software units or other components creates an integrated software component. With large software development projects, *integration testing* often includes software from many developers. Integration and testing may be accomplished in several levels:

- Integrating software units into software program components

- Integrating software program components into software subsystem components

- Integrating software subsystem components into the software system

Depending on the organization and the size of the project, integration testing may be performed by the developers or by a separate integration testing team. The focus of integration testing is on the interfaces and interactions between the integrated components or units. Since the individual units are already tested at the unit level, integration testing can maintain this focus without the distraction of an excessive amount of unit-level defects. To continue the analogy used above, integration testing focuses on making sure the mortar between the bricks is good and that the wall is solid.

System testing is "testing conducted on a complete, integrated system to evaluate the system's compliance with its specified requirements" (ISO/IEC 2009). This system may be an aggregation of software, hardware, or both that is treated as a single entity for the purpose of system testing, as well as operational use after release. To finish the analogy, system testing focuses on the functionality and quality of the entire house.

Acceptance testing is a special type of system testing performed by or for the acquirer (customer) of the software to demonstrate that the as-built software performs in accordance with the acceptance criteria. Typically, the acceptance test criteria are defined in a set of acceptance tests and agreed to as part of the contract (or other early agreement between the development organization and the customers). Acceptance tests are designed to provide a mechanism for formal acceptance of the software as it transitions into operations.

Certification testing is also a special type of system testing that is done by a third party (an organization other than the supplier or acquirer of the software). Certification test criteria and any standards that the software must meet should be defined and agreed to in advance. Contractual agreements between the supplier and acquirer may call for certification testing in place of or in addition to acceptance testing. A software development organization may also voluntarily seek some form of certification for their products for marketing or other purposes.

Functional Testing

Functional testing focuses on testing the functional requirements of the software— "what the software is supposed to do." Functional testing strategies include:

- Testing each individual function

- Testing usage scenarios

- Testing to the operational profile

To test each individual function, the tester decomposes and analyzes functional requirements and partitions the functionality into logical components (commands, actions, menu options). For each component, make a list of detailed functions and subfunctions that need to be tested, as illustrated in the example in Figure 22.10.

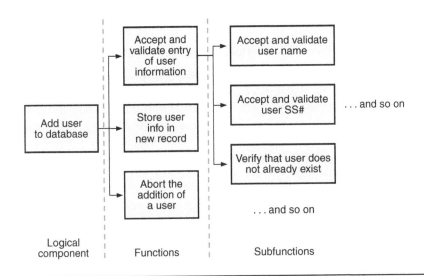

Figure 22.10   Function and subfunction list—example.

According to Whittaker (2003), "functional software testing is about intelligence." First, the testers must become familiar with the environment in which each function/subfunction operates. This involves identifying "users" of that function or subfunction from outside the software being tested. As illustrated in Figure 22.11, there are four classes of users that need to be considered.

- *Humans and hardware.* Human users can not interface directly with the software. Instead they must communicate using hardware devices (for example, keyboard, mouse, or button) whose inputs are processed by device drivers. Software may also interface directly with hardware without human interaction.

- *Operating system.* The operating system user provides memory and file pointers. Operating systems provide a set of functions needed and used by most applications (for example, time and date functions), and provide the necessary linkages to control a computer's hardware.

- *File systems.* File system users read, write, and store data in binary or text format. Files are used to store persistent data as opposed to internally stored global or local data structures (for example, integers, characters, arrays, strings, stacks, queues, pointers) that only exist while the program that defined them is executing. Because file contents are easily corrupted and are also easy to change from outside the confines of the applications that create and process them, the tester must be concerned with testing issues such as how the software handles:

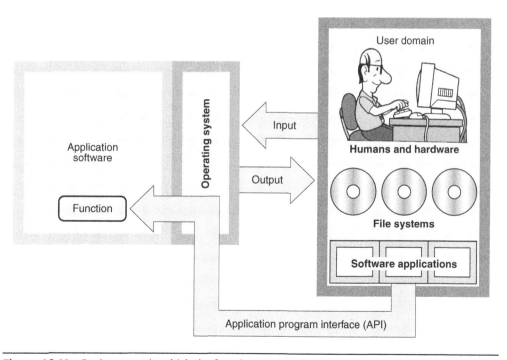

Figure 22.11   Environment in which the function operates.

- Corrupt data (for example, wrong type, incorrectly formatted, field delimiters misplaced, fields in the wrong order, file too large for the system under test to handle)

- A privileged user changing the permissions of a file while another user is editing the file contents

- *Software applications.* Other software programs (for example, databases, runtime libraries, applications) that supply inputs and receive outputs. Testers should consider:

  - Data that is passed to the application, return values and error codes, and failure scenarios of external resources

  - Databases, math libraries, and any other external resource the application may link to or communicate with for potential failure

  - Environment issues (for example, congested networks, busy or slow responses)

Once the environmental users for the function/subfunction are identified, the tester must explore the capabilities of each function/subfunction as it relates to each of those users. For example:

- *What inputs, both valid and invalid, can each user provide the function/subfunction?* The tester first tests to ensure that valid input values are handled appropriately. The tester then tests to ensure that the software prevents invalid input from being accepted or that the software handles it correctly.

- *What outputs does the function/subfunction send to each user?* The tester must test to ensure that the function responds to specific conditions, inputs, and events with output of the right form, fit, and function. For example, if the user hits the print command from a word processor, the appropriate document is sent to the printer (function), it is formatted correctly (form), and the right number of pages printed (fit). The tester must also test to ensure that the function does not respond with outputs unless the proper conditions, inputs, or events occur. For example, the word processor doesn't send the document to the printer when the "open" function is activated or when no function at all has been selected.

- *What data are stored or retrieved because of interactions with each user?* The tester must test to ensure that data are stored and retrieved in the proper formats and structures. Data structures should be tested to ensure that data could be appropriately added, read, and deleted from them. Testers should test to make sure that overflowing of the data structures couldn't occur. Testers should also consider other data system–related issues including data integrity and data control (for example, security, refresh, backup, and recovery).

- *What computation(s) are done because of interactions with each user?* Testers should think about what computations occur and how they might overflow (or underflow), or how they might interact or share data poorly with other computations or features.

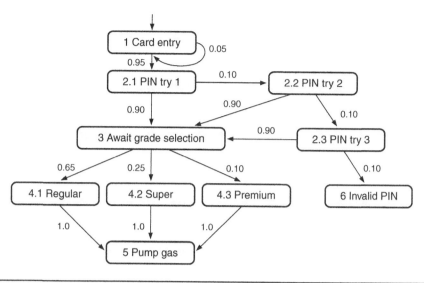

Figure 22.12 Decision tree—example.

To test usage scenarios, the tester chains together individual tests, from testing of the functions/subfunctions, into test scenarios that test start-to-finish user interactions with the system. Each feature may work independently, but they may not "play well together" to get real work accomplished for the users.

Testers perform *operational profile testing* in order to flush out the areas where defects are most likely to impact the reliability of the software. To perform operational profile testing, the tester must identify the different threads through the software. A thread is a sequential set of usage steps through the software that a user takes. For example, as illustrated in the decision tree in Figure 22.12, one thread would be to enter the credit card correctly the first time, enter the PIN correctly the first time, and then select and pump regular gas. A different thread would repeat these steps except for selecting and pumping premium gas. A third thread would be to enter the card correctly but take two tries before entering the PIN correctly and selecting and pumping regular gas. Once the threads have been identified, probabilities must be assigned to the paths out of any given state. The sum of all of the probabilities for paths out of any given state must be 1. For example, in the decision tree in Figure 22.12:

- For the "card entry" state: putting the card in correctly is assigned a 95% (0.95) probability and putting the card in incorrectly is assigned a 5% (0.05) probability

- For the "await grade selection" state: selecting regular gas is assigned a 65% (0.65) probability, selecting super gas is assigned a 25% (0.25) probability, and selecting premium gas is assigned a 10% (0.10) probability

The probability of a given thread is calculated by multiplying the assigned probabilities on that thread together. Those threads with the highest probability are the most frequently traversed threads. For example, again using the example in Figure 22.12:

- Thread #1 through states 1, 2.1, 3, 4.1, and 5 = $.95 \times .90 \times .65 \times 1 \approx 55.58\%$
- Thread #2 through states 1, 2.1, 3, 4.2, and 5 = $.95 \times .90 \times .25 \times 1 \approx 21.38\%$
- Thread #3 through states 1, 2.1, 3, 4.3, and 5 = $.95 \times .90 \times .10 \times 1 \approx 8.56\%$
- Thread #4 through states 1, 2.1, 2.2, 3, 4.3, and 5 = $.95 \times .10 \times .90 \times .10 \times 1$ $\approx 0.85\%$
- Thread #5 through states 1, 2.1, 2.2, 2.3, 3, 4.1, and 5 = $.95 \times .10 \times 10 \times .90 \times .65 \times 1 \approx 0.56\%$
- And so on

Using this example, if 1000 tests are going to be executed, operational profile testing would sample 556 (1000 × 55.58%) of those tests as variations on thread #1, for example, using different types of cards, different valid PINs and pumping different amounts of gas. A sample of 212 tests would be executed as variations on thread #2, 86 tests would be executed as variations on thread #3, and so on through each possible thread.

Performance, Environmental Load, Volume, and Stress Testing

The objective of *performance testing* is to determine if the system has any problems meeting its performance requirements for throughput (number of transactions per time unit), response time, or capacities (for example, the number of simultaneous users, of terminals or transactions). Performance testing is typically done at the system level under full environmental load. Typically, software can perform to specification when not much is going on. The performance of some software applications may degrade at full volume, with multiple users interacting with the software and other applications running in the background taking up system resources. Performance tests should be performed after the software is relatively problem free.

Environmental load testing evaluates the software's performance capabilities (throughputs, response times, and capacities) under normal load conditions, as illustrated in Figure 22.13.

Volume testing is a special type of environmental load testing that subjects the software to heavy loads over long periods of time and evaluates the software's capability. For example, does the software have any problems handling the maximum required volumes of data, transactions, users, and peripherals over several days or weeks?

Stress testing is another special type of environmental load testing that subjects the software to surges or spikes in load over short periods of time, and evaluates the software's performance. For example, is the software able to appropriately deal with jumping from no load to a spike of maximum data, transactions, or users? Stress testing can involve testing for excess load. For example, if the requirement states that the maximum capacity that a telecommunication switch can handle is 10,000, does the software appropriately handle a spike to 11,000 calls by reporting the appropriate messages ("all lines are currently busy, please call back later") or does it result in an inappropriate failure condition?

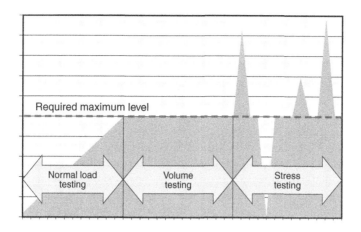

Figure 22.13   Load, stress, and volume testing.

Resource Utilization Testing

The objective of *resource utilization testing* is to determine if the system uses resources (for example, memory or disk space) at levels that exceed requirements or if the software has any problems when needed resource levels fluctuate or when resources are busy or unavailable. To perform resource utilization testing, the testers must evaluate objectives or requirements for resource availability. By testing the software with inadequate resources or by saturating resources with artificially induced overloads, the tester can help force resource-related exception conditions. Other resource-related testing considerations include whether the software can appropriately handle hardware or resource failures like:

- Full disk, directory, memory area, print queue, message queue, stack

- Disk not in drive, out of service, missing

- Printer off-line, out of paper, out of ink, jammed, or missing

- Extended memory not present or not responding

Usability Testing

The objective of *usability testing* is to ensure that the software matches the user's actual work style and determines whether the software has any areas that will be difficult or inconvenient for the users. The characteristics of usability include:

- *Accessibility.* Can users enter, navigate, and exit with relative ease?

- *Responsiveness.* Can users do what they want, when they want?

- *Efficiency.* Can users do what they want in a minimum amount of time or steps?

- *Comprehensibility.* Do users understand the product structure, its help system, and its documentation?

- *Aesthetics.* Are the screens, reports, and other user interfaces pleasing to the user's senses?

- *Ease of use.* How intuitive is the software use?

- *Ease of learning.* How intuitive is it to learn how to use the software?

When designing tests for usability, the tester has to consider the different potential users of the system including novice users, occasional users, different types of typical users, power users, enterprise users (for example, drivers from a taxi fleet or a trucking company that have special requirements for pay-at-the pump software), database administrators (DBAs), or operators. These different types of users may interpret usability very differently. Features that make the system user-friendly to novice or infrequent users may drive power users nuts. Take the "paper clip" help character in Microsoft Word as an example.

Having different types of actual users work with the software and then observing their responses is a method that is often used for usability testing. Usability tests can include having these users perform freeform, unplanned tasks as part of the testing process. This includes the user just working with the system in a manner that reflects how they actually expect to work with the system. The users may also be asked to perform predefined, written scripts containing step-by-step instructions for the user to follow. This method ensures better coverage but may not effectively reflect the user's actual work patterns. Using a preliminary prototype or mock-up rather than the final product can provide a mechanism for conducting usability testing earlier in the life cycle. Conducting and observing beta testing or field trials on the product at the actual user's site or in the actual environment where the system will be used can also be used to perform usability testing.

Worst-Case Testing

One type of *worst-case testing* is an extension of boundary testing. Boundary testing investigates the boundaries of each input variable separately by exploring the minimum value, one below the minimum, the maximum value, and one above the maximum. If multiple variables are needed as inputs to the software, all of the other variables are input at their normal values. For example, if a software function has two inputs x with boundaries at 0 and 5 and y with boundaries at 20 and 50, boundary testing would first boundary-test variable x with y set to its typical value. Then variable x would be set to its typical value and variable y would be boundary-tested.

Worst-case testing explores the boundaries of multiple input variables in combination at their boundary values. To continue the example above with the two inputs x and y, worst-case testing would require 16 test cases:

1. $x = -1$ and $y = 19$
2. $x = -1$ and $y = 20$
3. $x = -1$ and $y = 50$
4. $x = -1$ and $y = 51$
5. $x = 0$ and $y = 19$

6. $x = 0$ and $y = 20$

7. $x = 0$ and $y = 50$

8. $x = 0$ and $y = 51$

9. $x = 5$ and $y = 19$

10. $x = 5$ and $y = 20$

11. $x = 5$ and $y = 50$

12. $x = 5$ and $y = 51$

13. $x = 6$ and $y = 19$

14. $x = 6$ and $y = 20$

15. $x = 6$ and $y = 50$

16. $x = 6$ and $y = 51$

Another type of worst-case testing is to execute testing under worst-case resource conditions, for example, with the minimum allowable amount of memory, bandwidth, processing speed or network speed, or with the maximum volume of users, peripherals, or other applications running in the background. Performance requirements are a particular concern when testing under worst-case conditions.

Exploratory Testing

In *exploratory testing*, also known as *artistic testing*, the testers design and execute tests at the same time based on the knowledge gained as they are testing the software. Unlike preplanned testing where tests are written well in advance based on the software specifications, in exploratory testing the testers use the information they learn about the product as they are testing it to create additional tests. Unlike ad hoc testing, exploratory testing is not just wandering around the software randomly, it is a systematic exploration of the software based on experience-testing the software and the testers consciously thinking about what they don't know but want to find out. Also unlike ad hoc testing, the exploratory tester should "always write down what you do and what happens when you run exploratory tests" (Kaner 1999).

Exploratory testing is based on the tester's intuition, experience, and observations. For example, a tester runs the preplanned set of test cases for a function and everything matches the expected results, but things just don't seem right. Based on this judgment, the tester creates additional test cases to further investigate the feature and identify problems. Another example would be when the tester does find several problems in an area of the code but believes there are still more to find, even though all the preplanned test cases have been executed. Again, the tester creates additional test cases to explore the feature further, trying to confirm or refute their suspicions.

Exploratory testing can also leverage off of risk-based testing. For example, if a feature is expected to be low-risk, few planned test cases may be written for that feature. The exploratory tester can quickly investigate the low-risk feature to find out if they can find problems that might cause a reassessment of that feature's risk. On the other hand, for features that are expected to be high-risk, time should be reserved in the schedule to plan for additional exploratory testing of those features.

Regression Testing

Regression testing is concerned with how fixes or updates to software affect the unchanged portions of the software or hardware. Regression testing is "selective retesting of a system or component to verify that modifications have not caused unintended effects and that the system or component still complies with its specified requirements" (ISO/IEC 2009).

Regression analysis is the activity of examining a proposed software change and determining the depth and breadth of the effects the proposed change could have on the software. It is the determination of how extensively a change needs to be tested and how many already-executed test cases will need to be re-executed.

Regression analysis must balance the risk of releasing the software with undiscovered defects and the software's quality and integrity requirements against the cost of a more extensive testing effort.

Of course, the first testing step when software has been changed is to test the changes. Both white-box and black-box testing strategies can be used to test the units, components, and features that changed. Regression analysis is then used to determine how extensively other parts of the software should be retested. When deciding what other white-box regression tests to execute, consider units/components that share the same local or global variables or that directly call or are called by the unit/component changed. More rigorous regression testing might also consider going to a second level, as illustrated in Figure 22.14. This more rigorous testing includes testing the units/components that call or are called by the unit/component that call or are called by the unit/component changed. When deciding what other black-box regression tests to execute, consider functions that:

- Perform similar functions or are closely associated with the changed functions

- Interface with the same external device(s) or user(s)

- Access the same external data or databases

The final step in regression testing is to execute the regression test suite. The regression test suite can include both white-box and black-box tests that are always repeated no matter what changes in the software. Candidate tests for the regression test suite are tests for the units/components and functions that:

- *Are mission-critical to the success of the software.* For example, if everything else fails, the "save" command in a word processor or the "self-destruct" in a missile system must work.

- *Are defect-prone.* Software that has been defect-prone in the past is more likely to be defect-prone in the future.

- *Are the most used (operational profile).* Defects in areas of the software that are used most extensively will impact more users.

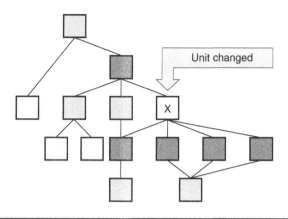

Unit changed

Figure 22.14   Test what changed.

- *Contain patches.* Since patches are temporary fixes, it is very easy to make a mistake when adding a patch back into a new software build.

Tests that are included in the regression test suite are prime candidates for automation because those tests will be rerun many times (every time the software is changed).

5. TESTS OF SUPPLIER COMPONENTS AND PRODUCTS

> Determine appropriate levels of testing for integrating third-party components and products. (Apply)
>
> **Body of Knowledge VI.B.5**

When a supplier-provided component or product is incorporated into a software system, it must be tested to the same level of rigor as other parts of that software system (that is, decisions about testing supplier software should be based on risk analysis and the level of integrity required). If a supplier-provided component or product is used to develop, build, or test the software system, it must also be tested to ensure that it does not cause problems in the software being developed. Supplier-provided components or products should be treated as an extended part of the primary development organization. The adequacy of the supplier's development and test process should be prequalified and then monitored throughout the effort. Supplier processes do not necessarily have to mirror the acquirer's process but need to achieve the same quality criteria for development and testing.

Throughout the software development process the supplier should be performing V&V activities. Depending on the acquirer's relationship to that supplier, the amount of visibility the acquirer has into those activities may vary. For example, for commercial off-the-shelf (COTS) software, the acquirer may have no way of determining the extent to which the supplier tested their software. On the other hand, with custom-built software, the acquirer might be an active participant in some supplier testing activities or at least have access to the test results and reports.

As part of product acceptance, the acquirer should conduct acceptance testing against negotiated acceptance criteria, which are included in the supplier contract or agreement to ensure that the delivered products meet all agreed-to requirements. The acquirer may also want to conduct alpha or beta testing. If the supplier's software is being integrated as part of a larger product, it should be integration tested and system tested as part of that larger system. Black-box strategies are usually necessary for this testing since access to the software source code is typically not available.

As with other testing activities, risk should be considered when scoping any COTS testing effort. For example, for COTS software where the mainstream functionality is being utilized, less testing may be required because this functionality has already been validated extensively through operational use. However, if more fringe functionality is being used or if this is a newly released COTS product, more extensive testing may be appropriate. If the COTS software is being integrated into the software system, it should be integration tested and system tested as part of that larger system. As with any supplier-supplied software, black-box strategies are usually necessary for this testing since access to the software source code is typically not available. If the COTS software is being used to develop or test the software being developed, risk-based validation should be used to ensure that it performs as required. Any customization or wraparounds that are done for the COTS software should also be tested.

For some projects, the customers may also be supplying software that will be integrated into the software system. If this is the case, this customer-supplied software must also be tested to the same level of rigor as other parts of the software system.

6. TEST COVERAGE SPECIFICATIONS

> Evaluate the adequacy of specifications such as functions, states, data and time domains, interfaces, security, and configurations that include internationalization and platform variances. (Evaluate)
>
> **Body of Knowledge VI.B.6**

Test coverage looks at the completeness of the testing. Test coverage maps the tests to some attribute of the software unit, component, or product being tested. These attributes can be attributes of the specification, as discussed in this section, or attributes of the code, as discussed in the next section.

Requirements Coverage

Requirements coverage looks at the mapping of tests to each of the uniquely identified requirements in the specification. Traceability is one of the primary mechanisms to ensure that all of the functional and other product requirements from the specification are covered. Every requirement should trace forward to one or more tests that will be used to evaluate the complete and correct implementation of that requirement. Requirements coverage metrics can be used to monitor progress toward complete coverage during the testing activities. The requirements coverage metric is the percentage of the requirements that trace forward to at least one test case.

A *test matrix*, also called a *system verification matrix*, is another tool for ensuring that each requirement is appropriately tested. A test matrix traces each requirement to the method that will be used to test it, as illustrated in Table 22.6. Initially, a test matrix is used to plan the testing strategy for each requirement as shown in the table. As test design progresses, additional detail can be added to the matrix to include more information about the specific approach to be taken. In this example, the methods include:

- *Inspection.* Evaluation of the requirements is done through visual examination or static analysis of the products (for example, source code or documentation) rather than through dynamic execution. Examples of the types of requirements that would be inspected are:

  - Product physical characteristics (for example, the screen will be blue)

  - Standards (for example, adherence to specified coding or commenting standards)

  - Specified languages or algorithms (for example, the software will be written in C++ or the data items will be sorted using a bubble sort)

- *Demonstration.* Evaluation of the requirements is done through the use of black-box techniques. Examples of the types of requirements that would be demonstrated are:

  - Functional requirements

Table 22.6 Test matrix–example.

Number	Requirement	Methods
R103	The system responds to all user commands and data entries within three seconds	Demonstration
R200	The software shall store all currently active transactions in memory to allow access if the storage media fails	Execution
R397	The source code shall be written in C++	Inspection
R560	The system shall calculate sales tax at current tax rates	Analysis
R50	The system shall work with all credit cards issued by all banks	Not testable

  – Performance-type requirements (for example, throughput, speed, response times, capacity)

  – Security- or safety-type requirements

  – Usability-type requirements

- *Execution.* Evaluation of the requirements is done through the use of white-box techniques. Examples of the types of requirements that would be tested in this manner include most design constraint–type requirements, including internal communication protocol requirements or internal data storage or format requirements.

- *Analysis.* Evaluation of the requirements that necessitate the use of independent calculations or other analytical techniques in addition to either white-box or black-box testing techniques. Examples of the types of requirements that would be evaluated through analysis are:

  – Requirements that include calculations (for example, calculating payroll withholding, calculating monthly sales totals)

  – Requirements that include statistical techniques (for example, means, standard deviations, confidence intervals)

- *Not testable.* Requirements that can not be evaluated because:

  – They are not really software requirements (for example, project constraints like delivery schedules)

  – It is not possible to test them with the current resources (for example, requirements that are not finite or not measurable)

An advantage of creating a test matrix early in the life cycle is the identification of non-testable requirements like R50 in Table 22.6 before they propagate into other software work products. Non-testable requirements and other issues discovered during the creation of the test matrix should be reported to the requirements analyst for resolution. It should be remembered that any requirement that is not tested is a source of risk because the implementation of that requirement may include undiscovered defects.

Functional Coverage

Of course 100 percent requirements coverage automatically achieves 100 percent coverage of all of the functional requirements. Another way to measure functional coverage from a user perspective is to look at the percentage of threads through the program that map to tests.

State Coverage

State coverage looks at the mapping of tests to the various states that the software can be in and the various transitions between those states to ensure that they are thoroughly tested. State testing is done to determine if the software:

- Switches correctly from valid state to valid state as specified

- Performs any state transitions that are not valid (moving to a state that is not a valid transition from the previous state)

- Loses track of its current state

- Mishandles inputs or other data while it is switching states

Data Domain Coverage

Data domain coverage looks at the mapping of tests to the various data domains in the software to ensure that they are thoroughly tested. Once the equivalency classes and boundaries for the inputs and output have been identified as defined previously, data domain coverage evaluates the percentage of those classes and boundaries that have test cases associated with them.

Another data domain coverage technique creates a list of all of the data items in the software. This can be done through evaluating the data dictionary or looking at the specification and identifying data items and structures. The CRUDL acronym can then be used to investigate coverage by ensuring that tests exist to evaluate any existing requirements or user needs for:

- C: The creation and initializations of each data item or structure

- R: The reading, querying, or displaying of each data item or structure

- U: The updating or refreshing of each data item or structure

- D: The deleting of each data item or structure

- L: The listing, summarizing, or tracking of each data item or structure in reports

Date and Time Domain Coverage

Date and time domain coverage looks at the mapping of tests to the various special date and/or time domains in the software to ensure that they are thoroughly tested. Date and time domain testing considers:

- Times of the day or special dates when the software is expected to perform differently. For example, performing background maintenance, refreshing data, and/or creating reports.

- Peak or minimum loads at certain times and/or dates

Date and time domain testing also considers whether the software appropriately handles special times and/or dates. For example:

- End of day, week, month, quarter, year, or century

- Holidays

- Daylight savings time change

- Leap year

- Time zone changes or international date line changes

Interface Coverage

An *interface* is a shared boundary across which information is passed. There are interfaces internal to the software between its units and components. There are also interfaces between the software and external entities (user/hardware, operating systems, file systems, and other software applications), as illustrated earlier in Figure 22.11. Interface coverage looks at the mapping of tests to the various identified interfaces to ensure that they are thoroughly tested. Integration testing typically focuses on ensuring interface coverage. Early levels of integration testing are focused on the software's internal interfaces. System integration looks at the assembly of hardware and software components and their external interfaces.

Security Coverage

The objective of *security testing* is to determine if the security of the system can be breached and to determine whether or not the software can handle the breaches or recover from them if security is breached. *Security coverage* looks at the mapping of tests to the various identified security issues to ensure that they are thoroughly tested.

Platform Configuration Coverage

The objective of *platform configuration testing* is to determine if the software has any problems handling all the required possible hardware and software configurations. *Platform configuration coverage* looks at the mapping of tests to the various possible platforms to ensure that the software is thoroughly tested on each platform. One method used for platform configuration coverage is to use a configuration test matrix as illustrated in the example in Table 22.7. In a configuration test matrix, all of the possible platforms are listed as column headers. In this example, that includes different operating systems that the software needs to run on. A list of tests is then listed down the rows. Each cell lists the status of that test on that platform:

- *Blank*. Indicates that the test has yet to be executed on that platform
- *Passed*. The test passed when it was executed on that platform
- *Failed*. The test failed when it was executed on that platform
- *N/A*. The test is not applicable or does not need to be executed on that platform

Internationalization Configuration Coverage

The objective of *internationalization testing*, also called *localization testing*, is to determine if the software has any problems related to transitioning it to other geographic locations. This includes adaptation to different languages, cultures, customs, and standards. The tester must be fluent in each language they will be using to test the system in order to ensure proper translation of screens, reports, error messages, help, and other items.

Table 22.7   Configuration test matrix.

Tests	W2K server	W2K advanced server	Microsoft NT 4	Windows 2003	Linux	Netware 6.0
ABC-1	Passed	Passed			N/A	N/A
ABC-2	Passed	Passed			N/A	N/A
AR-1	Passed	**Failed**			N/A	N/A
. . .						
XYZ-10	Passed				Passed	

Internationalization configuration coverage looks at the mapping of tests to the various possible geographic locations to ensure that the software is thoroughly tested on each location. Internationalization configuration coverage can also be tracked using a configuration test matrix, as illustrated in Table 22.7. However, in the case of internationalization, all of the possible locations are listed as column headers instead of the platforms. Test considerations in internationalization testing include:

- *Character sets.* Different character set are used in different countries. Ensure that the software uses the proper set.

- *Keyboards.* Keyboards should be tested with the software to ensure that they correctly interpret key codes according to the character set.

- *Text filters.* The software may accept only certain characters in a field. Test that the software allows and displays every character in the appropriate places.

- *Loading, saving, importing, and exporting high and low ASCII.* Save and read full character sets to every file format that the software supports. Display and print them to verify correctness.

- *Operating system language.* Check variances in wild card symbols, file name delimiters, and common operating system commands.

- *Hot keys.* Consider any underlined, bolded, or otherwise highlighted character in a menu item such as X in eXit. Do any hot keys from the original language have their old effect even though they do not appear in the localized menu?

- *Garbled in translation.* If the software builds messages from fragments, how does that appear in the localized version? Are there file names and data values inserted into an error message to make it more descriptive?

- *Expanding text.* Translated text expands and can overflow menus, dialog boxes, and internal storage, overwriting other code or data.

- *Spelling rules.* Spelling rules vary across dialects of the same language. For example, in the United States the word "organization" is spelled with a "z" where in England it is spelled "organisation." Does the spell-checker work correctly for the new location?

- *Hyphenation rules.* Rules are not the same across languages.

- *Sorting rules.* Character and word sorting rules vary from country to country (for example, sorting by last name, first name). The addition of special characters like letters with accents may not allow sorting using ASCII numeric order.

- *Case conversion.* Only in English is case conversion correctly done by adding or subtracting 32 to or from the letter. Look for case conversion issues in any search dialog or other text pattern matching functions.

- *Underscoring rules.* Underlining conventions differ between countries. It can be poor form to underscore punctuation, spaces, and other characters in some countries.

- *Printers.* Though most European printers are essentially the same as U.S. printers, differences can and do occur.

- *Paper size.* In different parts of the world, paper sizes differ—check that the default margins are correct for each size and that outputs to printers are formatted correctly.

- *Data format and setup.* For example, consider both the format and the numeric separators for time and date displays and money formats—where the USA puts a comma, others put a decimal point or a space. Many subroutines that the software links into may treat commas as separators between items in a list.

- *Rulers and measurements.* Rulers, tab dialogs, grids, and every measure of length, height, volume, or weight that is displayed must be in the correct unit of measure.

- *Culture-bound graphics.* Check clip art, tool icons, screens, manuals, and even packaging for culture-bound graphics.

- *Culture-bound outputs.* Calendar formats vary, the appearance of a standard invoice varies, and address formats differ, and so on.

7. CODE COVERAGE TECHNIQUES

> Identify and use techniques such as branch-to-branch, condition, domain, McCabe's cyclomatic complexity, boundary, etc.
>
> **Body of Knowledge VI.B.7**

Unlike threads, which are usage/functionality focused, *paths* refer to control flow-sequences through the internal structure of the software. There are typically many possible paths between the entry and exit of a typical software application. Every decision doubles the number of potential paths, every case statement multiplies the number of potential paths by the number of cases, and every loop multiplies the number of potential paths by the number of different iteration values possible for the loop. For example, a software unit with a loop that can be iterated from one to 100 times has 100 possible paths (once through the loop, twice through the loop, and so on, up to 100 times through the loop). Add an if-than-else statement inside that loop and that increases the number of paths to 200. Add a case statement with four possible choices inside the loop as well and there are 800 possible paths. Moving from the individual unit to the integration level, if this unit with 800 paths is integrated with a unit that only has two sequential if-than-else statements (four paths), there are now 3200 paths through these two units in combination.

Since there are rarely enough resources to test every path through a complex software application or even a complex individual unit, the tester uses white-box logic coverage techniques to systematically select the tests that are the most likely to help identify the yet undiscovered, relevant defect.

Statement, Decision, and Condition Coverage

To demonstrate the different statement, decision, and condition coverage techniques, the piece of nonsense code shown in Figure 22.15 will be used.

A *statement*, also called a *line*, is an instruction or a series of instructions that a computer carries out. *Statement coverage*, also called *line coverage*, is the extent that a given software unit/component's statements are exercised by a set of tests. Statement coverage is the least rigorous type of code coverage technique. To have complete statement coverage, each statement must be executed at least once. Table 22.8 illustrates that it only takes one test case to have statement coverage of the code in Figure 22.15. As long as input variables B and C are selected so that both decisions in this code are true, every statement is executed.

```
A = 300
if B > 40 and C < 100 then A = 1000
if B < 60 and C < 20 then A = 10
print A
```

Figure 22.15   Code–example.

Table 22.8   Statement coverage–example.

Test case #	Inputs		Expected output
	B	C	A
1	> 40 and < 60	< 20	10

A *decision* determines the branch path that the code takes. To have *decision coverage*, also called *branch coverage*, each statement is executed at least once and each decision takes all possible outcomes at least once. For example, if the decision is a Boolean expression, decision coverage requires test cases for both the true and false branches. If the decision is a case statement, decision coverage requires test cases that take each case branch. If decision coverage exists, then statement coverage also exists. Table 22.9 illustrates the test cases needed to have decision coverage of the code in Figure 22.15. The first test case results in the first decision being true and the second decision being false. The second test case results in the first decision being false and the second decision being true. Thus, these two test cases in combination provide decision coverage because the true and false paths are taken out of each decision.

A *condition* is a state that a decision is based on. To have *condition coverage*, each statement is executed at least once and each condition in a decision takes all possible outcomes at least once. If decision coverage exists, then statement coverage also exists. For the code in Figure 22.15 there are three conditions that the input variable B can have: B ≤ 40, 40 < B < 60, or B ≥ 60. There are also three conditions that input variable C can have: C < 20, 20 ≤ C < 100 or C ≥ 100. Table 22.10 illustrates one choice of test cases that combines these into condition coverage of the code in Figure 22.15.

Note that condition coverage does not always imply decision coverage. For example, in the set of test cases in Table 22.10, test case 1 results in the first decision being true and the second decision being false. Test cases 2 and 3 result in both decisions being false. Therefore, decision coverage has not been achieved because the true path has not been taken out of the second decision.

Table 22.9 Decision coverage–example.

Test case #	Inputs		Expected output
	B	C	A
1	≥ 60	< 20	1000
2	≤ 40	< 20	10

Table 22.10 Condition coverage–example.

Test case #	Inputs		Expected output
	B	C	A
1	≥ 60	< 20	1000
2	≤ 40	≥ 20 and < 100	300
3	> 40 and < 60	≥ 100	300

Table 22.11   Decision/condition coverage–example.

Test case #	Inputs		Expected output
	B	C	A
1	≥ 60	≥ 20 and < 100	1000
2	> 40 and < 60	< 20	10
3	≤ 40	≥ 100	300

Table 22.12   Multiple condition coverage–example.

Test case #	Inputs		Expected output
	B	C	A
1	≤ 40	< 20	10
2	≤ 40	≥ 20 and < 100	300
3	≤ 40	≥ 100	300
4	> 40 and < 60	< 20	10
5	> 40 and < 60	≥ 20 and < 100	1000
6	> 40 and < 60	≥ 100	300
7	≥ 60	< 20	1000
8	≥ 60	≥ 20 and < 100	1000
9	≥ 60	≥ 100	300

The next level of rigor is to have condition and decision coverage where each statement is executed at least once, each decision takes all possible outcomes at least once, and each condition in a decision takes all possible outcomes at least once. If decision/condition coverage exists, condition coverage, decision coverage, and statement coverage also all exist. Table 22.11 illustrates one choice of test cases that provides decision/condition coverage of the code in Figure 22.15.

To have *multiple condition coverage*, each statement is executed at least once and all possible combinations of condition outcomes in each decision occur at least once. Multiple condition coverage always results in condition, decision, and statement coverage as well. Multiple condition coverage is the most rigorous type of structural coverage testing. Table 22.12 illustrates a choice of test cases that provides multiple condition coverage of the code in Figure 22.15.

Domain and Boundary Testing

For structural testing, the conditions for the input variables define their *domains*, or *equivalence classes*. Once these domains are defined, sampling from these domains can be done when executing test cases. Boundary value testing can also be done by sampling values on the boundaries of these domains. For example, for input variable *B* the boundary values would be 39, 40, 60, and 61.

McCabe's Cyclomatic Complexity and Basis Path Testing

Basis path testing is a structural testing technique that identifies test cases based on the flows or independent logical paths that can be taken through the software. A *basis path* is a unique path through the software where no iterations are allowed. Basis paths are atomic-level paths, and all possible paths through the system are linear combinations of them. Basis path testing uses McCabe's *cyclomatic complexity* metric, which measures the complexity of a source code unit by examining the control flow structure. McCabe's cyclomatic complexity can be used to determine the testing required and tests needed to have coverage of the linearly independent paths (basis paths).

The first step in basis path testing is to draw a control flow graph. As illustrated in the example in Figure 22.16, this can be done directly from the source code or it can also be done from the detailed design.

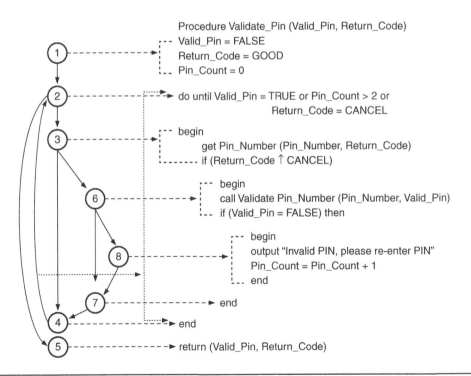

Figure 22.16 Control flow graph—example.

The second step in basis path testing is to calculate the McCabe's cyclomatic complexity from the control flow graph. There are actually three ways to calculate the cyclomatic complexity of a control flow graph.

- Cyclomatic complexity = Edges − Nodes + $2p$. For this example there are 10 edges, eight nodes, and there is only one part to the control flow graph ($p = 1$), so the cyclomatic complexity = $10 − 8 + (2 \times 1) = 4$

- Cyclomatic complexity = Number of regions in the control flow graph. For this example there are three enclosed regions plus the outside region, so cyclomatic complexity = 4.

Static analysis tools exist for drawing control flow graphs and/or calculating cyclomatic complexity from source code so that these processes do not have to be done manually.

The third step is to identify a set of basis paths. In this case, since the cyclomatic complexity is 4, there are four paths to identify. Path identification is accomplished by selecting the shortest, simplest path through the control flow graph. That is the path through nodes 1, 2, and 5 in this example. Then each subsequent path adds at least one new edge but adds the minimum number of new edges possible. Following this method, the second path in this example is the path through nodes 1, 2, 3, 4, 2, and 5, the third path is the path through nodes 1, 2, 3, 6, 7, 4, 2, and 5, and the fourth path is the path through nodes 1, 2, 3, 6, 8, 7, 4, 2, and 5.

The fourth step is to generate the test cases that will force execution of each path in the basis path set. To define the actual test cases, the tester refers back to the actual source code. The test cases for this example are:

Path 1: 1, 2, 5
Test case 1

Path 1 can not be tested stand-alone; however, since these edges are tested as part of path 2, 3, or 4 this test is not necessary

Path 2: 1, 2, 3, 4, 2, 5
Test case 2

Press cancel in response to the "enter PIN number" prompt

Path 3: 1, 2, 3, 6, 7, 4, 2, 5
Test case 3

Enter a valid PIN number on the first try

Path 4: 1, 2, 3, 6, 8, 7, 4, 2, 5
Test case 4

Enter an invalid PIN on the first try and a valid PIN on the second try

---

It should be noted that in order to follow path 4 this test case executes the loop a second time, so the path is actually 1, 2, 3, 6, 8, 7, 4, 2, 3, 6, 7, 4, 2, 5, but this test case covers all of the edges of the basis path.

8. TEST ENVIRONMENTS

Select and use simulations, test libraries,
drivers, stubs, harnesses, etc., and identify
parameters to establish a controlled test
environment in various situations. (Analyze)

Body of Knowledge VI.B.8

Test Beds

A *test bed* is an environment established and used for the execution of the tests. The goal here is to be able to create a test environment that matches the actual operating environment as closely as possible while providing the testers with a known platform to test from and providing the testers with visibility into test results. The test bed includes:

- *Hardware.* At a minimum this includes the hardware required to execute the software, and it may also include additional hardware that inputs information into or accepts outputs from the software being tested.

- *Instrumentation.* This may include oscilloscopes or other hardware or software equipment needed to probe the software or its behaviors during test execution. For example, it may include software that monitors memory or disk space utilization or coverage during test execution.

- *Simulators.* As discussed earlier, simulators are used to substitute for (simulate) missing or unavailable system components during test execution. Simulators mimic the behavior of these missing components in order to provide needed inputs to and accept output from the software being tested.

- *Software tools.* This may include automation tools, stubs, and drivers or other software tools used in testing, for example, debuggers or other tools that allow step-by-step execution or breakpoints to be inserted to "watch" code execution and examine variable and memory values. This also includes the operating system and cohabitating software (including database software or other interfacing software applications) used to run and test the software.

- *Other support elements.* For example, facilities and manuals.

Stubs

A *stub* is a software unit/component that usually minimally simulates the actions of a called (lower-level) unit/component that has not yet been integrated during top-down testing. Some required stubs need more than the minimal return response. For example, if the calling unit/component under test expects a calculation from the invoked stub, that calculation capability may need to be programmed into the stub, or the stub can simply set the returned variable(s). Table 22.13 shows an example of a very simple stub and its associated calling routine.

A stub can also be used when the software needs to talk to an external device in order to replace that device. For example, a stub could intercept the data that would normally be sent to a hardware device and automatically analyze that data against the expected values. This analysis can often be done more quickly and accurately by a stub than it can be manually, especially if the output is large or complex. For example, humans are not good at finding a single missing or incorrect data point in a long stream of data.

Drivers

A *driver* is a software unit/component that usually minimally simulates the actions of a calling (higher-level) unit/component that has not yet been integrated during bottom-up testing. The driver typically establishes the values that will be passed to the unit/component under test before calling it. Table 22.14 shows an example of a very simple driver and its associated called routine.

Table 22.13   Stub—example.

Stub:	Calling (higher-level) unit:
Procedure CALCULATE_TAX (taxes)	Procedure SALE_PROCESS
Return taxes	begin;
begin;	statement 1;
return $1.32;	statement 2;
end CALCULATE_TAX;	TAX = CALCULATE_TAX (taxes);
	statement 3;
	end SALE_PROCESS

Table 22.14   Driver—example.

Driver:	Called (lower-level) unit:
Procedure EXEC_DRV	Function MEAN_VALUE
begin;	(X1, X2 : FLOAT) return FLOAT
NUM1 = 15	begin
NUM2 = 25	return (X1 + X2)/2.0;
MEAN_VALUE(NUM1, NUM2);	end MEAN_VALUE
end EXEC_DRV;	

Part VI.B.8

More-complex test drivers can be used to mimic large amounts of data being entered manually. For example, a driver could mimic data entry streams coming from multiple keyboards simply by reading a predefined set of inputs from a data file and using them to emulate the keyboard entries.

Harnesses

At their most sophisticated, *test harnesses* can be used as a framework of software, tests, and test data used to automate the testing of a unit by executing a set of test cases and/or scripts under a variety of conditions and collecting, monitoring, and even evaluating the test results. The two primary parts of a test harness are the test execution engine and the repository of test cases and/or scripts.

Test Libraries

Test libraries are managed libraries that are used to control and track changes to test plans, test cases, test procedures, test scripts, and test data. These libraries act as repositories that can also facilitate the reuse of test products across products or product lines.

Controlled Test Environments

Sometimes the time to set up the test environment is trivial. However, according to Black (2004), "A complex test environment can take a long time and involve a lot of effort to set up and configure." Whatever the initial investment, it must be protected by managing and controlling the test environment as it is being utilized by the testers to execute their tests. The key here is to be able to restore the test environment to a known state with minimal effort because as tests are being executed unexpected events may occur that corrupt the data or the software being tested or cause issues with some other part of the test bed. After the software is released into operations, the test bed may also need to be reproduced to test the software after maintenance changes are made.

Test environment control policies and processes should be established and followed to ensure that the test bed is not interjecting false positives (issues that look like software problems but are actually test bed problems) or allowing software problems that should have been identified to be missed. The policies and procedures may include mechanisms for:

- Effectively controlling passwords and access

- Controlling, backing up, and restoring test data and databases

- Controlling, restoring, "freezing," or updating the software being tested so that the testers have a steady platform to test from

- Validating the test bed setup, the individual elements of the test bed, and their interoperability

- Requesting, approving, and implementing changes to the test bed's hardware, tool set, or other elements, including performing impact analysis and notifying impacted stakeholders of implemented changes

- Ensuring that testers are trained to use the test bed elements correctly and have access to user/operator manuals, help files, or other support documentation for test bed elements

- Providing support for the test bed's hardware, tool set, or other elements including service level agreements and escalation processes

- Maintaining licenses for purchased test bed elements

- Identifying the current versions, revisions, and calibrations for the test bed elements, including the software being tested

9. TEST TOOLS

> Identify and use utilities, diagnostics, and test management tools. (Apply)
>
> **Body of Knowledge VI.B.9**

Like any other software product, testing tools should go through verification and validation (V&V) prior to use. Requirements for the V&V of supplier-provided testing tools should be specified as part of acquisition plans. This may include requirements for supplier V&V activities as well as plans for acquirer conducted V&V (joint reviews, alpha, beta, and acceptance testing). Both supplier-provided and in-house-developed software testing tools should go through an appropriate level of rigorous V&V for the required integrity level/risk of the software they will be testing. This helps ensure that a tool does not indicate that the software passes tests that it actually failed. It also helps eliminate the waste caused when software developers spend time debugging reported software problems that were actually defects in the testing tools and not in the software.

Test Utilities

There are many test automation tools on the market that range from very simplistic capture-and-playback tools to fully programmable, integrated tool test tool suites. Stress and load tools induce various levels of environmental load into the software being tested.

There are also many simple tools used by testers to perform their work. These tools may or may not be parts of the test bed discussed previously. These include tools like:

- *Word processors.* Used for test plans, test reports, and other test documentation

- *Spreadsheets.* Used for test matrices, test metrics, to perform analysis calculations, and for other testing tasks

- *Checklist.* List of common defects and test heuristics so the testers remember to create tests for these items or features, or list of attributes or other characteristics to map to tests to ensure coverage

- *Database software.* Used to create test databases as inputs into testing, to query the databases of the software being tested to analyze test results, to record and track test data, and create test metrics (for example a test case database or a problems-reporting database)

- *Stopwatches, oscilloscopes, or other monitoring or probe devices.* Used to analyze test results

- *Random number generators.* Used to create random samples as test inputs

- *Video cameras or other recording devices.* Used to record usability testing sessions

Test Diagnostic Tools

Test diagnostic tools include a variety of static code analyzers that can be used to aid in test case design. For example, some static code analyzers can calculate a unit/component's cyclomatic complexity and even identify the inputs that should be used to test the basis paths. Static code analyzers can identify improper control flows, uninitialized variables, inconsistencies in data declarations or usage, redundant code, unreachable code, and overly complex code and thus eliminate defects before they need to be found using more expensive testing techniques. Cross-referencing code analyzers provide the information so that when a variable is modified in one section of code, the programmers and testers knows all the other places the software uses that variable and therefore might be impacted by the change. This is extremely helpful when analyzing the amount of regression testing needed after a change.

Test diagnostic tools include a variety of dynamic analyzers to aid in test execution. Examples of dynamic analysis tools include:

- Code coverage analyzers

- Resource utilization analyzers, for example, memory- or disk space–monitoring tools

- File comparison, screen capture, and comparison tools, and other tools used to capture and analyze the actual results of test execution against expected results

- Communication analyzers that allow the tester to view raw data moving across the network or other communication channels

- Debuggers, which are used to step through code or set breakpoints and to examine memory values during structural testing

Test Management Tools

Test planning tools include templates for various test documents, which allow the tester to focus on the content rather than the format of those documents. These may be as simple as templates in a word processor to sophisticated test management tools that allow test cases and procedures to be entered into test databases and linked with requirements, design elements, change requests, and problem reports to document traceability.

Test planning tools can also include project management tools used for the testing part of the project. These tools can aid in test estimation, creating test-related work breakdown structures, test scheduling and budgeting, and tracking and controlling the testing effort.

Problem-reporting tools and configuration management tools are also tools that support the management of the testing effort. For example, the configuration management status accounting tools should be able to identify for the testers what changed (and what didn't change) between the new software build they just received and the build they were previously testing.

Chapter 23

C. Reviews and Inspections

Identify and use desk-checks, peer reviews,
walk-throughs, Fagan and Gilb inspections,
etc. (Apply)

Body of Knowledge VI.C

The ISO/IEC *Systems and Software Engineering—Vocabulary* (ISO/IEC 2009) defines a *review* as "a process or meeting during which a work product, or set of work products, is presented to project personnel, managers, users, customers, or other interested parties for comment or approval." A *peer review* is a special type of technical review where one or more of the author's peers evaluate a work product to identify defects, to obtain a confidence level that the product meets its requirements, and/or to identify opportunities to improve that work product. The author of a work product is the person who either originally produced that work product or the person who is currently responsible for maintaining that work product. An inspection is the most formal type of peer review.

OBJECTIVES OF PEER REVIEWS

One of the primary objectives of peer reviews is to identify and remove defects in software work products as early in the software life cycle as possible. It can be very difficult for the author to find defects in their own work product. Most software practitioners have experienced situations where they hunt and hunt for that elusive defect and just can't find it. When they ask someone else to help, the other person takes a quick look at the work product and spots the defect almost instantly. That's the power of peer reviews.

Another objective of peer reviews is to provide confidence that the work product meets its requirements and the customers' needs. Peer reviews can check to make sure that all of the functional requirements and quality attributes have been adequately implemented in the design and code and are adequately being evaluated by the tests.

Peer reviews can be used to check the work product for compliance to standards. For example, the design can be peer reviewed to ensure that it matches modeling standards and notations, or the code can be reviewed to ensure that it complies with coding standards and naming conventions.

Peer reviews can also be used to identify areas for improvement (this does not mean "style" issues, if it is a matter of style, the author wins). However, peer reviewers can identify areas that make the software more efficient. For example, when reviewing a piece of source code, a reviewer might identify a more efficient sorting routine or method of removing redundant code or even identify areas where existing code can be reused. During a peer review, a tester might identify issues with the testability of a requirement or section of the design. Peer reviewers can also identify maintainability issues. For example, in a code review inadequate comments, hard-coded variable values, or confusing code indentation might be identified as areas for improvement.

BENEFITS OF PEER REVIEWS

The Software Engineering Institute's (SEI) Capability Maturity Model Integration (CMMI) for Development (SEI 2006) states, "Peer reviews are an important part of verification and are a proven mechanism for effective defect removal." The benefits of peer reviews, especially formal inspections, are well documented in the industry. For example, more defects are typically found using peer reviews than other verification and validation (V&V) methods. Capers Jones reports, "Within a single testing stage, you are unlikely to remove more than 35% of the errors in the tested work product. In contrast, design and code inspections typically remove between 50% and 70% of the defects present." Well-run inspections with highly experienced inspectors can obtain 90% defect removal effectiveness (Wiegers 2002). "Inspections can be expected to reduce defects found in field use by one or two orders of magnitude" (Gilb 1993).

It typically takes much less time per defect to identify defects during peer reviews than it does using any of the other defect detection techniques. For example, Kaplan reports that at IBM's Santa Teresa laboratory it took an average of 3.5 labor hours to find a major defect using code inspection while it took 15 to 25 hours to find a major defect during testing (Wiegers 2002). It also typically takes much less time to fix it because the defect is identified directly in the work product, which eliminates the need for time-consuming debugging activities. Peer reviews can also be used early in the life cycle on work products such as requirements and design specifications to eliminate defects before those defects propagate into other work products and become more expensive to correct.

Peer reviews can also be beneficial because they help provide opportunities for cross-training. Less-experienced practitioners can benefit from seeing what a high-quality work product looks like, such as when they help peer review the work of more experienced practitioners. More-experienced practitioners can provide engineering analysis and improvement suggestions that help transition knowledge when they peer review the work of less-experienced practitioners. Peer reviews also help spread product, project, and technical knowledge around the organization. For example, after a peer review, more than one practitioner is familiar with the reviewed work product and can potentially support it if its author is unavailable. Peer reviews of requirements and design documents aid in communications and help promote a common understanding that is beneficial in future development activities. For example, these peer reviews can help identify and clarify assumptions or ambiguities in the work products being reviewed.

Peer reviews can help establish shared workmanship standards and expectations. They can build a synergistic mind-set as the work products transition from individual to team ownership with the peer review.

Finally, peer reviews provide data that aid the team in assessing the quality and reliability of the work products. Peer review data can also be used to drive future defect prevention and process improvement efforts.

WHAT TO PEER REVIEW

Every work product that is created during software development can be peer reviewed. However, not every work product should be. Before a peer review is held, practitioners should ask the question, "Will it cost more to perform this peer review than the benefit of holding it is worth?" Peer reviews, like any other process activity, should always be value-added or they should not be held. Typically, every work product that is delivered to a customer or end user should be considered as a candidate for peer reviews. Examples include responses to requests for proposals, contracts, user manuals, requirements specifications, and, of course, the software and its subcomponents. In addition, any work product that is input to or has major influence in the creation of these deliverables should also be peer reviewed. For example, a low-level design, interface specification, or test case may never get directly delivered, but defects in those documents can have a major impact on the quality of the delivered software.

So what doesn't get peer reviewed? Actually many work products are created in the process of developing software that may not be candidates for peer reviews. For example, most quality records such as meeting minutes, status reports, and defect logs are typically not peer reviewed.

SELECTING PEER REVIEWERS

Peer reviewers are selected based on the type and nature of the work product. Reviewers should be peers of the author and possess enough technical or domain knowledge to allow for a thorough evaluation of the work product. For a peer review to be effective, the reviewers must also be available to put in the time and energy necessary to conduct the review. There are a variety of reasons why individuals might be unavailable to participate, including time constraints, the need to focus on higher-priority tasks, or the belief that they have inadequate domain/technical knowledge. If an "unavailable" individual is considered essential to the success of the peer review, this issue needs to be dealt with, to the satisfaction of that individual, prior to assigning them to participate in the peer review.

The general rule for peer reviews is that managers don't participate in peer reviews—they aren't peers. Peers are the people that are at the same level of authority in the organization as the work product's author. The principle is that if managers participate, then:

- Authors are more reluctant to have the products peer reviewed because the defects found might reflect badly on the author in the eyes of the manager

- Reviewers are more reluctant to report defects in front of managers and make their colleagues look bad—remembering that it might be their turn next

However, it isn't quite that simple. It depends a lot on the culture of the organization. For organizations where first-line managers are working managers (active members of the team) or where participative management styles prevail, having the immediate supervisor in the peer review may be a real benefit. They may possess knowledge and skills that are assets to the peer review team and the author. Individuals from one level above or below the author in the organizational level, as illustrated in Figure 23.1, can be considered as peer reviewers, but only if the author is comfortable with that selection. In other words—ask the author.

When talking about "peers" in a peer review, it doesn't mean "clones." In a requirements peer review where the author is a systems analyst, this does not necessarily limit the peer review team to just other systems analysts. Having reviewers with different perspectives increases the diversity on the peer review team. This diversity brings with it different perspectives that can increase the probability of finding additional defects and different kinds of defects. The reviewers should be selected to maximize this benefit by choosing diverse participants including:

- The author of the work product that is the predecessor to the work product that is being reviewed. "The predecessor perspective is important because one . . . goal is to verify that the work product satisfies its specification" (Wiegers 2002).

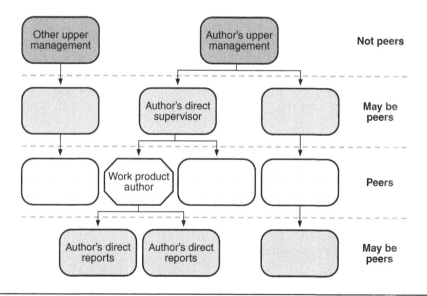

Figure 23.1   Selecting peer reviewers.

- Others with the same job as the author have the knowledge of the workmanship standards and best practices for the specific product. They are also most familiar with the common defects made in that type of work product.

- The authors of dependent (successor) work products and authors of interfacing work products have a strong vested interest in the quality of the work product. For example, consider inviting a designer and a tester to the requirements peer review. Not only will they help find defects but they are excellent candidates for looking at issues such as understandability, feasibility, and testability.

- Specialists may also be called on when special expertise can add to the effectiveness of the peer review (for example, security experts, GUI interface experts).

For most peer reviews, the peers are typically other members of the project team. However, for small projects or projects that have only a single person with a specialized skill set, it may be necessary to ask people from other projects to participate in the peer reviews.

As mentioned above, peer reviews are wonderful training grounds for teaching new people programming techniques, product and domain knowledge, processes, and other valuable information. However, too many trainees can also impact the efficiency and effectiveness of the peer review. There may also be several reasons why individuals may want to observe peer reviews. For example, an auditor may be observing to ensure that the peer review is being conducted in accordance with documented procedures, or an inspection moderator trainee may be observing an experienced moderator in action. Observers can be distracting to team members even if they aren't participating in the actual review. Limiting the number of trainees and observers in a peer review meeting to no more than one or two per meeting is recommended.

Management's primary responsibility to the peer review process is to champion that process by emphasizing its value and maintaining the organization's commitment to the process. To do this, management must understand that while the investment in peer reviews is required early in the project, their true benefits (their return on that investment) won't be seen until the later phases of the life cycle or even after the product is released. Management can champion peer reviews by:

- Ensuring adequate scheduling and resources for peer reviews

- Incorporating peer reviews into the project plans

- Ensuring that training is planned and complete for all software practitioners participating in peer reviews

- Advocating and supporting the usefulness of peer reviews through communications and encouragement

- Appropriately using data on the conduct and results of peer reviews

  • Being brave enough to stay away from the actual peer reviews unless specifically invited to participate

INFORMAL VERSUS FORMAL PEER REVIEWS

Peer reviews can vary greatly in their level of formality. At the most informal end of the peer review spectrum, a software practitioner can ask a colleague to, "Please take a look at this for me." These types of informal peer reviews are performed all the time. It is just good practice to get a second pair of eyes on a work product when the practitioner is having problems or needs a second opinion. As illustrated in Figure 23.2, these informal reviews are done ad hoc with no formal process, no preparation, no quality records or metrics. Defects are usually reported either verbally or as redlined mark-ups on a draft copy of the work product. Any rework that results from these informal peer reviews is up to the author's discretion.

On the opposite end of the spectrum is the formal peer review. In formal peer reviews, a rigorous process is documented, followed, and continuously improved with feedback from peer reviews as they are being conducted. Preparation before the peer review meeting is emphasized. Peer review participants have well-defined roles and responsibilities to fulfill during the review. Defects are formally recorded and that list of defects and a formal peer review report become quality records for the review. The author is responsible for the rework required to correct the reported defects and that rework is formally verified by either rereviewing the work product or through checking done by another member of the peer review team (for example, the inspection moderator). Metrics are collected and used as part of the

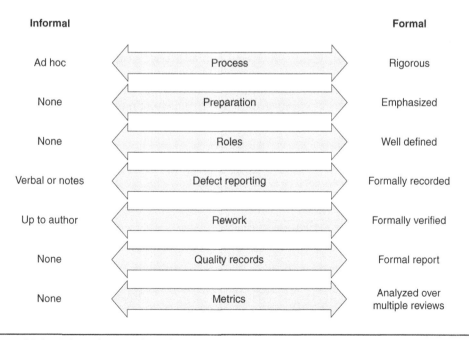

Figure 23.2   Informal versus formal peer reviews.

peer review process. Metrics are also used to analyze multiple reviews over time as a mechanism for process improvement and defect prevention.

TYPES OF PEER REVIEWS

There are different types of peer reviews called by many different names in the software industry. Peer reviews go by names such as *team reviews, technical reviews, walk-throughs, inspections, pair reviews, pass-arounds, ad hoc reviews, desk checks,* and others. However, the author has found that most of these can be classified into one of three major peer review types:

- Desk checks

- Walk-throughs

- Inspections

Figure 23.3 illustrates that while inspections are always very formal peer reviews, the level of formality in desk checks and walk-throughs varies greatly depending on the needs of the project, the timing of the reviews, and the participants involved.

The type of peer review that should be chosen depends on several factors. First, inspections are focused purely on defect detection. If one of the goals of the peer review is to provide engineering analysis and improvement suggestions (for example, reducing unnecessary complexity, suggesting alternative approaches, identifying poor methods or areas that can be made more robust), a desk check or walk-through should be used. The maturity of the work product being reviewed should also be considered when selecting the peer review type. Desk checks or walk-throughs can be performed very early in the life of the work product being reviewed. For example, as soon as the code has a clean compile or a document has been spell-checked. In fact, whiteboard walk-throughs can be used just to bounce around very early concepts before there even is a work product. However, inspections are performed once the author thinks the work product is done and ready to transition into the next phase or activity in development. Staff availability and location can also be a factor. If the peer review team is geographically dispersed,

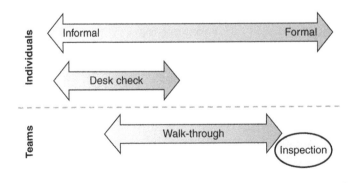

Figure 23.3 Types of peer reviews.

it can be much easier to perform desk checks than walk-throughs or inspections. Economic factors such as cost, schedule, and effort should also be considered. Team reviews tend to cost more and take longer than individuals reviewing separately. More-formal peer reviews also tend to cost more and take longer. However, the trade-off is the effectiveness of the reviews. Team peer reviews take advantage of team synergy to find more defects, and more-formal reviews also typically are more thorough and therefore more effective at identifying defects. The final factor to consider when choosing which type of peer review to hold is risk.

RISK-BASED PEER REVIEWS

Risk-based peer reviews are simply a type of risk-based V&V activity. Risk analysis should be performed on each work product that is being considered for peer review to determine the probability that yet-undiscovered, important defects exist in the software item and the potential impact of those defects if they escape the peer review. If there is both a low probability and a low impact, then an informal desk check may be appropriate, as illustrated in Figure 23.4. As the probability and impact increase, the type of appropriate peer review moves to more-formal desk check to informal walk-through to more-formal walk-through to formal inspection. For a very high-risk work product, having multiple peer reviews may be appropriate. For example, a product may be desk checked or have a walk-through early in development, and then be inspected late in its development just before it is released.

The number of people performing the peer review may also be varied based on risk. For very low-risk work products, having a single individual perform a desk check may be appropriate. For slightly higher-risk work products, it may be appropriate to have multiple people perform the desk check. For products worthy of an investment in an inspection, less risky work products may be assigned a smaller inspection team of two to four people and higher-risk products may be assigned an inspection team of five to seven people.

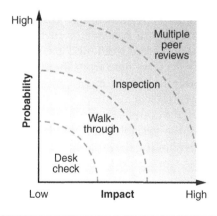

Figure 23.4   Risk-based selection of peer review types.

Risk-based peer reviews also embrace the law of diminishing returns. When a software work product is first peer reviewed, many of the defects that exist in the product are discovered with little effort. As additional peer reviews are held, the probability of discovering any additional defects decreases. At some point, the return-on-investment to discover those last few defects is outweighed by the cost of additional peer reviews.

DESK CHECKS

A *desk check* is the process where one or more peers of a work product's author review that work product individually. Desk checks can be done to detect defects in the work product and/or to provide engineering analysis. The formality used during the desk check process can vary. Desk checks can be the most informal of the peer review processes, or more-formal peer review techniques can be applied. A desk check can be a complete peer review process in and of itself or it can be used as part of the preparation step for a walk-through or inspection. The effectiveness of the desk check process is highly dependent on the skills of the individual reviewers and the amount of care and effort they invest in the review.

An informal desk check starts with the author of the work product requesting that one or more other individuals review the work product. These reviewers then evaluate the work product independently and feed back their comments to the author either verbally or by providing a copy of the work product that has been annotated (redlined) with their comments. This is typically done on the first draft of a document or after a clean compile of the code.

Desk checks can also be done in a more formal manner. For example, when a desk check is done as part of a review and approval cycle, a defined process may be followed with specific assigned roles (for example, software quality engineer or development manager) and formally recorded defects. These more-formal desk checks may result in specific quality records being kept, including formal peer review defect logs and/or formal written reports.

During a desk check, the reviewer shouldn't try to find everything in a single pass through the work product. This defuses the reviewer's focus, and fewer important defects and issues will be identified. Instead, the reviewer should make a quick first pass through the work product to get a general overview and understanding. This provides a context for further, more detailed review. The reviewer can then make a second detailed pass looking for issues in general. The reviewer can then select one item from the checklist or one area of focus and make a third pass through the document concentrating on reviewing just that one item. The reviewer can select another checklist item or focus area and make a fourth pass, and so on. For example, in a code review the review could concentrate on making sure that all the variables are initialized before they are used during one pass and focus on evaluating the error-handling in another pass. Making multiple passes through the work product is not considered rework (repeating work that is already done) because each pass looks at the work product from a different area of focus or emphasis.

One of the desk check techniques that the reviewers can use on their second, general pass through a work product is *mental execution*. Using the mental execution technique, the reviewer follows the flow of each path or thread through the work product instead of following the line-by-line order in which it is written. For example, in a design review the reviewer might follow each logical control flow through the design. In the review of a set of installation instructions, the reviewer might follow the flow of installation steps. A code review example might be to select a set of input data and follow the data flow through the source code.

In the *test case review technique*, the reviewer writes a set of test cases and uses those test cases to review the work product. This technique is closely associated with the mental execution technique since the reviewer usually doesn't have executable software so they have to mentally execute their test cases. The very act of trying to write test cases can help identify ambiguities in the work product and issues with the product's testability. By shifting from a "how does the product work" mentality to the "how can I break it" mentality of a tester, the reviewer may also identify areas that are "missing" from the work product (for example, requirements that have not been addressed, process alternatives or exceptions that are not implemented, missing error-handling code, or areas in the code where resources are not released properly). The test case review technique can be used for many different types of work products. For example, the reviewer can write test cases to a requirements specification, a high-level or low-level design element, source code, installation instruction, the user manual, and even to test cases themselves.

One of the real advantages of having a second set of eyes look at a work product is that they can see things that the author didn't consider. However, it is much harder to review what is missing from the work product than to review what is in the work product. One of the advantages of checklists is that they remind the reviewer to look for things that might not be there. Another technique is for the reviewer to brainstorm a list of things that might be missing based on the type of work product being reviewed.

For example, for a requirements document this list might include items such as:

- Missing requirements

- Assumptions that aren't documented

- Users or other stakeholders that aren't being considered

- Failure modes or error conditions that aren't being handled

- Special circumstances, alternatives, or exceptions that exist that aren't being considered

The goal of any peer review is to find as many important defects as possible within the time and resource constraints that exist. It is typically easier to find many small, insignificant defects such as typos and grammar problems than it is to find the major problems in the work product. In fact, if the reviewer starts finding many little defects, it is easy to get distracted by them. The reviewer should focus on finding important defects. If they notice minor defects or typos they should document them but then return their focus to looking for the "big stuff." If the reviewers just can't resist, they should make one pass though the document just to look for the small stuff and be done with it. This is why many organizations insist that all work products be spell-checked and/or run through code tools (for example, compilers) to ensure they are clean as possible so reviewers can avoid wasting time finding defects that could be more efficiently found with a tool.

It is the computer age, and reviewers can take advantage of the tools that computers provide them. One of these tools that can be used in a desk check is the search function. If the reviewer can get an electronic copy of the work product, they can search for keywords. For example, words such as "all," "usually," "sometimes," or "every" in a requirements document that may be indicators of areas that need further investigation. After a defect is identified, the search function can also be used to help identify other occurrences of that same defect. For example, when this book was being written, one of the reviewers pointed out that the term "recorder" was being used in some places and the term "scribe" in others to refer to the same inspection role. Since this might add a level of confusion, the search function was used to find all occurrences of the word "scribe" and changed them to "recorder." The moral here is, don't search manually for things that the computer can find much more quickly and accurately.

During desk checking, the work product should be compared against its predecessor for completeness and consistency. A work product's predecessor is the previous work product used as the basis for the creation of the work product being peer reviewed. Table 23.1 shows examples of work products and their predecessors.

Table 23.1 Work product predecessor—examples.

Work product being peer reviewed	Predecessor examples
Software requirements specification	System requirements specification, business requirements document, or marketing specification
Architectural (high-level) design	Software requirements specification
Detailed (low-level) design	Architectural (high-level) design
New source code	Detailed (low-level) design
Modified source code	Defect report, enhancement request, or modified detailed (low-level) design
Unit test cases	Source code or detailed (low-level) design
System test cases	Software requirements specification
Software quality assurance (SQA) plan	Software quality assurance (SQA) standard processes, or required SQA plan template
Work instructions	Standard process documentation
Response to request for proposal	Request for proposal

WALK-THROUGHS

A *walk-through* is the process where one or more peers of a work product's author meet with that author to review that work product as a team. A walk-through can be done to detect defects in the work product and/or to provide engineering analysis. Preparation before the walk-through meeting is less emphasized than it is in inspections. The effectiveness of the walk-through process is not only dependent on the skills of the individual reviewers and the amount of care and effort they invest in the review but on the synergy of the review team.

The formality used during the walk-through process can vary. An example of a very informal walk-through might be an author holding an impromptu "whiteboard" walk-through of an algorithm or other design element. In an informal walk-through there may be little or no preparation.

As illustrated in Figure 23.5, more-formal peer review techniques can also be applied to walk-throughs. In a more formal walk-through, preparation is done prior to the team meeting, typically through the use of desk checking. Preparation is usually left to the discretion of the individual reviewer and may range from little or no preparation to an in-depth study of the work product under review. During the walk-through meeting, the author presents the work product one section at a time and explains each section to the reviewers. The reviewers ask questions, make suggestions (engineering analysis), or report defects found. The recorder keeps a record of the discussion and any suggestions or defects identified. After the walk-through meeting, the recorder produces the minutes from the meeting and the author makes any required changes to the work product to incorporate suggestions and to correct defects.

While walk-throughs and inspections are both team-oriented peer review processes, there are significant differences between the two, as illustrated in

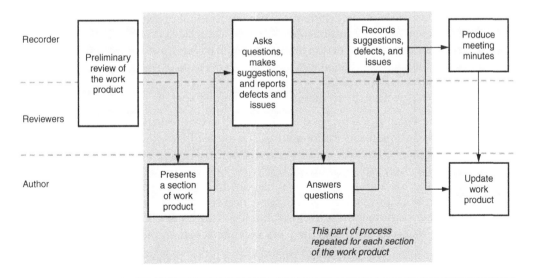

Figure 23.5   Formal walk-through process.

Walk-throughs		Inspections
• May be formal or informal	⟺	• Always formal
• Early in the work product's development	⟺	• When work product is ready to transition to next activity
• Engineering analysis and defect detection	⟺	• Exclusively focused on defect detection
• Author typically presents work product to team	⟺	• Separate reader role presents work product
• Preparation less emphasized	⟺	• Preparation very formal including kickoff meeting
• Metrics less emphasized	⟺	• Metrics use formalized
• Rework reponsibility of author (may be follow-up)	⟺	• Formal rework and follow-up process

Figure 23.6   Walk-throughs versus inspection.

Figure 23.6. However, many of the tools and techniques that will be discussed in the inspection section below can also be applied to walk-throughs depending on the amount of formality selected for the walk-through.

INSPECTIONS—THE PROCESS AND ROLES

An *inspection* is a very formal method of peer review where a team of peers, including the author, performs detailed preparation and then meets to examine a work product. The work product is typically inspected when the author thinks it is complete and ready for transition to the next phase or activity. The focus of an inspection is only on defect identification. Individual preparation using checklists and assigned roles is emphasized. Metrics are collected and used to determine entry criteria in the inspection meeting as well as for input into product or process improvement efforts. The inspection process consists of several distinct activities, as illustrated in Figure 23.7.

In an inspection, team members are assigned specific roles:

- The *author* is the original creator of the work product or the individual responsible for its maintenance. The author is responsible for initiating the inspection and working closely with the moderator throughout the inspection process. During the inspection meeting, the author acts as an inspector with the additional responsibility of answering questions about the work product. After the inspection meeting the author works with other team members to close all open issues. The author is responsible for all required rework to the work product based on the inspection findings.

- The *moderator,* also called the *inspection leader,* is the coordinator and leader of the inspection and is considered the "owner" of the process during the inspection. The moderator must possess strong facilitation,

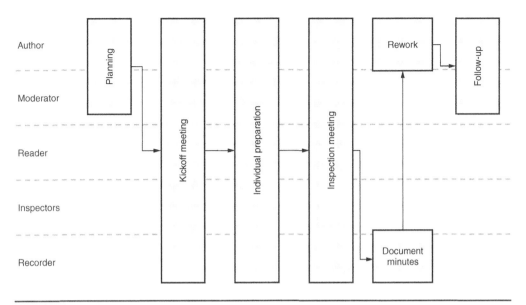

Figure 23.7   Inspection process.

coordination, and meeting management skills. The moderator should receive training on how to perform their duties and on the details of the inspection process. The moderator has the ultimate responsibility for ensuring that inspection metrics are collected and recorded in the inspection metrics database.

- During the inspection meeting, the *reader,* also called the *presenter,* describes one part or section of the work product at a time to the other inspection team members and then opens that section up for discussion. This item-by-item paraphrasing allows the added benefit of the author being able to hear how someone else interprets his or her work. Many times this interpretation leads to the author identifying additional defects during the meeting when the interpretation differs from the intended meaning. The reader's "interpretation often reveals ambiguities, hidden assumptions, inadequate documentation, style problems that hamper communications or outright errors" (Wiegers 2002). The reader must have the appropriate mixture of good presentation skills, product technical familiarity, and strong organizational skills. In Gilb-type inspections the reader is an optional role and the author presents the work product instead. In Fagan-type inspections the reader is a required role.

- The *recorder,* also called the *scribe,* is responsible for acting as the team's official record keeper. This includes recording the preparation and meeting metrics and all defects and open issues identified during the inspection meeting. Since the recorder is also acting as an inspector at the meeting, this person must be able to "multiplex" their time and should have solid writing skills.

- All of the members of the inspection team, including the author, moderator, and recorder are inspectors. The primary responsibility of the *inspectors* is to identify defects in the work product being inspected. During the preparation phase, the inspectors use desk check techniques to review the work product. They identify and note defects, questions, and other comments. During the inspection meeting, the inspectors work as a synergistic team. They actively listen to the reader paraphrasing each part of the work product to determine if their personal interpretation differs from the reader's. They ask questions, discuss issues, and report defects. Inspectors should continue to search for additional defects that were not logged prior to the meeting but that are discovered through the synergy of the team interaction. The observer role is optional in an inspection. The observer does not take an active role in the inspection but acts as a passive observer of the inspection activities. This may be done to learn about the work product or about the inspection process. It may also be done as part of an audit or other evaluation.

INSPECTIONS—PLANNING STEP

When the author completes a work product and determines that it is ready for inspection, the author initiates the inspection process by identifying a moderator for the inspection. There is typically a group of trained moderators available to each project from which the author can choose. The moderator works with the author to plan the inspection. The detailed process for the planning step is illustrated in Figure 23.8.

During the planning step, the moderator verifies that the inspection entry criteria are met before the inspection is officially started, and verifies that the work product is ready to be inspected. This may include doing a desk check of a sample of the work product to ensure that it is of appropriate quality to continue. Any fundamental deficiencies should be removed from the work product before the inspection process begins.

Inspection meetings should be limited to no more than two hours in length. If the work product is too large to be inspected in a two-hour meeting, the author and moderator partition the product into two or more subproducts and schedule separate inspections for each partition. The same inspection team should be used for each of these meetings, and a single kickoff meeting may be appropriate.

The moderator and author select the appropriate individuals to participate in the inspection and assign roles. As a general rule the inspection teams should be kept as small as possible and still meet the inspection objectives, including having the diversity needed to find different types of defects. A typical rule of thumb is no more than seven inspectors per meeting.

The author and moderator determine whether or not a kickoff meeting is necessary. A kickoff meeting should be held if the inspectors need information about the important features, assumptions, background, and/or context of the work product to effectively prepare for the inspection or if they need training on the inspection process. An alternative to holding a kickoff meeting is to include a summary of product overview information as part of the inspection package.

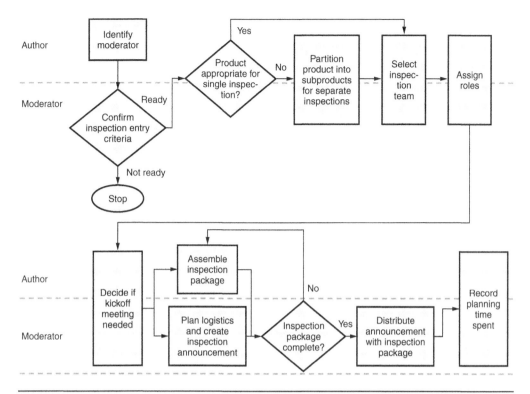

Figure 23.8 Inspection planning step process.

Decisions about when and where to hold the kickoff and inspection meetings should take the availability and location of the participants into consideration. The moderator should also make reservations for meeting rooms. The time and date of the inspection should be arranged such that each inspector has a minimum of two to three full working days to review the product in preparation for the inspection meeting. No more than two inspection meetings should be scheduled per day for the same inspectors, with a long break between those two meetings. Arranging the meeting logistics also means handling any special logistical arrangements, for example, if an overhead or LCD projector is needed for displaying sections of the work product or if the recorder needs access to a computer to record the meeting information directly into an inspection database.

The primary deliverable from inspection planning is the *inspection package,* which includes all of the materials needed by the inspection team members to adequately prepare for the inspection, including:

- The work product being inspected

- Inspection forms (for recording defects, questions, and issues)

- Copies of or pointers to related work products, for example:

  - Predecessor work product(s)

    – Related standard(s)

    – Work product checklist(s)

    – Traceability matrix

The inspection announcement should be delivered with the inspection package to all inspection team members far enough in advance of the meeting to allow for adequate preparation (typically a minimum of one day before the kickoff meeting and two to three days before the inspection meeting).

INSPECTIONS—KICKOFF MEETING STEP

The primary objective of the kickoff meeting, also called the *overview meeting*, is education. Some members of the inspection team may not be familiar with the work product being inspected or how it fits into the overall software product or customer requirements. The author gives a brief overview of the work product being inspected and answers any questions from the other team members. The product briefing section of the kickoff meeting is used to bring the team members up to speed on the scope, purpose, important functions, context, assumptions, and background of the work product being inspected.

The inspection process briefing section of the kickoff meeting is used to ensure that all of the inspection team members have the same understanding of the inspection process, roles, and assignments. If there are members of the inspection team that are not familiar with the inspection process, the kickoff meeting can also be used to provide remedial inspection process training to ensure that all the team members understand what's expected from them.

In addition to a general evaluation of the work product from their own perspective, it may be valuable to ask inspectors to focus on a special area or characteristic of the work product. For example, if security is an important aspect of the work product, an inspector could be assigned to specifically investigate that characteristic of the product. Assigning special focus areas has the benefit of ensuring that someone is covering that area while at the same time removing potential redundancy from the preparation process. The author is typically the best person to identify whether special areas of focus are appropriate for the work product under inspection. These areas of focus are typically assigned during the kickoff meeting.

INSPECTIONS—PREPARATION STEP

The real work of finding defects and issues in the work product begins with the preparation step. Utilizing the information supplied in the inspection package, each inspector evaluates the work product independently with the intent of identifying and documenting as many defects, issues, and questions as possible. Checklists are used during preparation to ensure that important items are investigated. However, inspectors should look outside the checklists for other defects as well. If the inspector was assigned a specific area of focus, they should evaluate the work product from that point of view in addition to doing their general inspection preparation. The author should be contacted if the questions an inspector has are severe enough to impact the inspector's ability to prepare for the inspection. Otherwise, questions should be documented and brought to the inspection meeting.

Preparation is also essential for the reader, who must plan and lay out the schedule for conducting the meeting, including how the work product will be separated into individual, small sections for presentation and discussion. The reader must determine how to paraphrase each section of the work product, make notes to facilitate that paraphrasing during the meeting, and then practice their paraphrasing so that it can be accomplished smoothly and quickly during the inspection meeting.

INSPECTIONS—INSPECTION MEETING STEP

The goal of the inspection meeting is to find and classify as many important defects as possible in the time allotted. As illustrated in Figure 23.9, the inspection meeting starts with the moderator requesting the preparation time, counts of defects by severity, and counts of questions/issues from each inspector. The moderator uses this information to determine whether or not all of the members of the inspection team are ready to proceed. If one or more team members are unprepared for the meeting, the moderator should reschedule the meeting for a later time or date and the inspection process returns to the preparation phase.

The moderator also uses this information to determine how to proceed with the inspection meeting. If there are a large number of major defects, questions, and issues to cover, the moderator may decide that only major items will be brought up in the first round of discussion. If there is time, a second pass through the work product can be made to discuss minor issues. Remember, the goal is to find as many important defects as possible in the time allotted. If there are that many major issues, the work product will probably require reinspection anyway. The recorder records the preparation time spent by each inspector, their defect counts by severity, and their issue/question counts.

After the moderator has reviewed any pertinent meeting procedures, the meeting is turned over to the reader. The moderator then assumes the role of an inspector but with an eye toward moderating the meeting from the perspective of ensuring that the inspection process is followed and that the inspection stays focused on the work product and not on the people. The reader begins with a call for global issues with the work product. Any issues discovered in the predecessor work products, standards, or checklists could also be reported at this time. The recorder should record these issues in the meeting minutes. After the meeting, the author should inform the appropriate responsible individuals of these defects. However, these defects are not recorded in the inspection log nor are they counted in the inspection defect count metrics.

The reader then paraphrases one small part of the work product at a time and calls for specific issues for that part of the product. The inspectors then ask questions and report issues and potential defects, and the author answers questions about the work product. Team discussion on each question, issue, or potential defect should be limited to answering the questions, discussing the issue, and identifying actual defects. Discussion of possible solutions should be deferred

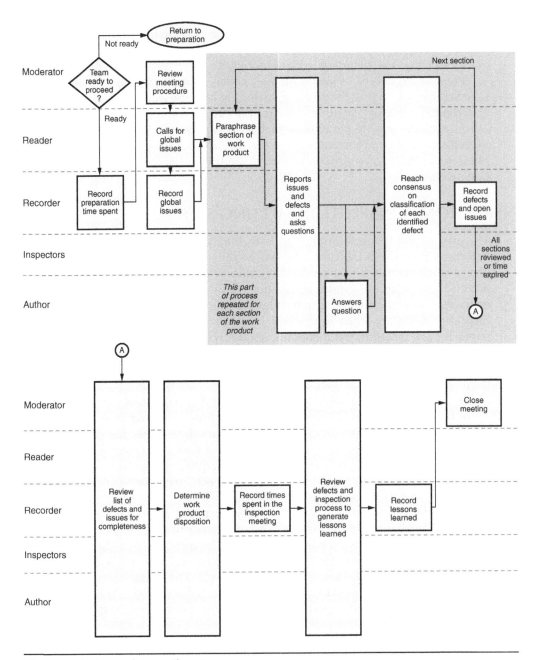

Figure 23.9   Inspection meeting step process.

until after the inspection meeting. The intent of the discussion is for the team to come to a consensus on the classification of each question, issue, or potential defect. A question, issue, or potential defect may be determined to be a nonissue or become a defect. If consensus can not be reached on the disposition of a question, issue, or potential defect within a reasonable period of time (less than two minutes), it is classified as an open issue and its resolution is assigned to the author. One or more other inspection team members can also be assigned to the open issue. The recorder documents all identified defects with their severities and types and open issues with their assignees.

After the last section of the work product has been discussed, the moderator resumes control of the meeting. If the meeting time has expired but all of the sections of the work product have not been covered, the inspection team should schedule a second inspection meeting to complete the inspection. If a second continuation meeting is needed, the moderator coordinates the logistics of that meeting. The recorder then reviews all of the defects and open issues. This is a verification step to ensure that everything has been recorded, that the description of each item is adequately documented, and that open issues are appropriately assigned.

The team then comes to consensus on the disposition of the work product. The work product dispositions include:

- *Pass.* If no major defects were identified, this disposition allows the author to make minor changes to correct typos without any required follow-up.

- *Fail—author rework.* The author performs the rework as necessary and that rework is verified by the moderator. (Note: based on the technical knowledge of the moderator, another member of the inspection team may be assigned to verify the rework.)

- *Fail—reinspect.* There were enough important defects or open issues that the work product should be reinspected after the rework is complete

- *Fail—reject.* The document has so many important defects or open issues that it is a candidate for reengineering

The defect-logging portion of the meeting is now complete. The recorder notes the end time of the inspection meeting and the total effort spent. As a final step in the inspection meeting process, the team spends the last few minutes of the meeting discussing suggestions for improving the inspection process. This step can provide useful information that can help continuously improve the inspection process. Examples of lessons learned might include:

- Improvement to inspection forms

- Improvement to the contents of the inspection package

- Items that should be added to the checklist or standards

- Defect types that need to be added or changed

- Effective techniques used during inspection that should be propagated to other inspections

- Ineffective techniques that need to be avoided in future inspections

- Systemic defect types found across multiple inspections that should be investigated

INSPECTIONS—POST-MEETING STEPS

After the meeting, the recorder documents and distributes the inspection meeting minutes. The payback for all the time spent in the other inspection activities comes during the rework phase when the quality of the work product is improved through the correction of all of the identified defects. The author is responsible for resolving all defects and documenting the corrective actions taken. The author also has the primary responsibility for ensuring that all open issues are handled during rework. The author works with any other team member(s) assigned to each open issue, either closing the open issue as resolved if it is determined that no defect exists or translating the open issue into one or more defect(s) and resolving those defects.

The purpose of the follow-up step is to verify defect resolution and to ensure that other defects were not introduced during the correction process. Follow-up also acts as a final check to ensure that all open issues have been appropriately resolved. Depending on the work product dispositions decided by the peer review team, the moderator may perform the follow-up step or a reinspection may be required.

SOFT SKILLS FOR PEER REVIEWS AND INSPECTIONS

One of the challenges the author faces during a peer review is to remain "egoless" during the process (especially in the meetings) and not become defensive or argumentative. An egoless approach enables an author to step back and accept improvement suggestions and acknowledge identified defects without viewing them as personal attacks on their professional abilities or their value as an individual. One way of doing this is for the author to think of the work product as transitioning from their personal responsibility to becoming the team's product when it is submitted for inspection. The other peer reviewers should also take an egoless approach and not try to prove how intelligent they are by putting down the work of the author, the comments of other reviewers, or the work product. During a peer review, everyone should treat the work product, the other review members, and especially the author with respect.

Focus throughout the peer review process should be on the product, not on people. One way of doing this is to use "I" and "it" messages—avoid the word "you" during discussions. For example, a reviewer might say, "I didn't understand this logic" or "the logic in this section of the document has a defect" rather than saying "you made a mistake in this logic." Another method is to word comments as neutral facts, positive critiques, or questions—not criticisms.

During the peer review meetings, team members should not interrupt each other. They should listen actively to what other team members say and build on the inputs from other reviewers to find more defects.

Don't force the author to acknowledge every defect. This can really beat the author down. Remember, the work product is the author's baby. The author has probably worked long and hard producing that work product. During a peer review, pointing out every defect is like telling the author that their baby is ugly. Making them acknowledge each defect is like making them admit in public that their baby is ugly. Assume that the author's silence indicates their agreement that the defect exists.

TECHNICAL REVIEWS

IEEE 1028 (2008a) states that the "purpose of a technical review is to evaluate a software product by a team of qualified personnel to determine its suitability for its intended use and identify discrepancies from specifications and standards." One of the primary differences between technical reviews and peer reviews is that managers and other individuals, including customers and users, are active participants in technical reviews. IEEE 1028 (2008a) defines the following major steps in the technical review process:

- *Planning.* The review leader plans the review, including identifying the members of the review team, assigning roles and responsibilities, handling scheduling and logistics for the review meeting, distributing the review package, and setting the review schedule.

- *Preparation.* Each review member reviews the work product and other inputs from the review package before the review meeting. These reviewers forward their comments and identified problems to the review leader, who classifies them and forwards them on to the author. The review leader also verifies that the reviewers are prepared for the meeting.

- *Examination.* One or more meetings are held to evaluate the software product and identify problems.

- *Rework/follow-up.* After the meeting, the review leader confirms that all of the action items assigned during the meeting are appropriately resolved.

Chapter 24

D. Test Execution Documentation

There are a variety of different kinds of test documents, as illustrated in Figure
24.1. Test planning documents include the verification and validation (V&V) plans,
test plans, and test design specifications. Test execution input documents include
test cases and test procedures. Planned test cases and procedures are defined and
written during test design activities. Additional test cases and test procedures
may also be defined and written during exploratory testing done at test execution

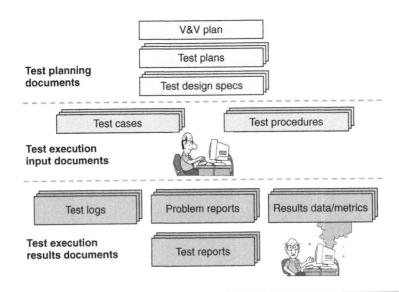

Figure 24.1 Types of testing documentation.

time. Test cases and procedures are utilized to run the tests during test execution activities. The results of test execution activities are documented in test logs, problem reports, test reports, and test data and metrics. The IEEE *Standard for Software and System Test Documentation* (IEEE 2008b) describes a set of basic software test documents. This standard recommends beneficial form and content for each of the individual test documents, not the required set of test documents.

Test results documentation is done throughout the test execution process to capture the results of the testing activities. This documentation is produced to capture the test execution process so that people can understand and benefit from what has occurred.

Test execution and results documentation is necessary because it records the testing process and helps software testers know what needs to be accomplished, where they are, what they have and have not tested, and how testing was done. This test documentation also helps maintainers and other engineers understand the testing performed by others and supports the repeatability of tests during debugging and regression testing. All test documentation should be an outgrowth of the normal testing process, not an end in itself. Experience is required to strike a proper balance between too much and too little test documentation.

TEST EXECUTION

Test execution is the process of actually executing the predefined tests or performing exploratory testing, and observing, analyzing, and recording the results. Test execution activities include setting up and validating the testing environment and using that environment to execute software tests. Testers execute the tests by running predefined test cases or procedures, or by performing exploratory testing. The testers document these test execution activities in the test log. If they are performing exploratory testing, the testers also document the tests as they are executing them. The testers analyze the actual test results by comparing them to the expected results. The objective of this analysis is to identify failures. The testers also look around to identify any other adverse side effects. For example, the expected results typically only describe what should happen rather than what should not happen. The test might say enter *xyz* information and the expected result is the display of a certain screen. It will not say, "The printer should not start spewing paper on the floor," but if the printer does start spewing paper, the tester should notice and report the anomaly.

If failures or other anomalous results are identified, the testers capture information they believe will help the developers identify the underlying defects (for example, screen captures, data values, database snap, memory dump shots). The testers will also attempt to repeat the failures or other anomalous results. The testers report the identified failures or other anomalies in problem reports if the test items are baselined items or directly to the item's author if the items are not baselined. For baselined items, the testers may need to participate in change control to "champion" their problem reports or provide additional information as needed. Testers may also need to work with developers as necessary to isolate defects if the developers can not reproduce the failures or other anomalous results. For example, developers may not be able to reproduce the problem because they do not have the same tools, hardware, simulators, databases, or other resources/configurations in the development environment as the testers are using in the test beds.

During the test execution process, testers report their ongoing status, which includes activities completed, effort expended, and test cases executed, passed, failed, and blocked. As developers provide updated software, the testers also test corrected defects and changes, perform regression analysis, and execute regression testing based on that analysis. Testing status reports, data, and metrics are used to track and control the ongoing test execution effort. Test metrics are also used to evaluate the completeness status of testing and the quality of the software products. Finally, at the end of each major testing cycle, the testers write a test report to summarize that cycle of testing.

TEST CASE

Test cases are the fundamental building blocks of testing and are the smallest test unit to be directly executed during testing. Test cases are typically used to test individual paths in a unit or individual functions or subfunctions of the software. Test cases define the items to be tested, how the test environment should be set up, what inputs to use, what the expected output is (including evaluation criteria), and the steps to execute the test. Each test case should have a unique identifier (number and/or name) so that it can be easily referenced. The IEEE *Standard for Software and System Test Documentation* (IEEE 2008b) also includes special procedural requirements and intercase dependencies as part of its test case specification outline.

Test cases can be defined in a document, in a spreadsheet, or using automated testing tools. The level of detail needed in a documented test case will vary based on the needs of the project and testing staff. For example, automated test cases may need less documentation than those run manually, unit level test cases may need less documentation than system test cases, test cases for a system used to search for library books may need less rigor than those for airplane navigation systems. Figure 24.2 illustrates two examples of test case documentation: one simple example for unit test cases and one more rigorously documented example for a system test case.

The input specification part of the test case defines the requirements for the inputs into the test case. To make the test case reusable for many different test scenarios, this specification should be as generic as possible. For example, instead of specifying a specific number such as 7 or 10, the input specification might read "input an integer between one and 10." The actual number chosen for each execution of the test case would be recorded as part of the test log information.

The expected output and evaluation criteria part of the test case defines the expected results from the execution of the software with the specified inputs. This includes specific outputs (for example, reports to the printer, flashing lights, error messages) and the criteria for evaluating those outputs (for example, for a report to the printer this might include the specific criteria for judging if the entire report was printed correctly and that all information on the report is correct).

The environmental needs (setup instructions) part of the test case defines any special test bed requirements for running the test case. For example, if it is a throughput-type requirement, there may be a need to attach a simulator that

Unit Test Case Example

Test case #	Inputs		Expected output
	Variable B	Variable C	Variable A
1	≥ 60	< 20	1000
2	≤ 40	≥ 20 and < 100	300
3	> 40 and < 60	≥ 100	300

System Test Case Example

Test case name	Save a file: test for invalid characters in file name	
Test equipment/ environment	PC with word processing software installed	
Test setup	Run the word processing software. Create a new document with a paragraph of text in it.	
Step number	Test execution steps and inputs	Expected result
1.	Left mouse-click on the Save File icon	Word processor displays the Save As window
2.	In the Filename field: enter a file name consisting of < 254 alphanumeric characters with one of the following characters somewhere in the file name: • Greater than sign (>) • Less than sign (<) • Quotation mark (") • Pipe symbol (I) • Colon (:) • Semicolon (;) Left-click the <Save> button	Error message: "The filename, location, or format is not valid. Type the filename and location in the correct format"
3.	Left-click the <OK> button on the error message Press <Escape> key to exit the Save function	Return to document screen

Figure 24.2 Test case–examples.

emulates multiple transaction inputs. Another example might be a requirement to run the test case while the temperature is over 140 degrees for reliability testing.

TEST PROCEDURE

Test procedures, also called *test scripts* or *test scenarios,* typically evaluate a sequence or set of features or functions by chaining together test cases to test a complete user scenario or thread within the software. For example, the "pay at the pump with a valid credit card" test procedure might chain together the following test cases:

- *Scan a readable card*—with a valid credit card as input

- *Validate a valid credit card with clearinghouse*—with valid credit card and merchant information as input

- *Select a valid gas grade*—with a regular gas grade as input

- *Pump gas*—with selected gallons of gas being pumped as input

- *Complete transaction with clearinghouse*—with cost of gas pumped amount as input

- *Prompt for receipt*—with selection of "yes" or "no" as input

- *Print receipt*—with information on this transaction as input (this test case would only be included if "yes" was selected in previous test case)

- *Complete transaction and store info*—with information on this transaction as input

Alternative procedures that would chain many of these same test cases together with other test cases might include test procedures such as "pay at the pump with a valid debit card," which would include the addition of an "accept valid PIN" test case after the first test case and use the "validate a valid debit card with clearing-house" test case in place of the second test case.

The documentation of a test procedure defines the purpose of the procedure, any special requirements, including environmental needs or tester skills, and the detailed instructional steps for setting up and executing the procedure. Each test procedure should have a unique identifier (number and/or name) so that it can be easily referenced. The IEEE *Standard for Software and System Test Documentation* (IEEE 2008b) says the procedural steps should include:

- Methods and formats for logging the test execution results.

- The setup actions.

- The steps necessary to start, execute, and stop the test procedure (basically the chaining together of the test cases and their inputs).

- Instructions for taking test measures.

- Actions needed to restore the test environment at the completion of the test procedure.

- If a test procedure might need to be suspended, that test procedure also includes steps for shutting down and restarting the procedure. Finally, the test procedure may also include contingency plans for dealing with risk associated with that procedure.

Test procedures, like test cases, can be defined in documents, in a spreadsheet, or using automated testing tools. Like test cases, the level of detail needed in a documented test procedure will also vary based on the needs of the project and testing staff.

TEST LOG

A *test log* is a chronological record that documents the execution of one or more test cases and/or test procedures in a testing session. The test log can be a very useful source of information for the programmer having trouble reproducing a reported problem or for the tester trying to replicate test results. For example, sometimes it is not the execution of the last test case or procedure that caused the failure but the sequence of multiple test cases or procedures. The log can be helpful in repeating those sequences exactly. It may also be important to understand the time of day or day of the week that the tests were executed or what other applications were running in the background at the time.

The test log should include generic information about the test execution session, including a description of the session, the specific configuration environment, the version and revision of the software being tested, and the tester(s) and observers (if any). The tester then logs the specifics about each test case or procedure executed, including the specific time and date, the specific input selected, any failures or other anomalies observed, and other observations or comments worthy of note. The log information can be logged into a document, a spreadsheet, directly into the test cases or procedures, or into a testing tool.

PROBLEM REPORT

A *problem report*, also called *anomaly report, defect report, failure report, trouble report,* or *change request,* documents a failure or other anomaly observed during the execution of the tests. The tester records information in the problem report about the identified failure or anomaly with enough detail so that the appropriate change control board can analyze its impact and make informed decisions, and so that the developers can investigate, replicate, and fix the problem, if necessary. Problem report descriptions should be specific enough to identify the defect. For example,

- *This:* Incomplete message packets input from the XYZ controller component do not time out after two seconds and report a communication error as stated in requirements R00124.

- *Not this:* The software hangs up.

Problem report descriptions should be neutral in nature and be stated in terms of observed facts, not opinions. Descriptions should treat the work product and its authors with respect. For example:

- *This:* When the user enters invalid data into one of the fields in form ABC, they receive the error message, "Error 397: Invalid Entry." This error message does not identify the specific field(s) that were incorrectly entered or provide enough guidance to the user to allow the identification and correction of mistakes.

- *Not this:* The error messages in this software are horrible.

Problem report descriptions should be written in a clear and easily understood manner. For example:

- *This:* Page 12, paragraph 2 of the user manual states "that the user should respond quickly . . ." This statement is ambiguous because the use of the term "quickly" does not indicate a specific, measurable response time.

- *Not this:* The use of vague terminology and nonspecific references in adverbial phrasing makes the interpretation of page 12, paragraph 2 of the user manual questionable at best and may lead to misinterpretations by the individuals responsible for translating its realization into actionable responses.

Each problem report should describe a single failure or anomaly and not combine multiple issues into a single report.

The contents and tracking of problem reports are further discussed in Chapter 28, "Configuration Control and Status Accounting." While problem reports can be documented on paper forms, most organizations use some kind of automated problem reporting or change request tool or database to document these reports and track them to resolution. A project's V&V plans should specify which problem reporting and tracking mechanisms are used by that project.

TEST RESULTS DATA AND METRICS

Test management and product and process quality metrics are fundamental to the tracking and controlling of the testing activities of the project as well as providing management with information to make better, informed decisions.

Test management metrics report the test activities' progress against the testing plan. Examples of test management metrics include test activity schedules planned versus actual, test effort planned versus actual, test costs budget versus actual, resource utilization planned versus actual, requirements (and test case) volatility, and testing staff turnover. These test management metrics reveal trends in current progress, indicate accuracy in test planning estimation, flag needed control actions, can be used to forecast future progress, and provide data to indicate the completeness of the testing effort.

Product quality metrics collected during testing can provide insight into the quality of the products being tested and the effectiveness of the testing activities, and provide data to indicate the completeness of the testing effort. Examples of product quality metrics include defect arrival rates, cumulative defects by status, and defect density.

Test process metrics can help evaluate the effectiveness and efficiency of the testing activities and identify opportunities for future process improvement. Examples of test process metrics include escapes, defect detection efficiency, cycle times, and productivity.

TEST REPORT

A *test report*, also called a *test summary report*, summarizes the results and conclusions from a cycle of testing or a designated set of testing activities. For example, there may be an integration test summary report for each subsystem, a system test summary report, an acceptance test summary report, or other reports as appropriate. Basically, at a minimum, every test plan should have an associated test report. A project's V&V plans should specify which test summary reports will be written for that project.

A test report includes a summary of the testing cycle or activities and their results, including any variances between what was planned and what was actually tested. The summary also includes an evaluation, by the testers, of the quality of the products that were tested and their readiness (and associated risks) to transition to the next stage of development or to be released into operations. The report also includes a detailed, comprehensive assessment of:

- The testing process against the criteria specified in the test plan, including a list of any units, components, features, and/or functions that were not adequately tested

- A list of identified problems:

  - If resolved—a description of their resolution

  - If unresolved—their associated risks, potential impacts, and work-arounds

- An evaluation of each item tested based on its pass/fail criteria and test results, including an assessment of its reliability (likelihood of future failure)

Finally, the test report includes a summary of test activities and information including testing budget actuals, effort and staffing actuals, number of test cases and procedures executed, and other information that would be beneficial to evaluating lessons learned and planning and estimating future testing efforts.

Chapter 25

E. Customer Deliverables

Assess the completeness of customer
deliverables, including packaged and hosted
or downloadable products, license keys and
user documentation, marketing and training
materials, etc. (Evaluate)

Body of Knowledge VI.E

Many different types of software work products may be delivered to the customers and/or end users. All of the deliverables should be verified and validated. Examples of these deliverables include:

- The *software* (executable and potentially the source code depending on contractual or other agreements)

- *Development documentation* (depending on contractual or other agreements, documents including the requirements, design, plans, reports, and metrics may be deliverable to the customers and/or users)

- *User/operator documentation* including:

  - Installation instructions

  - Operation/maintenance instructions or manuals

  - User manuals or help files

  - Release notes

- *Training and training materials*

- *Help desk support*

- *Marketing materials*

PEER REVIEWS

Peer reviews and technical reviews should be held to evaluate the completeness and quality of customer deliverables, including software, development documentation, user/operator documentation, training materials, and marketing materials.

DEVELOPMENT TESTING

Software products, including source code and executables, are tested by the development organization during various levels of testing including unit, integration, and system testing. During system testing, user/operator documentation and training materials are also typically tested to ensure that the documentation reflects the actual performance of the system. The installation of the system and its installation instructions should also be tested to ensure that the system is easy and efficient to install.

DEVELOPMENT AUDITS

In-process product audits can be used throughout the software development process to evaluate the completeness of software work products and their adherence to requirements and workmanship standards. Functional configuration audits can be conducted to verify that the development of a configuration item has been completed satisfactorily, that the item has achieved the performance and functional characteristics specified, and that its operational and support documents are complete and satisfactory. Physical configuration audits can be conducted to verify that the configuration item, as built, conforms to the technical documentation that defines it.

PILOTS

A pilot is an experimental execution of a product or service to a selected audience to provide assurance that the product or service has the potential to succeed when released. Customer deliverables such as training courses can be piloted to ensure the completeness and accuracy of the course content, presentation materials, and student notebooks. For example, members of the development, testing, or help desk teams might be selected to attend a pilot training class. Members of the actual user community might also attend the pilot with their full knowledge that it is a pilot run and that constructive feedback is requested. Other examples where pilots can also be useful are to verify the readiness of help desk services and Web sites for rollout to support the customers/users.

The readiness of help desk support can also be piloted. For example, near the end of testing, the testers have gained knowledge of the working software to the point where they should be able to identify areas where the end users may have difficulties. This knowledge could be used to create a sample set of possible user issues or questions. The testers could then pilot the help desk support by calling in and using these questions to determine the accuracy and completeness of the assistance they receive.

ORDERING, MANUFACTURING, SHIPPING

V&V activities for customer deliverables should include the process steps that lead up to the delivery of those software work products and services. This includes the evaluations of:

- *Ordering.* Is the process for ordering the system in place and functional? If the software can be ordered through the Web, are the supporting Web pages in place and has the online ordering process been validated?

- *Manufacturing.* Is manufacturing prepared to support the orders that are anticipated, including software and documentation replication?

- *Shipping.* Are there issues with shipping of the software product, such as geographical limitations or prerequisites? If the software will be delivered through the Web, are the Web pages in place and has the download process been validated?

One technique that can be useful for verifying these processes is to deliver a complete shipment package in-house first (preferably to someone who has the same level of knowledge about the system that the typical customer/user will have). This technique basically pilots these processes. This can help verify that the manufacturing (replication) process was successful, that all the needed parts (for example, software and documentation) were in the delivered package, and that the installation process can be successfully executed.

Checklists can be used during the ordering processes to ensure that all of the necessary items for a complete, working product have been considered during ordering. Checklists can also be used to validate that all ordered items have been packaged for shipment.

The manufacturing process for software is mostly a replication process. One mechanism for validating the replication process is to sample replicated product to ensure their completeness and quality. For example, copies of documentation could be sampled periodically as they are being printed, and reviewed to ensure their completeness and quality. Sample copies of replicated CDs or magnetic tapes could also be selected periodically. These samples could then be installed on test beds and smoke tests run to ensure their installability and quality. This can ensure that the copies can be read from devices other than those they were created on, for example, to catch issues with replication devices being out of calibration. Of course the calibration of replication devices should be checked regularly anyway.

Other mechanisms exist for verifying the replication of the software product. For example, most applications that perform electronic copying include verification steps that read back the information written to the media and perform a comparison to the written information. *Checksums,* also called *hash sums,* and *cyclic redundancy checks* (CRC) can be used to detect accidental errors that occur during transmittal (for downloadable packages) or replication. In the checksum or CRC process an algorithm is used to create a calculated value for the software package. After transmittal or replication, the value is recalculated for the transmitted or replicated copy. If the original and recalculated values do not match, accidental alteration of the data has occurred.

License keys, also called *product keys* or *CD keys,* are added during the manufacturing process to specifically identify the replicated software as an original, manufactured copy (and not an aftermarket, unauthorized copy). Typical license keys are a series of numbers and/or letters that are entered by the user during the software installation process. Some licensing keys are activated off-line through verification by the software itself. Other software packages require online activation and validation of their licensing keys.

INSTALLATION TESTING

Depending on the software (size, complexity, and criticality) and the needs of the customers and/or users, it may be advisable (or even required) for the supplier of the software to send testers to the operational site(s) to test to assure that the transported and installed software (or reassembled system) functions correctly. In other cases where the customers or end users perform the installation themselves, they may perform their own version of installation testing after the installation has occurred.

Using the original system or acceptance tests, or new tests specifically designed to evaluate the installation, installation testing is done by selecting a representative set of tests that will adequately verify that the installation of the software (or reassembly of the system) has not degraded its functionality or performance. As appropriate, installation testing should ensure that all software diagnostics are performed and that results are acceptable. The software diagnostics are built-in tests that evaluate certain parts of the system (for example, electronic components and printed circuit cards) and return status to the tester.

In addition, installation testing can be used to verify the license keys if they are used for the replication copies. These keys are used to identify that the replicated copy of the software product used for the installation is a valid original copy.

CUSTOMER/USER TESTING

In addition to installation testing described above, other types of testing typically performed by the customer/user include:

- *Acceptance testing* is done to evaluate the completed software against predefined criteria to provide the user, customer, or other authorized entity the information they need to determine whether to allow the software to be released into operations.

- *Alpha testing* is typically done by the customers/users of the software or their representatives at the supplier's facility or on a customer/user test bed. Alpha testing may be done on an intermediate version of the software that does not include all of the final releasable functionality.

- *Beta testing,* also called *first office verification* or *field-testing,* is done by the users in the actual operational environment with a prerelease software product or the software that is expected to be released unless major show-stoppers are identified. Beta testing is typically done with a limited set of customers/users before full general availability of the software. No matter how well specified and built the simulators are that are used during previous types of testing, there is nothing like testing the software in the actual target operational environment.

- *Operational testing* is performed once the software has been installed and is being executed by the actual users/operators, using normal operating processes and documentation. The objectives are to ensure that the software is operating correctly under normal operating conditions and to evaluate the effectiveness of the training the users/operators received. Operational testing can also be performed periodically during the ongoing use of the software in operations to ensure that no problems have crept in over a period of time, for example, that performance has not degraded from original baselined values.

Part VII

Software Configuration Management

The ISO/IEC *Systems and Software Engineering—Vocabulary* (ISO/IEC 2009) defines *configuration management* as "a discipline applying technical and administrative direction and surveillance to: identify and document the functional and physical characteristics of a configuration item, control changes to those characteristics, record and report change processing and implementation status, and verify compliance with specified requirements."

Software configuration management (SCM) is the process of applying configuration management tools and techniques throughout the software product life cycle to ensure the completeness, correctness, and integrity of software configuration items. SCM helps a project ensure and maintain the consistency between the software's requirements and the resulting software design, code, documentation, and other work products and the project's plans. One way of thinking about SCM is to consider it the inventory control system for software.

Most software systems today are made up of many different components and are built using many different tools. The larger the projects, the more components there typically are and the more people there are involved in creating, using, and sharing access to all of the components. SCM provides the mechanisms needed to identify those components, coordinate their interrelationships, and successfully build and release a set of deliverables. As Berczuk (2003) puts it, "The way teams communicate their work products to each other is through their SCM and version control practices."

As illustrated in Figure VII.1, there are four core activities that make up SCM:

- *Software configuration identification.* The partitioning of the software product into formally identified configuration items, components, and units, documenting their functional and physical characteristics, defining their acquisition points, and assigning unique identifiers to those items, components, and units

- *Software configuration control.* The systematic process that ensures that changes to baselined configuration items are properly identified, documented, evaluated for impact, approved by an appropriate level of authority, incorporated, and verified

- *Software configuration status accounting.* The recording and reporting of information needed to manage a configuration effectively, including the implementation status of the configuration items, components, and units and the status of proposed changes to those items, components, or units

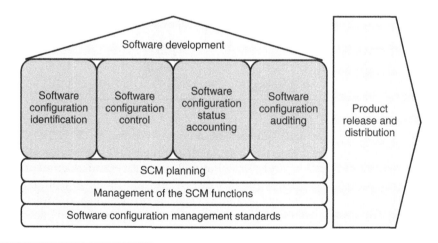

Figure VII.1 Software configuration management activities.

- *Software configuration auditing.* The independent evaluations to assess compliance with SCM processes and to assess the consistency of software configuration items with their documentation

In addition to these four major SCM activities, the Government Electronics and Information Technology Association (GEIA) *National Consensus Standard for Configuration Management* (EIA 2004) includes a fifth configuration management planning and management function. This SCM planning and management function includes:

- Establishing and documenting the SCM policies, standards, and processes for the organization

- Managing of the SCM functions, including establishing the SCM infrastructure, assigning SCM functional responsibilities, and providing SCM training

- Performing SCM planning for each project, including creating, documenting, and controlling SCM plans as appropriate for the needs of that project

- Monitoring the performance of SCM by suppliers

- Protecting the intellectual capital of the organization

- Establishing SCM metrics to monitor performance and provide input into SCM process improvement

All of these SCM activities create a strong foundation that supports the other software development activities so that they can be conducted in a stable, predictable, and efficient manner. This foundation also supports the ability to release and distribute high-quality, stable, and reproducible software products. Examples of risks (potential problems) associated with a lack of good SCM practices include:

- Inconsistencies between various software work products (for example, documentation that does not match the source code and/or executable)

- Missing source code or other software work products

- Unauthorized and unwanted changes to the software

- Inability to track when and why changes were made to the software and who made them

- Inability to integrate individual "working" software modules into "working" software products

- Uncertainty about what needs to be tested

- Working software that suddenly stops working, or fixed defects that reappear in subsequent builds

These risks can result in major negative consequences to software projects, including missed delivery deadlines, cost overruns, missing functionality or quality characteristic in deliverables, inefficient use of personnel and other resources, customer dissatisfaction, and even contract or regulatory violations.

Part VII

Chapter 26

A. Configuration Infrastructure

The *configuration infrastructure* provides the organizational structure, tools, and processes that create the discipline upon which a consistent and effective *software configuration management* (SCM) system can be built. The organizational structure requires project-level SCM groups and the specific assignment of SCM roles and responsibilities at the project level. It may also include the creation of an organizational-level SCM group with defined roles and responsibilities. The selection of the appropriate SCM tools and the establishment of SCM libraries, which support the established SCM system, greatly improve the ability to build, release, and distribute high-quality software products with the least amount of effort and allow organizations to retain and protect their intellectual capital.

1. CONFIGURATION MANAGEMENT TEAM

> Describe the roles and responsibilities
> of a configuration management group.
> (Understand)
>
> **Body of Knowledge VII.A.1**

Trained, qualified people are needed to perform the activities required to implement an effective SCM system both at an organizational level and at a project level. The number of people needed at each level depends on the size, complexity, and objectives of the organization and of the individual projects. In the case of large projects with hundreds of developers in geographically dispersed teams, with each team creating multiple software components, the project's SCM group might include several full-time specialists. For a small project, with a few colocated developers creating a limited increment of functionality, the SCM group may consist of one or more individuals performing the SCM activities as just one of their multiple project responsibilities.

Organizational-Level SCM Group Roles and Responsibilities

Many organizations establish an organizational-level SCM function to oversee the SCM system. This centralized SCM group may select industry standards and models as guidance for their SCM program to leverage good industry practices and keep from "reinventing the wheel." The organizational-level SCM group establishes, documents, and distributes standardized SCM policies, processes, and work instructions that can be shared across multiple projects.

The organizational-level SCM group defines, implements, and maintains an organizational-level SCM infrastructure, including:

- Standardized SCM tools

- Standardized SCM training

- Reuse libraries

- SCM databases and other historic SCM information

- Backup and disaster recovery mechanisms

Having a standardized SCM system and infrastructure benefits the organization by making it easier for individuals to move from project to project without a steep SCM learning curve. There may also be economy-of-scale benefits derived from having a few centralized experts that act as internal consultants to the projects rather than requiring expert individuals on each project. Centralizing certain SCM responsibilities provides mechanisms for transitioning lessons learned on individual projects into an integrated SCM system to improve practices across the organization. The organizational-level SCM group also performs SCM corrective actions and process improvement as needed.

Finally, an organizational-level SCM group provides a single conduit for management visibility and oversight of the organization's SCM system. For example, the organizational-level SCM group acts as the review and approval authority as projects tailor the standardized SCM processes. This ensures that key elements are not tailored out or modified inappropriately.

Project-Level SCM Group Roles and Responsibilities

A project-level SCM group is responsible for planning, implementing, and controlling the project-specific SCM activities. Organizations that establish an organizational-level SCM function also need people at the project level responsible for the project-specific SCM activities. This may be accomplished by having members of the organizational-level SCM group report on a dotted-line basis to the project or by having project-specific individuals assigned to SCM roles. For organizations that choose not to establish an organizational-level SCM function, the organizational-level responsibilities described above become additional activities that are delegated to the project-level SCM group members as appropriate.

Each project-level SCM group performs SCM planning for their project by defining how that project intends to implement and tailor the organizational-level SCM policies, standards, processes, work instructions, and infrastructure to the needs of their specific project. SCM planning defines the specific SCM roles,

Part VII.A.1

responsibilities, staffing, training, schedules, and budgets for performing the various project SCM activities. SCM planning determines how SCM will be managed for the project and the plans for communicating with SCM stakeholders. The identified configuration items and baselines the project will use to control their software products and product components are defined. The types, levels, and mechanisms of control required for each of those configuration items and baselines are also planned. The SCM planning includes selecting mechanisms for performing configuration status accounting and configuration audits. The SCM planning may also include plans for supplier work product control and for controlling external interfaces to the work products being developed by the project or its suppliers. Depending on the needs of the project, the SCM plans may be documented in a stand-alone document (that is, a software configuration management plan) or a section in one of the other project plans (for example, the project plans or the software quality assurance plans). Even if little formal planning documentation of the SCM is created (for example, on a project using agile methodologies), appropriate SCM decisions and plans still need to be made and communicated to project team members.

The project-level SCM group is responsible for ensuring that the SCM plans for that project are appropriately implemented and for tracking and controlling that implementation. These activities include:

- Implementing and/or tailoring organizational-level standardized SCM processes and work instructions or creating and implementing project-specific SCM processes and work instructions as appropriate

- Defining and implementing the project's SCM infrastructure needs, including needed libraries, and areas/partitions/customizations in SCM tools and databases

- Providing SCM inputs to project proposals to potential customers and requests for proposals to potential suppliers to ensure that all SCM requirements are being met

- Administering activities related to acquiring controlled configuration items

- Establishing project baselines

- Providing administrative support to the configuration control boards (CCBs)

- Ensuring that only authorized changes are made to baselined software

- Ensuring that all baseline changes are recorded in sufficient detail so that they can be reproduced or backed out

- Controlling commercial off-the-shelf (COTS) software, third-party software, customer-supplied products/components/documents and software tools as appropriate to the requirements of the project

- Supporting activities related to building the software configuration items/components from lower-level components/units

- Participating in or conducting software configuration audits

- Ensuring that configuration items, components, and units are appropriately stored and protected

- Providing a mechanism for exception resolution and deviations

- Advising the project team of SCM-related risks and problems, and providing solutions

Special SCM Roles and Responsibilities

In addition to the organizational-level and project-level SCM groups, there may be individuals who perform special SCM roles. These roles include the SCM managers, the SCM librarians, SCM toolsmiths, and software practitioners. Note that the roles and responsibilities of the configuration control board (CCB) as the change authorization authority are discussed in Chapter 28, "Configuration Control and Status Accounting."

SCM managers are responsible for managing the SCM groups at either the organizational or project level and for the overall success of the SCM program. This includes:

- Providing the overall strategic and tactical planning for the SCM function, establishing the SCM system and group goals and objectives, and approving project-level SCM plans

- Implementing, tracking, and controlling the SCM system, including reviewing the performance of the SCM system and its practices and tools, as well as the individual performance of SCM group members

- Ensuring that lessons learned are gathered and appropriate SCM preventive and corrective actions are implemented as needed

SCM librarians are responsible for establishing, coordinating, and ensuring the integrity of the controlled and static libraries for each project and for coordinating the reuse of software components between projects. SCM librarians may also be charged with performing backup and disaster recovery functions.

SCM toolsmiths, also called *tool administrators,* are responsible for the implementation and maintenance of the SCM tool set. These responsibilities include:

- Making recommendations on the tool selection process, testing and implementing the selected tools

- Updating the SCM tools as new versions become available

- Customizing the SCM tools to meet organizational and project requirements

- Automating of SCM activities through the use of the SCM tools and/or scripting routines

- Acting as subject matter experts that other project personnel can go to for answers to questions and problems about the SCM tools

Software practitioners include analysts, designers, programmers, testers, and suppliers who utilize the SCM program as part of their responsibilities in creating and maintaining the software products. The SCM responsibilities of software practitioners include:

- Identifying relevant configuration items

- Submitting those items for configuration control when they are baselined

- Maintaining bidirectional traceability information

- Using the information produced by the status accounting system to manage the configuration items

2. CONFIGURATION MANAGEMENT TOOLS

> Describe these tools as they are used for managing libraries, build systems, defect tracking systems, etc. (Understand)
>
> **Body of Knowledge VII.A.2**

Configuration management tools are used to automate the tedious and often error-prone work of manually performing the SCM activities of establishing and maintaining SCM libraries, controlling multiple versions of work products, creating software builds, reporting and tracking defects, and requesting and tracking change requests. This automation can improve development efficiency, decrease cycle times, allow software work products and product information to be easily shared across large and geographically dispersed groups, and increase the integrity of product information.

SCM tools can influence how an organization works. Therefore, tools should be selected that match the organization's SCM processes. An organization should not try to force-fit its processes to its SCM tools. If SCM process improvements are needed, they should be done in conjunction with selecting and/or upgrading the SCM tools that support those improvements. If the tool set is cumbersome or doesn't match the way software practitioners and others do their work, they will often find ways to work around the tools or circumvent the controls provided by the tools.

SCM Library and Version Control Tools

SCM library tools include the tools used to establish, maintain, and manage the various SCM libraries. These tools may range from simple scripts that are run to create static archives or nightly backups to sophisticated version control tools used to establish and manage the controlled libraries.

Version control tools handle the storage of multiple versions of individual configuration items. The tool assigns a unique identifier to each version of each configuration item (and its units and components) so that they can be referenced and retrieved as needed. Typically, the versions are stored as either forward or backward deltas to conserve space. In a backward delta system, the latest version of the item is saved along with the deltas between it and the previous versions. A forward delta system saves the original version and deltas going forward. For example, if the fifth version of a source code module were retrieved in a forward delta system, the tool would take the original file and apply four deltas to it to create the fifth version.

Version control tools typically have some kind of labeling mechanism that allows baselined versions of configuration items to be identified and related to other items in the same baseline. For example, when a new baseline is created, all of the work products (for example, source code modules and documents) included in that baseline are labeled with that baseline's identifier. More-sophisticated version control systems include automated promotion management as software development moves through the various life cycle phases.

Integrated version control tools work in conjunction with change management and build tools so that the correct versions of the appropriate configuration items are used when new builds are created.

For Web applications, content management tools may be more appropriate than version control tools. Content management tools provide the ability to manage versions of the content as it evolves, including the ability to create, review/edit, publish, and view the content.

SCM Build Tools

A *software build* is the process of combining software configuration units and components into higher-level components or items. For example, as illustrated in Figure 26.1, a build process is used to convert individual software source code files into one or more software executables that can be run on a computer. *SCM build tools* include:

- *Compilers* that convert high-level language source code into object code.

- *Assemblers* that convert assembly language source code into object code.

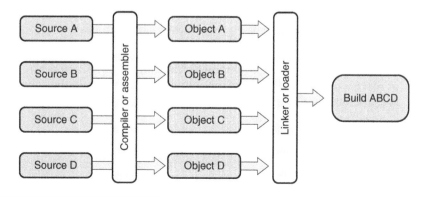

Figure 26.1 Software build.

- *Linkers* or *loaders* that combine and convert object code modules into the software executable.

- *Build scripts* used to automate build processes that would otherwise require people to perform multiple manual operations. Build scripts can be expanded to perform tasks in addition to basic builds, including the running of automated test scripts and the deployment of the build into the production environment.

- *Virus detection and removal tools.*

Build tools capture the details about the build and build process so that the build can be reproduced as needed. For example, these details would include what version of each component was used and what switches or options were used for the tools (for example, for the complier or linker).

SCM Change Management Tools

Change management tools automate the change control processes through which changes are requested, impact analysis is performed, change requests are approved or disapproved, and approved change requests are tracked through implementation, verification, and closure. Change management applies to both reported defects (failures) and enhancement requests (requirements changes). Some organizations use multiple defect tracking and/or enhancement request tools while other organizations use a single integrated change management tool to track both defects and enhancement requests. Depending on their sophistication, these change management tools are used to:

- Request changes (for example, to request enhancements or to report problems or other anomalies), including documenting the associated information.

- Notify the appropriate individuals and disseminate information when a change is requested.

- Facilitate virtual change control board meetings and impact analysis reviews.

- Identify and track the statuses of change requests as they are worked to resolution, documenting each step in the change process.

- Notify the appropriate individuals of status changes to each change request. For example, a development lead might be notified when one or more work products have been updated to incorporate the change and are ready for approval, or a tester might be notified when the change is ready for testing.

Through integration with the version control tool, the change management tool can:

- Identify individuals authorized to check out controlled configuration items for change, thus helping to ensure that only authorized changes are being made to controlled items

- Support change management across parallel, concurrent, or distributed development through automated merging of changes into items in other branches

SCM Status Accounting Tools

SCM tools can automatically provide much of the information required for good status accounting and traceability that would otherwise require a monumental manual effort to document and maintain. *SCM status accounting tools* harvest the data recorded in the other SCM tools (for example, version control tools, build tools, change management tools) to provide ad hoc information queries and standardized reports. This data and information supports management and engineering decision-making processes, including software metrics and measurement. This status accounting information also supports the ability to perform SCM audits.

3. LIBRARY PROCESSES

Describe dynamic, static, and controlled processes used in library systems and related procedures, such as check-in/check-out, merge changes, etc. (Understand)

Body of Knowledge VII.A.3

There is a dichotomy in SCM. On one side, individual developers need the flexibility necessary to do creative work, to modify code to try out what-if scenarios, and to make mistakes, learn from them, and evolve better software solutions. On the other side, teams need stability to allow code to be shared with confidence, to create builds and perform testing in a consistent environment, and to ship high-quality products with confidence. This requires an intricate balance to be maintained. Too much flexibility can result in problems including unauthorized and/or unwanted changes, the inability to integrate software components, uncertainty about what needs to be tested, and working programs that suddenly stop working. On the other hand, enforcing too much stability can result in costly bureaucratic overhead, delays in delivery, and may even require developers to ignore the process in order to get their work done.

One of the ways that SCM supports this need for both flexibility and stability is through the use of different *SCM libraries*. The number and kinds of libraries used in SCM will vary based on the size, criticality, and requirements of each project. The contents of each library will also vary based on the types and formats of the various configuration entities identified. There are four kinds of SCM libraries:

- Dynamic library
- Controlled library

- Static library

- Backup library

For each library used by a project, SCM planning should identify the name and type of the library, the information retention method (for example, online or off-line, media used, tool used), the control mechanisms, and the retention policies and procedures.

Dynamic Library

A *dynamic library*, also called a *development, programmer's,* or *working library*, is used to hold configuration entities that are currently being worked on by the software practitioner (for example, developers, testers, or other project personnel). Each practitioner typically has one or more dynamic libraries under their personal control that are used as personal work areas. The contents of a dynamic library are not considered to be under configuration control.

The dynamic library provides a mechanism for creating private working copies of new work products or obtaining copies of baselined work products approved for modification. Utilizing these copies, the developers can create new work products or make changes to existing products without affecting anyone else or impacting the integrity of the controlled copies. This gives the developer the flexibility needed to:

- Create work products

- Prototype changes

- Conduct tests and attempt to re-create problems

- Modify the code to facilitate debugging

- Make temporary changes to try out potential corrections

- Conduct trial-and-error experiments

Another example of a dynamic library is the work area used by testers for test execution. This allows tests to be performed that might cause failures that corrupt the software or data without impacting the work of other software practitioners. This dynamic test library is under the control of the tester.

Controlled Library

A *controlled library*, also called a *master* or *system library*, is used for managing current controlled configuration items and baselines, and controlling changes to those items and baselines. The controlled library contains configuration units, components, and items that have been acquired and placed under formal control. The controlled library may be made up of one or more actual libraries, directories, or repositories depending on the needs of the project. For example, different libraries might be used to store different types of configuration items (for example, source code, documentation, hardware drawings). The controlled libraries may also be implemented as areas inside a tool, such as a version control tool.

The controlled library is used to share work products with other members of the project team. Software practitioners can freely obtain "read-only" copies of the units, components, or items from the controlled library and move them into their dynamic libraries. However, the appropriate authority must authorize changes to work products in the controlled library. Work products from the controlled library are used to create software builds from a "known" environment for testing and for release to the users.

Static Library

A *static library*, also called a *software repository* or *software product baseline library*, is used to archive important baselines, including those released into operations. Static libraries can also be used to archive ("freeze") various intermediate baselines as appropriate during the development process. Items in the static libraries can be accessed through read-only mechanisms and are not modifiable.

Backup Library

A *backup library* contains duplicates of the versions of the software and associated components, data, and documentation at the time that the copies were made. Backups are performed on a periodic basis to ensure that the intellectual capital of the organization is protected. For example, if important files are accidentally deleted, a feature has been modified and needs to be rolled back to a previous version, or if a hard disk crashes, backed-up versions can be retrieved.

SCM Library Process: Creating a New Software Work Product

A dynamic library is used when new work products are created. For example, as illustrated in Figure 26.2, the library process steps to create a new work product include:

Step 1. The author creates and saves a new software work product ABC in a dynamic library. Examples of work products include a source code module, a document, a test case or procedure, a data file, or a build script.

Step 2. The author reviews and/or tests the newly created work product and makes whatever modifications are necessary to correct any defects found. This review process might include peer reviews or other reviews involving other software practitioners.

Step 3. When the author is satisfied that the work product is ready to share and the appropriate level of approval has been obtained, the author checks work product ABC into the controlled library and a unique identifier is assigned to indicate the name of the work product and its version (for example, ABC 1.0).

Once a new work product has been checked in to the controlled library it is under formal change control and can only be modified through formal change control processes.

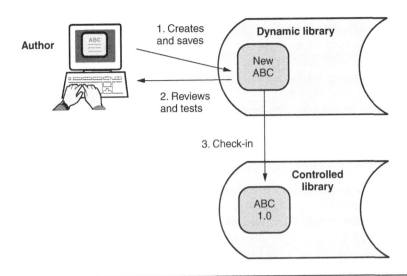

Figure 26.2 Creating a new software work product.

The check-in process includes the capturing of information about the work product, including:

- Descriptive information about the work product, including initial creation information and subsequent change information when the work product is checked out and back in as a modified version in the future

- Check-in date and time and who performed the check-in

- File access permissions

SCM Library Process: Creating a Software Build

While software builds can be created in a dynamic library, official software builds are created from the information in a controlled library. This is done so that the build is created from controlled entities in a controlled environment where build information is captured to ensure that the build is reproducible. For example, as illustrated in Figure 26.3, the library process steps to creating a software build include:

Step 1. The builder executes the build script using controlled units or components as inputs. The builder may be a person creating the build manually, or the build may be created automatically. Automatic builds may be done on a periodic basis, for example, every hour. Special events may also be used to initiate an automatic build, for example, when a new version of any of a set of specified components is checked in to the controlled library.

Step 2. The output of this execution is the software build, which is assigned a unique identifier.

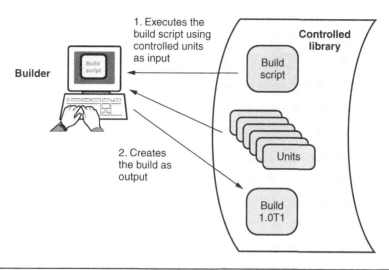

Figure 26.3   Creating a software build.

SCM Library Process: Testing a Software Build

Assuming that the tester has already created a set of test work products (for example, test cases, procedures, scripts, data) and checked them into the controlled library, the library process steps for testing a software build include:

Step 1.   A tester checks out read-only copies of the build and test work products from the controlled library into the dynamic library used for testing. If testing is automated as part of an integrated build script, the script would move the build and appropriate test work products to the dynamic library.

Step 2.   The tester or the automated script executes one or more tests and the results are either observed or recorded. An evaluation is then performed to determine if the actual results of the test matched the expected results. If the test is performed automatically, any anomalies encountered are reported to the appropriate individual(s).

Step 3.   For manual testing, the tester reports any problems encountered during testing with either the build or the test work products into the change request (problem reporting) database. For automated testing, the person receiving the anomaly report interprets that report and reports problems into the change request database as appropriate.

Figure 26.4 illustrates this process for manual testing performed by a tester.

SCM Library Process: Modifying a Controlled Work Product

Once the appropriate level of authority approves a change request (for example, problem report or enhancement request), one or more controlled work products

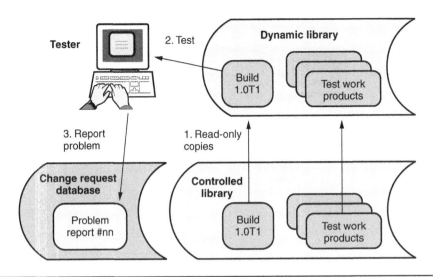

Figure 26.4 Testing a software build.

are updated to incorporate that approved change. The library process steps to modify an existing controlled work product include:

Step 1. As illustrated in Figure 26.5, the assigned author checks out a copy of each work product that needs to be updated from the controlled library into a dynamic library based on an analysis of the approved change request. The controlled library locks each work product checked out for modification so that other team members know that it is being updated. This allows other team members to retrieve read-only copies but not check these work products out for modification. Note that some tools are sophisticated enough to allow for concurrent development and will enable developer reconciliation of multiple changes as copies of updated work products are checked back into the controlled library.

Step 2. As illustrated in Figure 26.6, the author then makes the required changes to the copies of each checked-out work product based on the approved change request. The author saves these corrected copies into the dynamic library. The author then reviews and/or tests the updated work product and makes whatever modifications are necessary to correct any defects found.

Step 3. As illustrated in Figure 26.7, the author checks each updated work product back into the controlled library, and an updated version number is assigned as appropriate. As it is checked in, the control library unlocks each work product so that both the previous and the new versions of those work products are available for future modification. The author updates the work product library information as each product is checked in and should also update the change request with new status information.

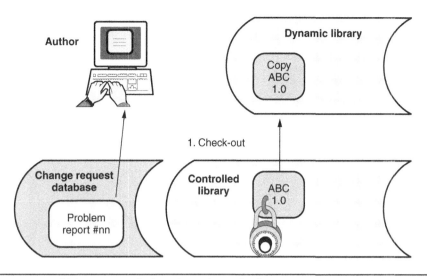

Figure 26.5   Modifying a controlled work product–check-out process.

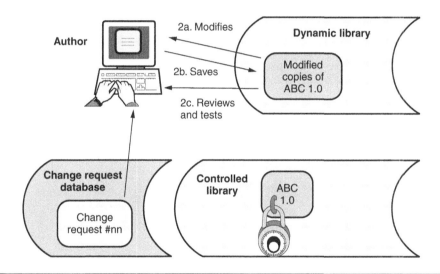

Figure 26.6   Modifying a controlled work product–modification process.

SCM Library Process: Branching

Consider the main codeline example in Figure 26.8. Each label in this example represents the versions of a set of configuration units that were used to create a build. Assume label 2 represents a build that has been released into operations and label 3 represents a build that is currently under test and that contains new functionality updates to configuration units CU #1 and CU #2. A problem report comes in from operations. The label 2 build is debugged and a defect is found in version 4 of configuration unit CU #1. Version 4 can not just be fixed and checked back in as version 8 because that would lose the new functionality and/or corrections added

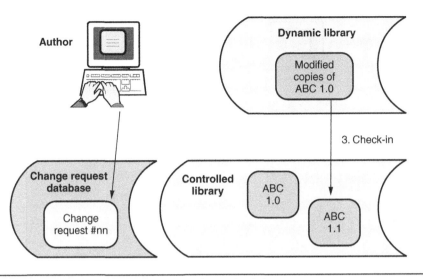

Figure 26.7 Modifying a controlled work product–check-in process.

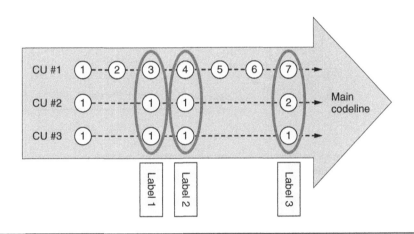

Figure 26.8 Main codeline–example.

in versions 5, 6, and 7. On the other hand, the defect can not just be fixed in version 7 to create a new build for operations (assuming that the defect even still exists in version 7 after the changes that have been made) for reasons including the fact that the new functionality in version 7:

- May not be completely tested

- May have dependencies on other updated work products

- Should not be given away for free

Branching the codeline can give the flexibility needed to support multiple versions of the product at the same time. As illustrated in Figure 26.9, a new codeline can

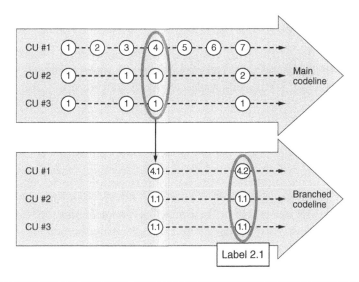

Figure 26.9   Branching—example.

be created from all of the work products in label 2. For example, version 4 of configuration unit CU #1 is copied into the branched codeline, becoming version 4.1, and version 1 of configuration unit CU #2 becomes version 1.1, and so on. Version 4.1 of configuration unit CU #1 can then be checked out and modified to correct the defect. It is then checked back in as version 4.2. The corrective build label 2.1 can now be created and released into production containing the fix to the reported problem. At the same time new development can continue on the main codeline.

Another example of where a branched codeline might be useful is to "freeze" a version of the product build for a testing cycle. Critical fixes that allow testing to continue can be done to the branched codeline while new development continues on the main codeline. Branching may also be used to create customized versions of work products or for concurrent, parallel development that allows multiple people to work on the same files at the same time. Branches can be taken from the original codeline, or branches can be taken from other branches. However, caution should be used when branching is implemented. Branching is the most complex of the library processes. Without a strong and disciplined branching strategy, chaos can quickly take over with multiple copies of many configuration items needing to be supported. A well-structured branching approach that minimizes the number of active branches at any given time reduces complexity.

One useful branching strategy is to ensure that new development is always done on the main codeline (or trunk). The advantage of this is that the branched product releases or other branches off the main codeline are relatively temporary in nature. Once testing is complete on a frozen branch or once a released version of the product is no longer supported in operations, its associated branch can be archived as necessary and removed in order to minimize the number of branches off the main codeline.

SCM Library Process: Merging

Consider the defect that was corrected in the production release label 2.1 build discussed in the last section. The current operations problem was solved with this corrective release. If this defect also exists in configuration unit CU #1 versions 5, 6, and 7 and it is not corrected, there is a risk that a future release of the product may bring back an old problem, resulting in a very unhappy customer. One answer to this is to check out version 7 of configuration unit CU #1, edit the file to make the same correction a second time, and check it back in as version 8. Another answer is called *merging,* taking two or more versions of a work product and combining them into a single new version. In the example above, version 4.2 (with the correction) could be merged with version 7 (with the new functionality) to create a new version 8, as illustrated in Figure 26.10. Of course, merging can be done in the opposite direction, with changes being merged from the main codeline into items on a branched codeline.

Merging can also be used to combine functionality added on several concurrent, parallel development branches back into the main codeline. One possibility when doing this is that the multiple developers changed the same work product. If this is the case, several variations can arise:

- *The functionality added by the various developers does not conflict and can simply be merged.* For example, one developer adds the ability to add a customized logo to a report, and another developer adds a graph to the report. These changes do not affect each other so no conflict exists in the merge.

- *The functionality added by the various developers creates a merge conflict but that conflict can be corrected through blending.* In this case, one change may supersede the others. For example, one developer adds a logo to the report and another developer adds a customizable logo. Since the static logo

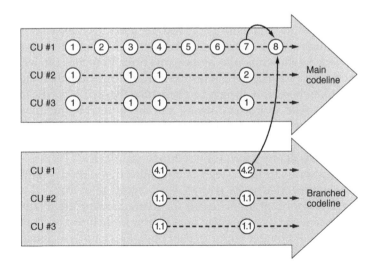

Figure 26.10 Merging—example.

can be added as a customized logo, the customized logo change may be chosen to supersede the other change. Changes may also be blended during a merge. In this logo example, the static logo change added by the first developer might be blended by adding it as the default to the customizable logo change.

- *The functionality added by the various developers creates a merge conflict and blending can not be used to correct the conflict.* In this case, decisions will have to be made to prioritize the changes and select one over the others, or additional changes will have to be made to incorporate the intent of all changes.

In any case, once the merge is accomplished, the resulting new version should be tested to ensure that the merge did not result in new defects that were not identified during the merge analysis process.

Chapter 27

B. Configuration Identification

Software *configuration identification* is the software configuration management (SCM) activity that involves the partitioning of the software product into a hierarchy of controllable configuration items and the associated configuration components and configuration units used to produce them. According to Keyes (2004), "effective configuration identification is a prerequisite for the other configuration management activities (for example, configuration control, status accounting, auditing), which all use the products of configuration identification." Configuration identification activities include:

- Documenting of the functional and physical characteristics for each configuration item, component, and unit

- Defining the acquisition points and criteria of each configuration item, component, and unit

- Assigning unique identifiers to each item, component, and unit (and their versions and revisions)

Software configuration identification also includes defining the project baselines, their contents, and mechanisms used to establish those baselines.

Software configuration identification is the first of the four core activities of SCM to be done by the project because it is the prerequisite for performing software configuration control, status accounting, and auditing.

1. CONFIGURATION ITEMS

Describe configuration items
(documentation, software code, equipment,
etc.), identification methods (naming
conventions, versioning schemes, etc.),
and when baselines are created and used.
(Understand)

Body of Knowledge VII.B.1

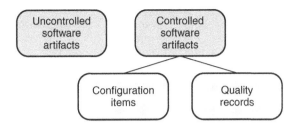

Figure 27.1   Levels of software work product control.

The software development process produces many different software work products. Software work products are any tangible output, artifact, or specific measurable accomplishment from the software development activity or process. Examples of software work products include source code, models, electronic files, documents, databases, reports, metrics, logs, and services. As illustrated in Figure 27.1, these work products may be controlled at various levels. In fact, some work products are temporary, so they are never placed under any kind of control. Examples of temporary software artifacts include printed program listings with the programmer's handwritten annotations or a recorder's personal notes from a meeting that are later used as input to the formal meeting minutes.

Software work products that are controlled fall into two major categories. The first category is called *quality records*. Work products designated as quality records must be controlled, but are not considered to be under formal SCM. For example, for most projects it would be considered overkill to report a correction to a set of meeting minutes by opening up a change request in the change request tool and formally approving and tracking that change to closure. In fact, no formal change control process is typically implemented for quality records. Procedures should be established, however, to define the controls for the identification, storage, protection, retrieval, retention time, and disposition of quality records. Quality records should also remain legible, readily identifiable, and retrievable (ISO 2008).

The second category of controlled software work products is called *configuration items*. A configuration item, also called a *computer software configuration item* (CSCI), is a work product placed under SCM and treated as a single entity. "In practice, a CI is a stand-alone, test-alone, use-alone element of the software that requires control during development and subsequent use in the field" (Berlack 1992).

Software Product Partitioning

A first step in configuration identification is the partitioning of the software product into a hierarchy of controllable configuration items, components, and units. As illustrated in Figure 27.2, *configuration items* can be made up of other work products called *configuration components*, which in turn can be made up of other work products called *configuration units*. For example, the entire system can be treated as a configuration item that is made up of various configuration components including equipment and/or software subsystems. Those components can

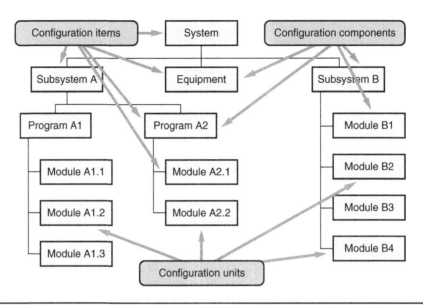

Figure 27.2 Configuration identification hierarchy.

be made up of configuration units including programs and individual software modules. However, from a different perspective, each software subsystem can be designated a configuration item and controlled separately. In this case, each software subsystem is made up of configuration components including software programs and/or individual software modules. In fact, even the individual software modules can be designated as configuration items.

Because of the high risk of direct impact on the customers/end users if issues arise, externally delivered work products should always be designated as configuration items. Examples of externally delivered work products can include:

- Software executables (and the software components/units used to create them)

- System data files and databases

- Commercial off-the-shelf (COTS) or third-party software included in or delivered with the software system

- User and operational documentation (user/operations manuals, help files, installation instructions, release descriptions/notes)

- Training materials

The project may also designate other internal software work products and data as configuration items. For example, good requirements management practices dictate that the requirements and design specifications should be configuration items. Other examples include plans (project, quality, verification and validation, test, and SCM plans), test cases, test procedures, test data, and test automation products, and project-level process and work instruction documentation. Customer-supplied equipment, software, or documentation used in the development of the software work products should also be considered for designation as configuration items.

"Tools and other capital assets of the project's work environment" and "other items that are used in creating and describing these work products" (SEI 2006) should be considered for placement under configuration control to ensure that past versions of the work products can be re-created and maintained as necessary. When multiple versions of the software are supported in the field that were built using different versions of these tools, designating these tools as configuration items may be particularly important. If a tool is designated as a configuration item, both the tool's executable and its associated documentation (for example, user manuals) should be placed under SCM. Other considerations may include keeping tool licenses up to date, maintaining copies of tool certifications if applicable, and maintaining a history of tool updates and customizations. Examples of support tools that should be considered for placement under SCM include:

- Compilers, assemblers, linkers, loaders, scripts, and other build tools

- Operating systems

- Word processors and other documentation tools

- Computer-aided software engineering (CASE) tools, testing tools, and SCM tools

- Simulation and modeling tools

According to the IEEE *Standard for Software Configuration Management Plans* (IEEE 2005) the SCM plans shall:

- "Identify the project configuration items and their structure at each project control point."

- "State how each configuration item and its versions are to be uniquely named and describe the activities performed to define, track, store, and retrieve configuration items."

Another approach is to have the list of configuration items and their relationship to each other automated using the SCM tools. Whatever approach is used, conscious decisions need be made about what should be considered configuration items so that important items are not forgotten.

Multiple technical factors should be taken into consideration when partitioning the software into configuration items, components, and units. These factors include:

- *Product architecture.* The partitioning of the software product into configuration items, components, and units typically reflects the architectural structure of the product. This means that each software product as a whole should have a unique identifier, and each component or unit that makes up the product should also have a unique identifier.

- *Reuse.* Partitioning should consider whether a component or unit is being reused by multiple subsystems or by multiple products. For example, if part of a work product has high reuse and another part of that same work product is not being reused, it may be appropriate to break the work product into two configuration items. If the configuration item already exists in another product and is being reused in this product, it has already been established as a configuration item.

- *Documentation hierarchy.* Each document in the documentation hierarchy must have a unique identifier. There must also be a mechanism for identifying the interrelationships between the documents and between the documents and the configuration items, components, and units.

- *Requirements allocation and traceability.* Traceability is used to track the relationship between the requirements and the configuration items, components, and units to which those requirements are allocated.

- *Change and dependencies.* Another factor to consider is whether or not a work product is expected to have a high level of change over time. For example, if part of a work product is expected to have a high rate of change and another part of that same work product is expected to have little or no change, it may be appropriate to break that work product into two configuration items. Work products that are dependent on each other (that is, if a change to one product would mandate changes to other products) would typically be grouped together.

Multiple managerial factors should also be taken into consideration when partitioning the software into configuration items, components, and units. These factors include:

- *Scope and magnitude.* The larger and more complex the software system is and the more people involved, the more rigorous and stringent the SCM system typically is that supports the development and maintenance processes, and the more complex the software product hierarchy will be.

- *Author assignment.* If different authors are working on different parts of the same work product, it may be appropriate to break it into separate configuration items. This may be especially important for geographically dispersed authors.

- *Authority and responsibility.* The role and level of responsibility required to review and approve a software entity typically influences the product's partitioning. For example, the team lead may have the authority to approve the completion and acquisition of a configuration unit while it may require a technical or project manager to approve the completion and acquisition of a configuration component and the director of software development to approve the completion and acquisition of a configuration item. Whether or not more than one group might use a work product should also be taken into consideration.

- *Planning and estimation.* The structure of the configuration items, components, and units may also parallel the work breakdown structure used to plan and estimate the software development project and maintenance effort. The choice of an incremental or evolutionary development life cycle may also guide product partitioning.

- *Need for visibility.* Configuration items, components, and units are used to track the progress and completeness of the work. The more visibility that is needed into the status of software work products, the more detailed the configuration hierarchy must be. For example, the work product's criticality to the project should be considered.

- *COTS or supplier work products.* If an item, component, or unit is procured off the shelf or is produced by a supplier, it will impact the configuration items available. For example, there may only be an executable and user manual to place under SCM and not individual source code modules.

Functional and Physical Characteristics

The functional and physical characteristics of a configuration item are described in or pointed to by its associated metadata. "Metadata is a database concept that means the data about the data stored in the database" (Hass 2003). In the case of a configuration item, metadata is used to define the characteristics of the configuration item, including its name, its description, its author, its version/revision history information, its status, and other information as specified. Again, for many projects this metadata is documented inside the configuration management tools. Physical characteristics of a configuration item are defined by the metadata through maintaining references to other related configuration items that describe those characteristics. For example, the metadata for a software source code module might include references to the detailed design document that defines its internal structure or to external interface specifications. There must also be a mechanism for identifying what versions of each component or unit make up each version of each configuration item. For example, the metadata for a software user manual might include references to all of the chapters (other physical configuration components) and their versions that are part of that manual.

The metadata defines the functional characteristics of a configuration item by maintaining references to related specifications that describe those characteristics. For example, the metadata for a software build might include a reference to the software requirements specification that describes its functional characteristics, or the metadata for a software source code module might include traceability back to the requirements that were allocated to it.

Acquisition Points

Defining when each configuration item is *acquired* (that is, placed under configuration control) is also important. Quality gates are used to approve the acquiring of a configuration item and its placement under configuration control (see Figure 27.3). Examples of quality gates include the successful completion of:

- A peer review (for example, desk check, inspection, walk-through)

- A test activity

- A project review (for example, phase gate review, major milestone review)

- An independent product analysis or audit

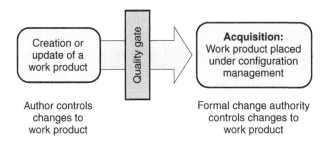

Figure 27.3 Configuration item acquisition.

The software configuration management planning should define the acquisition point, associated quality gate, and acceptance criteria for each configuration item. The earlier the acquisition point is in the life of a configuration item, the more rigorous the level of control and the more formal the communication about changes to that item must be, which results in more stability. The later the acquisition point, the easier and quicker it is to make changes, resulting in more flexibility. The higher the risk that changes to a configuration item will create potential issues, the earlier in the life cycle the acquisition point is established for that configuration item.

For example, consider a source code module. If the acquisition point is set after peer review, then all defects found in unit, integration, and system test must go through formal change control. The peer review acquisition point may be too early for most projects, but, for example, if a project has an independent verification and validation (IV&V) team that does unit testing, it may provide the formality needed for the IV&V and development teams to communicate effectively. For many projects, an acquisition point for source code may be more appropriately set after unit test or integration test depending on when the handoff takes place to a testing group outside development. For small development teams with high levels of internal communications, it may even be appropriate for the acquisition point to be set at the point of product release, so that only defects reported from operations (production) are subject to formal change control.

For other configuration items, such as requirements or design specifications, the successful completion of the peer review or of a major phase gate or milestone review may be the appropriate acquisition point. These points act as internal release points where the specification moves from creation by its authors to use by other members of the project team (for example, development, test, and/or technical publications), so the need for more control (stability) and more formal communication about changes and their impacts may be desirable.

Identification Methods

Another role of software configuration identification is to define an identification schema and naming conventions for assigning a unique *identifier* to each configuration item, component, and unit and their various versions and revisions.

There may be several identification schema used for configuration identification. For example, different schema might be used for different types of configuration items (for example, code modules, builds, documents). According to Leon (2005), "a good identification scheme should:

- Facilitate the storage, retrieval, tracking, reproduction, and distribution of the configuration items

- Make it possible to understand the relationship between the configuration items from their names"

In its simplest form, the filename used to save the configuration item can be used to uniquely identify it. For example, when it was first created, this chapter was saved in a file named *Part 7 Configuration Management—Chapter 27 Configuration Identification 01.00.doc*, with the version number 01.00 embedded in the file name to indicate that this was the first revision of this chapter and that there were, as yet, no corrective revisions. As the first round of reviewing occurs, the second two-digit number is incremented as reviewer comments are incorporated to change the chapter to create a new filename. If there are major rewrites to this chapter to include new information, the first two-digit number indicating the chapter version is incremented to create a new filename.

Within the controlled library, configuration items, components, or units may be labeled with a unique filename or other identifier. Most projects use SCM tools that automatically assign an incremented version/revision number every time a configuration item or a new copy of an existing item is checked in to the tool. As illustrated in Figure 27.4, for example, the three configuration units have unique names CU #1, CU #2, and CU #3. They also have identifiers that indicate when they changed. As illustrated in Figure 27.4, for example, CU#1 has changed seven times with version/revision identifiers 1–7 while CU#2 has changed only once with version/revision identifiers 1 and 2 and CU #3 has not changed because it is still at version/revision 1.

A project typically has multiple configuration items, components, and units checked in to one or more control libraries. There are times when it is desirable to identify relationships between these configuration entities, for example, to identify the set of configuration items and their version/revisions that make up

Part VII.B.1

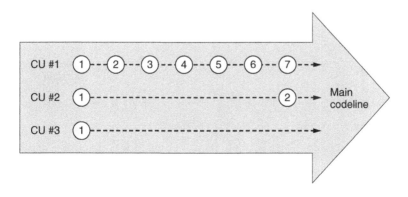

Figure 27.4 Configuration unit identification scheme—example.

a baseline or to identify all the configuration units and components to be used in a build. These associations are accomplished using *labeling*, also called *tagging*. Most configuration management tools have functionality to automate the labeling process.

Figure 27.5 illustrates a very simple example of labeling, where work products are only labeled in a single library. In this example, label 3 associates version/revision 7 of configuration unit #1 with version/revision 2 of configuration unit #2 and version/revision 1 of configuration unit #3. Notice that the same version/revision of a work product can have more than one label. In this example, version/revision 1 of configuration unit #3 has labels 1, 2, and 3 associated with it. More-complex labeling associates work products across multiple controlled libraries and can select specified items from each library.

The labels in Figure 27.5 are version/revision-type labels, which associate the specific versions/revisions of the work products with the time the labels were created. A version/revision-type label might be useful, for example, when associating the specific versions/revisions of the source code modules that were built into a specific software build.

Another type of labeling is file labeling, where a set of files are associated without specifying their specific versions/revisions. Rules are then used to identify which versions/revisions are to be used at any given time. A simple example of these rules would be to use the latest version/revision of each file whenever the label is used. A file-type label might be useful, for example, when associating the source code modules that should be used when automatically creating builds on a periodic basis. The automation would then build the latest versions/revisions of each source code module into the new executable it creates each time it runs.

As illustrated in Figure 27.6, when branching occurs, version/revision numbers must reflect that branching and indicate the branching relationships. In this identification scheme example, an extension was added to both the version/revision number and label number to show the relationships. That is, CU #1 version/revision 4.1 was copied from CU #1 version/revision 4, CU #2 1.1 was copied from CU #2 1, CU #3 1.1 was copied from CU #3 1, and label 2.1 is an

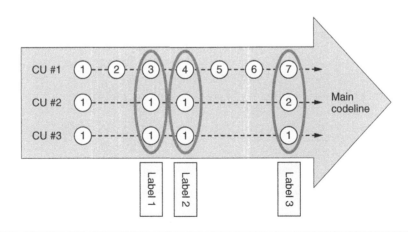

Figure 27.5 Labeling—example.

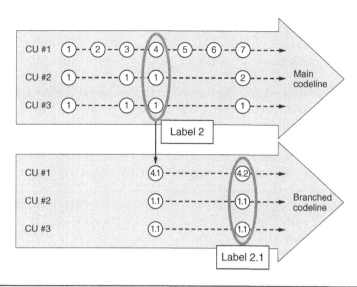

Figure 27.6   Branching identification scheme—example.

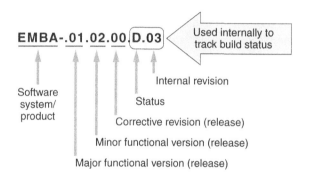

Figure 27.7   Build identification scheme—example.

updated version/revision of label 2. Again, modern SCM tools support labeling and dynamic branching and merging functions.

Figure 27.7 illustrates an example of a software build identification scheme. This scheme assigns an alphanumeric name to the software system/product, in this case EMBA. There is a two-digit indicator of the major functional version (release) of the build, in this case 01 (indicating that this is the first major release of this product). This major functional version indicator is incremented when a new major functional version build is created. There is a two-digit indicator of the minor functional version (release) of the build, in this case 02 (indicating that this is the second minor release of this product). This minor functional version indicator is incremented when a new minor functional version build is created, for example, when the first build is created for the third incremental release against major release 01. There is a two-digit indicator of the corrective revision (release) of the build, in this case 00 (indicating that there are no corrective releases against this build). This corrective revision indicator is incremented when a new corrective revision build is created, such as when a service pack build correcting defects found during operations is created for major release 01 and minor release 02 of this product.

The final letter and two-digit number in this identification scheme are used as build status counters internally within the development organization. In this case D.03 indicates that this is the third developmental testing build of the product. Figure 27.8 illustrates an example of how this build status counter might be used during development. In this example, the letter D indicates that the build is being used for developmental testing, and the two-digit internal revision number is incremented each time a new developmental testing build is created. The final developmental testing build EMBA-.01.02.00.D.nn becomes the first system testing build EMBA-.01.02.00.S.01 when it passes through a quality gate (for example, successful completion of a "ready to system test" review). The final system testing build, EMBA-.01.02.00.S.nn, becomes the first beta testing build, EMBA-.01.02.00.B.01, when it passes through a quality gate (for example, successful completion of a "ready to beta test" review). The final beta testing build EMBA-.01.02.00.B.nn becomes the released build EMBA-.01.02.00 when it passes through a quality gate (for example, successful completion of a ready-to-ship review). Note that the internal status indicator is dropped when the build is released to operations. Many SCM tools include mechanisms for automatically assigning identifiers

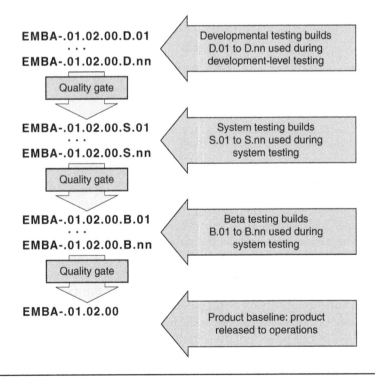

Figure 27.8   Build identification scheme–internal build status example.

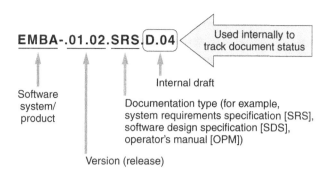

Figure 27.9 Document identification scheme—example.

to individual configuration items and builds. It is recommended that the project simply use the identification schema from their selected tools and not reinvent a different one without specific value-added reasons.

As a final example, Figure 27.9 illustrates an example of a document identification scheme. In this example the alphanumeric software system/product name (EMBA), the two-digit major functional version, and the two-digit minor functional version (01.02) link the document back to the software release associated with the document. There is also a three-character acronym that indicates the type of document, in this example SRS indicating that the document is a system requirements specification. There is also an internal status indicator letter and number that indicate the internal revisions of the document, in this case, D.04 indicating the fourth developmental revision of the document.

It should be noted that these are just examples of some of the many possible schema that can be used to assign unique identifiers to configuration items, units, and components and their versions/revisions.

Baselines

A baseline is a well-defined reference point that represents a snapshot of a configuration item (including all of its component parts) or a set of configuration items at a specific point in the development life cycle. "A baseline is a set of specifications or work products that has been formally reviewed and agreed on, that thereafter serves as a basis for further development or delivery, and that can only be changed through change control procedures" (SEI 2006). Prior to baselining, the author of a configuration item can make changes to a work product quickly and informally. After baselining, changes to configuration items can only be made through formal change-control procedures. As illustrated in Figure 27.10, there are four different types of baselines: functional baselines, allocated baselines, developmental baselines, and product baselines.

According to the IEEE *Standard for Software Configuration Management Plans* (IEEE 2005), the SCM plans "shall define how baselines are to be created, in terms of the following:

- The event that creates the baseline

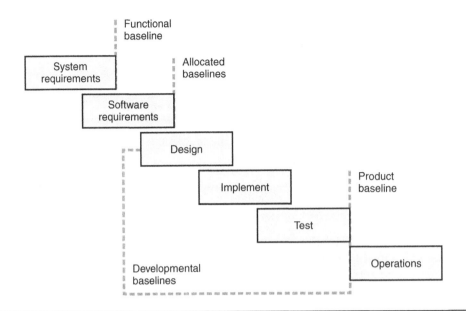

Figure 27.10 Types of baselines.

- The items that are to be controlled in the baseline
- The procedures used to establish and change the baseline
- The authority required to approve changes to the approved baselined documents"

The *functional baseline* is typically established upon the completion and approval of the technical specification (system requirements) for the product. The functional baseline is an agreement between the customer (or the marketing function), the organization developing the system, and other stakeholders about the needed features and functions of the system. The functional baseline becomes the basis for technical planning, designing, coding, and testing of the product, and for project management planning. It also provides a basis for verification and validation planning and for product validation. Examples of configuration items that might be included in the functional baseline include the business needs document, stakeholder-level requirements (for example, user cases, usage scenarios, or user stories), system requirements specifications, external interface specifications, acceptance test plans and specifications, and the project charter and initial project plan.

Once the system-level requirements are allocated down to the highest-level configuration components (equipment and software subsystems), the *allocated baselines* are typically established upon the completion and approval of the technical specification (equipment and software requirements) for each of those subsystems. For example, an allocated baseline would be established for each software component of the system when its software requirements specification was approved. There could also be one or more equipment-allocated baselines for each equipment component (for example, each item of hardware) in the system.

The *developmental baselines* are intermediate baselines established throughout the software development process. Typically, these baselines are under the control of the development organization and are controlled at a lower level of authority than other baselines. For example, an architectural design developmental baseline might be established with the approval of the architectural design. This architectural design baseline might include the architectural design specification, the integration test plan and specification, and the software system test cases and procedures. Another example might be a source code developmental baseline that is established with the successful completion of the unit test of that code. This source code baseline might include the low-level design specification for that code, the source code module (and associated data or other files), unit test cases and procedures, and automated unit-level test scripts.

The *product baseline,* also called the *production baseline,* "snapshots" the product as it is delivered to the users for use in operations and the maintenance parts of the life cycle. The contents of the product baseline may include configuration items promoted from the functional, allocated, and developmental baselines, as appropriate, and released software and documentation deliverables. The product baseline is also when the support tool–type configuration items are typically baselined. The highest level of change authority typically controls the product baseline.

2. SOFTWARE BUILDS

> Describe the relationship between software builds and configuration management functions, and describe methods for controlling builds (automation, new versions, etc.). (Understand)
>
> **Body of Knowledge VII.B.2**

A software build is the process of combining software configuration components and units into configuration components or items. The resulting executable software work product is also called a build. According to the ISO/IEC *Systems and Software Engineering—Vocabulary* (ISO/IEC 2009), a *build* is "an operational version of a system or component that incorporates a specified subset of the capabilities that the final product will provide."

The build process includes all of the activities associated with the processing of source files to create one or more derived final target files (builds). According to Bays (1999), these "build activities can be broken down into several key actions:

- Dependency checking
- Source compilation
- Executable linking

Part VII.B.2

- Occasionally some form of data file generation"

Guaranteeing the ability to produce high-quality, consistent, and complete builds may be the most important role of SCM after protecting the configuration items from loss and unauthorized change.

Build Automation

In order to ensure that the same build processes are followed consistently every time a build is performed, without the possibility of human errors, the build process should be automated as much as possible. Automation also allows builds to occur more often, providing more-timely feedback as changes are made to the software and automation, and eliminates the need for rigorous documentation of what files, options, and so on, were used since this information is typically documented as part of the automation. The build process is automated using a command file called a *build script*, which specifies:

- The components of the build (source and derived)
  - Their versions
  - Their locations in the configuration libraries
- The build tools, including compilers, assemblers, linkers, loaders, and build scripts
  - Their versions
  - The required setting for options and environmental parameters
- Pointers to the appropriate macros, libraries, and other files to be included
  - Their versions
  - Their locations in the configuration libraries

For example, for IBM mainframes these command files (build scripts) are usually JCL files, in UNIX they are shell scripts, and for C++ they are make files. These build scripts are typically designated as configuration items themselves and placed under configuration control to ensure the reproducibility of the build process. The resulting builds (target files) are also configuration items and should be considered new versions whenever the source files for the build have been modified or the build script has been modified in any way.

Build Reproducibility

Software builds must be reproducible in order to release high-quality, consistent, and complete product, and to debug and correct reported problems found during testing and in operations. For a build to be reproducible, a standardized development environment with known elements is a necessity. The source files used to create the build must also have a known configuration, which is why official builds are created using configuration items (source files) from controlled libraries. Many SCM tools make build reproducibility a trivial event if the appropriate decisions are made and tool capabilities are appropriately implemented.

To verify that a build is reproducible, an attempt is made to reproduce that build and then compare the original build with the test build. Ideally, these two builds are created on completely separate systems, where the test system's runtime, development, and build environments have been newly instanced using the specifications defined for those environments. The resulting test build is then compared with the original build using one or more of the following tests:

1. *Same file and directory contents.* This test compares the listings of the files and directory paths in both source trees to verify that they are identical.

2. *Identical source file contents.* This test compares the contents of each pair of source files to verify that they are identical in both trees.

3. *Same size target files.* This test compares the target files to verify that they are identical in size.

4. *Byte-for-byte identical target files.* This test compares the contents of the target files to verify that they are identical in both trees.

5. *Byte-for-byte identical intermediate files.* This test compares the contents of each pair of intermediate files to verify that they are identical in both trees (Bays 1999).

These last two tests can be problematic in some systems because of complications including:

• Compilation date and time stamps being embedded in the files

• Compilers that leave garbage in uninitialized variables

Part VII.B.2

Chapter 28

C. Configuration Control and Status Accounting

Software *configuration control* is "the systematic process that ensures that changes to a baseline are properly identified, documented, evaluated for impact, approved by an appropriate level of authority, incorporated into all impacted work products and verified" (MIL-HDBK 2001). Software configuration control procedures include:

- Mechanisms for placing configuration items under control

- Mechanisms for requesting and documenting changes to controlled configuration items

- Mechanisms for informing affected stakeholders of the change request and soliciting their input to the impact analysis

- Requirements for performing impact analysis for each requested change or set of changes

- An authority for making decisions on accepting or rejecting a requested change

- Mechanisms for informing affected stakeholders of the decision to accept, defer, or reject the change and for obtaining their commitment to the change if it is accepted

- Mechanisms for tracking requested changes from submission through final disposition (rejection or completion of the change)

- Mechanisms for verifying the change

- Controls for ensuring that unauthorized change does not occur

- Mechanisms for obtaining deviations and waivers

There is a dichotomy in software configuration control. On one side, individual developers need the flexibility necessary to do creative work, to modify code to try out what-if scenarios, and to make mistakes, learn from them, and evolve better software solutions. On the other side, teams need stability to allow code to be shared with confidence, to create builds and perform testing in a consistent environment, and to ship high-quality products with confidence. This requires an intricate balance to be maintained. Too much flexibility can result in problems including unauthorized and/or unwanted changes, the inability to integrate software components, uncertainty about what needs to be tested, and working programs that suddenly stop working. On the other hand, enforcing too much stability can result in costly bureaucratic overhead or delays in delivery, and may even require developers to ignore the process in order to get their work done.

How much flexibility can a project afford when it comes to controlling changes to software products and components? How much stability does a project need? The answer to this, like many questions in software development, depends on risk. The choice isn't really between complete flexibility (anyone can change anything at any time) and complete stability (everything is locked down so that change only happens through rigorous control processes). As the software product is being created, reviewed, tested internally to development, independently tested, and finally released, components of that product can move through a continuum from complete flexibility, through various levels of more rigorous control, to stability at shipment to operations. Risk-based analysis can be used to make decisions about the levels and types of control, the processes and mechanisms used to implement that control, and the number of levels of control authority that are appropriate for each software configuration item. These configuration control decisions should be documented as part of each project's software configuration management (SCM) plans.

The basic trade-off trilogy between cost, schedule (cycle time), and the integrity of the software product exists for the configuration control decisions just like it does for software project management. If the rigor and formality of the configuration control process is increased in order to increase the integrity of the software product, this typically also increases the costs and cycle time for making change. When analyzing these trade-offs, consideration should be given to the total lifetime of the software product, including:

- Initial development costs and schedules for delivering the required product functionality, quality, reliability, safety, security, and so on

- Corrective, adaptive, preventive, and perfective maintenance costs and schedules

- Operational costs of the software product in the field such as training people to use the software, as well as the cost of using it

- Internal and external failure costs and other impacts if the software has problems

Configuration status accounting is the record-keeping activity within SCM. It provides management, software practitioners, and other stakeholders with the information they need to:

- Appropriately manage the configuration items and baselines

- Track the status of configuration items and baselines

- Perform informed change request impact analysis

- Effectively and efficiently track approved changes to resolution and verify those changes

- Ensure that unauthorized changes are not occurring

- Produce version description documentation (release notes)
- Evaluate the integrity of the software products and the effectiveness of the implementation of SCM practices
- Analyze and improve the software processes, products, and services

1. ITEM, BASELINE, AND VERSION CONTROL

Describe processes for documentation control, tracking item changes, version control, etc., that are used to manage various configurations, and describe processes used to manage configuration item dependencies in software builds and versioning. (Understand)

Body of Knowledge VII.C.1

Chapter 27, "Configuration Identification," talked about three different levels of control: uncontrolled software artifacts, quality records, and configuration items. Of these three levels, only configuration items are placed under configuration control. As illustrated in Figure 28.1, there are two types of control for these configuration items: change control and document control.

Change Control

Change control is the more rigorous level of configuration control and therefore provides a higher level of stability for configuration items controlled at that level.

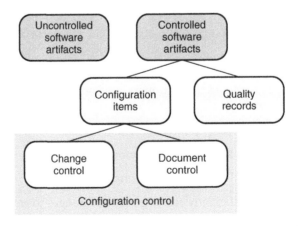

Figure 28.1   Types of software configuration control.

Change control proactively manages changes by reviewing each proposed change before it is implemented and allowing only authorized changes to be made to the configuration items. Higher-risk configuration items are typically placed under this level of control. Examples of configuration items that are typically controlled through change control include requirements, interface, and design specifications, and source code.

Figure 28.2 illustrates the change control process. When an author is assigned to create a new configuration item, that author can make any changes necessary to create and update that product as it is being created and verified (for example, peer reviewed and, in the case of source code, unit tested depending on the acquisition point). At some point, however, that configuration item is acquired (baselined for internal use) and placed under configuration control. As that configuration item is being used internally, including additional verification and validation, or as it is used in operations, problems or enhancements may be identified. The change control process requires that each of these problems or enhancements that require change to baselined configuration items be formally documented in a change request and that the appropriate configuration control board (CCB) review that request and determine its disposition. If the CCB defers the change request to a later time, the change request goes into a wait state and comes back to the CCB for additional review at the designated time. If the CCB disapproves the change request, the CCB communicates the reasons for that disapproval to the appropriate parties. If the CCB approves the change request, one or more authors are assigned

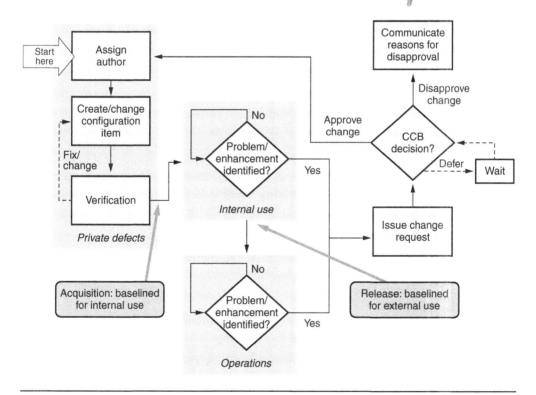

Figure 28.2 Change control process.

to make the changes to the configuration items impacted by the requested change. The authors can update their assigned configuration items as needed to implement the approved change. However, if while they are implementing the approved change, another defect or enhancement is identified, that new defect or enhancement must be documented in another change request that goes back through the change control process.

Document Control

Document control is a less rigorous level of configuration control than change control and can therefore be used for less risky configuration items. Lower-risk configuration items are typically placed under this level of control. Examples of configuration items that are typically controlled through document control include plans (project, software quality assurance, verification and validation, test, SCM), test cases and test procedures, project-specific process and work instruction documentation, release notes, and training materials. Notice that not all documents are controlled at the document level. For example, as mentioned previously, requirements, interface, and design specifications are typically controlled using change control.

As illustrated in Figure 28.3, after the initial version of the configuration item is acquired and placed under document control, all subsequent changes are made to a draft (for example, non-released or preliminary) version of the configuration item. That updated draft must go through a review cycle and be formally approved by the appropriate level of CCB before it is released for use. Once an updated version of the configuration item is released for use, procedures should be in place to ensure that obsolete versions of the configuration item are removed from use. If the obsolete versions must remain available for reference, then they should be clearly marked to indicate that they are not the most current versions of the configuration item. The document control process is more reactive in managing change than the more formal change control process because it reviews the changed configuration items after the changes are implemented in draft form. Document control, however, allows for more flexibility because multiple changes can be made to the same draft and all of those changes are approved together as a set when the draft document is approved. Document control also allows problems or enhancements found while making other changes to be implemented in the same draft without going through an additional approval cycle first.

As mentioned earlier, the trade-off between cost, schedule (cycle time), and the integrity of the software product should be considered when making configuration control decisions. An organization can increase the rigor and formality of the configuration control process in order to increase the integrity of the software product; however, this typically also increases the costs and cycle time for making change.

When considering these trade-offs, the organization should consider the total lifetime of the product, including:

- Requirements for product quality, reliability, safety, security, and so on

- Initial development costs and schedules

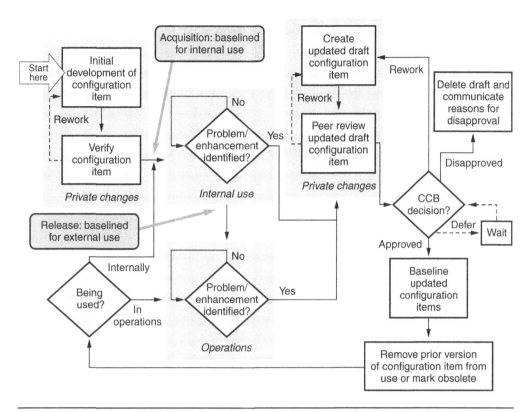

Figure 28.3 Document control process.

- Corrective, adaptive, preventive, and perfective maintenance costs and schedules

- Operational costs and overall costs of ownership

- Internal and external failure costs and other impacts

Many a software company has focused on just optimizing the initial software development to the long-term detriment of the software products and processes.

Tracking Item Changes

Different mechanisms can be used to place configuration items under control and for requesting and tracking changes to those items. At their simplest, these mechanisms can be completely manual. For example, as illustrated in Figure 28.4, if a configuration item is being controlled manually, the change made to each version or revision of the document might be manually documented in a change history section of the configuration item (or in a separate, related change history document). The configuration item itself may be controlled using manual directories. First by moving the item being changed from a manually controlled directory into the author's personal dynamic library while it is being changed, verified, and

Part VII.C.1

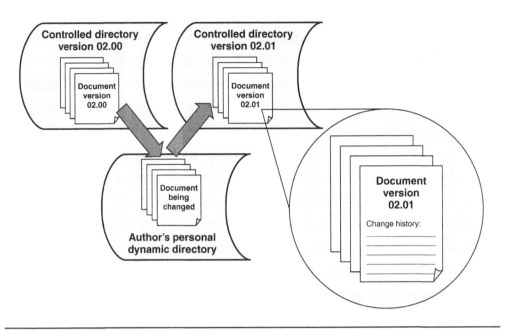

Figure 28.4   Manual tracking of item changes.

approved. Then by moving it back into another (or the same) manually controlled directory while manually marking it with the updated version/revision.

More-complex mechanisms used to place configuration items under control and for requesting and tracking changes to those items can include automated version control and change management tools. Change management tools can allow for the recording and reporting of the change request from origination through screening, impact analysis, CCB disposition, and the correction and verification of approved changes. Depending on the degree of integration with the version control tool, the change management tool can either include fields that point to configuration items and their version being updated to implement approved changes or there can be a sharing of information and links between these tools. These tools can also provide controls that help ensure that unauthorized changes do not occur. For example, the version control tool might include a required field for either the requirement identifier or change request identifier when a new version of a baselined configuration item is being checked into the tool.

Version Control

A *version* of a configuration item, component, or unit has a defined set of functionality. For example, there may be a version of a software executable that is being created to add two new features to the software product. To implement these two new features may require new versions of multiple lower-level configuration items, components, or units, for example, a new requirements specification, an updated architecture, several updated or new detailed designs and software source code modules, new test cases, or an updated user manual.

As these new or updated configuration items, components, and units go through the development process, each of them may have multiple revisions. A *revision* makes changes to the configuration item to correct defects without affecting functionality. For example, assume that a new version of source code module ABC is updated from the previous version to implement part of a new feature. After this new version of module ABC is acquired, a defect is found during integration testing. A new revision of this version of module ABC is created to correct this defect. If a second defect is found later in integration or system testing, a second revision of this version of module ABC is created, and so on, with a new revision being created for each subsequent correction (or set of corrections done at the same time). As illustrated in Figure 27.8, page 510, similar revision can occur to a version of the software build as it is rebuilt throughout the development life cycle as defects are found and corrected.

A release is the promotion of a version of a configuration item for distribution outside development for use in operations by the end users. A *version description document* (VDD), also called *release notes*, is created to describe the release and its contents, including the changes (new features or defect corrections) made since the last release and a list of any known issues with the release and their workarounds.

Configuration Item Dependencies

The real benefit of version control comes from maintaining the dependencies between versions/revisions of higher-level configuration items and the associated versions/revisions of lower-level configuration items, components, and units used to create or describe them. For example, as illustrated in Figure 28.5, each version/revision of each configuration item, component, and unit has dependencies with the version/revisions of the requirements, architectural design, and detailed design specifications that describe its physical and functional characteristics and with the test cases, procedures, and scripts used to test it. Each software build has dependencies with the version/revisions of the:

- Requirements, architectural design, and detailed design specifications that describe its physical and functional characteristics

- Configuration items, components, and/or units used to build it

- Tools, macros, libraries, and platform used to assemble/compile those configuration items, components, and/or units and to create the build

- Test cases, procedures, and scripts used to test it

- User documentation (for example, user manuals, operation manuals, help files, version description documents, installation instructions) used to support it in operations

- Target platforms and environments it is targeted to run on

All of these dependencies should be considered when analyzing the impact of a requested change and implementing that change. Changes to these dependencies must be documented when approved changes are implemented.

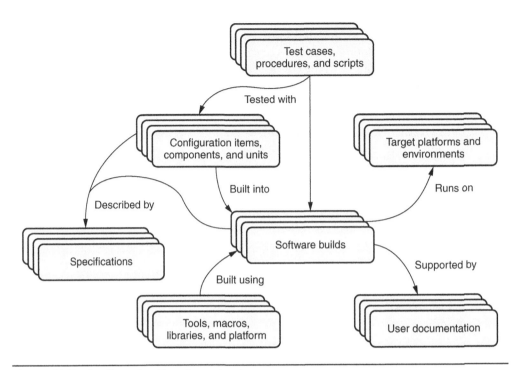

Figure 28.5 Configuration item dependencies.

2. CONFIGURATION CONTROL BOARD (CCB)

> Describe the roles and responsibilities of the
> CCB and its members and the procedures
> they use. (Understand)
>
> **Body of Knowledge VII.C.2**

Configuration control boards (CCBs), also called *change control boards* (CCBs), *change authority boards* (CABs), or *engineering change boards* (ECBs), are the formal change authorities that make decisions on configuration control issues. CCBs provide the authority for approving/differing/disapproving changes to configuration items and baselines. They provide visibility into the configuration control processes and ensure communication with impacted stakeholders. Multiple levels of CCBs may exist for a project. However, at any specific time, each configuration item or baseline has a single CCB assigned as its owner. As changes are requested, the CCB with ownership for the impacted entities ensures that the stakeholders impacted by those changes are informed of the requests and have an opportunity to provide input into the impact analysis. Based on the impact analysis, the CCB then makes a decision about the disposition of the requested change (accept, reject, or defer) and informs the impacted stakeholders of their decision. For approved changes, the owning CCB facilitates resource allocation to the effort of implementing and verifying the changes. The CCB also provides a vehicle for ensuring that requested changes are tracked to resolution and ensuring that unauthorized changes are not occurring. At any given CCB meeting, multiple change requests may be reviewed, analyzed for impact, dispositioned, tracked, or resolved. By performing these activities, CCBs play an integral role in keeping the software development process under control.

CCB Member Roles and Responsibilities

In addition to the responsibilities of the CCB as a team, individual members of the CCB perform special CCB roles including CCB leader, CCB members, CCB screener, and CCB recorder. In the case where a single individual acts as the entire CCB, that individual is responsible for all of these roles and their responsibilities.

The CCB *leader* (chair) is responsible for planning and leading the CCB meetings. This includes handling logistics, setting priorities, making assignments, and performing other leadership activities. The CCB leader is typically responsible for escalating change requests and other issues to a higher-level CCB or management as necessary.

Individual CCB *members* are responsible for representing their constituency groups in the CCB meetings. This includes ensuring that their groups are informed of change requests and the CCB's disposition of those requests. The members act as their group's voice in impact analysis discussion and other decisions. Members may also be responsible for tracking approved changes assigned to their groups, for reporting their status back to the CCB, and for ensuring that those changes are implemented and verified.

CCB *screener* is an optional role that is responsible for reviewing submitted change requests (or changed documents) and checking their correctness and completeness prior to CCB review. This can help increase the efficiency and effectiveness of the CCB meetings by ensuring that the CCB has adequate information to work from. This can also aid in the timely disposition of change requests. For example, if the CCB only meets weekly and rejects a change request because more information is needed from its originator, it will be another week before the request will be reconsidered.

The CCB *recorder* is the record keeper for the CCB. The recorder is responsible for recording/distributing the CCB minutes. The recorder may also be responsible for recording CCB information in change request records (for example, CCB dispositions, CCB updates to change request priorities or problem severities, impact analysis information, and implementation assignments).

How a CCB conducts its business can vary widely. For example, depending on the CCB charter, CCB members may have voting privileges or may be required to come to consensus on CCB decisions. In other cases the CCB leader may be the final decision-making authority with input from the CCB members. Also, depending on its charter, the scope of the CCB's decision-making authority may vary from being limited to a single software component to encompassing the entire system.

CCBs may meet on a periodic basis (for example, daily during the system test cycle) or on an as needed basis (for example, after product release, the leader may only call a meeting when one or more changes are requested). These and other decisions about the conduct of each CCB should be determined based on multiple factors including management structure, customer requirements, and risk.

CCB Process: Change Control

Figure 28.6 illustrates a typical process for requesting, dispositioning, and resolving a requested change to a configuration item under change control. The actual steps in the process for any given project should be defined and documented in (or pointed to by) the project's SCM plans.

Step 1: The individual requesting the change submits a formal change request for CCB review and disposition. This can be accomplished through multiple techniques, for example, through the completion and submission of a hard-copy change request form or through opening and submitting a change request in the change management tool. A requested change may be submitted to correct an identified problem (defect, problem, anomaly, or issue report) or to request the implementation of one or more new or changed requirements (enhancement request).

Step 2: Optionally, the CCB has someone assigned as a screener to perform an initial review of the requested change. If the change request has been inadequately completed (for example, required fields were left blank or the description of the change does not include enough detail), the screener sends the change request

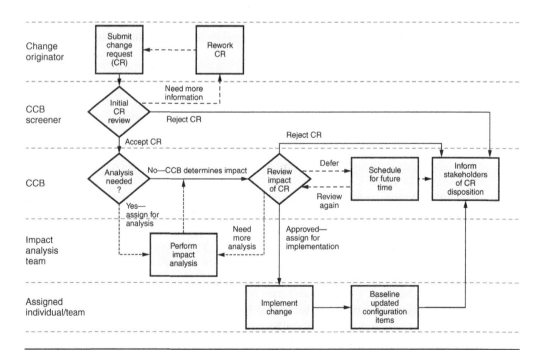

Figure 28.6   Configuration control board processes for change control.

back to its originator with a description of the additional information needed. The screener may also have the authority to reject certain types of change requests (for example, ones that are the result of operator error or that are duplicates of other requests). If the change request is rejected, the appropriate stakeholders, including the originator of the change request, are informed of the reasons for rejection. If the change request passed screening, it is assigned to a CCB meeting. In the case of critical change requests, the screener may request the convening of a special CCB meeting.

Step 3: During the CCB meeting, the CCB reviews each requested change and decides if they have the appropriate people in the meeting and adequate information to review the impact of the requested change. If not, the change request may be assigned to an impact analysis team for further investigation. This team analyzes the impact of the requested change and contacts affected stakeholders to elicit opinions and additional information as needed. The impact analysis team reports their findings back to the CCB at a future CCB meeting.

Step 4: The CCB reviews the impact of each change request by either analyzing the change request themselves and/or reviewing the report from the impact analysis team. If the CCB needs more information, the change request is sent back to the impact analysis team with a description of the additional information needed. Once they have adequate information, the CCB decides on the disposition of the change request. If the change request is deferred, it is scheduled for a future version of the product and will come back to the CCB for review as part of that version. If the change request is deferred or rejected, the appropriate stakeholders, including the originator of the change request, are informed of the reasons for deferral or rejection.

Step 5: If the change request is approved, it is assigned to one or more individuals or teams to incorporate the requested change into the appropriate configuration items, and then to verify those changes. After that change has been implemented and verified, baselines are updated for any modified configuration items.

CCB Process: Document Control

Figure 28.7 illustrates a typical process for requesting, dispositioning, and resolving a requested change to a configuration item under document control. Again, the actual steps in the process for any given project should be defined and documented in (or pointed to by) the project's SCM plans.

Step 1: After one or more changes have been incorporated into a draft version of a configuration item under document control and verified, the updated configuration item is submitted for CCB review and disposition. These changes may correct one or more identified defects and/or implement one or more new or changed requirements (enhancements). The changes should be adequately documented (for example, in a change history or through redlining of the configuration item) so that the CCB can quickly identify the requested changes.

Step 2: Optionally, the CCB has someone assigned as a screener to perform an initial review of the updated configuration item. If the screener identifies defects or other issues, the screener can send the configuration item back to the originator

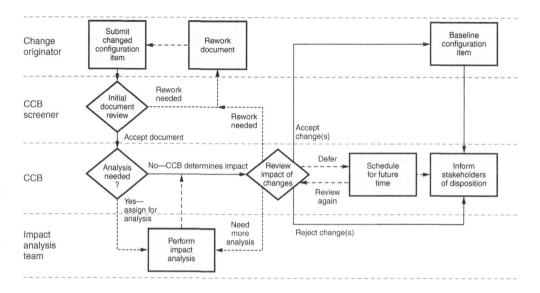

Figure 28.7 Configuration control board processes for document control.

for rework. If the configuration item passed screening, it is assigned to a CCB meeting. In the case of critical configuration items, the screener may request the convening of a special CCB meeting.

Step 3: During the CCB meeting, the CCB reviews each updated configuration item and decides if they have the appropriate people in the meeting and adequate information to review the impact of the implemented changes. If not, that configuration item is assigned to an impact analysis team for further investigation. This team analyzes the impact of the implemented changes and contacts affected stakeholders to elicit opinions and additional information as needed. This team then reports their findings back to the CCB at a future CCB meeting.

Step 4: The CCB reviews the impacts to each updated configuration item by either analyzing the updated configuration items themselves and/or reviewing the report from the impact analysis team. If the CCB needs more information, the configuration item is sent back to the impact analysis team with a description of the additional information needed. Once they have adequate information, the CCB decides on the disposition of the updated configuration item. The CCB can send the changed configuration item back to the change originator for rework, accept or reject the change(s), or defer the change(s) to a later time. If the change(s) are deferred, the document is rescheduled for CCB review at a future date. The appropriate stakeholders, including the originator of the change request, are informed of the configuration item's disposition.

Step 5: If the changed configuration item is approved, baselines are updated for that configuration item.

Impact Analysis

When analyzing the impact of a change, multiple factors should be considered, including factors beyond the scope of the immediate project. This is particularly true since the change could impact an item that is reused in multiple products. Factors to consider during impact analysis include:

- *Size and breadth of the change.*

  - Number of configuration items, components, or units touched by the change

  - Number of software products and/or versions of a software product that include those configuration items, components, or units

  - Number of new/changed/deleted function points, lines of code, requirements, or pages of documentation

- *Complexity of the change.* Number and complexity of new/changed/ deleted configuration items, components, or units required to implement the change

- *Severity of the change.* What is the impact of this change on the customer? If the change is required to fix a defect, how critical is the impact of the defect on the functioning of the software or system?

- *Schedule impacts.*

  - New tasks added to the schedule to implement the change and their estimated duration

  - Impacts on other tasks or dependencies

  - Overall impact to duration of the critical path

  - Availability of people and other resources to implement the change

- *Cost impacts.* Potential costs or savings from making the change

- *Effort impacts.* Estimated effort to implement the change

- *Technical impacts.*

  - The change's impact on the functionality of the software

  - Future product consequences of the change (for example, quality, maintainability, reliability, performance, security, safety, portability, efficiency)

  - Critical computer resource impacts (for example, memory, channel capacity)

- *Relationships to other changes.*

  - Supersede or eliminate need for other changes

  - Dependencies on other changes

  - Economies of packaging the changes with other previously approved changes to the same work products

- *Testing requirements.*

- Number of new/changed/deleted test cases required

- Regression testing requirements

- Special testing resource requirements (for example, test beds or simulators)

- *Benefits.* Special advantages to be gained from adding this change (for example, political, marketplace advantage, or customer satisfaction benefits)

When assessing the size and breadth of the change, bidirectional traceability plays a major role. If a change is requested because of a change in the business or user environment (for example, a business objective, stakeholder requirement, or standard has changed), then if good forward traceability has been maintained, that change can be traced forward to the associated requirements and all of the configuration items, components, and units that are impacted by that change. This greatly reduces the amount of effort required to do a thorough job of impact analysis. It also reduces the risk that one of the affected work products is forgotten, resulting in an incomplete implementation of the change and a defect being introduced.

Backward traceability is beneficial when a defect is identified in one of the work products. For example, as illustrated in Figure 28.8, if the code unit XYZ has a defect, the traceability matrix can be used to help determine the root cause of that defect. In this example, it is not just a code defect, the defect also traces back to a defect in the associated design and requirement.

If design and/or requirements defects are discovered during this analysis, what other work products might be impacted by the defect? (One more time back to forward traceability to ensure a complete analysis.) Figure 28.9 continues this example by illustrating the use of this forward traceability analysis. In this example, the defective requirements traced forward to two additional design elements Y, which had the defect, and Z, which did not. The requirements also traced forward to two training models, one of which had the defect. Tracing from the two design elements X and Y with defects also uncovered two additional source code units X02 and Y02 that had defects.

Multiple Levels of CCBs

As a configuration item moves through the software development life cycle, the balance between the need for flexibility and stability typically shifts. For example, when a source code module is first created, the developer requires a high level of flexibility to experiment, create, and perfect that module. Since the module has not been acquired and no one else is using it, the need for stability is nil. As that source code module moves through the life cycle and is integrated into larger and larger system components and/or is used by more and more stakeholders, the need for more rigorous control and communications (stability) increases.

One mechanism for addressing this need to shift the balance from more flexible to more stable as a configuration item moves through the life cycle is to

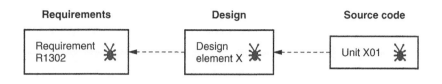

Figure 28.8   Using backward traceability for defect analysis—example.

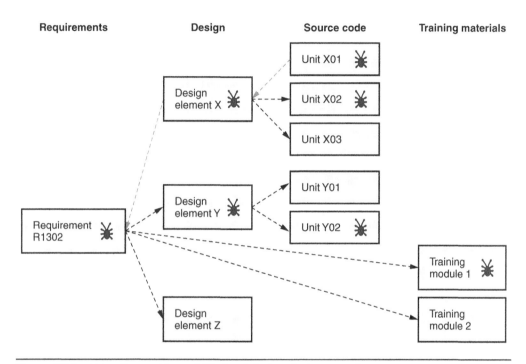

Figure 28.9   Using forward traceability for defect analysis—example.

create multiple levels of CCBs. Having multiple levels of CCBs allows small changes of limited scope and impact to be approved at lower levels of authority while major changes that impact multiple stakeholders or multiple work products can be escalated to higher-level CCBs that have broader scope and involve all affected parties.

To continue the source code module example, as illustrated in Figure 28.10, the developer can change a newly created source code module as necessary. When it is initially acquired, a team-level CCB could be assigned change control authority for that module because typically only team members need to be consulted when the code changes at that level. As illustrated in Figure 28.11, the membership of the team-level CCB might be limited to only the software architect/designer and the software engineers on the team. Since this CCB has limited members who work closely together, they can usually meet and make decisions quickly.

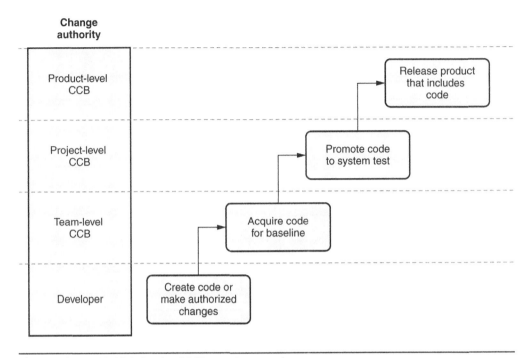

Figure 28.10 Multiple levels of CCBs–code example.

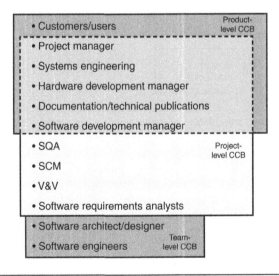

Figure 28.11 Membership of multiple levels of CCBs.

Once system testing starts, the source code module is promoted to the project-level CCB (see Figure 28.10). Changes to that source code module at this phase of the life cycle may impact software written by other teams, the hardware, and/or the documentation, as well as the work of the testers, software configuration management, software quality assurance, and other specialists. Changes this late in the life cycle may also impact project schedules, costs, effort, and risks. The membership in the project-level CCB expands to include representatives from the various stakeholders that may be impacted (see Figure 28.9). In this example, the individual team architect/designer and software engineers are not members of the project-level CCB but may be called on to participate in CCB activities as subject matter experts if their software designs or code are impacted by the requested changes.

Finally, when the product from this example is released into production, the source code module is promoted to the product-level CCB, along with all of the other configuration items that become part of the product baseline (see Figure 28.10). Again, the membership of the CCB changes to include the customer/user representative and management-level personnel who are making business decisions about the longer-term direction of the product (see Figure 28.11). CCB meetings at this level typically happen much less frequently, however, and to attempt to control lower-level products early in their life cycle with this level of CCB would add an extreme time burden that would probably grind software development to a halt.

Not every configuration item needs to start at the same level of CCB. Higher-risk configuration items should be assigned to higher-level CCBs when they are acquired. For example, as illustrated in Figure 28.12, the software requirements specification (SRS) for this project could go directly under the control of the project-level CCB when it is acquired because of the wider impact that changes to requirements may have across the project. The SRS is promoted to the product-level CCB along with all of the other configuration items that become part of the product baseline when the product is released into production.

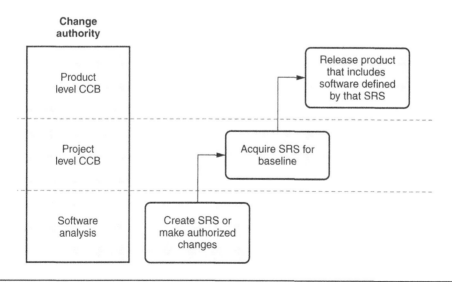

Figure 28.12   Multiple levels of CCBs—software requirements specification (SRS) example.

The project's SCM plans should define the promotion points and associated quality gates for each type of identified configuration item, as well as the formal change authority that owns the configuration item at each level of acquisition/ promotion.

3. CONCURRENT DEVELOPMENT

> Describe the use of configuration management control principles in concurrent development processes. (Understand)
>
> **Body of Knowledge VII.C.3**

Concurrent development occurs when two or more versions of a software product are in development and/or are being supported as releases in operations at the same time. The SCM processes of check-in, check-out, labeling, branching, and merging all support the configuration control of concurrent development.

To illustrate the use of these processes in supporting concurrent development, let's walk through an example. In this example, Figure 28.13 depicts the evolution graph for a software product that is currently undergoing concurrent development. Assume a decision was made to use incremental development for each major release of the product. Version 1.0.0 might represent the first incremental version of the product. As development progresses, Version 1.0.0 moves into testing, and the next increment, Version 1.1.0, starts development. As Version 1.0.0 is released, Version 1.1.0 transitions into testing, and development starts on the third increment, Version 1.2.0. After the release of Version 1.1.0, a problem is discovered

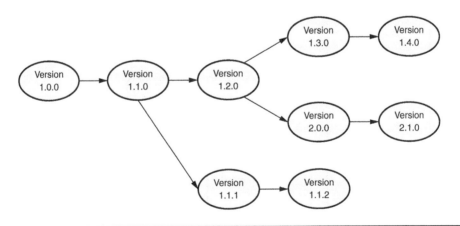

Figure 28.13   Software product evolution graph—example.

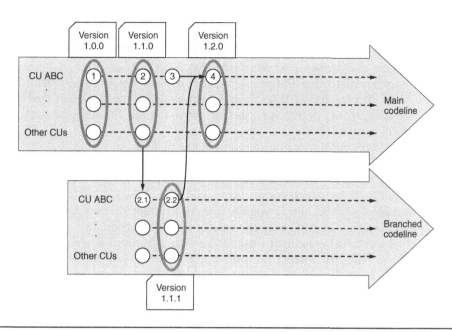

Figure 28.14   Software unit versioning–example 1.

in that version. The problem is fixed in the corrective release Version 1.1.1, and that fix is merged into Version 1.2.0, which is still in development.

Figure 28.14 demonstrates how an individual configuration unit ABC might be affected by this example. The initial controlled Version 1 of ABC was checked in to the main codeline when it was acquired, and later labeled as part of Version 1.0.0 of the software product when that product was released. Version 1 of ABC was checked out, new functionality was added to it, and it was checked in as Version 2. Version 2 of ABC was checked out, new functionality was added to it as part of the development of Version 1.2.0 of the product, and it was checked in as Version 3 of ABC. Version 2 of ABC was labeled as part of Version 1.1.0 of the software product when it was released. The problem discovered in the released product Version 1.1.0 was debugged and it was determined that this problem originated in Version 2 of ABC. In order to correct this problem, the codeline was branched, and Version 2.1 of ABC was created, and the problem was fixed in Version 2.2 of ABC. After testing, Version 2.2 of ABC was labeled as part of product Version 1.1.1 when it was released. It was also determined that the defect also existed in Version 3 of ABC, so Version 4 of ABC was created by merging the fix from Version 2.2 of ABC into Version 3 of ABC. It should be noted that the branched codeline is created for the corrective release. The expectation is that this branch will eventually be retired (terminated) when this release is no longer supported in operations. Ongoing development continues as part of the main codeline, with branches being as temporary as possible.

To continue with the example, as Version 1.2.0 moves on to testing and becomes stable, a decision is made to not only use Version 1.2.0 as the basis for incremental

Version 1.3.0 but also as the basis to start the first increment of the next major release, Version 2.0.0. A problem is found in Version 2.0.0 that was introduced and fixed in that version. Another problem is also discovered in Version 1.1.1 and it is determined that the problem originated in Version 1.1.0 but didn't get propagated into version 1.2.0 because the problem area was overwritten by new code that was created in that version. Corrective release Version 1.1.2 is created to fix this problem.

Figure 28.15 continues the demonstration of how an individual configuration unit ABC might be affected by this decision and these problems. In order to use Version 1.2.0 as a basis for both the incremental Version 1.3.0 and the new major Version 2.0.0, the codeline was branched, and Version 4.1 of ABC was created from Version 4 of ABC and labeled as part of product Version 1.3.0 when it was released. Version 4 of ABC was checked out, new functionality was added to it as part of the development of product Version 2.0.0, and it was checked in as Version 5 of ABC. To correct the problem that was found during Version 2.0.0

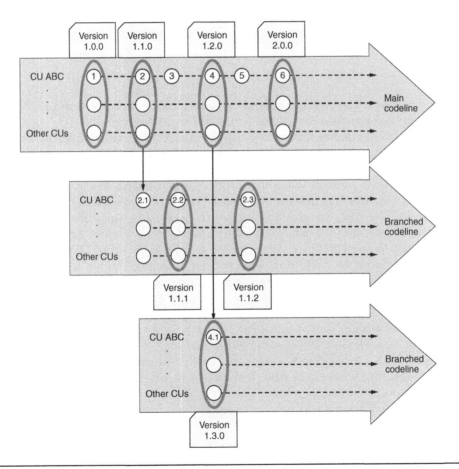

Figure 28.15 Software unit versioning—example 2.

development, Version 5 of ABC was checked out and that problem was corrected, and a new Version 6 of ABC was checked in. Version 6 of ABC was later labeled as part of product Version 2.0.0 when it was released. To correct the problem that was isolated to Version 1.1.1, Version 2.2 of ABC was checked out, corrected, and checked back in as version 2.3 of ABC. Version 2.3 of ABC was labeled as part of the corrective release of product Version 1.1.2 when it was released.

As development continues to progress, new functionality is added to Version 1.3.0 to create the new incremental product Version 1.4.0. The latest change to the product in development was to merge the changes from product Versions 1.3.0 and 1.4.0 into Version 2.0.0 to create the next increment of the product, Version 2.1.0. Figure 28.16 demonstrates how the individual configuration unit ABC might be affected by these changes. Version 4.1 of ABC was checked out, new functionality was added to it as part of the development of product Version 1.4.0, and it was checked in as Version 4.2 of ABC. Version 4.2 of ABC was labeled as part of product Version 1.4.0 when that product build was done and it moved into

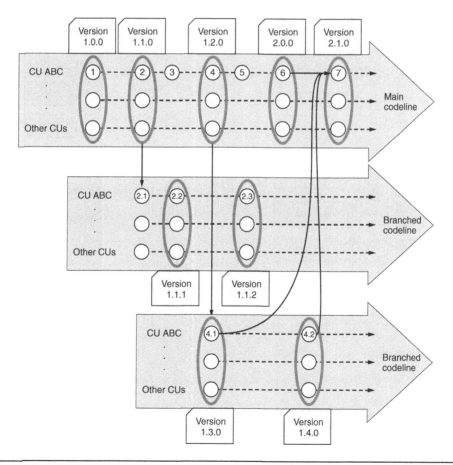

Figure 28.16   Software unit versioning—example 3.

Part VII.C.3

testing. Changes from Versions 4.1 and 4.2 of ABC were merged with Version 6 of ABC to create Version 7 of ABC, which was checked in. Version 7 of ABC was labeled as part of product Version 2.1.0 when that product build was done and it moved into testing.

Another major consideration of concurrent development and supporting concurrent releases in the field is the need to perform more extensive impact analysis when changes are requested. For example, assume that all of the released versions of the software product from Figure 28.16 are still being used by one or more end users in operations, except for Versions 1.4.0 and 2.1.0, which are still in concurrent development. The left side of Figure 28.17 illustrates the "build into" relationships between the versions of configuration unit ABC and the versions of the product. A problem (bug) is reported from operations by an end user that is currently using Version 1.2.0. Performing the initial debugging and impact analysis determines that this problem is the result of a defect in Version 4 of ABC. Since there are concurrent releases and development, impact analysis must be

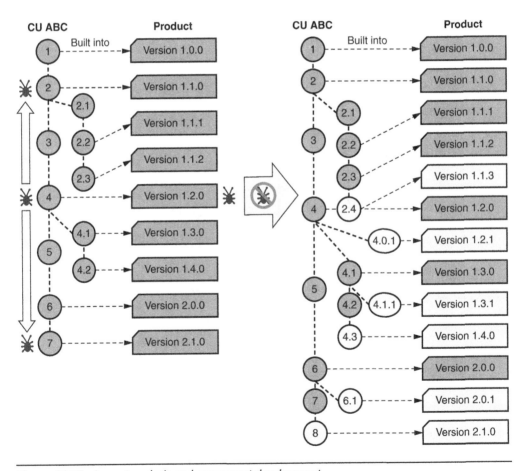

Figure 28.17 Impact analysis and concurrent development.

performed to determine which version of ABC originated the defect (in this example it originated in Version 2 of ABC) and if it exists in any subsequent versions (in this example it exists in all versions through Version 7 of ABC). Therefore, the defect impacts all product versions from 1.1.0 through 2.1.0. Assuming that the CCB determines that the defect is a serious enough problem to require corrective releases, a branch would be created for corrective Version 1.2.1, and Version 4.1 would be checked out, the defect corrected, and checked in to the new branch as version 4.0.1 (note that the version numbering used here and elsewhere in this example will depend on the version numbering schema being implemented). As illustrated on the right side of Figure 28.17, this correction would be merged into Versions 2.3, 4.1, 4.2, 6, and 7 of ABC to create corrected Versions 2.4, 4.1.1, 4.3, 6.1, and 8 of ABC, respectively. These updated versions of ABC would then be built into corrective releases of the product in Versions 1.1.3, 1.2.1, 1.3.1, and 2.0.1. The updates would also be built into updated revisions of the product in Versions 1.4.0 and 2.1.0 currently in test.

To further complicate this example, let's assume that a new version of the compiler was introduced between product Versions 1.1.0 and 1.2.0 and that a new version of the operating system is being used for major release Version 2.0.0 and its increments. This complication is the reason why software development tools should be considered as configuration items. The prior version of the compiler would be needed to build product Version 1.1.3, and the prior version of the operating system would be needed to both build and test product Versions 1.1.3, 1.2.1, 1.3.1, and 1.4.0. Again, these considerations should be included in the impact analysis.

Finally, to extend the complexity of the impact analysis even further, consider the fact that configuration unit ABC might be reused in multiple products, each of which have multiple releases being supported in operations and/or multiple versions in concurrent development. This simple example demonstrates why a good SCM tool that automates the identification, branching, and merging functions is essential for most software development projects.

4. STATUS ACCOUNTING

> Discuss various processes for establishing, maintaining, and reporting the status of configuration items. (Understand)
>
> **Body of Knowledge VII.C.4**

Configuration status accounting is the SCM activity that involves the recording and reporting of data and information needed to manage the software configuration. It includes data collection and recording activities and report-generation activities.

Data Collection and Recording

The configuration status accounting data is collected and recorded while performing the other SCM, software development, testing, and release management activities. For example, the originator typically collects the following change request information when a change request is created and records this information in the change management tool (or on a change request form):

- Change request identifier
- Summary
- Originator of the CR and their contact information
- Severity/priority
- Creation date
- Product/version reported against
- Detailed description
  - For enhancement requests include a requirements statement
  - For problem reports provide a description of the problem including:
    - Inputs
    - Steps to reproduce
    - Expected results
    - Environment
    - Actual results
    - Attempts to repeat
    - Anomalies
    - Phase detected
    - Occurence date and time
    - Tester/user and observer(s)

Additional information about the change request is collected and recorded as that change request progresses through the change request process. For example, as the change request is reviewed by the CCB its impact analysis information, implementation priority, and CCB disposition (approved, rejected, or deferred) are collected and recorded. For deferred change requests, the deferral data or target release may also be collected and recorded. For change requests approved by the CCB, the software practitioner(s) assigned to implement the change collect and record:

- Its resolution description
- Effort to debug and implement the change

- A list of (or links to) the configuration items, components, or units modified to implement the change

For problem reports, the software practitioner might also record the problem's work-around and root cause information (for example, the phase in which the problem was introduced and the type of problem). As the change is incorporated into one or more software builds, those build identifiers are collected and recorded. As the change is tested, the effort to test and the pass/fail status for each level of testing for each build is collected and recorded. As the change request passes through the change request process, its history may also be recorded, including dates and times of data modifications or status changes, what was modified/changed, and who made each modification/change.

The types of status accounting data being collected depend on the information needs of the organization and its projects. Other examples of SCM data include:

- *Configuration item metadata* (for example, current author, current approval authority, approved versions, associated change request status, implementation status for approved changes) collected when configuration items are checked in/out of control libraries, when branches or labels are created, or when merges are performed

- *Build metadata* (for example, build dates, versions/revisions of build contents, versions/revisions of tools and their options used to create the build) collected when builds are created

- *Baseline metadata* (for example, baseline dates, versions/revisions of baseline contents, authority that approved the baseline) collected when baselines are created or changed

- *Configuration item dependencies and interrelationship data* (see Figures 28.5, 28.16, and 28.17) collected when baselines are created or changed

- *Release management data* (for example, release dates and product warranty/ licensing data) collected when products are released

- *Configuration management deviations and waivers data* collected when deviations and waivers are created, processed, and approved

- *Software configuration management–related project data* (for example, effort, cost, schedule, and cycle time data) collected as part of project execution and tracking

- *Site installation history data* (for example, what release(s) were installed on each site on what date, and site configuration history data) collected as new/updated releases are installed or as site configurations are installed/updated

According to the IEEE *Standard for Software Configuration Management Plans* (IEEE 2005), the SCM plan "should include information on the following:

- What data elements and SCM metrics are to be tracked and reported for baselines and changes

- What types of status accounting reports are to be generated and their frequency

- How information is to be collected, stored, processed, reported, and protected from loss

- How access to the status data is to be controlled"

The configuration status accounting data can be collected and recorded manually (for example, in the change history of a document, in a build report, on a site installation form, or even in a spreadsheet containing a bidirectional traceability matrix). Configuration status accounting data can be automated through the use of various tools and databases (for example, the library and version control tools, build tools. change management tools, or the project management tools).

Status Reporting

Configuration status reporting should include both standardized reports and metrics and the ability to create ad hoc queries of the configuration status accounting data to extract additional information as needed. Depending on the requirements of the organization and/or project and the resulting types of configuration data being collected, a configuration status accounting system should be able to provide answers to questions including:

- How many configuration items, components, and units exist?

- What is the status of each version/revision of each configuration item, component, and unit at any specific time?

- Which version/revisions of which configuration units constitute a specific version of each configuration component, and which version/ revisions of which configuration components/units constitute a specific version of each configuration item?

- How do the versions/revisions of each configuration item, component, and unit differ?

- Which versions of which products are affected by a given configuration item, component, or unit revision?

- What documents support each version of each configuration item/ component/unit?

- What hardware and/or software dependencies exist for each configuration item/component/unit?

- What are the contents of each baseline, and when was that baseline created?

- What tools and options/switches within those tools were used to create each build?

- Which releases of which products are installed at which sites, and what is the installation history of each site?

- Which configuration item, component, unit versions/revisions are affected by a specific change request?

- What is the impact and status of each change request?

- How many product problems were reported/fixed in each version of each build/release?

Chapter 29

D. Configuration Audits

> Define and distinguish between functional
> and physical configuration audits and
> how they are used in relation to product
> specifications. (Understand)
>
> **Body of Knowledge VII.D**

Software configuration management (SCM) audits provide independent, objective assurance that the SCM processes are being complied with, that the software configuration items are being built as required, and, at production, that the software products are ready to be released. Using standardized checklists, tailored to the specifics of each project, for these SCM audits can make them more effective, efficient, and consistent, as well as aiding in continual process improvement. Three types of SCM audits are typically performed:

- *Functional configuration audit (FCA).* An independent evaluation of the completed software products to determine their conformance to their requirements specification(s) in terms of completeness, performance, and functional characteristics.

- *Physical configuration audit (PCA).* An independent evaluation of each configuration item to determine its conformance to the technical documentation that defines it.

- *In-process SCM audits.* Ongoing independent evaluations conducted throughout the life cycle to provide information about compliance to SCM policies, plans, processes, and systems, about the effectiveness of the SCM practices, and about the conformance of configuration items to their requirements and workmanship standards.

According to the IEEE *Standard for Software Configuration Management Plans* (IEEE 2005), the SCM plans for the performance of SCM audits should include objectives, the configuration items under audit, schedules, procedures for conducting the audits and for recording deficiencies, audit participants, required documentation that needs to be available to support the audit, and approval criteria. The audit plan may also include activities, responsibilities, and resource allocations.

Functional and physical configuration audits are covered in this chapter. In-process SCM audits are simply a specific type of process audit. Audits, including process audits, are discussed in Chapter 8, "Audits." Examples of in-process SCM audits include auditing the:

- Software configuration management practices against the defined SCM processes (for example, auditing the configuration control board [CCB] practices against defined CCB processes or auditing product release practices against defined product release processes)

- Contents of a project's controlled library to ensure that only authorized changes have been incorporated into baselined configuration items and that those changes were verified

FUNCTIONAL CONFIGURATION AUDIT (FCA)

According to the ISO/IEC *Systems and Software Engineering—Vocabulary* (ISO/IEC 2009), a functional configuration audit (FCA) is "an audit conducted to verify that:

- The development of a configuration item has been completed satisfactorily

- The item has achieved the performance and functional characteristics specified in the functional or allocated configuration identification

- Its operational and support documents are complete and satisfactory"

A functional configuration audit is performed to provide an independent evaluation that the as-built, as-tested system/software and its deliverable documentation meet the specified functional, performance, quality attributes, and other requirements. Typically, the FCA is conducted just before the final "ready to beta test" or "ready to ship" review and provides input information into those reviews. An FCA is essentially an independent review of the system/software's verification and validation data to ensure that the deliverables meet their completion and/or quality requirements and that they are sufficiently mature for transition into either beta testing or production, depending on where in the life cycle the FCA is conducted.

Table 29.1 illustrates an example of an FCA checklist and proposes possible objective evidence-gathering techniques for each example checklist item. While several suggested evidence-gathering techniques are listed for each checklist item, the level of rigor chosen for the audit will dictate which of these techniques (or other techniques) will actually be used. The level of rigor chosen for each SCM audit should be based on a trade-off analysis of cost/schedule/product and risk. For example, when evaluating whether the code implements all and only the specified requirements, a less rigorous approach would be to evaluate the traceability matrix while a more rigorous audit might examine actual code samples, comparing them and against their allocated requirements.

Table 29.1 Example FCA checklist items and evidence-gathering techniques.

FCA checklist item	Suggestions for evidence-gathering techniques
1. Does the code implement all and only the documented software/system requirements?	• Evaluate requirements-to–source code forward and backward traceability information (for example, traceability matrix or trace tags) for completeness and to ensure that only authorized functionality has been implemented. • Sample a set of requirements and, using the traceability information, review the associated code for implementation completeness and consistency. • Sample a set of approved enhancement requests and review their resolution status (or if approved for change, evaluate their associated code for implementation completeness and consistency).
2. Can each system/software requirement be traced forward into tests (test cases, procedures, scripts) that verify that requirement?	• Evaluate requirements-to-tests traceability information (for example, traceability matrix or trace tags) for completeness. • Sample a set of requirements and, using the traceability information, review the associated test documentation (for example, test plans, defined tests) for adequacy of verification by ensuring the appropriate level of test coverage for each requirement.
3. Are comprehensive system/software testing complete, including functional testing, interface testing, and the testing of required quality attributes (performance, usability, safety, security, and so on)?	• Review approved verification and validation reports for accuracy and completeness. • Evaluate approved test documentation (for example, test plans, defined tests) against test results data (for example, test logs, test case status, test metrics) to ensure adequate test coverage of the requirements and system/software during test execution. • Execute a sample set of test cases to ensure that the observed results match those recorded in the test reporting documentation to evaluate accuracy of test results.
4. Are all the problems reported during testing adequately resolved (or the appropriate waivers/deviations obtained and known defects with work-arounds documented in the release notes)?	• Review a sample set of approved test problem report records for evidence of adequate resolution. • Sample a set of test problem report records and review their resolution status (or if approved for change, evaluate their associated code for implementation completeness and consistency). • Review regression test results data (for example, test logs, test case execution outputs/status, test metrics) to ensure adequate test coverage after defect correction.

Continued

Table 29.1   *Continued.*

FCA checklist item	Suggestions for evidence-gathering techniques
5. Is the deliverable documentation consistent with the requirements and the as-built system/software?	• Review minutes and defect resolution information from peer reviews of deliverable documentation for evidence of consistency. • Evaluate approved test documentation (for example, test plans, defined tests) against test results data (for example, test logs, test case execution outputs/status, test metrics) to ensure adequate test coverage of the deliverable documentation during test execution. • Review a sample set of updates to previously delivered documents to ensure consistency with requirements and as-built system/software.
6. Are the findings from peer reviews incorporated into the software deliverables (system/software and/or documentation)?	• Review records from major milestone/phase gate reviews that verified the resolution of peer review defects. • Review a sample set of peer review records for evidence of the resolution of all identified defects. • Review a sample set of minutes from peer reviews and evaluate the defect lists against the associated work products to ensure that the defects were adequately resolved.
7. Have approved corrective actions been implemented for all findings from in-process SCM audits?	• Evaluate findings from SCM audit reports against their associated corrective action status. • Re-audit against findings from in-process SCM audits to verify implementation of corrective actions.

PHYSICAL CONFIGURATION AUDIT (PCA)

According to the ISO/IEC *Systems and Software Engineering—Vocabulary* (ISO/IEC 2009), a physical configuration audit (PCA) is "an audit conducted to verify that each configuration item, as built, conforms to the technical documentation that defines it." A PCA verifies that:

- All items identified as being part of the configuration are present in the product baseline

- The correct version and revision of each item is included in the product baseline

- Each item corresponds to information contained in the baseline's configuration status report

A PCA is performed to provide an independent evaluation that the software, as implemented, has been described adequately in the documentation that will be delivered with it and that the software and its documentation have been captured in the SCM database and are ready for delivery. Finally, the PCA may also be used to evaluate adherence to legal obligations, including licensing and export compliance requirements.

The PCA is typically held either in conjunction with the FCA or soon after the FCA (once any issues identified during the FCA are resolved). A PCA is essentially a review of the software configuration status accounting data to ensure that the software products and their deliverable documentation are appropriately baselined and properly built prior to release to beta testing or production, depending on where in the life cycle the PCA is conducted.

Table 29.2 illustrates an example of a PCA checklist and proposes possible objective evidence-gathering techniques for each item.

Table 29.2 Example PCA checklist items and evidence-gathering techniques.

PCA checklist item	Suggestions for evidence-gathering techniques
1. Has each nonconformance or noncompliance from the FCA been resolved?	• Review findings from the FCA audit report, associated corrective actions, follow-up and verification records, to evaluate adequacy of actions taken (or verify that appropriate approved waivers/deviations exist).
2. Have all of the identified configuration items (for example, source code, documentation, and so on) been baselined?	• Sample a set of configuration items and evaluate them against configuration status accounting records.
3. Has the software been built from the correct components and in accordance with the specification?	• Evaluate the build records against the configuration status accounting information to ensure that the correct version and revision of each module was included in the build. • Evaluate any patches/temporary fixes made to the software to ensure their completeness and correctness. • Sample a set of design elements from the architectural design and trace them to their associated detailed design elements and source code. Compare those elements with the build records to evaluate them for completeness and consistency with the as-built software. • Sample a set of configuration items and re–peer review them to ensure that their physical characteristics match their documented specifications.

Continued

Table 29.2   Example PCA checklist items and evidence-gathering techniques.

PCA checklist item	Suggestions for evidence-gathering techniques
4. Is the deliverable documentation set complete?	• Evaluate the master copy of each document against the configuration status accounting information to ensure that the correct version and revision of each document subcomponent (for example, chapter, section, figure) is included in the document. • Sample the set of copied documents ready for shipment and review them for completeness and quality against the master copy. • Evaluate the version description document against the build records for completeness and consistency. • Compare the current build records to the build records from the last release to identify changed components. Evaluate this list of changed components against the version description document to evaluate the version description document's completeness and consistency.
5. Does the actual system delivery media conform to its specification and is it frozen to prevent further change? Has the delivery media been appropriately marked/labeled?	• Evaluate the items on the master media against the required software deliverables (executables, help files, data) to ensure that the correct versions and revisions were included. • Rebuild a sample set of software deliverables from the SCM repository and compare them with those on the delivery media to ensure that the controlled configuration items match those built into the deliverables. • Sample a set of copied media ready for shipment and review them for completeness and quality against the master media. • Sample a set of copied media ready for shipment and review their marking/labeling against specification.
6. Do the deliverables for shipment match the list of required deliverables?	• Evaluate the packing list against the list of documented deliverables to ensure completeness. • Sample a set of ready-to-ship packages and evaluate them against the packing list to ensure that media (for example, CD, disks, tape), documentation, and other deliverables are included in each package.
7. Have all third-party licensing requirements been met?	• Evaluate the build records against configuration status accounting information to identify third-party components and license information to confirm that adequate numbers of licenses exist.
8. Have all export compliance requirements been met?	• Evaluate the build records against configuration status accounting information to identify components with export restrictions and confirmed export compliance.

STANDARDIZED CHECKLISTS

Standardized checklists, such as the examples in this chapter, can be created for SCM audits. Advantages of using standardized checklists include:

- Providing guidance to audit team members, the auditees, and management to help achieve consistency, uniformity, completeness, and continuity of the application of the SCM audit process and SCM practices

- Reducing the effort involved in preparing for each audit

- Providing a basis for analyzing lessons learned from previous audits, which can then be incorporated into those standardized checklists to improve future audits as part of continual process improvement

- Providing a set of training aids to promote common understanding

Prior to each audit, these standardized checklists should be reviewed and updated as necessary to ensure that they reflect any changes made in the SCM standards, policies, processes, or plans since the last audit was conducted. These generic checklists should also be supplemented and tailored to the exact circumstances of each individual project. For example, if the corrective actions against prior audit findings are being verified with the current audit, specific checklist items for those actions may be added to the checklist. Another example might be the auditing of small projects where certain optional processes do not apply. Only processes required for that specific project should be included in its audit checklist. "Optional" or "not applicable" processes should either be identified as such or removed from the checklist.

Chapter 30

E. Product Release and Distribution

T he primary focus of software quality is to ensure that quality is being built into software products and services throughout the software development project. However, eventually the development portion of the project ends and it becomes time to release the software products and services and distribute them into operations. Depending on the project, there may also be a need to distribute interim or preliminary releases to the customers or users, for example, releases into beta testing or other evaluation and feedback releases.

As with any other process, defects can be introduced during the release process that can impact the quality and reliability of the product or services during operations. Therefore, the software quality engineer (SQE) must be familiar with the release and distribution processes in order to help define these process, evaluate their effectiveness and efficiency, help identify issues and process improvement opportunities, and perform other release and distribution quality-related activities.

1. PRODUCT RELEASE

> Review product release processes (planning, scheduling, defining hardware and software dependencies, etc.) and assess their effectiveness. (Evaluate)
>
> **Body of Knowledge VII.E.1**

Types of Releases

There are two major types of product releases. The first type of release is a *corrective release*, also called a *service pack* or *patch release*. As illustrated in Figure 30.1, a corrective release is done to deliver defect corrections into operations in a timely manner. Typically, this is done when the defects are deemed to be critical enough (have a large enough impact on the users) that they can not wait until the next scheduled feature release of the product. This type of release may not be appropriate or even allowed for some software products (for example, biomedical products).

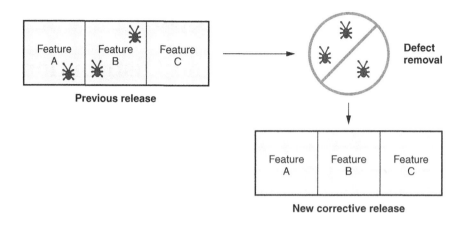

Figure 30.1   Corrective release.

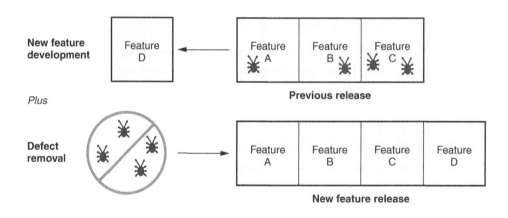

Figure 30.2   Feature release.

The second type of release is a *feature release,* which is done primarily to deliver new features or functionality to the user. However, as illustrated in Figure 30.2, defects may also be corrected as part of a feature release.

Release Planning and Scheduling

The release planning starts by defining the scope of the version/revision that will eventually become the release through utilizing requirements engineering practices to select the initial set of requirements for the new, changed, or deleted functionality that will be included (for a feature release) and using configuration control activities to determine which problems will be corrected (for either a feature or corrective release). The release process continues through design and implementation to create the software version/revision, including the associated user documentation, to implement those requirements and correct those problems. During that implementation, changes to the scope are managed through requirements management activities and configuration control activities as additional enhancements are requested and/or new problems are discovered. Throughout the implementation process, verification and validation activities are used to ensure that the selected scope meets the specified requirements and stakeholder needs.

Once the software version/revision, including its associated user documentation, has been completely implemented, final packaging is done, version description documentation is created, and final verification and validation activities are performed, including functional and physical configuration audits. A "ready to ship" review is then conducted as a final quality gate before promoting the software version/revision to a release.

The major release planning and scheduling activities are related to the replication and delivery of the release into operations. Release and distribution can be as trivial a process as installing a software package on a single computer or as complex as delivering multiple products and services to hundreds, thousands, or in some cases even millions of customers around the globe. In complex systems with dependencies between various software applications and hardware components, release planning and scheduling may require coordination of multiple product releases so that all of the system components that share changed dependencies are installed together. Release planning and scheduling includes the following:

- Determining the contents of the releasable unit (for example, is it the release of a single software application or does it include multiple software/hardware product releases coordinated together as a single releasable unit? Are services like training bundled into the release unit or are they separate release units?)

- Coordinating with distributors, customers, and/or users on the logistics of rollout, including:

  – What release units will be delivered

  – Quantities for each release unit

  – Delivery dates for each release unit

  – Delivery location for each release unit

  – Delivery mechanism for each release unit

- Documenting release plans (for example, schedules, budgets, staffing, and other resource requirements, quality plans, communication plans, and risk management plans)

- Negotiating, contracting, and coordinating deliveries from suppliers, as necessary

- Handling legal issues (for example, licensing and export regulations)

- Conducting preinstallation and installation site visits, as appropriate

- Defining responsibilities for and performing installation and installation testing

- Defining and implementing back-out plans as necessary

- Configuring and customizing the released units to specific user/site requirements

- Training help desk and other support personnel, as well as training customers/users

- Negotiating service level agreements, and scaling up help desk and other support activities as appropriate

Version Description Documentation

Each delivered release should include version description documentation, also called *release notes,* that describes the new version/revision of the software. This documentation should define:

- The environmental requirements needed to execute the software, including the operating system version(s) and hardware/software dependencies

- Installation instructions and post-installation testing instructions

- A list of new features, functions, or other enhancements added with this release (for feature releases)

- A list of the defects previously reported from operations that are corrected with this release

- A list of known defects, problems, or limitations in the release including work-arounds if they are available

- Contact information for obtaining technical assistance or reporting problems

Release Packaging

Release packaging defines what is included on the media that is used to transition the software into operations. According to Bays (1999), there are three types of release packaging:

- *Full release.* The media contents is capable of completing a full installation of the product

- *Partial release.* The media contents is limited to only making modifications—to add, modify, or remove portions of the full release—but requires a full release to already be installed

- *Patch.* The media contains a temporary fix to a specific release through a modification made directly to an object or executable, which avoids the need to rebuild the product, or a temporary fix to the source itself

As illustrated in Figure 30.3, various types of packaging may be appropriate over the lifetime of the product in the field. For example, the initial release of the product must always be a full release. Subsequent corrective releases can be

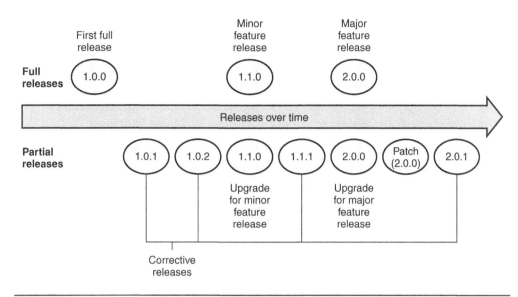

Figure 30.3   Packaging of releases over time.

accomplished through partial releases and/or patches since only minimal changes are typically being made. Installing partial releases is typically much less time-consuming than installing a full release. When minor or major feature releases are ready for delivery, they may be packaged as both partial releases, to allow existing operational sites the efficiencies of partial installation, and as full releases for use at any new operational sites. This allows the new sites to install a complete version without the need to install the initial full release and then all of its subsequent partial releases.

Because of their temporary nature and because patches to the object or executable code are often done manually, patching can be risky. For example, as illustrated in Figure 30.4, a patch might be made to the executable code in operations to temporarily correct (put a band-aid on) a critical field problem. However, the defect was only fixed in the executable and not in the actual source code. Without good configuration management, the defective source code might be built into a future software version. When that version is subsequently released into operations, the user might reencounter that same critical bug. This scenario is the reason that regression testing should include the testing of all patches until they have been permanently corrected in the source code.

Internationalization, also called *localization,* is an issue that may also impact how the software is packaged. For example, there may have to be separate packages for each different geographic location (internationalization).

Replication, Delivery, and Installation

The purpose of replication, delivery, and installation is to provide the users of the software with everything they need to successfully install and use the software

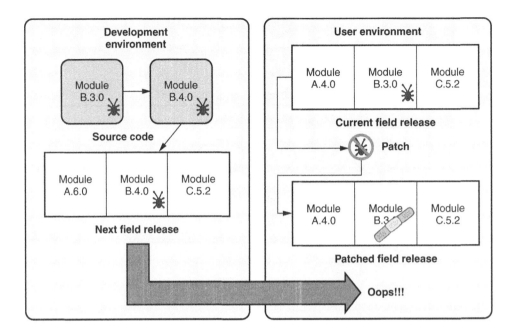

Figure 30.4   The problem with patching.

product. Part of project planning is defining the external deliverable that will be included in each release. This planning should include coming to agreement with the customer on:

- What software products or services will be delivered

- Quantities for each product or service

- Delivery dates for each product or service

- Delivery location for each product or service

- Delivery mechanism for each product or service

Replication is the process of making copies of the software deliverables for delivery to the customer. *Delivery* is the process of actually getting those deliverables to the users. *Installation* is the process of integrating the software into its operational environment for use by the end user.

To expand on the delivery concept, there are several vehicles that can be used to deliver the products into operations, including intermediate installation media, direct-access media, personal delivery, and electronic transfer. When *intermediate installation media* is used to deliver the software product, that product is copied onto some form of intermediate media (for example, CD, floppy, magnetic tape). This intermediate media is then delivered into operations where the software product is installed from that media onto the target system. These installations can be performed by the customer, user, or their representative, or by supplier personnel sent to the operational site. The intermediate media is not needed after it is installed, except for additional installation or reinstallation activities. *Direct-access media* (for example, EPROMS, hard-copy documentation, and in some cases CDs) contains a product that is used in operations as is, without the need for installation. The primary advantage of direct-access media is that it doesn't take up space on the target computer system itself. The primary disadvantage is that the media has to be present to run. For deliverables such as training or customer support, supplier personnel may personally deliver the product directly to the customer or users. The software products may also be delivered via electronic transfer, for example, using the Internet, bulletin boards, or network-mounted file systems. The benefits of electronic transfer include reduced costs and immediate availability.

While the primary focus of software quality is on development (building quality into the software), a supplier's organization can not completely ignore the replication, delivery, and installation process. For example, if the hardware used to replicate the delivery media is out of calibration or the media is damaged during shipment, the resulting copies may prove to be unreadable when they are received. Therefore, from a quality perspective the replication process and delivery vehicles need to be verified, at least on a sampling basis. Verification should be done to ensure that the master source media used in the replication process are free from viruses before copies are made. During replication, checksums can be used to ensure that duplication errors did not result in the target media having different content than the master source media being copied. On a sampling basis, the resulting media should also be checked on a different hardware device to ensure that calibration issues have not occurred.

The copied media are also subject to corruption in transit and/or storage and therefore need appropriate protection. Again, periodic sampling can be used to verify that corruptions have not occurred during the delivery process.

The installation should also be verified to ensure that everything was installed properly and that the system is functioning correctly. This verification is typically done by whoever installed the software.

Another technique for verifying the entire replication, delivery, and installation process is to deliver a complete release package in-house first (preferably to someone who has the same level of knowledge about the system as the typical installer). This person utilizes the deliverables to install the software and ensure that it works in the target environment. This helps verify that the replication process was successful, that all the needed deliverables (software, databases, documentation) were in the delivered release package, and that the installation process can be successfully executed.

Hardware and Software Dependencies

Hardware dependencies exist when the current release of the software is not backward-compatible with the hardware used to run previous versions of the software. For example, a new version of the software is created to implement a feature set to control a new widget added to the hardware system. If that software can not be run on older versions of the hardware that have not been upgraded to include the new widget, then a hardware dependency exists.

Software dependencies exist when the current release of the software is not backward-compatible with:

- *The software platform used to run previous versions of the software.* For example, the new software version uses features available only in the newest version of the operating system and will not run on previous versions of the operating system.

- *Other software that interfaced with the previous version of the software.* For example, the new software version implements a new communications protocol that is also implemented in the new XYZ software and can not communicate with the previous XYZ version.

- *Data files that were accessed by a previous version of the software.* For example, the new software implements changes to the format of the accessed data files and can not use the older versions of the data files.

Release Support

Rarely do the software supplier's responsibilities end when the release is delivered. The release must also be supported during its operational lifetime. The level and duration of this support depends on a service level agreement between the supplier and the acquirer of the product, which may include:

- The ability for the acquirer to obtain additional copies of the release package as more operational sites are created (continued replication, delivery, and installation support)

- Product and process implementation and customization

- Ongoing operational testing

- Technical support for the release as it is being used in operations, including the ability of users to:

  - Get their questions answered

  - Report problems or issues and have them resolved in a timely manner

2. ARCHIVAL PROCESSES

> Review the source and release archival processes (backup planning and scheduling, data retrieval, archival of build environments, retention of historical records, offsite storage, etc.) and assess their effectiveness. (Evaluate)
>
> **Body of Knowledge VI.E.2**

Backups

Disasters happen. Hard disks fail or become corrupted, important files are inadvertently deleted, and buildings burn down. When computer files are lost under circumstances such as these, they are often gone for good, or recovery costs can be huge. Backing up the developer's working libraries, all of the versions/revisions of the controlled configuration items, components, and units, the status accounting information, and quality records is the single most important thing an organization can do to allow for quick recovery from these disasters.

Backups can be made on a periodic basis or on an event-driven basis (for example, when a static library is created) depending on:

- Criticality of the work products kept in the library and the impact if they are lost

- Level of change activity

- Reliability of the system on which the electronic assets are stored

Depending on these considerations, many organizations choose to back up their active (non-archived) electronic assets on a nightly basis. This ensures that no more than a day's worth of work is lost if a disaster happens. These backups are typically done after hours because there may be a need to freeze those assets and not allow change during the backup process. Care must be taken to ensure that all appropriate entities are being backed up. For example, the organization may have a policy that electronic assets are stored in libraries on the shared network server and not kept on personal computers or laptops that may not be included in the official nightly backups. According to Kenefick (2003), "this has the double problem-solving ability of protecting the developer's work in between check-ins and providing access to the code should the developer be absent."

Backup libraries can be stored on-site for quick recovery, but copies should also be stored off-site for disaster recovery. For each project, the SCM plan should identify the backup and disaster-recovery plans and processes.

Another consideration in executing backups is the media used for those backups. This can be especially critical for long-term (multiyear) archiving of electronic assets. For example, years ago, organizations used eight-inch floppy disks for backups. Those floppies started deteriorating, becoming brittle and unreadable after a year or so. This required someone to be assigned to copying archived information onto new floppies on a periodic basis to prevent the possibility of losing corporate assets. Today debates are going on as to how long CDs will last before deteriorating. Just a few years ago, some organizations used Zip drives or floppy disks as their backup media. Today they may not even have the hardware necessary to read that type of media.

When the software is released, an archive should be created of the software product baseline into a static library. For example, according to the IEEE *Standard for Software Configuration Management Plans* (IEEE 2005), "master copies of code and documentation shall be maintained for the life of the software product." All of the configuration items necessary to re-create the development environment (including the hardware, tools, operating system), as well as the software product itself, should be archived. The goal is to be able to re-create and maintain the released software and its components. Other considerations may include maintaining the appropriate licenses to continue to use any purchased software that is part of or used to support the released software.

Quality Records

Quality records provide the evidence that the appropriate quality activities took place and that the execution of those activities met required standards. Examples of quality records include:

- Minutes from meetings (reviews, configuration control boards, audits, and so on)

- Reports (technical review, managerial review, test, audit, status, metrics, and so on)

- Change requests, action item lists, corrective action reports, and so on

- Test logs, engineering notebooks, completed checklists, and so on

- Completed forms (purchase orders, approval forms, and so on)

While they are not considered configuration items under configuration management, quality records must also be identified, controlled, and stored so that they are protected from loss or damage (so they remain legible) and easily retrievable when needed. For each type of quality record, the retention period should be specified as part of the quality management system documentation. For example, typical retention periods might be "a minimum of the duration of the project plus two years" or "a minimum of the active use of the release in operations plus one year." The reason the retention period should be specified as "at a minimum" is to allow the organization to prune older quality records from active retention on a periodic basis. At the same time this keeps auditors from reporting issues when they find quality records that have been retained for longer than an absolute specified retention period (for example, "the completion of the project plus one year").

Control of quality records procedures should also specify what is done with those records after the retention period has expired. Are they simply thrown away, do they need to be disposed of in some secure manner (for example, through shredding), or are they moved into long-term archival storage, and if so, for how long? Control of quality records procedures may also need to be implemented in a manner that is in compliance with any applicable regulatory requirements or industry standards (for example, ISO 9001) depending on the needs of the organization.

In addition to quality records, other organizational process assets from the project may also be archived when the software is released (for example, tailored life cycles, processes, or work instructions, contracts, customer letters or e-mails, project plans, or other work products that were not designated as configuration items and lessons learned).

Appendix A

Software Quality Engineer
Certification Body of Knowledge

The following is an outline of topics that constitute the Body of Knowledge for Software Quality Engineer

The topics in this Body of Knowledge include additional detail in the form of subtext explanations and the cognitive level at which the questions will be written. This information will provide useful guidance for both the Examination Development Committee and the candidates preparing to take the exam. The subtext is not intended to limit the subject matter or be all-inclusive of what might be covered in an exam. It is intended to clarify the type of content to be included in the exam. The descriptor in parentheses at the end of each entry refers to the highest cognitive level at which the topic will be tested. A more comprehensive description of cognitive levels is provided at the end of this page.

I. *General Knowledge* (16 questions)

A. *Quality principles.*

1. *Benefits of software quality.* Describe the benefits that software quality engineering can have at the organizational level. (Understand)

2. *Organizational and process benchmarking.* Use benchmarking at the organizational, process, and project levels to identify and implement best practices. (Apply)

B. *Ethical and legal compliance.*

1. *ASQ Code of Ethics.* Determine appropriate behavior in situations requiring ethical decisions, including identifying conflicts of interest, recognizing and resolving ethical issues, etc. (Evaluate)

2. *Legal and regulatory issues.* Define and describe the impact that issues such as copyright, intellectual property rights, product liability, data privacy, the Sarbanes-Oxley Act, etc., can have on software development. (Understand)

C. *Standards and models.* Define and describe the following standards and assessment models: ISO 9000 standards, IEEE software standards, and the SEI Capability Maturity Model Integrated (CMMI). (Understand)

D. *Leadership skills.*

1. *Organizational leadership.* Use leadership tools and techniques, such as organizational change management, knowledge-transfer, motivation, mentoring and coaching, recognition, etc. (Apply)

2. *Facilitation skills.* Use various approaches to manage and resolve conflict. Use negotiation techniques and identify possible outcomes. Use meeting management tools to maximize performance. (Apply)

3. *Communication skills.* Use various communication elements (e.g., interviewing and listening skills) in oral, written, and presentation formats. Use various techniques for working in multi-cultural environments, and identify and describe the impact that culture and communications can have on quality. (Apply)

E. *Team skills.*

1. *Team management.* Use various team management skills, including assigning roles and responsibilities, identifying the classic stages of team development (forming, storming, norming, performing, adjourning), monitoring and responding to group dynamics, and working with diverse groups and in distributed work environments. (Apply))

2. *Team tools.* Use decision-making and creativity tools, such as brainstorming, nominal group technique (NGT), multi-voting, etc. (Apply)

II. *Software Quality Management* (26 questions)

A. *Quality management system.*

1. *Quality goals and objectives.* Design quality goals and objectives for programs, projects, and products that are consistent with business objectives. Develop and use documents and processes necessary to support software quality management systems. (Create)

2. *Customers and other stakeholders.* Describe and distinguish between various stakeholder groups, and analyze the effect their requirements can have on software projects and products. (Analyze)

3. *Planning.* Design program plans that will support software quality goals and objectives. (Evaluate)

4. *Outsourcing.* Determine the impact that acquisitions, multi-supplier partnerships, outsourced services, and other external drivers can have on organizational goals and objectives, and design appropriate criteria for evaluating suppliers and subcontractors. (Analyze)

B. *Methodologies.*

1. *Cost of quality (COQ).* Analyze COQ categories (prevention, appraisal, internal failure, external failure) and their impact on products and processes. (Evaluate)

2. *Process improvement models.* Define and describe elements of lean tools and the six sigma methodology, and use the plan–do–check–act (PDCA) model for process improvement. (Apply)

3. *Corrective action procedures.* Evaluate corrective action procedures related to software defects, process nonconformances, and other quality system deficiencies. (Evaluate)

4. *Defect prevention.* Design and use defect prevention processes such as technical reviews, software tools and technology, special training, etc. (Evaluate)

C. *Audits.*

1. *Audit types.* Define and distinguish between various audit types, including process, compliance, supplier, system, etc. (Understand)

2. *Audit roles and responsibilities.* Identify roles and responsibilities for audit participants: client, lead auditor, audit team members and auditee. (Understand)

3. *Audit process.* Define and describe the steps in conducting an audit, developing and delivering an audit report, and determining appropriate follow-up activities. (Apply)

III. *Systems and Software Engineering Processes* (27 questions)

A. *Lifecycles and process models.* Evaluate various software development lifecycles (iterative, waterfall, etc.) and process models (V-model, Feature Driven Development, Test Driven Development, etc.) and identify their benefits and when they should be used. (Evaluate)

B. *Systems architecture.* Identify and describe various architectures, including embedded systems, client–server, n-tier, web, wireless, messaging, collaboration platforms, etc., and analyze their impact on quality. (Analyze)

C. *Requirements engineering.*

1. *Requirements types.* Define and describe various types of requirements, including feature, function, system, quality, security, safety, regulatory, etc. (Understand)

2. *Requirements elicitation.* Describe and use various elicitation methods, including customer needs analysis, use cases, human factors studies, usability prototypes, joint application development (JAD), storyboards, etc. (Apply)

3. *Requirements analysis.* Identify and use tools such as data flow diagrams (DFDs), entity relationship diagrams (ERDs), etc., to analyze requirements. (Apply)

D. *Requirements management.*

1. *Participants.* Identify various participants who have a role in requirements planning, including customers, developers, testers, the quality function, management, etc. (Understand)

2. *Requirements evaluation.* Assess the completeness, consistency, correctness, and testability of requirements, and determine their priority. (Evaluate)

3. *Requirements change management.* Assess the impact that changes to requirements will have on software development processes for all types of lifecycle models. (Evaluate)

4. *Bidirectional traceability.* Use various tools and techniques to ensure bidirectional traceability from requirements elicitation and analysis through design and testing. (Apply)

E. *Software analysis, design, and development*

1. *Design methods.* Identify the steps used in software design and their functions, and define and distinguish between software design methods such as object-oriented analysis and design (OOAD), structured analysis and design (SAD), and patterns. (Understand)

2. *Quality attributes and design.* Analyze the impact that quality-related elements (safety, security, reliability, usability, reusability, maintainability, etc.) can have on software design. (Analyze)

3. *Software reuse.* Define and distinguish between software reuse, reengineering, and reverse engineering, and describe the impact these practices can have on software quality. (Understand)

4. *Software development tools.* Select the appropriate development tools to use for modeling, code analysis, etc., and analyze the impact they can have on requirements management and documentation. (Analyze)

5. *Software development methods.* Define and describe principles such as pair programming, extreme programming, cleanroom, formal methods, etc., and their impact on software quality. (Understand)

F. *Maintenance management.*

1. *Maintenance types.* Describe the characteristics of corrective, adaptive, perfective, and preventive maintenance types. (Understand)

2. *Maintenance strategy.* Describe various factors affecting the strategy for software maintenance, including service-level agreements (SLAs), short- and long-term costs, maintenance releases,

product discontinuance, etc., and their impact on software quality. (Understand)

IV. *Project Management* (24 questions)

   A. *Planning, scheduling, and deployment.*

      1. *Project planning.* Use forecasts, resources, schedules, task and cost estimates, etc., to develop project plans. (Apply)

      2. *Project scheduling.* Use PERT charts, critical path method (CPM), work breakdown structure (WBS), Scrum, burn-down charts, and other tools to schedule and monitor projects. (Apply)

      3. *Project deployment.* Use various tools, including milestones, objectives achieved, task duration, etc., to set goals and deploy the project. (Apply)

   B. *Tracking and controlling*

      1. *Phase transition control.* Use phase transition control tools and techniques such as entry/exit criteria, quality gates, Gantt charts, integrated master schedules, etc. (Apply)

      2. *Tracking methods.* Calculate project-related costs, including earned value, deliverables, productivity, etc., and track the results against project baselines. (Apply)

      3. *Project reviews.* Use various types of project reviews such as phase-end, management, and retrospectives or post-project reviews to assess project performance and status, to review issues and risks, and to discover and capture lessons learned from the project. (Apply)

      4. *Program reviews.* Define and describe various methods for reviewing and assessing programs in terms of their performance, technical accomplishments, resource utilization, etc. (Understand)

   C. *Risk management.*

      1. *Risk management methods.* Use risk management techniques (assess, prevent, mitigate, transfer) to evaluate project risks. (Evaluate)

      2. *Software security risks.* Evaluate risks specific to software security, including deliberate attacks (hacking, sabotage, etc.), inherent defects that allow unauthorized access to data, and other security breaches, and determine appropriate responses to minimize their impact. (Evaluate)

      3. *Safety and hazard analysis.* Evaluate safety risks and hazards related to software development and implementation and determine appropriate steps to minimize their impact. (Evaluate)

V. *Software Metrics and Analysis* (24 questions)

A. *Metrics and measurement theory*

1. *Terminology.* Define and describe metrics and measurement terms including reliability, internal and external validity, explicit and derived measures, etc. (Understand)

2. *Basic measurement theory and statistics.* Define the central limit theorem, and describe and use mean, median, mode, standard deviation, variance, and range. Apply appropriate measurement scales (nominal, ordinal, ratio, interval) in various situations. (Apply)

3. *Psychology of metrics.* Describe how metrics and measuring affect the people whose work is being measured and how people affect the ways in which metrics are used and data are gathered. (Understand)

B. *Process and product measurement.*

1. *Software metrics.* Use metrics to assess various software attributes such as size, complexity, number of defects, the amount of test coverage needed, requirements volatility, and overall system performance. (Apply)

2. *Process metrics.* Measure the effectiveness and efficiency of software using functional verification tests (FVT), cost, yield, customer impact, defect detection, defect containment, total defect containment effectiveness (TDCE), defect removal efficiency (DRE), process capability and efficiency, etc. (Apply)

3. *Metrics reporting tools.* Use various metric representation tools, including dashboards, stoplight charts, etc., to report results efficiently. (Apply)

C. *Analytical techniques.*

1. *Sampling.* Define and distinguish between sampling methods (e.g., random, stratified, cluster) as used in auditing, testing, product acceptance, etc. (Understand)

2. *Data collection and integrity.* Describe the importance of data integrity from planning through collection and analysis, and apply various techniques to ensure its quality, accuracy, completeness, and timeliness. (Apply)

3. *Quality analysis tools.* Describe and use classic quality tools (flowcharts, Pareto charts, cause-and-effect diagrams, control charts, histograms, etc.) and problem-solving tools (affinity and tree diagrams, matrix and activity network diagrams, root cause analysis, etc.) in a variety of situations. (Apply)

VI. *Software Verification and Validation (V&V)* (27 questions)

   A. *Theory.*

      1. *V&V methods.* Select and use V&V methods, including static analysis, structural analysis, mathematical proof, simulation, etc., and analyze which tasks should be iterated as a result of modifications. (Analyze)

      2. *Software product evaluation.* Use various evaluation methods on documentation, source code, test results, etc., to determine whether user needs and project objectives have been satisfied. (Analyze)

   B. *Test planning and design.*

      1. *Test strategies.* Select and analyze test strategies (test-driven design, good-enough, risk-based, time-box, top-down, bottom-up, black-box, white-box, simulation, automation, etc.) for various situations. (Analyze)

      2. *Test plans.* Develop and evaluate test plans and procedures, including system, acceptance, validation, etc., to determine whether project objectives are being met. (Create)

      3. *Test designs.* Select and evaluate various test designs, including fault insertion, fault-error handling, equivalence class partitioning, boundary value, etc. (Evaluate)

      4. *Software tests.* Identify and use various tests, including unit, functional, performance, integration, regression, usability, acceptance, certification, environmental load, stress, worst-case, perfective, exploratory, system, etc. (Apply)

      5. *Tests of supplier components and products.* Determine appropriate levels of testing for integrating third-party components and products. (Apply)

      6. *Test coverage specifications.* Evaluate the adequacy of specifications such as functions, states, data and time domains, interfaces, security, and configurations that include internationalization and platform variances. (Evaluate)

      7. *Code coverage techniques.* Identify and use techniques such as branch-to-branch, condition, domain, McCabe's cyclomatic complexity, boundary, etc. (Apply)

      8. *Test environments.* Select and use simulations, test libraries, drivers, stubs, harnesses, etc., and identify parameters to establish a controlled test environment in various situations. (Analyze)

      9. *Test tools.* Identify and use utilities, diagnostics, and test management tools. (Apply)

   C. *Reviews and inspections.* Identify and use desk-checks, peer reviews, walk-throughs, Fagan and Gilb inspections, etc. (Apply)

D. *Test execution documentation.* Review and evaluate documents such as defect reporting and tracking records, test completion metrics, trouble reports, input/output specifications, etc. (Evaluate)

E. *Customer deliverables.* Assess the completeness of customer deliverables, including packaged and hosted or downloadable products, license keys and user documentation, marketing and training materials, etc. (Evaluate)

VII. *Software Configuration Management* (16 questions)

A. *Configuration infrastructure.*

1. *Configuration management team.* Describe the roles and responsibilities of a configuration management group. (Understand) [NOTE: The roles and responsibilities of the configuration control board (CCB) are covered in area VII.C.2.]

2. *Configuration management tools.* Describe these tools as they are used for managing libraries, build systems, defect tracking systems, etc. (Understand)

3. *Library processes.* Describe dynamic, static, and controlled processes used in library systems and related procedures, such as check-in/check-out, merge changes, etc. (Understand)

B. *Configuration identification.*

1. *Configuration items.* Describe configuration items (documentation, software code, equipment, etc.), identification methods (naming conventions, versioning schemes, etc.), and when baselines are created and used. (Understand)

2. *Software builds.* Describe the relationship between software builds and configuration management functions, and describe methods for controlling builds (automation, new versions, etc.). (Understand)

C. *Configuration control and status accounting.*

1. *Item, baseline, and version control.* Describe processes for documentation control, tracking item changes, version control, etc., that are used to manage various configurations, and describe processes used to manage configuration item dependencies in software builds and versioning. (Understand)

2. *Configuration control board (CCB).* Describe the roles and responsibilities of the CCB and its members and the procedures they use. (Understand) [NOTE: The roles and responsibilities of the configuration management team are covered in area VII.A.1.]

3. *Concurrent development.* Describe the use of configuration management control principles in concurrent development processes. (Understand)

       4. *Status accounting.* Discuss various processes for establishing, maintaining, and reporting the status of configuration items. (Understand)

    D. *Configuration audits.* Define and distinguish between functional and physical configuration audits and how they are used in relation to product specifications. (Understand)

    E. *Product release and distribution.*

       1. *Product release.* Review product release processes (planning, scheduling, defining hardware and software dependencies, etc.) and assess their effectiveness. (Evaluate)

       2. *Archival processes.* Review the source and release archival processes (backup planning and scheduling, data retrieval, archival of build environments, retention of historical records, offsite storage, etc.) and assess their effectiveness. (Evaluate)

LEVELS OF COGNITION
BASED ON *BLOOM'S TAXONOMY*—REVISED (2001)

In addition to *content* specifics, the subtext for each topic in this BOK also indicates the intended *complexity level* of the test questions for that topic. These levels are based on "Levels of Cognition" (from *Bloom's Taxonomy*—Revised, 2001) and are presented below in rank order, from least complex to most complex.

Remember

Recall or recognize terms, definitions, facts, ideas, materials, patterns, sequences, methods, principles, etc.

Understand

Read and understand descriptions, communications, reports, tables, diagrams, directions, regulations, etc.

Apply

Know when and how to use ideas, procedures, methods, formulas, principles, theories, etc.

Analyze

Break down information into its constituent parts and recognize their relationship to one another and how they are organized; identify sublevel factors or salient data from a complex scenario.

Evaluate

Make judgments about the value of proposed ideas, solutions, etc., by comparing the proposal to specific criteria or standards.

Create

Put parts or elements together in such a way as to reveal a pattern or structure not clearly there before; identify which data or information from a complex set is appropriate to examine further or from which supported conclusions can be drawn.

Glossary

acceptance—The formal acknowledgement of the customer and/or user's willingness to receive and use the external product deliverables.

acceptance criteria—The minimum level of quality required before the product can pass through a quality gate including release into operations.

acceptance test—Formal black-box testing, typically conducted prior to delivery to verify that the product(s) meet predefined and agreed-to acceptance criteria. The objective is to allow the customer and/or users to make a determination of whether to accept the system or software.

access control—The security safeguards and mechanisms put in place to permit authorized access while detecting and denying unauthorized access.

accessibility—A quality criterion describing the ease with which the system and its information can be accessed.

accident—"An unplanned event or series of events that result in death, injury, illness, environmental damage, or damage to or loss of equipment or property" (IEEE 1994).

accountability—The ability to trace access to the software or performance of software activities to the responsible party (for example, to a user or other software system).

accuracy—A quality attribute describing the level of precision, correctness, and/or freedom from error in the calculations and outputs of the software.

acquirer—The individuals or groups that are customers or users of the software.

acquisition or **acquire**—The process of obtaining software through in-house development, through the purchase of commercial off-the-shelf (COTS) software, through development by a third-party vendor or through a combination of these methods. The point at which each baseline and each configuration item, component, and unit is initially brought under configuration control).

activity—A cohesive, individual unit of work that must be accomplished to complete a project. The lowest-level unit of work in the work breakdown structure.

activity diagram—An analysis model that illustrates a dynamic activity-oriented view of the software product's functions.

activity network—A diagram that shows all of the activities of a project and their predecessor/successor relationships.

actor—Entities outside the scope of the system under consideration that interact with that system in a use case.

ACWP (actual value)—An earned value metric of the *actual cost of work performed.* (Also called actual value.)

adaptive maintenance—"Modification of a software product, performed after delivery, to keep a software product usable in a changed environment" (IEEE 2006).

adjourning—The phase of team development where the team accomplishes its mission, shuts down its efforts, and disbands.

affinity diagram—An analysis and problem-solving tool whose purpose is to organize a large number of ideas into significant categories or groups.

agile methods—A set of loosely affiliated software development methods and techniques including eXtreme programming, scrum, feature-driven development, test-driven development, Crystal, and lean.

allocated baseline—The baseline created when a product-level requirements specification for a system component (for example, a software requirements specification) and its associated configuration items are acquired.

alpha testing—Testing that is typically done by the customers and/or users of the software or their representatives at the supplier's facility or on a user test bed.

ambiguous—Capable of being interpreted or understood in two or more senses or contexts.

analysis—A verification and validation technique where individuals or teams perform in-depth assessments of the requirements or other software products.

appraisal costs of quality—All of the costs of quality that involve finding defects in the products, processes, or services, including peer reviews, testing, audits, pilots, and quality metrics.

approval—Agreement from a designated authority or set of stakeholders that a product, process, service, or information artifact (for example, a report or completed form) meets its requirements and is ready for implementation, transition to the next phase of development, or use.

architectural design—For a system, the process of defining the collection of hardware, software, and manual components of a system and the interfaces between those components. For software, the process of defining the components of the software (including subsystem, program, module, data, and/or procedural elements) and the interfaces between them. (Also called high-level design.)

architectural design review—A phase gate review meeting held at the transition from architectural design (high-level design) to detailed design. (Also called a preliminary design review [PDR].)

archive or **archival**—The act of placing work products, quality records, or data into historical storage, typically for a specified period of time, so that they can be retrieved and used if needed.

arrival rate—The rate that problem reports or corrective action requests are opened over time.

ASQ—American Society for Quality.

assembler—A software configuration management build tool that converts assembly language source code into object code.

assumption—An assertion, evaluation, or educated guess about how various factors or characteristics in the future will impact a project or task.

attack—An attempt to gain unauthorized access or compromise the software's integrity, availability, or confidentiality.

attribute—A measurable property or characteristic of an entity.

audit—"A systematic, independent, and documented process for obtaining audit evidence and evaluating it objectively to determine the extent to which the audit criteria are fulfilled" (Russell 2005). "An independent evaluation of a software product, process, or set of processes to assess compliance with specifications, standards, contractual agreements, or other criteria" (IEEE 2008a).

audit criteria—The agreed-to objective requirements, policies, standards, or processes against which conformance or compliance are evaluated during an audit. (Also called audit evaluation criteria or audit requirements.)

audit objectives—The defined reasons (purpose) for conducting the audit.

audit program—An overarching program planned as part of an organization's quality management system to ensure that required audits are performed regularly and audits of critical elements are performed more freqently.

audit report—The formal documented results of an audit.

audit scope—The established boundaries of the audit that identify the exact items, groups, locations, and/or activities to be examined.

audit trail—The documented records of software's access and use that provide the information needed for accountability.

auditee—The organization or individual being audited.

auditee management—The management of the organization being audited.

auditor or **audit team**—The team of one or more individuals conducting the audit including the lead auditor.

auditor management—The management of the individual(s) who plan and conduct the audit.

author—The individual who created the work product or who is currently responsible for maintaining the work product.

availability—A quality attribute describing the extent to which the software or a service is available for use when needed.

backup—The act of duplicating the software and its associated components, units, data, and documentation at a specific time typically used to protect organizational intellectual capital and assets from loss or corruption.

backup library—A software configuration management library used to contain duplicates of the versions of organizational intellectual capital and assets.

baseline—"A specification or product that has been formally reviewed and agreed upon, that thereafter serves as the basis for further development, and that can be changed only through formal change control procedures" (ISO/IEC 2009). An agreed-to project plan including schedule dates, effort estimates, resources and costs that is used to compare progress (plan versus actuals).

basis path testing—A white-box testing technique using cyclomatic complexity to ensure that all of the linearly independent paths are tested.

BCWP—An earned value metric of the *budgeted cost of work performed*. (Also called earned value.)

BCWS—An earned value metric of the *budgeted cost of work scheduled*. (Also called planned value.)

benchmarking—The process of identifying, understanding, adopting, and adapting outstanding practices and processes from organizations, anywhere in the world, to help an organization improve the performance of its processes, projects, products, and/or services.

beta test—A type of black-box testing that is typically performed by a selected subset of customers or users in an actual operational environment prior to the release of the software to general availability.

black-box testing—A form of testing that validates the external features of the software without regard to its internal structure.

bottom-up—An integration and testing strategy where testing starts with the lowest-level units or components in the calling tree being tested and tests it using drivers. The higher-level software items and their drivers are then integrated one or more at a time, replacing these drivers.

boundary value—A test design method for selecting test cases that examine the values on or around the boundaries of the equivalence classes or other boundaries in the software.

brainstorming—An analysis and problem-solving tool whose purpose is to have a team generate lists of creative ideas in a short period of time through free association and by reserving critical judgment.

branching—The software configuration management process of creating a new codeline containing one or more configuration items that are duplicated from an existing codeline in a controlled library.

budget—A planned sequence of expenditures (for example, dollars or engineering effort) over time with costs assigned to specific activities.

build—"An operational version of a system or component that incorporates a specified subset of the capabilities that the final product will provide" (ISO/IEC 2009). The resulting executable software product.

business requirements—The business problems to be solved or the business opportunities to be addressed by the software product

business rules—The specific policies, standards, practices, regulations, and guidelines that define how the stakeholders do business.

capacity—A measure of the maximum amount of activities, actions, or events that can be concurrently handled by the software or system.

cause-and-effect diagram—A type of tree diagram that is used to explore the multiple causes of a problem or potential causes of a risk. (Also called a fishbone diagram or an Ishikawa diagram.)

cause-effect graphing (CEG)—A model used to help design productive test cases by using a simplified digital-logic circuit (combinatorial logic network) graph.

central limit theorem—A theorem that states that irrespective of the shape of the distribution of the populations or universe, the distribution of average values of samples drawn from that universe will tend toward a normal distribution as the sample size grows without bound.

certification testing—A special type of system testing that is done by a third party.

change—An addition, deletion, or modification to the software (for example, to the concept, requirements, design, code, or documentation). Any modification to an existing policy, system, process, product, or system.

change agent—An individual or team assigned the primary responsibility to plan and manage the change process.

change control—The process by which a change to a formally controlled configuration item, component, unit, or baseline is requested, documented, evaluated, approved, or rejected by the change control board, scheduled, tracked through implementation if approved, and verified prior to its acquisition.

change request (CR)—A formally documented request to make a modification, correction, or enhancement to a controlled configuration item, component, unit, or baseline.

check sheet—An analysis and problem-solving tool used to collect data to create a frequency distribution.

check-in—The process of placing a configuration item into a controlled library.

checklist—A list of yes/no questions or elements used to ensure that all items are considered during an activity (for example, a checklist of criteria evaluated in an audit or a checklist of common errors to be reviewed in an inspection).

check-out—The process of obtaining an official copy of a configuration item from the controlled library.

class—In object-oriented programming, a category (classification) of objects or object types that defines all of the common properties of the different objects that belong to it.

class diagram—An analysis model that looks at the objects the system is modeling and the operations that pertain to those objects. A class diagram defines class information and the interrelationship between classes in a software product.

clean-room methodology—A software development strategy based on incremental development and certification of a pipeline of user-function increments into the final product.

client—The individual who has the authority to initiate an audit and who is a primary customer of the audit results. (Also called the audit's customer or initiator.)

client/server—A two-tier network architecture in which each computer or process on the network is either a client or a server.

closing meeting of an audit—The last step in the execution phase of an audit where the lead auditor presents the results of the audit to the auditee management and other audit stakeholders.

cluster sampling—A statistical sampling method where the population that is being sampled is divided into groups called clusters and each cluster is as heterogeneous as possible to match the population. (Also called block sampling.)

CMMI—SEI's Capability Maturity Model Integration

coaching—"A form of mentoring that involves expert knowledge and skill in the subject matter being coached" (SEI 2002).

COCOMO and **COCOMO II models**—Constructive Cost Model for project estimating.

codeline—A sequence of versions and revisions of the same configuration item that does not include any branching.

cohesion—A measure of the extent to which a component performs a single task or function.

collaboration platforms—A system archetecture that provides components and services to enable people to find information, communicate, and work together regardless of geographic dispersion.

common cause variation—When the root cause of the statistically improbable variation in a process can be attributed to normal, expected variation in the process due to typical causes including influences from people, machinery, environmental factors, materials, measurements, or methods.

communications—Activities involving the transmitting and receiving of information between individuals.

compiler—A software configuration management build tool that converts high-level language source code into object code.

complete or **completeness**—A quality attribute that describes the extent to which a system or software configuration item fully implements all of its allocated requirements.

complexity—A quality attribute that describes the amount or degree of data and/or structural intricacy or interrelationships that makes the software more difficult to understand.

compliance—The degree to which a software practitioner, supplier, or organization has met an agreed-to set of requirements or other measurable criteria.

conciseness or **concision**—A quality attribute describing the degree to which a function has been implemented in the minimum amount of code or documentation has been implemented in the minimum about of verbiage.

concurrent development—When two or more versions of a software product are in development and/or are being supported as releases in operations at the same time.

condition coverage—A white-box testing coverage technique where each statement is executed at least once and each condition in a decision takes all possible outcomes at least once.

confidence level—The probability that a value or number is correct or that a prediction matches its actual future value.

configuration audit—One of the four basic activities of software configuration management. An evaluation that provides independent, objective assurance that the software configuration management processes are being complied with, that the software configuration items are being built as required, and at production, that the software products are ready to be released.

configuration component (CC)—A distinguishable part of the configuration item. Configuration items are made up of configuration components, which are made up of configuration units.

configuration control—"The systematic process that ensures that changes to a baseline are properly identified, documented, evaluated for impact, approved by an appropriate level of authority, incorporated into all impacted work products, and verified" (MIL-HDBK 2001).

configuration control board (CCB)—The authority responsible for evaluating and approving, deferring, or disapproving proposed changes to a formally controlled configuration item and for ensuring implementation of approved changes. (Also called change control board [CCB] or change authority board [CAB] or engineering change board [ECB].)

configuration coverage—Testing analysis that looks at the mapping of tests to the various hardware and software configurations that the software can execute on to ensure that they are thoroughly tested.

configuration identification—One of the four basic activities of software configuration management. The partitioning of the software product into configuration items, components, and units, documenting their functional and physical characteristics, defining their acquisition, assigning unique identifiers to those items, components, and units, and establishing baselines.

configuration item (CI)—A work product placed under configuration management and treated as a single entity. Configuration items are made up of configuration components, which are made up of configuration units.

configuration management—"A discipline applying technical and administrative direction and surveillance to identify and document the functional and physical characteristics of a configuration item, control changes to those characteristics, record and report change processing and implementation status, and verify compliance with specified requirements" (ISO/IEC 2009).

configuration status accounting—One of the four basic activities of software configuration management. The recording and reporting on the implementation status of configuration items, components, and units and the status of proposed changes to those items, components, or units.

configuration testing or **platform configuration coverage**—A type of testing whose objective is to determine if the system or software has any problems handling all the required hardware and software configurations.

configuration unit (CU)—A distinguishable part (unit) of the configuration component or configuration item. The smallest individual entity that is part of a system or work product. For example, a single software module that is discrete and identifiable with respect to compiling. Configuration items are made up of configuration components, which are made up of configuration units.

conflict—A state in which the needs, values, or interests of one or more individuals are in perceived or actual opposition with each other.

conflict of interest—Conflict that occurs when a person in a position of trust has competing professional or personal interests that may make it difficult for that individual to perform his or her duties in an impartial or unbiased manner.

conformance—The degree to which a product or service has met an agreed-to set of requirements or other measurable criteria.

consistency—A quality attribute describing the extent to which strict and uniform adherence has been maintained to prescribed symbols, notations, terminology, and conventions.

constraint—A limit or condition on the project, product, or process that must be met.

context-free questions—Questions that minimize the amount of context included in the question so that they do not limit the scope of the responses.

contingency plan—A set of activities that are planned in advance to handle a problem and are taken only if the risk actually turns into a problem.

contract—A binding, legal agreement between two parties (for example, a supplier and an acquirer).

control chart—A graphical mechanism used to control an attribute of a process over time by identifying improbable patterns that may indicate that the process is out of control.

control flow graph—A graphical representation of the flow of control through a software component or unit.

controlled library—A software configuration management library used for managing current controlled configuration items and baselines, and controlling change to those items and baselines. (Also called the master library or system library.)

conversion—A type of tort lawsuit that might be applied to software. Conversion would be involved if the software were intentionally designed to steal from the customer or destroy property. Conversion only involves tangible personal property.

copyright—A legal mechanism for protect original written works, such as books or software, from being copied without permission.

corrective action—Actions taken to eliminate the root cause of a nonconformance, noncompliance, defect, or other issue in order to prevent future recurrence.

corrective action request (CAR)—A formally documented request to make a modification, correction, or enhancement to a policy, standard, or process.

corrective maintenance—"The reactive modification of a software product performed after delivery to correct discovered problems" (IEEE 2006).

corrective release—An interim release that is done to deliver defect corrections to the users in a timely manner.

correctness—The degree to which the system, software, or documentation is free from defects, meets the specified requirements, and meets the users' needs.

cost—The total monetary amount spent to perform an activity or project, or to create a product.

cost/benefit analysis—An evaluation in which the costs for a product, process, project, or activity are matched against the anticipated value of its benefits to make a determination (for example, whether to acquire a product, implement a process, or start or continue a project).

cost driver—A factor or characteristic that exerts a strong influence on software effort, costs, or productivity.

cost of quality—A measurement of the total cost of software quality that includes the sum of the costs of preventing defects, finding defects, and the costs of internal and external software failures (for example, fixing defects, corrective maintenance, customer technical support, unhappy customers).

cost performance index (CPI)—An earned value metric defined as the earned value divided by the actual value (BCWP/ACWP).

cost variance—An earned value metric defined as the earned value minus the actual value (BCWP – ACWP).

COTS—Commercial off-the-shelf software.

coupling—A measure of the degree to which an individual module or component is interconnected to other modules or components within the system. The more coupled a module or component is, the higher the probability that changes to the module or component will impact other parts of the system.

critical computer resources—Resources including memory capacity, disk space, processor usage, communications capacity, and so on, needed for the development platform, the test platforms, or the target platform.

critical path—The longest path through the activities network that defines the shortest amount of time it will take to complete the project. All of the activities on the critical path must be completed on schedule for the project to be completed on schedule.

customer—The individuals who select, request, purchase, and/or pay for the product, process, or project.

customer satisfaction—A measure of the extent to which the customer is happy with the products, services, or results received.

cycle time—A measure of the amount of calendar time it takes to go from the start to the completion of a process or activity.

cyclomatic complexity—A measure of the number of linearly independent paths through a module.

dashboard—A set of multiple metrics displayed together to provide a complete picture of the status of a process, product, or service.

data domain coverage or **data domain testing**—Testing analysis that looks at the mapping of tests to the various data domains in the software to ensure that they are thoroughly tested.

data flow diagram (DFD)—A graphical representation of how data flows through and is transformed by the system or software.

data privacy—Issues that exist whenever personal information is collected, transmitted, and/or stored by the software.

data requirements—Requirements that define the specific data items or data structures that must be included as part of the software product.

date-time domain coverage or **date-time domain testing**—Testing analysis that looks at the mapping of tests to the various date and time domains in the software to ensure that they are thoroughly tested.

debug—The process of finding and analyzing a suspected defect (fault) in a software product to identify the root cause of a failure.

decision coverage—A white-box testing coverage technique where each statement is executed at least once and each decision takes all possible outcomes at least once. (Also called branch coverage.)

decision criteria— "Thresholds, targets, or patterns used to determine the need for action or further investigation or to describe the level of confidence in a given result" (ISO/IEC 2002).

decision tree—A tree diagram that illustrated the decisions that are made by the software.

decoupled—A lack of coupling.

defect—A fault that exists in the software, which if not corrected could cause the software to fail or produce incorrect results.

defect containment effectiveness—A measure of the effectiveness of defect detection techniques to keep defects from escaping into later phases or into operations.

defect density—A measure that normalizes the number of defects by size so that comparisons can be made between software entities of different sizes.

defect removal effectiveness (DRE) or **defect detection efficiency**—A measure of the effectiveness of our defect detection techniques in finding both defects introduced in the phase and in finding defects that "escaped" from previous phases.

defect severity—An ordinal scale metric that measures the impact of the defect on the successful operation or use of the software.

deliverable—A work product that is delivered internally or released and delivered to operations (to the software's users). In process definition, the tangible, physical objects or specific measurable accomplishments that are the outcomes of the tasks or verification steps.

delivery—The process of actually getting the software and its associated documentation into the operational environment for use by the user.

Delphi and **wideband Delphi**—Expert judgment–based estimation techniques.

denial of service—Any action or security attack that prevents authorized access to software or that prevents any part of software from functioning.

dependency—An interrelationship existing between components in a system or between systems where their versions must be coordinated to avoid interoperability problems or other conflicts. An interrelationship existing between two project activities where the start or finish of one task is dependant on the starting or finishing of the other task.

derived measure—Measures that are calculated using a mathematical combination of two or more explicit measures or other derived measures. (Also called a complex metric.)

design—Translation of the product requirements into the architecture and detailed design that define how the software will be implemented, including defining the components, units, interfaces, and data internal to the software system.

design constraint—A requirement that defines a limitation on the choices that the developers can make when implementing the software or system.

design pattern—A description of "a design structure that solved a particular design problem within a specific context and amid 'forces' that may have an impact on the manner in which the pattern is applied and used" (Pressman 2005).

design predicate approach—An integration testing technique that uses integration complexity to ensure that all of the paths through the calling tree are tested.

desk audit—An audit conducted at the auditor's desk.

desk check—A peer review method where one or more individuals other than the author examines a work product independently and feeds back comments to the author.

detailed design—The process of refining and expanding the architectural design to contain more detailed descriptions of the processing logic, data structures, and data definitions, to the extent that the design is sufficiently complete to implement.

detailed design review—A phase gate review meeting held at the transition from detailed design to implementation (code and unit test). There may be multiple detailed design reviews, one for each of the major design elements. (Also called critical design review [CDR].)

detection—A philosophy that focuses on finding and fixing defects that exist in a product or service before it is released into operations. The process of finding and fixing defect that have caused process problems.

developers—Individuals and groups that are part of the organization that develops and/or maintains the software.

developmental baseline—A baseline created when a configuration item and its associated configuration components, units, and/or documentation are acquired during the development process.

deviation—A written approval from the appropriate body of authority to depart from a policy, standard, or other requirement for a specific period of time or for a specific work product version.

direct-access media—Delivery media containing a software product that the target system can use as is, without the need for installation onto a target platform.

disaster recovery plan—A documented contingency plan of actions to be taken if a catastrophe occurs (for example, if a hard disk crashes or a building where software development is being done burns down).

distributors—The individuals and groups that distribute the software to the customers or users.

DMADV model—A Six Sigma model (define, measure, analyze, design, verify) used to define new processes and products or to perform evolutionary improvement on existing processes to achieve Six Sigma quality levels. (Also called design for Six Sigma [DFSS].)

DMAIC model—A Six Sigma model (define, measure, analyze, improve, control) used to improve existing processes that are not performing at the required level through incremental improvement.

document control—A level of formal change control where one or more requested changes are made to a draft copy of a baselined configuration item followed by change control board (CCB) approval before the modified version or revision is acquired.

domain analysis—Black-box testing techniques that divide the input and output domains into equivalency classes.

driver—A temporary piece of source code used as a replacement for a calling module when performing bottom-up integration and integration testing. A driver is used to invoke a lower-level module under test and may also provide test inputs to that module and report the results.

duration—The length of calendar time it takes to complete an activity.

dynamic analysis—Methods of performing V&V by evaluating a software component or product by executing it and comparing the actual results to expected results. Examples of dynamic analysis testing, simulation, and piloting.

dynamic library—A software configuration management library used to hold configuration entities that are currently being worked on by software practitioners. This typically includes new work products or existing work product that are being modified or tested. The dynamic library is the software practitioner's work area and is under the control of that practitioner. (Also called a development, programmer's, or working library.)

earned value or **earned value management (EVM)**—A measure of the value of work performed so far. Earned value "uses the original estimates and progress to date to show whether the actual costs incurred are on budget and whether the tasks are ahead or behind the baselined plan" (Project 2000).

efficiency—A quality attribute describing the extent to which the software can perform its functions while utilizing minimal amounts of computing resources (for example, memory, or disk space).

effort—The amount of human work that is required to complete an activity or project.

EIA—Electronic Industries Association.

electronic transfer—Delivery of software products via the Internet, bulletin boards, and network mounted file systems.

embedded system—A system where the software is embedded as part of a complete device that includes hardware and/or mechanical components.

encryption algorithm—Set of mathematically expressed rules for rendering data unintelligible by executing a series of conversions controlled by a key.

enhancement—A change made to an existing software product to add additional functionality or capability, adapt it to a changing environment, or to enhance its quality attributes.

enhancement request—A change request reported to add an enhancement to the software.

entity—In measurement, the person, place, thing, process, or time period being measured.

entity relationship diagram (ERD)—A graphical representation of how the data objects in a system relate to each other.

entry criteria—The activities that must be completed, resources that must be in place, or measurable conditions that must be met prior to starting an activity or phase.

environment—The combination of all external policies, procedures, culture, conditions, people, organizations, objects, or other systems that affect the development, operation, and/or maintenance of the software.

environmental factors—All of the elements that surround the project including items such as organizational culture, infrastructure, tools, and existing staff.

equivalence class partitioning—A test design method where the input and/or output domains are divided into subsets of values that are assumed to be handled identically by the software.

error—A human action or mistake that results in the software containing a defect. In measurement, the difference that occurs when the number or symbol (also called the measurement signal, measured value, or data item) differs from the actual value that would be mapped to the attribute of the entity in a perfect world.

error guessing—A black-box testing technique where the tester selects test cases based on the typical types of errors that are made by the programmers or that are input into the software from users, interfacing software, and/or hardware.

escape—A defect that evades one or more defect detection techniques (was not identified) and that moves on to the next process or phase in the life cycle.

escort—An individual or individuals assigned to accompany the auditor(s) during objective evidence-gathering activities and serve as liaison between the audit team and the auditees.

estimate or **estimation**—The predicted future value of a software or project characteristic or attribute (for example, size, cost, effort, schedule, quality, reliability).

ETVX—A methodology for process definition where the entry criteria, tasks, verification, and exit criteria are defined.

event—A specific time, typically at the start or finish of an activity.

event/response table—An analysis model used to list the events that affect the software product and the software product responses to those events based on the state of the software product or one of its components.

evolutionary change—Changes that replace the existing systems, processes, and/or products with better ones.

evolutionary development or **evolutionary model**—A software life cycle model where the product is developed in multiple releases over time based on inputs from the utilization of that software in operations.

executable—A stand-alone software work product that can be run directly on a computer. (Also called a build.)

exit criteria—The activities that must be completed, resources that must be in place, or measurable conditions that must be met before an activity or phase can be considered finished. (Also called completion criteria or acceptance criteria.)

expert judgment—A set of estimation and forecasting techniques based on the judgment of the subject matter experts.

explicit knowledge—Knowledge that is transmitted in a formal manner through various documents, artifacts, or books.

explicit measure—Metrics that are measured directly. (Also called a metric primitive, direct metric, or base measure.)

exploratory testing—Testing where the tester designs and execute tests at the same time, based on the knowledge gained as they are testing the software. (Also called artistic testing.)

external attribute—A characteristic or property of an entity that can be measured only in terms of the entity's relationship to its environment.

external audit—An evaluation performed by a group outside the organization being audited. (Also called second-party audit or third-party audit.)

external failure costs of quality—All the costs of quality that involve handling and correcting a failure that has occurred once the product or service is in operations.

external interface requirements—Requirements for the information flow across shared interfaces to hardware, humans, other software applications, the operating system, and file systems outside the boundaries of the software product being developed.

extranet—An intranet web architecture that has various levels of accessibility to authorized outsiders.

extreme programming (XP)—An agile method that focuses on (as opposed to process improvement techniques like lean or project management techniques like scrum) software development techniques.

extrinsic motivation—"Satisfaction of psychological or material needs by others through incentives or rewards" (Westcott 2006).

facilitated requirements workshops—Facilitated meetings that bring together cross-functional groups of stakeholders to produce specific software requirements work products.

facilitator—An individual who creates an environment in which others can direct their own learning and/or work.

failure—An occurrence of the software not meeting its requirements or intended usage while it is being executed.

failure mode effects and criticality analysis (FMECA)—Activities involving the analysis of possible software failures, the effects of those failures, and the critically of those effects.

fan-in—In procedural language, a measure of the number of modules that directly call a module. In object-oriented development, a measure of the number of classes that a class directly inherits from.

fan-out—In procedural language, a measure of the number of modules that are directly called by another module. In object-oriented development, a measure of the number of classes that directly inherit from a class.

fault—A defect in a software work product.

fault insertion—The process of intentionally adding a known number of defects to the software for the purpose of estimating the number of unknown defects remaining in the software. (Also called fault seeding.)

fault tolerance—A quality attribute describing the extent to which the software can detect and handle defects, invalid inputs, or erroneous states from the environment in which it operates (for example, hardware failures, invalid or interrupted data communications) without failure. (Also called exception handling, fault-error handling, robustness, or error tolerance.)

feasible or **feasability**—Something that can be implemented using available technologies, techniques, tools, resources, and personnel within the specified cost and schedule constraints.

feature driven development (FDD)—An agile development methodology for implementing software functionality that is based on breaking the requirements down into small client-valued pieces of functionality and iteratively implementing them.

feature release—A release done primarily to deliver new features or functionality to the user. Defects can also be corrected as part of a feature release.

finding—Any nonconformance, noncompliance, observation, process improvement opportunity, best practice, or other fact worthy of reporting as a result of an audit activity.

firewall—A mechanism for preventing unauthorized access to a network.

firmware—Software that is embedded into and becomes part of a hardware device (for example in an EPROM).

first-party audit—An audit that an organization performs on itself. (Also called an internal audit.)

first-pass yield—A measure of the effectiveness of defect prevention techniques.

flexibility—A quality attribute describing the ease with which the software can be modified or customized by the user.

flowchart—A graphical representation of the inputs, actions, and outputs of a process.

focus groups—Small groups of representative users (typical users) brought together to elicit information and opinions about a product and its requirements.

follow-up audit—A re-audit of one or more elements that had previous nonconformances.

force field analysis—An analysis and problem-solving tool whose purpose is to identify driving forces that help move toward reaching the goal and restraining forces inhibiting movement toward the goal.

forecasting—The predicted future value of a software or project characteristic or a period of time (for example, staffing needs, resource needs, and project risks and opportunities).

formal methods—A set of mathematics-based techniques for the specification, development, and verification of software-intensive systems.

forming—The first stage of team development when the team is initially brought together or when new members are added to an existing team.

fraud—A type of tort lawsuit that might be applied to software. The seller of the software knowingly misrepresented the capabilities of the product.

full release—Packaging of a release that is capable of completing a full installation of the product.

function points—A measurement of software size in terms of its functionality.

functional baseline—The baseline created when a system requirement and associated configuration items are acquired.

functional configuration audit—"An audit conducted to verify that the development of a configuration item has been completed satisfactorily, the item has achieved the performance and functional characteristics specified, and its operational and support documents are complete and satisfactory" (ISO/IEC 2009).

functional requirements—Stakeholder- or product-level requirements that define the capabilities of the software (what the software must do) to satisfy the business requirements.

functional testing—Testing to evaluate the extent to which the software meets its functional requirements.

functionality—A quality attribute describing the extent to which the software can perform all of the functions required by the user.

Gantt chart—A bar chart used to show the scheduled calendar time and duration for each activity in a project and the actual calendar time and duration used.

goal/question/metric paradigm—A mechanism for defining a goal-based measurement program through the selection of metrics that provide information to answer questions about the achievement or progress toward achieving goals.

gold-plating—Functionality that it added to the software product that is not necessary to meet the business or user objectives and therefore does not add value for the stakeholders.

good enough software—A strategy where analysis is done to make conscious, logical decisions about the trade-offs between the level of quality and integrity that the stakeholders need in the software, and the basic economic fact that increasing software quality and integrity typically costs more and takes longer.

gray-box testing—A blending of white-box and black-box testing strategies that primarily focuses on interfaces and interactions at various levels as units are integrated into programs, programs into subsystems, and subsystems into the software system.

guidelines—A suggested practice, method, or instructions that are considered good practice but are not mandatory.

hacker or **hacking**—An unauthorized user who attempts to or gains access into a software product, an information system, or data.

haphazard sampling or **pseudo random sampling**—A nonstatistical sampling technique where samples are selected based on convenience but preferably should still be chosen as randomly as possible.

hardware dependency—A dependency that exists when the current release of the software is not backward compatible with the hardware used to run previous versions of the software.

Hawthorne effect—The fact that the simple act of measurement, which give attention (demonstrated interest by management) to the attributes being measured, causes workers to endeavor to make those measurements improve.

hazard analysis—The identification and analysis of potential risks that could cause harm (for example, personal injury, property or environmental damage, negative impacts to the health or safety of the society).

histogram—A bar chart that shows the distribution (shape) of a set of data.

human factors studies—Studies that consider the ways in which the human users of a software system will interact with the software.

IDEAL—The software process improvement approach developed by the Software Engineering Institute (SEI). IDEAL is an acronym for each of the five stages in the model: initiating, diagnosing, establishing, acting, leveraging (McFeeley 1996).

identifier—A unique label associated with a configuration item, component, unit, or baseline, or one of their versions or revisions.

IEC—International Electrotechnical Commission.

IEEE—Institute of Electrical and Electronics Engineers.

IFPUG—International Function Point User's Group.

impact analysis—The analysis of the impacts a requested change would have on the software product, process, service, and/or project.

incremental change—Changes made to improve the existing systems, processes, and/or products to make them better

incremental development or **incremental model**—A software life cycle model based on the process of constructing increasingly larger subsets of the software's requirements.

independent test team—An organization responsible for testing the software that is both technically and managerially separated from the organization responsible for the development of the software.

information hiding—In object-oriented programming, the hiding of an object's internal structure from its surroundings.

information radiator—A Crystal practice where forms of (displayed) project documentation are used or placed in areas where people can easily see them.

informative workspace—An extreme programming practice where the workspace is used to communicate important, active information.

inheritance—In object-oriented programming, a relationship between classes that allows the definition of a new class based on the definition of an existing class.

in-process audit—An audit of a process as it is being implemented.

input—The tangible, physical objects that are input into and utilized during the process. Data or other items that come into a software system or component from outside its boundary.

inspection—A formal method of peer review where a team of peers, including the author, meets to examine a work product.

inspectors—Individuals participating in an inspection.

installability—A quality attribute describing the ease with which the software product can be installed on the target platform.

installation—The process of integrating the software into its operational environment for use by the users.

integrated master schedule—A summarization of the statuses of the lower-level subprojects into a higher-level project view.

integrated product team (IPT)—A cross-functional team formed for the specific purpose of delivering an integrated product that was produced by more than one organization (for example, partially developed in-house and partially developed by one or more suppliers).

integration—"The process of fitting together the various components of a system so that the entire system works as a whole" (Jones 1994).

integration complexity—A measure of the number of linearly independent paths through a calling tree.

integration testing—The testing of the combination of two or more software or hardware units or components in order to determine if there are any problems with their interfaces, logical communications, or other interactions.

intellectual property—A legal area that includes inventions and ideas of the human mind, such as books, music, artwork, and software.

interface—A shared boundary across which information is passed.

intermediate installation media—Delivery media that requires an installation of the software product onto the target system.

internal attribute—A property or characteristic of an entity that can be measured in terms of the entity by itself.

internal audit—An audit that an organization performs on itself. (Also called a first-party audit.)

internal failure costs of quality—Internal failure costs are all the costs of quality that involve handling and correcting a failure that has occurred in-house before the product or service has been made available to the customer.

international configuration coverage or **international configuration testing**—Testing analysis that looks at the mapping of tests to the various international configurations that the software can have to ensure that they are thoroughly tested. (Also called localization coverage or localization testing.)

Internet—A Web architecture made up of a global network connecting millions of computers.

interoperability—A quality attribute describing the degree to which the software functions properly and shares resources with other software applications or hardware operating in the same environment

interrelationship digraph—An analysis and problem-solving tool whose purpose is to organize ideas and define the ways in which ideas influence each other.

interval scale measurement—For interval scale measurements, the exact distance between the scales is known. This allows the mathematical operations of addition and subtraction to be applied to interval scale measurement values. However, there is no zero point in the interval scale, so multiplication and division do not apply.

interview—A technique for gathering information through the process of one or more individuals (interviewers) asking questions and evaluating the answers provided by one or more other people (interviewees).

intranet—A web architecture made up of a connected network that resides behind a firewall and is only accessible to people within the organization.

intrinsic motivation—"A self-motivating process where an individual obtains reinforcement through personally valuing characteristics of the situation itself" (Westcott 2006).

ISO—International Organization for Standardization

iterative model—An iterative software development process model where steps or activities are repeated multiple times.

joint applications development (JAD)—A facilitated team-based requirements development technique. (Also called a facilitated requirements workshop.)

judgmental sampling—A nonstatistical sampling technique where the person doing the sample uses his or her knowledge or experience to select the items to be sampled.

Kano model—A model showing the relationship between customer satisfaction and product quality.

Kiviat chart—A circular chart where each "spoke on the wheel" represents a metric with the metric's value plotted on that spoke. (Also called a polar chart, radar chart, or spider chart.)

KLOC—Thousand (K) lines of code (LOC).

labeling—The software configuration management process of creating a unique identifier (label) and using it to create an association between a set of configuration items in one or more controlled libraries. (Also called tagging.)

lead auditor—The person responsible for leading the audit team and conducting the audit.

lean—A set of agile software development techniques including eliminating waste, amplifying learning, deciding as late as possible, delivering as early as possible, empowering the team, building integrity in, and seeing the whole.

legibility—A quality criterion that describes the ease with which the software source code or documentation can be read and accurately interpreted.

lessons learned—Knowledge gained from reflecting on activities, processes, or projects after they have been implemented, through performing root cause analysis of identified issues or defects, or through other empirical analysis methods that is used to prevent future problems.

life cycle—A high-level representation of the software development process, which provides a framework for the detailed definition of the process and defines the stages (phases) through which software development moves.

lines of code (LOC)—A metric for the size of a software component. A count of the number of physical or logical lines of source code in a software component.

linker or **loader**—A software configuration management build tool that combines and converts object code modules into the software executable.

load/volume/stress testing—Performance testing techniques used to determine if the system has any problems dealing with normal level, maximum level, and excess levels of capacity.

maintainability—A quality attribute describing the ease with which a software system or one of its components can be modified. "The ease with which a software system or component can be modified to change or add capabilities, correct faults or defects, improve performance or other attributes, or adapt to a changed environment" (ISO/IEC 2009).

maintenance—The activities involved in modifying the software after it has been released.

malicious code—An unauthorized process or funtion programmed into the software with the intention of adversely impacting its confidentiality, integrity, or availability.

malpractice—A type of tort lawsuit that might be applied to software. The software's author (or the program itself) provides unreasonably poor professional services.

management review—A project review held to provide senior management awareness of and visibility into project activities.

manager—"A person that provides technical and administrative direction and control to those performing tasks or activities within the manager's area of responsibility. The traditional functions of a manager include planning, organizing, directing, and controlling work within an area of responsibility" (SEI 2006).

mapping system—The rules or units of measure for mapping numbers and symbols onto the attributes of entities. (Also called measurement method or counting criteria.)

matrix diagram—An analysis and problem-solving tool whose purpose is to analyze the correlations between two groups of items.

mean—The arithmetic average of the numbers in the data set.

mean time to change—A maintainability metric that measures the average amount of effort it takes to make a change to the software.

mean time to fix—A maintainability metric that measures the average amount of effort it takes to fix a defect that has been identified in the software.

measurement—"The process by which numbers or symbols are assigned to attributes of entities in the real world in such a way as to describe them according to clearly defined rules" (Fenton 1997).

median—The middle value when the numbers in a data set are arranged according to size.

mentoring—The act of a more experienced individual forming a relationship with a less experienced individual in order to help that individual develop or improve his or her skill set, performance, knowledge, or other capability.

merging—The software configuration management process of taking two or more versions or revisions of a work product and combining them into a single new version or revision.

messaging systems architecture—An architecture designed to accept messages from or deliver messages to other systems.

method—In object-oriented programming, a piece of software code that implements an operation.

metric model—The equation used to calculate a derived measure.

metrics—The systematic application of measurement-based techniques to software products, processes, and services to provide engineering and management information that can be used to improve those software products, processes, and services (based on Goodman 1993).

migration—Porting of the software to another environment.

milestone—A significant event that marks progress in a project, usually representing the completion of a major phase of work.

mistake—"A human action that produced an incorrect result" (ISO/IEC 2009).

mode—The value that occurs most often in the data set

model—An abstract representation of an item or process from a particular point of view.

moderator—The role in an inspection process that is responsible for ensuring that the inspection process is correctly implemented by the inspectors.

modularity—A quality attribute describing the extent to which the software is partitioned into independent modules, where each module is constructed to work with the other modules without being involved with the detailed internal structure of those other modules.

motivation—The set of feelings or reasons that determines the extent to which an individual will engage in a particular activity or behavior.

multiple condition coverage—A white-box testing coverage technique where each statement is executed at least once and all possible combinations of condition outcomes in each decision occur at least once.

multivoting—A team decision-making technique where each team member casts multiple votes to aid in the selection process.

negligence—A type of tort lawsuit that might be applied to software. The producer of the software failed to take steps that a reasonable software producer would take, and because of this failure the software injured a customer or his or her property.

negotiation—Communication designed to come to an agreement, resolve a dispute, determine a course of action, or satisfy various interests.

nominal group techniques—Structured, team-based analysis and problem-solving techniques used to explore issues and determine solutions.

nominal scale measurement—The simplest form of measurement is classification (one-to-one mapping) where its type categorizes the attribute of the entity. Nominal scale does not make any assumptions about order or sequence.

nonconformance or **noncompliance**—A type of audit finding that is a nonfulfillment of a specific objective criteria.

nonfunctional requirements—Product-level requirements that define the specific characteristic that the software must possess in order to fulfill the quality attribute requirements.

norming—A stage of team development when the team is coming to agreement on their methods of operations and norms for conducting their business.

n-tier architectures—n-tiered architectures break the application into two or more tiers or layers. A client/server architecture is an example of a two-tiered architecture.

object—A self-contained element in object-oriented programming that has both data associated with it and associated procedures to manipulate the data.

objective evidence—"Information, which can be proven true, based on facts obtained through observation, measurement, test, or other means" (Russell 2005).

objectivity—The absence of bias that will influence results.

object-oriented analysis and design (OOD)—Analyzes and specifies the design in terms of the objects that the system is modeling and the operations that pertain to those objects.

observation—Any item worthy of note to management (both positive and negative) that does not rise to the level of a nonconformance.

offshore—A type of outsourcing where the supplier is located in a different country than the acquirer.

open-ended questions—Questions that require more than a few words to answer (for example, who, what, when, where, why, and how type questions).

opening meeting of an audit—A meeting at the beginning of the audit execution step between the audit team and the auditee organization. The objectives of this meeting include introducing the audit team, reviewing the conduct of the audit, reviewing audit logistics, and making sure the auditee understands what to expect from the audit.

operation—In object-oriented programming, an action that can be applied to an object to obtain a certain effect.

operational profile testing—A black-box testing method where the number of tests done on each thread is weighted based on its usage in the expected operational environment

operations—The phase of the software life cycle when the software is available for use by all of its customers. (Also called the production phase, operation phase, maintenance phase, or general availability [GA].)

opportunity—A possibility of a positive outcome occurring during a project that will impact the success of that project. (Also called a positive risk.)

ordering—The activities involved in ordering copies of the software product.

ordinal scale measurement—The ordinal scale classifies the attribute of the entity by order. However, there are no assumptions made about the magnitude of the differences between categories.

organizational change management—The management of technology transfers and other changes to the organization's methods, processes, and systems so the organization can grow and improve in order to stay competitive.

organizational process assets—Artifacts that represent organizational learning and knowledge and are considered "useful to those who are defining, implementing, and managing processes in the organization" (SEI 2006).

output—The tangible, physical objects that are output from a process. Data or other items that come from a software system or component and are communicated outside its boundary.

outsourcing—The development or maintenance of all or part of a software product by a supplier outside the primary development organization.

packaging—Mechanisms for delivery of a release.

pair programming—An agile technique where two people work together, one of whom is constantly reviewing what the other is developing.

Pareto analysis—The process of ranking problems or categories based on their frequency of occurrence or the size of their impact in order to determine which of many possible opportunities to pursue first.

Pareto chart—A bar chart where the height of each bar indicates the frequency or impact of problems or categories.

partial release—Packaging of a release that requires a full release to already be installed.

patch—A modification made directly to an object program without changing the source code (avoids reassembling or recompiling). A temporary fix to the source or object code.

patent—A legal mechanism for protecting ideas by providing "exclusive rights for novel inventions for a limited period of time" (Futrell 2002).

path—A control flow sequence through the internal structure of the software

peer review—A static analysis technique for evaluating the form, structure, and content of a document, source code, or other work product using examination rather then execution.

perfective maintenance—"Improvements in the software's performance or functionality, for example, in response to user suggestions or requests" (ISO/IEC 2009).

performance—A quality attribute describing the levels of performance (for example, capacity, throughput, response times) required from the software.

performance measures—Measures of the ability of the software to perform its functions (for example, response time, throughput, number of transactions, accuracy, frequency).

performance testing—A type of testing whose objective is to determine if the system has any problems meeting its performance requirements for throughput, response time, number of simultaneous users, number of terminals supported, and so on.

performing—A stage of team development when the team is in high-performance mode and everyone knows how to work together effectively.

phase—A logical group of related activities that constitute a major step in a software project or life cycle. A major segment or component of a software life cycle.

phase containment effectiveness—A measure of the effectiveness of defect detection techniques in identifying defects in the same phase as they were introduced.

phase gate review—Reviews used to verify the successful completion of a project phase or milestone. (Also called phase transition reviews or milestone reviews.)

physical configuration audit—"An audit conducted to verify that each configuration item, as built, conforms to the technical documentation that defines it" (ISO/IEC 2009).

pilot—A verification and validation technique where the product or process is analyzed during a trial run.

plan–do–check–act model—A process improvement model. (Also called the Shewhart cycle or the Deming circle.)

PMI—Project Management Institute.

policy—"A governing principle typically used as the basis for regulations, procedures, or standards and generally stated by the highest authority in the organization" (Humphrey 1989).

polymorphism—In object-oriented programming, a mechanism that allows the sender of a stimulus (or message) to not need to know the receiving instance's class so that receiving instance can belong to an arbitrary class.

portability—A quality attribute describing the effort required to migrate the software to a different platform or environment.

post-conditions—Specific, measurable conditions that must be met before the use case is considered complete.

post-project review—A project review held at the end of a project (or at the end of one of the project's phases or activities) to evaluate what went right on the project (phase or activity) that needs to be repeated on future projects and what went wrong that could be improved on in the future. (Also called postmortem or project retrospective.)

preconditions—Specific, measurable conditions that must be met before the use case can be initiated.

prevention—A quality philosophy that focuses on keeping defects out of the product, service, or process.

prevention costs of quality—Prevention costs are all the costs of quality that involve keeping defects from getting into the software products, processes, and services.

preventive maintenance—"Modification of a software product after delivery to detect and correct latent faults in the software product before they manifest as failures" (IEEE 2006).

prioritization graph—An X-Y graph used to prioritize items by order of importance based on two criteria.

prioritization matrix—A tool used to rank items in order of priority based on a set of weighted criteria.

problem report—A change request created to report an issue or anomaly in the software.

problem resolution—The process that deals with correcting specific instances of a problem in one or more software products.

procedure—"A course of action to be taken to perform a given task" (ISO/IEC 2009).

process—The step-by-step sequence of actions that must be carried out to complete an activity. A definable, repeatable, measurable sequence of tasks used to produce a quality product.

process architecture—The definition of the ordering of the individual processes, their interactions and interdependencies, of work product flows between the processes, and their interfaces to external processes.

process audit—An in-depth evaluation of a process or set of processes.

process flow diagram—A graphical representation of the flow of control through the tasks and verification steps in a process and the roles responsible for each task or verification step.

process improvement—The planned and systematic set of all actions and activities needed to identify, plan, implement, track, and control improvements to a process.

process metric—A metric designed to report one or more measures that provide information about a process.

process owner—The group or individual responsible for making decisions about the process.

process stakeholder—Individuals or groups who affect or are affected by a software process and therefore have some level of influence over the requirements for that process.

product audit—An evaluation of a product to examine its conformance to the product specification, performance, and other standards or the customer's requirements.

product backlog—In scrum, a prioritized list of unimplemented product requirements (features).

product baseline—The baseline created when the product is released into operations. (Also called the production baseline.)

product licensing—A legal mechanism for granting the license holder the right to either use or redistribute one or more copies of copyrighted products without breaking copyright law.

product limitations—A definition of items that will not be included in the product.

product metric—A metric designed to report one or more measures that provide information about a work product.

product owner—The scrum role that represents the project stakeholders, is responsible for project funding, and controls and prioritizes the product backlog.

product scope—A definition of what will be included in the product, thus defining the boundaries of the product.

product stakeholder—Individuals or groups who affect or are affected by a software product and therefore have some level of influence over the requirements for that product.

product vision—The definition of how the new or updated software product bridges the gap between the current state and the desired future state needed to take advantage of a business opportunity or solve a business problem.

production—Activities involving the creation of master media and the replication of that media.

productivity—A measure of the effectiveness and efficiency of executing a process typically modeled in terms of the size or amount of work product produced per unit of time.

program—"A group of related projects managed in a coordinated way to obtain benefits and control not available from managing them individually" (PMI 2008).

program review—A review meeting that involves gathering and consolidating status information from the individual project being managed together as a group or program.

project—"A temporary endeavor undertaken to create a unique product, service, or result" (PMI 2008).

project audit—An audit of the processes used to plan, implement, track, control, and close a project to evaluate the processes' conformance to documented instructions or standards. A project audit also looks at the effectiveness of the project management process in meeting the intended goals or objectives, and the adequacy and effectiveness of the process controls.

project charter—The document that formally authorizes the project and is created during project initiation.

project closure—The processes and activities involving the termination of a project.

project execution—The processes and activities involved in implementing and deploying the project. (Also called project deployment.)

project initiation—The processes and activities involved in starting a project, including defining the project's charter

project management—The planning and management of strategies and tactics of a project to direct the intent of the project, plan actions, activities, risks, resources and responsibilities, guide the ongoing project activities, and anticipate and prepare for change.

project monitoring and controlling—The processes and activities involved in tracking the actual results of the project's implemented actions and activities against the established plans, controlling significant deviation from the expected plans, and making any changes required to keep the project in line with its objectives. (Also called project tracking and control.)

project objectives—The defined list of intended outcomes for the project.

project plan—The planning documentation that describes how the organization's project management policies, standards, processes, work instructions, and infrastructure will be implemented and tailored to meet the needs of an individual project, including specific activities, responsibilities, resource and budget allocations, tactics, tools, and methods. This information may be in a single project plan or separated into multiple planning documents (for example, software quality assurance plan, verification and validation plan, software configuration management plan).

project planning—The processes and activities involved in planning the project.

project reviews—Various types of reviews intended to track the progress of the project and identify issues.

project scope—The amount of work being done on the project.

project stakeholder—"Persons and organizations . . . that are actively involved in the project, or whose interests may be positively or negatively affected by the execution or completion of the project" (PMI 2008).

project team review—A project review with project team members held to monitor the current status and results of the project against the project's documented estimates, plans, commitments, and requirements and to identify project issues in a timely manner so that effective action can be taken.

promotion—A transition in the level of authority needed to approve changes to a controlled configuration item, component, unit, or baseline.

proof of correctness—"A formal technique used to prove mathematically that a computer program satisfies its specified requirements" (ISO/IEC 2009). (Also called mathematical proofs.)

prototype—A partial, preliminary, or mock-up version of the software product used to elicit, analyze, and validate requirements.

quality—1. "The degree to which a system, component, or process meets specified requirements. 2. Ability of a product, service, system, component, or process to meet customer or user needs, expectations, or requirements. 3. The totality of characteristics of an entity that bear on its ability to satisfy stated and implied needs. 4. Conformity to user expectations, conformity to user requirements, customer satisfaction, reliability, and level of defects present. 5. The degree to which a set of inherent characteristics fulfils requirements" (ISO/ IEC 2009).

quality assurance—The planned and systematic set of all actions and activities needed to provide adequate confidence that:

- A work product conforms to its requirements

- The organization's quality management system (or each individual process) is adequate to meet the organization's quality goals and objectives, is appropriately planned, is being followed, and is effective and efficient

quality attributes—Stakeholder-level requirements that define the characteristics that the software must possess to be considered a high-quality product by one or more stakeholders.

quality engineering—The planned and systematic set of all actions and activities needed to define, plan, and implement the quality management system.

quality function deployment (QFD)—A quality management technique for evaluating the user's needs against product requirements.

quality gate—A quality checkpoint or review that a work product must pass through in order to be acquired or to transition to the next project activity.

quality goals—Specific targets established to institutionalize quality-related activities into every aspect of the organization and its key business practices.

quality improvement—The planned and systematic set of all actions and activities needed to identify, plan, implement, track, and control improvements to the quality management system.

quality management system (QMS)—The aggregate of the organization's quality-related organizational structure, policies, processes, work instructions, plans, supporting tools, and infrastructure.

quality manual—Formal documentation of an organization's quality management system, including its quality policy.

quality objectives—Specific, measurable, achievable, realistic, and time-framed objectives needed to achieve quality goals.

quality plan—Planning documentation that defines the specifics for how a project (program or product) intends to implement and tailor the organization's quality management system to meet the needs of an individual project, including specific activities, responsibilities, resource and budget allocations, tactics, tools, and methods.

quality policy—The formally documented statement of the overall intentions and direction of an organization with regard to quality, as formally expressed by top management.

quality record—An artifact that provides the objective evidence that the appropriate quality and process activities took place and that the execution of those activities met required standards, policies, procedures, and/or specifications. Examples of quality records include meeting minutes, logs, change requests, completed forms, completed checklists, formal sign-off or approval pages, reports, and metrics.

quality system audit—An evaluation of an organization's existing quality program's conformance to company policies, contractual commitments, industry standards, and/or regulatory requirements.

race condition—When one event should follow a second event but in actuality occurs first.

random sampling—A sampling procedure where a sample of size n is drawn from the population in such a way that every possible element has the same chance of being selected.

range—The difference between the maximum and minimum values in a data set.

rapid application development (RAD)—"An incremental software development process model that achieves extremely short development cycle through the use of component-based construction" (Pressman 2001).

ratio scale measurement—The ratio scale is an interval scale with an absolute or nonarbitrary zero point. All mathematical operations can be applied to ratio scale measurement values including multiplication and division.

reader—The role in an inspection process that is responsible for presenting the work product to the other inspectors during the meeting.

ready-to-ship review—A phase gate review held at the transition from the final test cycle to deployment of the completed system for use by the end users. (Also called a ready-to-release review.)

recognition—The act of acknowledging and/or rewarding individuals for their performance or behavior.

recorder—The person in a meeting who is responsible for keeping the record of that meeting. (Also called the scribe or secretary.)

recovery—The ability to restore a previous state of the software products, data, or development environment from its backup

reengineering—The process of rebuilding existing software products to create a product with added functionality, better performance and reliability, and improved maintainability.

regression analysis—The activity of examining a proposed software change and determining the depth and breadth of the effects the proposed change could have on the software to determine of how extensively a change needs to be tested and the software needs to be retested.

regression testing—"Selective retesting of a system or component to verify that modifications have not caused unintended effects and that the system or component still complies with its specified requirements" (ISO/IEC 2009).

regulation—"A rule, law, or instruction, typically established by some legislative or regulatory body with penalties for noncompliance" (Humphrey 1989).

release—Certain promotions of the configuration item that are distributed outside development.

reliability—A quality attribute describing the extent to which the software can perform its functions without failure for a specified period of time under specified conditions. "The ability of a system or component to perform its required functions under stated conditions for a specified period of time" (ISO/IEC 2009).

reliable metric—A metric is reliable if it can be used by different people (or the same person multiple times) with the same result.

replication—The process of making copies of the software and its associated documentation for shipment to the customers or users.

requirement—A capability, attribute, or design constraint of the software that provides value to or is needed by a stakeholder.

requirements analysis—The requirements development activity that involves evaluating and modeling the information gathered from the product's stakeholders to identify gaps, conflicts, and other issues that require additional elicitation, to organize that information into requirements, and to prioritize those requirements.

requirements churn—The level of change occurring in the baselined requirements. (Also called requirement volatility or scope creep.)

requirements development—All of the activities involved in eliciting, analyzing, specifying, and validating the requirements.

requirements elicitation—The requirements development activity that includes all of the activities involved in identifying the requirement's stakeholders, selecting representatives from each stakeholder class, and collecting information to determine the needs of each class of stakeholders

requirements engineering—A disciplined, process-oriented approach to the definition, documentation, and maintenance of software requirements throughout the software development life cycle

requirements management—The activities employed to ensure that the system and software requirements are maintained in accordance with all applicable rules, regulations, standards, procedures, and so on, and that only authorized changes are made to those requirements once they are baselined.

requirements review—A phase gate review held at the transition from the requirements phase into the high-level or architectural design phase.

requirements specification—The requirements development activities that involve documenting the requirements into one or more specification or other documents.

requirements validation—The requirements development activities that involve evaluating the requirements for completeness, correctness, consistency, feasibility, finiteness, measurability, maintainability, and other quality criteria.

resource utilization—A measure of the average or maximum amount of a given resource (for example, memory, disk space, bandwidth) used by the software to perform a function or activity.

resource utilization testing—A type of testing whose objective is to determine if the system uses resources (for example, memory, disk space) at levels that exceed requirements.

response time—A measure of the average or maximum amount of calendar time required to respond to a stimulus (for example, user command, input from another software application or hardware signal).

retirement—The time at which the support of a particular release of the software or the entire software product is terminated.

return on investment (ROI)—A measure of the ratio between the profits received from an activity or project and its cost.

reusability or reuse—A quality attribute describing the extent to which one or more components of a software product can be reused when developing other software products.

reverse engineering—The software design and interface information is re-created from the source code.

review—"A process or meeting during which a work product, or set of work products, is presented to project personnel, managers, users, customers, or other interested parties for comment or approval" (ISO/IEC 2009).

revision—A change to a configuration item, component, or unit that corrects one or more defects but does not incorporate any new functionality or features.

rework—Repetition of work that has already been completed because of unsatisfactory results.

risk—"The likelihood of an event, hazard, threat, or situation occurring and its undesirable consequences" (IEEE 2006a).

risk analysis—The activities involving exploring the context of each risk, assigning a probability, loss, and time frame to each risk, and prioritizing the risks.

risk exposure (RE)—The expected value of the loss associated with the risk calculated by multiplying the risk likelihood by the risk loss.

risk identification—The activities involving the identification and communication of risks.

risk loss—The cost (for example, dollars, effort hours, or schedule slippage) to the project if the risk actually turns into a problem. The impact or jeopardy to the project if the problem occurs. (Also called risk impact.)

risk management process—The process for identifying, analyzing, planning for, taking action against, and tracking risks.

risk mitigation actions—A set of planned activities intended to handle a risk by reducing the probability that the risk will turn into a problem or by reducing the loss to the project if the problem does occur. (Also called risk containment actions or risk-handling activities.)

risk probability—The likelihood that the risk will turn into a major problem.

risk reduction leverage (RRL)—The benefit-to-cost ratio for a given risk reduction plan.

risk tracking—The activities involving tracking the risk until it is closed.

role—The individual or group responsible for one or more tasks, verification steps, or activities that are part of a process or plan.

root cause analysis—The process of assessing sets of product defects or process problems to identify their systemic cause(s).

run chart—An analytical tool that plots data arranged in time sequence.

safety—A quality attribute describing the ability to use the software without adverse impact to individuals, property, the environment, or society.

safety testing—A type of testing whose objective is to determine if the system is safe.

safety-critical software—Software that can result in an accident, that is intended to mitigate the results of an accident, or that is intended to recover from the results of an accident.

sampling—A mechanism for using only part of the entire population to estimate attributes of that population.

scatter diagram—An x-y plot of one variable versus another. One variable, called the independent variable, is typically plotted on the x-axis. The second variable, called the dependent variable, is typically plotted on the y-axis. Scatter diagrams are used to investigate whether the independent variable is causing changes in the dependent variable.

schedule or **scheduling**—The length of calendar time planned for the performance of a process or a project.

schedule performance index (SPI)—An earned value metric defined as the earned value divided by the planned value (BCWP / BCWS).

schedule variance—An earned value metric defined as the earned value minus the planned value (BCWP – BCWS).

SCM librarians—The role responsible for establishing, coordinating, and ensuring the integrity of the software configuration management controlled libraries and static libraries for each project and for reuse of software components between projects

SCM manager—The role responsible for managing the software configuration management activities and software configuration management group.

SCM toolsmith—The role responsible for the implementation and maintenance of the software configuration management tool set.

scope—In project management, the quantity of the work done during the project to produce outputs with the required functionality and quality. In product management, the boundaries of that project.

scrum—A set of agile techniques that emphasize project management.

scrum master—The scrum role that is responsible for the scrum process and fitting scrum into the organization.

scrum planning meeting—A meeting held to select the items from the product backlog to form a specific set (sprint backlog) of features and process improvement items for implementation in the next sprint. (Also called the sprint planning meeting.)

scrum team—The scrum role that includes the members of a self-managed, cross-functional team that is responsible for turning each sprint backlog into a deliverable software increment.

second-party audit—An audit performed by a customer (or an organization contracted by a customer) on its supplier.

security—A quality attribute describing the probability that an attack of a specific type will be detected, repelled, or handled by the software.

security coverage or **security testing**—A type of testing whose objective is to determine if the security of the system can be breached.

SEI—Software Engineering Institute.

SEI's Capability Maturity Model Integration (CMMI)—Software Engineering Institute's models for analyzing organizational process maturity or individual process capability.

sequence diagram—An analysis model that records in detail how objects interact over time to perform a task by describing the messages that pass between them.

service level agreement (SLA)—A formally negotiated agreement between two parties (typically, the maintainer and the acquirer of the software) that defines the agreed-upon level of service to be provided.

shipping—The activities involved in packaging and shipping the software product to the end user or customer.

simulator—A mechanism used to imitate the real-world environment, for example, during testing.

situational leadership—Methods where the style of leadership selected depends on the situation or context.

Six Sigma—The Greek letter sigma (σ) is the statistical symbol for standard deviation. Therefore Six Sigma literally means six standard deviations away from the mean. Or no more than 3.4 defects per million opportunities. As a quality strategy, Six Sigma has evolved into a comprehensive and flexible road map for both continuous (DMAIC) and evolutionary (DMADV) process improvement.

slack—"The amount of calendar time that an activity can be delayed before it begins to impact the project's finish date" (Lewis 1995).

SLIM—Software life cycle management model for project estimation.

software architecture—The architecture composed of software-level components, interfaces between those components, and the functions to be interchanged.

software assurance—Activities involving the assurance that the software is safe and secure.

software configuration management (SCM)—The process of applying configuration management tools and techniques throughout the software product life cycle to ensure the completeness, correctness, and integrity of software configuration items.

software dependency—A dependency that exists when the current release of the software is not backward compatible with the software platform used to run previous versions of the software, other software that interfaced with the previous version of the software, or data files that were accessed by previous versions of the software.

source code—Assembly language or higher-level language statements defining a set of instructions to be followed by the computer after translation into machine language.

special cause variation—When the root cause of the statistically improbable variation in a process can be attributed to one or more special factors outside the normal expected variation in the process.

spiral model—A software life cycle model that is a risk-based model that expands on the structure of a waterfall model with details including the exploration of alternatives, prototyping, risk management, and planning.

sponsor—A senior leader or manager who has the position and authority to legitimize and champion a project, team, or change initiative.

sprint—In scrum, a single iteration through the development cycle.

sprint backlog—In scrum, a prioritized list of product requirements (features) that are planned for implementation during the current sprint.

sprint retrospective—A meeting held after the sprint review meeting to address needed process improvements.

sprint review meeting—A meeting held with stakeholders to review the output of the sprint and determine what to do next.

stakeholder—Any individual or group who affects or are affected by a software product, project, or process and therefore have some level of influence over the requirements for that software product, project, or process.

standard—"The formal mandatory requirements developed and used to prescribe consistent approaches to development" (SEI 2006).

standard deviation—A measure of the variability in a data set

state coverage or **state testing**—Testing analysis that looks at the mapping of tests to the various state transitions that can occur in the software to ensure that they are thoroughly tested.

state transition diagram or table—A representation of the behavior of a system by depicting its states and the events that cause the system to change states.

statement coverage—Structured testing analysis that looks at the mapping of tests to the various instructions or a series of instructions that a computer carries out to ensure that they are thoroughly tested.

static analysis—Methods of performing V&V by evaluating a software component or product without executing that component. Examples of static analysis techniques include peer reviews, proofs of correctness, and code analysis tools (for example, compilers, complexity analyzers).

static library—A software configuration management library used to archive important baselines, including those released into operations. The static library is used for the control, preservation, and retrieval of master media. (Also called the software repository or software product baseline library.)

stoplight chart—A chart that provides a red, yellow, and green signal to the user of the metric to aid in the interpretation of the measurement.

storming—A stage of team development when the team members are aware that they are going to have to change to make the team work together and there is a period of resistance to that change.

storyboards—Pictorial sequences used in requirements engineering to describe the human user interfaces.

stratified sampling—A sampling procedure where individual elements are first classified into non-overlapping groups (strata) and then random samples are selected from each group.

stress testing—A type of environmental load testing that subjects the software to surges or spikes in load over short periods of time and evaluates the software's performance.

strict product liability—A type of tort lawsuit that might be applied to software. The software caused injury or property damage because it is dangerously defective.

structural complexity—The complexity of the interactions between the modules in a calling structure (or in the case of object-oriented development between the classes in an inheritance tree).

structured analysis and design (SAD) or **structured analysis and design techniques (SADT)**—"A collection of guidelines for distinguishing between good designs and bad designs, and a collection of techniques, strategies, and heuristics that generally lead to good design" (Yourdon 1979).

structuredness—A quality criterion that describes the degree to which the system or computer program adheres to specific rules based on structured programming constructs (for example, single entry and exit points, no "go to" statements, sequential logic).

stub—A temporary piece of source code used as a replacement for a called module when performing top-down integration and integration testing.

supplier—Individuals and/or groups that are part of the organization that develops and/or maintains the software for the acquirer or are part of the organization that distributes the software to the acquirer.

supplier qualification audit—A second-party audit to evaluate the supplier's quality system to determine whether the supplier has the capability to produce products and/or services of the required quality level prior to selecting that supplier to perform work.

supplier surveillance audit—Ongoing second-party audits of a current supplier's systems, processes, projects, and/or products to ensure their continued capability to produce products and/or services of the required quality level.

supportability—A quality attribute describing the ease with which the technical support staff can isolate and resolve software issues reported by end users.

system architecture—The highest level of design. The architecture composed of system-level components, interfaces between those components, and the functions to be interchanged.

system audits—Audits conducted on management systems that evaluate all of the policies, processes, and work instructions, supporting plans and activities, training, and other components of those systems. An in-depth evaluation of an entire system (for example, a quality management system, environmental system, or safety system).

system requirements—Requirements for the entire system (as opposed to software requirements).

system testing—"Testing conducted on a complete, integrated system to evaluate the system's compliance with its specified requirements" (ISO/IEC 2009).

systematic sampling—A sampling procedure where every *n*th sample from the randomly sorted list is selected as the sample, starting with a random sample number *n* from the first *k* elements.

tacit knowledge—Knowledge gained through experience rather than through formal reading or education.

tailoring—Altering or adapting the standardized policies, processes, or work instructions to meet the specific objectives, constraints, needs, and/or requirements of a project, program, or product.

tasks—In process definition, the individual steps or activities that must be performed to implement the process and create the resulting product.

taxonomy—A categorized list of items (for example a risk taxonomy).

team—A group of two or more people working together toward a common goal.

team champion—A senior member of management who selects and defines the team's mission, scope, and goals, setting the vision and chartering the team.

team leader—The person responsible for managing the team.

technical review—Reviews of a software work product from a technical perspective.

template—A predefined layout used to create a new document, page, or other entity of the same design, pattern, format, or style.

test automation—The use of software to automate the activities of test design, test execution, and the capturing and analysis of test results.

test bed—An environment established and used for the execution of tests including hardware, instrumentation, simulators, software tools, and other support elements.

test coverage—An evaluation to determine how completely a set of testing exercised all of the software.

testability or **testable**—A quality attribute describing the effort required to perform tests on the software. There exists a reasonably cost-effective way to determine that the software satisfies the requirement.

test-driven development or **test-driven design (TDD)**—An agile iterative development methodology where software functionality is implemented based on first writing the test cases that the code must pass.

testing—A verification and validation method that involves the execution of all or part of the software in an attempt to detect the defects that exist in that software or to obtain a confidence level that the requirements are met. "The process of operating a system or component under specified conditions, observing or recording the results, and making an evaluation of some aspect of the system or component" (ISO/IEC 2009).

test-readiness review—A phase gate review held at the beginning of a major test cycle.

third-party audit—An audit performed on an organization by an external auditor other than their customer.

thread—A sequential set of usage steps through the software that a user takes.

throughput—A measure of the amount of work performed by a software system over a period of time (for example, transactions per hour, jobs per day).

time-box—In project management, a fixed amount of calendar time allocated to complete a given task.

time-box testing—A testing strategy where the calendar time for testing is fixed and the scope of the testing effort must be adjusted to fit inside that time-box.

top-down—An integration and testing strategy where testing starts with the highest-level unit or component in the section of the calling tree being tested, and tests it using stubs. The lower-level software items and their stubs are then integrated, one or more at a time, replacing the stubs.

tort lawsuits—"A wrongful act other than a breach of contract that injures another and for which the law imposes civil liabilities" (Futrell 2002).

total defect containment effectiveness (TDCE)—A metric that measures the effectiveness of defect detection techniques in identifying defects before the product is released into operation.

trace tags—Unique identifiers used in the subsequent work products to identify backward traceability to the predecessor document.

traceability or **traceable**—"The degree to which a relationship can be established between two or more products of the development process, especially products having a predecessor–successor or master–subordinate relationship to one another" (ISO/IEC 2009).

traceability matrix—A table that defines bidirectional traceability information.

tracing—An audit technique that follows the path of the chronological progress of a software module either forward or backward through its life cycle transactions.

trademark—A legal mechanism for branding products or services and distinguishing them from other similar products or services in the marketplace.

tree diagram—An analysis and problem-solving tool whose purpose is to break down or stratify ideas into progressively more detail.

Unified Modeling Language (UML)—A standardized set of models for object-oriented analysis.

unit testing—Testing that verifies that the individual software unit (component, module) meets its specification as defined in the detailed design and the requirements that are allocated to that unit.

usability—A quality attribute describing the amount of effort that the users must expend to learn and use the software.

usability testing—A type of testing whose objective is to determine if the system has any areas that will be difficult or inconvenient for the users.

use case diagram—A graphical representation of use cases and their interactions with users and their interrelationships with each other.

use cases—Scenarios created to describe the threads of usage for the system or software to be implemented.

user—Person or group that utilizes the functionality of the software. A primary user executes the software directly while a secondary user utilizes one or more outputs from the software without personally executing the software.

user or operator documentation—The set of documentation delivered to the users and/or operators that conveys the system instructions for understanding, installing, using, and maintaining the software.

user stories—A mechanism for capturing a stakeholder need in a way that acts as a reminder to have a future discussion about that need.

V&V—Verification and validation.

valid metric—A metric is internally valid if it measures what we expect it to measure. A metric is externally valid (also called predictive validity) if the metric results can be generalized or transferred to other populations or conditions.

validation—The "confirmation, through the provision of objective evidence, that the requirements for a specific intended use or application have been fulfilled" (ISO/IEC 2009). The process used "to demonstrate that a product or product component fulfills its intended use when placed in its intended environment" (SEI 2006).

value stream mapping—A lean technique used to trace a product from raw materials to use in order to determine areas were wastes can be eliminated.

variance—A measure of the variation in a data set equal to the square of the standard deviation.

verification—"The process of evaluating a system or component to determine whether the products of a given development phase satisfy the conditions imposed at the start of that phase" (ISO/IEC 2009). The process used to "ensure that selected work products meet their specified requirements" (SEI 2006).

verification and validation (V&V) sufficiency—Analysis that balances the risk that the software still has undiscovered defects and the potential loss associated with those defects against the cost of performing additional V&V activities and the benefits of additional V&V activities.

verification and validation task iteration—The repeating of one or more previously executed V&V activities.

verification steps—In process definition, the mechanisms used to ensure that the tasks are performed as required and that the deliverables meet required quality levels.

version—A configuration item, component, or unit with a defined set of functionality.

version control—The procedures and tools necessary to manage the different versions of the configuration items and software products.

version description document—A deliverable document that describes the released version of a software product, including an inventory of system or component parts, new or changed features or functionality, known defects and their work-arounds, and other information about that version. (Also called release notes.)

V-model—A software life cycle model that is a variation on the waterfall model that highlights the relationship between the testing phases and the products produced in the early life cycle phases.

volume testing—A type of environmental load testing that subjects the software to heavy loads over long periods of time and evaluates the software's capability.

vulnerability—Weakness in the software that could be exploited to cause a breach in security.

walk-throughs—A method of peer review where a team of peers meets with the author to examine a work product and provide feedback.

waste—Anything that does not add, or gets in the way of adding, value as perceived by the customer

waterfall model—A software life cycle model where each phase proceeds from start to finish before the next phase is started.

white-box testing—A form of testing that exercises the internal structure of a software component in order to detect defects. (Also called structural, clear box, or glass box testing.)

wireless systems architecture—The architecture of a computer system that is not tethered via cabling to a network.

W-model—A software life cycle model that is a variation on the waterfall model that has two paths (or crossing V's), each one representing the life cycle for a separate organization or team during development (the developers and the independent verification and validation team).

work breakdown structure (WBS)—"A method of subdividing the project work into smaller and smaller increments to permit accurate estimates of duration, resources, and costs" (Lewis 1995). A type of tree diagram that is a hierarchical decomposition of the project into subprojects, tasks, and subtasks.

work instructions—Specific, detailed instructions for implementing a process in a specific environment (for example, instructions, guidelines, checklists, forms, and templates).

work product—A tangible output, artifact, or specific measurable accomplishment that is a result of a software development activity or process. Examples of these artifacts include source code, models, electronic files, documents, databases, reports, metrics, logs, and services.

worst-case testing—A testing technique that utilizes worst-case scenarios based on boundaries.

References

Ambler, Scott W. 2002. *Agile Modeling: Effective Practices for eXtreme Programming and the Unified Process.* New York: John Wiley & Sons.

American Society for Quality. 2008. *Certified Software Quality Engineer Body of Knowledge* (available on the ASQ Web site).

Anand, Sanjay. 2006. *Sarbanes-Oxley Guide for Financial and Information Technology Professionals.* Hoboken, New Jersey: John Wiley & Sons.

Arter, Dennis. 1994. *Quality Audits for Improvement Performance,* Second Edition. Milwaukee: ASQ Quality Press.

Arthur, Lowell Jay. 1985. *Measuring Programmer Productivity and Software Quality.* New York: John Wiley & Sons.

Astels, David. 2003. *Test-Driven Development: A Practical Guide,* Second Edition. Upper Saddle River, NJ: Prentice Hall PTR.

Astels, David, Granville Miller, and Miroslav Novak. 2002. *A Practical Guide to eXtreme Programming.* Upper Saddle River, NJ: Prentice Hall.

Baker, Sunny, and Kim Baker. 1998. *The Complete Idiot's Guide to Project Management.* New York: Alpha Books.

Bass, Len, Paul Clements, and Risk Kazman. 2003. *Software Architecture in Practice,* Second Edition. SEI Series in Software Engineering. Boston: Addison-Wesley.

Bays, Michael E. 1999. *Software Release Methodology.* Upper Saddle River, NJ: Prentice Hall PTR.

Beck, Kent (with Cynthia Andres). 2005. *Extreme Programming Explained: Embrace Change,* Second Edition. Boston: Addison-Wesley.

Berczuk, Stephan P. 2003. *Software Configuration Management Patterns: Effective Teamwork, Practical Integration.* Boston: Addison-Wesley.

Berlack, H. Ronald. 1992. *Software Configuration Management.* Hoboken, NJ: John Wiley & Sons.

Bernstein, Albert J., and Sydney Craft Rozen. 1990. *Dinosaur Brains: Dealing with All Those Impossible People at Work.* New York: Ballantine Books.

Black, Rex. 2004. *Critical Testing Processes: Plan, Prepare, Perform, Perfect.* Boston: Addison-Wesley Professional.

Blohowiak, Donald. 1992. *Mavericks! How to Lead Your Staff to Think Like Einstein, Create Like da Vinci, and Invent Like Edison.* Homewood, IL: Business One Irwin.

Boehm, Barry. 1981. *Software Engineering Economics.* Englewood Cliffs, NJ: Prentice Hall.

———. 1988. "A Spiral Model of Software Development and Enhancement." *IEEE Computer* (May).

———. 1989. *Tutorial: Software Risk Management.* Los Alamitos, CA: IEEE Computer Society.

615

Boehm, Barry, Chris Abts, A. Winsor Brown, Sunita Chulani, Bradford K. Clark, Ellis Horowitz, Ray Madachy, Donald J. Reifer, and Bert Steece. 2000. *Software Cost Estimation with COCOMO II.* Upper Saddle River, NJ: Prentice Hall PTR.

Brooks, Fredrick. 1995. *Mythical Man-Month: Essays on Software Engineering,* Anniversary Edition. Boston: Addison-Wesley Professional.

Campanella, Jack. 1990. *Principles of Quality Costs: Principles, Implementation, and Use,* Second Edition. Milwaukee: ASQC Quality Press.

CMU/SEI. 1992. Robert E. Park, with the Size Subgroup of the Software Metrics Definition Working Group and the Software Process Measurement Project Team. *Software Size Measurement: A Framework for Counting Source Statements.* Technical Report. Carnegie-Mellon University, Software Engineering Institute, ESC-TR-92-020 (September 1992). (Available on the SEI Web site.)

CNSS. 2006. *National Information Assurance (IA) Glossary.* Ft. Meade, MD: Committee on National Security Systems (CNSS): CNSS Instruction No. 4009, Revised June 2006.

Coad, Peter, and Edward Yourdon. 1990. *Object-Oriented Analysis,* Second Edition. Englewood Cliffs, NJ: Yourdon Press Computing Series.

Cockburn, Alistair. 2002. *Agile Software Development.* Boston: Addison-Wesley.

———. 2005. *Crystal Clear: A Human-Powered Methodology for Small Teams.* Boston: Addison-Wesley.

DAC. 1981. *The DACS Glossary: A Bibliography of Software Engineering Terms.* Compiled from the literature by Shirley A. Gloss-Soler under contract to Rome Air Development Center, Griffiss Air Force Base, March, 1981.

Daughtrey, Taz. 2002. *Fundamental Concepts for the Software Quality Engineer.* Milwaukee: ASQ Quality Press.

DeMarco, Tom. 2001. *Slack.* New York: Broadway Books.

DeMarco, Tom, and Timothy Lister. 1999. *Peopleware—Productive Projects and Teams,* Second Edition. New York: Dorset House.

———. 2003. *Waltzing with Bears: Managing Risk on Software Projects.* New York: Dorset House.

DePree, Max. 1989. *Leadership Is an Art.* New York: Dell.

Derby, Esther, Diana Larsen, and Ken Schwaber. 2006. *Agile Retrospectives: Making Good Teams Great.* Raleigh, NC: The Pragmatic Bookshelf.

Dorofee, Audrey J., Julie A. Walker, Christopher J. Alberts, Ronald P. Higuera, Richard L. Murphy, and Ray C. Williams. 1996. *Continuous Risk Management Guidebook.* Pittsburgh: Carnegie Mellon University, Software Engineering Institute.

Down, Alex, Michael Coleman, and Peter Absolon. 1994. *Risk Management for Software Projects.* London: McGraw-Hill.

Dunn, Robert. 1990. *Software Quality, Concepts, and Plans.* Englewood Cliffs, NJ: Prentice Hall.

EIA. 2004. ANSI/EIA-649-2004, *National Consensus Standard for Configuration Management.* Arlington, VA: Electronic Industries Alliance (EIA).

Fenton, Norman E., and Shari Lawrence Pfleeger. 1997. *Software Metrics: A Rigorous and Practical Approach,* Second Edition. London: PWS Publishing.

Futrell, Robert T., Donald F. Shafer, and Linda Isabell Shafer. 2002. *Quality Software Project Management.* Upper Saddle River, NJ: Prentice Hall PTR.

Gamma, Erich, Richard Helm, Ralph Johnson, and John M. Vlissides. 1994. *Design Patterns: Elements of Reusable Object-Oriented Software.* Upper Saddle River, NJ: Addison-Wesley Professional.

Gilb, Tom. 1988. *Principles of Software Engineering Management.* Wokingham, England: Addison-Wesley.

———. 1993. *Software Inspections.* Wokingham, England: Addison-Wesley.

Goodman, Paul. 1993. *Practical Implementation of Software Metrics.* London: McGraw-Hill.

Gottesdiener, Ellen. 2002. *Requirements by Collaboration.* Boston: Addison-Wesley.

Grady, Robert. 1992. *Practical Software Metrics for Project Management and Process Improvement.* Englewood Cliffs, NJ: Prentice Hall PTR.

GSAM. 2000. Department of the Air Force, Software Technology Support Center. *Guidelines for Successful Acquisition and Management of Software-Intensive Systems: Weapon Systems, Command and Control Systems.* Management Information Systems (GSAM) Version 3.0, May 2000.

Hall, Elaine M. 1998. *Managing Risk: Methods for Software Systems Development.* Reading, MA: Addison-Wesley.

Hass, Anne Mette Jonassen. 2003. *Configuration Management Principles and Practices.* Boston, MA: Addison-Wesley.

Hersey, Paul. 1984. *The Situational Leader.* Escondido, CA: Warner Books.

Humphrey, Watts S. 1989. *Managing the Software Process.* Reading, MA: Addison-Wesley.

IEEE. 1994. IEEE Standards Software Engineering, *IEEE Standard for Software Safety Plans,* IEEE Std. 1228-1994. New York: The Institute of Electrical and Electronics Engineers.

———. 1996. IEEE Standards Software Engineering, *IEEE Guideline for Developing System Requirements Specifications,* IEEE Std. 1228-1996 (reaffirmed 2002). New York: The Institute of Electrical and Electronics Engineers.

———. 1998. IEEE Standards Software Engineering, *IEEE Standards for Software Project Management Plans,* IEEE Std. 1058-1998. New York: The Institute of Electrical and Electronics Engineers.

———. 1998a. IEEE Standards Software Engineering, *IEEE Standards for Verification and Validation Plans,* IEEE Std. 1059-1998. New York: The Institute of Electrical and Electronics Engineers (withdrawn).

———. 1998b. IEEE Standards Software Engineering, *IEEE Guide for Information Technology—System Definition—Concept of Operations (ConOps),* IEEE Std. 1362-1998 (reaffirmed 2007). New York: The Institute of Electrical and Electronics Engineers.

———. 1998c. IEEE Standards Software Engineering, *IEEE Recommended Practice for Software Requirements Specifications,* IEEE Std. 830-1998. New York: The Institute of Electrical and Electronics Engineers.

———. 1998d. IEEE Standards Software Engineering, *IEEE Standards for Software Quality Metrics Methodology,* IEEE Std. 1061-1998 (reaffirmed 2004). New York: The Institute of Electrical and Electronics Engineers.

———. 2002. IEEE Standards Software Engineering, *IEEE Standard for Software Quality Assurance Plans,* IEEE Std. 730-2002. New York: Institute of Electrical and Electronics Engineers.

———. 2004. IEEE Standards Software Engineering, *IEEE Standard for Software Verification and Validation,* IEEE Std. 1012-2004. New York: The Institute of Electrical and Electronics Engineers.

———. 2005. IEEE Standards Software Engineering, *IEEE Standard for Software Configuration Management Plans,* IEEE Std. 828-2005. New York: The Institute of Electrical and Electronics Engineers.

———. 2006. IEEE Standards Software Engineering, ISO/IEC 14764:2006, *Standard for Software Engineering—Software Life Cycle Processes—Maintenance.* New York: The Institute of Electrical and Electronics Engineers.

———. 2006a. IEEE Standards Software Engineering, ISO/IEC 16085, *Standard for Software Engineering—Software Life Cycle Processes—Risk Management.* New York: The Institute of Electrical and Electronics Engineers.

———. 2008. IEEE Software Engineering Standard Status Report, September 2008, (available at http://standards.ieee.org/software/). New York: The Institute of Electrical and Electronics Engineers.

———. 2008a. IEEE Standards Software Engineering, *IEEE Standard for Software Reviews and Audits,* IEEE Std. 1028-2008. New York: The Institute of Electrical and Electronics Engineers.

————. 2008b. IEEE Standards Software Engineering, *IEEE Standard for Software Test Documentation*, IEEE Std. 829-2008. New York: The Institute of Electrical and Electronics Engineers.

————. 2008c. IEEE Standards Software Engineering, *Systems and Software Engineering—Software Life Cycle Processes*, IEEE Std. 12207-2008. New York: The Institute of Electrical and Electronics Engineers.

ISO. 2008. American National Standard, *Quality Management Systems—Requirements*, ANSI/ISO/ASQ Q9001-2008. Milwaukee: American Society for Quality.

ISO/IEC. 2002. ISO/IEC 15939:2002 (E), International Standard, *Software Engineering—Software Measurement Process*. Geneva.

ISO/IEC. 2009. ISO/IEC FDIS 24765 *Systems and Software Engineering—Vocabulary*, (this standard is in the formal approval stage at the time of this publication). Montréal, Québec.

Jeffries, Ron. 2001. "Essential XP: Card, Conversation, and Confirmation." *XP Magazine* (August 3).

Jones, Capers. 1986. *Programming Productivity*. New York: McGraw-Hill.

————. 1994. *Assessment and Control of Software Risks*. Upper Saddle River, NJ: Yourdon Press, Prentice Hall.

————. 2008. *Applied Software Measurement: Global Analysis of Productivity and Quality*, Third Edition. New York: McGraw Hill.

Juran, Joseph M. 1999. *Juran's Quality Handbook*, Fifth Edition. New York: McGraw-Hill.

Kan, Stephen. 2003. *Metrics and Models in Software Quality Engineering*, Second Edition. Boston: Addison-Wesley.

Kaner, Cem, Jack Faulk, and Hung Quoc Nguyen. 1999. *Testing Computer Software*, Second Edition. New York: Wiley Computer Publishing, John Wiley & Sons.

Kasse, Tim, and Patricia A. McQuaid. 2000. "Software Configuration Management for Project Leaders," *Software Quality Professional* 2, no. 4 (September).

Kenefick, Sean. 2003. *Real World Software Configuration Management*. Berkeley, CA: APress.

Kerth, Norm L. 2001. *Project Retrospectives: A Handbook for Team Reviews*. New York: Dorset House.

Keyes, Jessica. 2004. *Software Configuration Management*. Boca Raton: Auerbach Publications.

Krasner, Herb. 1998. "Using the Cost of Quality Approach for Software," *CrossTalk—The War on Bugs* 11, no. 11 (November). (Available on the CrossTalk Web site.)

Kruchten, Philippe. 2000. *The Rational Unified Process: an Introduction*. Reading, MA: Addison-Wesley.

Lauesen, Soren. 2002. *Software Requirements: Styles and Techniques*. London: Addison-Wesley.

Leffingwell, Dean, and Don Widrig. 2000. *Managing Software Requirements: A Unified Approach*. Reading, MA: Addison-Wesley.

Leon, Alexis. 2005. *Software Configuration Management Handbook*, Second Edition. Boston: Artech House.

Lewis, James P. 1995. *The Project Manager's Desk Reference—A Comprehensive Guide to Project Planning, Scheduling, Evaluation, Control, and Systems*. New York: McGraw-Hill.

Loeb, Marshal, and Stephen Kindel. 1999. *Leadership for Dummies*. Foster City, CA: IDG Books Worldwide.

Martin, Robert C. 2003. *Agile Software Development: Principles, Patterns, and Practices*. Upper Saddle River, NJ: Prentice Hall.

McConnell, Steve. 1996. *Rapid Development: Taming Wild Software Schedules*. Redmond, WA: Microsoft Press.

McFeeley, Bob. 1996. *IDEAL: A User's Guide for Software Process Improvement*, CMU/SEI-96-HB-001. (Available on the SEI Web site.)

McGregor, John D., and David A. Sykes. 2001. *A Practical Guide to Testing Object-Oriented Software.* Boston: Addison-Wesley.

MIL-HDBK. 2001. *Military Handbook—Configuration Management Guidance.* MIL-HDBK-61A(SE), Department of Defense, February 7. Washington, DC.

Myers, Glenford J. 2004. *The Art of Software Testing,* Second Edition. Hoboken, NJ: John Wiley & Sons.

Ould, Martyn A. 1990. *Strategies for Software Engineering: The Management of Risk and Quality.* Chichester, England: John Wiley & Sons.

OWASP. 2009. *Some Proven Application Security Principles.* OWASP Web site. (Available at http://www.owasp.org/index.php/Category:Principle.)

Pande, Peter S., Robert P. Neuman, and Roland R. Cavanagh. 2000. *The Six Sigma Way.* New York: McGraw-Hill.

Petchiny, Maj. Nicko. 1998. *Object Oriented Testing.* PowerPoint Presentation. (Available at www.cs.queensu.ca.)

PMI. 2005. PMI Global Standard, *Practice Standard for Earned Value Management.* Newton Square, PA: Project Management Institute.

———. 2008. PMI Global Standard, *Project Management Body of Knowledge (PMBOK) Guide,* Version Four. Newton Square, PA: Project Management Institute.

Poppendieck, Mary, and Tom Poppendieck. 2003. *Lean Software Development: An Agile Toolkit.* Boston: Addison-Wesley.

Pressman, Roger. 2001. *Software Engineering: A Practitioner's Approach,* Fifth Edition. Boston: McGraw-Hill.

———. 2005. *Software Engineering: A Practitioner's Approach,* Sixth Edition. New York: McGraw-Hill.

Project 2000. *User's Guide*—Microsoft Project 2000. Microsoft Corporation.

Putnam, Lawrence H., and Ware Myers. 1992. *Measures for Excellence—Reliable Software on Time, within Budget.* Englewood Cliffs, NJ: Yourdon Press.

———. 2003. *Five Core Metrics: The Intelligence behind Successful Software Management.* New York: Dorset House.

Pyzdek, Thomas. 2000. *Quality Engineering Handbook.* New York: Marcel Dekker.

———. 2001. *The Six Sigma Handbook.* New York: McGraw-Hill, Quality Publishing Tucson.

Roberts, Wess. 1987. *Leadership Secrets of Attila the Hun.* New York: Warner Books.

Rothman, Johanna. 2007. *Manage It! Your Guide to Modern, Pragmatic Project Management.* Raleigh, NC: The Pragmatic Bookshelf.

Russell, J.P., editor. 2005. ASQ Quality Audit Division, *The ASQ Auditing Handbook,* Third Edition. Milwaukee: ASQ Quality Press.

Scholtes, Peter R., Brian L. Joiner, Barbara J. Steibel. 2003. *The Team Handbook,* Third Edition. Madison, WI: Oriel.

Schulmeyer, G. Gordon, and James McManus, editors. 1998. *Handbook of Software Quality Assurance,* Third Edition. Upper Saddle River, NJ: Prentice Hall PTR.

Schwaber, Ken, and Mike Beedle. 2002. *Agile Software Development with Scrum.* Upper Saddle River, NJ: Prentice Hall.

Schwaber, Ken, and Mike Cohn. 2007. From a Scrum Master training class given January 16–17, 2007 in Orlando, Florida.

SEI. 1993. Marvin J. Karr, et al., "Taxonomy-Based Risk Identification," CMU/SEI-93-TR-6, Software Engineering Institute, Carnegie Mellon University, Pittsburgh, PA, (available on the SEI Web site).

————. 1995. Capability Maturity Model (CMM), Version 1.2, Carnegie Mellon University Software Engineering Institute, Pittsburgh, PA (available on the SEI Web site).

————. 2002. People Capability Maturity Model (P-CMM), Version 2.0, Carnegie Mellon University Software Engineering Institute, Pittsburgh, PA 15213-3890, CMU/SEI-2001-MM-001, (available on the SEI Web site).

————. 2006. Capability Maturity Model Integration (CMMI) for Development, Version 1.2, Carnegie Mellon University Software Engineering Institute, Pittsburgh, PA 15213-3890, CMU/SEI-2006-TR-008, ESC-TR-2006-008 (available on the SEI Web site).

————. 2007. Capability Maturity Model Integration (CMMI) for Acquisition, Version 1.2, CMU/SEI-2007-TR-017, ESC-TR-2007-017, CMMI Product Team, Software Engineering Institute, November (available on the SEI Web site).

SPR. 1995. *Software Productivity Research (SPR): A Functional Metrics Course*. Burlington, MA: Software Productivity Research.

Takeuchi, H., and I. Nonaka. 1986. "The New Product Development Game," *Harvard Business Review* Jan/Feb.: 137–146.

————. 1995. *The Knowledge Creating Company*. New York: Oxford University Press.

Thayer, Richard, editor. 1997. *Software Engineering Project Management*. Los Alamitos, CA: IEEE Computer Society.

Toastmasters International. 1990. *How to Listen Effectively*. Mission Viejo, CA: Toastmasters International.

UML. 2003. OMG Unified Modeling Language Specification Version 1.5, Object Management Group (OMG), March 2003, formal/03-03-01, (available on the OMG Web site).

USC. 1999. USC COCOMO II Reference Manual, University of Sothern California, Center for Systems and Software Engineering, updated 2/05/1999, (available on the COCOMO Web site).

Vienneau, Robert L., and Milton Johns. 2008. "Introduction to U.S. Intellectual Property (IP) Law," *SoftwareTech News, The Data & Acquisition Center for Software (DACS)* 11, no. 2 (August). (Available at www.softwaretechnews.com.)

Weinberg, Gerald. 1997. *Quality Software Management, Volume 4: Anticipating Change*. New York: Dorset House Publishing.

Westcott, Russell T., editor. 2006. ASQ Quality Management Division. *The Certified Manager of Quality/Organizational Excellence Handbook*, Third Edition. Milwaukee: ASQ Quality Press.

Whittaker, James A. 2003. *How to Break Software: A Practical Guide to Testing*. New York: Addison-Wesley.

Wiegers, Karl E. 2002. *Peer Reviews in Software*. Boston: Addison-Wesley.

————. 2003. *Software Requirements*, Second Edition. Redmond, WA: Microsoft Press.

————. 2004. *In Search of Excellent Requirements*. Process Impact.

Yourdon, Edward, and Larry Constantine. 1979. *Structured Design: Fundamentals of a Discipline of Computer Program and Systems Design*. Englewood Cliffs, NJ: Prentice Hall.

WEB SITES

ACM. Association for Computer Machinery; http://www.acm.org
Agile Alliance. Agile Alliance; http://www.agilealliance.com
APLN. Agile Project Leadership Network; http://www.apln.org
ASQ. American Society for Quality; http://www.asq.org
ASQ. Software Division; http://www.asq.org/divisions-forums/software
Baldrige. Malcolm Baldrige National Quality Award; http://www.quality.nist.gov
COCOMO. Constructive Cost Model; http://sunset.usc.edu/csse/research/COCOMOII

Crossroads. http://www.cmcrossroads.com

Crosstalk. Crosstalk: The Journal of Defense Software Engineering; http://stsc.hill. af.mil/crosstalk

Dilbert. The Dilbert Zone; http://www.dilbert.com

DMAIC. Six Sigma DMAIC Quick Reference; http://www.isixsigma.com/ library/ content/six_sigma_dmaic_quickref_define.asp

ESPRIT. European Strategic Programme of Research and Development in Information Technology; http://cordis.europa.eu/esprit

FDD. Feature-driven development; http://www.nebulon.com/fdd

IEEE. Institute of Electrical and Electronics Engineers; http://www.ieee.org

IEEE. Computer Society; http://www2.computer.org

IFPUG. International Function Point User's Group; http://www.ifpug.org

IIA. The Institute of Internal Auditors; http://www.theiia.org

ISBSG. International Software Benchmarking Standards Group; http://www.isbsg.org

ISO. International Organization for Standardization; http://www.iso.org

ITIL. IT Service Management Institute—Information Technology Infrastructure Library (ITIL); http://www.itsmi.com

ITMPI. The IT Metrics and Productivity Institute; http://www.itmpi.org

NASA. Software Assurance, NASA Goddard Space Flight Center; http://sw-assurance. gsfc.nasa.gov

OMG. Object Management Group; http://www.omg.org

OWASP. Open Web Application Security Project (OWASP); http://www.owasp.org

PMI. Project Management Institute; http://www.pmi.org

PSM. Practical Software and System Measurement; http://www.psmsc.com

Scrum. Scrum Alliance; http://www.scrumalliance.org

SEI. Software Engineering Institute; http://www.sei.cmu.edu

SPMN. Software Program Managers Network; http://www.spmn.com

STQE. Software Testing and Quality Engineering; http://www.stickyminds.com

SwA. Software Assurance: Community Resources and Information Clearing House. Sponsored by the US Department of Homeland Security Cyber Security Division; https://buildsecurityin.us-cert.gov/swa/

SWEBOK. Software Engineering Body of Knowledge; http://www.swebok.org

Westfall Team. The Westfall Team; http://www.westfallteam.com

Wikipedia. http://www.wikipedia.org

XPE. Extreme programming (XP)—embedded; http://www.xp-embedded.com

XPP. Extreme programming; www.xprogramming.com

Index

Belong to the Quality Community!

Established in 1946, ASQ is a global community of quality experts in all fields and industries. ASQ is dedicated to the promotion and advancement of quality tools, principles, and practices in the workplace and in the community.

The Society also serves as an advocate for quality. Its members have informed and advised the U.S. Congress, government agencies, state legislatures, and other groups and individuals worldwide on quality-related topics.

Vision

By making quality a global priority, an organizational imperative, and a personal ethic, ASQ becomes the community of choice for everyone who seeks quality technology, concepts, or tools to improve themselves and their world.

ASQ is...

- More than 90,000 individuals and 700 companies in more than 100 countries

- The world's largest organization dedicated to promoting quality

- A community of professionals striving to bring quality to their work and their lives

- The administrator of the Malcolm Baldrige National Quality Award

- A supporter of quality in all sectors including manufacturing, service, healthcare, government, and education

- YOU

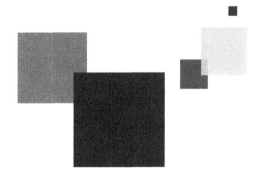

Visit www.asq.org for more information.

ASQ Membership

Research shows that people who join associations experience increased job satisfaction, earn more, and are generally happier*. ASQ membership can help you achieve this while providing the tools you need to be successful in your industry and to distinguish yourself from your competition. So why wouldn't you want to be a part of ASQ?

Networking

Have the opportunity to meet, communicate, and collaborate with your peers within the quality community through conferences and local ASQ section meetings, ASQ forums or divisions, ASQ Communities of Quality discussion boards, and more.

Professional Development

Access a wide variety of professional development tools such as books, training, and certifications at a discounted price. Also, ASQ certifications and the ASQ Career Center help enhance your quality knowledge and take your career to the next level.

Solutions

Find answers to all your quality problems, big and small, with ASQ's Knowledge Center, mentoring program, various e-newsletters, *Quality Progress* magazine, and industry-specific products.

Access to Information

Learn classic and current quality principles and theories in ASQ's Quality Information Center (QIC), *ASQ Weekly* e-newsletter, and product offerings.

Advocacy Programs

ASQ helps create a better community, government, and world through initiatives that include social responsibility, Washington advocacy, and Community Good Works.

Visit www.asq.org/membership for more information on ASQ membership.

*2008, The William E. Smith Institute for Association Research

ASQ Certification

ASQ certification is formal recognition by ASQ that an individual has demonstrated a proficiency within, and comprehension of, a specified body of knowledge at a point in time. Nearly 150,000 certifications have been issued. ASQ has members in more than 100 countries, in all industries, and in all cultures. ASQ certification is internationally accepted and recognized.

Benefits to the Individual
- New skills gained and proficiency upgraded
- Investment in your career
- Mark of technical excellence
- Assurance that you are current with emerging technologies
- Discriminator in the marketplace
- Certified professionals earn more than their uncertified counterparts
- Certification is endorsed by more than 125 companies

Benefits to the Organization
- Investment in the company's future
- Certified individuals can perfect and share new techniques in the workplace
- Certified staff are knowledgeable and able to assure product and service quality

Quality is a global concept. It spans borders, cultures, and languages. No matter what country your customers live in or what language they speak, they demand quality products and services. You and your organization also benefit from quality tools and practices. Acquire the knowledge to position yourself and your organization ahead of your competition.

Certifications Include
- Biomedical Auditor – CBA
- Calibration Technician – CCT
- HACCP Auditor – CHA
- Pharmaceutical GMP Professional – CPGP
- Quality Inspector – CQI
- Quality Auditor – CQA
- Quality Engineer – CQE
- Quality Improvement Associate – CQIA
- Quality Technician – CQT
- Quality Process Analyst – CQPA
- Reliability Engineer – CRE
- Six Sigma Black Belt – CSSBB
- Six Sigma Green Belt – CSSGB
- Software Quality Engineer – CSQE
- Manager of Quality/Organizational Excellence – CMQ/OE

Visit www.asq.org/certification to apply today!

ASQ Training

Classroom-based Training

ASQ offers training in a traditional classroom setting on a variety of topics. Our instructors are quality experts and lead courses that range from one day to four weeks, in several different cities. Classroom-based training is designed to improve quality and your organization's bottom line. Benefit from quality experts; from comprehensive, cutting-edge information; and from peers eager to share their experiences.

Web-based Training

Virtual Courses

ASQ's virtual courses provide the same expert instructors, course materials, interaction with other students, and ability to earn CEUs and RUs as our classroom-based training, without the hassle and expenses of travel. Learn in the comfort of your own home or workplace. All you need is a computer with Internet access and a telephone.

Self-paced Online Programs

These online programs allow you to work at your own pace while obtaining the quality knowledge you need. Access them whenever it is convenient for you, accommodating your schedule.

Some Training Topics Include

- Auditing
- Basic Quality
- Engineering
- Education
- Healthcare
- Government
- Food Safety
- ISO
- Leadership
- Lean
- Quality Management
- Reliability
- Six Sigma
- Social Responsibility

Visit www.asq.org/training for more information.